FORD ESCAPE
2001-07 REPAIR MANUAL

MW01484801

CHILTON'S

Covers all U.S. and Canadian models of
Ford Escape, Mazda Tribute & Mercury Mariner

Does not include information specific to hybrid models

by Mike Stubblefield

CHILTON *Automotive Books*

PUBLISHED BY **HAYNES NORTH AMERICA**, Inc.

Manufactured in USA
© 2003, 2009 Haynes North America, Inc.
ISBN 13: 978 156392 700 3
ISBN 10: 1 56392 700 4
Library of Congress Control No. 2009930743

Haynes Publishing Group
Sparkford Nr Yeovil
Somerset BA22 7JJ England

Haynes North America, Inc
861 Lawrence Drive
Newbury Park
California 91320 USA

ABCDE
FGHIJ
KLMNO
PQ

6M2

Contents

2002 Ford Escape

ACKNOWLEDGMENTS

   Wiring diagrams originated by Valley Forge Technical Information Services. Technical writers who contributed to this project include Rob Maddox, Ralph Rendina and John Wegmann.

   While every attempt is made to ensure that the information in this manual is correct, no liability can be accepted by the authors or publishers for loss, damage or injury caused by any errors in, or omissions from, the information given.

About this manual

ITS PURPOSE

The purpose of this manual is to help you get the best value from your vehicle. It can do so in several ways. It can help you decide what work must be done, even if you choose to have it done by a dealer service department or a repair shop; it provides information and procedures for routine maintenance and servicing; and it offers diagnostic and repair procedures to follow when trouble occurs.

We hope you use the manual to tackle the work yourself. For many simpler jobs, doing it yourself may be quicker than arranging an appointment to get the vehicle into a shop and making the trips to leave it and pick it up. More importantly, a lot of money can be saved by avoiding the expense the shop must pass on to you to cover its labor and overhead costs. An added benefit is the sense of satisfaction and accomplishment that you feel after doing the job yourself.

USING THE MANUAL

The manual is divided into Chapters. Each Chapter is divided into numbered Sections. Each Section consists of consecutively numbered paragraphs.

At the beginning of each numbered Section you will be referred to any illustrations which apply to the procedures in that Section. The reference numbers used in illustration captions pinpoint the pertinent Section and the Step within that Section. That is, illustration 3.2 means the illustration refers to Section 3 and Step (or paragraph) 2 within that Section.

Procedures, once described in the text, are not normally repeated. When it's necessary to refer to another Chapter, the reference will be given as Chapter and Section number. Cross references given without use of the word "Chapter" apply to Sections and/or paragraphs in the same Chapter. For example, "see Section 8" means in the same Chapter.

References to the left or right side of the vehicle assume you are sitting in the driver's seat, facing forward.

Even though we have prepared this manual with extreme care, neither the publisher nor the author can accept responsibility for any errors in, or omissions from, the information given.

➡ NOTE

A *Note* provides information necessary to properly complete a procedure or information which will make the procedure easier to understand.

❄❄ CAUTION

A *Caution* provides a special procedure or special steps which must be taken while completing the procedure where the Caution is found. Not heeding a Caution can result in damage to the assembly being worked on.

❄❄ WARNING

A *Warning* provides a special procedure or special steps which must be taken while completing the procedure where the Warning is found. Not heeding a Warning can result in personal injury.

Introduction

This manual covers the Ford Escape, Mazda Tribute and Mercury Mariner. The available engines are:

The 2.0L Zetec in-line four-cylinder engine, 2.3L in-line four-cylinder engine and the 3.0L Duratec V6 engine.

The engine drives the front wheels through either a five-speed manual or a four-speed automatic transaxle via independent driveaxles. On 4WD models the rear wheels are also propelled, via a driveshaft, rear differential, and two rear driveaxles.

Suspension is independent at all four wheels, MacPherson struts being used at the front end and trailing arms, control arms, coil springs and telescopic shock absorbers at the rear. The rack-and-pinion steering unit is mounted on the suspension crossmember.

The brakes are disc at the front and drums at the rear, with power assist standard. Some models are equipped with an optional Anti-lock Brake System (ABS).

Vehicle identification numbers

Modifications are a continuing and unpublicized process in vehicle manufacturing. Since spare parts manuals and lists are compiled on a numerical basis, the individual vehicle numbers are essential to correctly identify the component required.

VEHICLE IDENTIFICATION NUMBER (VIN)

This very important identification number is stamped on a plate attached to the dashboard inside the windshield on the driver's side of the vehicle (see illustration). The VIN also appears on the Vehicle Certificate of Title and Registration. It contains information such as where and when the vehicle was manufactured, the model year and the body style.

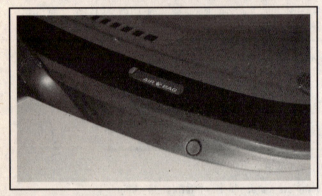

The Vehicle Identification Number (VIN) is visible through the driver's side of the windshield

Location of the Manufacturer's Certification Regulation label

MANUFACTURER'S CERTIFICATION REGULATION LABEL

The Manufacturer's Certification Regulation label is attached to the driver's side door end or post (see illustration). The label contains the name of the manufacturer, the month and year of production, the Gross Vehicle Weight Rating (GVWR), the Gross Axle Weight Rating (GAWR) and the certification statement.

VIN MODEL YEAR CODE

Counting from the left, the model year code letter designation is the 10th character. On all models covered by this manual the model year codes are:

```
1 .................................... 2001
2 .................................... 2002
3 .................................... 2003
4 .................................... 2004
5 .................................... 2005
6 .................................... 2006
```

ENGINE NUMBER

On four-cylinder models, the engine identification number is stamped into a machined pad on the front-side of the engine under the exhaust manifold.

On V6 models, the engine identification number is stamped into a machined pad on the right end (driver's side) of the engine block (see illustration).

Location of the engine identification number - V6 engine

Buying parts

Replacement parts are available from many sources, which generally fall into one of two categories - authorized dealer parts departments and independent retail auto parts stores. Our advice concerning these parts is as follows:

Retail auto parts stores: Good auto parts stores will stock frequently needed components which wear out relatively fast, such as clutch components, exhaust systems, brake parts, tune-up parts, etc. These stores often supply new or reconditioned parts on an exchange basis, which can save a considerable amount of money. Discount auto parts stores are often very good places to buy materials and parts needed for general vehicle maintenance such as oil, grease, filters, spark plugs, belts, touch-up paint, bulbs, etc. They also usually sell tools and general accessories, have convenient hours, charge lower prices and can often be found not far from home.

Authorized dealer parts department: This is the best source for parts which are unique to the vehicle and not generally available elsewhere (such as major engine parts, transmission parts, trim pieces, etc.).

Warranty information: If the vehicle is still covered under warranty, be sure that any replacement parts purchased - regardless of the source - do not invalidate the warranty!

To be sure of obtaining the correct parts, have engine and chassis numbers available and, if possible, take the old parts along for positive identification.

Maintenance techniques, tools and working facilities

MAINTENANCE TECHNIQUES

There are a number of techniques involved in maintenance and repair that will be referred to throughout this manual. Application of these techniques will enable the home mechanic to be more efficient, better organized and capable of performing the various tasks properly, which will ensure that the repair job is thorough and complete.

Fasteners

Fasteners are nuts, bolts, studs and screws used to hold two or more parts together. There are a few things to keep in mind when working with fasteners. Almost all of them use a locking device of some type, either a lockwasher, locknut, locking tab or thread adhesive. All threaded fasteners should be clean and straight, with undamaged threads and undamaged corners on the hex head where the wrench fits. Develop the habit of replacing all damaged nuts and bolts with new ones. Special locknuts with nylon or fiber inserts can only be used once. If they are removed, they lose their locking ability and must be replaced with new ones.

Rusted nuts and bolts should be treated with a penetrating fluid to ease removal and prevent breakage. Some mechanics use turpentine in a spout-type oil can, which works quite well. After applying the rust penetrant, let it work for a few minutes before trying to loosen the nut or bolt. Badly rusted fasteners may have to be chiseled or sawed off or removed with a special nut breaker, available at tool stores.

If a bolt or stud breaks off in an assembly, it can be drilled and removed with a special tool commonly available for this purpose. Most automotive machine shops can perform this task, as well as other repair procedures, such as the repair of threaded holes that have been stripped out.

Flat washers and lockwashers, when removed from an assembly, should always be replaced exactly as removed. Replace any damaged washers with new ones. Never use a lockwasher on any soft metal surface (such as aluminum), thin sheet metal or plastic.

Fastener sizes

For a number of reasons, automobile manufacturers are making wider and wider use of metric fasteners. Therefore, it is important to be able to tell the difference between standard (sometimes called U.S. or SAE) and metric hardware, since they cannot be interchanged.

All bolts, whether standard or metric, are sized according to diameter, thread pitch and length. For example, a standard 1/2 - 13 x 1 bolt is 1/2 inch in diameter, has 13 threads per inch and is 1 inch long. An M12 - 1.75 x 25 metric bolt is 12 mm in diameter, has a thread pitch of 1.75 mm (the distance between threads) and is 25 mm long. The two bolts are nearly identical, and easily confused, but they are not interchangeable.

In addition to the differences in diameter, thread pitch and length, metric and standard bolts can also be distinguished by examining the bolt heads. To begin with, the distance across the flats on a standard bolt head is measured in inches, while the same dimension on a metric bolt is sized in millimeters (the same is true for nuts). As a result, a standard wrench should not be used on a metric bolt and a metric wrench should not be used on a standard bolt. Also, most standard bolts have slashes radiating out from the center of the head to denote the grade or strength of the bolt, which is an indication of the amount of torque that can be applied to it. The greater the number of slashes, the greater the strength of the bolt. Grades 0 through 5 are commonly used on automobiles. Metric bolts have a property class (grade) number, rather than a slash, molded into their heads to indicate bolt strength. In this case, the higher the number, the stronger the bolt. Property class numbers 8.8, 9.8 and 10.9 are commonly used on automobiles.

Strength markings can also be used to distinguish standard hex nuts from metric hex nuts. Many standard nuts have dots stamped into one side, while metric nuts are marked with a number. The greater the number of dots, or the higher the number, the greater the strength of the nut.

Metric studs are also marked on their ends according to property class (grade). Larger studs are numbered (the same as metric bolts), while smaller studs carry a geometric code to denote grade.

It should be noted that many fasteners, especially Grades 0 through 2, have no distinguishing marks on them. When such is the case, the only way to determine whether it is standard or metric is to measure the thread pitch or compare it to a known fastener of the same size.

Standard fasteners are often referred to as SAE, as opposed to metric. However, it should be noted that SAE technically refers to a non-metric fine thread fastener only. Coarse thread non-metric fasteners are referred to as USS sizes.

Since fasteners of the same size (both standard and metric) may have different strength ratings, be sure to reinstall any bolts, studs or nuts removed from your vehicle in their original locations. Also, when replacing a fastener with a new one, make sure that the new one has a strength rating equal to or greater than the original.

Tightening sequences and procedures

Most threaded fasteners should be tightened to a specific torque value (torque is the twisting force applied to a threaded component such as a nut or bolt). Overtightening the fastener can weaken it and cause it to break, while undertightening can cause it to eventually come loose. Bolts, screws and studs, depending on the material they are made of and their thread diameters, have specific torque values, many of which are noted in the Specifications at the end of each Chapter. Be sure to follow the torque recommendations closely. For fasteners not assigned a specific torque, a general torque value chart is presented here as a guide. These torque values are for dry (unlubricated) fasteners threaded into steel or cast iron (not aluminum). As was previously mentioned, the size and grade of a fastener determine the amount of torque that can safely be applied to it. The figures listed here are approximate for Grade 2 and Grade 3 fasteners. Higher grades can tolerate higher torque values.

Fasteners laid out in a pattern, such as cylinder head bolts, oil pan bolts, differential cover bolts, etc., must be loosened or tightened in sequence to avoid warping the component. This sequence will normally be shown in the appropriate Chapter. If a specific pattern is not given, the following procedures can be used to prevent warping.

Initially, the bolts or nuts should be assembled finger-tight only. Next, they should be tightened one full turn each, in a criss-cross or diagonal pattern. After each one has been tightened one full turn, return to the first one and tighten them all one-half turn, following the same

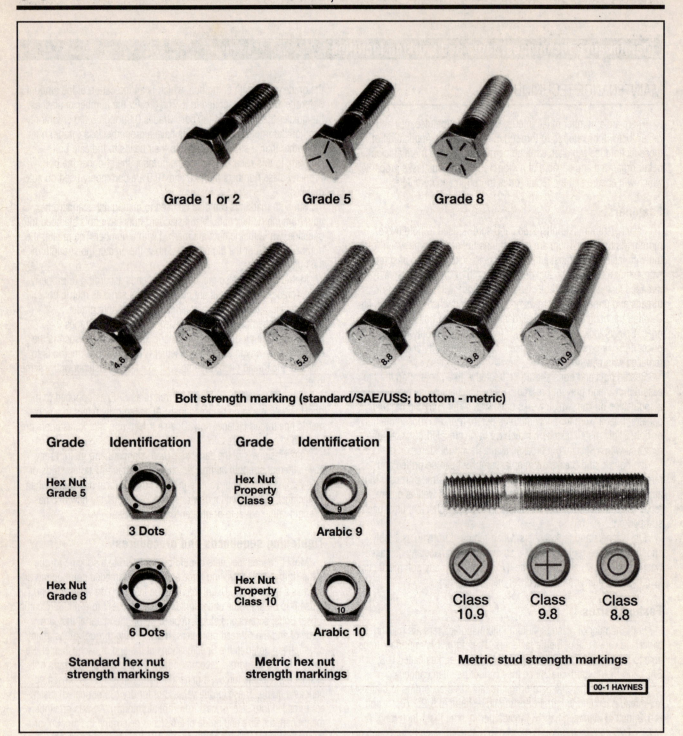

Grade 1 or 2   Grade 5   Grade 8

Bolt strength marking (standard/SAE/USS; bottom - metric)

Grade	Identification
Hex Nut Grade 5	3 Dots
Hex Nut Grade 8	6 Dots

Standard hex nut strength markings

Grade	Identification
Hex Nut Property Class 9	Arabic 9
Hex Nut Property Class 10	Arabic 10

Metric hex nut strength markings

Class 10.9   Class 9.8   Class 8.8

Metric stud strength markings

00-1 HAYNES

pattern. Finally, tighten each of them one-quarter turn at a time until each fastener has been tightened to the proper torque. To loosen and remove the fasteners, the procedure would be reversed.

Component disassembly

Component disassembly should be done with care and purpose to help ensure that the parts go back together properly. Always keep track of the sequence in which parts are removed. Make note of special characteristics or marks on parts that can be installed more than one way, such as a grooved thrust washer on a shaft. It is a good idea to lay the

disassembled parts out on a clean surface in the order that they were removed. It may also be helpful to make sketches or take instant photos of components before removal.

When removing fasteners from a component, keep track of their locations. Sometimes threading a bolt back in a part, or putting the washers and nut back on a stud, can prevent mix-ups later. If nuts and bolts cannot be returned to their original locations, they should be kept in a compartmented box or a series of small boxes. A cupcake or muffin tin is ideal for this purpose, since each cavity can hold the bolts and nuts from a particular area (i.e. oil pan bolts, valve cover bolts, engine

Metric thread sizes

	Ft-lbs	Nm
M-6	6 to 9	9 to 12
M-8	14 to 21	19 to 28
M-10	28 to 40	38 to 54
M-12	50 to 71	68 to 96
M-14	80 to 140	109 to 154

Pipe thread sizes

	Ft-lbs	Nm
1/8	5 to 8	7 to 10
1/4	12 to 18	17 to 24
3/8	22 to 33	30 to 44
1/2	25 to 35	34 to 47

U.S. thread sizes

	Ft-lbs	Nm
1/4 - 20	6 to 9	9 to 12
5/16 - 18	12 to 18	17 to 24
5/16 - 24	14 to 20	19 to 27
3/8 - 16	22 to 32	30 to 43
3/8 - 24	27 to 38	37 to 51
7/16 - 14	40 to 55	55 to 74
7/16 - 20	40 to 60	55 to 81
1/2 - 13	55 to 80	75 to 108

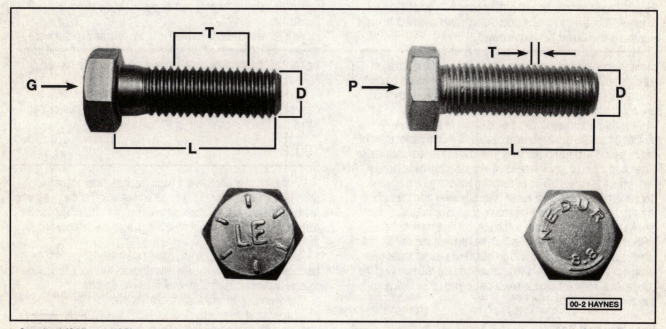

Standard (SAE and USS) bolt dimensions/grade marks

G Grade marks (bolt strength)
L Length (in inches)
T Thread pitch (number of threads per inch)
D Nominal diameter (in inches)

Metric bolt dimensions/grade marks

P Property class (bolt strength)
L Length (in millimeters)
T Thread pitch (distance between threads in millimeters)
D Diameter

mount bolts, etc.). A pan of this type is especially helpful when working on assemblies with very small parts, such as the carburetor, alternator, valve train or interior dash and trim pieces. The cavities can be marked with paint or tape to identify the contents.

Whenever wiring looms, harnesses or connectors are separated, it is a good idea to identify the two halves with numbered pieces of masking tape so they can be easily reconnected.

Gasket sealing surfaces

Throughout any vehicle, gaskets are used to seal the mating surfaces between two parts and keep lubricants, fluids, vacuum or pressure contained in an assembly.

Many times these gaskets are coated with a liquid or paste-type gasket sealing compound before assembly. Age, heat and pressure can sometimes cause the two parts to stick together so tightly that they are

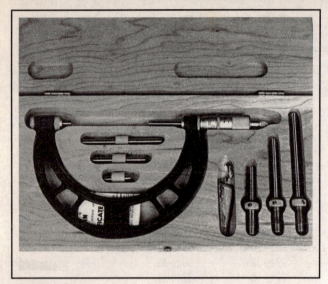

Micrometer set

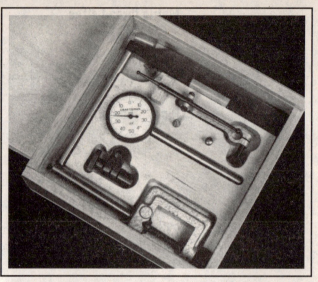

Dial indicator set

very difficult to separate. Often, the assembly can be loosened by striking it with a soft-face hammer near the mating surfaces. A regular hammer can be used if a block of wood is placed between the hammer and the part. Do not hammer on cast parts or parts that could be easily damaged. With any particularly stubborn part, always recheck to make sure that every fastener has been removed.

Avoid using a screwdriver or bar to pry apart an assembly, as they can easily mar the gasket sealing surfaces of the parts, which must remain smooth. If prying is absolutely necessary, use an old broom handle, but keep in mind that extra clean up will be necessary if the wood splinters.

After the parts are separated, the old gasket must be carefully scraped off and the gasket surfaces cleaned. Stubborn gasket material can be soaked with rust penetrant or treated with a special chemical to soften it so it can be easily scraped off. A scraper can be fashioned from a piece of copper tubing by flattening and sharpening one end. Copper is recommended because it is usually softer than the surfaces to be scraped, which reduces the chance of gouging the part. Some gaskets can be removed with a wire brush, but regardless of the method used, the mating surfaces must be left clean and smooth. If for some reason the gasket surface is gouged, then a gasket sealer thick enough to fill scratches will have to be used during reassembly of the components. For most applications, a non-drying (or semi-drying) gasket sealer should be used.

Hose removal tips

✳✳ WARNING:

If the vehicle is equipped with air conditioning, do not disconnect any of the A/C hoses without first having the system depressurized by a dealer service department or a service station.

Hose removal precautions closely parallel gasket removal precautions. Avoid scratching or gouging the surface that the hose mates against or the connection may leak. This is especially true for radiator hoses. Because of various chemical reactions, the rubber in hoses can bond itself to the metal spigot that the hose fits over. To remove a hose, first loosen the hose clamps that secure it to the spigot. Then, with slip-joint pliers, grab the hose at the clamp and rotate it around the

spigot. Work it back and forth until it is completely free, then pull it off. Silicone or other lubricants will ease removal if they can be applied between the hose and the outside of the spigot. Apply the same lubricant to the inside of the hose and the outside of the spigot to simplify installation.

As a last resort (and if the hose is to be replaced with a new one anyway), the rubber can be slit with a knife and the hose peeled from the spigot. If this must be done, be careful that the metal connection is not damaged.

If a hose clamp is broken or damaged, do not reuse it. Wire-type clamps usually weaken with age, so it is a good idea to replace them with screw-type clamps whenever a hose is removed.

TOOLS

A selection of good tools is a basic requirement for anyone who plans to maintain and repair his or her own vehicle. For the owner who has few tools, the initial investment might seem high, but when compared to the spiraling costs of professional auto maintenance and repair, it is a wise one.

To help the owner decide which tools are needed to perform the tasks detailed in this manual, the following tool lists are offered: *Maintenance and minor repair, Repair/overhaul and Special*.

The newcomer to practical mechanics should start off with the *maintenance and minor repair* tool kit, which is adequate for the simpler jobs performed on a vehicle. Then, as confidence and experience grow, the owner can tackle more difficult tasks, buying additional tools as they are needed. Eventually the basic kit will be expanded into the repair and overhaul tool set. Over a period of time, the experienced do-it-yourselfer will assemble a tool set complete enough for most repair and overhaul procedures and will add tools from the special category when it is felt that the expense is justified by the frequency of use.

Maintenance and minor repair tool kit

The tools in this list should be considered the minimum required for performance of routine maintenance, servicing and minor repair work. We recommend the purchase of combination wrenches (box-end and open-end combined in one wrench). While more expensive than open end wrenches, they offer the advantages of both types of wrench.

Combination wrench set (1/4-inch to 1 inch or 6 mm to 19 mm)

Adjustable wrench, 8 inch
Spark plug wrench with rubber insert
Spark plug gap adjusting tool
Feeler gauge set
Brake bleeder wrench
Standard screwdriver (5/16-inch x 6 inch)
Phillips screwdriver (No. 2 x 6 inch)
Combination pliers - 6 inch

Hacksaw and assortment of blades
Tire pressure gauge
Grease gun
Oil can
Fine emery cloth
Wire brush
Battery post and cable cleaning tool
Oil filter wrench

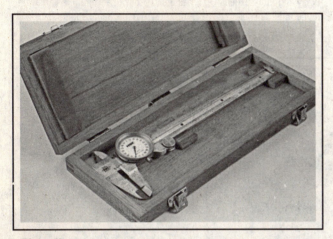

Dial caliper

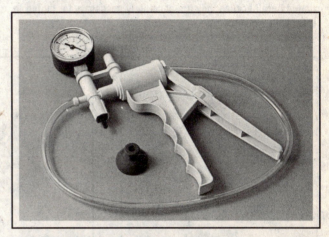

Hand-operated vacuum pump

Timing light

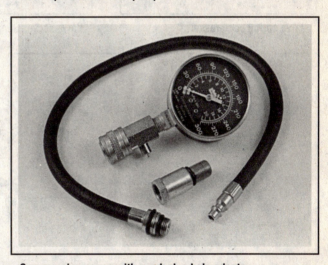

Compression gauge with spark plug hole adapter

Damper/steering wheel puller

General purpose puller

Hydraulic lifter removal tool

Funnel (medium size)
Safety goggles
Jackstands (2)
Drain pan

➡**Note: If basic tune-ups are going to be part of routine maintenance, it will be necessary to purchase a good quality stroboscopic timing light and combination tachometer/dwell meter. Although they are included in the list of special tools, it is mentioned here because they are absolutely necessary for tuning most vehicles properly.**

Repair and overhaul tool set

These tools are essential for anyone who plans to perform major repairs and are in addition to those in the maintenance and minor repair tool kit. Included is a comprehensive set of sockets which, though expensive, are invaluable because of their versatility, especially when various extensions and drives are available. We recommend the 1/2-inch drive over the 3/8-inch drive. Although the larger drive is bulky and more expensive, it has the capacity of accepting a very wide range of large sockets. Ideally, however, the mechanic should have a 3/8-inch drive set and a 1/2-inch drive set.

Valve spring compressor

Valve spring compressor

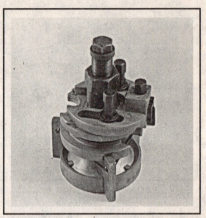

Ridge reamer

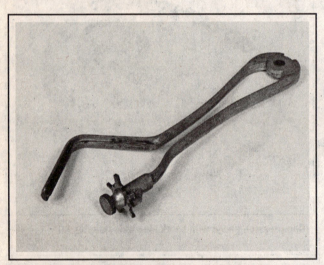

Piston ring groove cleaning tool

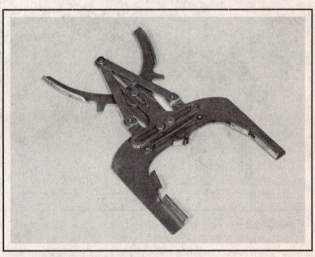

Ring removal/installation tool

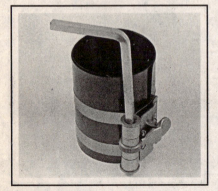

Ring compressor

Cylinder hone

Brake hold-down spring tool

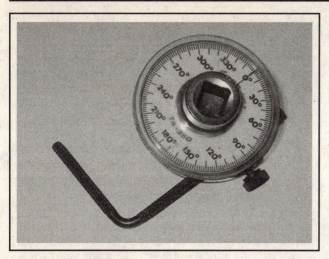

Torque angle gauge

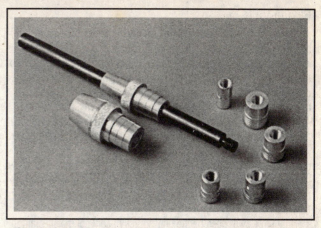

Clutch plate alignment tool

Socket set(s)
Reversible ratchet
Extension - 10 inch
Universal joint
Torque wrench (same size drive as sockets)
Ball peen hammer - 8 ounce
Soft-face hammer (plastic/rubber)
Standard screwdriver (1/4-inch x 6 inch)
Standard screwdriver (stubby - 5/16-inch)
Phillips screwdriver (No. 3 x 8 inch)
Phillips screwdriver (stubby - No. 2)
Pliers - vise grip
Pliers - lineman's
Pliers - needle nose
Pliers - snap-ring (internal and external)
Cold chisel - 1/2-inch
Scribe
Scraper (made from flattened copper tubing)
Centerpunch
Pin punches (1/16, 1/8, 3/16-inch)
Steel rule/straightedge - 12 inch
Allen wrench set (1/8 to 3/8-inch or 4 mm to 10 mm)
A selection of files
Wire brush (large)
Jackstands (second set)
Jack (scissor or hydraulic type)

➡**Note: Another tool which is often useful is an electric drill with a chuck capacity of 3/8-inch and a set of good quality drill bits.**

Special tools

The tools in this list include those which are not used regularly, are expensive to buy, or which need to be used in accordance with their manufacturer's instructions. Unless these tools will be used frequently, it is not very economical to purchase many of them. A consideration would be to split the cost and use between yourself and a friend or friends. In addition, most of these tools can be obtained from a tool rental shop on a temporary basis.

This list primarily contains only those tools and instruments widely available to the public, and not those special tools produced by the vehicle manufacturer for distribution to dealer service departments. Occasionally, references to the manufacturer's special tools are included in the text of this manual. Generally, an alternative method of doing the job without the special tool is offered. However, sometimes there is no alternative to their use. Where this is the case, and the tool cannot be purchased or borrowed, the work should be turned over to the dealer service department or an automotive repair shop.

Valve spring compressor
Piston ring groove cleaning tool
Piston ring compressor
Piston ring installation tool
Cylinder compression gauge
Cylinder ridge reamer
Cylinder surfacing hone
Cylinder bore gauge
Micrometers and/or dial calipers
Hydraulic lifter removal tool
Balljoint separator
Universal-type puller
Impact screwdriver
Dial indicator set
Stroboscopic timing light (inductive pick-up)
Hand operated vacuum/pressure pump
Tachometer/dwell meter
Universal electrical multimeter
Cable hoist
Brake spring removal and installation tools
Floor jack

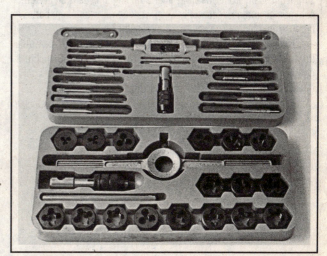

Tap and die set

Buying tools

For the do-it-yourselfer who is just starting to get involved in vehicle maintenance and repair, there are a number of options available when purchasing tools. If maintenance and minor repair is the extent of the work to be done, the purchase of individual tools is satisfactory. If, on the other hand, extensive work is planned, it would be a good idea to purchase a modest tool set from one of the large retail chain stores. A set can usually be bought at a substantial savings over the individual tool prices, and they often come with a tool box. As additional tools are needed, add-on sets, individual tools and a larger tool box can be purchased to expand the tool selection. Building a tool set gradually allows the cost of the tools to be spread over a longer period of time and gives the mechanic the freedom to choose only those tools that will actually be used.

Tool stores will often be the only source of some of the special tools that are needed, but regardless of where tools are bought, try to avoid cheap ones, especially when buying screwdrivers and sockets, because they won't last very long. The expense involved in replacing cheap tools will eventually be greater than the initial cost of quality tools.

Care and maintenance of tools

Good tools are expensive, so it makes sense to treat them with respect. Keep them clean and in usable condition and store them properly when not in use. Always wipe off any dirt, grease or metal chips before putting them away. Never leave tools lying around in the work area. Upon completion of a job, always check closely under the hood for tools that may have been left there so they won't get lost during a test drive.

Some tools, such as screwdrivers, pliers, wrenches and sockets, can be hung on a panel mounted on the garage or workshop wall, while others should be kept in a tool box or tray. Measuring instruments, gauges, meters, etc. must be carefully stored where they cannot be damaged by weather or impact from other tools.

When tools are used with care and stored properly, they will last a very long time. Even with the best of care, though, tools will wear out if used frequently. When a tool is damaged or worn out, replace it. Subsequent jobs will be safer and more enjoyable if you do.

HOW TO REPAIR DAMAGED THREADS

Sometimes, the internal threads of a nut or bolt hole can become stripped, usually from overtightening. Stripping threads is an all-too-common occurrence, especially when working with aluminum parts, because aluminum is so soft that it easily strips out.

Usually, external or internal threads are only partially stripped. After they've been cleaned up with a tap or die, they'll still work. Sometimes, however, threads are badly damaged. When this happens, you've got three choices:

1) *Drill and tap the hole to the next suitable oversize and install a larger diameter bolt, screw or stud.*

2) *Drill and tap the hole to accept a threaded plug, then drill and tap the plug to the original screw size. You can also buy a plug already threaded to the original size. Then you simply drill a hole to the specified size, then run the threaded plug into the hole with a bolt and jam nut. Once the plug is fully seated, remove the jam nut and bolt.*

3) *The third method uses a patented thread repair kit like Heli-Coil or Slimsert. These easy-to-use kits are designed to repair damaged threads in straight-through holes and blind holes. Both are available as kits which can handle a variety of sizes and thread patterns. Drill the hole, then tap it with the special included tap. Install the Heli-Coil and the hole is back to its original diameter and thread pitch.*

Regardless of which method you use, be sure to proceed calmly and carefully. A little impatience or carelessness during one of these relatively simple procedures can ruin your whole day's work and cost you a bundle if you wreck an expensive part.

WORKING FACILITIES

Not to be overlooked when discussing tools is the workshop. If anything more than routine maintenance is to be carried out, some sort of suitable work area is essential.

It is understood, and appreciated, that many home mechanics do not have a good workshop or garage available, and end up removing an engine or doing major repairs outside. It is recommended, however, that the overhaul or repair be completed under the cover of a roof.

A clean, flat workbench or table of comfortable working height is an absolute necessity. The workbench should be equipped with a vise that has a jaw opening of at least four inches.

As mentioned previously, some clean, dry storage space is also required for tools, as well as the lubricants, fluids, cleaning solvents, etc. which soon become necessary.

Sometimes waste oil and fluids, drained from the engine or cooling system during normal maintenance or repairs, present a disposal problem. To avoid pouring them on the ground or into a sewage system, pour the used fluids into large containers, seal them with caps and take them to an authorized disposal site or recycling center. Plastic jugs, such as old antifreeze containers, are ideal for this purpose.

Always keep a supply of old newspapers and clean rags available. Old towels are excellent for mopping up spills. Many mechanics use rolls of paper towels for most work because they are readily available and disposable. To help keep the area under the vehicle clean, a large cardboard box can be cut open and flattened to protect the garage or shop floor.

Whenever working over a painted surface, such as when leaning over a fender to service something under the hood, always cover it with an old blanket or bedspread to protect the finish. Vinyl covered pads, made especially for this purpose, are available at auto parts stores.

Jacking and towing

JACKING

WARNING:

The jack supplied with the vehicle should only be used for changing a tire or placing jackstands under the frame. Never work under the vehicle or start the engine while this jack is being used as the only means of support.

The vehicle should be on level ground. Place the shift lever in Park, if you have an automatic, or Reverse if you have a manual transaxle. Block the wheel diagonally opposite the wheel being changed. Set the parking brake.

Remove the spare tire and jack from stowage. Remove the wheel cover and trim ring (if so equipped) with the tapered end of the lug nut wrench by inserting and twisting the handle and then prying against the back of the wheel cover. Loosen, but do not remove, the lug nuts (one-half turn is sufficient).

Place the scissors-type jack under the vehicle and adjust the jack height until it engages with the proper jacking point. There is a front and rear jacking point on each side of the vehicle (see illustrations).

Turn the jack handle clockwise until the tire clears the ground. Remove the lug nuts and pull the wheel off. Replace it with the spare.

Install the lug nuts with the beveled edges facing in. Tighten them snugly. Don't attempt to tighten them completely until the vehicle is lowered or it could slip off the jack. Turn the jack handle counterclockwise to lower the vehicle. Remove the jack and tighten the lug nuts in a diagonal pattern.

Install the cover (and trim ring, if used) and be sure it's snapped into place all the way around.

Stow the tire, jack and wrench. Unblock the wheels.

TOWING

Two-wheel drive models can be towed from the front with the front wheels off the ground, using a wheel lift type tow truck. If towed from the rear, the front wheels must be placed on a dolly. Four-wheel drive models must be towed with all four wheels off the ground. A sling-type tow truck cannot be used, as body damage will result. The best way to tow the vehicle is with a flat-bed car carrier.

In an emergency the vehicle can be towed a short distance with a cable or chain attached to one of the towing eyelets located under the front or rear bumpers. The driver must remain in the vehicle to operate the steering and brakes (remember that power steering and power brakes will not work with the engine off).

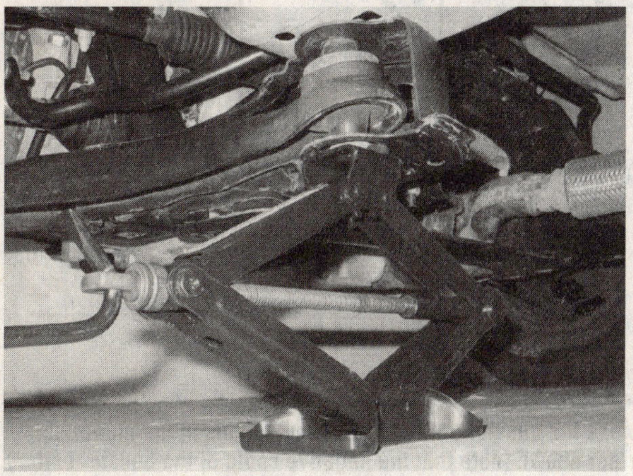

Front jacking location (place the jack head under the control arm rear mounting bolt)

Rear jacking location (place the jack head under the protrusion on the trailing arm)

Booster battery (jump) starting

Observe these precautions when using a booster battery to start a vehicle:

a) *Before connecting the booster battery, make sure the ignition switch is in the Off position.*

b) *Turn off the lights, heater and other electrical loads.*

c) *Your eyes should be shielded. Safety goggles are a good idea.*

d) *Make sure the booster battery is the same voltage as the dead one in the vehicle.*

e) *The two vehicles MUST NOT TOUCH each other!*

f) *Make sure the transaxle is in Neutral (manual) or Park (automatic).*

g) *If the booster battery is not a maintenance-free type, remove the vent caps and lay a cloth over the vent holes.*

Connect the red jumper cable to the positive (+) terminals of each battery (see illustration).

Connect one end of the black jumper cable to the negative (-) terminal of the booster battery. The other end of this cable should be connected to a good ground on the vehicle to be started, such as a bolt or bracket on the body.

Start the engine using the booster battery, then, with the engine running at idle speed, disconnect the jumper cables in the reverse order of connection.

➡**Note: On vehicles equipped with an automatic transaxle, if the battery has been run down or disconnected, the Powertrain Control Module (PCM) must relearn its idle and fuel mixture trim strategy for optimum drivability and performance (see Chapter 5, Section 1 for this procedure).**

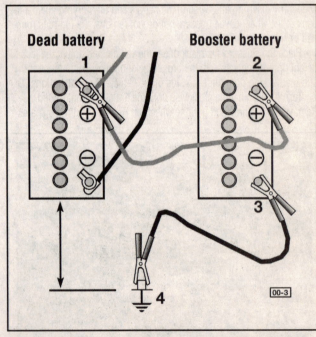

Make the booster battery cable connections in the numerical order shown (note that the negative cable of the booster battery is NOT attached to the negative terminal of the dead battery)

CONVERSION FACTORS

Length (distance)

Inches (in)	X	25.4	= Millimeters (mm)	X 0.0394	= Inches (in)
Feet (ft)	X	0.305	= Meters (m)	X 3.281	= Feet (ft)
Miles	X	1.609	= Kilometers (km)	X 0.621	= Miles

Volume (capacity)

Cubic inches (cu in; in³)	X	16.387	= Cubic centimeters (cc; cm³)	X 0.061	= Cubic inches (cu in; in³)
Imperial pints (Imp pt)	X	0.568	= Liters (l)	X 1.76	= Imperial pints (Imp pt)
Imperial quarts (Imp qt)	X	1.137	= Liters (l)	X 0.88	= Imperial quarts (Imp qt)
Imperial quarts (Imp qt)	X	1.201	= US quarts (US qt)	X 0.833	= Imperial quarts (Imp qt)
US quarts (US qt)	X	0.946	= Liters (l)	X 1.057	= US quarts (US qt)
Imperial gallons (Imp gal)	X	4.546	= Liters (l)	X 0.22	= Imperial gallons (Imp gal)
Imperial gallons (Imp gal)	X	1.201	= US gallons (US gal)	X 0.833	= Imperial gallons (Imp gal)
US gallons (US gal)	X	3.785	= Liters (l)	X 0.264	= US gallons (US gal)

Mass (weight)

Ounces (oz)	X	28.35	= Grams (g)	X 0.035	= Ounces (oz)
Pounds (lb)	X	0.454	= Kilograms (kg)	X 2.205	= Pounds (lb)

Force

Ounces-force (ozf; oz)	X	0.278	= Newtons (N)	X 3.6	= Ounces-force (ozf; oz)
Pounds-force (lbf; lb)	X	4.448	= Newtons (N)	X 0.225	= Pounds-force (lbf; lb)
Newtons (N)	X	0.1	= Kilograms-force (kgf; kg)	X 9.81	= Newtons (N)

Pressure

Pounds-force per square inch (psi; lbf/in²; lb/in²)	X	0.070	= Kilograms-force per square centimeter (kgf/cm²; kg/cm²)	X 14.223	= Pounds-force per square inch (psi; lbf/in²; lb/in²)
Pounds-force per square inch (psi; lbf/in²; lb/in²)	X	0.068	= Atmospheres (atm)	X 14.696	= Pounds-force per square inch (psi; lbf/in²; lb/in²)
Pounds-force per square inch (psi; lbf/in²; lb/in²)	X	0.069	= Bars	X 14.5	= Pounds-force per square inch (psi; lbf/in²; lb/in²)
Pounds-force per square inch (psi; lbf/in²; lb/in²)	X	6.895	= Kilopascals (kPa)	X 0.145	= Pounds-force per square inch (psi; lbf/in²; lb/in²)
Kilopascals (kPa)	X	0.01	= Kilograms-force per square centimeter (kgf/cm²; kg/cm²)	X 98.1	= Kilopascals (kPa)

Torque (moment of force)

Pounds-force inches (lbf in; lb in)	X	1.152	= Kilograms-force centimeter (kgf cm; kg cm)	X 0.868	= Pounds-force inches (lbf in; lb in)
Pounds-force inches (lbf in; lb in)	X	0.113	= Newton meters (Nm)	X 8.85	= Pounds-force inches (lbf in; lb in)
Pounds-force inches (lbf in; lb in)	X	0.083	= Pounds-force feet (lbf ft; lb ft)	X 12	= Pounds-force inches (lbf in; lb in)
Pounds-force feet (lbf ft; lb ft)	X	0.138	= Kilograms-force meters (kgf m; kg m)	X 7.233	= Pounds-force feet (lbf ft; lb ft)
Pounds-force feet (lbf ft; lb ft)	X	1.356	= Newton meters (Nm)	X 0.738	= Pounds-force feet (lbf ft; lb ft)
Newton meters (Nm)	X	0.102	= Kilograms-force meters (kgf m; kg m)	X 9.804	= Newton meters (Nm)

Vacuum

Inches mercury (in. Hg)	X	3.377	= Kilopascals (kPa)	X 0.2961	= Inches mercury
Inches mercury (in. Hg)	X	25.4	= Millimeters mercury (mm Hg)	X 0.0394	= Inches mercury

Power

Horsepower (hp)	X	745.7	= Watts (W)	X 0.0013	= Horsepower (hp)

Velocity (speed)

Miles per hour (miles/hr; mph)	X	1.609	= Kilometers per hour (km/hr; kph)	X 0.621	= Miles per hour (miles/hr; mph)

Fuel consumption*

Miles per gallon, Imperial (mpg)	X	0.354	= Kilometers per liter (km/l)	X 2.825	= Miles per gallon, Imperial (mpg)
Miles per gallon, US (mpg)	X	0.425	= Kilometers per liter (km/l)	X 2.352	= Miles per gallon, US (mpg)

Temperature

Degrees Fahrenheit = (°C x 1.8) + 32

Degrees Celsius (Degrees Centigrade; °C) = (°F - 32) x 0.56

*It is common practice to convert from miles per gallon (mpg) to liters/100 kilometers (l/100km), where mpg (Imperial) x l/100 km = 282 and mpg (US) x l/100 km = 235

FRACTION/DECIMAL/MILLIMETER EQUIVALENTS

DECIMALS TO MILLIMETERS

Decimal	mm	Decimal	mm
0.001	0.0254	0.500	12.7000
0.002	0.0508	0.510	12.9540
0.003	0.0762	0.520	13.2080
0.004	0.1016	0.530	13.4620
0.005	0.1270	0.540	13.7160
0.006	0.1524	0.550	13.9700
0.007	0.1778	0.560	14.2240
0.008	0.2032	0.570	14.4780
0.009	0.2286	0.580	14.7320
		0.590	14.9860
0.010	0.2540		
0.020	0.5080		
0.030	0.7620		
0.040	1.0160	0.600	15.2400
0.050	1.2700	0.610	15.4940
0.060	1.5240	0.620	15.7480
0.070	1.7780	0.630	16.0020
0.080	2.0320	0.640	16.2560
0.090	2.2860	0.650	16.5100
		0.660	16.7640
0.100	2.5400	0.670	17.0180
0.110	2.7940	0.680	17.2720
0.120	3.0480	0.690	17.5260
0.130	3.3020		
0.140	3.5560		
0.150	3.8100		
0.160	4.0640	0.700	17.7800
0.170	4.3180	0.710	18.0340
0.180	4.5720	0.720	18.2880
0.190	4.8260	0.730	18.5420
		0.740	18.7960
0.200	5.0800	0.750	19.0500
0.210	5.3340	0.760	19.3040
0.220	5.5880	0.770	19.5580
0.230	5.8420	0.780	19.8120
0.240	6.0960	0.790	20.0660
0.250	6.3500		
0.260	6.6040		
0.270	6.8580	0.800	20.3200
0.280	7.1120	0.810	20.5740
0.290	7.3660	0.820	21.8280
		0.830	21.0820
0.300	7.6200	0.840	21.3360
0.310	7.8740	0.850	21.5900
0.320	8.1280	0.860	21.8440
0.330	8.3820	0.870	22.0980
0.340	8.6360	0.880	22.3520
0.350	8.8900	0.890	22.6060
0.360	9.1440		
0.370	9.3980		
0.380	9.6520		
0.390	9.9060		
		0.900	22.8600
0.400	10.1600	0.910	23.1140
0.410	10.4140	0.920	23.3680
0.420	10.6680	0.930	23.6220
0.430	10.9220	0.940	23.8760
0.440	11.1760	0.950	24.1300
0.450	11.4300	0.960	24.3840
0.460	11.6840	0.970	24.6380
0.470	11.9380	0.980	24.8920
0.480	12.1920	0.990	25.1460
0.490	12.4460	1.000	25.4000

FRACTIONS TO DECIMALS TO MILLIMETERS

Fraction	Decimal	mm	Fraction	Decimal	mm
1/64	0.0156	0.3969	33/64	0.5156	13.0969
1/32	0.0312	0.7938	17/32	0.5312	13.4938
3/64	0.0469	1.1906	35/64	0.5469	13.8906
1/16	0.0625	1.5875	9/16	0.5625	14.2875
5/64	0.0781	1.9844	37/64	0.5781	14.6844
3/32	0.0938	2.3812	19/32	0.5938	15.0812
7/64	0.1094	2.7781	39/64	0.6094	15.4781
1/8	0.1250	3.1750	5/8	0.6250	15.8750
9/64	0.1406	3.5719	41/64	0.6406	16.2719
5/32	0.1562	3.9688	21/32	0.6562	16.6688
11/64	0.1719	4.3656	43/64	0.6719	17.0656
3/16	0.1875	4.7625	11/16	0.6875	17.4625
13/64	0.2031	5.1594	45/64	0.7031	17.8594
7/32	0.2188	5.5562	23/32	0.7188	18.2562
15/64	0.2344	5.9531	47/64	0.7344	18.6531
1/4	0.2500	6.3500	3/4	0.7500	19.0500
17/64	0.2656	6.7469	49/64	0.7656	19.4469
9/32	0.2812	7.1438	25/32	0.7812	19.8438
19/64	0.2969	7.5406	51/64	0.7969	20.2406
5/16	0.3125	7.9375	13/16	0.8125	20.6375
21/64	0.3281	8.3344	53/64	0.8281	21.0344
11/32	0.3438	8.7312	27/32	0.8438	21.4312
23/64	0.3594	9.1281	55/64	0.8594	21.8281
3/8	0.3750	9.5250	7/8	0.8750	22.2250
25/64	0.3906	9.9219	57/64	0.8906	22.6219
13/32	0.4062	10.3188	29/32	0.9062	23.0188
27/64	0.4219	10.7156	59/64	0.9219	23.4156
7/16	0.4375	11.1125	15/16	0.9375	23.8125
29/64	0.4531	11.5094	61/64	0.9531	24.2094
15/32	0.4688	11.9062	31/32	0.9688	24.6062
31/64	0.4844	12.3031	63/64	0.9844	25.0031
1/2	0.5000	12.7000	1	1.0000	25.4000

Automotive chemicals and lubricants

A number of automotive chemicals and lubricants are available for use during vehicle maintenance and repair. They include a wide variety of products ranging from cleaning solvents and degreasers to lubricants and protective sprays for rubber, plastic and vinyl.

CLEANERS

Carburetor cleaner and choke cleaner is a strong solvent for gum, varnish and carbon. Most carburetor cleaners leave a dry-type lubricant film which will not harden or gum up. Because of this film it is not recommended for use on electrical components.

Brake system cleaner is used to remove brake dust, grease and brake fluid from the brake system, where clean surfaces are absolutely necessary. It leaves no residue and often eliminates brake squeal caused by contaminants.

Electrical cleaner removes oxidation, corrosion and carbon deposits from electrical contacts, restoring full current flow. It can also be used to clean spark plugs, carburetor jets, voltage regulators and other parts where an oil-free surface is desired.

Demoisturants remove water and moisture from electrical components such as alternators, voltage regulators, electrical connectors and fuse blocks. They are non-conductive and non-corrosive.

Degreasers are heavy-duty solvents used to remove grease from the outside of the engine and from chassis components. They can be sprayed or brushed on and, depending on the type, are rinsed off either with water or solvent.

LUBRICANTS

Motor oil is the lubricant formulated for use in engines. It normally contains a wide variety of additives to prevent corrosion and reduce foaming and wear. Motor oil comes in various weights (viscosity ratings) from 0 to 50. The recommended weight of the oil depends on the season, temperature and the demands on the engine. Light oil is used in cold climates and under light load conditions. Heavy oil is used in hot climates and where high loads are encountered. Multi-viscosity oils are designed to have characteristics of both light and heavy oils and are available in a number of weights from 0W-20 to 20W-50.

Gear oil is designed to be used in differentials, manual transmissions and other areas where high-temperature lubrication is required.

Chassis and wheel bearing grease is a heavy grease used where increased loads and friction are encountered, such as for wheel bearings, ball-joints, tie-rod ends and universal joints.

High-temperature wheel bearing grease is designed to withstand the extreme temperatures encountered by wheel bearings in disc brake equipped vehicles. It usually contains molybdenum disulfide (moly), which is a dry-type lubricant.

White grease is a heavy grease for metal-to-metal applications where water is a problem. White grease stays soft under both low and high temperatures (usually from -100 to +190-degrees F), and will not wash off or dilute in the presence of water.

Assembly lube is a special extreme pressure lubricant, usually containing moly, used to lubricate high-load parts (such as main and rod bearings and cam lobes) for initial start-up of a new engine. The assembly lube lubricates the parts without being squeezed out or washed away until the engine oiling system begins to function.

Silicone lubricants are used to protect rubber, plastic, vinyl and nylon parts.

Graphite lubricants are used where oils cannot be used due to contamination problems, such as in locks. The dry graphite will lubricate metal parts while remaining uncontaminated by dirt, water, oil or acids. It is electrically conductive and will not foul electrical contacts in locks such as the ignition switch.

Moly penetrants loosen and lubricate frozen, rusted and corroded fasteners and prevent future rusting or freezing.

Heat-sink grease is a special electrically non-conductive grease that is used for mounting electronic ignition modules where it is essential that heat is transferred away from the module.

SEALANTS

RTV sealant is one of the most widely used gasket compounds. Made from silicone, RTV is air curing, it seals, bonds, waterproofs, fills surface irregularities, remains flexible, doesn't shrink, is relatively easy to remove, and is used as a supplementary sealer with almost all low and medium temperature gaskets.

Anaerobic sealant is much like RTV in that it can be used either to seal gaskets or to form gaskets by itself. It remains flexible, is solvent resistant and fills surface imperfections. The difference between an anaerobic sealant and an RTV-type sealant is in the curing. RTV cures when exposed to air, while an anaerobic sealant cures only in the absence of air. This means that an anaerobic sealant cures only after the assembly of parts, sealing them together.

Thread and pipe sealant is used for sealing hydraulic and pneumatic fittings and vacuum lines. It is usually made from a Teflon compound, and comes in a spray, a paint-on liquid and as a wrap-around tape.

CHEMICALS

Anti-seize compound prevents seizing, galling, cold welding, rust and corrosion in fasteners. High-temperature anti-seize, usually made with copper and graphite lubricants, is used for exhaust system and exhaust manifold bolts.

Anaerobic locking compounds are used to keep fasteners from vibrating or working loose and cure only after installation, in the absence of air. Medium strength locking compound is used for small nuts, bolts and screws that may be removed later. High-strength locking compound is for large nuts, bolts and studs which aren't removed on a regular basis.

Oil additives range from viscosity index improvers to chemical treatments that claim to reduce internal engine friction. It should be noted that most oil manufacturers caution against using additives with their oils.

Gas additives perform several functions, depending on their chemical makeup. They usually contain solvents that help dissolve gum and varnish that build up on carburetor, fuel injection and intake parts. They also serve to break down carbon deposits that form on the inside surfaces of the combustion chambers. Some additives contain upper cylinder lubricants for valves and piston rings, and others contain chemicals to remove condensation from the gas tank.

MISCELLANEOUS

Brake fluid is specially formulated hydraulic fluid that can withstand the heat and pressure encountered in brake systems. Care must be taken so this fluid does not come in contact with painted surfaces or plastics. An opened container should always be resealed to prevent contamination by water or dirt.

Weatherstrip adhesive is used to bond weatherstripping around doors, windows and trunk lids. It is sometimes used to attach trim pieces.

Undercoating is a petroleum-based, tar-like substance that is designed to protect metal surfaces on the underside of the vehicle from corrosion. It also acts as a sound-deadening agent by insulating the bottom of the vehicle.

Waxes and polishes are used to help protect painted and plated surfaces from the weather. Different types of paint may require the use of different types of wax and polish. Some polishes utilize a chemical or abrasive cleaner to help remove the top layer of oxidized (dull) paint on older vehicles. In recent years many non-wax polishes that contain a wide variety of chemicals such as polymers and silicones have been introduced. These non-wax polishes are usually easier to apply and last longer than conventional waxes and polishes.

Safety first!

Regardless of how enthusiastic you may be about getting on with the job at hand, take the time to ensure that your safety is not jeopardized. A moment's lack of attention can result in an accident, as can failure to observe certain simple safety precautions. The possibility of an accident will always exist, and the following points should not be considered a comprehensive list of all dangers. Rather, they are intended to make you aware of the risks and to encourage a safety conscious approach to all work you carry out on your vehicle.

ESSENTIAL DOS AND DON'TS

DON'T rely on a jack when working under the vehicle. Always use approved jackstands to support the weight of the vehicle and place them under the recommended lift or support points.

DON'T attempt to loosen extremely tight fasteners (i.e. wheel lug nuts) while the vehicle is on a jack - it may fall.

DON'T start the engine without first making sure that the transmission is in Neutral (or Park where applicable) and the parking brake is set.

DON'T remove the radiator cap from a hot cooling system - let it cool or cover it with a cloth and release the pressure gradually.

DON'T attempt to drain the engine oil until you are sure it has cooled to the point that it will not burn you.

DON'T touch any part of the engine or exhaust system until it has cooled sufficiently to avoid burns.

DON'T siphon toxic liquids such as gasoline, antifreeze and brake fluid by mouth, or allow them to remain on your skin.

DON'T inhale brake lining dust - it is potentially hazardous (see Asbestos below).

DON'T allow spilled oil or grease to remain on the floor - wipe it up before someone slips on it.

DON'T use loose fitting wrenches or other tools which may slip and cause injury.

DON'T push on wrenches when loosening or tightening nuts or bolts. Always try to pull the wrench toward you. If the situation calls for pushing the wrench away, push with an open hand to avoid scraped knuckles if the wrench should slip.

DON'T attempt to lift a heavy component alone - get someone to help you.

DON'T rush or take unsafe shortcuts to finish a job.

DON'T allow children or animals in or around the vehicle while you are working on it.

DO wear eye protection when using power tools such as a drill, sander, bench grinder, etc. and when working under a vehicle.

DO keep loose clothing and long hair well out of the way of moving parts.

DO make sure that any hoist used has a safe working load rating adequate for the job.

DO get someone to check on you periodically when working alone on a vehicle.

DO carry out work in a logical sequence and make sure that everything is correctly assembled and tightened.

DO keep chemicals and fluids tightly capped and out of the reach of children and pets.

DO remember that your vehicle's safety affects that of yourself and others. If in doubt on any point, get professional advice.

STEERING, SUSPENSION AND BRAKES

These systems are essential to driving safety, so make sure you have a qualified shop or individual check your work. Also, compressed suspension springs can cause injury if released suddenly - be sure to use a spring compressor.

AIRBAGS

Airbags are explosive devices that can CAUSE injury if they deploy while you're working on the vehicle. Follow the manufacturer's instructions to disable the airbag whenever you're working in the vicinity of airbag components.

ASBESTOS

Certain friction, insulating, sealing, and other products - such as brake linings, brake bands, clutch linings, torque converters, gaskets, etc. - may contain asbestos or other hazardous friction material. Extreme care must be taken to avoid inhalation of dust from such products, since it is hazardous to health. If in doubt, assume that they do contain asbestos.

FIRE

Remember at all times that gasoline is highly flammable. Never smoke or have any kind of open flame around when working on a vehicle. But the risk does not end there. A spark caused by an electrical short circuit, by two metal surfaces contacting each other, or even by static electricity built up in your body under certain conditions, can ignite gasoline vapors, which in a confined space are highly explosive. Do not, under any circumstances, use gasoline for cleaning parts. Use an approved safety solvent.

Always disconnect the battery ground (-) cable at the battery before working on any part of the fuel system or electrical system. Never risk spilling fuel on a hot engine or exhaust component. It is strongly recommended that a fire extinguisher suitable for use on fuel and electrical fires be kept handy in the garage or workshop at all times. Never try to extinguish a fuel or electrical fire with water.

FUMES

Certain fumes are highly toxic and can quickly cause unconsciousness and even death if inhaled to any extent. Gasoline vapor falls into this category, as do the vapors from some cleaning solvents. Any draining or pouring of such volatile fluids should be done in a well ventilated area.

When using cleaning fluids and solvents, read the instructions on the container carefully. Never use materials from unmarked containers.

Never run the engine in an enclosed space, such as a garage. Exhaust fumes contain carbon monoxide, which is extremely poisonous. If you need to run the engine, always do so in the open air, or at least have the rear of the vehicle outside the work area.

THE BATTERY

Never create a spark or allow a bare light bulb near a battery. They normally give off a certain amount of hydrogen gas, which is highly explosive.

Always disconnect the battery ground (-) cable at the battery before working on the fuel or electrical systems.

If possible, loosen the filler caps or cover when charging the battery from an external source (this does not apply to sealed or maintenance-free batteries). Do not charge at an excessive rate or the battery may burst.

Take care when adding water to a non maintenance-free battery and when carrying a battery. The electrolyte, even when diluted, is very corrosive and should not be allowed to contact clothing or skin.

Always wear eye protection when cleaning the battery to prevent the caustic deposits from entering your eyes.

HOUSEHOLD CURRENT

When using an electric power tool, inspection light, etc., which operates on household current, always make sure that the tool is correctly connected to its plug and that, where necessary, it is properly grounded. Do not use such items in damp conditions and, again, do not create a spark or apply excessive heat in the vicinity of fuel or fuel vapor.

SECONDARY IGNITION SYSTEM VOLTAGE

A severe electric shock can result from touching certain parts of the ignition system (such as the spark plug wires) when the engine is running or being cranked, particularly if components are damp or the insulation is defective. In the case of an electronic ignition system, the secondary system voltage is much higher and could prove fatal.

HYDROFLUORIC ACID

This extremely corrosive acid is formed when certain types of synthetic rubber, found in some O-rings, oil seals, fuel hoses, etc. are exposed to temperatures above 750-degrees F (400-degrees C). The rubber changes into a charred or sticky substance containing the acid. *Once formed, the acid remains dangerous for years. If it gets onto the skin, it may be necessary to amputate the limb concerned.*

When dealing with a vehicle which has suffered a fire, or with components salvaged from such a vehicle, wear protective gloves and discard them after use.

Troubleshooting

CONTENTS

This section provides an easy reference guide to the more common problems which may occur during the operation of your vehicle. These problems and their possible causes are grouped under headings denoting various components or systems, such as Engine, Cooling system, etc. They also refer you to the chapter and/or section which deals with the problem.

Remember that successful troubleshooting is not a mysterious black art practiced only by professional mechanics. It is simply the result of the right knowledge combined with an intelligent, systematic approach to the problem. Always work by a process of elimination, starting with the simplest solution and working through to the most complex - and never overlook the obvious. Anyone can run the gas tank dry or leave the lights on overnight, so don't assume that you are exempt from such oversights.

Finally, always establish a clear idea of why a problem has occurred and take steps to ensure that it doesn't happen again. If the electrical system fails because of a poor connection, check the other connections in the system to make sure that they don't fail as well. If a particular fuse continues to blow, find out why - don't just replace one fuse after another. Remember, failure of a small component can often be indicative of potential failure or incorrect functioning of a more important component or system.

ENGINE

1 Engine will not rotate when attempting to start

1 Battery terminal connections loose or corroded (Chapter 1).
2 Battery discharged or faulty (Chapters 1 and 5).
3 Automatic transaxle not completely engaged in Park (Chapter 7) or clutch pedal not completely depressed (Chapter 6).
4 Broken, loose or disconnected wiring in the starting circuit (Chapters 5 and 12).
5 Starter motor pinion jammed in flywheel ring gear (Chapter 5).
6 Starter solenoid faulty (Chapter 5).
7 Starter motor faulty (Chapter 5).
8 Ignition switch faulty (Chapter 12).
9 Starter pinion or flywheel teeth worn or broken (Chapter 5).

2 Engine rotates but will not start

1 Fuel tank empty.
2 Battery discharged (engine rotates slowly) (Chapter 5).
3 Battery terminal connections loose or corroded (Chapter 1).
4 Leaking fuel injector(s), faulty fuel pump, pressure regulator, etc. (Chapter 4).
5 Broken or stripped timing belt (Chapter 2A) or broken timing chain (Chapter 2B).
6 Ignition components damp or damaged (Chapter 5).
7 Worn, faulty or incorrectly gapped spark plugs (Chapter 1).
8 Broken, loose or disconnected wiring in the starting circuit (Chapter 5).
9 Broken, loose or disconnected wires at the ignition coil or faulty coil (Chapter 5).
10 Defective crankshaft or camshaft sensor (Chapter 6).

3 Engine hard to start when cold

1 Battery discharged or low (Chapter 1).
2 Malfunctioning fuel system (Chapter 4).

3 Faulty coolant temperature sensor or intake air temperature sensor (Chapter 6).
4 Faulty ignition system (Chapter 5).

4 Engine hard to start when hot

1 Air filter clogged (Chapter 1).
2 Fuel not reaching the fuel injection system (Chapter 4).
3 Corroded battery connections, especially ground (Chapter 1).
4 Faulty coolant temperature sensor or intake air temperature sensor (Chapter 6).

5 Starter motor noisy or excessively rough in engagement

1 Pinion or flywheel gear teeth worn or broken (Chapter 5).
2 Starter motor mounting bolts loose or missing (Chapter 5).

6 Engine starts but stops immediately

1 Loose or faulty electrical connections at ignition coil or alternator (Chapter 5).
2 Insufficient fuel reaching the fuel injector(s) (Chapters 1 and 4).
3 Vacuum leak at the gasket between the intake manifold/plenum and throttle body (Chapter 4).

7 Oil puddle under engine

1 Oil pan gasket and/or oil pan drain bolt washer leaking (Chapter 2).
2 Oil pressure sending unit leaking (Chapter 2).
3 Valve cover leaking (Chapter 2).
4 Engine oil seals leaking (Chapter 2).
5 Oil pump housing leaking (Chapter 2).

8 Engine lopes while idling or idles erratically

1 Vacuum leakage (Chapters 2 and 4).
2 Leaking EGR valve (Chapter 6).
3 Air filter clogged (Chapter 1).
4 Malfunction in the fuel injection or engine control system (Chapters 4 and 6).
5 Leaking head gasket (Chapter 2).
6 Timing belt or chain and/or sprockets worn (Chapter 2).
7 Camshaft lobes worn (Chapter 2).

9 Engine misses at idle speed

1 Spark plugs worn or not gapped properly (Chapter 1).
2 Faulty spark plug wires (Chapter 1).
3 Vacuum leaks (Chapter 1).
4 Incorrect ignition timing (Chapter 1).
5 Uneven or low compression (Chapter 2).
6 Problem with the fuel injection system (Chapter 4).

10 Engine misses throughout driving speed range

1 Fuel filter clogged and/or impurities in the fuel system (Chapters 1 and 4).
2 Low fuel pressure (Chapter 4).
3 Faulty or incorrectly gapped spark plugs (Chapter 1).
4 Leaking spark plug wires (Chapters 1 or 5).
5 Faulty emission system components (Chapter 6).
6 Low or uneven cylinder compression pressures (Chapter 2).

7   Weak or faulty ignition system (Chapter 5).

8   Vacuum leak in fuel injection system, intake manifold, air control valve or vacuum hoses (Chapters 4 and 6).

11   Engine stumbles on acceleration

1   Spark plugs fouled (Chapter 1).

2   Problem with fuel injection or engine control system (Chapters 4 and 6).

3   Fuel filter clogged (Chapters 1 and 4).

4   Intake manifold air leak (Chapters 2 and 4).

5   Problem with the emissions control system (Chapter 6).

12   Engine surges while holding accelerator steady

1   Intake air leak (Chapter 4).

2   Fuel pump or fuel pressure regulator faulty (Chapter 4).

3   Problem with the fuel injection system (Chapter 4).

4   Problem with the emissions control system (Chapter 6).

13   Engine stalls

1   Idle speed incorrect (Chapter 1).

2   Fuel filter clogged and/or water and impurities in the fuel system (Chapters 1 and 4).

3   Distributor components damp or damaged (Chapter 5).

4   Faulty emissions system components (Chapter 6).

5   Faulty or incorrectly gapped spark plugs (Chapter 1).

6   Faulty spark plug wires (Chapter 1).

7   Vacuum leak in the fuel injection system, intake manifold or vacuum hoses (Chapters 2 and 4).

14   Engine lacks power

1   Obstructed exhaust system (Chapter 4).

2   Defective spark plug wires or faulty coil (Chapters 1 and 5).

3   Faulty or incorrectly gapped spark plugs (Chapter 1).

4   Problem with the fuel injection system (Chapter 4).

5   Plugged air filter (Chapter 1).

6   Brakes binding (Chapter 9).

7   Automatic transaxle fluid level incorrect (Chapter 1).

8   Clutch slipping (Chapter 8).

9   Fuel filter clogged and/or impurities in the fuel system (Chapters 1 and 4).

10   Emission control system not functioning properly (Chapter 6).

11   Low or uneven cylinder compression pressures (Chapter 2).

15   Engine backfires

1   Emission control system not functioning properly (Chapter 6).

2   Problem with the fuel injection system (Chapter 4).

3   Vacuum leak at fuel injector(s), intake manifold, air control valve or vacuum hoses (Chapters 2 and 4).

4   Valve clearances incorrectly set and/or valves sticking (Chapter 2).

16   Pinging or knocking engine sounds during acceleration or uphill

1   Incorrect grade of fuel.

2   Fuel injection system faulty (Chapter 4).

3   Improper or damaged spark plugs or wires (Chapter 1).

4   Knock sensor defective (Chapter 6).

5   EGR valve not functioning (Chapter 6).

6   Vacuum leak (Chapters 2 and 4).

17   Engine runs with oil pressure light on

1   Low oil level (Chapter 1).

2   Idle rpm below specification (Chapter 1).

3   Short in wiring circuit (Chapter 12).

4   Faulty oil pressure sender (Chapter 2).

5   Worn engine bearings and/or oil pump (Chapter 2).

18   Engine diesels (continues to run) after switching off

1   Idle speed too high (Chapter 1).

2   Excessive engine operating temperature (Chapter 3).

ENGINE ELECTRICAL SYSTEMS

19   Battery will not hold a charge

1   Alternator drivebelt defective or not adjusted properly (Chapter 1).

2   Battery electrolyte level low (Chapter 1).

3   Battery terminals loose or corroded (Chapter 1).

4   Alternator not charging properly (Chapter 5).

5   Loose, broken or faulty wiring in the charging circuit (Chapter 5).

6   Short in vehicle wiring (Chapter 12).

7   Internally defective battery (Chapters 1 and 5).

20   Alternator light fails to go out

1   Faulty alternator or charging circuit (Chapter 5).

2   Alternator drivebelt defective or out of adjustment (Chapter 1).

3   Alternator voltage regulator inoperative (Chapter 5).

21   Alternator light fails to come on when key is turned on

1   Warning light bulb defective (Chapter 12).

2   Fault in the printed circuit, dash wiring or bulb holder (Chapter 12).

FUEL SYSTEM

22   Excessive fuel consumption

1   Dirty or clogged air filter element (Chapter 1).

2   Emissions system not functioning properly (Chapter 6).

3   Fuel injection system not functioning properly (Chapter 4).

4   Low tire pressure or incorrect tire size (Chapter 1).

23   Fuel leakage and/or fuel odor

1   Leaking fuel feed or return line (Chapters 1 and 4).

2   Tank overfilled.

3   Evaporative canister filter clogged (Chapters 1 and 6).

4   Problem with the fuel injection system (Chapter 4).

COOLING SYSTEM

24   Overheating

1   Insufficient coolant in system (Chapter 1).

2 Water pump drivebelt defective or out of adjustment (Chapter 1).
3 Radiator core blocked or grille restricted (Chapter 3).
4 Thermostat faulty (Chapter 3).
5 Electric coolant fan inoperative or blades broken (Chapter 3).
6 Expansion tank cap not maintaining proper pressure (Chapter 3).

25 Overcooling

1 Faulty thermostat (Chapter 3).
2 Inaccurate temperature gauge sending unit (Chapter 3).

26 External coolant leakage

1 Deteriorated/damaged hoses; loose clamps (Chapters 1 and 3).
2 Water pump defective (Chapter 3).
3 Leakage from radiator core or coolant reservoir (Chapter 3).
4 Engine drain or water jacket core plugs leaking (Chapter 2).

27 Internal coolant leakage

1 Leaking cylinder head gasket (Chapter 2).
2 Cracked cylinder bore or cylinder head (Chapter 2).

28 Coolant loss

1 Too much coolant in reservoir (Chapter 1).
2 Coolant boiling away because of overheating (Chapter 3).
3 Internal or external leakage (Chapter 3).
4 Faulty radiator cap (Chapter 3).

29 Poor coolant circulation

1 Inoperative water pump (Chapter 3).
2 Restriction in cooling system (Chapters 1 and 3).
3 Water pump drivebelt defective/out of adjustment (Chapter 1).
4 Thermostat sticking (Chapter 3).

CLUTCH

30 Pedal travels to floor - no pressure or very little resistance

1 Master or release cylinder faulty (Chapter 8).
2 Hose/pipe burst or leaking (Chapter 8).
3 Connections leaking (Chapter 8).
4 No fluid in reservoir (Chapter 8).
5 If fluid level in reservoir rises as pedal is depressed, master cylinder center valve seal is faulty (Chapter 8).
6 If there is fluid on dust seal at master cylinder, piston primary seal is leaking (Chapter 8).
7 Broken release bearing or fork (Chapter 8).
8 Faulty pressure plate diaphragm spring (Chapter 8).

31 Fluid in area of master cylinder dust cover and on pedal

Rear seal failure in master cylinder (Chapter 8).

32 Fluid on release cylinder

Release cylinder plunger seal faulty (Chapter 8).

33 Pedal feels spongy when depressed

Air in system (Chapter 8).

34 Unable to select gears

1 Faulty transaxle (Chapter 7).
2 Faulty clutch disc or pressure plate (Chapter 8).
3 Faulty release lever or release bearing (Chapter 8).
4 Faulty shift lever assembly or control cables (Chapter 8).

35 Clutch slips (engine speed increases with no increase in vehicle speed)

1 Clutch plate worn (Chapter 8).
2 Clutch plate is oil soaked by leaking rear main seal (Chapters 2 and 8).
3 Clutch plate not seated (Chapter 8).
4 Warped pressure plate or flywheel (Chapter 8).
5 Weak diaphragm springs (Chapter 8).
6 Clutch plate overheated. Allow to cool.

36 Grabbing (chattering) as clutch is engaged

1 Oil on clutch plate lining, burned or glazed facings (Chapter 8).
2 Worn or loose engine or transaxle mounts (Chapter 2).
3 Worn splines on clutch plate hub (Chapter 8).
4 Warped pressure plate or flywheel (Chapter 8).
5 Burned or smeared resin on flywheel or pressure plate (Chapter 8).

37 Transaxle rattling (clicking)

1 Release lever loose (Chapter 8).
2 Clutch plate damper spring failure (Chapter 8).

38 Noise in clutch area

1 Fork shaft improperly installed (Chapter 8).
2 Faulty bearing (Chapter 8).

39 Clutch pedal stays on floor

1 Clutch master cylinder piston binding in bore (Chapter 8).
2 Broken release bearing or fork (Chapter 8).

40 High pedal effort

1 Piston binding in bore (Chapter 8).
2 Pressure plate faulty (Chapter 8).
3 Incorrect size master or release cylinder (Chapter 8).

MANUAL TRANSAXLE

41 Knocking noise at low speeds

1 Worn driveaxle constant velocity (CV) joints (Chapter 8).
2 Worn side gear shaft counterbore in differential case (Chapter 7A).*

42 Noise most pronounced when turning

Differential gear noise (Chapter 7A).*

43   Clunk on acceleration or deceleration

1   Loose engine or transaxle mounts (Chapter 2).
2   Worn differential pinion shaft in case.*
3   Worn side gear shaft counterbore in differential case (Chapter 7A).*
4   Worn or damaged driveaxle inboard CV joints (Chapter 8).

44   Clicking noise in turns

Worn or damaged outboard CV joint (Chapter 8).

45   Vibration

1   Rough wheel bearing (Chapter 10).
2   Damaged driveaxle (Chapter 8).
3   Out-of-round tires (Chapter 1).
4   Tire out of balance (Chapters 1 and 10).
5   Worn CV joint (Chapter 8).

46   Noisy in neutral with engine running

1   Damaged input gear bearing (Chapter 7A).*
2   Damaged clutch release bearing (Chapter 8).

47   Noisy in one particular gear

1   Damaged or worn constant mesh gears (Chapter 7A).*
2   Damaged or worn synchronizers (Chapter 7A).*
3   Bent reverse fork (Chapter 7A).*
4   Damaged fourth speed gear or output gear (Chapter 7A).*
5   Worn or damaged reverse idler gear or idler bushing (Chapter 7A).*

48   Noisy in all gears

1   Insufficient lubricant (Chapter 7A).
2   Damaged or worn bearings (Chapter 7A).*
3   Worn or damaged input gear shaft and/or output gear shaft (Chapter 7A).*

49   Slips out of gear

1   Worn or improperly adjusted linkage (Chapter 7A).
2   Transaxle loose on engine (Chapter 7A).
3   Shift linkage does not work freely, binds (Chapter 7A).
4   Input gear bearing retainer broken or loose (Chapter 7A).*
5   Dirt between clutch cover and engine housing (Chapter 7A).
6   Worn shift fork (Chapter 7A).*

50   Leaks lubricant

1   Side gear shaft seals worn (Chapter 7).
2   Excessive amount of lubricant in transaxle (Chapters 1 and 7A).
3   Loose or broken input gear shaft bearing retainer (Chapter 7A).*
4   Input gear bearing retainer O-ring and/or lip seal damaged (Chapter 7A).*

51   Locked in gear

Lock pin or interlock pin missing (Chapter 7A).*

Although the corrective action necessary to remedy the symptoms described is beyond the scope of this manual, the above information should be helpful in isolating the cause of the condition so that the owner can communicate clearly with a professional mechanic.

AUTOMATIC TRANSAXLE

→**Note: Due to the complexity of the automatic transaxle, it is difficult for the home mechanic to properly diagnose and service this component. For problems other than the following, the vehicle should be taken to a dealer or transmission shop.**

52   Fluid leakage

1   Automatic transaxle fluid is a deep red color. Fluid leaks should not be confused with engine oil, which can easily be blown onto the transaxle by air flow.
2   To pinpoint a leak, first remove all built-up dirt and grime from the transaxle housing with degreasing agents and/or steam cleaning. Then drive the vehicle at low speeds so air flow will not blow the leak far from its source. Raise the vehicle and determine where the leak is coming from. Common areas of leakage are:

   a)   Dipstick tube (Chapters 1 and 7)
   b)   Transaxle oil lines (Chapter 7
   c)   Speed sensor (Chapter 6
   d)   Driveaxle oil seals (Chapter 7).

53   Transaxle fluid brown or has a burned smell

Transaxle fluid overheated (Chapter 1).

54   General shift mechanism problems

1   Chapter 7, Part B, deals with checking and adjusting the shift linkage on automatic transaxles. Common problems which may be attributed to poorly adjusted linkage are:

   a)   Engine starting in gears other than Park or Neutral.
   b)   Indicator on shifter pointing to a gear other than the one actually being used.
   c)   Vehicle moves when in Park.

2   Refer to Chapter 7B for the shift linkage adjustment procedure.

55   Transaxle slips, shifts roughly, is noisy or has no drive in forward or reverse gears

There are many probable causes for the above problems, but the home mechanic should be concerned with only one possibility - fluid level. Before taking the vehicle to a repair shop, check the level and condition of the fluid as described in Chapter 1. Correct the fluid level as necessary or change the fluid and filter if needed. If the problem persists, have a professional diagnose the cause.

DRIVEAXLES

56   Clicking noise in turns

Worn or damaged outboard CV joint (Chapter 8).

57   Shudder or vibration during acceleration

1   Excessive toe-in (Chapter 10).
2   Worn or damaged inboard or outboard CV joints (Chapter 8).
3   Sticking inboard CV joint assembly (Chapter 8).

58   Vibration at highway speeds

1   Out-of-balance front wheels and/or tires (Chapters 1 and 10).

2 Out-of-round front tires (Chapters 1 and 10).
3 Worn CV joint(s) (Chapter 8).

BRAKES

➡Note: Before assuming that a brake problem exists, make sure that:

a) The tires are in good condition and properly inflated (Chapter 1).
b) The front end alignment is correct.
c) The vehicle is not loaded with weight in an unequal manner.

59 Vehicle pulls to one side during braking

1 Incorrect tire pressures (Chapter 1).
2 Front end out of alignment (have the front end aligned).
3 Front, or rear, tire sizes not matched to one another.
4 Restricted brake lines or hoses (Chapter 9).
5 Malfunctioning drum brake or caliper assembly (Chapter 9).
6 Loose suspension parts (Chapter 10).
7 Excessive wear of brake shoe or pad material or disc/drum on one side (Chapter 9).
8 Contamination (grease or brake fluid) of brake shoe or pad material or disc/drum on one side (Chapter 9).

60 Noise (high-pitched squeal when the brakes are applied)

Front brake pads worn out. Replace pads with new ones immediately (Chapter 9).

61 Brake roughness or chatter (pedal pulsates)

1 Excessive lateral runout (Chapter 9).
2 Uneven pad wear (Chapter 9).
3 Defective disc (Chapter 9).

62 Excessive brake pedal effort required to stop vehicle

1 Malfunctioning power brake booster (Chapter 9).
2 Partial system failure (Chapter 9).
3 Excessively worn pads or shoes (Chapter 9).
4 Piston in caliper or wheel cylinder stuck or sluggish (Chapter 9).
5 Brake pads or shoes contaminated with oil or grease (Chapter 9).
6 Brake disc grooved and/or glazed (Chapter 9).
7 New pads or shoes installed and not yet seated. It will take a while for the new material to seat against the disc or drum.

63 Excessive brake pedal travel

1 Partial brake system failure (Chapter 9).
2 Insufficient fluid in master cylinder (Chapters 1 and 9).
3 Air trapped in system (Chapter 9).

64 Dragging brakes

1 Incorrect adjustment of brake light switch (Chapter 9).
2 Master cylinder pistons not returning correctly (Chapter 9).
3 Restricted brakes lines or hoses (Chapter 9).
4 Incorrect parking brake adjustment (Chapter 9).

65 Grabbing or uneven braking action

1 Malfunction of proportioning valve (Chapter 9).

2 Binding brake pedal mechanism (Chapter 9).
3 Contaminated brake linings (Chapter 9).

66 Brake pedal feels spongy when depressed

1 Air in hydraulic lines (Chapter 9).
2 Master cylinder mounting bolts loose (Chapter 9).
3 Master cylinder defective (Chapter 9).

67 Brake pedal travels to the floor with little resistance

1 Little or no fluid in the master cylinder reservoir caused by leaking caliper or wheel cylinder piston(s) (Chapter 9).
2 Loose, damaged or disconnected brake lines (Chapter 9).

68 Parking brake does not hold

Parking brake linkage improperly adjusted (Chapter 9).

SUSPENSION AND STEERING SYSTEMS

➡Note: Before attempting to diagnose the suspension and steering systems, perform the following preliminary checks:

a) Tires for wrong pressure and uneven wear.
b) Steering universal joints from the column to the rack and pinion for loose connectors or wear.
c) Front and rear suspension and the rack and pinion assembly for loose or damaged parts.
d) Out-of-round or out-of-balance tires, bent rims and loose and/or rough wheel bearings.

69 Vehicle pulls to one side

1 Mismatched or uneven tires (Chapter 10).
2 Broken or sagging springs (Chapter 10).
3 Wheel alignment incorrect. Have the wheels professionally aligned.
4 Front brake dragging (Chapter 9).

70 Abnormal or excessive tire wear

1 Wheel alignment out-of-specification. Have the wheels aligned.
2 Sagging or broken springs (Chapter 10).
3 Tire out-of-balance (Chapter 10).
4 Worn strut damper (Chapter 10).
5 Overloaded vehicle.
6 Tires not rotated regularly.

71 Wheel makes a thumping noise

1 Blister or bump on tire (Chapter 10).
2 Improper strut damper action (Chapter 10).

72 Shimmy, shake or vibration

1 Tire or wheel out-of-balance or out-of-round (Chapter 10).
2 Loose or worn wheel bearings (Chapter 10).
3 Worn tie-rod ends (Chapter 10).
4 Worn balljoints (Chapters 1 and 10).
5 Excessive wheel runout (Chapter 10).
6 Blister or bump on tire (Chapter 10).

73   Hard steering

1   Lack of lubrication at balljoints and/or tie-rod ends (Chapter 10).
2   Wheel alignment out-of-specifications. Have the wheels professionally aligned.
3   Low tire pressure(s) (Chapter 1).
4   Worn steering gear (Chapter 10).

74   Poor returnability of steering to center

1   Lack of lubrication at balljoints and tie-rod ends (Chapter 10).
2   Binding in balljoints (Chapter 10).
3   Binding in steering column (Chapter 10).
4   Lack of lubricant in steering gear assembly (Chapter 10).
5   Wheel alignment out-of-specifications. Have the wheels professionally aligned.

75   Abnormal noise at the front end

1   Lack of lubrication at balljoints and tie-rod ends (Chapters 1 and 10).
2   Damaged strut mounting (Chapter 10).
3   Worn control arm bushings or tie-rod ends (Chapter 10).
4   Loose stabilizer bar (Chapter 10).
5   Loose wheel nuts (Chapter 1).
6   Loose suspension bolts (Chapter 10).

76   Wander or poor steering stability

1   Mismatched or uneven tires (Chapter 10).
2   Lack of lubrication at balljoints and tie-rod ends (Chapters 1 and 10).
3   Worn strut assemblies (Chapter 10).
4   Loose stabilizer bar (Chapter 10).
5   Broken or sagging springs (Chapter 10).
6   Wheels out of alignment. Have the wheels professionally aligned.

77   Erratic steering when braking

1   Wheel bearings worn (Chapter 10).
2   Broken or sagging springs (Chapter 10).
3   Leaking wheel cylinder or caliper (Chapter 10).
4   Warped rotors or drums (Chapter 10).

78   Excessive pitching and/or rolling around corners or during braking

1   Loose stabilizer bar (Chapter 10).

2   Worn strut dampers or mountings (Chapter 10).
3   Broken or sagging springs (Chapter 10).
4   Overloaded vehicle.

79   Suspension bottoms

1   Overloaded vehicle.
2   Sagging springs (Chapter 10).

80   Cupped tires

1   Front wheel or rear wheel alignment out-of-specifications. Have the wheels professionally aligned.
2   Worn strut dampers or shock absorbers (Chapter 10).
3   Wheel bearings worn (Chapter 10).
4   Excessive tire or wheel runout (Chapter 10).
5   Worn balljoints (Chapter 10).

81   Excessive tire wear on outside edge

1   Inflation pressures incorrect (Chapter 1).
2   Excessive speed in turns.
3   Wheel alignment incorrect (excessive toe-in). Have professionally aligned.
4   Suspension arm bent or twisted (Chapter 10).

82   Excessive tire wear on inside edge

1   Inflation pressures incorrect (Chapter 1).
2   Wheel alignment incorrect (toe-out). Have professionally aligned.
3   Loose or damaged steering components (Chapter 10).

83   Tire tread worn in one place

1   Tires out-of-balance.
2   Damaged or buckled wheel. Inspect and replace if necessary.
3   Defective tire (Chapter 1).

84   Excessive play or looseness in steering system

1   Wheel bearing(s) worn (Chapter 10).
2   Tie-rod end loose (Chapter 10).
3   Steering gear loose (Chapter 10).
4   Worn or loose steering intermediate shaft U-joint (Chapter 10).

85   Rattling or clicking noise in steering gear

1   Steering gear loose (Chapter 10).
2   Steering gear defective.

Notes

1

TUNE-UP AND ROUTINE MAINTENANCE

Typical engine compartment components (V6 engine)

1	Brake fluid reservoir	5	Automatic transaxle fluid dipstick	9	Power steering fluid reservoir
2	Fuse/relay block	6	Engine oil dipstick	10	Battery
3	Air filter housing	7	Radiator hose	11	Windshield washer fluid reservoir
4	Coolant reservoir	8	Engine oil filler cap		

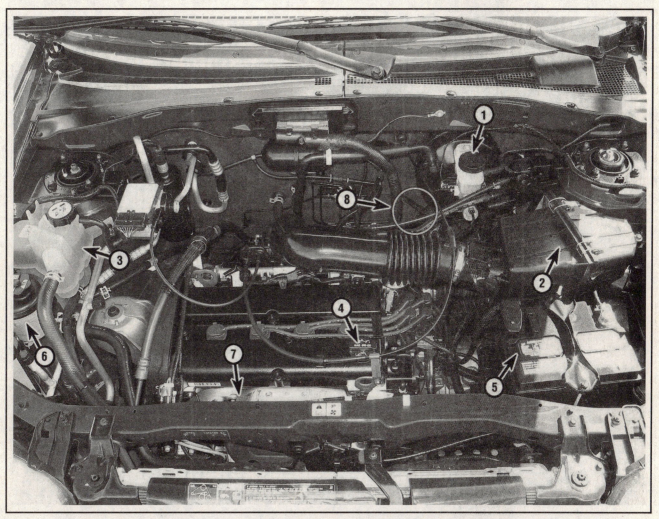

Typical engine compartment components (four-cylinder engine)

1	Brake/clutch fluid reservoir	4	Engine oil filler cap	7	Engine oil dipstick (not visible in this photo)
2	Air filter housing	5	Battery		
3	Coolant reservoir	6	Power steering fluid reservoir	8	Automatic transmission dipstick location

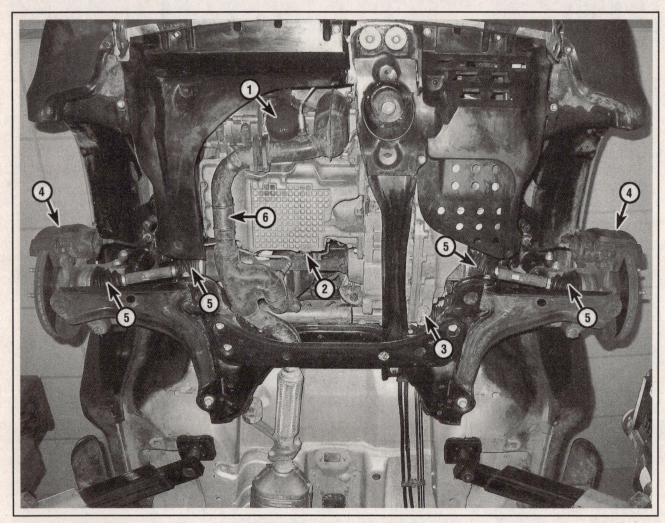

Typical engine underside components (V6 engine)

1	Engine oil filter	3	Automatic transaxle drain plug	5	Driveaxle boot
2	Engine oil drain plug	4	Front disc brake caliper	6	Exhaust pipe

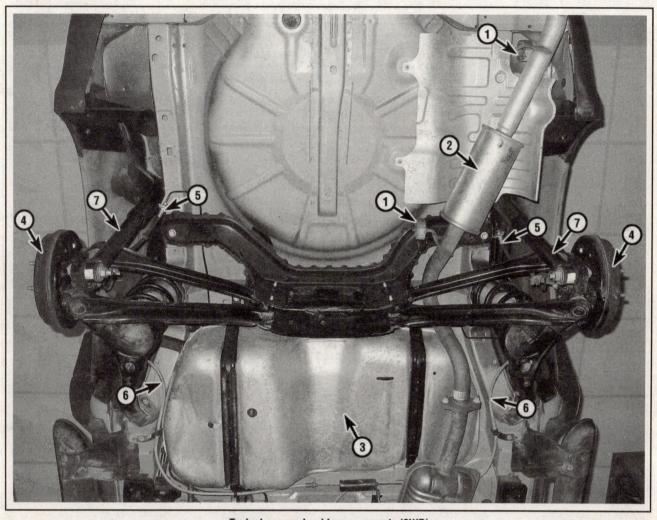

Typical rear underside components (2WD)

1	Exhaust system hanger	3	Fuel tank	5	Brake hose	7	Shock absorber
2	Muffler	4	Rear drum brake assembly	6	Parking brake cable		

Typical rear underside components (4WD)

1 Driveshaft   2 Driveaxle boot   3 Differential   4 Differential filler plug

1 Ford Escape and Mazda Tribute maintenance schedule

The maintenance intervals in this manual are provided with the assumption that you, not the dealer, will be doing the work. These are the minimum maintenance intervals recommended by the factory for vehicles that are driven daily. If you wish to keep your vehicle in peak condition at all times, you may wish to perform some of these procedures even more often. Because frequent maintenance enhances the efficiency, performance and resale value of your car, we encourage you to do so. If you drive in dusty areas, tow a trailer, idle or drive at low speeds for extended periods or drive for short distances (less than four miles) in below freezing temperatures, shorter intervals are also recommended.

When your vehicle is new, it should be serviced by a factory authorized dealer service department to protect the factory warranty. In many cases, the initial maintenance check is done at no cost to the owner.

EVERY 250 MILES OR WEEKLY, WHICHEVER COMES FIRST

Check the engine oil level (Section 4)
Check the engine coolant level (Section 4)
Check the brake and clutch fluid level (Section 4)
Check the windshield washer fluid level (Section 4)
Check the power steering fluid level (Section 4)
Check the automatic transaxle fluid level (Section 4)
Check the tires and tire pressures (Section 5)

EVERY 3000 MILES OR 3 MONTHS, WHICHEVER COMES FIRST

All items listed above plus:
Change the engine oil and oil filter (Section 6)

EVERY 7500 MILES OR 6 MONTHS, WHICHEVER COMES FIRST

All items listed above plus:
Inspect (and replace, if necessary) the windshield wiper blades (Section 7)
Check and service the battery (Section 8)
Check the cooling system (Section 9)
Rotate the tires (Section 10)
Check the seat belts (Section 11)

EVERY 15,000 MILES OR 12 MONTHS, WHICHEVER COMES FIRST

All items listed above plus:
Check all underhood hoses (Section 12)
Inspect the brake system (Section 13)*
Inspect the suspension and steering components (Section 14)*
Check the fuel system (Section 15)
Check the manual transaxle lubricant level (Section 16)
Check the transfer case lubricant level (4WD models) (Section 17)
Check (and replace, if necessary) the air filter (Section 18)*
Check the driveaxle boots (Section 19)

EVERY 30,000 MILES OR 24 MONTHS, WHICHEVER COMES FIRST

All items listed above plus:
Check the exhaust system (Section 20)
Replace the fuel filter (Section 21)
Service the cooling system (drain, flush and refill) (Section 22)
Change the brake fluid (Section 23)
Check/adjust the engine drivebelts (Section 24)
Replace the automatic transaxle fluid (Section 25)**
Replace the manual transaxle lubricant (Section 26)
Replace the rear differential lubricant (4WD) (Section 27)
Replace the transfer case lubricant (4WD) (Section 28)

EVERY 60,000 MILES OR 48 MONTHS, WHICHEVER COMES FIRST

Replace the Positive Crankcase Ventilation (PCV) valve (four-cylinder engines) (Section 29)
Check (and replace, if necessary) the spark plugs (conventional, non-platinum or iridium type) (Section 30)
Check the ignition coils (V6 engines and 2005 and later four-cylinder engines) (Section 31)
Inspect (and replace, if necessary) the spark plug wires (2004 and earlier four-cylinder engines) (Section 32)
Check and adjust the valve clearances (four-cylinder engines) (see Chapter 2A)
Inspect (and replace, if necessary) the engine timing belt (four-cylinder engines) (see Chapter 2A)

EVERY 90,000 MILES

Replace the engine timing belt (four-cylinder engines) (See Chapter 2A)

EVERY 100,000 MILES

Replace the spark plugs (platinum-tipped type) (Section 30)
Positive crankcase ventilation (PCV) replacement (V6 engines) (see Chapter 6)

This item is affected by "severe" operating conditions as described below. If your vehicle is operated under "severe" conditions, perform all maintenance indicated with an asterisk (*) at 3000 mile/3 month intervals. Severe conditions are indicated if you mainly operate your vehicle under one or more of the following conditions:

Operating in dusty areas
Towing a trailer
Idling for extended periods and/or low speed operation
Operating when outside temperatures remain below freezing and when most trips are less than 4 miles

** If operated under one or more of the following conditions, change the manual or automatic transaxle fluid and differential lubricant every 15,000 miles:

In heavy city traffic where the outside temperature regularly reaches 90-degrees F (32-degrees C) or higher
In hilly or mountainous terrain

2   Introduction

This Chapter is designed to help the home mechanic maintain the Ford Escape, Mazda Tribute and Mercury Mariner with the goals of maximum performance, economy, safety and reliability in mind.

Included is a master maintenance schedule, followed by procedures dealing specifically with each item on the schedule. Visual checks, adjustments, component replacement and other helpful items are included. Refer to the accompanying illustrations of the engine compartment and the underside of the vehicle for the locations of various components.

Servicing the vehicle, in accordance with the mileage/time maintenance schedule and the step-by-step procedures will result in a planned maintenance program that should produce a long and reliable service life. Keep in mind that it is a comprehensive plan, so maintaining some items but not others at the specified intervals will not produce the same results.

As you service the vehicle, you will discover that many of the procedures can - and should - be grouped together because of the nature of the particular procedure you're performing or because of the close proximity of two otherwise unrelated components to one another.

For example, if the vehicle is raised for chassis lubrication, you should inspect the exhaust, suspension, steering and fuel systems while you're under the vehicle. When you're rotating the tires, it makes good sense to check the brakes since the wheels are already removed. Finally, let's suppose you have to borrow or rent a torque wrench. Even if you only need it to tighten the spark plugs, you might as well check the torque of as many critical fasteners as time allows.

The first step in this maintenance program is to prepare yourself before the actual work begins. Read through all the procedures you're planning to do, then gather up all the parts and tools needed. If it looks like you might run into problems during a particular job, seek advice from a mechanic or an experienced do-it-yourselfer.

OWNER'S MANUAL AND VECI LABEL INFORMATION

Your vehicle owner's manual was written for your year and model and contains very specific information on component locations, specifications, fuse ratings, part numbers, etc. The Owner's Manual is an important resource for the do-it-yourselfer to have; if one was not supplied with your vehicle, it can generally be ordered from a dealer parts department.

Among other important information, the Vehicle Emissions Control Information (VECI) label contains specifications and procedures for applicable tune-up adjustments and, in some instances, spark plugs (see Chapter 6 for more information on the VECI label). The information on this label is the exact maintenance data recommended by the manufacturer. This data often varies by intended operating altitude, local emissions regulations, month of manufacture, etc.

This Chapter contains procedural details, safety information and more ambitious maintenance intervals than you might find in manufacturer's literature. However, you may also find procedures or specifications in your Owner's Manual or VECI label that differ with what's printed here. In these cases, the Owner's Manual or VECI label can be considered correct, since it is specific to your particular vehicle.

3   Tune-up general information

The term tune-up is used in this manual to represent a combination of individual operations rather than one specific procedure.

If, from the time the vehicle is new, the routine maintenance schedule is followed closely and frequent checks are made of fluid levels and high wear items, as suggested throughout this manual, the engine will be kept in relatively good running condition and the need for additional work will be minimized.

More likely than not, however, there will be times when the engine is running poorly due to lack of regular maintenance. This is even more likely if a used vehicle, which has not received regular and frequent maintenance checks, is purchased. In such cases, an engine tune-up will be needed outside of the regular routine maintenance intervals.

The first step in any tune-up or diagnostic procedure to help correct a poor running engine is a cylinder compression check. A compression check (see Chapter 2C) will help determine the condition of internal engine components and should be used as a guide for tune-up and repair procedures. If, for instance, a compression check indicates serious internal engine wear, a conventional tune-up will not improve the performance of the engine and would be a waste of time and money. Because of its importance, the compression check should be done by someone with the right equipment and the knowledge to use it properly.

The following procedures are those most often needed to bring a generally poor running engine back into a proper state of tune.

MINOR TUNE-UP

Check all engine related fluids (Section 4)
Clean, inspect and test the battery (Section 8)
Check the cooling system (Section 9)
Check all underhood hoses (Section 12)
Check the fuel system (Section 15)
Check the air filter (Section 18)

MAJOR TUNE-UP

All items listed under Minor tune-up, plus . . .
Replace the air filter (Section 18)
Replace the fuel filter (Section 21)
Check the drivebelt (Section 24)
Replace the PCV valve (Section 29)
Replace the spark plugs (Section 30)

4 Fluid level checks (every 250 miles or weekly)

1   Fluids are an essential part of the lubrication, cooling, brake and windshield washer systems. Because the fluids gradually become depleted and/or contaminated during normal operation of the vehicle, they must be periodically replenished. See *Recommended lubricants and fluids* at the end of this Chapter before adding fluid to any of the following components.

➡**Note: The vehicle must be on level ground when fluid levels are checked.**

ENGINE OIL

♦ **Refer to illustrations 4.2a, 4.2b, 4.4 and 4.6**

2   The oil level is checked with a dipstick, which is attached to the engine block (see illustrations). The dipstick extends through a metal tube down into the oil pan.

3   The oil level should be checked before the vehicle has been driven, or about 5 minutes after the engine has been shut off. If the oil is checked immediately after driving the vehicle, some of the oil will remain in the upper part of the engine, resulting in an inaccurate reading on the dipstick.

4   Pull the dipstick out of the tube and wipe all the oil from the end with a clean rag or paper towel. Insert the clean dipstick all the way back into the tube and pull it out again. Note the oil at the end of the dipstick. At its highest point, the level should be between the MIN and MAX marks on the dipstick (see illustration).

5   It takes one quart of oil to raise the level from the MIN mark to the MAX mark on the dipstick. Do not allow the level to drop below the MIN mark or oil starvation may cause engine damage. Conversely, overfilling the engine (adding oil above the MAX mark) may cause oil fouled spark plugs, oil leaks or oil seal failures. Maintaining the oil level above the MAX mark can cause excessive oil consumption.

6   To add oil, remove the filler cap from the valve cover (see illustration). After adding oil, wait a few minutes to allow the level to stabilize, then pull out the dipstick and check the level again. Add more oil if required. Install the filler cap and tighten it by hand only.

7   Checking the oil level is an important preventive maintenance step. A consistently low oil level indicates oil leakage through damaged seals, defective gaskets or past worn rings or valve guides. If the oil looks milky in color or has water droplets in it, the cylinder head gasket(s) may be blown or the head(s) or block may be cracked. The

4.2a The oil dipstick is located on the forward side of the engine on V6 engines

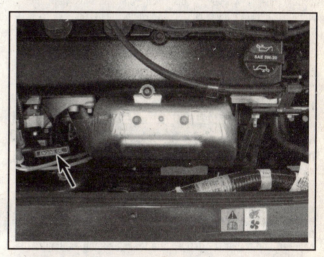

4.2b On four-cylinder engines the oil dipstick is located on the forward side of the engine next to the exhaust manifold

4.6 The oil filler cap is located on the valve cover - always make sure the area around the opening is clean before unscrewing the cap to prevent dirt from contaminating the engine (V6 engine shown)

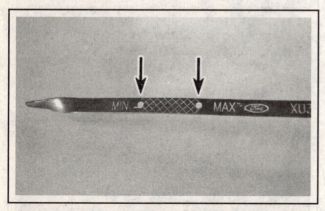

4.4 The oil level should be in the safe range - if it's below the MIN of ADD mark, add enough oil to bring it up to or near the MAX or FULL mark

4.8 The cooling system expansion tank is located at the right side of the engine compartment

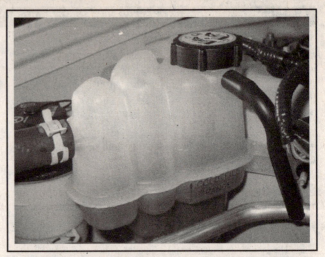

4.9 When the engine is cold, the engine coolant level should be at the COLD FULL mark

engine should be checked immediately. The condition of the oil should also be checked. Whenever you check the oil level, slide your thumb and index finger up the dipstick before wiping off the oil. If you see small dirt or metal particles clinging to the dipstick, the oil should be changed (see Section 6).

ENGINE COOLANT

♦ Refer to illustrations 4.8 and 4.9

❄❄ WARNING:

Do not allow antifreeze to come in contact with your skin or painted surfaces of the vehicle. Flush contaminated areas immediately with plenty of water. Don't store new coolant or leave old coolant lying around where it's accessible to children or pets - they're attracted by its sweet smell. Ingestion of even a small amount of coolant can be fatal! Wipe up garage floor and drip pan spills immediately. Keep antifreeze containers covered and repair cooling system leaks as soon as they're noticed.

8   All vehicles covered by this manual are equipped with a pressurized coolant recovery system. A plastic expansion tank located at the front of the engine compartment is connected by a hose to the radiator (see illustration). As the engine heats up during operation, the expanding coolant fills the tank.

9   The coolant level in the tank should be checked regularly.

❄❄ WARNING:

Do not remove the expansion tank cap to check the coolant level when the engine is warm! The level in the tank varies with the temperature of the engine. When the engine is cold, the coolant level should be at the COLD FULL mark on the reservoir. If it isn't then remove the cap from the tank and add a 50/50 mixture of ethylene glycol based antifreeze and water (see illustration).

10   Drive the vehicle, let the engine cool completely then recheck the coolant level. Don't use rust inhibitors or additives. If only a small amount of coolant is required to bring the system up to the proper level, water can be used. However, repeated additions of water will

dilute the antifreeze and water solution. In order to maintain the proper ratio of antifreeze and water, always top up the coolant level with the correct mixture. An empty plastic milk jug or bleach bottle makes an excellent container for mixing coolant.

11   If the coolant level drops consistently, there may be a leak in the system. Inspect the radiator, hoses, filler cap, drain plugs and water pump (see Section 9). If no leaks are noted, have the expansion tank cap pressure tested by a service station.

12   If you have to remove the expansion tank cap wait until the engine has cooled completely, then wrap a thick cloth around the cap and unscrew it slowly, stopping if you hear a hissing noise. If coolant or steam escapes, let the engine cool down longer, then remove the cap.

13   Check the condition of the coolant as well. It should be relatively clear. If it's brown or rust colored, the system should be drained, flushed and refilled. Even if the coolant appears to be normal, the corrosion inhibitors wear out, so it must be replaced at the specified intervals.

BRAKE AND CLUTCH FLUID

♦ Refer to illustrations 4.14 and 4.15

14   The brake master cylinder is mounted on the front of the power

4.14 The clutch master cylinder is located next to the brake master cylinder and the two share a common reservoir

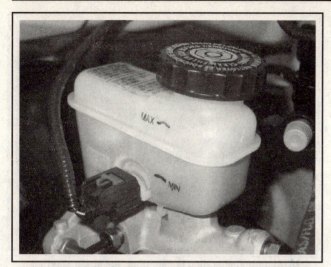

4.15 The brake fluid level should be kept between the MIN and MAX marks on the translucent plastic reservoir; the same reservoir contains the clutch fluid and is connected to the clutch master cylinder by a hose

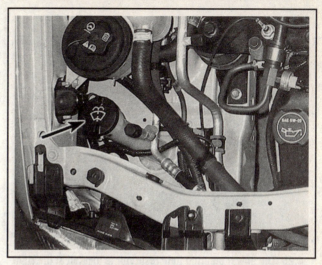

4.22 The windshield/rear window washer fluid reservoir is located in the right front corner of the engine compartment

booster unit in the engine compartment. The hydraulic clutch master cylinder used on manual transaxle vehicles is located next to the brake master cylinder (see illustration).

15 The brake master cylinder and the clutch master cylinder share a common reservoir. To check the fluid level of either system, simply look at the MAX and MIN marks on the brake fluid reservoir (see illustration).

16 If the level is low, wipe the top of the reservoir cover with a clean rag to prevent contamination of the brake system before lifting the cover.

17 Add only the specified brake fluid to the reservoir (refer to *Recommended lubricants and fluids* at the end of this Chapter or to your owner's manual). Mixing different types of brake fluid can damage the system. Fill the brake master cylinder reservoir only to the MAX line.

✳ WARNING:

Use caution when filling the reservoir - brake fluid can harm your eyes and damage painted surfaces. Do not use brake fluid that is more than one year old or has been left open. Brake fluid absorbs moisture from the air. Excess moisture can cause a dangerous loss of braking.

18 While the reservoir cap is removed, inspect the master cylinder reservoir for contamination. If deposits, dirt particles or water droplets are present, the system should be drained and refilled.

19 After filling the reservoir to the proper level, make sure the lid is properly seated to prevent fluid leakage.

20 The fluid in the brake master cylinder will drop slightly as the brake pads at each wheel wear down during normal operation. If the master cylinder requires repeated replenishing to keep it at the proper level, this is an indication of leakage in the brake or clutch system, which should be corrected immediately. If the brake system shows an indication of leakage check all brake lines and connections, along with the calipers, wheel cylinders and booster (see Section 13 for more information). If the hydraulic clutch system shows an indication of leakage check all clutch lines and connections, along with the clutch release cylinder (see Chapter 8 for more information).

21 If, upon checking the brake or clutch master cylinder fluid level, you discover the reservoir empty or nearly empty, the systems should be bled (see Chapters 8 and 9).

WINDSHIELD WASHER FLUID

▸ **Refer to illustration 4.22**

22 Fluid for the windshield washer system is stored in a plastic reservoir located at the right front of the engine compartment (see illustration).

23 In milder climates, plain water can be used in the reservoir, but it should be kept no more than 2/3 full to allow for expansion if the water freezes. In colder climates, use windshield washer system antifreeze, available at any auto parts store, to lower the freezing point of the fluid. Mix the antifreeze with water in accordance with the manufacturer's directions on the container.

✳ CAUTION:

Do not use cooling system antifreeze - it will damage the vehicle's paint.

POWER STEERING FLUID

▸ **Refer to illustrations 4.25 and 4.28**

24 Check the power steering fluid level periodically to avoid steering system problems, such as damage to the pump.

✳ CAUTION:

DO NOT hold the steering wheel against either stop (extreme left or right turn) for more than five seconds. If you do, the power steering pump could be damaged.

25 The power steering reservoir, located at the right side of the engine compartment (see illustration), has MIN and MAX fluid level

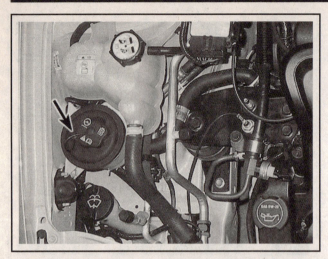

4.25 The power steering fluid reservoir is located at the right side of the engine compartment next to the windshield washer fluid reservoir

marks on the side. The fluid level can be seen without removing the reservoir cap.

26 Park the vehicle on level ground and apply the parking brake.

27 Run the engine until it has reached normal operating temperature. With the engine at idle, turn the steering wheel back and forth about 10 times to get any air out of the steering system. Shut the engine off with the wheels in the straight-ahead position.

28 Note the fluid level on the side of the reservoir. It should be between the two marks (see illustration).

29 Add small amounts of fluid until the level is correct.

✳✳ CAUTION:

Do not overfill the reservoir. If too much fluid is added, remove the excess with a clean syringe or suction pump.

30 Check the power steering hoses and connections for leaks and wear.

AUTOMATIC TRANSAXLE FLUID

▶ **Refer to illustrations 4.34a and 4.34b**

31 The level of the automatic transaxle fluid should be carefully

4.28 At normal operating temperature, the power steering fluid level should be between the MAX and MIN marks

maintained. Low fluid level can lead to slipping or loss of drive, while overfilling can cause foaming, loss of fluid and transaxle damage.

32 The transaxle fluid level should only be checked when the transaxle is hot (at its normal operating temperature). If the vehicle has just been driven over 10 miles (15 miles in a frigid climate), and the fluid temperature is 160 to 175-degrees F, the transaxle is hot.

✳✳ CAUTION:

If the vehicle has just been driven for a long time at high speed or in city traffic in hot weather, or if it has been pulling a trailer, an accurate fluid level reading cannot be obtained. Allow the fluid to cool down for about 30 minutes.

33 If the vehicle has not just been driven, park the vehicle on level ground, set the parking brake and start the engine. While the engine is idling, depress the brake pedal and move the selector lever through all the gear ranges, beginning and ending in Park.

34 With the engine still idling, remove the dipstick from its tube (see illustration). Check the level of the fluid on the dipstick (see illustration) and note its condition.

35 Wipe the fluid from the dipstick with a clean rag and reinsert it back into the filler tube until the cap seats.

36 Pull the dipstick out again and note the fluid level. The fluid level

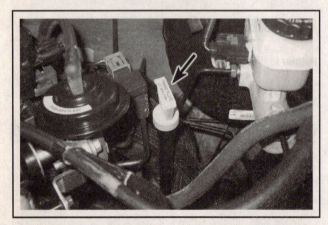

4.34a The automatic transaxle dipstick is located at the rear of the engine compartment

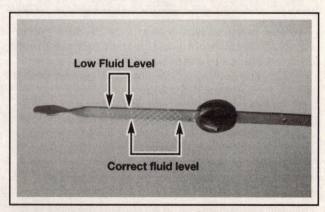

4.34b At operating temperature, the automatic transaxle fluid level should be kept in the cross-hatched area of the dipstick

should be in the operating temperature range (the cross-hatched area). If the level is at the low side of either range, add the specified automatic transmission fluid through the dipstick tube with a funnel.

37 Add just enough of the recommended fluid to fill the transaxle to the proper level. It takes about one pint to raise the level from the low mark to the high mark when the fluid is hot, so add the fluid a little at a time and keep checking the level until it is correct.

38 The condition of the fluid should also be checked along with the level. If the fluid at the end of the dipstick is black or a dark reddish brown color, or if it emits a burned smell, the fluid should be changed (see Section 25). If you are in doubt about the condition of the fluid, purchase some new fluid and compare the two for color and smell.

5 Tire and tire pressure checks (every 250 miles or weekly)

▶ **Refer to illustrations 5.2, 5.3, 5.4a, 5.4b and 5.8**

1 Periodic inspection of the tires may spare you the inconvenience of being stranded with a flat tire. It can also provide you with vital information regarding possible problems in the steering and suspension systems before major damage occurs.

2 The original tires on this vehicle are equipped with 1/2-inch wide bands that will appear when tread depth reaches 1/16-inch, at which point they can be considered worn out. Tread wear can be monitored with a simple, inexpensive device known as a tread depth indicator (see illustration).

3 Note any abnormal tread wear (see illustration). Tread pattern irregularities such as cupping, flat spots and more wear on one side than the other are indications of front end alignment and/or balance problems. If any of these conditions are noted, take the vehicle to a tire shop or service station to correct the problem.

4 Look closely for cuts, punctures and embedded nails or tacks. Sometimes a tire will hold air pressure for a short time or leak down

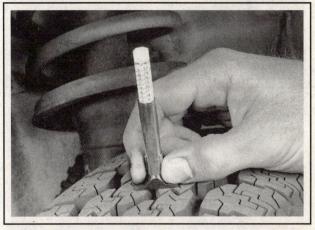

5.2 A tire tread depth indicator should be used to monitor tire wear - they are available at auto parts stores and service stations and cost very little

UNDERINFLATION

CUPPING

Cupping may be caused by:
- Underinflation and/or mechanical irregularities such as out-of-balance condition of wheel and/or tire, and bent or damaged wheel.
- Loose or worn steering tie-rod or steering idler arm.
- Loose, damaged or worn front suspension parts.

OVERINFLATION

INCORRECT TOE-IN OR EXTREME CAMBER

FEATHERING DUE TO MISALIGNMENT

5.3 This chart will help you determine the condition of your tires, the probable cause(s) of abnormal wear and the corrective action necessary

5.4a If a tire loses air on a steady basis, check the valve core first to make sure it's snug (special inexpensive wrenches are commonly available at auto parts stores)

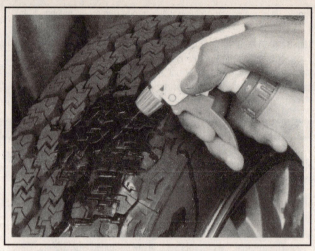

5.4b If the valve core is tight, raise the corner of the vehicle with the low tire and spray a soapy water solution onto the tread as the tire is turned slowly - slow leaks will cause small bubbles to appear

very slowly after a nail has embedded itself in the tread. If a slow leak persists, check the valve stem core to make sure it is tight (see illustration). Examine the tread for an object that may have embedded itself in the tire or for a "plug" that may have begun to leak (radial tire punctures are repaired with a plug that is installed in a puncture). If a puncture is suspected, it can be easily verified by spraying a solution of

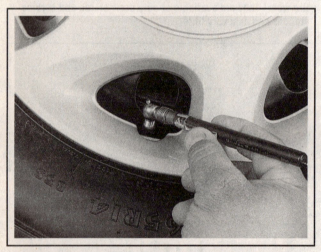

5.8 To extend the life of your tires, check the air pressure at least once a week with an accurate gauge (don't forget the spare!)

soapy water onto the puncture area (see illustration). The soapy solution will bubble if there is a leak. Unless the puncture is unusually large, a tire shop or service station can usually repair the tire.

5 Carefully inspect the inner sidewall of each tire for evidence of brake fluid leakage. If you see any, inspect the brakes immediately.

6 Correct air pressure adds miles to the life span of the tires, improves mileage and enhances overall ride quality. Tire pressure cannot be accurately estimated by looking at a tire, especially if it's a radial. A tire pressure gauge is essential. Keep an accurate gauge in the glove compartment. The pressure gauges attached to the nozzles of air hoses at gas stations are often inaccurate.

7 Always check tire pressure when the tires are cold. Cold, in this case, means the vehicle has not been driven over a mile in the three hours preceding a tire pressure check. A pressure rise of four to eight pounds is not uncommon once the tires are warm.

8 Unscrew the valve cap protruding from the wheel or hubcap and push the gauge firmly onto the valve stem (see illustration). Note the reading on the gauge and compare the figure to the recommended tire pressure shown on the tire placard on the driver's side door. Be sure to reinstall the valve cap to keep dirt and moisture out of the valve stem mechanism. Check all four tires and, if necessary, add enough air to bring them up to the recommended pressure.

9 Don't forget to keep the spare tire inflated to the specified pressure (refer to the pressure molded into the tire sidewall).

6   Engine oil and filter change (every 3000 miles or 3 months)

▶ **Refer to illustrations 6.2, 6.7, 6.12 and 6.15**

1 Frequent oil changes are the most important preventive maintenance procedures that can be done by the home mechanic. As engine oil ages, it becomes diluted and contaminated, which leads to premature engine wear.

2 Make sure that you have all the necessary tools before you begin this procedure (see illustration). You should also have plenty of rags or newspapers handy for mopping up oil spills.

3 Access to the oil drain plug and filter will be improved if the vehicle can be lifted on a hoist, driven onto ramps or supported by jackstands.

❊❊ **WARNING:**

Do not work under a vehicle supported only by a jack - always use jackstands!

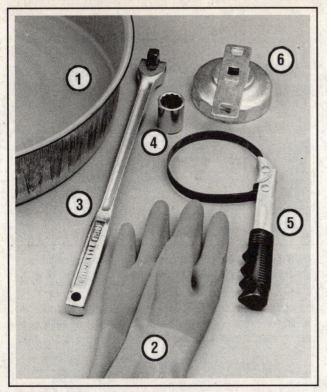

6.2 These tools are required when changing the engine oil and filter

1   **Drain pan** - *It should be fairly shallow in depth, but wide in order to prevent spills*
2   **Rubber gloves** - *When removing the drain plug and filter, it is inevitable that you will get oil on your hands (the gloves will prevent burns)*
3   **Breaker bar** - *Sometimes the oil drain plug is pretty tight and a long breaker bar is needed to loosen it*
4   **Socket** - *To be used with the breaker bar or a ratchet (must be the correct size to fit the drain plug)*
5   **Filter wrench** - *This is a metal band-type wrench, which requires clearance around the filter to be effective*
6   **Filter wrench** - *This type fits on the bottom of the filter and can be turned with a ratchet or beaker bar (different size wrenches are available for different types of filters)*

4   If you haven't changed the oil on this vehicle before, get under it and locate the oil drain plug and the oil filter. The exhaust components will be warm as you work, so note how they are routed to avoid touching them when you are under the vehicle.

5   Start the engine and allow it to reach normal operating temperature - oil and sludge will flow out more easily when warm. If new oil, a filter or tools are needed, use the vehicle to go get them and warm up the engine/oil at the same time. Park on a level surface and shut off the engine when it's warmed up. Remove the oil filler cap from the valve cover.

6   Raise the vehicle and support it on jackstands. Make sure it is safely supported!

7   Being careful not to touch the hot exhaust components, position a drain pan under the plug in the bottom of the engine, then remove the plug (see illustration). It's a good idea to wear a rubber glove while unscrewing the plug the final few turns to avoid being scalded by hot oil.

6.7 Use a proper size box-end wrench or socket to remove the oil drain plug and avoid rounding it off

6.12 Use an oil filter wrench to remove the filter (V6 engine shown)

8   It may be necessary to move the drain pan slightly as oil flow slows to a trickle. Inspect the old oil for the presence of metal particles.

9   After all the oil has drained, wipe off the drain plug with a clean rag. Any small metal particles clinging to the plug would immediately contaminate the new oil.

10 Clean the area around the drain plug opening, reinstall the plug and tighten it securely, but don't strip the threads.

11 Move the drain pan into position under the oil filter.

12 Loosen the oil filter by turning it counterclockwise with a filter wrench (see illustration). Any standard filter wrench will work.

13 Once the filter is loose, use your hands to unscrew it from the block. Just as the filter is detached from the block, immediately tilt the open end up to prevent the oil inside the filter from spilling out.

14 Using a clean rag, wipe off the mounting surface on the block. Also, make sure that none of the old gasket remains stuck to the mounting surface. It can be removed with a scraper if necessary.

15 Compare the old filter with the new one to make sure they are the same type. Smear some engine oil on the rubber gasket of the new filter and screw it into place (see illustration). Overtightening the filter

will damage the gasket, so don't use a filter wrench. Most filter manufacturers recommend tightening the filter by hand only. Normally they should be tightened 3/4-turn after the gasket contacts the block, but be sure to follow the directions on the filter or container.

16 Remove all tools and materials from under the vehicle, being careful not to spill the oil in the drain pan, then lower the vehicle.

17 Add new oil to the engine through the oil filler cap. Use a funnel to prevent oil from spilling onto the top of the engine. Pour four quarts of fresh oil into the engine. Wait a few minutes to allow the oil to drain into the pan, then check the level on the dipstick (see Section 4 if necessary). If the oil level is in the OK range, install the filler cap.

18 Start the engine and run it for about a minute. While the engine is running, look under the vehicle and check for leaks at the oil pan drain plug and around the oil filter. If either one is leaking, stop the engine and tighten the plug or filter slightly.

19 Wait a few minutes, then recheck the level on the dipstick. Add oil as necessary to bring the level into the OK range.

20 During the first few trips after an oil change, make it a point to check frequently for leaks and proper oil level.

21 The old oil drained from the engine cannot be reused in its present state and should be disposed of. Check with your local auto parts store, disposal facility or environmental agency to see if they will accept the oil for recycling. After the oil has cooled it can be drained

6.15 Lubricate the oil filter gasket with clean engine oil before installing the filter on the engine

into a container (capped plastic jugs, topped bottles, milk cartons, etc.) for transport to one of these disposal sites. Don't dispose of the oil by pouring it on the ground or down a drain!

7   Windshield wiper blade inspection and replacement (every 7500 miles or 6 months)

▶ **Refer to illustrations 7.4a and 7.4b**

1 The windshield wiper and blade assembly should be inspected periodically for damage, loose components and cracked or worn blade elements.

2 Road film can build up on the wiper blades and affect their efficiency, so they should be washed regularly with a mild detergent solution.

3 If the wiper blade elements are cracked, worn or warped, or no longer clean adequately, they should be replaced with new ones.

4 Lift the arm assembly away from the glass for clearance, press on the release lever, then slide the wiper blade assembly out of the hook in the end of the arm (see illustrations).

5 Attach the new wiper to the arm. Connection can be confirmed by an audible click.

7.4a To release the blade holder, push the release pin . . .

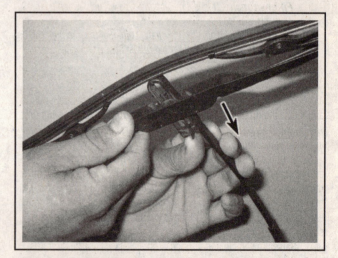

7.4b . . . and pull the wiper blade in the direction of the arrow to separate it from the arm

8   Battery check, maintenance and charging (every 7500 miles or 6 months)

◆ **Refer to illustrations 8.1, 8.6a, 8.6b, 8.7a, 8.7b and 8.8**

✳✳ WARNING:

Certain precautions must be followed when checking and servicing the battery. Hydrogen gas, which is highly flammable, is always present in the battery cells, so keep lighted tobacco and all other open flames and sparks away from the battery. The electrolyte inside the battery is actually diluted sulfuric acid, which will cause injury if splashed on your skin or in your eyes. It will also ruin clothes and painted surfaces. When removing the battery cables, always detach the negative cable first and hook it up last!

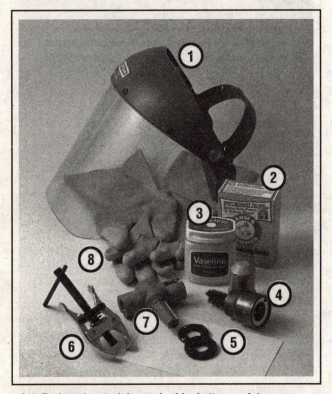

8.1 Tools and materials required for battery maintenance

1   *Face shield/safety goggles* - *When removing corrosion with a brush, the acidic particles can easily fly up into your eyes*
2   *Baking soda* - *A solution of baking soda and water can be used to neutralize corrosion*
3   *Petroleum jelly* - *A layer of this on the battery posts will help prevent corrosion*
4   *Battery post/cable cleaner* - *This wire brush cleaning tool will remove all traces of corrosion from the battery posts and cable clamps*
5   *Treated felt washers* - *Placing one of these on each post, directly under the cable clamps, will help prevent corrosion*
6   *Puller* - *Sometimes the cable clamps are very difficult to pull off the posts, even after the nut/bolt has been completely loosened. This tool pulls the clamp straight up and off the post without damage*
7   *Battery post/cable cleaner* - *Here is another cleaning tool which is a slightly different version of number 4 above, but it does the same thing*
8   *Rubber gloves* - *Another safety item to consider when servicing the battery; remember that's acid inside the battery*

1   A routine preventive maintenance program for the battery in your vehicle is the only way to ensure quick and reliable starts. But before performing any battery maintenance, make sure that you have the proper equipment necessary to work safely around the battery (see illustration).

2   There are also several precautions that should be taken whenever battery maintenance is performed. Before servicing the battery, always turn the engine and all accessories off and disconnect the cables from the negative terminal of the battery (see Chapter 5).

3   The battery produces hydrogen gas, which is both flammable and explosive. Never create a spark, smoke or light a match around the battery. Always charge the battery in a ventilated area.

4   Electrolyte contains poisonous and corrosive sulfuric acid. Do not allow it to get in your eyes, on your skin on your clothes. Never ingest it. Wear protective safety glasses when working near the battery. Keep children away from the battery.

5   Note the external condition of the battery. If the positive terminal and cable clamp on your vehicle's battery is equipped with a rubber protector, make sure that it's not torn or damaged. It should completely cover the terminal. Look for any corroded or loose connections, cracks in the case or cover or loose hold-down clamps. Also check the entire length of each cable for cracks and frayed conductors.

6   If corrosion, which looks like white, fluffy deposits (see illustration) is evident, particularly around the terminals, the battery should be removed for cleaning. Loosen the cable clamp bolts with a wrench, being careful to remove the ground cable first, and slide them off the terminals (see illustration). Then disconnect the hold-down clamp bolt and nut, remove the clamp and lift the battery from the engine compartment.

7   Clean the cable clamps thoroughly with a battery brush or a terminal cleaner and a solution of warm water and baking soda (see illustration). Wash the terminals and the top of the battery case with the same solution but make sure that the solution doesn't get into the battery. When cleaning the cables, terminals and battery top, wear safety goggles and rubber gloves to prevent any solution from coming in contact with your eyes or hands. Wear old clothes too - even diluted, sulfu-

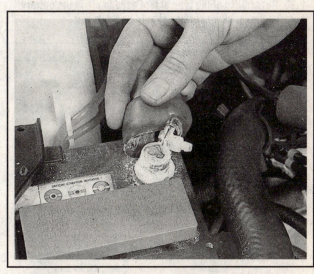

8.6a Battery terminal corrosion usually appears as light, fluffy powder

8.6b Removing a cable from the battery post with a wrench - sometimes a pair of special battery pliers are required for this procedure if corrosion has caused deterioration of the nut hex (always remove the ground (-) cable first and hook it up last!)

8.7b Regardless of the type of tool used to clean the battery posts, a clean, shiny surface should be the result

8.8 Make sure the battery hold-down fasteners are tight

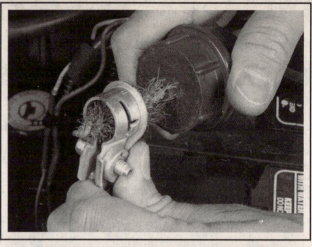

8.7a When cleaning the cable clamps, all corrosion must be removed (the inside of the clamp is tapered to match the taper on the post, so don't remove too much material)

ric acid splashed onto clothes will burn holes in them. If the terminals have been extensively corroded, clean them up with a terminal cleaner (see illustration). Thoroughly wash all cleaned areas with plain water.

8   Make sure that the battery tray is in good condition and the hold-down clamp fasteners are tight (see illustration). If the battery is removed from the tray, make sure no parts remain in the bottom of the tray when the battery is reinstalled. When reinstalling the hold-down clamp bolts, do not overtighten them.

9   Information on removing and installing the battery can be found in Chapter 5. If you disconnected the cable(s) from the negative and/or positive battery terminals, the powertrain control module (PCM) must relearn its idle and fuel trim strategy for optimum driveability and performance (see Chapter 5, Section 1 for this procedure). Information on jump starting can be found at the front of this manual.

CLEANING

10 Corrosion on the hold-down components, battery case and surrounding areas can be removed with a solution of water and baking soda. Thoroughly rinse all cleaned areas with plain water.

11 Any metal parts of the vehicle damaged by corrosion should be covered with a zinc-based primer, then painted.

CHARGING

※※ WARNING:

When batteries are being charged, hydrogen gas, which is very explosive and flammable, is produced. Do not smoke or allow open flames near a charging or a recently charged battery. Wear eye protection when near the battery during charging. Also, make sure the charger is unplugged before connecting or disconnecting the battery from the charger.

12 Slow-rate charging is the best way to restore a battery that's discharged to the point where it will not start the engine. It's also a good way to maintain the battery charge in a vehicle that's only driven a few miles between starts. Maintaining the battery charge is particularly

important in the winter when the battery must work harder to start the engine and electrical accessories that drain the battery are in greater use.

13 It's best to use a one or two-amp battery charger (sometimes called a "trickle" charger). They are the safest and put the least strain on the battery. They are also the least expensive. For a faster charge, you can use a higher amperage charger, but don't use one rated more than

1/10th the amp/hour rating of the battery. Rapid boost charges that claim to restore the power of the battery in one to two hours are hardest on the battery and can damage batteries not in good condition. This type of charging should only be used in emergency situations.

14 The average time necessary to charge a battery should be listed in the instructions that come with the charger. As a general rule, a trickle charger will charge a battery in 12 to 16 hours.

9 Cooling system check (every 7,500 miles or 6 months)

♦ **Refer to illustration 9.4**

1 Many major engine failures can be caused by a faulty cooling system.

2 The engine must be cold for the cooling system check, so perform the following procedure before the vehicle is driven for the day or after it has been shut off for at least three hours.

3 Remove the pressure-relief cap from the expansion tank at the right side of the engine compartment. Clean the cap thoroughly, inside and out, with clean water. The presence of rust or corrosion in the expansion tank means the coolant should be changed (see Section 22). The coolant inside the expansion tank should be relatively clean and transparent. If it's rust colored, drain the system and refill it with new coolant.

4 Carefully check the radiator hoses and the smaller diameter heater hoses (see illustrations in Chapter 3). Inspect each coolant hose along its entire length, replacing any hose which is cracked, swollen or deteriorated (see illustration). Cracks will show up better if the hose is squeezed. Pay close attention to hose clamps that secure the hoses to cooling system components. Hose clamps can pinch and puncture hoses, resulting in coolant leaks.

5 Make sure that all hose connections are tight. A leak in the cooling system will usually show up as white or rust colored deposits on the area adjoining the leak. If wire-type clamps are used on the hoses, it may be a good idea to replace them with screw-type clamps.

6 Clean the front of the radiator and air conditioning condenser with compressed air, if available, or a soft brush. Remove all bugs, leaves, etc. embedded in the radiator fins. Be extremely careful not to damage the cooling fins or cut your fingers on them.

7 If the coolant level has been dropping consistently and no leaks are detectable, have the expansion tank cap and cooling system pressure checked at a service station.

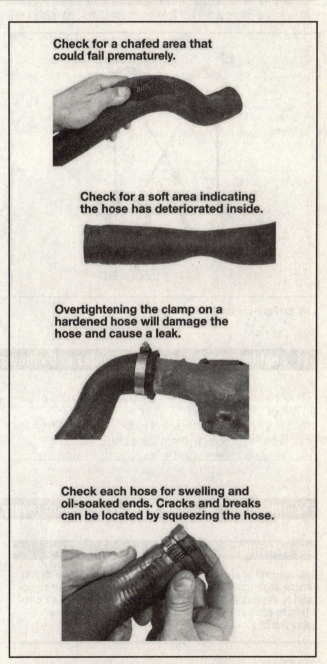

Check for a chafed area that could fail prematurely.

Check for a soft area indicating the hose has deteriorated inside.

Overtightening the clamp on a hardened hose will damage the hose and cause a leak.

Check each hose for swelling and oil-soaked ends. Cracks and breaks can be located by squeezing the hose.

9.4 **Hoses, like drivebelts, have a habit of failing at the worst possible time - to prevent the inconvenience of a blown radiator or heater hose, inspect them carefully as shown here**

10 Tire rotation (every 7,500 miles or 6 months)

◆ **Refer to illustrations 10.2a and 10.2b**

1   The tires should be rotated at the specified intervals and whenever uneven wear is noticed. Since the vehicle will be raised and the tires removed anyway, check the brakes also (see Section 13).

2   Radial tires must be rotated in a specific pattern (see illustrations). If your vehicle has a compact spare tire, don't include it in the rotation pattern.

3   Refer to the information in *Jacking and towing* at the front of this manual for the proper procedure to follow when raising the vehicle and changing a tire. If the brakes must be checked, don't apply the parking brake as stated.

4   The vehicle must be raised on a hoist or supported on jackstands to get all four wheels off the ground. Make sure the vehicle is safely supported!

5   After the rotation procedure is finished, check and adjust the tire pressures as necessary and be sure to check the lug nut tightness.

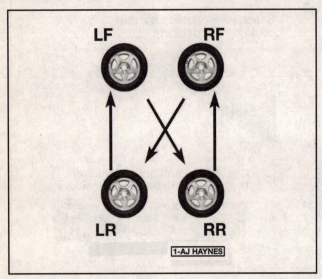

10.2a Four-tire rotation pattern

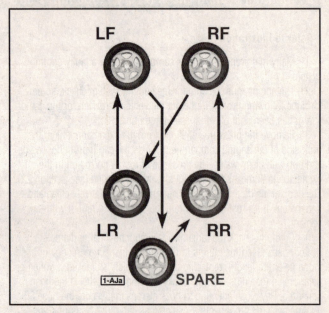

10.2b Five tire rotation pattern

11 Seat belt check (every 7,500 miles or 6 months)

1   Check seat belts, buckles, latch plates and guide loops for obvious damage and signs of wear.

2   See if the seat belt reminder light comes on when the key is turned to the Run or Start position. A chime should also sound.

3   The seat belts are designed to lock up during a sudden stop or impact, yet allow free movement during normal driving. Make sure the retractors return the belt against your chest while driving and rewind the belt fully when the buckle is unlatched.

4   If any of the above checks reveal problems with the seat belt system, replace parts as necessary.

12 Underhood hose check and replacement (every 15,000 miles or 12 months)

❊❊ **WARNING:**

Replacement of air conditioning hoses must be left to a dealer service department or air conditioning shop that has the equipment to depressurize the system safely. Never remove air conditioning components or hoses until the system has been depressurized.

GENERAL

1   High temperatures under the hood can cause deterioration of the rubber and plastic hoses used for engine, accessory and emission systems operation. Periodic inspection should be made for cracks, loose clamps, material hardening and leaks.

2   Information specific to the cooling system hoses can be found in Section 9.

3   Most (but not all) hoses are secured to the fittings with clamps. Where clamps are used, check to be sure they haven't lost their tension, allowing the hose to leak. If clamps aren't used, make sure the hose has not expanded and/or hardened where it slips over the fitting, allowing it to leak.

PCV SYSTEM HOSE

4   To reduce hydrocarbon emissions, crankcase blow-by gas is vented through the PCV valve in the rocker arm cover to the intake

manifold via a rubber hose on most models. The blow-by gases mix with incoming air in the intake manifold before being burned in the combustion chambers.

5   Check the PCV hose for cracks, leaks and other damage. Disconnect it from the valve cover and the intake manifold and check the inside for obstructions. If it's clogged, clean it out with solvent.

VACUUM HOSES

6   It's quite common for vacuum hoses, especially those in the emissions system, to be color coded or identified by colored stripes molded into them. Various systems require hoses with different wall thickness, collapse resistance and temperature resistance. When replacing hoses, be sure the new ones are made of the same material.

7   Often the only effective way to check a hose is to remove it completely from the vehicle. If more than one hose is removed, be sure to label the hoses and fittings to ensure correct installation.

8   When checking vacuum hoses, be sure to include any plastic T-fittings in the check. Inspect the fittings for cracks and the hose where it fits over each fitting for distortion, which could cause leakage.

9   A small piece of vacuum hose (1/4-inch inside diameter) can be used as a stethoscope to detect vacuum leaks. Hold one end of the hose to your ear and probe around vacuum hoses and fittings, listening for the "hissing" sound characteristic of a vacuum leak.

✳✳ WARNING:

When probing with the vacuum hose stethoscope, be careful not to come into contact with moving engine components such as drivebelts, the cooling fan, etc.

FUEL HOSE

✳✳ WARNING:

Gasoline is flammable, so take extra precautions when you work on any part of the fuel system. Don't smoke or allow open flames or bare light bulbs near the work area, and don't work in a garage where a gas-type appliance (such as a water heater or clothes dryer) is present. Since fuel is carcinogenic, wear latex gloves when there's a possibility of being exposed to fuel, and, if you spill any fuel on your skin, rinse it off immediately with

soap and water. Mop up any spills immediately and do not store fuel-soaked rags where they could ignite. The fuel system is under constant pressure, so, if any fuel lines are to be disconnected, the fuel pressure in the system must be relieved first (see Chapter 4 for more information). When you perform any kind of work on the fuel system, wear safety glasses and have a Class B type fire extinguisher on hand.

10   The fuel lines are usually under pressure, so if any fuel lines are to be disconnected be prepared to catch spilled fuel.

✳✳ WARNING:

Your vehicle is equipped with fuel injection and you must relieve the fuel system pressure before servicing the fuel lines. Refer to Chapter 4 for the fuel system pressure relief procedure.

11   Check all flexible fuel lines for deterioration and chafing. Check especially for cracks in areas where the hose bends and just before fittings, such as where a hose attaches to the fuel pump, fuel filter and fuel injection unit.

12   When replacing a hose, use only hose that is specifically designed for your fuel injection system.

13   Spring-type clamps are sometimes used on fuel return or vapor lines. These clamps often lose their tension over a period of time, and can be "sprung" during removal. Replace all spring-type clamps with screw clamps whenever a hose is replaced. Some fuel lines use spring-lock type couplings, which require a special tool to disconnect. See Chapter 4 for more information on this type of coupling.

METAL LINES

14   Sections of metal line are often used for fuel line between the fuel pump and the fuel injection unit. Check carefully to make sure the line isn't bent, crimped or cracked.

15   If a section of metal fuel line must be replaced, use seamless steel tubing only, since copper and aluminum tubing do not have the strength necessary to withstand vibration caused by the engine.

16   Check the metal brake lines where they enter the master cylinder and brake proportioning unit (if used) for cracks in the lines and loose fittings. Any sign of brake fluid leakage calls for an immediate thorough inspection of the brake system.

13 Brake check (every 15,000 miles or 12 months)

✳✳ WARNING:

Dust created by the brake system is harmful to your health. Never blow it out with compressed air and don't inhale any of it. An approved filtering mask should be worn when working on brakes. Do not, under any circumstances, use petroleum-based solvents to clean brake parts. Use brake system cleaner only!

1   The brakes should be inspected every time the wheels are removed or whenever a defect is suspected. Indications of a potential brake system problem include the vehicle pulling to one side when the brake pedal is depressed, noises coming from the brakes when they

are applied, excessive brake pedal travel, a pulsating pedal and leakage of fluid, usually seen on the inside of the tire or wheel.

➡Note: It is normal for a vehicle equipped with an Anti-lock Brake System (ABS) to exhibit brake pedal pulsations during severe braking conditions.

DISC BRAKES

◆ **Refer to illustration 13.5**

2   Disc brakes can be visually checked without removing any parts except the wheels. Remove the hub caps (if applicable) and loosen the

13.5 You will find an inspection hole like this in each caliper through which you can view the thickness of remaining friction material for the inner pad

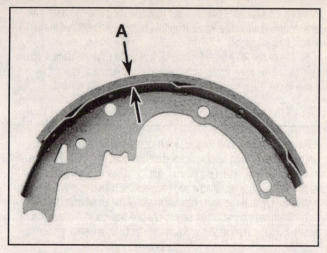

13.14 If the lining is bonded to the brake shoe, measure the lining thickness from the outer surface to the metal shoe, as shown here; if the lining is riveted to the shoe, measure from the lining outer surface to the rivet head

wheel lug nuts a quarter turn each.

3   Raise the vehicle and place it securely on jackstands.

❄❄ WARNING:

Never work under a vehicle that is supported only by a jack!

4   Remove the wheels. Now visible is the disc brake caliper which contains the pads. There is an outer brake pad and an inner pad. Both must be checked for wear.

➡Note: Usually the inner pad wears faster than the outer pad.

5   Measure the thickness of the outer pad at each end of the caliper and the inner pad through the inspection hole in the caliper body (see illustration). Compare the measurement with the limit given in this Chapter's Specifications; if any brake pad thickness is less than specified, then all brake pads must be replaced (see Chapter 9).

6   If you're in doubt as to the exact pad thickness or quality, remove them for measurement and further inspection (see Chapter 9).

7   Check the disc for score marks, wear and burned spots. If any of these conditions exist, the disc should be removed for servicing or replacement (see Chapter 9).

8   Before installing the wheels, check all the brake lines and hoses for damage, wear, deformation, cracks, corrosion, leakage, bends and twists, particularly in the vicinity of the rubber hoses and calipers.

9   Install the wheels, lower the vehicle and tighten the wheel lug nuts to the torque given in this Chapter's Specifications.

DRUM BRAKES

◆ **Refer to illustrations 13.14 and 13.17**

10 Remove the hub caps (if applicable) and loosen the wheel lug nuts a quarter turn each.

11 Raise the rear of the vehicle and support it securely on jackstands.

❄❄ WARNING:

Never work under a vehicle that is supported only by a jack!

Block the front wheels to prevent the vehicle from rolling, however, do not apply the parking brake or it will lock the drums in place. Remove the rear wheels.

12 Remove the brake drum as described in Chapter 9.

13 With the drum removed, carefully clean off any accumulations of dirt and dust using brake system cleaner.

❄❄ WARNING:

DO NOT blow the dust out with compressed air and don't inhale any of it.

14 Measure the thickness of the lining material on both leading and trailing brake shoes (see illustration). Compare the measurement with the limit given in this Chapter's Specifications, if any brake shoe thickness is less than specified, then all brake shoes must be replaced (see Chapter 9).

15 Inspect the brake shoes for uneven wear patterns, cracks, glazing

13.17 Carefully peel back the wheel cylinder boot and check for leaking fluid indicating that the cylinder must be replaced or rebuilt

and delamination and replace if necessary. If the shoes have been saturated with brake fluid, oil or grease, this also necessitates replacement (see Chapter 9).

16 Make sure all the brake assembly springs are connected and in good condition.

17 Check the brake wheel cylinder for signs of fluid leakage. Carefully pry back the rubber dust boots on the wheel cylinder (see illustration). Any leakage here is an indication that the wheel cylinders must be overhauled immediately (see Chapter 9). Also, check all hoses and connections for signs of leakage.

18 Clean the inside of the drum with brake system cleaner. Again, be careful not to breathe the dust.

19 Inspect the inside of the drum for cracks, score marks, deep scratches and "hard spots" which will appear as small discolored areas. If imperfections cannot be removed with fine emery cloth, the drum must be taken to an automotive machine shop for resurfacing.

20 Repeat the procedure for the remaining wheel.

21 Install the wheels, lower the vehicle and tighten the wheel lug nuts to the torque given in this Chapter's Specifications.

PARKING BRAKE

22 Slowly pull up on the parking brake and count the number of clicks you hear until the handle is up as far as it will go. The adjustment is correct if you hear the specified number of clicks (see this Chapter's Specifications). If you hear more or fewer clicks, it's time to adjust the parking brake (see Chapter 9).

23 An alternative method of checking the parking brake is to park the vehicle on a steep hill with the engine running (so you can apply the brakes if necessary) with the parking brake set and the transaxle in Neutral. If the parking brake cannot prevent the vehicle from rolling, it needs adjustment (see Chapter 9).

14 Steering and suspension check (every 15,000 miles or 12 months)

▶ Refer to illustrations 14.4, 14.10 and 14.11

➡Note: For detailed illustrations of the steering and suspension components, refer to Chapter 10.

WITH THE WHEELS ON THE GROUND

1 With the vehicle stopped and the front wheels pointed straight ahead, rock the steering wheel gently back and forth. If freeplay is excessive, a front wheel bearing, steering shaft universal joint or lower arm balljoint is worn or the steering gear is out of adjustment or broken. Refer to Chapter 10 for the appropriate repair procedure.

2 Other symptoms, such as excessive vehicle body movement over rough roads, swaying (leaning) around corners and binding as the steering wheel is turned, may indicate faulty steering and/or suspension components.

3 Check the shock absorbers by pushing down and releasing the vehicle several times at each corner. If the vehicle does not come back to a level position within one or two bounces, the shocks/struts are worn and must be replaced. When bouncing the vehicle up and down, listen for squeaks and noises from the suspension components.

4 Check the shock absorbers for evidence of fluid leakage (see illustration). A light film of fluid is no cause for concern. Make sure that any fluid noted is from the shocks and not from some other source. If leakage is noted, replace the shocks as a set.

5 Check the shocks to be sure they are securely mounted and undamaged. Check the upper mounts for damage and wear. If damage or wear is noted, replace the shocks as a set (front and rear).

6 If the shocks must be replaced, refer to Chapter 10 for the procedure.

UNDER THE VEHICLE

7 Raise the vehicle with a floor jack and support it securely on jackstands. See *Jacking and towing* at the front of this book for the proper jacking points.

8 Check the tires for irregular wear patterns and proper inflation.

14.4 Check the shocks for leakage at the indicated area

See Section 5 in this Chapter for information regarding tire wear and Chapter 10 for information on wheel bearing replacement.

9 Inspect the universal joint between the steering shaft and the steering gear housing. Check the steering gear housing for lubricant leakage. Make sure that the dust seals and boots are not damaged and that the boot clamps are not loose. Check the steering linkage for looseness or damage. Check the tie-rod ends for excessive play. Look for loose bolts, broken or disconnected parts and deteriorated rubber bushings on all suspension and steering components. While an assistant turns the steering wheel from side to side, check the steering components for free movement, chafing and binding. If the steering components do not seem to be reacting with the movement of the steering wheel, try to determine where the slack is located.

10 Check the balljoints for wear by trying to move each control arm up and down with a pry bar (see illustration) to ensure that its balljoint

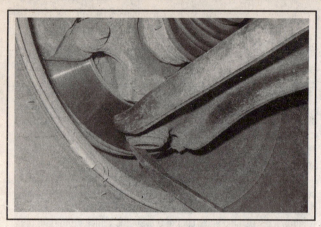

14.10 To check a balljoint for wear, try to pry the control arm up and down to make sure there is no play in the balljoint (if there is, replace it)

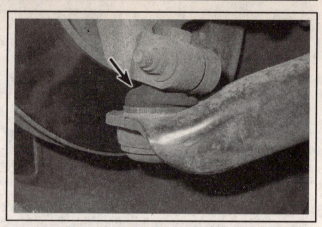

14.11 Check the balljoint boot for damage also

has no play. If any balljoint does have play, replace it. See Chapter 10 for the balljoint replacement procedure.

11 Inspect the balljoint boots for damage and leaking grease (see

illustration). Replace the balljoints with new ones if they are damaged (see Chapter 10).

12 At the rear of the vehicle, inspect the suspension arm bushings for deterioration. Additional information on suspension components can be found in Chapter 10.

15 Fuel system check (every 15,000 miles or 12 months)

✳✳ WARNING:

Gasoline is flammable, so take extra precautions when you work on any part of the fuel system. Don't smoke or allow open flames or bare light bulbs near the work area, and don't work in a garage where a gas-type appliance (such as a water heater or clothes dryer) is present. Since fuel is carcinogenic, wear latex gloves when there's a possibility of being exposed to fuel, and, if you spill any fuel on your skin, rinse it off immediately with soap and water. Mop up any spills immediately and do not store fuel-soaked rags where they could ignite. When you perform any kind of work on the fuel system, wear safety glasses and have a Class B type fire extinguisher on hand. The fuel system is under constant pressure, so, before any lines are disconnected, the fuel system pressure must be relieved (see Chapter 4).

1 If you smell gasoline while driving or after the vehicle has been sitting in the sun, inspect the fuel system immediately.

2 Remove the fuel filler cap and inspect if for damage and corrosion. The gasket should have an unbroken sealing imprint. If the gasket is damaged or corroded, install a new cap.

3 Inspect the fuel feed line for cracks. Make sure that the connections between the fuel lines and the fuel injection system and between the fuel lines and the in-line fuel filter are tight.

✳✳ WARNING:

Your vehicle is fuel injected, so you must relieve the fuel system pressure before servicing fuel system components. The fuel system pressure relief procedure is outlined in Chapter 4.

4 Since some components of the fuel system - the fuel tank and part of the fuel feed line, for example - are underneath the vehicle, they can be inspected more easily with the vehicle raised on a hoist. If that's not possible, raise the vehicle and support it on jackstands.

5 With the vehicle raised and safely supported, inspect the gas tank and filler neck for punctures, cracks and other damage. The connection between the filler neck and the tank is particularly critical. Sometimes a rubber filler neck will leak because of loose clamps or deteriorated rubber. Inspect all fuel tank mounting brackets and straps to be sure that the tank is securely attached to the vehicle.

✳✳ WARNING:

Do not, under any circumstances, try to repair a fuel tank (except rubber components). A welding torch or any open flame can easily cause fuel vapors inside the tank to explode.

6 Carefully check all rubber hoses and metal lines leading away from the fuel tank. Check for loose connections, deteriorated hoses, crimped lines and other damage. Repair or replace damaged sections as necessary (see Chapter 4).

16 Manual transaxle lubricant level check (every 15,000 miles or 12 months)

1 The manual transaxle does not have a dipstick. To check the fluid level, raise the vehicle and support it securely on jackstands. On the front side of the transaxle housing you will see a plug. Remove it. If the lubricant level is correct, it should be up to the lower edge of the hole.

2 If the transaxle needs more lubricant (if the level is not up to the

hole), use a syringe or a gear oil pump to add more. Stop filling the transaxle when the lubricant begins to run out the hole.

3 Install the plug and tighten it securely. Drive the vehicle a short distance, then check for leaks.

17 Transfer case lubricant level check (every 15,000 miles or 12 months)

◆ **Refer to illustration 17.2**

1   Raise the vehicle and support it securely on jackstands.
2   Using a ratchet or breaker bar, unscrew the check/fill plug from the transfer case (see illustration).
3   Use your little finger to reach inside the housing to feel the lubricant level. The level should be at or near the bottom of the plug hole. If it isn't, add the recommended lubricant through the plug hole with a syringe or squeeze bottle.
4   Install and tighten the plug. Check for leaks after the first few miles of driving.

17.2 Remove the check/fill plug and use your finger as a dipstick to check the transfer case lubricant level.

18 Air filter check and replacement (every 15,000 miles or 12 months)

◆ **Refer to illustrations 18.1a and 18.1b**

1   The air filter is located inside a housing at the left (driver's) side of the engine compartment. To remove the air filter, loosen the clamp securing the inlet tube to the air filter cover, release the clamps that secure the two halves of the air cleaner housing together, then separate the cover halves and remove the air filter element (see illustrations).
2   Inspect the outer surface of the filter element. If it is dirty, replace it. If it is only moderately dusty, it can be reused by blowing it clean from the back to the front surface with compressed air. Because it is a pleated paper type filter, it cannot be washed or oiled. If it cannot be cleaned satisfactorily with compressed air, discard and replace it. While the cover is off, be careful not to drop anything down into the housing.

✳ CAUTION:

Never drive the vehicle with the air cleaner removed. Excessive engine wear could result and backfiring could even cause a fire under the hood.

3   Wipe out the inside of the air cleaner housing.
4   Place the new filter into the air cleaner housing, making sure it seats properly.
5   Installation of the housing is the reverse of removal.

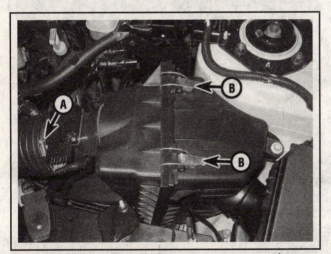

18.1a Loosen the intake hose clamp (A), then unlatch these clips (B) . . .

18.1b . . . pull the cover out of the way and lift the element out

19 Driveaxle boot check (every 15,000 miles or 12 months)

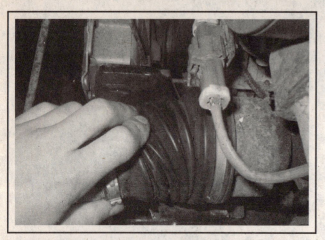

19.2 Flex the driveaxle boots by hand to check for cracks and/or leaking grease

▶ **Refer to illustration 19.2**

1   The driveaxle boots are very important because they prevent dirt, water and foreign material from entering and damaging the constant velocity (CV) joints. Oil and grease can cause the boot material to deteriorate prematurely, so it's a good idea to wash the boots with soap and water. Because it constantly pivots back and forth following the steering action of the front hub, the outer CV boot wears out sooner and should be inspected regularly.

2   Inspect the boots for tears and cracks as well as loose clamps (see illustration). If there is any evidence of cracks or leaking lubricant, they must be replaced as described in Chapter 8.

20 Exhaust system check (every 30,000 miles or 24 months)

▶ **Refer to illustration 20.2**

1   With the engine cold (at least three hours after the vehicle has been driven), check the complete exhaust system from the engine to the end of the tailpipe. Ideally, the inspection should be done with the vehicle on a hoist to permit unrestricted access. If a hoist isn't available, raise the vehicle and support it securely on jackstands.

2   Check the exhaust pipes and connections for evidence of leaks, severe corrosion and damage. Make sure that all brackets and hangers are in good condition and tight (see illustration).

3   At the same time, inspect the underside of the body for holes, corrosion, open seams, etc. which may allow exhaust gases to enter the passenger compartment. Seal all body openings with silicone or body putty.

4   Rattles and other noises can often be traced to the exhaust system, especially the mounts and hangers. Try to move the pipes, muffler and catalytic converter. If the components can come in contact with the body or suspension parts, secure the exhaust system with new mounts.

5   Check the running condition of the engine by inspecting inside the end of the tailpipe. The exhaust deposits here are an indication of engine state-of-tune. If the pipe is black and sooty or coated with white

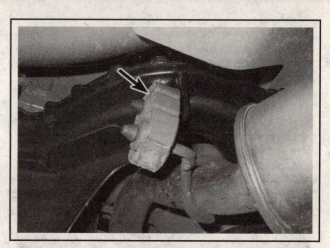

20.2 Be sure to check each exhaust system rubber hanger for damage

deposits, the engine may need a tune-up, including a thorough fuel system inspection and adjustment.

21 Fuel filter replacement (every 30,000 miles or 24 months)

▶ **Refer to illustrations 21.1 and 21.4**

❈❈ **WARNING:**

Gasoline is extremely flammable, so take extra precautions when you work on any part of the fuel system. Don't smoke or allow open flames or bare light bulbs near the work area, and don't work in a garage where a gas-type appliance (such as a water heater or clothes dryer) is present. Since fuel is carcinogenic, wear latex gloves when there's a possibility of being exposed to fuel, and, if you spill any fuel on your skin, rinse it off immediately with soap and water. Mop up any spills immediately and do not store fuel-soaked rags where they could ignite. When you perform any kind of work on the fuel system, wear safety glasses and have a Class B type fire extinguisher on hand.

21.1 The fuel filter is located in front of the fuel tank

21.4 Use a small screwdriver to pry off the fuel line fitting retaining clips at both ends of the filter

1   The fuel filter is mounted under the vehicle on the right side, in front of the gas tank (see illustration).

2   Relieve the fuel system pressure (see Chapter 4).

3   If necessary, raise the vehicle and support it securely on jackstands. Inspect the fittings at both ends of the filter to see if they're clean. If more than a light coating of dust is present, clean the fittings before proceeding.

4   Release the clips holding the fuel lines to the filter (see illustration).

5   Detach the fuel hoses, one at a time, from the filter. Be prepared for fuel spillage.

6   After the lines are detached, check the fittings for damage and distortion. If they were damaged in any way during removal, new ones must be used when the lines are reattached to the new filter (if new clips are packaged with the filter, be sure to use them in place of the originals).

7   Remove the fuel filter from the mounting clamp, while noting the direction the fuel filter is installed.

8   Install the new filter in the same direction. Carefully push each hose onto the filter until it's seated against the collar on the fitting, then install the clips. Make sure the clips are securely attached to the hose fittings - if they come off, the hoses could back off the filter and a fire could result!

9   Start the engine and check for fuel leaks.

22 Cooling system servicing (draining, flushing and refilling) (every 30,000 miles or 24 months)

♦ **Refer to illustrations 22.4, 22.5 and 22.10**

※※ **WARNING:**

Do not allow antifreeze to come in contact with your skin or painted surfaces of the vehicle. Rinse off spills immediately with plenty of water. Antifreeze is highly toxic if ingested. Never leave antifreeze lying around in an open container or in puddles on the floor; children and pets are attracted by its sweet smell and may drink it. Check with local authorities about disposing of used antifreeze. Many communities have collection centers which will see that antifreeze is disposed of safely. Never dump used antifreeze on the ground or pour it into drains.

※※ **CAUTION:**

Do not mix coolants of different colors. Doing so might damage the cooling system and/or the engine. The manufacturer specifies either a green colored coolant or a yellow colored coolant to be used in these systems. Read the warning label in the engine compartment for additional information.

➡**Note: Non-toxic antifreeze is now manufactured and available at local auto parts stores, but even this type must be disposed of properly.**

1   Periodically, the cooling system should be drained, flushed and refilled to replenish the antifreeze mixture and prevent formation of rust and corrosion, which can impair the performance of the cooling system and cause engine damage. When the cooling system is serviced, all hoses and the expansion tank cap should be checked and replaced if necessary.

DRAINING

2   Apply the parking brake and block the wheels. If the vehicle has just been driven, wait several hours to allow the engine to cool down before beginning this procedure.

3   Once the engine is completely cool, remove the expansion tank cap.

4   Move a large container under the radiator drain to catch the

22.4 The radiator drain fitting is located at the bottom of the radiator - before opening the valve, push a short length of rubber hose onto the plastic fitting to prevent the coolant from splashing

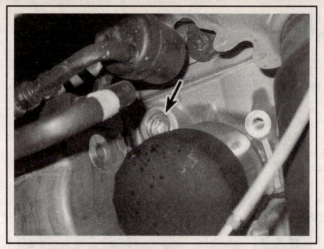

22.5 On the V6 engine, remove the engine block drain plugs from both sides of the engine

coolant. Attach a length of hose to the drain fitting to direct the coolant into the container, then open the drain fitting (a pair of pliers may be required to turn it) (see illustration).

5   After the coolant stops flowing out of the radiator, move the container under the engine block drain plug(s) and allow the coolant in the block to drain (see illustration).

6   While the coolant is draining, check the condition of the radiator hoses, heater hoses and clamps (refer to Section 9 if necessary). Replace any damaged clamps or hoses.

7   Reinstall the block drain plugs and tighten them securely.

FLUSHING

8   Once the system has completely drained, remove the thermostat housing from the engine (see Chapter 3), then reinstall the housing without the thermostat. This will allow the system to be thoroughly flushed.

9   Disconnect the upper hose from the radiator.

10 Place a garden hose in the upper radiator inlet and flush the system until the water runs clear at the upper radiator hose (see illustration).

11 Severe cases of radiator contamination or clogging will require removing the radiator (see Chapter 3) and reverse flushing it. This involves inserting the hose in the bottom radiator outlet to allow the clean water to run against the normal flow, draining out through the top. A radiator repair shop should be consulted if further cleaning or repair is necessary.

12 When the coolant is regularly drained and the system refilled with the correct coolant mixture there should be no need to employ chemical cleaners or descalers.

REFILLING

13 Close and tighten the radiator drain.

14 Place the heater temperature control in the maximum heat position.

15 Slowly add new coolant (a 50/50 mixture of water and antifreeze) to the expansion tank until the level is at the COLD FULL mark on the expansion tank.

16 Leave the expansion tank cap off and run the engine in a well-ventilated area until the thermostat opens (coolant will begin flowing through the radiator and the upper radiator hose will become hot).

17 Turn the engine off and let it cool. Add more coolant mixture to bring the level to the COLD FULL mark on the expansion tank.

18 Squeeze the upper radiator hose to expel air, then add more coolant mixture if necessary. Replace the expansion tank cap.

19 Start the engine, allow it to reach normal operating temperature and check for leaks. Also, set the heater and blower controls to the maximum setting and check to see that the heater output from the air ducts is warm. This is a good indication that all air has been purged from the cooling system.

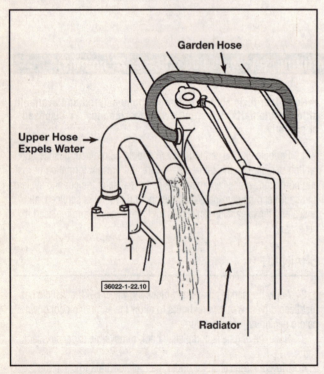

22.10 With the thermostat removed, disconnect the upper radiator hose and flush the radiator and engine block with a garden hose

23 Brake fluid change (every 30,000 miles or 24 months)

※ WARNING:

Brake fluid can harm your eyes and damage painted surfaces, so use extreme caution when handling or pouring it. Do not use brake fluid that has been standing open or is more than one year old. Brake fluid absorbs moisture from the air. Excess moisture can cause a dangerous loss of braking effectiveness.

1   At the specified intervals, the brake fluid should be drained and replaced. Since the brake fluid may drip or splash when pouring it, place plenty of rags around the master cylinder to protect any surrounding painted surfaces.

2   Before beginning work, purchase the specified brake fluid (see *Recommended lubricants and fluids* at the end of this Chapter).

3   Remove the cap from the master cylinder reservoir.

4   Using a hand suction pump or similar device, withdraw the fluid from the master cylinder reservoir.

5   Add new fluid to the master cylinder until it rises to the base of the filler neck.

6   Bleed the brake system as described in Chapter 9 at all four brakes until new and uncontaminated fluid is expelled from the bleeder screw. Be sure to maintain the fluid level in the master cylinder as you perform the bleeding process. If you allow the master cylinder to run dry, air will enter the system.

7   Refill the master cylinder with fluid and check the operation of the brakes. The pedal should feel solid when depressed, with no sponginess.

※ WARNING:

Do not operate the vehicle if you are in doubt about the effectiveness of the brake system.

24 Drivebelt check and replacement (every 30,000 miles or 24 months)

ACCESSORY DRIVEBELT

1   A single serpentine drivebelt is located at the front of the engine and plays an important role in the overall operation of the engine and its components. Due to its function and material make up, the belt is prone to wear and should be periodically inspected. The serpentine belt drives the alternator, power steering pump, water pump (four-cylinder models) and air conditioning compressor. Although the belt should be inspected at the recommended intervals, replacement may not be necessary for more than 100,000 miles.

Check

▶ Refer to illustrations 24.2 and 24.4

2   Since the drivebelt is located very close to the right-hand side of the engine compartment, it is possible to gain better access by raising the front of the vehicle and removing the right-hand wheel, then unbolting the lower splash shield from the underbody (see illustration).

Be sure to support the front of the vehicle securely on jackstands.

3   With the engine stopped, inspect the full length of the drivebelt for cracks and separation of the belt plies. It will be necessary to turn the engine (using a wrench or socket and bar on the crankshaft pulley bolt) in order to move the belt from the pulleys so that the belt can be inspected thoroughly. Twist the belt between the pulleys so that both sides can be viewed. Also check for fraying, and glazing which gives the belt a shiny appearance. Check the pulleys for nicks, cracks, distortion and corrosion.

4   Note that it is not unusual for a ribbed belt to exhibit small cracks in the edges of the belt ribs, and unless these are extensive or very deep, belt replacement is not essential (see illustration).

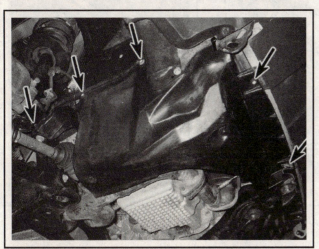

24.2 Remove the lower splash shield to gain access to the drivebelt

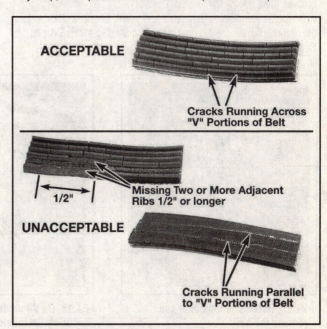

24.4 Small cracks in the underside of a V-ribbed belt are acceptable - lengthwise cracks, or missing pieces that cause the belt to make noise, are cause for replacement

24.6 Rotate the tensioner arm to relieve belt tension

Replacement

▶ Refer to illustration 24.6

5   To remove the drivebelt, loosen the right front wheel lug nuts, then raise the front of the vehicle and support it on jackstands. Remove the right front wheel and remove the lower splash shield from the underbody.

6   Note how the drivebelt is routed, then remove the belt from the pulleys. If you're working on a four-cylinder engine, use a wrench on the tensioner center bolt and turn the tensioner clockwise to release the drivebelt tension. If you're working on a V6 engine, insert a 3/8-inch drive ratchet or breaker bar into the tensioner hole and pull the handle clockwise to release the drivebelt tension (see illustration).

7   Fit the new drivebelt onto the crankshaft, alternator, power steering pump, and air conditioning compressor pulleys, as applicable, then turn the tensioner counterclockwise and locate the drivebelt on the pulley. Make sure that the drivebelt is correctly seated in all of the pulley grooves, then release the tensioner.

8   Install the lower splash shield and wheel, then lower the car to the ground. Tighten the lug nuts to the torque listed in this Chapter's Specifications.

WATER PUMP DRIVEBELT (V6 ENGINE)

Replacement

▶ Refer to illustration 24.10

9   The water pump drivebelt is located at the left end of the engine and is driven by a pulley attached to the end of the front cylinder bank intake camshaft. The belt and pulley are protected by a cover.

10   To replace the belt, remove the cover (see illustration 4.1 in Chapter 2, Part B), rotate the tensioner clockwise and remove the belt (see illustration). Slowly release the tensioner.

11   Route the new belt over the pulleys, again rotating the tensioner to allow the belt to be installed, then release the belt tensioner. Make sure the belt is positioned properly on the pulleys. Reinstall the cover and tighten the fasteners securely.

TENSIONER REPLACEMENT

12   Remove the drivebelt as described previously.

Accessory drivebelt tensioner

▶ Refer to illustration 24.13

13   On four-cylinder models, remove the two bolts securing the tensioner to the engine block. On V6 models, remove the bolt in the center of the tensioner, then detach the tensioner from the engine (see illustration).

14   Installation is the reverse of removal. Be sure to tighten the tensioners bolt(s) to the torque listed in this Chapter's Specifications.

Water pump drivebelt tensioner (V6 engine)

▶ Refer to illustration 24.15

15   Unscrew the bolt securing the tensioner, then remove the tensioner (see illustration).

16   Installation is the reverse of removal. Be sure to tighten the tensioner bolts to the torque listed in this Chapter's Specifications.

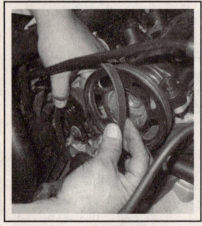

24.10 Rotate the tensioner and remove the belt

24.13 On V6 models, remove the bolt securing the tensioner to the block

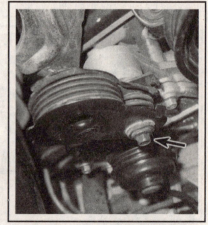

24.15 Remove the bolt securing the water pump drivebelt tensioner

25 Automatic transaxle fluid change (every 30,000 miles or 24 months)

◆ **Refer to illustration 25.6**

1   The automatic transaxle fluid should be changed at the recommended intervals.

2   Before beginning work, purchase the specified transmission fluid (see *Recommended lubricants and fluids* at the end of this chapter).

3   Other tools necessary for this job include jackstands to support the vehicle in a raised position, wrenches, drain pan capable of holding at least four quarts, newspapers and clean rags.

4   The fluid should be drained immediately after the vehicle has been driven. Hot fluid is more effective than cold fluid at removing built up sediment.

✳✳ WARNING:

Fluid temperature can exceed 350-degrees F in a hot transaxle. Wear protective gloves.

5   After the vehicle has been driven to warm up the fluid, raise the front of the vehicle and support it securely on jackstands.

✳✳ WARNING:

Never work under a vehicle that is supported only by a jack!

Remove the transaxle splash shield for access to the transaxle drain plug.

6   Place the drain pan under the drain plug in the transaxle pan and remove the drain plug (see illustration). Be sure the drain pan is in position, as fluid will come out with some force. Once the fluid is drained, reinstall the drain plug securely. Measure the amount of fluid

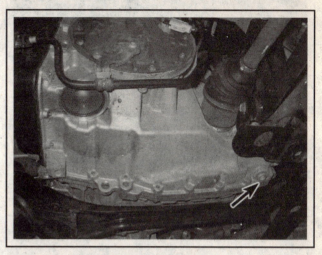

25.6 Remove the transaxle drain plug

drained and write down this figure for reference when refilling.

7   Lower the vehicle

8   With the engine off, add new fluid to the transaxle through the dipstick tube (see *Recommended lubricants and fluids* for the recommended fluid type). Begin the refill procedure by initially adding 1/3 of the amount drained. Then, with the engine running, add 1/2-pint at a time (cycling the shifter through each gear position between additions) until the level is correct on the dipstick.

9   Repeat Steps 5 through 8 once to flush any contaminated fluid from the torque converter.

10 Before final installation of the transaxle drain plug, apply Teflon tape to the threads.

26 Manual transaxle lubricant change (every 30,000 miles or 24 months)

1   Raise the vehicle and support it securely on jackstands.

2   Move a drain pan, rags, newspapers and wrenches under the transaxle.

3   Remove the transaxle fill plug on the front of the case and the drain plug at the bottom of the case, then allow the lubricant to drain into the pan.

4   After the lubricant has drained completely, reinstall the drain

plug and tighten it securely.

5   Using a hand pump, syringe or funnel, fill the transaxle with the specified lubricant until it is level with the lower edge of the filler hole. Reinstall the fill plug and tighten it securely.

6   Lower the vehicle.

7   Drive the vehicle for a short distance, then check the drain and fill plugs for leakage.

27 Differential lubricant change (4WD models) (every 30,000 miles or 24 months)

DRAIN

1   This procedure should be performed after the vehicle has been driven so the lubricant will be warm and therefore flow out of the differential more easily.

2   Raise the vehicle and support it securely on jackstands.

3   The easiest way to drain the differential(s) is to remove the lubricant through the filler plug hole with a suction pump. If the differential cover gasket is leaking, it will be necessary to remove the cover to drain the lubricant (which will also allow you to inspect the differential).

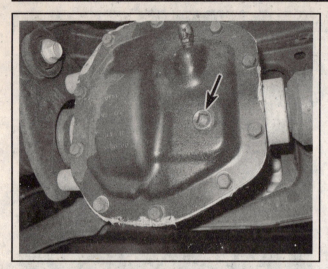

27.4 Rear differential check/fill plug

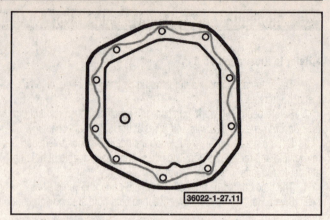

27.11 Apply a continuous thin bead of RTV sealant to the cover

CHANGING THE LUBRICANT WITH A SUCTION PUMP

▶ **Refer to illustration 27.4**

4 Remove the filler plug from the differential (see illustration).

5 Insert the flexible hose.

6 Work the hose down to the bottom of the differential housing and pump the lubricant out.

CHANGING THE LUBRICANT BY REMOVING THE COVER

▶ **Refer to illustration 27.11**

7 Move a drain pan, rags, newspapers and wrenches under the vehicle.

8 Remove the bolts on the lower half of the cover. Loosen the bolts on the upper half and use them to loosely retain the cover. Allow the oil to drain into the pan, then completely remove the cover.

9 Using a lint-free rag, clean the inside of the cover and the accessible areas of the differential housing. As this is done, check for chipped gears and metal particles in the lubricant, indicating that the differential should be more thoroughly inspected and/or repaired.

10 Thoroughly clean the gasket mating surfaces of the differential housing and the cover plate. Use a gasket scraper or putty knife to remove all traces of the old gasket.

11 Apply a thin bead of RTV sealant to the cover flange (see illustration). Make sure the bolt holes align properly then install the cover and tighten the fasteners to the torque listed in this Chapter's Specifications.

REFILL

12 Use a hand pump, syringe or funnel to fill the differential housing with the specified lubricant until it's level with the bottom of the filler plug hole.

13 Install the fill plug and tighten it securely.

28 Transfer case lubricant change (4WD models) (every 30,000 miles or 24 months)

28.3a First remove the transfer case check/fill plug . . .

▶ **Refer to illustrations 28.3a and 28.3b**

1 Drive the vehicle for at least 15 minutes to warm the lubricant in the case. Perform this warm-up procedure with 4WD engaged, if possible.

2 Raise the vehicle and support it securely on jackstands.

3 Remove the check/fill plug, then the drain plug and allow the old lubricant to drain completely (see illustrations).

4   After the lubricant has drained completely, reinstall the plug and tighten it securely.

5   Fill the case with the specified lubricant until it is level with the lower edge of the filler hole.

6   Install the check/fill plug and tighten it securely.

7   Drive the vehicle for a short distance, then check the drain and fill plugs for leakage.

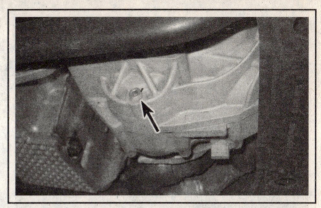

28.3b . . . then remove the transfer case drain plug

29 Positive Crankcase Ventilation (PCV) valve replacement (four-cylinder models) (every 60,000 miles or 48 months)

➡**Note 1: For additional information on the PCV system, the PCV valve on V6 models and the oil separators on both engines, refer to Chapter 6.**

➡**Note 2: This Section applies to models with four-cylinder engines only.**

1   The PCV valve is located in the valve cover.

2   Start the engine and allow it to idle, then disconnect the PCV valve from the valve cover and feel for vacuum at the end of the valve. If vacuum is felt, the PCV valve/system is working properly (see Chapter 6 for additional PCV system information).

3   If no vacuum is felt, remove the valve and check for vacuum at the hose. If vacuum is present at the hose but not at the valve, replace the valve. If no vacuum is felt at the hose, check for a plugged or cracked hose between the PCV valve and the intake plenum.

4   Check the rubber grommet in the valve cover for cracks and distortion. If it's damaged, replace it.

5   If the valve is clogged, the hose might also be plugged. Remove the hose between the valve and the intake manifold and clean it with solvent.

6   After cleaning the hose, inspect it for damage, wear and deterioration. Make sure it fits snugly on the fittings.

7   If necessary, install a new PCV valve.

30 Spark plug check and replacement (see Maintenance schedule for service intervals)

▶ **Refer to illustrations 30.2, 30.5a, 30.5b, 30.7a, 30.7b, 30.7c, 30.7d, 30.9, 30.10, 30.11a and 30.11b**

1   On these vehicles the spark plugs are located at the top of the engine.

2   In most cases, the tools necessary for spark plug replacement include a spark plug socket which fits onto a ratchet (spark plug sockets are padded inside to prevent damage to the porcelain insulators on the new plugs), various extensions and a gap gauge to check and adjust the gaps on the new plugs (see illustration). A torque wrench should be used to tighten the new plugs.

3   The best approach when replacing the spark plugs is to purchase the new ones in advance, adjust them to the proper gap and replace the plugs one at a time. When buying the new spark plugs, be sure to obtain the correct plug type for your particular engine. This information can be found in the *Specifications* Section at the end of this Chapter or in the factory owner's manual.

4   Allow the engine to cool completely before attempting to remove any of the plugs. These engines are equipped with aluminum cylinder heads, which can be damaged if the spark plugs are removed when the engine is hot. While you are waiting for the engine to cool, check the new plugs for defects and adjust the gaps.

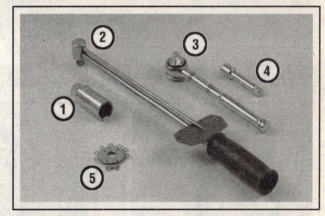

30.2 Tools required for changing spark plugs

1   *Spark plug socket* - This will have special padding inside to protect the spark plug porcelain insulator

2   *Torque wrench* - Although not mandatory, use of this tool is the best way to ensure that the plugs are tightened properly

3   *Ratchet* - Standard hand tool to fit the plug socket

4   *Extension* - Depending on model and accessories, you may need special extensions and universal joints to reach one or more of the plugs

5   *Spark plug gap gauge* - This gauge for checking the gap comes in a variety of styles. Make sure the gap for your engine is included

30.5a Spark plug manufacturers recommend using a tapered thickness gauge when checking the gap - slide the thin side into the gap and turn it until the gauge just fills the gap, then read the thickness on the gauge - do not force the tool into the gap or use the tapered portion to widen a gap

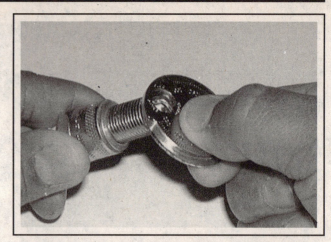

30.5b To change the gap, bend the side electrode only, using the adjuster hole in the tool, and be very careful not to crack or chip the porcelain insulator surrounding the center electrode

30.7a V6 models are equipped with individual coils which must be removed to access the spark plugs

5   The gap is checked by inserting the proper-thickness gauge between the electrodes at the tip of the plug (see illustration). The gap between the electrodes should be the same as the one specified on the *Emissions Control Information* label or in this Chapter's Specifications. The gauge should just slide between the electrodes with a slight amount of drag. If the gap is incorrect, use the adjuster on the gauge body to bend the curved side electrode slightly until the proper gap is obtained (see illustration). If the side electrode is not exactly over the center electrode, bend it with the adjuster until it is. Check for cracks in the porcelain insulator (if any are found, the plug should not be used).

➡Note: We recommend using a tapered thickness gauge when checking platinum- or iridium-type spark plugs. Other types of gauges may scrape the thin coating from the electrodes, thus dramatically shortening the life of the plugs. However, if dual-electrode spark plugs are used, a wire-type gauge will have to be used.

6   On V6 engines, remove the engine cover and intake manifold (see Chapter 2 Part B).

7   Some engines are equipped with individual ignition coils which must be removed first to access the spark plugs (see illustrations). On other engines, remove the spark plug wire from one spark plug. Pull

30.7b To remove the coils, disconnect the electrical connector . . .

30.7c . . . and remove the coil retaining screw . . .

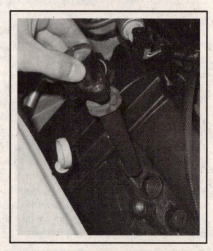

30.7d . . . then pull straight up and out to remove the coil

only on the boot at the end of the wire - do not pull on the wire. A plug wire removal tool should be used if available.

8   If compressed air is available, use it to blow any dirt or foreign material away from the spark plug hole. The idea here is to eliminate the possibility of debris falling into the cylinder as the spark plug is removed.

9   Place the spark plug socket over the plug and remove it from the engine by turning it in a counterclockwise direction (see illustration).

10 Compare the spark plugs with this chart to get an indication of the general running condition of the engine.

11 Apply a small amount of anti-seize compound to the spark plug threads (see illustration). Install one of the new plugs into the hole until you can no longer turn it with your fingers, then tighten it with a torque wrench (if available) or the ratchet. It is a good idea to slip a short length of rubber hose over the end of the plug to use as a tool to thread it into place (see illustration). The hose will grip the plug well enough to turn it, but will start to slip if the plug begins to cross-thread in the hole - this will prevent damaged threads and the accompanying repair costs.

12 On V6 engines, before pushing the ignition coil onto the end of the plug, inspect the ignition coil following the procedures outlined in

30.9 Use a ratchet and extension to remove the spark plugs

Section 31. On four-cylinder engines, inspect the plug wire following the procedures outlined in Section 32.

13 Repeat the procedure for the remaining spark plugs.

A **normally worn** spark plug should have light tan or gray deposits on the firing tip.

A **carbon fouled** plug, identified by soft, sooty, black deposits, may indicate an improperly tuned vehicle. Check the air cleaner, ignition components and engine control system.

An **oil fouled** spark plug indicates an engine with worn piston rings and/or bad valve seals allowing excessive oil to enter the chamber.

This spark plug has been **left in the engine too long**, as evidenced by the extreme gap- Plugs with such an extreme gap can cause misfiring and stumbling accompanied by a noticeable lack of power.

A **physically damaged** spark plug may be evidence of severe detonation in that cylinder. Watch that cylinder carefully between services, as a continued detonation will not only damage the plug, but could also damage the engine.

A **bridged or almost bridged** spark plug, identified by a build-up between the electrodes caused by excessive carbon or oil build-up on the plug.

30.10 Inspect the spark plug to determine engine running conditions

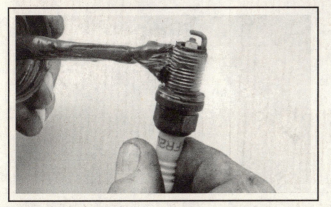

30.11a Apply a thin coat of anti-seize compound to the spark plug threads

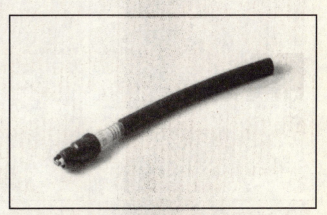

30.11b A length of snug-fitting rubber hose will save time and prevent damaged threads when installing the spark plugs

31   Ignition coil check (V6 engines and 2005 and later four-cylinder engines) (every 60,000 miles or 48 months)

1   Remove the ignition coils (see illustrations 30.7b and 30.7c). Clean the coil(s) with a dampened cloth and dry them thoroughly.

2   Inspect each coil, for cracks, damage and carbon tracking. If damage exists, replace the coil.

32   Spark plug wire check and replacement (2004 and earlier four-cylinder engines) (every 60,000 miles or 48 months)

1   The spark plug wires should be checked at the recommended intervals or whenever new spark plugs are installed.

2   Begin this procedure by making a visual check of the spark plug wires while the engine is running. In a darkened garage (make sure there is adequate ventilation) or at night while using a flashlight, start the engine and observe each plug wire. Be careful not to come into contact with any moving engine parts. If possible, use an insulated or non-conductive object to wiggle each wire. If there is a break in the wire, you will see arcing or a small blue spark coming from the damaged area. Secondary ignition voltage increases with engine speed and sometimes a damaged wire will not produce an arc at idle speed. Have an assistant press the accelerator pedal to raise the engine speed to approximately 2000 rpm. Check the spark plug wires for arcing as stated previously. If arcing is noticed, replace all spark plug wires.

3   Perform the following checks with the engine OFF. The wires should be inspected one at a time to prevent mixing up the order that is essential for proper engine operation.

➡**Note: Due to the short length of the spark plug wire, always disconnect the spark plug wire from the ignition coil pack first.**

4   With the engine cool, disconnect the spark plug wire from the ignition coil pack. Pull only on the boot at the end of the wire; don't pull on the wire itself. Use a twisting motion to free the boot/wire from the coil. Disconnect the same spark plug wire from the spark plug, using the same twisting method while pulling on the boot. Disconnect the spark plug wire from any retaining clips as necessary and remove it from the engine.

5   Check inside the boot for corrosion, which will look like a white, crusty powder (don't mistake the white dielectric grease used on some plug wire boots for corrosion protection).

6   Now push the wire and boot back onto the end of the spark plug. It should be a tight fit on the plug end. If not, remove the wire and use a pair of pliers to carefully crimp the metal connector inside the wire boot until the fit is snug.

7   Now push the wire and boot back into the end of the ignition coil terminal. It should be a tight fit in the terminal. If not, remove the wire and use a pair of pliers to carefully crimp the metal connector inside the wire boot until the fit is snug.

8   Now, using a cloth, clean each wire along its entire length. Remove all built-up dirt and grease. As this is done, inspect for burned areas, cracks and any other form of damage. Bend the wires in several places to ensure that the conductive material inside hasn't hardened. Repeat the procedure for the remaining wires.

9   If new spark plug wires are required, purchase a complete set for your particular engine. The terminals and rubber boots should already be installed on the wires. Replace the wires one at a time to avoid mixing up the firing order and make sure the terminals are securely seated on the coil pack and the spark plugs.

10 Attach the plug wire to the new spark plug and to the ignition coil pack using a twisting motion on the boot until it is firmly seated. Attach the spark plug wire to any retaining clips to keep the wires in their proper location on the valve cover.

Specifications

Recommended lubricants and fluids

➡Note: Listed here are manufacturer recommendations at the time this manual was written. Manufacturers occasionally upgrade their fluid and lubricant specifications, so check with your local auto parts store for current recommendations.

Engine oil	
Type	API "certified for gasoline engines"
Viscosity	SAE 5W-20
Fuel	Unleaded gasoline, 87 octane
Automatic transaxle fluid	MERCON® automatic transmission fluid.

❊❊ CAUTION:

Do not use Mercon® V or dual usage Mercon®/Mercon® V automatic transmission fluid.

Manual transaxle lubricant	SAE 75W-90 gear oil
Transfer case (4WD models)	
With automatic transaxle	SAE 75W-140
With manual transaxle	SAE 80W-90 Premium Rear Axle Lubricant
Rear differential lubricant (4WD models)	SAE 80W-90 Premium Rear Axle Lubricant
Brake fluid	DOT 3 brake fluid
Clutch fluid	DOT 3 brake fluid
Engine coolant*	50/50 mixture of Motorcraft Premium Engine Coolant (green colored) or Motorcraft Premium Gold Engine Coolant (yellow colored) and distilled water
Power steering system	MERCON® automatic transmission fluid

❊❊ CAUTION:

Do not mix coolants of different colors. Doing so might damage the cooling system and/or the engine. The manufacturer specifies either a green colored coolant or a yellow colored coolant to be used in these systems, depending on what was originally installed in the vehicle.

Capacities*

Engine oil (including filter)	
Four-cylinder engine	4.5 qts (4.25 liters)
V6 engine	
2004 and earlier models	5.5 qts (5.2 liters)
2005 and later models	6.0 qts (5.7 liters)
Coolant	
Four-cylinder engine	Up to 7.0 qts (6.6 liters)
V6 engine	Up to 10.5 qts (10.0 liters)
Automatic transaxle (dry fill)	Up to 10.0 qts (9.5 liters)

➡Note: Since this is a dry-fill specification, the amount required during a routine fluid change will be substantially less. The best way to determine the amount of fluid to add during a routine fluid change is to measure the amount drained. Begin the refill procedure by initially adding 1/3rd of the amount drained. Then, with the engine running, add 1/2-pint at a time (cycling the shifter through each gear position between additions) until the level is correct on the dipstick. It is important to not overfill the transaxle. You will, however, need to purchase a few extra quarts, since the fluid replacement procedure involves flushing the torque converter (see Section 25).

Manual transaxle	
2WD models	Up to 2.85 qts (2.7 liters)
4WD models	Up to 2.32 qts (2.2 liters)
Transfer case (4WD models)	
With automatic transaxle	Up to 12 ounces (0.35 liters)
With manual transaxle	Up to 12 ounces (0.35 liters)
Rear differential (4WD models)	Up to 1.47 qts (1.4 liters)

*All capacities approximate. Add as necessary to bring up to appropriate level.

Ignition system

Spark plug type and gap

Type

    Four-cylinder engine

        Cylinders 1 and 3 .... Motorcraft AZFS-32F or equivalent

        Cylinders 2 and 4 .... Motorcraft AZFS-32FE or equivalent

    V6 engine .... Motorcraft AWSF-32F or equivalent

Gap

    2.0L four-cylinder engine .... 0.048 to 0.052 inch (1.22 to 1.32 mm)

    2.3L four-cylinder engine .... 0.054 inch (1.37 mm)

    V6 engine .... 0.052 to 0.056 inch (1.3 to 1.4 mm)

Engine firing order

    Four-cylinder engine 1-3-4-2

    V6 engine 1-4-2-5-3-6

Cylinder location and coil terminal arrangement (four-cylinder engine)

Cylinder location (V6 engine)

Valve clearances (engine cold)

Four-cylinder engine

    2.0L intake valve .... 0.004 to 0.007 inch (0.11 to 0.18 mm)

    2.3L intake valve .... 0.008 to 0.011 inch (0.22 to 0.28 mm)

    2.0L exhaust valve .... 0.010 to 0.013 inch (0.27 to 0.34 mm)

    2.3L exhaust valve .... 0.010 to 0.013 inch (0.27 to 0.33 mm)

V6 engine .... No adjustment required

Clutch pedal

Freeplay .... 0.22 to 0.59 inch (5.58 to 15 mm)

Height .... 8.35 to 8.54 inches (212 to 217 mm)

Brakes

Disc brake pad lining thickness (minimum) ..... 1/8 inch (3 mm)

Drum brake shoe lining thickness (minimum) ... 1/16 inch (1.5 mm)

Parking brake adjustment .... 3 to 5 clicks

Torque specifications	Ft-lbs (unless otherwise indicated)	Nm

➡**Note: One foot-pound (ft-lb) of torque is equivalent to 12 inch-pounds (in-lbs) of torque. Torque values below approximately 15 ft-lbs are expressed in inch-pounds, since most foot-pound torque wrenches are not accurate at these smaller values.**

	Ft-lbs	Nm
Engine oil drain plug		
Four-cylinder engine	18	25
V6 engine	19	26
Automatic transaxle drain plug	20	27
Manual transaxle drain plug	35	47
Rear differential cover bolts (4WD)	17	23
Rear differential check/fill plug (4WD)	20	27
Spark plugs	132 in-lbs	15
Drivebelt tensioner bolts		
Four-cylinder engine	18	25
V6 engine	18	25
Water pump drivebelt tensioner mounting bolt		
(V6 engine)	89 in-lbs	10
Wheel lug nuts	98	133

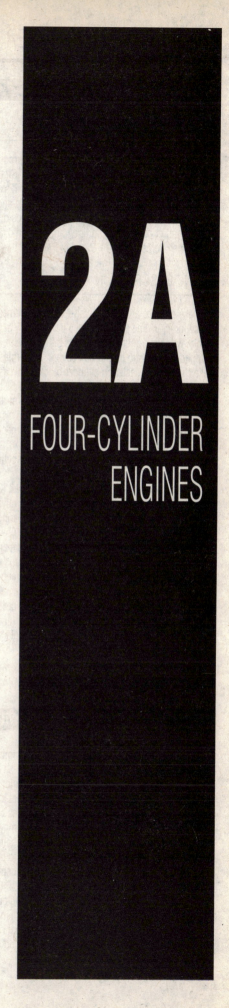

2A
FOUR-CYLINDER ENGINES

Section

Reference to other Chapters

1 General information

HOW TO USE THIS CHAPTER

This Part of Chapter 2 is devoted to repair procedures possible while the engine is still installed in the vehicle. Since these procedures are based on the assumption that the engine is installed in the vehicle, if the engine has been removed from the vehicle and mounted on a stand, some of the preliminary dismantling steps outlined will not apply.

Information concerning engine/transaxle removal and replacement and engine overhaul, can be found in Part C of this Chapter.

ENGINE DESCRIPTION

These engines are sixteen-valve, double overhead camshaft (DOHC), four-cylinder, in-line type, mounted transversely at the front of the vehicle, with the transmission on its left-hand end. The 2.0L engine is equipped with plastic timing belt covers, a fiberglass-reinforced plastic intake manifold, a cast-iron cylinder block/crankcase and aluminum cylinder head. The 2.0L engine also includes a cast aluminum alloy lower crankcase that is bolted to the underside of the engine block, with a pressed-steel oil pan bolted under that. This arrangement offers greater rigidity than the normal oil pan arrangement, and helps to reduce engine vibration.

The 2.3L engine incorporates an aluminum cylinder head and an aluminum cylinder block.

The two camshafts are driven by a timing belt (2.0L engine), or timing chain (2.3L engines), each operating eight valves via conventional cam followers. Each camshaft rotates in five bearings that are line-bored directly in the cylinder head and the (bolted-on) bearing caps. This means that the bearing caps are not available separately from the cylinder head, and must not be interchanged with caps from another engine.

In addition to the features of the 2.0L Zetec engine, the 2.3L engine incorporates an all aluminum timing chain cover, engine block and oil pan. The bottom end of the engine is non-serviceable; this includes the pistons, connecting rods, crankshaft and engine block. Any failure of any one of these components will require replacement of the entire engine block/crankcase as an assembly.

When working on this engine, note that Torx-type (both male and female heads) and hexagon socket (Allen head) fasteners are widely used. A good selection of sockets, with the necessary adapters, will be required, so that these can be unscrewed without damage and, on reassembly, tightened to the torque wrench settings specified.

LUBRICATION SYSTEM

Lubrication is by means of an eccentric-rotor trochoidal pump, which is mounted on the crankshaft right-hand end, and draws oil through a strainer located in the oil pan. The pump forces oil through an externally-mounted full-flow cartridge-type filter. From the filter, the oil is pumped into a main gallery in the cylinder block/crankcase, from where it is distributed to the crankshaft (main bearings) and cylinder head.

The connecting rod bearings are supplied with oil via internal drillings in the crankshaft. Each piston crown is cooled by a spray of oil directed at its underside by a jet. These jets are fed by passages off the crankshaft oil supply galleries, with spring-loaded valves to ensure that the jets open only when there is sufficient pressure to guarantee a good oil supply to the rest of the engine components. Where the jets are not installed, separate blanking plugs are provided so that the passages are sealed, but can be cleaned at overhaul.

The cylinder head is provided with two oil galleries, one on the intake side and one on the exhaust, to ensure constant oil supply to the camshaft bearings and cam followers. A retaining valve (inserted into the cylinder head's top surface, in the middle, on the intake side) prevents these galleries from being drained when the engine is switched off. The valve incorporates a ventilation hole in its upper end, to allow air bubbles to escape from the system when the engine is restarted.

While the crankshaft and camshaft bearings receive a pressurized supply, the camshaft lobes and valves are lubricated by splash, as are all other engine components.

2 Repair operations possible with the engine in the vehicle

Many major repair operations can be accomplished without removing the engine from the vehicle.

Clean the engine compartment and the exterior of the engine with some type of degreaser before any work is done. It will make the job easier and help keep dirt out of the internal areas of the engine.

Depending on the components involved, it may be helpful to remove the hood to improve access to the engine as repairs are performed (refer to Chapter 11 if necessary). Cover the fenders to prevent damage to the paint. Special pads are available, but an old bedspread or blanket will also work.

If vacuum, exhaust, oil or coolant leaks develop, indicating a need for gasket or seal replacement, the repairs can generally be made with the engine in the vehicle. The intake and exhaust manifold gaskets, oil pan gasket, camshaft and crankshaft oil seals and cylinder head gasket

are all accessible with the engine in place.

Exterior engine components, such as the intake and exhaust manifolds, the oil pan, the oil pump, the water pump, the starter motor, the alternator and the fuel system components can be removed for repair with the engine in place.

Since the camshaft(s) and cylinder head can be removed without pulling the engine, valve component servicing can also be accomplished with the engine in the vehicle. Replacement of the timing belt or chain and sprockets is also possible with the engine in the vehicle.

In extreme cases caused by a lack of necessary equipment, repair or replacement of piston rings, pistons, connecting rods and rod bearings is possible with the engine in the vehicle. However, this practice is not recommended because of the cleaning and preparation work that must be done to the components involved.

3　Top Dead Center (TDC) for Number 1 piston - locating

♦ **Refer to illustrations 3.4, 3.5a, 3.5b, 3.6, 3.7a, 3.7b and 3.7c**

1　Top dead center (TDC) is the highest point of the cylinder that each piston reaches as the crankshaft turns. Each piston reaches its TDC position at the end of its compression stroke, and then again at the end of its exhaust stroke. For the purpose of engine timing, TDC on the compression stroke for the Number 1 piston is used. The Number 1 cylinder is at the timing belt end of the engine. Proceed as follows.

2　Disconnect the cable from the battery negative terminal (see Chapter 5).

3　Remove all the spark plugs as described in Chapter 1, then remove the valve cover as described in Section 4.

4　Loosen the right front wheel lug nuts, raise the front of the vehicle and support it securely on jackstands, then remove the wheel. Remove the fender splash shield. Using a wrench or socket on the crankshaft pulley bolt, rotate the crankshaft clockwise until the intake valves for the Number 1 cylinder have opened and just closed again.

➡ **Note: Double-check the TDC notch on the crank-shaft with the alignment mark on the lower crankcase (above oil pan) (see illustration).**

5　The camshafts each have a machined slot at the transaxle end of the engine. Both slots will be completely horizontal, and at the same height as the cylinder head machined surface, when the engine is at TDC on the Number 1 cylinder. Ford service tool 303-465 is used to check this position, and to positively locate the camshafts in position. Fortunately, a substitute tool can be made from a strip of metal 5 mm thick. While the strip's thickness is critical, its length and width are not, but should be approximately 180 to 230 mm long by 20 to 30 mm wide (see illustrations).

6　A TDC timing hole is provided on the front of the cylinder block to permit the crankshaft to be located more accurately at TDC. The blanking plug is located behind the catalytic converter, and access is not easy - also, take care against burning if the engine is still warm (see illustration).

7　Unscrew the timing pin blanking plug and screw in the timing pin (Ford service tool 303-574). This tool is obtainable from Ford dealers or a tool supplier. An alternative pin can be made from an M10 diameter bolt, cut down so that the length from the underside of the bolt head to the tip is exactly 63.4 mm (see illustrations). It may be necessary to slightly turn the crankshaft either way (remove the tool from the camshafts first) to be able to fully insert the timing pin.

8　Turn the engine forwards slowly until the crankshaft comes into

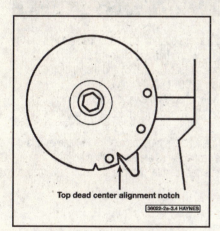

3.4　Align the Top Dead Center (TDC) notch with the casting on the lower crankcase

3.5a　Turn the engine so that the camshaft end slots are aligned . . .

3.5b　. . . then insert the metal strip into the slots to locate and set the shafts to TDC

3.6　Remove the timing hole blanking plug - catalytic converter removed for clarity

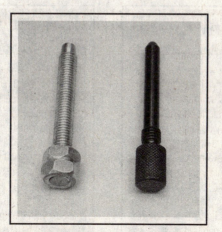

3.7a　Home-made (left) and factory (right) timing pins

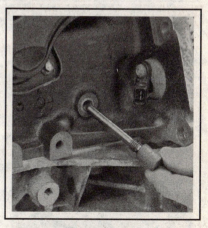

3.7b　Insert the timing pin in the hole . . .

contact with the timing pin - in this position, the engine is set to TDC on the Number 1 cylinder.

9   Before rotating the crankshaft again, make sure that the timing pin is removed. When operations are complete, do not forget to install the blanking plug.

10 If the timing pin is not available, insert a length of wooden dowel (about 150 mm/ 6 in long) or similar into the Number 1 spark plug hole until it rests on the piston crown. Turn the engine back from its TDC position, then forward (taking care not to allow the dowel to be trapped in the cylinder) until the dowel stops rising - the piston is now at the top of its compression stroke and the dowel can be removed.

11 There is a 'dead' area around TDC (as the piston stops rising, pauses and then begins to descend) which makes it difficult to find the exact location of TDC by this method; if accuracy is required, either carefully establish the exact mid-point of the dead area (perhaps by using a dial gauge and probe), or refer to Step 5.

12 Once the Number 1 cylinder has been positioned at TDC on the compression stroke, TDC for any of the other cylinders can then be located by rotating the crankshaft clockwise 180° at a time and following the firing order (see this Chapter's Specifications).

3.7c . . . and screw it fully into position

13 Reconnect the battery. After you're done, the Powertrain Control Module (PCM) must relearn its idle and fuel trim strategy for optimum driveability and performance (see Chapter 5, Section 1).

4   Valve cover - removal and installation

▶ **Refer to illustrations 4.3, 4.8a and 4.8b**

REMOVAL

1   Disconnect the battery cable from the negative battery terminal (see Chapter 5).

2   Remove the air intake duct from the air filter housing (see Chapter 4).

3   Remove the spark plug wires from the spark plugs (see illustration). On the 2.3L engine, remove the ignition coil assemblies from the spark plugs.

4   Disconnect the accelerator cable and the cruise control actuator cable from the throttle valve (see Chapter 4).

5   Disconnect the catalytic converter monitor connector and the heated oxygen sensor connector (see Chapter 6). Remove the connectors from the bracket.

6   Remove the wiring harness support nuts from the studs on the valve cover and position the wiring harness off to the side.

7   Remove the ignition coil (see Chapter 5) and the ignition coil bracket from the valve cover (2001 to 2004 only).

8   Working progressively, unscrew the valve cover retaining bolts, noting the (captive) spacer sleeve and rubber seal, then withdraw the cover (see illustrations).

9   Discard the cover gasket. This must be replaced whenever it is disturbed. Check that the sealing faces are undamaged and that the rubber seal at each bolt hole is serviceable. Replace any worn or damaged seals.

INSTALLATION

10 On installation, clean the cover and cylinder head gasket faces carefully, then install a new gasket onto the valve cover, ensuring that it

4.3 Twist the spark plug wire boots, then remove the plug wires from the spark plugs

4.8a Remove the retaining bolts and . . .

4.8b . . . lift off the valve cover from the cylinder head

is located correctly by the rubber seals and spacer sleeves.

11 Install the cover to the cylinder head, ensuring as the cover is tightened that the gasket remains seated.

12 Working in a diagonal sequence from the center outwards, first tighten the cover bolts by hand only. Once all the bolts are hand-tight, go around once more in sequence, and tighten the bolts to the torque listed in this Chapter Specifications.

13 On 2004 and earlier four-cylinder models, install the spark plug wires, clipping them into place so that they are correctly routed; each is numbered and can also be identified by the numbering on its respective coil terminal. On other models, install the ignition coils.

14 Reconnect the battery. After you're done, the Powertrain Control Module (PCM) must relearn its idle and fuel trim strategy for optimum driveability and performance (see Chapter 5, Section 1).

15 On completion, run the engine and check for signs of oil leakage.

5   Valve clearances - checking and adjustment

2.0L ENGINE

➡**Note: Note that while checking the valve clearances is an easy operation, changing the shims requires the use of a Ford special tool - owners may prefer to have this work carried out by a Ford dealer.**

Checking

▶ **Refer to illustration 5.3**

1 Remove the valve cover as described in Section 4.

2 Set the number 1 cylinder to TDC on the compression stroke as described in Section 3. The intake and exhaust cam lobes of the number 1 cylinder will be pointing upwards (though not vertical) and the valve clearances can be checked.

3 Working on each valve in turn, measure the clearance between the base of the cam lobe and the shim using feeler gauges (see illustration). Record the thickness of the blade required to give a firm sliding fit on all four valves of the Number 1 cylinder.

4 Now turn the crankshaft clockwise through 180 degrees so that the valves of cylinder Number 3 are pointing upwards. Measure and record the valve clearances for cylinder number 3. The clearances for cylinders 4 and 2 can be measured after turning the crankshaft through 180° each time. Any measured valve clearances that do not fall in the specified range (see Specifications) must be adjusted.

Adjustment

➡**Note: Use of the Ford special tool is highly recommended, as the design of the camshafts and cylinder head and the lack of space mean that it would not be possible to use a screwdriver or similar tool to depress the cam follower without serious risk of damage to the cylinder head. The only alternative is to measure the clearances very carefully several times each, record the clearances measured, and take the average as determining the true value. Access can then be gained to the shims by removing the camshafts (see Section 12) so that all relevant shims can be changed without the need for special tools. This approach requires very careful, methodical work if the camshafts are not to be removed and replaced several times.**

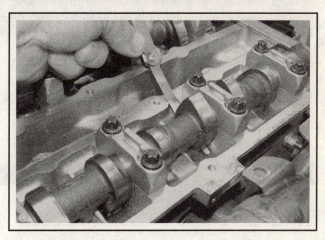

5.3 Check the valve clearances with a feeler gauge of the specified thickness

5 If adjustment is required, the shim thicknesses must be changed by depressing the cam follower and removing the old shim, then fitting a new one.

6 Before changing a shim, the piston for the relevant cylinder needs to be lowered from its TDC position by turning the crankshaft approximately 90 degrees clockwise. If this is not done, the piston will be too close to the valve to allow the cam follower to be depressed, and there is a risk of the valve being bent.

7 Ford technicians use service tool 303-350, which is bolted onto the cylinder head above each camshaft in turn using two of the camshaft bearing cap bolt locations - a spacer 8 x 12 mm (or equivalent thickness of 8 mm washers) may be required to allow the tool to be bolted onto the head. Locate the operating end of the tool onto the cam follower and operate the handle to depress the cam follower.

8 Take great care not to scratch or otherwise damage the cam follower and its housing. Remove the shim with a small screwdriver or magnetic probe, taking care not to scratch or damage the cam follower, then slowly release the pressure applied to the tool. Do not rotate the camshaft while a shim is removed - the risk of damage to the cam lobe and/or cam follower is too great.

9 Record the thickness of the shim (in mm) which is engraved on the side facing away from the camshaft. If the marking is missing or illegible, a micrometer will be needed to establish shim thickness.

10 If the valve clearance was too small, a thinner shim must be installed. If the clearance was too large, a thicker shim must be installed. When the shim thickness and the valve clearance are known, the required thickness of the new shim can be calculated as follows:

Sample calculation - clearance too small

Desired clearance (A) = 0.15 mm
Measured clearance (B) = 0.09 mm
Shim thickness found (C) = 2.55 mm
Thickness required (D) = C + B - A = 2.49 mm

Sample calculation - clearance too large

Desired clearance (A) = 0.30 mm
Measured clearance (B) = 0.36 mm
Shim thickness found (C) = 2.19 mm
Thickness required (D) = C + B - A = 2.25 mm

11 Depress the cam follower again, and press the correct shim into the recess in the cam follower with the thickness marking facing downwards. Ensure that the shim is properly located in the cam follower, and apply a smear of clean oil to it.

12 When all the clearances of the first cylinder's valves have been set, rotate the crankshaft through two full turns clockwise to settle the shims. Return the cylinder to TDC on the compression stroke and recheck the valve clearances. Repeat the procedure from Step 10 onwards if any are still incorrect.

13 Repeat the process for the remaining cylinders, turning the crankshaft to bring each in turn first to the TDC position and then 90 degrees after TDC, as described above.

14 It will be helpful for future adjustment if a record is kept of the thickness of the shims fitted at each position. The shims required can be purchased in advance once the clearances and the existing shim thicknesses are known. It is permissible to interchange shims between cam followers to achieve the correct clearances, but it is not advisable to turn the camshaft with any shims removed, since there is a risk that the cam lobe will jam in the empty cam follower.

15 When all the clearances are correct, remove the tool, then install the valve cover as described in Section 4.

2.3L ENGINE

16 On these engines the valve clearances are checked the same way as on the 2.0L engine, but instead of removable shims to set the proper clearance, cam followers with heads of differing thicknesses are available to set the desired clearance. The same formula used to calculate shim thickness is used to calculate desired follower head thickness (see Step 10). To change the cam followers, the camshafts have to be removed (see Section 12).

6 Intake manifold - removal and installation

REMOVAL

1 Relieve the fuel system pressure (see Chapter 4).
2 Disconnect the cable from the negative battery terminal (see Chapter 5).
3 Remove the air intake hose (see Chapter 4).
4 Disconnect the accelerator cable and, if equipped, the cruise control cable from the throttle lever arm (see Chapter 4).
5 Remove the fuel rail, fuel pressure regulator and fuel injectors as a single assembly (see Chapter 4).
6 Remove the breather hose and the PCV valve from the intake manifold (see Chapter 6).
7 Remove the ignition wires and disconnect the ignition coil harness connector (see Chapter 5).
8 Disconnect the vacuum lines from the intake manifold and label them for correct reassembly.
9 Disconnect the PCM harness connector (see Chapter 6).
10 Disconnect the cylinder head temperature (CHT) sensor connector (see Chapter 6). Detach the harness from the clip and separate the harness from the intake manifold.
11 Remove the alternator (see Chapter 5).
12 Remove the EGR valve (see Chapter 6).
13 If you're planning to replace or service the intake manifold, remove the throttle body (see Chapter 4).
➤Note: If you're simply removing the intake manifold plenum to remove or service the cylinder head, it's not necessary to remove the throttle body from the intake manifold plenum.

14 Remove the intake manifold support bracket.
15 Remove the intake manifold fasteners and washers and then remove the intake manifold and the manifold gasket.

INSPECTION

16 Using a straightedge and feeler gauge, check the intake manifold mating surface for warpage. Check the intake manifold surface on the cylinder head also. If the warpage on either surface exceeds the limit listed in this Chapter's Specifications, the intake manifold and/or the cylinder head must be resurfaced at an automotive machine shop or, if the warpage is too excessive for resurfacing, replaced.

INSTALLATION

17 Using a new manifold gasket, install the intake manifold. Tighten the bolts and nuts in several stages, working from the center out, to the torque listed in this Chapter's Specifications.
18 Installation is otherwise the reverse of removal.
19 Reconnect the battery. After you're done, the Powertrain Control Module (PCM) must relearn its idle and fuel trim strategy for optimum driveability and performance (see Chapter 5, Section 1).

7   Exhaust manifold - removal and installation

✳✳ WARNING:

Allow the engine to cool completely before beginning this procedure.

REMOVAL

▸ **Refer to illustration 7.5**

1   Raise the vehicle and place it securely on jackstands.

2   Remove the exhaust pipe and the catalytic converter (see Chapter 4). Remove and discard the old flange gasket.

3   Remove the dipstick tube bracket bolt and lift the assembly from the engine compartment.

4   Unplug the electrical connector for the oxygen sensor and then remove the oxygen sensor from the exhaust manifold (see Chapter 6).

5   Remove the exhaust manifold heat shield (see illustration).

6   Remove the exhaust manifold mounting bolts and then remove the exhaust manifold and the old manifold gasket.

7.5 Remove the heat shield mounting bolts

INSPECTION

7   Inspect the exhaust manifold for cracks and any other obvious damage. If the manifold is cracked or damaged in any way, replace it.

8   Using a wire brush, clean up the threads of the exhaust manifold bolts and then inspect the threads for damage. Replace any bolts that have thread damage.

9   Using a scraper, remove all traces of gasket material from the mating surfaces and inspect them for wear and cracks.

✳✳ CAUTION:

When removing gasket material from any surface, especially aluminum, be very careful not to scratch or gouge the gasket surface. Any damage to the surface may leak after reassembly. Gasket removal solvents are available from auto parts stores and may prove helpful.

10   Using a straightedge and feeler gauge, inspect the exhaust manifold mating surface for warpage. Check the exhaust manifold surface on the cylinder head also. If the warpage on any surface exceeds the limits listed in this Chapter's Specifications, the exhaust manifold and/or cylinder head must be replaced or resurfaced at an automotive machine shop.

INSTALLATION

11   Coat the threads of the exhaust manifold bolts and studs with an anti-seize compound. Install a new gasket, install the manifold and install the fasteners. Tighten the bolts and nuts in several stages, working from the center out, to the torque listed in this Chapter's Specifications.

12   The remainder of installation is the reverse of removal. When you're done, be sure to run the engine and check for exhaust leaks.

8   Crankshaft pulley - removal and installation

2.0L ENGINE

Removal

▸ **Refer to illustrations 8.4a and 8.4b**

1   Remove the drivebelt (see Chapter 1).

2   If the pulley is being removed as part of another procedure such as timing belt replacement, it will be easier to set the engine to TDC now (see Section 3) before removing the crankshaft pulley bolt.

➡**Note: NEVER use the timing pin as a means of locking the crankshaft - it is not strong enough for this, and will shear off. Always ensure that the timing pin is removed before the crankshaft pulley bolt (or similar fasteners) is slackened or tightened.**

3   The crankshaft must now be held or locked to prevent its rotation while the pulley bolt is unscrewed. There are two recommended procedures. One method is to use a chain wrench around the crankshaft pulley with a piece of rubber or old drivebelt material under the chain to prevent any damage to the pulley. Another method to prevent crankshaft rotation is to lock the flywheel by removing the starter (see Chapter 5)

8.4a Unscrew and remove the pulley bolt . . .

and wedging a screwdriver in the flywheel/driveplate ring gear teeth.

4   Unscrew the pulley bolt and remove the pulley (see illustrations).

8.4b . . . and remove the crankshaft pulley

36071-2B-7.5 HAYNES

8.10 The crankshaft pulley holding tool installed

8.16 Installing the M6 bolt to verify TDC

Installation

5   Installation is the reverse of the removal procedure. Ensure that the pulley's keyway is aligned with the crankshaft's locating key. Tighten the pulley bolt to the torque setting listed in this Chapter's Specifications. Lock the crankshaft using the same method as for loosening.

2.3L ENGINE

Removal

▶ **Refer to illustration 8.10**

❋❋ CAUTION:

Once the crankshaft pulley is loosened, the crankshaft (timing) sprocket will be loosened as well. The engine is considered out-of-time at this point. The installation procedure in this Section must be followed exactly to re-time the engine properly. Severe engine damage may occur otherwise.

6   Remove the cooling fan and shroud (see Chapter 3).
7   Remove the auxiliary drivebelt (see Chapter 1).
8   Remove the valve cover (see Section 4)
9   Set the engine to TDC (see Section 3).
10 The crankshaft must be held to prevent its rotation while the pulley bolt is unscrewed. A special tool to hold the crankshaft pulley is needed for this (see illustration), and is available at most auto supply stores or equipment rental locations. A suitable equivalent can be fabricated from a length of strap steel.

❋❋ CAUTION:

Use of a pry bar or similar tool can damage the crankshaft pulley.

11 Insert the service tool into the spaces in the front face of the pulley to hold it in place while turning the crankshaft pulley bolt with a large wrench or socket/breaker-bar combination.

❋❋ CAUTION:

Failure to hold the crankshaft pulley securely while removing the pulley bolt could result in engine damage. Moreover, NEVER

rely on the timing pin or the camshaft service tool as a means of locking the crankshaft - they are designed for calibration only. Engine damage could occur by not using these tools for their intended purpose.

12 Unscrew the pulley bolt and remove the holding tool.
13 Remove the pulley and label or mark which side is installed towards the engine.

Installation

▶ **Refer to illustrations 8.16 and 8.25**

14 Lightly coat the crankshaft front seal with clean engine oil, then install the crankshaft pulley.

➡**Note: If the seal shows signs of leakage, you may want to replace it before installing the crankshaft pulley (see Section 16).**

15 Install a new crankshaft pulley bolt and hand tighten only. Attempt to closely align the hole in the pulley with the threaded hole in the timing chain cover.
16 Install a crankshaft pulley alignment bolt (M6 x 18 mm) through the pulley and into the front engine cover. Rotate the pulley as necessary to do this (see illustration).

➡**Note: This aligns the pulley correctly with the crankshaft.**

17 Insert the large holding tool into the pulley and tighten the crankshaft pulley bolt to the torque listed in this Chapter's Specifications.
18 Remove the crankshaft pulley holding tool and the threaded

8.25 The camshaft alignment tool installed

crankshaft alignment bolt from the pulley and front engine cover.

19 Remove the timing pin from the cylinder block.

20 Remove the camshaft alignment tool.

21 Rotate the engine clockwise two complete revolutions by turning the crankshaft pulley bolt with a wrench or large socket.

22 Rotate the engine again to achieve TDC (see Section 3).

➡**Note: Rotate the engine in the clockwise direction only.**

23 Install the timing pin into the cylinder block.

24 Install the crankshaft pulley alignment bolt (M6 x 18 mm). If it cannot be installed, the crankshaft pulley must be removed and aligned so that it can. Repeat Steps 14 through 23 until crankshaft pulley align-

ment is correct.

25 With the crankshaft pulley alignment bolt (M6 x 18 mm) installed, install the camshaft alignment tool and check the position of the camshafts (see illustration). If the tool cannot be installed, the engine timing must be corrected by repeating Steps 14 through 24.

26 The correct engine timing is achieved when the camshaft alignment tool, timing pin and the crankshaft pulley alignment bolt tool can be placed simultaneously.

27 Once correct engine timing is achieved, remove all the alignment tools and bolts and install the timing pin plug.

28 The remainder of installation is the reverse of removal.

9 Timing belt - removal, inspection and installation (2.0L engine)

REMOVAL

▶ **Refer to illustrations 9.12, 9.14a, 9.14b, 9.17, 9.19a, 9.19b, 9.20, 9.21, 9.24a, 9.24b and 9.25**

1 Disconnect the battery cable from the negative battery terminal (see Chapter 5).

2 Remove the air intake duct from the air filter housing (see Chapter 4).

3 Remove the spark plugs (see Chapter 5).

4 Disconnect the accelerator cable and the cruise control actuator cable from the throttle valve (see Chapter 4).

5 Disconnect the catalytic converter monitor connector and the heated oxygen sensor connector (see Chapter 6). Remove the connectors from the bracket.

6 Remove the wiring harness support nuts from the studs on the valve cover and position the wiring harness off to the side.

7 Remove the valve cover (see Section 4).

8 Drain the coolant (see Chapter 1). Remove the coolant pipe mounting bolts and position the coolant pipe off to the side.

9 Loosen the right front wheel lug nuts. Raise the vehicle and secure it on jackstands.

10 Remove the front wheel and front fender splash shield on the timing belt side of the engine compartment.

11 Position the engine at TDC for number 1 (see Section 3).

➡**Note: NEVER use the timing pin as a means of locking the crankshaft - it is not strong enough for this, and will shear off. Always ensure that the timing pin is removed before the crank-**

9.12 Unbolt and remove the water pump pulley

shaft pulley bolt (or similar fasteners) is slackened or tightened. Follow the recommended procedure in Section 8 for locking the flywheel.

12 Remove the three water pump pulley bolts (see Chapter 3). Separate the water pump pulley from the timing belt cover (see illustration).

13 Remove the crankshaft pulley (see Section 8).

14 Remove the bolts from the lower timing belt cover (see illustrations).

15 Connect a hoist or an engine support fixture to the engine (see Chapter 2C). Alternatively, a floor jack and block of wood can be positioned under the oil pan to support the engine.

16 Remove the upper engine mount next to the timing belt cover (see Section 18).

9.14a Unscrew the bolts . . .

9.14b . . . and remove the timing belt lower cover

9.17 Unscrew and remove the engine mount studs

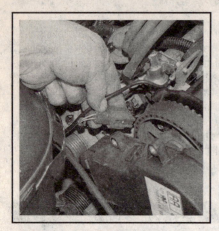

9.19a Disconnect the harness connector next to the upper timing belt cover

9.19b Remove the bolts and lift off the upper timing belt cover

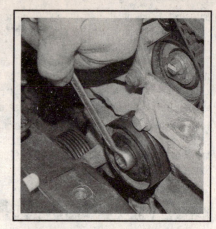

9.20 Remove the bolt for the idler pulley

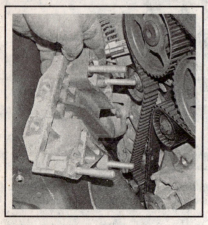

9.21 Remove the engine mount bracket

9.24a Unscrew the bolt . . .

9.24b . . . then unhook and remove the timing belt tensioner

17 Remove the studs from the engine mount bracket (see illustration).

18 Remove the knock sensor electrical connector from the upper timing belt cover (see Chapter 6).

19 Remove the upper timing belt cover (see illustrations).

20 Remove the accessory drivebelt idler pulley bolt and pulley from the timing belt cover (see illustration).

21 Remove the engine mount bracket (see illustration).

22 Before removing the timing belt, note that Ford service tool 303-376 will be needed (see Section 3), to set the camshafts to their TDC position. Fortunately, a substitute tool can be made from a strip of metal 5 mm thick (while the strip's thickness is critical, its length and width are not, but should be approximately 180 to 230 mm long by 20 to 30 mm wide) (see illustration 3.5b).

23 If the timing belt is to be re-used (and this is not recommended), mark it with paint to indicate its direction of rotation, clockwise, viewed from the timing belt end of the engine.

24 Loosen the timing belt tensioner bolt and turn the tensioner clockwise, using an Allen key in the hole provided. Now unscrew the bolt and unhook the tensioner from the inner shield (see illustrations).

25 Ensuring that the sprockets are turned as little as possible, slide the timing belt off the sprockets and pulleys, and remove it (see illustration).

26 If the timing belt is not being installed right now or if the belt is being removed as part of another procedure, such as cylinder head removal, temporarily install the engine right-hand mount and tighten the bolts securely.

INSPECTION

27 If the old belt is likely to be reinstalled, check it carefully for any signs of uneven wear, splitting, cracks especially at the roots of the belt teeth.

9.25 When removing the timing belt, ensure the sprockets do not turn

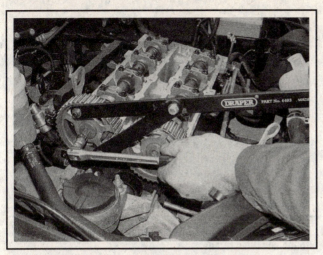

9.32 Use a sprocket holding tool while loosening the camshaft sprocket bolts

9.38a Use an Allen key to set the tensioner pointer in the center of the square window. . .

28 Even if a new belt is to be installed, check the old one for signs of oil or coolant. If evident, trace the source of the leak and rectify it, then clean the engine timing belt area and related components to remove all traces of oil or coolant. Do not simply install a new belt in this instance, or its service life will be greatly reduced, increasing the risk of engine damage if it fails in service.

29 Always replace the belt if there is the slightest doubt about its condition. As a precaution against engine damage, the belt must be replaced as a matter of course at the intervals given in Chapter 1; if the car's history is unknown, the belt should be replaced irrespective of its apparent condition whenever the engine is overhauled.

30 Similarly check the belt tensioner, replacing it if there is any doubt about its condition. Check also the sprockets and pulleys for signs of wear or damage (and particularly cracking), and ensure that the tensioner and guide pulleys rotate smoothly on their bearings; replace any worn or damaged components.

➡Note: It is considered good practice by many professional mechanics to replace tensioner and guide pulley assemblies as a matter of course, whenever the timing belt is replaced.

INSTALLATION

▶ Refer to illustrations 9.32, 9.38a and 9.38b

31 Without turning the crankshaft more than a few degrees, check that the engine is still set to TDC on the Number 1 cylinder (see Section 3).

32 The TDC position of the camshafts must now be set, and for this, the camshaft sprocket bolts must be loosened. A holding tool will be required to prevent the camshaft sprockets from rotating while their bolts are slackened and retightened; either obtain Ford service tool 303-465, or fabricate a substitute as follows. Find two lengths of steel strip, one approximately two feet long and the other about eight inches long, and three bolts with nuts and washers; one nut and bolt forming the pivot of a forked tool, with the remaining nuts and bolts at the tips of the 'forks', to engage with the sprocket spokes (see illustration).

➡Note: Do not use the camshaft TDC alignment tool (whether genuine Ford or not) to prevent rotation while the camshaft sprocket bolts are loosened or tightened; the risk of damage to the camshaft concerned and to the cylinder head is far too great. Use only a holding tool applied directly to the sprockets,

as described.

33 Loosen the camshaft sprocket bolts, ensuring that the camshafts are turned as little as possible as this is done. The bolts should be loose enough that the sprockets are free to turn on the shafts. It is essential that the bolts are left loose until the timing belt has been installed and tensioned, otherwise the valve timing will not be accurate.

34 The tool described in Step 22 is now required. Rest the tool on the cylinder head mating surface, and slide it into the slots in the opposite end (transaxle side) of both camshafts. The tool should slip snugly into both slots while resting on the cylinder head mating surface. If one camshaft is only slightly out of alignment, rotate the camshaft gently and carefully until the tool will fit. Once the camshafts are set at TDC, the positions of the sprockets are less important - they can move independently of the camshafts, to allow the timing belt to be accurately aligned with the teeth on the sprockets.

35 When installing the belt, note that the tensioner must not be installed until after the belt is fully positioned around the sprockets and pulley(s).

36 Install the timing belt; if the original is being reinstalled, ensure that the marks and notes made on removal are followed, so that the belt is installed to run in the same direction. Starting at the crankshaft sprocket, work counterclockwise around the guide pulley(s) and camshaft sprockets. Ensure that the belt teeth engage correctly with those on the sprockets.

➡Note: The crankshaft gear does not have alignment marks to verify TDC position. Instead it will be necessary to install the crankshaft pulley and check the alignment mark with the relief mark on the case (see Section 3).

37 Any slack in the belt should be kept on the tensioner side - the 'front' run must be kept tensioned, without altering the position of the crankshaft or the camshafts. If necessary, the camshaft sprockets can be turned slightly in relation to the camshafts (which remain fixed by the aligning tool).

38 When the timing belt is correctly installed on the sprockets and guide pulley(s), the belt tensioner can be installed. Hook the tensioner into the timing belt inner shield, and insert the bolt loosely. Using the Allen key, turn the tensioner counterclockwise until the arrow (Type A) (see illustrations) or fork (Type B) is aligned with the mark or square hole on the bracket, then tighten the tensioner bolt to its specified torque.

➡Note 1: There are two types of indicators on the tensioner. Type A uses an arrow that aligns with the dot in the square box. Type B uses a fork that aligns with a mark directly in the middle of the two prongs on the fork.

➡Note 2: The timing belt tensioner automatically adjusts the tension by internal spring forces - checking the tension once set, for instance, by depressing or twisting the timing belt, will not give a meaningful result.

39 Tighten both camshaft sprocket bolts to the torque listed in this Chapter's Specifications, holding the sprockets stationary using the tool described in Step 32.

40 Remove the camshaft aligning tool and the timing pin (see Section 3). Temporarily install the crankshaft pulley, and rotate the crankshaft through two full turns clockwise to settle and tension the timing belt, returning it to TDC. Check that the timing pin can be fully installed, then install the camshaft aligning tool; it should slip into place. If the checks are not correct, go back to Step 31 and perform the timing procedures again.

41 If one camshaft is slightly out of line, attach the forked holding tool to its sprocket (see Step 32), adjust its position as required, and check that any slack created in the belt has been taken up by the tensioner. Rotate the crankshaft two turns clockwise and install the camshaft aligning tool to check that it now fits as it should. If all is well, proceed to Step 43.

42 If either camshaft is significantly out of line, use the holding tool described in Step 32 above to prevent its sprocket from rotating while its retaining bolt is loosened - the camshaft can then be rotated carefully until the camshaft aligning tool will slip into place. Take care not to disturb the relationship of the sprocket to the timing belt. Without disturbing the sprocket's new position on the camshaft, tighten the sprocket bolt to the torque listed in this Chapter's Specifications. Remove the camshaft aligning tool and timing pin, and rotate the crank-

9.38b . . . then hold it while the tensioner bolt is tightened to the specified torque

shaft two more turns clockwise, and install the tool to check that it now fits as it should.

43 The remainder of the reassembly procedure is the reverse of removal, noting the following points:

a) Make sure that the timing pin and camshaft aligning tool are removed.

b) When replacing the engine right-hand mount, remember to install the timing belt upper cover.

c) Tighten all fasteners to the specified torque settings.

44 After you reconnect the battery, the Powertrain Control Module (PCM) must relearn its idle and fuel trim strategy for optimum driveability and performance (see Chapter 5, Section 1).

10 Timing chain cover and timing chain and tensioner - removal and installation

TIMING CHAIN COVER

Removal

▸ Refer to illustration 10.3

1 Disconnect the negative battery cable (see Chapter 5).
2 Remove the crankshaft pulley (see Section 8).
3 Disconnect the crankshaft position (CKP) sensor electrical connector (see illustration). Move the wiring harness away from the engine cover by removing the harness retainers.

4 Remove the (CKP) sensor (see Chapter 6).

➡Note: Unfortunately with this engine, anytime this sensor is removed, a new sensor must be installed. The new sensor is packaged with a special sensor alignment tool that is critical for installation.

5 Remove the drivebelt and the tensioner (see Chapter 1).
6 Remove the water pump pulley (see Chapter 3).
7 Disconnect the electrical connector to the power steering pressure switch. The switch is located on a high-pressure hose within the power steering system.
8 Remove the single bolt on the lower left corner of the power steering pump and move the pump aside.
9 Remove the bolts and the engine cover.

Installation

▸ Refer to illustration 10.10

10 Installation is the reverse of removal noting the following:

a) Clean the mating surfaces of all material.

➡Note: Be careful not to gouge or use any abrasives on the mating surfaces.

b) Install the engine cover within four minutes of applying a 2.5 mm bead of RTV sealant.

10.3 The crankshaft position (CKP) sensor is located adjacent to the crankshaft pulley

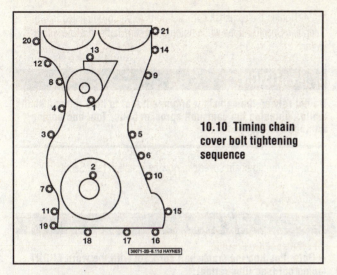

10.10 Timing chain cover bolt tightening sequence

c) Tighten all bolts to the specified torque settings (using a three-stage sequence - see Specifications) and also using the sequence pattern provided (see illustration).

d) Be sure to re-time the engine as described in Section 8 and also use a new crankshaft position sensor which includes the necessary alignment tool.

TIMING CHAIN AND TENSIONER

Removal

▶ **Refer to illustrations 10.13a and 10.13b**

11 Apply the parking brake, then carefully jack up the front of the vehicle and support the lifted portion on jackstands.

12 Remove the timing chain cover (see Section 7).

13 Carefully compress the timing chain tensioner and place a pin (a drill bit or paper clip will work) into the hole to hold it in the compressed position (see illustration).

➡**Note: The tensioner contacts the right-hand chain guide.**

✳✳ CAUTION:

Compress only the round plunger on the tensioner and not the ratchet mechanism. The ratchet is next to the plunger and has square sides. If the ratchet needs to be reset, do the following (see illustration):

a) Remove the tensioner and place it lightly in a vise using the plunger and tensioner housing.

b) Place a pick-type tool in the hole closest to the ratchet to relieve the tension on the ratchet mechanism.

c) While holding the pick tool in place, move the ratchet back into the tensioner, then install a pin into the other hole to keep the plunger and ratchet compressed.

d) Remove the tensioner from the vise.

14 Remove the two tensioner mounting bolts and then the tensioner itself.

15 Remove the loose timing chain guide (right). Remove the timing chain.

16 The left chain guide and camshaft sprockets can now be removed if necessary (see Section 10).

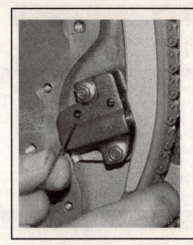

10.13a Compressing the timing chain tensioner and placing the lock pin

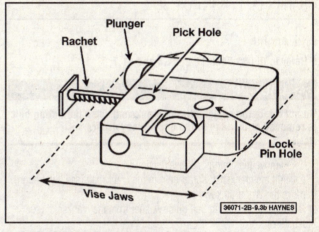

10.13b Timing chain tensioner details

Installation

▶ **Refer to illustration 10.22**

17 Remove the camshaft alignment tool (if installed).

18 Loosen both camshaft sprocket bolts but don't remove them. Use a wrench on the hexagonal area of the camshaft to hold it while turning the camshaft sprocket bolt.

➡**Note: The hexagonal portion of the camshaft is located just after the second lobe from the front.**

10.22 Compressing the tensioner to release the lock pin

❋❋ CAUTION:

Damage to the valves or pistons may occur if the camshafts are rotated during this procedure.

19 Install the left chain guide (if removed).
20 Install the timing chain.
21 Install the right chain guide.
22 Install the timing chain tensioner and tighten the fasteners to the torque listed in this Chapter's Specifications. Then remove the pin to release the tensioner to engage the chain guide (see illustration).
23 Install the camshaft alignment tool.

24 Tighten the camshaft sprocket bolts to the torque listed in this Chapter's Specifications while holding the camshafts in place with a wrench.

❋❋ CAUTION:

Do not rely on the camshaft alignment tool to hold the camshafts while tightening the camshaft sprocket bolts. Tool and engine damage may occur.

25 The timing chain cover can now be installed (see Section 8).

11 Engine front oil seals - replacement

CRANKSHAFT FRONT OIL SEAL

2.0L engine

▶ Refer to illustrations 11.2, 11.3 and 11.7

❋❋ CAUTION:

Do not rotate the camshaft(s) or crankshaft when the timing belt is removed or damage to the engine may occur.

1 Remove the timing belt (see Section 9).
2 Pull the crankshaft sprocket from the crankshaft (see illustration). Remove the Woodruff key.
3 Remove the timing belt guide washer from the crankshaft (see illustration).
4 Wrap the tip of a small screwdriver with tape. Working from below the right inner fender, use the screwdriver to pry the seal out of its bore. Take care to prevent damaging the oil pump assembly, the crankshaft and the seal bore.
5 Thoroughly clean and inspect the seal bore and sealing surface on the crankshaft. Minor imperfections can be removed with emery cloth. If there is a groove worn in the crankshaft sealing surface from contact with the seal, installing a new seal will probably not stop the leak.
6 Lubricate the new seal with engine oil and drive the seal into place with a hammer and an appropriate size socket.
7 The remaining steps are the reverse of removal.

➡**Note: Position the crankshaft sprocket with the word FRONT facing out (see illustration).**

8 Reinstall the timing belt and covers (see Section 9).
9 Run the engine and check for oil leaks.

2.3L engine

▶ Refer to illustrations 11.14 and 11.15

10 Remove the crankshaft pulley (see Section 8).
11 Use a screwdriver or hook tool to carefully pry out the seal.

➡**Note: Be careful not to damage the timing chain cover bore where the seal is seated or the nose and sealing surface of the crankshaft.**

12 Another procedure for removing the seal is to drill a small hole on each side of the seal and place a self-tapping screw in each hole. Use these screws as a means of pulling the seal out without having to pry on it.
13 Wipe the sealing surfaces in the engine cover and on the crankshaft. Clean and coat them with clean engine oil.
14 Start installing the new seal by pressing it into the timing chain cover (see illustration).
15 Once started, use a seal driver or a suitable socket of the correct size to carefully drive the seal squarely into place (see illustration).
16 The seal should be flush with the engine cover and remain square when installed.
17 Coat the lip of the seal (where it contacts the crankshaft) with clean engine oil.
18 Install the crankshaft pulley (see Section 8).

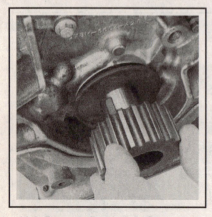

11.2 Remove the crankshaft sprocket from the crankshaft

11.3 Remove the timing belt guide washer

11.7 Make sure the FRONT mark on the crankshaft sprocket is facing out

11.14 Make certain that the oil seal is kept square as it is placed in the bore

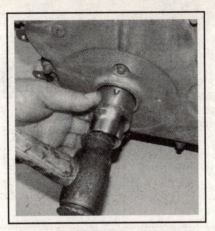

11.15 A socket of the correct size can be used to install the new seal

11.21 Remove the camshaft sprocket from the camshaft

CAMSHAFT OIL SEALS

♦ Refer to illustrations 11.21, 11.24a and 11.24b

❊❊ CAUTION:

Do not rotate the camshaft(s) or crankshaft when the timing belt is removed or damage to the engine may occur.

11.24a Install the seal with the lip toward the journal

19 Position the engine at TDC for number 1 piston (see Section 3).

20 Remove the timing belt (see Section 9).

21 Remove the camshaft sprocket bolts (see illustration 9.32). Then, remove the sprockets from the camshafts (see illustration).

22 Note how far the seal is seated in the bore, then carefully pry it out with a small screwdriver. Don't scratch the bore or damage the camshaft in the process. If the camshaft is damaged, the new seal will end up leaking.

23 Clean the bore and coat the outer edge of the new seal with engine oil or multi-purpose grease. Also lubricate the seal lip.

24 Using a socket with an outside diameter slightly smaller than the outside diameter of the seal, carefully drive the new seal into place with a hammer (see illustrations). Make sure it's installed squarely and driven in to the same depth as the original.

25 Set the camshafts to their TDC positions by inserting the tool shown in illustration 3.5b into the slots in the ends of the cam-shafts.

26 Install the camshaft sprockets. Tighten the bolts to the torque listed in this Chapter's Specifications, using the tool shown in illustration 9.32 to prevent the camshafts from turning.

27 Reinstall the timing belt (see Section 9).

28 Run the engine and check for oil leaks at the camshaft seal.

11.24b Tap the seal into the housing using a large socket

12 Camshafts and cam followers - removal, inspection and installation

REMOVAL

♦ Refer to illustrations 12.3, 12.4a, 12.4b, 12.5a and 12.5b

1 Remove the timing belt as described in Section 9.

2 Remove the camshaft sprockets as described in Section 11. While both sprockets are the same and could be interchanged, it is good working practice to mark them so that each sprocket is reinstalled to its original location.

3 All the camshaft bearing caps have a single-digit identifying number etched on them. The exhaust camshaft's bearing caps are numbered in sequence from 0 (right-hand cap) to 4 (left-hand cap); the intake's are

12.3 Location of the camshaft bearing designations

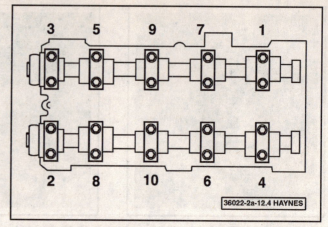

12.4a Camshaft bearing cap loosening sequence (2.0L engine) - loosen each pair of bolts on the designated bearing cap in sequence

numbered from 5 (right-hand cap) to 9 (left-hand cap). Each cap is to be fitted so that its numbered side faces outwards, to the front (exhaust) or to the rear (intake) (see illustration). If no marks are present, or they are hard to see, make your own - the bearing caps must be reinstalled in their original positions.

4 Working in the sequence shown, loosen the camshaft bearing cap bolts progressively by half a turn at a time (see illustrations). Work only as described, to release gradually and evenly the pressure of the valve springs on the caps.

5 Withdraw the caps, noting their markings and the presence of the locating dowels, then remove the camshafts and withdraw their oil seals (see illustrations). The intake camshaft can be identified by the reference lobe for the camshaft position sensor; therefore, there is no need to mark the camshafts.

6 Obtain sixteen small, clean containers, and number them 1 to 16. Using a rubber suction tool (such as a valve-lapping tool), withdraw each cam follower in turn and place them in the containers. Do not interchange the cam followers, or the rate of wear will be greatly increased. Make sure the shims remain with their corresponding cam followers, to ensure correct installation.

INSPECTION

◆ **Refer to illustrations 12.8 and 12.11**

7 With the camshafts and cam followers removed, check each for signs of obvious wear (scoring, pitting, etc) and for roundness and replace if necessary.

8 Measure the outside diameter of each cam follower - take measurements at the top and bottom of each cam follower, then a second

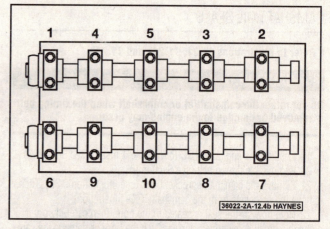

12.4b Camshaft bearing cap loosening sequence (2.3L engine) - loosen each pair of bolts on the designated bearing cap in sequence

set at right-angles to the first; if any measurement is significantly different from the others, the cam follower is tapered or oval (as applicable) and must be replaced (see illustration). If the necessary equipment is available, measure the inside diameter of the corresponding cylinder head bore. No manufacturer's specifications were available at time of

12.5a Remove the bearing caps . . .

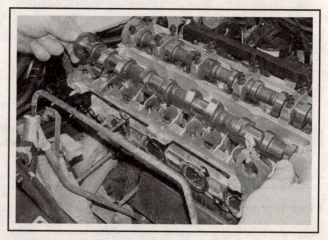

12.5b . . . then lift out the camshafts

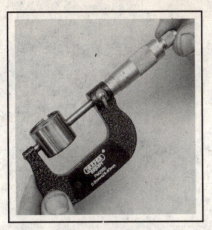

12.8 Measure the cam follower outside diameter at several points

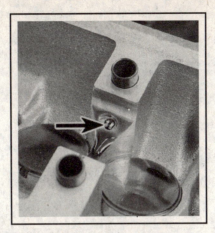

12.11 Check that the camshaft bearing oilways are not blocked with debris

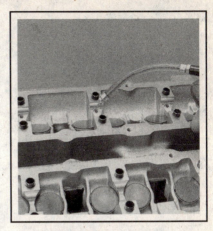

12.20a Lubricate the camshaft bearing surfaces . . .

writing; if the cam followers or the cylinder head bores are excessively worn, new cam followers and/or a new cylinder head may be required.

9   If the engine's valve components have sounded noisy, it may be just that the valve clearances need adjusting. Although this is part of the routine maintenance schedule in Chapter 1, the extended checking interval and the need for dismantling or special tools may result in the task being overlooked.

10 Visually examine the camshaft lobes for score marks, pitting, galling (wear due to rubbing) and evidence of overheating (blue, discolored areas). Look for flaking away of the hardened surface layer of each lobe. If any such signs are evident, replace the component concerned.

11 Examine the camshaft bearing journals and the cylinder head bearing surfaces for signs of obvious wear or pitting. If any such signs are evident, consult an automotive machine shop for advice. Also check that the bearing oilways in the cylinder head are clear (see illustration).

12 Using a micrometer, measure the diameter of each journal at several points. If the diameter of any one journal is less than the specified value, replace the camshaft.

13 To check the bearing journal running clearance, remove the cam followers, use a suitable solvent and a clean lint-free rag to carefully clean all bearing surfaces, then install the camshafts and bearing caps with a strand of Plastigage across each journal. Tighten the bearing cap bolts in the given sequence (see Installation) to the specified torque setting (do not rotate the camshafts), then remove the bearing caps and use the scale provided to measure the width of the compressed strands. Scrape off the Plastigage with your fingernail or the edge of a credit card - don't scratch or nick the journals or bearing caps.

12.20b . . . then install the camshafts . . .

14 If the running clearance of any bearing is found to be worn to beyond the specified service limits, install a new camshaft and repeat the check; if the clearance is still excessive, the cylinder head must be replaced.

15 To check camshaft endplay, remove the cam followers, clean the bearing surfaces carefully and install the camshafts and bearing caps. Tighten the bearing cap bolts to the specified torque wrench setting, then measure the endplay using a dial indicator mounted on the cylinder head so that its tip bears on the camshaft right-hand end.

16 Tap the camshaft fully towards the gauge, zero the gauge, then tap the camshaft fully away from the gauge and note the gauge reading. If the endplay measured is found to be at or beyond the specified service limit, install a new camshaft and repeat the check; if the clearance is still excessive, the cylinder head must be replaced.

INSTALLATION

♦ **Refer to illustrations 12.20a, 12.20b, 12.20c, 12.21, 12.22a, 12.22b, 12.23a, 12.23b, 12.29a and 12.29b**

17 As a precaution against the valves hitting the pistons when the camshafts are replaced, remove the timing pin and turn the engine approximately 90-degrees (1/4-turn) back from the TDC position - this will move all the pistons an equal distance down the bores. This is only a precaution - if the engine is known to be at TDC on the Number 1 cylinder, and the camshafts are replaced as described below, valve-to-piston contact should not occur.

18 On reassembly, liberally oil the cylinder head cam follower bores and the cam followers. Carefully install the cam followers to the cylinder head, ensuring that each cam follower is replaced to its original bore, and is the correct way up. Some care will be required to guide the cam followers squarely into their bores. Make sure that the shims are installed in their previously-noted positions.

19 It is highly recommended that new camshaft oil seals are installed. The new seals are installed after the caps are tightened - see Section 11.

20 Liberally oil the camshaft bearings (not the caps) and lobes. Ensuring that each camshaft is in its original location, install the camshafts, locating each so that the slot in its left-hand end is approximately parallel to, and just above, the cylinder head mating surface (see illustrations). Check that, as each camshaft is laid in position, the metal strip TDC setting tool will fit into the slot.

12.20c . . . ensuring that the slot at the transmission end is approximately horizontal

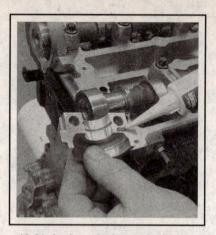

12.21 Apply sealant to each of the bearing caps at the timing belt end

12.22a Apply a little oil to the camshaft surface . . .

21 Ensure that the locating dowels are pressed firmly into their recesses and check that all mating surfaces are completely clean, unmarked and free from oil. Apply a thin film of suitable sealant (Ford recommends a sealant to specification WSK-M2G348-A5) to the mating surfaces of each camshaft's right-hand bearing cap (see illustration).

22 Apply a little oil to the camshaft as shown, then install each of the camshaft bearing caps to its previously-noted position, so that its numbered side faces outwards, to the front (exhaust) or to the rear (intake) (see illustrations).

23 Ensuring that each cap is kept square to the cylinder head as it is tightened down and working in the sequence shown, tighten the camshaft bearing cap bolts slowly and by one turn at a time, until each cap touches the cylinder head (see illustrations).

24 Next, using the same sequence, tightening the bolts to the Step 1 torque listed in this Chapter's Specifications.

25 With all the bolts tightened to the Step 1 torque, tighten them to the Stage 2 torque listed in this Chapter's Specifications.

26 Wipe off all surplus sealant, so that none is left to find its way into any oilways. Follow the sealant manufacturer's instructions as to the time needed for curing; usually, at least an hour must be allowed between application of the sealant and starting the engine (including turning the engine for further reassembly work).

27 Once the caps are fully tightened, it makes sense to check the valve clearances before proceeding - assuming that the Ford tool

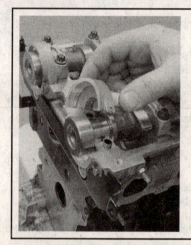

12.22b . . . then install the camshaft bearing caps

described in Section 5 is not available, the camshafts have to be removed to allow any of the shims to be changed. Turning the camshafts with the timing belt removed carries a risk of the valves hitting the pistons, so (if not already done) remove the timing pin and turn the crankshaft 90° counterclockwise first. Set the camshafts to TDC on the Number 1 cylinder using the setting tool (see Section 3) to establish a starting point, then proceed as described in Section 5 (see illustration 3.5b). When all the clearances have been checked, bring the crankshaft back to TDC, and install the timing pin.

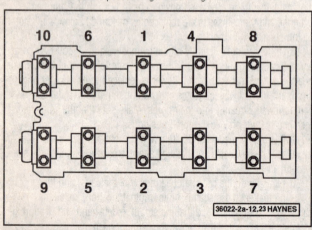

12.23a Camshaft bearing cap tightening sequence (2.0L engine)

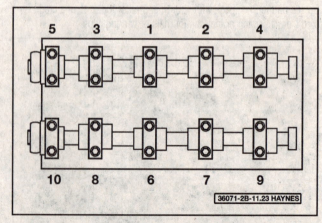

12.23b Camshaft bearing cap tightening sequence (2.3L engine)

12.29a Install the camshaft sprockets . . .

12.29b . . . and secure with the retaining bolts, tightened only loosely at this stage

28 Install new camshaft oil seals as described in Section 11.

29 Using the marks and notes made on dismantling to ensure that each is replaced to its original camshaft, install the sprockets to the camshafts, tightening the retaining bolts loosely (see illustrations).

30 The remainder of the reassembly procedure, including replacement of the timing belt and setting the valve timing, is as described in Section 9. On completion (if not already done), check and adjust the valve clearances as described in Section 5.

31 After you reconnect the battery, the Powertrain Control Module (PCM) must relearn its idle and fuel trim strategy for optimum driveability and performance (see Chapter 5, Section 1).

13 Cylinder head - removal and installation

❊❊ WARNING:

Wait until the engine is completely cool before beginning this procedure.

REMOVAL

◆ **Refer to illustrations 13.12, 13.14, 13.16, 13.18, 13.19 and 13.20**

1 Relieve the fuel pressure (see Chapter 4).

2 Disconnect the battery cable from the negative battery terminal (see Chapter 5).

3 Remove the intake duct from the air filter housing (see Chapter 4).

4 Disconnect the accelerator cable (see Chapter 4) and cruise control cable, if equipped.

5 Drain the cooling system (see Chapter 1).

6 Remove the timing belt (see Section 9) or timing chain (see Section 10).

7 Remove the camshafts (see Section 12).

8 Temporarily install the valve cover, to protect the top of the engine until the cylinder head bolts are removed.

9 Disconnect the camshaft position sensor (see Chapter 6).

10 Remove the fuel rail and injectors as a complete assembly (see Chapter 4).

11 Remove the alternator and its mounting bracket (see Chapter 5).

12 Remove the thermostat housing from the cylinder head (see illustration).

13 Remove the intake manifold (see Section 6).

14 Remove the nut and detach the dipstick tube from the cylinder head (see illustration).

15 Remove the exhaust manifold (see Section 7).

16 Remove the bolt from the power steering hose support bracket (see illustration) and position the hose off to the side.

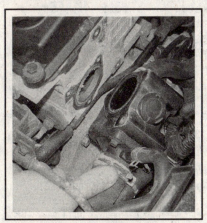

13.12 Remove the thermostat housing from the cylinder head

13.14 Remove the nut that secures the dipstick tube

13.16 Unbolt this power steering fluid pipe bracket

13.18 Unbolt the power steering pump bracket

13.19 Remove the cylinder head bolts - note the head bolt uses a Torx socket

13.20 Lift off the cylinder head

17 If an engine support fixture or hoist is being used to hold the engine up (for timing belt removal), reinstall the engine mount bracket and engine mount, then remove the hoist or support fixture. If a floor jack and block of wood is being used to support the engine, it can remain in place.

18 Remove the power steering pump mounting bracket (see illustration).

19 Loosen the ten cylinder head bolts progressively and by half a turn at a time (see illustration), working in the reverse order of the tightening sequence (see illustrations 13.35a and 13.35b).

❋❋ CAUTION:

The head bolts are torque-to-yield bolts that must be replaced with new ones on installation.

20 Lift the cylinder head from the engine compartment (see illustration).

21 If the head is stuck, be careful how you choose to free it. Remember that the cylinder head is made of aluminum alloy, which is easily damaged. Striking the head with tools carries the risk of damage, and the head is located on two dowels, so its movement will be limited. Do not, under any circumstances, pry the head between the mating surfaces, as this will certainly damage the sealing surfaces for the gasket, leading to leaks. Try rocking the head free, to break the seal, taking care not to damage any of the surrounding components.

22 Once the head has been removed, recover the gasket from the two dowels, and discard it.

INSPECTION

23 The mating faces of the cylinder head and cylinder block must be perfectly clean before replacing the head. Use a hard plastic or wood scraper to remove all traces of gasket and carbon.

24 Take particular care during the cleaning operations, as aluminum alloy is easily damaged. Also, make sure that the carbon is not allowed to enter the oil and water passages - this is particularly important for the lubrication system, as carbon could block the oil supply to the engine's components.

25 To prevent carbon entering the gap between the pistons and bores, smear a little grease in the gap. After cleaning each piston, use

13.27 Location of the cylinder head locating dowels

a small brush to remove all traces of grease and carbon from the gap, then wipe away the remainder with a clean rag.

26 Check the mating surfaces of the cylinder block and the cylinder head for nicks, deep scratches and other damage. If slight, they may be removed carefully with a file. Also check the cylinder head gasket surface and the cylinder block gasket surface with a precision straight-edge and feeler gauges. If either surface exceeds the warpage limit listed in this Chapter's Specifications, the manufacturer states that the component out of specification must be replaced. If the gasket mating surface of your cylinder head or block is out of specification or is severely nicked or scratched, you may want to consult with an automotive machine shop for advice.

INSTALLATION

♦ **Refer to illustrations 13.27, 13.30a, 13.30b, 13.34, 13.35a, 13.35b and 13.47**

27 Wipe clean the mating surfaces of the cylinder head and cylinder block. Check that the two locating dowels are in position in the cylinder block (see illustration).

28 The cylinder head bolt holes must be free from oil or water. This is most important, because a hydraulic lock in a cylinder head bolt hole can cause a fracture of the block casting when the bolt is tightened.

13.30a Position the head gasket over the dowels

13.30b The head gasket teeth must be positioned at the front of the block

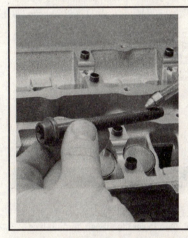

13.34 Apply a light coat of oil to the cylinder head bolt threads

(thread size) studs approximately 90 mm long, with a screwdriver slot cut in one end - you can use two of the old cylinder head bolts with their heads cut off. Screw these guide studs, screwdriver slot upwards to permit removal, into the bolt holes at diagonally-opposite corners of the cylinder block surface; ensure that approximately 70 mm of stud protrudes above the gasket.

33 Install the cylinder head, sliding it down the guide studs (if used) and locating it on the dowels. Unscrew the guide studs (if used) when the head is in place.

34 Coat the threads with a light oil - do not apply more than a light film of oil (see illustration). Install the cylinder head bolts carefully, and screw them in by hand only until finger-tight.

35 Working progressively and in the sequence shown, first tighten all the bolts to the specified Step 1 torque setting listed in this Chapter's Specifications (see illustrations).

2.0L engine

36 With all the bolts tightened to Step 1, tighten them in sequence to the Step 2 torque setting.

37 Step 3 involves tightening the bolts through an angle, rather than to a torque. Each bolt in sequence must be rotated through the specified angle - special angle gauges are available from tool outlets (see illustration), but a 90° angle is equivalent to a quarter-turn, and this is easily judged by assessing the start and end positions of the socket handle or torque wrench.

38 Once all the bolts have been tightened to Step 3, no subsequent tightening is necessary.

29 The new head gasket is selected according to a number cast on the front face of the cylinder block, in front of the Number 1 cylinder. Consult a Ford dealer or your parts supplier for details.

30 Position a new gasket over the dowels on the cylinder block surface, so that the TOP mark is uppermost; where applicable, the teeth must protrude towards the front of the vehicle (see illustrations).

31 Temporarily install the crankshaft pulley and rotate the crankshaft counterclockwise so that the Number 1 cylinder's piston is lowered to approximately 20 mm before TDC, thus avoiding any risk of valve/piston contact and damage during reassembly.

32 As the cylinder head is such a heavy and awkward assembly to install, it is helpful to make up a pair of guide studs from two 10 mm

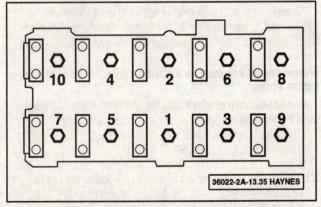

13.35a Cylinder head bolt tightening sequence (2.0L engine)

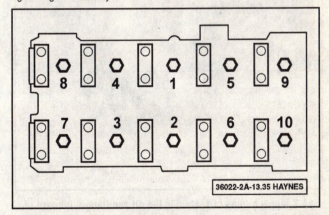

12.35b Cylinder head bolt tightening sequence (2.3L engine)

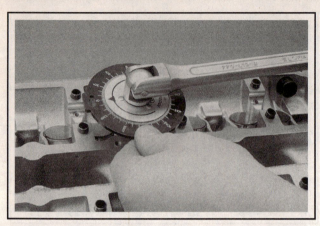

13.37 You can use a torque angle gauge, or you can carefully note the starting and stopping points of the wrench handle

2.3L engine

39 On these engines there are five tightening stages, the final two using the angle torque method (see illustration 13.37).

40 Before proceeding with replacement, turn the crankshaft forwards to TDC, and check that the setting tools described in Section 3 can be inserted. Do not turn the engine more than necessary while the timing belt is removed, or the valves may hit the pistons - for instance, if the engine is accidentally turned past the TDC position, turn it back slightly and try again - do not rotate the crankshaft a full turn.

41 Replacement of the other components removed is a reversal of removal, noting the following points:

a) Install the catalytic converter with reference to Chapter 4 if necessary, using new gaskets.

b) Install the camshafts as described in Section 12, and the timing belt or timing chain as described in Section 9 or 10.

c) Tighten all fasteners to the specified torque, where given, and use new gaskets.

d) Ensure that all hoses and wiring are correctly routed, and that hose clips and wiring connectors are securely installed.

e) Refill the cooling system as described in Chapter 1.

f) Check all disturbed joints for signs of oil or coolant leakage once the engine has been restarted and warmed-up to normal operating temperature.

42 After you reconnect the battery, the Powertrain Control Module (PCM) must relearn its idle and fuel trim strategy for optimum driveability and performance (see Chapter 5, Section 1).

14 Oil pan - removal and installation

REMOVAL

1 Raise the vehicle and support it on jackstands (see Jacking and Towing).

2 Drain the engine oil (see Chapter 1), then clean and install the engine oil drain plug, tightening it to the torque listed in the Chapter 1 Specifications. Remove and discard the oil filter, so that it can be replaced with the oil.

3 Remove the catalytic converter from the exhaust system (see Chapter 6).

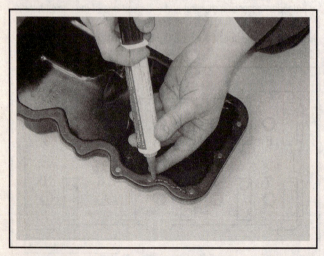

14.7 Apply a bead of sealant to the oil pan flange, inboard of the bolt holes

4 Progressively unscrew the oil pan retaining bolts. Use a rubber mallet to loosen the oil pan seal, then lower the oil pan, turning it as necessary to clear the exhaust system.

5 Unfortunately, the use of sealant can make removal of the oil pan more difficult. Be careful when prying between the mating surfaces, otherwise they will be damaged, resulting in leaks when finished. With care, a putty knife can be used to cut through the sealant.

INSTALLATION

► **Refer to illustration 14.7**

6 Thoroughly clean and degrease the mating surfaces of the lower engine block/crank-case and oil pan, removing all traces of sealant, then use a clean rag to wipe out the oil pan.

7 Apply a 1/8-inch wide bead of sealant to the oil pan flange so that the bead is approximately 3/16-inch from the outside edge of the flange. Make sure the bead is around the inside edge of the bolt holes (see illustration).

➡**Note: The oil pan must be installed within 7 minutes of applying the sealant.**

8 Install the oil pan bolts, tightening them to the Step 1 torque listed in this Chapter's Specifications, in a criss-cross pattern.

9 When all the oil pan bolts have been tightened to Step 1, tighten them again in sequence to the Step 2 setting.

10 Lower the vehicle to the ground. Wait at least 1 hour for the sealant to cure, or whatever time is indicated by the sealant manufacturer, before refilling the engine with oil. Trim off the excess sealant with a sharp knife. Install a new oil filter with reference to Chapter 1.

15 Oil pump - removal, inspection and installation

2.0L ENGINE

Removal

✳✳ WARNING:

The air conditioning system is under high pressure. DO NOT loosen any fittings or remove any components until after the system has been discharged. Air conditioning refrigerant must be properly discharged into an EPA-approved container at a dealership service department or an automotive air conditioning repair facility. Always wear eye protection when disconnecting air conditioning system fittings.

➡Note: While this task is theoretically possible when the engine is in place in the vehicle, in practice, it requires so much preliminary dismantling and is so difficult to carry out due to the restricted access, that owners are advised to remove the engine from the vehicle first (see Chapter 2C). Note, however, that the oil pump pressure relief valve can be removed with the engine in place (see Step 11).

1 Have the air conditioning system discharged (see the **Warning** above).

2 Remove the timing belt (see Section 9), then withdraw the crankshaft sprocket and the guide washer behind it, noting which way the

15.9a Remove the oil pump cover . . .

guide washer is installed (see Section 10).

3 Remove the oil pan (see Section 14).

4 Unscrew the two bolts securing the oil pump pick-up tube to the base of the lower crankcase, and withdraw it. Discard the gasket.

5 Remove the air conditioning compressor (see Chapter 3). Remove the air conditioning bracket bolts and remove it from the lower section of the engine block.

6 Remove the timing belt tensioner (see Section 9).

7 Progressively unscrew and remove the bolts securing the lower crankcase to the base of the engine block and the transaxle. Remove the lower crankcase, and recover any spacer washers, noting where they are installed, as these must be used on replacement. Remove the gasket, and remove any traces of sealant at the joint with the oil pump.

8 Unbolt the pump from the engine block. Withdraw and discard the gasket, then remove the crankshaft right-hand oil seal. Thoroughly clean and degrease all components, particularly the mating surfaces of the pump, the oil pan and the engine block.

Inspection

◆ Refer to illustrations 15.9a, 15.9b, 15.12, 15.13, 15.14a and 15.14b

9 Unscrew the Torx screws and remove the pump cover plate; noting any identification marks on the rotors, withdraw the rotors (see illustrations).

10 Inspect the rotors for obvious signs of wear or damage, and replace if necessary. If either rotor, the pump body, or its cover plate are scored or damaged, the complete oil pump assembly must be replaced.

11 The oil pressure relief valve can be disassembled, if required, without disturbing the pump. With the vehicle parked on firm level ground, apply the parking brake securely and raise its front end, supporting it securely on jackstands. Remove the front right-hand wheel and fender splash shield to provide access to the oil pressure relief valve.

12 Unscrew the threaded plug and recover the valve spring and plunger (see illustration).

13 Reassembly is the reverse of the disassembly procedure; ensure the spring and valve are reinstalled the correct way and tighten the threaded plug securely (see illustration).

14 When reassembling the oil pump, oil the housing and components as they are installed; tighten the oil pump cover bolts securely (see illustrations).

15.9b . . . and withdraw the rotors, noting which way they are facing

15.12 Oil pump pressure relief valve components (seen with oil pump removed)

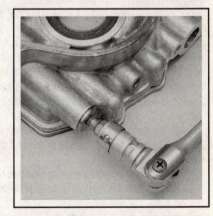

15.13 Tighten the relief valve cover plug securely

15.14a Oil the housing and rotors as they are installed

15.14b Tighten the oil pump cover bolts securely

15.16a Place the new gasket into position . . .

15.16b . . . then install the oil pump and the bolts, tightening them finger tight only at this stage

15.17 Check the alignment of the oil pump with the crankcase

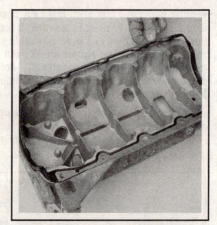

15.21a Install the new gasket . . .

Installation

◆ Refer to illustrations 15.16a, 15.16b, 15.17, 15.21a, 15.21b, 15.22, 15.23, 15.24a, 15.24b and 15.24c

15 The oil pump must be primed on installation, by pouring clean engine oil into it and rotating its inner rotor a few turns.

16 Rotate the pump's inner rotor to align with the flats on the crankshaft, then install the pump (and new gasket) and insert the bolts, tightening them lightly at first (see illustrations).

17 Using a suitable straight-edge and feeler gauges, check that the pump is both centered exactly around the crankshaft and aligned squarely so that its (oil pan) mating surface is exactly the same amount between 0.012 and 0.031-inch (0.30 to 0.80 mm) below that of the cylinder block/crankcase on each side of the crankshaft (see illustration). Being careful not to disturb the gasket, move the pump into the correct position and tighten its bolts to the torque listed in this Chapter's Specifications.

18 Check that the pump is correctly located; if necessary, unbolt it again and repeat the full procedure to ensure that the pump is correctly aligned.

19 Install a new oil pump housing seal (see Section 10).

20 Apply a little RTV sealant to the joints between the oil pump and cylinder block.

➥**Note: Once this sealant has been applied, the lower crankcase must be installed and the bolts fully tightened within 7 minutes.**

21 Install the new gasket in place, then raise the lower crankcase

15.21b . . . then install the lower crankcase

into position and loosely secure with the bolts (see illustrations).

22 The lower crankcase must now be aligned with the cylinder block before the bolts are tightened. Using a straight-edge and feeler gauges, check the alignment of the end faces (see illustration).

23 Tighten the lower crankcase bolts, in sequence, to the specified torque, ensuring that the alignment with the cylinder block is not lost (see illustration).

24 Using grease to stick the gasket in place on the pump, install

15.22 Check the alignment of the lower crankcase and engine block

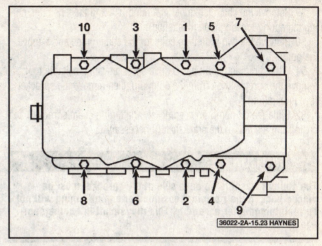

15.23 Lower crankcase bolt tightening sequence (2.0L engine)

the pickup/strainer pipe, tightening the retaining bolts to the specified torque (see illustrations).

25 The remainder of reassembly is the reverse of the removal procedure; refer to the relevant text for details where required.

2.3L engine

▸ Refer to illustrations 15.28, 15.29 15.31 and 15.33

➡Note: Removing the oil pump on this engine requires engine removal. Refer to Chapter 2C for the engine removal procedure. Also, the oil pump is serviced as a complete unit without any sub-assembly or internal inspection.

26 With the engine removed, remove the timing chain (see Section 9).

27 Remove the oil pan.

28 Remove the oil pick-up mounting bolts and then remove the pick-up tube (see illustration).

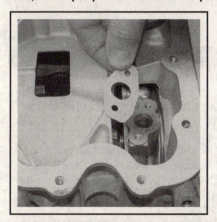

15.24a Using a new gasket . . .

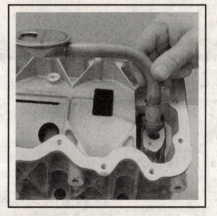

15.24b . . . install the oil pump pickup/strainer pipe . . .

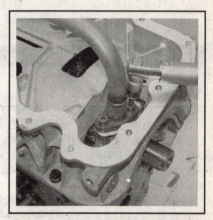

15.24c . . . and tighten the bolts to the specified torque

15.28 The oil pump pick-up tube is held by two mounting bolts

15.29 The tensioner is secured by one mounting bolt while the guide is held by two

15.31 Using a holding tool on the oil pump drive sprocket to remove the retaining bolt

29 Remove the chain tensioner mounting bolt and the tensioner, noting the spring location (see illustration).

30 Remove the two mounting bolts for the chain guide and remove the guide.

31 While holding the oil pump drive sprocket with a suitable tool, remove the sprocket bolt from the oil pump, then remove the sprocket (see illustration).

32 Slide the oil pump drive sprocket (and timing chain sprocket) and chain from the end of the crankshaft (if necessary).

❈❈ CAUTION:

The special washers on each side of the sprocket must be placed back in their original positions or engine timing will not be maintained after assembly. This may result in engine damage or failure.

15.33 Remove the four mounting bolts for the oil pump

33 Remove the oil pump mounting bolts, then remove the pump (see illustration).

34 Installation is the reverse of removal noting the following points:

a) *Replace all gaskets with new ones.*

b) *Tighten the oil pump mounting bolts to the torque listed in this Chapter's Specifications in a criss-cross pattern.*

c) *After installing the engine, refill the crankcase with oil and the*

cooling system with the proper type and mixture of antifreeze (see Chapter 1).

d) *Be certain to check for any oil warning lights in the instrument panel after the vehicle has been started and idling.*

16 Flywheel - removal, inspection and installation

REMOVAL

1   Remove the transaxle as described in Chapter 7A. Now is a good time to check components such as oil seals and replace them if necessary.

2   Remove the clutch as described in Chapter 8. Now is a good time to check or replace the clutch components and release bearing.

3   Use a center-punch or paint to make alignment marks on the flywheel and crankshaft to make replacement easier - the bolt holes are slightly offset, and will only line up one way, but making a mark eliminates the guesswork (and the flywheel is heavy).

4   Hold the flywheel stationary using one of the following methods:

a) *If an assistant is available, insert one of the transaxle mounting bolts into the cylinder block, and have the assistant engage a wide-bladed screwdriver with the starter ring gear teeth while the bolts are loosened.*

b) *Alternatively, a piece of angle-iron can be engaged with the ring gear, and located against the transaxle mounting bolt.*

5   Loosen and remove each bolt in turn and ensure that new replacements are obtained for reassembly. These bolts are subjected to severe stresses and so must be replaced, regardless of their apparent condition, whenever they are disturbed.

6   Remove the flywheel, remembering that it is very heavy - do not drop it.

INSPECTION

7   Clean the flywheel to remove grease and oil. Inspect the surface

for cracks, rivet grooves, burned areas and score marks. Light scoring can be removed with emery cloth. Check for cracked and broken ring gear teeth. Lay the flywheel on a flat surface and use a straight-edge to check for warpage.

8   Clean and inspect the mating surfaces of the flywheel and the crankshaft. If the oil seal is leaking, replace it (see Section 17) before replacing the flywheel. If the engine has covered a high mileage, it may be worth installing a new seal as a matter of course, given the amount of work needed to access it.

9   While the flywheel is removed, carefully clean its inboard face, particularly the recesses that serve as the reference points for the crankshaft speed/position sensor. Clean the sensor's tip and check that the sensor is securely fastened.

INSTALLATION

♦ **Refer to illustrations 16.10a, 16.10b and 16.11**

10 On installation, ensure that the engine/transaxle adapter plate is in place (where necessary), then install the flywheel on the crankshaft so that all bolt holes align - it will fit only one way - check this using the marks made on removal. Install the new bolts, tightening them by hand (see illustrations).

11 Lock the flywheel by the method used on dismantling. Working in a diagonal sequence to tighten them evenly and increasing to the final amount in two or three stages, tighten the new bolts to the torque listed in this Chapter's Specifications (see illustration).

12 The remainder of reassembly is the reverse of the removal procedure

16.10a Place the flywheel into position . . .

16.10b . . . and secure with the new bolts

16.11 Tighten the flywheel bolts to the specified torque

17 Rear main oil seal - replacement

1   The one-piece rear main oil seal is pressed into rear main oil seal carrier mounted. Remove the transaxle (see Chapter 7), the clutch components (see Chapter 8) and the flywheel (see Section 16).

➡Note: The rear main oil seal carrier is not to be removed with the engine in the vehicle. Observe that the oil seal is installed flush with the seal carrier and the lip of the oil pan.

2.0L ENGINE

2   Pry out the old seal with a flat-blade screwdriver.

✳✳ CAUTION:

To prevent an oil leak after the new seal is installed, be very careful not to scratch or otherwise damage the crankshaft sealing surface or the bore in the engine block.

3   Clean the crankshaft and seal bore in the block thoroughly and de-grease these areas by wiping them with a rag soaked in lacquer thin-

ner or acetone. Lubricate the lip of the new seal and the outer diameter of the crankshaft with engine oil. Make sure the edges of the new oil seal are not rolled over.

4   Position the new seal onto the crankshaft.

➡Note: When installing the new seal, if so marked, the words THIS SIDE OUT on the seal must face out, toward the rear of the engine. Use a special rear main oil seal installation tool or a socket with the exact diameter of the seal to drive the seal in place. Make sure the seal is not off-set; it must be flush along the entire circumference of the seal carrier.

5   The remainder of installation is the reverse of removal.

2.3L ENGINE

▶ Refer to illustration 17.13

6   Remove the oil pan (see Section 13).

7   Unbolt the oil seal and carrier.

8   Clean the mating surface for the oil seal carrier on the cylinder block and the crankshaft. Carefully remove and polish any burrs or raised edges on the crankshaft that may have caused the seal to fail.

9   Lightly coat the inside lip of the new seal with clean engine oil. Then, use a thin (but durable) two-inch wide plastic strip (or a two-liter plastic beverage bottle cut to size) around the inside circumference of the seal to act as a liner for installation.

10   With the plastic seal liner in place, carefully move the new oil seal and carrier into position by sliding it onto the contact surface of the crankshaft.

11   Install the oil seal carrier bolts and finger tighten them while holding the carrier in place.

12   Carefully remove the plastic liner or bottle so that the new seal contacts the crankshaft mating surface correctly.

13   Tighten the oil seal carrier to the torque listed in this Chapter's Specifications using the proper sequence (see illustration).

14   The seal is now fully installed. Be sure to check for signs of oil leakage when the engine is operable.

17.13 Rear oil seal carrier tightening sequence (2.3L engine)

36071-2B-16.18 HAYNES

18 Engine mounts - check and replacement

1 Engine mounts seldom require attention, but broken or deteriorated mounts should be replaced immediately or the added strain placed on the driveline components may cause damage or wear.

CHECK

2 During the check, the engine must be raised slightly to remove the weight from the mounts.

3 Raise the vehicle and support it securely on jackstands, then position a jack under the engine oil pan. Place a large wood block between the jack head and the oil pan to prevent oil pan damage, then carefully raise the engine just enough to take the weight off the mounts.

✳✳ WARNING:

DO NOT place any part of your body under the engine when it's supported only by a jack!

18.9 Remove the bolts and lift the engine mount upper bracket off the engine mount

4 Check the mounts to see if the rubber is cracked, hardened or separated from the metal backing. Sometimes the rubber will split right down the center.

5 Check for relative movement between the mount plates and the engine or frame. Use a large screwdriver or pry bar to attempt to move the mounts. If movement is noted, lower the engine and tighten the mount fasteners.

6 Rubber preservative may be applied to the mounts to slow deterioration.

REPLACEMENT

◗ **Refer to illustration 18.9**

➡**Note: Refer to Chapter 7 for information on the transaxle mounts.**

7 Disconnect the battery cable from the battery negative terminal (see Chapter 5), then raise the vehicle and support it securely on jackstands (if not already done).

8 Place a floor jack under the engine with a wood block between the jack head and oil pan and raise the engine slightly to relieve the weight from the mounts.

9 Remove the fasteners and detach the mount from the frame and engine (see illustration).

✳✳ CAUTION:

Do not disconnect more than one mount at a time, except during engine removal.

10 Installation is the reverse of removal. Use thread locking compound on the mount bolts and be sure to tighten them securely.

11 After you reconnect the battery, the Powertrain Control Module (PCM) must relearn its idle and fuel trim strategy for optimum driveability and performance (see Chapter 5, Section 1).

Specifications

General

2.0L engine

Engine type	Four-cylinder, in-line, DOHC
Displacement	121 cubic inches (1989 cc)
Engine VIN code	B
Bore	3.34 inches (84.8 mm)
Stroke	3.46 inches (88.0 mm)
Compression ratio	9.6:1
Compression	See Chapter 2C
Firing order	1-3-4-2
Oil pressure	See Chapter 2C

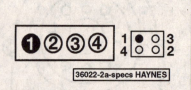

Cylinder/coil terminal locations four-cylinder engine

2.3L engine

Engine type	Four cylinder, in line DOHC
Displacement	2.3 L 140 cubic inches (2261 cc)
Engine VIN code	Z
Bore	3.44 inches (87.5 mm)
Stroke	3.70 (94.0 mm)
Compression ratio	9.7: 1
Compression	See Chapter 2C
Firing order	1-3-4-2
Oil pressure	See Chapter 2C

Camshafts

2.0L engine

Lobe height	
Intake	0.350 inch (8.9 mm)
Exhaust	0.343 inch (8.7 mm)
Bearing journal diameter	1.022 to 1.023 inches (25.96 to 25.98 mm)
Endplay	0.003 to 0.009 inch (0.080 to 0.220 mm)

2.3L engine

Lobe height	
Intake	0.324 inch (8.35 mm)
Exhaust	0.307 inch (7.8 mm)
Bearing journal diameter	0 982 inch (24.97 mm)
Endplay	0.003 to 0.009 inches (0.9 to 0.24 mm)

Valve clearances (cold)

2.0L engine

Intake	0.004 to 0.007 inch (0.11 to 0.18 mm)
Exhaust	0.011 to 0.013 inch (0.27 to 0.34 mm)

2.3L engine

Intake	0.008 to 0.011 inches (0.22 to 0.28 mm)
Exhaust	0.11 to 0.13 inches (0.27 to 0.33 mm)

Warpage limits

Cylinder head gasket surfaces (head and block)	0.002 inch (0.05 mm)
Intake and exhaust manifolds	0.008 inch (0.20 mm)

Torque specifications

	Ft-lbs (unless otherwise indicated)	Nm

➡ **Note: One foot-pound (ft-lb) of torque is equivalent to 12 inch-pounds (in-lbs) of torque. Torque values below approximately 15 ft-lbs are expressed in inch-pounds, since most foot-pound torque wrenches are not accurate at these smaller values.**

	Ft-lbs (unless otherwise indicated)	Nm
Camshaft bearing cap bolts		
2.0L engine		
Step 1	89 in-lbs	10
Step 2	168 in-lbs	19
2.3L engine		
Step 1	62 in-lbs	7
Step 2	144 in-lbs	16
Camshaft sprocket bolts	50	68
Crankshaft pulley bolt	85	115

Torque specifications (continued)   Ft-lbs (unless otherwise indicated)   Nm

➡Note: One foot-pound (ft-lb) of torque is equivalent to 12 inch-pounds (in-lbs) of torque. Torque values below approximately 15 ft-lbs are expressed in inch-pounds, since most foot-pound torque wrenches are not accurate at these smaller values.

	Ft-lbs	Nm
Cylinder head bolts - 2.0L engine (in sequence - see illustration 13.35a)		
Step 1	15	20
Step 2	30	40
Step 3	Tighten an additional 90-degrees	
Cylinder head bolts - 2.3L engine		
(in sequence - see illustration 13.35b)		
Step 1	44 in-lbs	5
Step 2	132 in-lbs	15
Step 3	33	44
Step 4	Tighten an additional 90-degrees	
Step 5	Tighten an additional 90-degrees	
Valve cover bolts	80 in-lbs	9
Exhaust manifold nuts and bolts (2.0L engine)	144 in-lbs	16
Exhaust Manifold/Catalytic converter (2.3L engine)	35	47
Flywheel bolts	83	112
Intake manifold nuts and bolts	156 in-lbs	18
Lower crankcase-to-engine block		
(in sequence - see illustration 15.23)	22	30
Oil pick-up pipe bolts	89 in-lbs	10
Oil pump-to-cylinder block bolts (2.0L engine)		
Step 1	53 in-lbs	6
Step 2	Tighten an additional 45-degrees	
Oil pan-to-lower crankcase (2.0L engine)		
Step 1	53 in-lbs	6
Step 2	105 in-lbs	12
Oil pan-to-bellhousing bolts (2.3L engine)	35	48
Oil pan-to-timing chain cover bolts (2.3L engine)	89 in-lbs	10
Oil pan-to-engine block bolts (2.3L engine)	18	25
Oil pump (2.3L engine)		
Oil pump mounting bolts		
Step 1	89 in-lbs	10
Step 2	15	20
Oil pump pick-up tube bolts	89	10
Sprocket bolt	18	25
Oil pump chain tensioner bolt	89 in-lbs	10
Timing belt covers (2.0L engine)		
Upper cover bolts	71 in-lbs	8
Middle cover bolts	37	50
Lower cover bolts	71 in-lbs	8
Timing belt guide pulley bolt (2.0L engine)	18	25
Timing chain guide bolts (2.3L engine)	89 in-lbs	10
Timing belt tensioner pulley bolt (2.0L engine)	18	25
Timing chain tensioner bolts (2.3L engine)	89 in-lbs	10
Timing chain cover bolts (2.3L engine)		
8 mm bolts	89 in-lbs	10
13 mm bolts	35	48

2B

V6 ENGINE

Section

1 General information

This part of Chapter 2 covers in-vehicle repairs for the 3.0 liter Overhead Camshaft (OHC) V6 Duratec engine. This version of the 3.0L V6 engine features an aluminum engine block and aluminum cylinder heads with dual overhead camshafts and four valves per cylinder.

All information on engine removal and installation, as well as general overhaul procedures, is in Part C of Chapter 2.

The following repair procedures are based on the assumption that the engine is installed in the vehicle. If the engine has been removed and mounted on a stand, many of the Steps in this part of Chapter 2 will not apply.

In this chapter, "left" and "right" are used to describe locations on the engine. These directions are in relation to the vehicle overall from the position of sitting in the driver's seat. So, "left" means the driver's side, and "right" means the passenger's side of the vehicle.

2 Repair operations possible with the engine in the vehicle

Many major repairs can be done without removing the engine from the vehicle. Clean the engine compartment and the exterior of the engine with a pressure washer or degreaser solvent before doing any work. Cleaning the engine and engine compartment will make repairs easier and help to keep dirt out of the engine.

It may help to remove the hood for better access to the engine. (Refer to Chapter 11, if necessary.)

If the engine has vacuum, exhaust, oil, or coolant leaks that indicate the need for gasket replacement, repairs can usually be done with the engine in the vehicle. The intake and exhaust manifold gaskets, the timing chain cover gasket, the oil pan gasket, crankshaft oil seals, and cylinder head gaskets are all accessible with the engine in the vehicle.

Exterior engine components, such as the intake and exhaust manifolds, the oil pan, the water pump, the starter motor, the alternator, and many fuel system components also can be serviced with the engine installed.

Because the cylinder heads can be removed without pulling the engine, valve train components can be serviced with the engine in the vehicle. The timing chain and sprockets also can be replaced without removing the engine, although clearance is very limited.

In some cases - caused by a lack of equipment - pistons, piston rings, connecting rods, and rod bearings can be replaced with the engine in the vehicle. This is not recommended, however, because of the cleaning and preparation that must be done to the parts involved.

3 Top Dead Center (TDC) for number one piston - locating

♦ Refer to illustrations 3.6a and 3.6b

➡**Note: Although this engine does not have a distributor, timing marks on the crankshaft pulley and a stationary pointer on the engine front cover will help you to locate Top Dead Center (TDC) for cylinders 1 and 5.**

1   Top Dead Center (TDC) is the highest point in the cylinder that each piston reaches as it travels upward when the crankshaft turns. Each piston reaches TDC on the compression stroke and on the exhaust stroke, but TDC usually refers to piston position on the compression stroke.

2   Positioning one or more pistons at TDC is an essential part of many procedures such as rocker arm removal, valve adjustment, and timing chain replacement.

3   To place any piston at TDC, turn the crankshaft using one of the methods described below. When you look at the front of the engine (right side of the engine compartment), crankshaft rotation is clockwise.

⁕⁕ **WARNING:**

Before using any of the following methods to turn the crankshaft, be sure the transaxle is in Park. Also disconnect the ignition wiring harness connector from the side of the coil pack assembly.

a)   *The best way to turn the crankshaft is to use a socket and breaker bar on the crankshaft pulley bolt on the front of the crankshaft.*

b)   *You also can use a remote starter switch connected to the S (switch) and B (battery) terminals of the starter relay. Operate the remote switch in short intervals until the piston is close to TDC. Then use a socket and breaker bar for the final rotation to TDC.*

c)   *If an assistant is available to operate the ignition switch in short intervals, you can rotate the crankshaft until the piston is close to TDC. Then use a socket and breaker bar for the final rotation to TDC.*

4   Remove the spark plug from number 1 cylinder and install a compression gauge in its place (see Chapter 5).

5   Rotate the crankshaft by one of the methods described in Step 3, until a compression reading is indicated on the gauge. The piston should be approaching TDC.

6   Continue turning the crankshaft with a socket and breaker bar until the notch in the crankshaft pulley is aligned with the TDC mark on the front cover (see illustrations). At this point, the number one cylin-

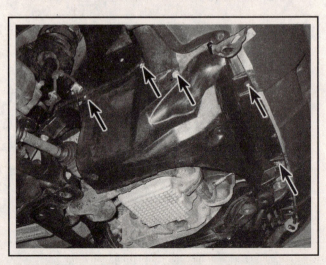

3.6a Remove the inner fender splash shield mounting bolts

3.6b To position the number 1 piston at TDC, position the crankshaft pulley keyway at 11 o'clock and align the mark on the pulley with the mark on the engine front cover

der is at TDC on the compression stroke. If the marks aligned but there was no compression, the piston was on the exhaust stroke. Continue rotating the engine until compression is indicated.

7   If you go past TDC, rotate the engine backwards (counterclockwise) until the timing marks indicate that the piston is before TDC. Then rotate the crankshaft clockwise until the marks align. Final rotation should always be clockwise to remove slack from the timing chains and ensure that the piston is truly at TDC.

8   After the number one piston is at TDC on the compression stroke, TDC for any of the remaining cylinders can be located by turning the crankshaft and following the firing order (refer to the Specifications). Divide the crankshaft pulley into three equal sections with chalk marks at three points, each indicating 120-degrees of crankshaft rotation. For example, rotating the engine 120-degrees past TDC for number 1 piston will place the engine at TDC for cylinder number 4. Refer to the firing order for the remaining cylinder numbers.

4   Valve covers - removal and installation

▶ **Refer to illustration 4.1**

1   Remove the engine access cover (see illustration).

FRONT (LEFT-SIDE) VALVE COVER

▶ **Refer to illustrations 4.2, 4.8a, 4.8b, 4.10, 4.11a and 4.11b**

2   Disconnect the crankcase ventilation tube (see illustration).

3   Remove the ignition coils (see Chapter 5) from the top of the valve cover.

4   Disconnect the wiring harness from the valve cover and position it off to the side.

5   Remove the engine lifting brackets.

6   Remove the bolt from the power steering pump hose bracket and position the hose off to the side.

7   Loosen the valve cover bolts gradually and evenly until all are loose. Follow the reverse of the tightening sequence (see illustration 4.15). Remove the valve cover fasteners and lift the valve cover off the engine.

8   Remove and discard the valve cover gaskets and spark plug tube

4.1 Remove the engine access cover mounting nuts

seals (see illustrations). Install new gaskets and seals during reassembly.

9   Inspect the valve cover and cylinder head sealing surfaces for

4.2 Disconnect the crankcase ventilation tube from the front valve cover

4.8a Remove and discard the old valve cover gasket - it must be replaced during assembly to prevent leakage

4.8b Remove and discard the spark plug tube seals from the valve cover

4.10 Press the new gasket into the groove in the valve cover, making sure it isn't twisted

nicks or other damage. Clean the sealing surfaces with clean solvent and a shop towel.

10 Install a new valve cover gasket, making sure the gasket is properly seated in the groove (see illustration). Also install new spark plug tube seals.

11 Apply a 5/16-inch bead of RTV sealant at the locations shown (see illustrations).

12 Lower the valve cover into position, making sure that the gaskets stay in place. Install the cover fasteners and tighten them gradually and evenly to the torque listed in this Chapter's Specifications.

13 Reconnect the wiring harness to the bracket studs.

14 Reconnect the crankcase ventilation tube to the valve cover.

15 Tighten the valve cover bolts to the torque listed in this Chapter's Specifications. Follow the correct torque sequence (see illustration).

16 The remaining installation is the reverse of removal.

REAR (RIGHT-SIDE) VALVE COVER

▶ **Refer to illustration 4.27**

17 Remove the upper intake manifold (see Section 5).

18 Remove the ignition coils (see Chapter 5) from the top of the valve cover.

19 Remove the oxygen sensor wiring harness cover and position the

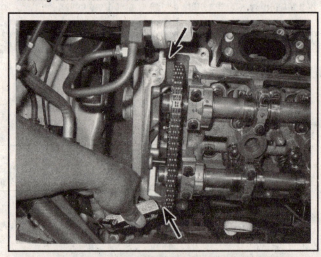

4.11a Apply a 5/16-inch bead of RTV sealant to the seams of the engine front cover/cylinder head . . .

oxygen sensor connectors and the wiring harness off to the side.

20 Remove the radio/ignition interference capacitor from the base of the alternator.

21 Disconnect the crankcase ventilation tube.

4.11b . . . and the camshaft seal retainer/cylinder head

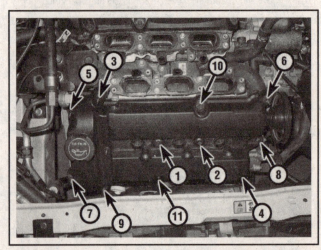

4.15 Valve cover bolt tightening sequence for the left valve cover (front)

22 Loosen the valve cover fasteners gradually and evenly, until all fasteners are loose. Follow the reverse of the tightening sequence (see illustration 4.27). Then, unscrew and remove the fasteners. Lift the valve cover off the cylinder head.

23 Remove and discard the valve cover gaskets and spark plug tube seals (see illustrations 4.8a and 4.8b). Install new gaskets and seals during reassembly.

24 Inspect the valve cover and cylinder head sealing surfaces for nicks or other damage. Clean the sealing surfaces with clean solvent and a shop towel.

25 Install a new valve cover gasket, making sure the gasket is properly seated in the groove (see illustration 4.10). Also install new spark plug tube seals.

26 Apply a 5/16-inch bead of RTV sealant to the two locations where the valve cover contacts the cylinder head (see illustration 4.11a).

27 Install the valve cover fasteners and tighten them gradually and evenly to the torque listed in this Chapter's Specifications. Follow the correct torque sequence (see illustration).

28 Reinstall all wiring harnesses and brackets.

29 Reinstall the ignition coils (see Chapter 5).

30 Install the upper intake manifold (see Section 5).

31 The remaining installation is the reverse of removal.

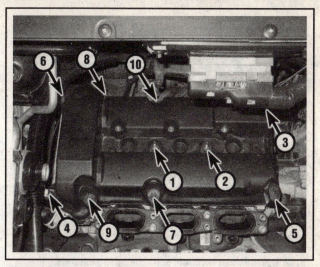

4.27 Valve cover bolt tightening sequence for the right valve cover (rear)

5 Intake manifold - removal and installation

UPPER INTAKE MANIFOLD

Removal

▸ **Refer to illustration 5.14**

1 Disconnect the cable from the negative battery terminal (see Chapter 5).

2 Remove the air filter housing intake duct (see Chapter 4).

3 Remove the engine access cover (see illustration 4.1).

4 Disconnect the accelerator cable and the cruise control cable, if equipped (see Chapter 4).

5 Disconnect the throttle position sensor (TPS) and the idle air control (IAC) valve connectors (see Chapter 4).

6 Disconnect the EGR valve vacuum hose and the EGR pipe (see Chapter 6).

7 Disconnect the EGR valve vacuum regulator solenoid connector (see Chapter 6).

8 Disconnect the vapor management valve (see Chapter 6).

9 Disconnect the vacuum lines and electrical connectors from the upper intake manifold. Be sure to mark them with tape to insure correct reassembly.

10 Disconnect the power steering pressure sensor from the power steering pump.

11 Remove the transaxle vent hose bracket and position the hose off to the side.

12 Remove the wire harness bracket nut and position the wiring harness off to the side.

13 Loosen the upper intake manifold bolts. Follow the opposite of the tightening sequence (see illustration 5.17).

14 Remove and discard the upper intake manifold gaskets (see illustration).

Installation

▸ **Refer to illustration 5.17**

❉ **CAUTION:**

Be very careful when scraping on aluminum engine parts. Aluminum is soft and gouges easily. Severely gouged parts may require replacement.

15 If the gasket was leaking, check the mating surfaces for warpage. Check carefully around the mounting points of components such as the IAC valve and the EGR pipe. Replace the manifold if it is cracked or badly warped.

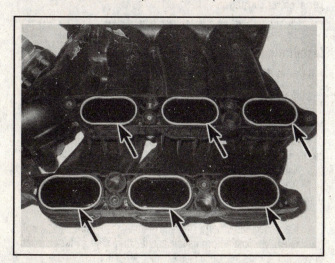

5.14 Remove the gaskets from the upper intake manifold

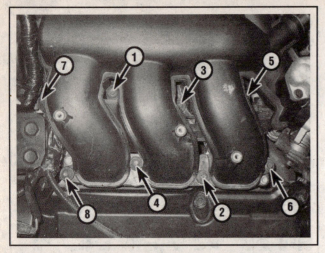

5.17 Upper intake manifold bolt tightening sequence

16 Install new gaskets. If the mating surfaces are clean and flat, a new gasket will ensure the joint is sealed. Don't use any kind of sealant on any part of the fuel system or intake manifold.

17 Locate the upper manifold on the lower manifold and install the fasteners. Tighten the fasteners in three or four steps in the sequence shown (see illustration) to the torque listed in this Chapter's Specifications.

18 Install the remaining parts in the reverse order of removal.

19 Before starting the engine, check the accelerator cable for correct adjustment and the throttle linkage for smooth operation.

20 Reconnect the battery. After you're done, the Powertrain Control Module (PCM) must relearn its idle and fuel trim strategy for optimum driveability and performance (see Chapter 5, Section 1).

21 When the engine is fully warm, check for fuel and vacuum leaks. Road test the vehicle and check for proper operation of all components.

LOWER INTAKE MANIFOLD

Removal

▶ **Refer to illustration 5.29**

22 Relieve the fuel pressure (see Chapter 4).

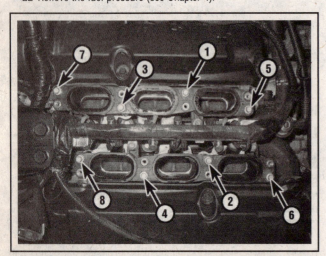

5.33 Lower intake manifold bolt tightening sequence

5.29 Remove the gaskets from the lower intake manifold

23 Disconnect the cable from the battery negative terminal (see Chapter 5).

24 Remove the upper intake manifold (see Steps 1 through 14).

25 Disconnect the fuel line from the fuel rail (see Chapter 4).

26 Disconnect the fuel injection electrical connectors from the fuel injectors (see Chapter 4). Move the injector wiring harness out of the way.

27 Disconnect the vacuum hose from the fuel pressure regulator.

28 To prevent warpage, loosen the eight lower manifold bolts gradually and evenly in the reverse of the tightening sequence until all are loose (see illustration 5.33). Then, remove the bolts.

29 Lift the lower intake manifold off the engine. Remove and discard the manifold gaskets (see illustration).

30 Carefully clean all gasket material from the manifold and cylinder head mating surfaces. Don't nick, scratch or gouge the sealing surfaces.

✳✳ CAUTION:

Be very careful when scraping on aluminum engine parts. Aluminum is soft and gouges easily. Severely gouged parts may require replacement. Inspect all parts for cracks or other damage. If the manifold gaskets were leaking, check the mating surfaces for warpage.

Installation

▶ **Refer to illustration 5.33**

31 Install new lower intake manifold gaskets on the cylinder heads.

32 Place the lower manifold into position on the cylinder heads. Make sure the gaskets are not dislodged.

33 Install the lower manifold bolts. Tighten the bolts gradually and evenly, in the sequence shown (see illustration), to the torque listed in this Chapter's Specifications.

34 The remainder of installation is the reverse of the removal procedure. Tighten the fasteners to the torque listed in this Chapter's Specifications.

35 Reconnect the battery. After you're done, the Powertrain Control Module (PCM) must relearn its idle and fuel trim strategy for optimum driveability and performance (see Chapter 5, Section 1).

6   Exhaust manifolds - removal and installation

✳✳ WARNING:

Allow the engine to cool completely before beginning this procedure.

FRONT (LEFT-SIDE) EXHAUST MANIFOLD

▶ **Refer to illustration 6.7**

✳✳ WARNING:

The engine and exhaust system must be completely cool before performing this procedure.

1   Disconnect the cable from the negative battery terminal (see Chapter 5).

2   Disconnect the electrical connector for the oxygen sensor and the catalytic converter monitor (see Chapter 6).

3   Loosen the right front wheel lug nuts, then raise the front of the vehicle and support it securely on jackstands. Remove the wheel, then remove the fender splash shield.

4   Remove the exhaust crossover pipe (see Chapter 4).

5   Remove the drivebelt (see Chapter 1).

6   Remove the air conditioning compressor bolts and position the compressor off to the side. Do not disconnect the refrigerant lines from the compressor.

7   Remove the six nuts securing the exhaust manifold (see illustration). Remove and discard the manifold gasket.

8   Using a scraper, remove all old gasket material and carbon deposits from the manifold and cylinder head mating surfaces.

✳✳ CAUTION:

Be very careful when scraping on aluminum engine parts. Aluminum is soft and gouges easily. Severely gouged parts may require replacement. If the gasket was leaking, check the manifold for warpage and have it resurfaced if necessary.

9   Install a new manifold gasket over the cylinder head studs. Lightly oil the stud threads with clean engine oil before installation. Install the manifold and the nuts.

10 Tighten the nuts in three or four steps, in a spiral pattern starting with the center fasteners, to the torque listed in this Chapter's Specifications.

11 The remainder of installation is the reverse of the removal procedure.

12 Start and run the engine and check for exhaust leaks. The Powertrain Control Module (PCM) must relearn its idle and fuel trim strategy for optimum driveability and performance (see Chapter 5, Section 1).

REAR (RIGHT-SIDE) EXHAUST MANIFOLD

▶ **Refer to illustration 6.18**

13 Disconnect the cable from the negative battery terminal (see Chapter 5).

14 Remove the EGR pipe from the exhaust manifold (see Chapter 6).

15 Remove the alternator (see Chapter 5).

16 Remove the oxygen sensor (see Chapter 6).

17 Remove the nuts from the exhaust manifold flange and separate the crossover pipe from the manifold (see Chapter 4).

18 Remove the six exhaust manifold mounting nuts and remove the manifold from the engine (see illustration). Remove and discard the manifold gasket.

19 Using a scraper, remove all gasket material and carbon deposits from the exhaust manifold and cylinder head mating surfaces.

✳✳ CAUTION:

Be very careful when scraping on aluminum engine parts. Aluminum is soft and gouges easily. Severely gouged parts may require replacement. If the gasket was leaking, check the manifold for warpage and have it resurfaced if necessary.

20 Install a new manifold gasket over the cylinder head studs. Lightly oil the stud threads with clean engine oil before installation. Install the manifold and the nuts.

21 Tighten the nuts in three or four steps, in a spiral pattern starting with the center fasteners, to the torque listed in this Chapter's Specifications.

22 Complete the installation by reversing the removal procedure.

23 Start and run the engine and check for exhaust leaks. The Powertrain Control Module (PCM) must relearn its idle and fuel trim strategy for optimum driveability and performance (see Chapter 5, Section 1).

6.7 Remove the front exhaust manifold mounting nuts - three nuts hidden from view

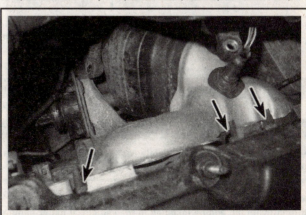

6.18 The rear exhaust manifold mounting nuts are difficult to access (not all are visible here)

7 Crankshaft pulley and front oil seal - removal and installation

REMOVAL

▶ Refer to illustrations 7.5a, 7.5b and 7.7

1   Disconnect the cable from the negative battery terminal (see Chapter 5).
2   Loosen the right front wheel lug nuts. Raise the front of the vehicle and support it securely on jackstands, then remove the wheel.
3   Remove the fender splash shield.
4   Remove the drivebelt (see Chapter 1).
5   Remove the driveplate access cover and hold the ring gear teeth with a large screwdriver or prybar to prevent the crankshaft from turning (see illustrations).
6   Remove the crankshaft pulley retaining bolt.
7   Using a suitable puller, remove the crankshaft pulley (see illustration).

❋❋ CAUTION:

Use a puller designed to remove a crankshaft pulley. Such a puller has bolts that screw into the holes in the center of the pulley. Do not use a gear puller or any puller that grips the outer circumference of the pulley. Such a puller will destroy the pulley.

8   Using a seal puller, remove the seal from the engine front cover. Note the orientation of the sealing lip so that the new seal will be installed in the same direction.

INSTALLATION

9   Inspect the front cover and the pulley seal surface for nicks, burrs, or other roughness that could damage the new seal. Correct as necessary.
10 Lubricate the new seal with clean engine oil and install it in the engine front cover with a suitable seal driver. Be sure that the lip of the seal faces inward. If a seal driver is unavailable, carefully tap the seal into place with a large socket and hammer until it's flush with the front cover surface.
11 Apply RTV sealant to the keyway and inner bore of the pulley and lubricate the outer sealing surface of the pulley with clean engine oil. Then align the pulley keyway with the crankshaft key and install the pulley with a suitable pulley installation tool (available at auto parts stores). If such a tool is unavailable, start the pulley onto the crankshaft with a soft-faced mallet and finish the installation by tightening the retaining bolt. Tighten the bolt to the torque listed in this Chapter's Specifications.
12 Reinstall the remaining parts in the reverse order of removal. Tighten the wheel lug nuts to the torque listed in the Chapter 1 Specifications.
13 Reconnect the battery, then start the engine and check for oil leaks.
14 The Powertrain Control Module (PCM) must relearn its idle and fuel trim strategy for optimum driveability and performance (see Chapter 5, Section 1).

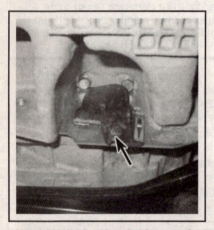

7.5a To keep the crankshaft from turning, remove the driveplate access cover . . .

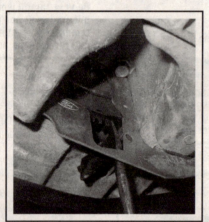

7.5b . . . engage the ring gear teeth with a large screwdriver or prybar

7.7 Remove the crankshaft pulley with a bolt-type puller

8 Engine front cover - removal and installation

❋❋ WARNING:

Wait until the engine is completely cool before beginning this procedure.

➡Note: Because of a lack of clearance, this procedure is very difficult with the engine installed in the vehicle. If major engine work is being performed, it may be easier to remove the engine from the vehicle (see Chapter 2C).

REMOVAL

▶ Refer to illustrations 8.11, 8.15 and 8.16

1   Disconnect the cable from the negative battery terminal (see Chapter 5).
2   Loosen the right front wheel lug nuts. Raise the front of the vehicle and support it securely on jackstands, then remove the wheel.
3   Drain the engine oil (see Chapter 1).

8.11 Disconnect the camshaft position sensor (A) and the crankshaft position sensor (B)

4   Remove the drivebelt (see Chapter 1).
5   Remove the drivebelt tensioner from the front cover.
6   Remove the valve covers (see Section 4).
7   Remove the alternator and alternator mounting bracket (see Chapter 5).
8   Remove the crankshaft pulley (see Section 7).
9   Drain the cooling system (see Chapter 1) and remove the coolant expansion tank (see Chapter 3).
10 Remove the power steering pump (see Chapter 10).
11 Disconnect the crankshaft position sensor (see illustration).
12 Disconnect the camshaft position sensor (see Chapter 6).
13 Remove the oil pan (see Section 12).
14 If necessary, loosen the air conditioning compressor mounting bolts and move the compressor aside as required for access to the engine cover.

❖❖ WARNING:

The air conditioning system is under high pressure. Do not disconnect the hoses from the compressor.

Remove or disconnect any remaining wires, hoses, clamps, or brackets that will interfere with engine cover removal.

8.16 Lift off the front cover

8.15 Remove the cover fasteners - note the locations of all studs and bolts for installation reference

15 Loosen the engine cover fasteners gradually and evenly; then remove the fasteners (see illustration).
➥Note: Draw a sketch of the engine cover and cover fasteners. Identify the location of all stud bolts for installation in their original locations.
16 Remove the front cover (see illustration).
17 Remove and discard the cover-to-cylinder block gaskets.

INSTALLATION

❖ **Refer to illustrations 8.20 and 8.23**

18 Inspect and clean all sealing surfaces of the engine front cover and the block.

❖❖ CAUTION:

Be very careful when scraping on aluminum engine parts. Aluminum is soft and gouges easily. Severely gouged parts may require replacement.

19 If necessary, replace the crankshaft seal in the front cover.
20 Apply a bead of RTV sealant approximately 1/8-inch wide at the locations shown (see illustration).

8.20 Apply a bead of RTV sealant at the locations shown

21 Install a new front cover gasket on the engine block. Make sure the gasket fits over the alignment dowels.

22 Install the front cover and cover fasteners. Make sure the fasteners are in their original locations. Tighten the fasteners by hand until the cover is contacting the block and cylinder heads around its entire periphery.

23 Following the correct sequence (see illustration), tighten the bolts to the torque listed in this Chapter's Specifications.

24 Install the drivebelt and tensioner. Tighten the tensioner pulley to the torque listed in this Chapter's Specifications.

25 Install the oil pan (see Section 12).

26 Install the crankshaft pulley (see Section 7).

27 Connect the wiring harness connectors to the camshaft and crankshaft position sensors.

28 Install the power steering pump and hoses (see Chapter 10).

29 Reinstall the remaining parts in the reverse order of removal.

30 Fill the crankcase with the recommended oil (see Chapter 1). Fill the power steering reservoir with the correct fluid and refill the cooling system.

31 Reconnect the battery, then start the engine and check for leaks. The Powertrain Control Module (PCM) must relearn its idle and fuel trim strategy for optimum driveability and performance (see Chapter 5, Section 1).

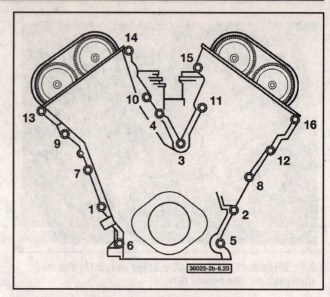

8.23 Engine front cover bolt tightening sequence

---

9   Timing chains, tensioners, and chain guides - removal, inspection, and installation

➡ **Note: Because of a lack of clearance, this procedure is very difficult with the engine installed in the vehicle. If major engine work is being performed, it may be easier to remove the engine from the vehicle (see Chapter 2C).**

REMOVAL

▶ **Refer to illustrations 9.2, 9.4a, 9.4b, 9.5, 9.6, 9.7, 9.8a, 9.8b and 9.10.**

1   Remove the engine front cover (see Section 8). Slide the crankshaft position sensor trigger wheel off the crankshaft.

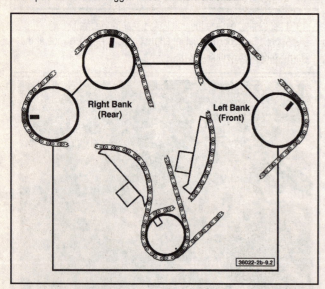

9.2 Positions of the camshaft sprocket timing marks and the crankshaft keyway with the engine set at TDC for the number one piston

✳✳ **CAUTION:**

The pulse (trigger) wheel cannot be interchanged with another engine. Note the exact position of the pulse wheel to insure correct reassembly. Remove the spark plugs (see Chapter 1).

2   Install the crankshaft pulley retaining bolt, then use a wrench on the bolt to turn the crankshaft clockwise and place the crankshaft keyway at the 11 o'clock position. TDC number 1 is the starting position and the ending position for this procedure. Verify TDC by observing the index marks on the front of the camshaft sprockets. If the number 1 cylinder is at TDC, the index mark on the front (left) bank exhaust camshaft will be directly UP (12 o'clock) in relation to the cylinder head surface and the intake camshaft index mark will be horizontal (9 o'clock) to the cylinder head (see illustration). If not, turn the crankshaft exactly one full turn and again position the crankshaft keyway at 11 o'clock.

✳✳ **CAUTION:**

Turning the crankshaft counterclockwise can cause the timing chains to bind and damage the chains, sprockets and tensioners. Turn the crankshaft only clockwise.

3   Recheck the marks on the sprockets. If they are aligned and the keyway is at 11 o'clock, the number 1 cylinder is at TDC on the compression stroke. Continue to turn the crankshaft clockwise until the keyway is at the 3 o'clock position, which will set the camshafts on the rear cylinder head in their "neutral" position.

4   Remove the two bolts securing the timing chain tensioner for the rear chain. Remove the tensioner, then remove the tensioner arm (see illustrations). Mark all parts that will be reused so they can be reinstalled in their original locations.

9.4a Remove the bolts securing the rear timing chain tensioner and remove the tensioner . . .

5   Lift the rear timing chain from the sprockets and remove the chain (see illustration).

6   Remove the bolts securing the rear chain guide and remove the guide (see illustration).

7   Slide the sprocket for the rear timing chain off the crankshaft

9.4b . . . then slide the tensioner arm off its pivot

(see illustration).

8   Rotate the crankshaft 600-degrees (1-2/3 turns) clockwise, until the keyway is in the 11 o'clock position, setting the camshafts in the front cylinder head in their neutral position. Remove the front timing chain tensioner mounting bolts. Remove the tensioner and tensioner arm (see illustrations).

9.5 Lift the rear timing chain off the sprockets and remove the chain

9.6 Remove the bolts securing the rear timing chain guide, then remove the guide

9.7 Remove the rear timing chain sprocket from the crankshaft

9.8a Remove the bolts that secure the front timing chain tensioner, then remove the tensioner . . .

9.8b . . . and remove the tensioner arm

9.10 Remove the bolts securing the front timing chain guide and remove the guide

9   Lift the front timing chain off the sprockets and remove the chain.
10   Remove the chain guide mounting bolts and remove the front chain guide (see illustration). If necessary, slide the crankshaft sprocket for the front timing chain off the crankshaft.

INSPECTION

➡ **Note: Do not mix parts from the front and rear timing chains and tensioners. Keep the parts separate.**

11   Clean all parts with clean solvent. Dry with compressed air, if available.
12   Inspect the chain tensioners and tensioner arms for excessive wear or other damage.
13   Inspect the timing chain guides for deep grooves, excessive wear, or other damage.
14   Inspect the timing chain for excessive wear or damage.
15   Inspect the camshaft and crankshaft sprockets for chipped or broken teeth, excessive wear, or damage.
16   Replace any component that is in questionable condition.

INSTALLATION

⬧ **Refer to illustration 9.32**

17   The timing chain tensioners must be fully compressed and locked in place before chain installation. To prepare the chain tensioners for installation:
a) *Insert a small screwdriver into the access hole in the tensioner and release the pawl mechanism.*
b) *Compress the plunger into the tensioner housing until the plunger tip is below the plate on the pawl.*
c) *Hold the plunger in the compressed position and rotate the plunger one-half turn so the plunger can be removed. Remove the plunger and plunger spring.*
d) *Drain the oil from the tensioner housing and plunger.*
e) *Lubricate the tensioner housing, spring and plunger with clean engine oil. Insert the plunger spring into the tensioner housing. Install the plunger into the housing and push it in until fully compressed. Then, turn the plunger 180-degrees and use a small screwdriver to push back the pawl mechanism into contact with the plunger.*
f) *With the plunger compressed, insert a 1/16-inch drill bit or a*

straightened paper clip into the small hole above the pawl mechanism to hold the plunger in place.
g) *Repeat this procedure for the other tensioner.*

18   If removed, install the crankshaft sprocket for the front timing chain. Make sure the crankshaft keyway is still at 11 o'clock.
19   Look at the index marks on the sprockets of the front bank intake and exhaust camshafts. The marks should be at 9 o'clock (intake) and at 12 o'clock (exhaust) (see illustration 9.2). If not, reposition the camshafts.

❊❊ CAUTION:

The timing chains have three links that are a different color than the rest of the links. When installed, the colored links on the chain must be aligned with the index marks on the camshaft and crankshaft sprockets (see illustration 9.2).

20   Install the front timing chain guide. Tighten the mounting bolts to the torque listed in this Chapter's Specifications.
21   Install the front timing chain around the camshaft and crankshaft sprockets. Make sure the index marks on the sprockets are aligned and the colored links of the chain.
22   Install the front tensioner arm over its pivot dowel. Seat the tensioner arm firmly on the cylinder head and block.
23   Install the front timing chain tensioner assembly (see illustrations 9.8a and 9.8b). Be sure the tensioner plunger is fully compressed and locked in place. Tighten the tensioner mounting bolts to the torque listed in this Chapter's Specifications. Verify that the colored links of the timing chain are aligned with the index marks on the camshaft and crankshaft sprockets, and the crankshaft keyway is at 11 o'clock. If not, remove the timing chain and repeat the installation procedure.
24   Install the crankshaft sprocket for the rear timing chain on the crankshaft (see illustration 9.7).
25   Rotate the crankshaft clockwise until the crankshaft keyway is in the 3 o'clock position. This will correctly position the pistons for installation of the rear timing chain.
26   Install the rear timing chain guide. Tighten the mounting bolts to the torque listed in this Chapter's Specifications.
27   Double-check the position of the rear camshafts so the index marks on the sprockets are at (approximately) 3 o'clock (intake) and at 12 o'clock (exhaust).

> **❋❋ CAUTION:**
>
> The timing chains have three links that are a different color than the rest of the links. When installed, the colored links on the chain must be aligned with the index marks on the camshaft and crankshaft sprockets.

28 Install the rear timing chain around the camshaft and crankshaft sprockets. Make sure the colored links of the chain are aligned with the index marks on the front of the camshaft and crankshaft sprockets.

29 Install the rear tensioner arm over its pivot dowel. Seat the tensioner arm firmly on the cylinder head and block.

30 Install the rear timing chain tensioner (see illustrations 9.4a and 9.4b). Be sure the tensioner plunger is fully compressed and locked in place. Tighten the tensioner mounting bolts to specification. Verify that the colored links of the timing chain are aligned with the index marks on the camshaft and crankshaft sprockets, and the crankshaft keyway is at 3 o'clock. If not, remove the timing chain and repeat the installation procedure.

31 Remove the drill bits or wires (locking pins) from the timing chain tensioners.

32 Rotate the crankshaft counterclockwise back to the 11 o'clock position (the Number 1 TDC position). Verify the timing marks on the camshafts sprockets and the crankshaft sprocket with the colored links (see illustration 9.2).

33 Install the crankshaft position sensor pulse (trigger) wheel on the crankshaft.

> **❋❋ CAUTION:**
>
> Make sure the pulse wheel is installed with the crankshaft key in the slot marked "20-25-34Y-30M."

34 Rotate the engine by hand and verify that there is no binding. If any resistance is felt, STOP; double-check your work and find out why.

35 Install the engine front cover (see Section 8).

36 Reinstall the remaining parts in the reverse order of removal.

37 Fill the crankcase with the recommended oil (see Chapter 1). Fill the power steering reservoir with the correct fluid and refill the cooling system.

38 Reconnect the battery, then start the engine and check for leaks. The Powertrain Control Module (PCM) must relearn its idle and fuel trim strategy for optimum driveability and performance (see Chapter 5, Section 1).

10 Camshafts, hydraulic lash adjusters and rocker arms - removal inspection, and installation

REMOVAL

▶ **Refer to illustrations 10.3, 10.5, 10.6 and 10.10**

1 Remove the timing chains (see Section 9).

➡**Note: If you're only removing the camshafts from the rear bank cylinder head, you only have to remove the rear timing chain. If you're removing the camshafts from the front bank cylinder head, both timing chains will have to be removed.**

Rear bank cylinder head

2 Note the location of each camshaft cap. Use a marker on each cap or notes on paper or cardboard if they're not marked. Do not mix any of the camshaft caps.

3 Following the sequence shown (see illustration), gradually loosen the bolts that secure the camshaft bearing caps to the cylinder head, then remove the camshaft caps. It may be necessary to tap the caps lightly with a soft-faced mallet to loosen them from the locating dowels.

> **❋❋ CAUTION:**
>
> The camshaft bearing caps and cylinder heads are numbered to identify the locations of the caps. The caps must be installed in their original locations. Keep all parts from each camshaft together; never mix parts from one camshaft with those for another.

4 Mark the intake and exhaust camshafts to prevent reinstalling them in the wrong locations, then lift the camshafts straight up and out of the cylinder head.

5 Mark the positions of the rocker arms so they can be reinstalled in their original locations, then remove the rocker arms (see illustration).

6 Place the rocker arms in a suitable container so they can be separated and identified (see illustration).

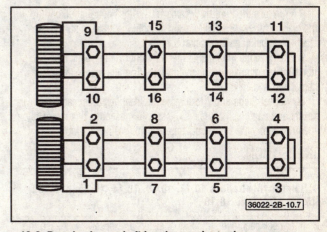

10.3 Rear bank camshaft bearing cap loosening sequence

10.5 Remove the rocker arms

10.6 Place all the parts in a container so they can be separated and identified for installation in their original locations

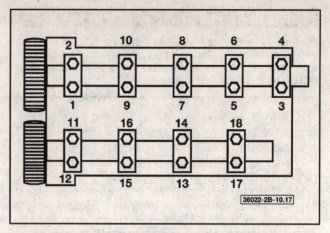

10.10 Front bank camshaft bearing cap loosening sequence

7   Lift the hydraulic lash adjusters from their bores in the cylinder head. Identify and separate the adjusters so they can be reinstalled in their original locations.

Front bank cylinder head

8   To place the front bank camshafts in the neutral position turn the crankshaft 1-2/3 turns (clockwise) until the crankshaft keyway is at 11 o'clock (see illustration 9.2).

9   Remove the timing chain for the front cylinder bank (see Section 9). Also remove the oil seal retainer from the rear of the intake camshaft.

10 Repeat Steps 3 to 7 to remove the front (left side) camshafts, rocker arms and lash adjusters. Be sure to loosen the bearing caps on the front camshafts in the sequence shown (see illustration).

INSPECTION

▶ Refer to illustrations 10.11, 10.13, 10.14, 10.15a, 10.15b, 10.16, 10.17 and 10.18

11 Check each hydraulic lash adjuster for excessive wear, scoring, pitting, or an out-of-round condition (see illustration). Replace as necessary.

12 Measure the outside diameter of each adjuster at the top and bottom of the adjuster. Then take a second set of measurements at a right angle to the first. If any measurement is significantly different from the others, the adjuster is tapered or out of round and must be replaced. If the necessary equipment is available, measure the diameter of the lash adjuster and the inside diameter of the corresponding cylinder head bore. Subtract the diameter of the lash adjuster from the bore diameter to obtain the oil clearance. Compare the measurements obtained to those given in this Chapter's Specifications. If the adjusters or the cylinder head bores are excessively worn, new adjusters or a new cylinder head, or both, may be required. If the valve train is noisy, particularly if the noise persists after a cold start, you can suspect a faulty hydraulic adjuster.

13 Inspect the rocker arms for signs of wear or damage. The areas of wear are the tip that contacts the valve stem, the socket that contacts the lash adjuster and the roller that contacts the camshaft (see illustration).

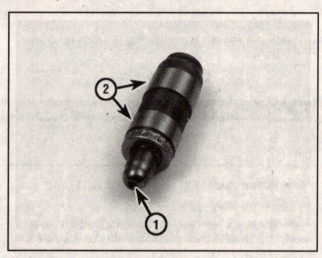

10.11 Inspect the lash adjusters for signs of excessive wear or damage, such as pitting, scoring or signs of overheating (bluing or discoloration), where the tip contacts the rocker arm (1) and the side surfaces that contact the bore in the cylinder head (2)

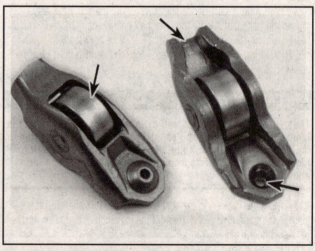

10.13 Check the roller surface (left arrow) of the rocker arm and the areas where the valve stem and lash adjuster contact the rocker arm (right arrows)

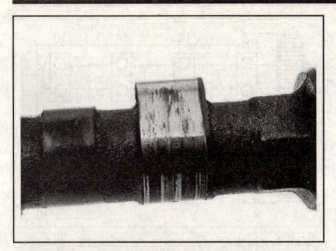

10.14 Check the cam lobes for pitting, excessive wear, and scoring. If scoring is excessive, as shown here, replace the camshaft

10.15a Measure the camshaft lobe height (greatest dimension) . . .

10.15b . . . and subtract the camshaft lobe base circle diameter (smallest dimension) to obtain the lobe lift specification

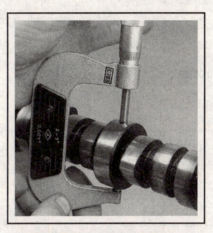

10.16 Measure each journal diameter with a micrometer. If any journal is less than the specified minimum, replace the camshaft

10.17 Lay a strip of Plastigage on each camshaft journal, in line with the camshaft

14 Examine the camshaft lobes for scoring, pitting, galling (wear due to rubbing), and evidence of overheating (blue, discolored areas). Look for flaking of the hardened surface layer of each lobe (see illustra-

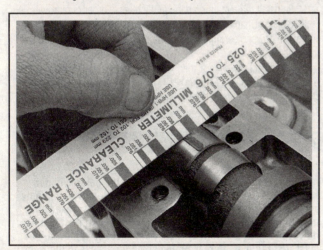

10.18 Compare the width of the crushed Plastigage to the scale on the package to determine the journal oil clearance

tion). If any such wear is evident, replace the camshaft.

15 Calculate the camshaft lobe lift by measuring the lobe height and the diameter of the base circle of the lobe (see illustrations). Subtract the base circle measurement from the lobe height to determine the lobe lift. If the lobe lift is less than that listed in this Chapter's Specifications the camshaft lobe is worn and should be replaced.

16 Inspect the camshaft bearing journals and the cylinder head bearing surfaces for pitting or excessive wear. If any such wear is evident, replace the component concerned. Using a micrometer, measure the diameter of each camshaft bearing journal at several points (see illustration). If the diameter of any journal is less than specified, replace the camshaft.

17 To check the bearing journal oil clearance, remove the rocker arms and hydraulic lash adjusters (if not already done), use a suitable solvent and a clean lint-free rag to clean all bearing surfaces, then install the camshafts and bearing caps with a piece of Plastigage across each journal (see illustration). Tighten the bearing cap bolts to the specified torque. Don't rotate the camshafts.

18 Remove the bearing caps and measure the width of the flattened Plastigage with the Plastigage scale (see illustration). Scrape off the Plastigage with your fingernail or the edge of a credit card. Don't scratch or nick the journals or bearing caps.

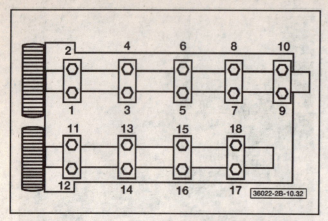

10.25 Front bank camshaft bearing cap tightening sequence

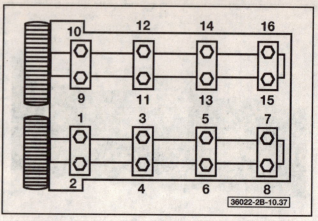

10.31 Rear bank camshaft bearing cap tightening sequence

19 If the oil clearance of any bearing is worn beyond the specified service limit, install a new camshaft and repeat the check. If the clearance is still excessive, replace the cylinder head.

20 To check camshaft endplay, remove the hydraulic lash adjusters, clean the bearing surfaces carefully, and install the camshafts and bearing caps. Tighten the bearing cap bolts to the specified torque, then measure the endplay using a dial indicator mounted on the cylinder head so that its tip bears on the camshaft end.

21 Lightly but firmly tap the camshaft fully toward the gauge, zero the gauge, then tap the camshaft fully away from the gauge and note the gauge reading. If the measured endplay is at or beyond the specified service limit, install a new camshaft thrust cap and repeat the check. If the clearance is still excessive, the camshaft or the cylinder head must be replaced.

INSTALLATION

◆ **Refer to illustrations 10.25 and 10.31**

Front bank cylinder head

22 Make sure the crankshaft keyway is at the 11 o'clock position (see illustration 9.2).

23 Lubricate the rocker arms and hydraulic lash adjusters with engine assembly lubricant or fresh engine oil. Install the adjusters into their original bores, then install the rocker arms in their correct locations.

24 Similarly lubricate the camshafts and install them in their correct locations.

25 Install the camshaft bearing caps in their correct locations. Install the cap bolts and tighten by hand until snug. Then, install the camshaft thrust caps and bolts. Tighten the bolts in four to five steps, following the sequence shown (see illustration) to the torque listed in this Chap-

ter's Specifications.

26 Install the seal retainer and a new seal over the left end of the intake camshaft. Tighten the bolts to the torque listed in this Chapter's Specifications.

27 Install the front timing chain sprocket on the crankshaft. Then install the front timing chain guide, the chain, and the tensioner (see Section 9).

28 Turn the crankshaft clockwise and position the crankshaft keyway at 3 o'clock.

Rear bank cylinder head

29 Lubricate the rocker arms and hydraulic lash adjusters with engine assembly lubricant or fresh engine oil. Install the adjusters into their original bores, then install the rocker arms in their correct locations.

30 Similarly lubricate the camshafts and install them in their correct locations.

31 Install the camshaft bearing caps in their correct locations. Install the cap bolts and tighten by hand until snug. Then, install the camshaft thrust caps and bolts. Tighten the bolts in four to five steps, following the sequence shown (see illustration) to the torque listed in this Chapter's Specifications.

32 Install the rear timing chain, chain guide and tensioner (see Section 9).

33 Install the engine front cover (see Section 8).

34 Reinstall the remaining parts in the reverse order of removal.

35 Refer to Chapter 1 and fill the crankcase with the recommended oil; fill the power steering reservoir with the correct fluid and refill the cooling system.

36 Reconnect the battery, then start the engine and check for leaks. The Powertrain Control Module (PCM) must relearn its idle and fuel trim strategy for optimum driveability and performance (see Chapter 5, Section 1).

11 Cylinder heads - removal and installation

❊❊ **WARNING:**

Wait until the engine is completely cool before beginning this procedure.

➡ **Note:** The following instructions describe the steps necessary to remove both cylinder heads. If only one cylinder head

requires removal, disregard the steps for the other cylinder head. If just the rear cylinder head requires removal, you only need to remove the timing chain, camshafts, and rocker arms from the rear cylinder head; the front can remain installed. However, if just the front cylinder head must be removed, you must first remove the rear timing chain for access to the front chain. In this case, the rear camshafts and rocker arms can remain installed.

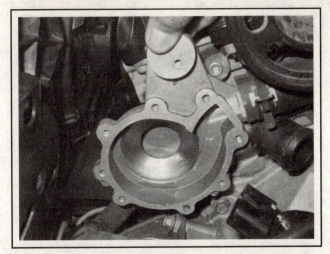

11.8 Remove the water pump housing from the left bank (front) cylinder head

REMOVAL

▶ **Refer to illustrations 11.8, 11.11a and 11.11b**

1 Relieve the fuel system pressure (see Chapter 4). Disconnect the cable from the negative battery terminal (see Chapter 5).

2 Drain the cooling system (see Chapter 1).

3 Remove the upper and lower intake manifolds (see Section 5).

4 Drain the engine oil (see Chapter 1). Remove the oil pan (see Section 12).

5 Remove the engine front cover (see Section 8).

6 Remove the timing chains, camshafts, rocker arms and lash adjusters as necessary (see Sections 9 and 10).

7 Remove the exhaust manifold(s) (see Section 6).

8 Remove the water pump (see Chapter 3) and the water pump housing (see illustration).

9 Remove the dipstick tube mounting bolt and lift the dipstick tube from the engine.

10 Disconnect the EGR valve pipe that connects the EGR valve to the rear exhaust manifold.

11 Remove the hoses and any electrical connectors from the coolant bypass tube. Remove the two fasteners securing the coolant bypass

11.11b . . . and remove the tube from the cylinder heads

11.11a Remove the coolant bypass tube mounting bolts . . .

tube (see illustrations). Then remove the tube.

12 Loosen each cylinder head bolt, one turn at a time, following the reverse order of the tightening sequence (see illustration 11.23a). When all cylinder head bolts are loose, remove and discard the bolts. New torque-to-yield cylinder head bolts must be used during installation.

13 Remove the cylinder head from the engine block and place it on a workbench.

✳✳ CAUTION:

If the cylinder head sticks to the block, pry only on a casting protrusion to prevent damaging the mating surfaces. Remove and discard the cylinder head gasket.

INSTALLATION

▶ **Refer to illustrations 11.21a and 11.21b**

14 The mating surfaces of the cylinder head and the block must be perfectly clean before installing the cylinder head. Clean the surfaces with a scraper, but be careful not to gouge the aluminum.

✳✳ CAUTION:

Be very careful when scraping on aluminum engine parts. Aluminum is soft and gouges easily. Severely gouged parts may require replacement.

15 Check the mating surfaces of the block and the cylinder head for nicks, deep scratches, and other damage. If slight, they can be removed carefully with a file; if excessive, machining may be the only alternative to replacement.

16 If you suspect warpage of the cylinder head gasket surface, use a straightedge to check it for distortion. If the gasket mating surface of your cylinder head or block is out of specification or is severely nicked or scratched, consult an automotive machine shop for advice.

17 Clean the mating surfaces of the cylinder head and block with a clean shop towel and solvent as needed.

18 Ensure that the two locating dowels are in position in the cylinder block and that all cylinder head bolt holes are free of oil, corrosion, or other contamination.

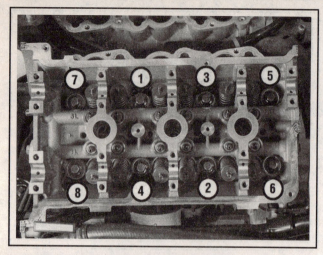

11.21a Cylinder head bolt TIGHTENING sequence

11.21b An angle gauge takes all the "guesswork" out of tightening the torque-to-yield cylinder head bolts

19 Install new cylinder head gaskets on the block, over the locating dowels.

20 Carefully install the cylinder heads. Use caution when lowering the cylinder heads onto the cylinder block to prevent damage to the cylinder heads or block. Make sure the cylinder heads fit properly over the locating dowels in the block.

21 Install new cylinder head bolts and turn down by hand until snug.

❈❈ CAUTION:

The cylinder head bolts are the torque-to-yield type and are stretched during tightening. Therefore, the original bolts must be discarded and new bolts installed during assembly.

Using a torque wrench and an angle gauge, tighten the cylinder head bolts in the sequence shown to the torque listed in this Chapter's Specifications (see illustrations).

➧Note: The method used for the cylinder head bolt tightening procedure is referred to as the "torque angle" or "torque-to-yield" method; follow the procedure exactly. Tighten the bolts using a torque wrench, then use a breaker bar and a special torque angle adapter (available at auto parts stores) to tighten the bolts the required angle.

22 Install the rest of the parts in the reverse order of removal. Tighten fasteners to the torque values listed in this Chapter's Specifications.

23 Refer to Chapter 1 and fill the engine with fresh engine oil, then fill the cooling system.

24 Reconnect the battery. After you're done, the Powertrain Control Module (PCM) must relearn its idle and fuel trim strategy for optimum driveability and performance (see Chapter 5, Section 1).

25 Start the engine and check for leaks.

12 Oil pan - removal and installation

REMOVAL

◆ **Refer to illustrations 12.8a and 12.8b**

1 Disconnect the cable from the negative battery terminal (see Chapter 5).

2 Raise the vehicle and support it securely on jackstands.

3 Drain the engine oil (see Chapter 1). Reinstall the oil drain plug and tighten it to the torque listed in the Chapter 1 Specifications, using a new gasket if necessary.

4 Remove the oil filter (see Chapter 1).

5 Disconnect the oxygen sensor connector(s) (see Chapter 6).

6 Refer to Chapter 4 and remove the crossover and flexible exhaust pipe and converter assembly from the vehicle.

➧Note: V6 engines are equipped with upstream catalytic converters designed integrally with the exhaust manifolds.

7 Remove the driveplate access cover.

8 Remove the bolts that secure the oil pan to the transaxle (see illustrations).

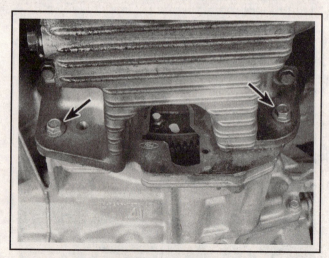

12.8a Remove these bolts that secure the oil pan to the transaxle . . .

12.8b . . . and these two in the recess at the rear of the pan

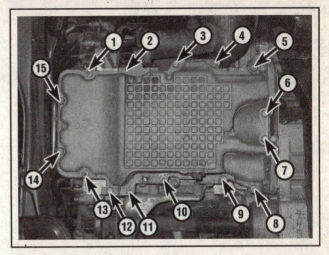

12.14 Oil pan bolt tightening sequence

9 Remove the oil pan fasteners and remove the oil pan. Note the location of any stud bolts.

10 Remove and discard the oil pan gasket. If necessary, remove the fasteners that secure the oil screen and pick-up tube and remove the screen and tube assembly.

11 Thoroughly clean the oil pan and cylinder block mating surfaces using lacquer thinner or acetone. The surfaces must be free of any residue that will keep the sealant from adhering properly. Clean the oil pan inside and out with solvent and dry with compressed air.

INSTALLATION

♦ **Refer to illustration 12.14**

12 If removed, install a new O-ring seal onto the oil pick-up tube. Install the tube and screen assembly and tighten the retaining fasteners to the torque listed in this Chapter's Specifications. Use a new self-locking nut to secure the pick-up tube support bracket. Tighten the nut to the torque listed in this Chapter's Specifications.

13 Install a new gasket on the oil pan. Apply a 1/8-inch bead of RTV sealant to the oil pan gasket in the area of the engine front cover-to-cyl-

inder block parting line.

14 Install the oil pan, being careful not to dislodge the pan gasket. Install the pan bolts and tighten by hand. Be sure to install any stud bolts in the locations noted during removal. Install the oil pan-to-transaxle bolts. Firmly push the oil pan against the transaxle and tighten the pan-to-transaxle bolts snugly. Then, tighten the oil pan bolts (see illustration) gradually and evenly, to the torque listed in this Chapter's Specifications.

15 The remainder of installation is the reverse of removal, noting the following items:

   a) Tighten all fasteners to the torque values listed in this Chapter's Specifications.
   b) Always replace any self-locking nuts disturbed on removal.
   c) Refer to Chapter 1 and fill the engine with fresh engine oil. Install a new oil filter.
   d) Refill the cooling system (see Chapter 1).
   e) Start the engine and check for leaks.

16 Reconnect the battery. After you're done, the Powertrain Control Module (PCM) must relearn its idle and fuel trim strategy for optimum driveability and performance (see Chapter 5, Section 1).

13 Oil pump - removal, inspection and installation

13.3 Remove the oil pump retaining bolts and pull the oil pump off the crankshaft

➡Note: Because of the difficulty of removing the oil pump, this job is best done as part of complete engine overhaul with the engine out of the vehicle.

REMOVAL

♦ **Refer to illustration 13.3**

1 Remove the oil pan and oil screen and pick-up tube assembly (see Section 12).

2 Remove the engine front cover (see Section 8), timing chains and crankshaft sprockets (see Section 9).

3 Loosen each of the four oil pump mounting bolts one turn. Then, gradually and evenly, loosen each bolt in several steps. When all bolts are loose, remove the bolts and oil pump (see illustration).

13.4 To disassemble the oil pump, remove the screws securing the pump cover to the pump body

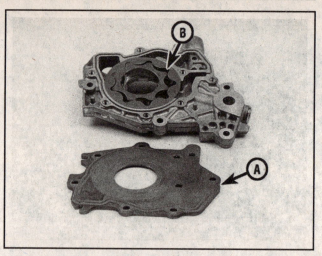

13.5 Remove the pump cover (A) and noting any identification marks on the rotors, remove the inner and outer rotors (B) from the pump body

INSPECTION

▶ **Refer to illustrations 13.4 and 13.5**

4   Remove the oil pump cover from the oil pump body (see illustration).

5   Note any identification marks on the rotors and withdraw the rotors from the pump body (see illustration).

6   Thoroughly clean and dry the components.

7   Inspect the rotors for obvious wear or damage. If either rotor, the pump body or the cover is scored or damaged, the complete oil pump assembly must be replaced.

8   If the oil pump components are in acceptable condition, dip the rotors in clean engine oil and install them into the pump body with any identification marks positioned as noted during disassembly.

9   Install the cover and tighten the screws securely.

INSTALLATION

▶ **Refer to illustration 13.11**

10 Rotate the oil pump inner rotor so it aligns with the flats on the crankshaft. Install the oil pump over the crankshaft and fit it firmly against the cylinder block.

11 Install the oil pump bolts and tighten by hand until snug. Tighten the bolts gradually and evenly, in sequence, to the torque listed in this Chapter's Specifications (see illustration).

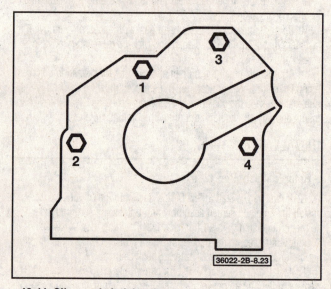

13.11 Oil pump bolt tightening sequence

12 Install the remainder of the components in the reverse order of removal.

13 Refer to Chapter 1 and fill the engine with fresh engine oil. Install a new oil filter. Refill the cooling system.

14 Start the engine and check for leaks.

14 Rear main oil seal - replacement

Refer to Chapter 2, Part A for the crankshaft rear oil seal replacement procedure.

15 Driveplate - removal and installation

This procedure is essentially the same as the flywheel removal procedure for the four-cylinder engine. Refer to Chapter 2, Part A and follow the procedure outlined there. However, use the bolt torque listed in this Chapter's Specifications.

16 Engine mounts - inspection and replacement

◆ **Refer to illustrations 16.1a and 16.1b**

This procedure is essentially the same as for the four cylinder engine. Refer to Chapter 2, Part A and follow the procedure outlined there but refer to the illustrations for this Section.

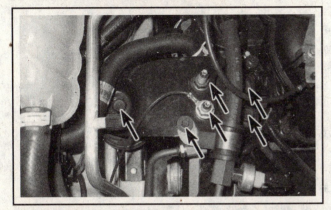

16.1a Remove the engine mount bracket bolts and separate the bracket from the engine and insulator

16.1b Remove the engine mount insulator bolts and separate the insulator from the engine compartment

Specifications

General

Engine type	Single overhead cam (SOHC) V6
Displacement	182 cubic inches (3.0 liters)
Engine VIN code	1
Bore	3.50 inches (89.0 mm)
Stroke	3.13 inches (79.5 mm)
Compression ratio	10:1
Compression	See Chapter 2C
Firing order	1-4-2-5-3-6
Oil pressure	See Chapter 2C

Cylinder location diagram - V6 engine

Camshafts

Lobe lift (intake and exhaust)	0.188 inch (4.79 mm)
Journal diameter	1.060 to 1.061 inches (26.936 to 26.962 mm)
Bearing inside diameter	1.062 to 1.063 inches (26.987 to 27.012 mm)
Journal-to-bearing oil clearance	
Standard	0.001 to 0.003 inch (0.025 to 0.076 mm)
Service limit	0.0047 (0.121 mm)
Endplay	
Standard	0.001 to 0.0064 inch (0.025 to 0.165 mm)
Service limit	0.0075 inch (0.190 mm)

Hydraulic lash adjuster

Diameter	0.6290 to 0.6294 inch (15.988 to 16.000 mm)
Lash adjuster-to-bore clearance	
Standard	0.0007 to 0.0027 inch (0.018 to 0.069 mm)
Minimum	0.0006 inch (0.016 mm)

Warpage limits

Head gasket surface warpage limit	0.005 inch (0.120 mm)

Torque specifications	**Ft-lbs (unless otherwise indicated)**	**Nm**

→Note: One foot-pound (ft-lb) of torque is equivalent to 12 inch-pounds (in-lbs) of torque. Torque values below approximately 15 ft-lbs are expressed in inch-pounds, since most foot-pound torque wrenches are not accurate at these smaller values.

Air conditioning compressor bolts	18	25
Air conditioning compressor bracket nuts		
Step 1	18	25
Step 2	Tighten an additional 90-degrees	
Camshaft bearing cap bolts	89 in-lbs	10
Camshaft oil seal retainer bolts	89 in-lbs	10
Crankshaft pulley bolt		
Step 1	86	120
Step 2	Loosen 360-degrees	
Step 3	37	50
Step 4	Tighten an additional 90-degrees	
Cylinder head bolts (in sequence - see illustration 11.21a)		
Step 1	30	40
Step 2	Tighten an additional 90-degrees	
Step 3	Loosen one full turn (360-degrees)	
Step 4	30	40
Step 5	Tighten an additional 90-degrees	
Step 6	Tighten an additional 90-degrees	
Drivebelt tensioner bolt	18	25
Driveplate-to-crankshaft bolts	59	80
Engine access cover	53 in-lbs	6
Engine front cover bolts (in sequence - see illustration 8.23)	18	25
Exhaust manifold nuts	15	20
Intake manifold assembly (in sequence - see illustrations 5.17 and 5.33)		
Upper intake manifold bolts	89 in-lbs	10
Lower intake manifold bolts	89 in-lbs	10
Oil pan bolts	18	25
Oil pan-to-transaxle bolts	30	40
Oil pump screen cover and tube bolts	89 in-lbs	10
Oil pump screen cover and tube nut		
Step 1	44 in-lbs	5
Step 2	Tighten an additional 45-degrees	
Oil pump-to-engine block bolts	89 in-lbs	10
Oil pan baffle bolts		
Step 1	44 in-lbs	5
Step 2	Tighten an additional 45-degrees	
Timing chain guide bolts	18	25
Timing chain tensioner bolts	18	25
Valve cover bolts (in sequence - see illustrations 4.15 and 4.27)	89 in-lbs	10

→ Note: Refer to Chapter 2, Part C for additional torque specifications.

Section

Reference to other Chapters

CHECK ENGINE light on - See Chapter 6

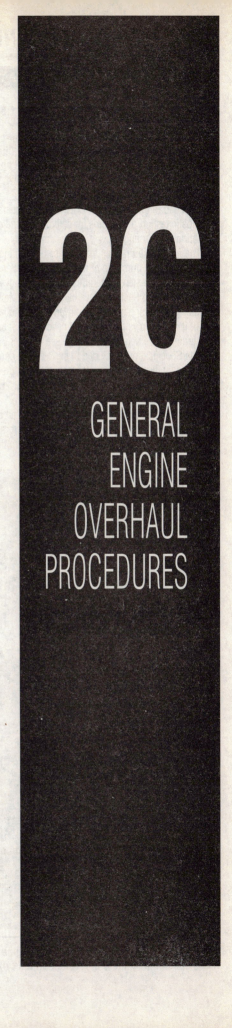

2C

GENERAL ENGINE OVERHAUL PROCEDURES

1 General information - engine overhaul

▶ **Refer to illustrations 1.1, 1.2, 1.3, 1.4, 1.5 and 1.6**

➡**Note: At the time of writing, the 2.3L four-cylinder engine was largely considered "un-rebuildable." Check with an automotive machine shop to see if aftermarket components and service techniques have been developed if your engine requires repair.**

Included in this portion of Chapter 2 are general information and diagnostic testing procedures for determining the overall mechanical condition of your engine.

The information ranges from advice concerning preparation for an overhaul and the purchase of replacement parts and/or components to detailed, step-by-step procedures covering removal and installation.

The following Sections have been written to help you determine whether your engine needs to be overhauled and how to remove and install it once you've determined it needs to be rebuilt. For information concerning in-vehicle engine repair, see Chapter 2A or 2B.

The Specifications included in this Part are general in nature and include only those necessary for testing the oil pressure and checking the engine compression. Refer to Chapter 2A or 2B for additional engine Specifications.

It's not always easy to determine when, or if, an engine should be completely overhauled, because a number of factors must be considered.

High mileage is not necessarily an indication that an overhaul is needed, while low mileage doesn't preclude the need for an overhaul. Frequency of servicing is probably the most important consideration. An engine that's had regular and frequent oil and filter changes, as well as other required maintenance, will most likely give many thousands of miles of reliable service. Conversely, a neglected engine may require an overhaul very early in its service life.

Excessive oil consumption is an indication that piston rings, valve seals and/or valve guides are in need of attention. Make sure that oil leaks aren't responsible before deciding that the rings and/or guides are bad. Perform a cylinder compression check to determine the extent of the work required (see Section 3). Also check the vacuum readings under various conditions (see Section 4).

Check the oil pressure with a gauge installed in place of the oil pressure sending unit and compare it to this Chapter's Specifications (see Section 2). If it's extremely low, the bearings and/or oil pump are probably worn out.

Loss of power, rough running, knocking or metallic engine noises, excessive valve train noise and high fuel consumption rates may also point to the need for an overhaul, especially if they're all present at the same time. If a complete tune-up doesn't remedy the situation, major mechanical work is the only solution.

An engine overhaul involves restoring the internal parts to the specifications of a new engine. During an overhaul, the piston rings are replaced and the cylinder walls are reconditioned (rebored and/or

1.1 An engine block being bored. An engine rebuilder will use special machinery to recondition the cylinder bores

1.2 If the cylinders are bored, the machine shop will normally hone the engine on a machine like this

1.3 A crankshaft having a main bearing journal ground

1.4 A machinist checks for a bent connecting rod, using specialized equipment

honed) (see illustrations 1.1 and 1.2). If a rebore is done by an automotive machine shop, new oversize pistons will also be installed. The main bearings, connecting rod bearings and camshaft bearings are generally replaced with new ones and, if necessary, the crankshaft may be reground to restore the journals (see illustration 1.3). Generally, the valves are serviced as well, since they're usually in less-than-perfect condition at this point. While the engine is being overhauled, other components, such as the starter and alternator, can be rebuilt or replaced as well. The end result should be similar to a new engine that will give many trouble free miles.

➡**Note: Critical cooling system components such as the hoses, drivebelts, thermostat and water pump should be replaced with new parts when an engine is overhauled. The radiator should be checked carefully to ensure that it isn't clogged or leaking (see Chapter 3). If you purchase a rebuilt engine or short block, some rebuilders will not warranty their engines unless the radiator has been professionally flushed. Also, we don't recommend overhauling the oil pump - always install a new one when an engine is rebuilt.**

Overhauling the internal components on today's engines is a difficult and time-consuming task which requires a significant amount of specialty tools and is best left to a professional engine rebuilder (see illustrations 1.4, 1.5 and 1.6). A competent engine rebuilder will handle the inspection of your old parts and offer advice concerning the reconditioning or replacement of the original engine, never purchase parts or have machine work done on other components until the block has been thoroughly inspected by a professional machine shop. As a general rule, time is the primary cost of an overhaul, especially since the vehicle may be tied up for a minimum of two weeks or more. Be aware that some engine builders only have the capability to rebuild the engine you bring them while other rebuilders have a large inventory of rebuilt exchange engines in stock. Also be aware that many machine shops could take as much as two weeks time to completely rebuild your engine depending on shop workload. Sometimes it makes more sense to simply exchange your engine for another engine that's already rebuilt to save time.

1.5 A bore gauge being used to check the main bearing bore

1.6 Uneven piston wear like this indicates a bent connecting rod

2 Oil pressure check

▶ **Refer to illustration 2.2a, 2.2b and 2.3**

1   Low engine oil pressure can be a sign of an engine in need of rebuilding. A "low oil pressure" indicator (often called an "idiot light") is not a test of the oiling system. Such indicators only come on when the oil pressure is dangerously low. Even a factory oil pressure gauge in the instrument panel is only a relative indication, although much better for driver information than a warning light. A better test is with a mechanical (not electrical) oil pressure gauge.

2   Locate the oil pressure sending unit on the engine block:

a) *On four-cylinder engines, the oil pressure sending unit is located on the rear of the block near the oil filter housing (see illustration).*

b) *On V6 engines, the sending unit is located near the oil filter housing behind the air conditioning compressor, on the front side of the block (see illustration).*

3   Unscrew the oil pressure sending unit and screw in the hose for your oil pressure gauge (see illustration). If necessary, install an adapter fitting. Use Teflon tape or thread sealant on the threads of the adapter and/or the fitting on the end of your gauge's hose.

4   Connect an accurate tachometer to the engine, according to the tachometer manufacturer's instructions.

5   Check the oil pressure with the engine running (normal operat-

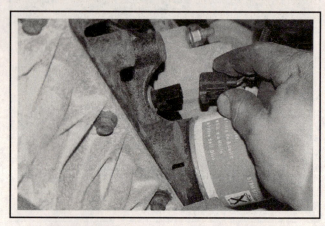

2.2a   On four-cylinder engines the oil pressure sending unit is located on the rear of the engine block near the oil filter housing

ing temperature) at the specified engine speed, and compare it to this Chapter's Specifications. If it's extremely low, the bearings and/or oil pump are probably worn out.

2.2b   On V6 engines the oil pressure sending unit is located on the front of the engine block behind the air conditioning compressor

2.3   The oil pressure can be checked by removing the sending unit and installing a pressure gauge in its place

3 Cylinder compression check

▶ **Refer to illustration 3.6**

1   A compression check will tell you what mechanical condition the upper end of your engine (pistons, rings, valves, head gaskets) is in. Specifically, it can tell you if the compression is down due to leakage caused by worn piston rings, defective valves and seats or a blown head gasket.

➡**Note: The engine must be at normal operating temperature and the battery must be fully charged for this check.**

2   Begin by cleaning the area around the spark plugs before you remove them (compressed air should be used, if available). The idea is to prevent dirt from getting into the cylinders as the compression check is being done.

3   Remove all of the spark plugs from the engine (see Chapter 1).

4   Block the throttle wide open.

5   Disconnect the primary (low voltage) wires from the coil pack (four-cylinder models) or the connectors at the ignition coils (V6 models) (see Chapter 5). Remove the fuel pump relay (see Chapter 4). The relays are located in the power distribution center in the engine compartment.

6   Install a compression gauge in the spark plug hole (see illustration).

7   Crank the engine over at least seven compression strokes and watch the gauge. The compression should build up quickly in a healthy engine. Low compression on the first stroke, followed by gradually increasing pressure on successive strokes, indicates worn piston rings.

A low compression reading on the first stroke, which doesn't build up during successive strokes, indicates leaking valves or a blown head gasket (a cracked head could also be the cause). Deposits on the undersides of the valve heads can also cause low compression. Record the highest gauge reading obtained.

8   Repeat the procedure for the remaining cylinders and compare the results to this Chapter's Specifications.

9   Add some engine oil (about three squirts from a plunger-type oil can) to each cylinder, through the spark plug hole, and repeat the test.

10   If the compression increases after the oil is added, the piston rings are definitely worn. If the compression doesn't increase significantly, the leakage is occurring at the valves or head gasket. Leakage past the valves may be caused by burned valve seats and/or faces or warped, cracked or bent valves.

11   If two adjacent cylinders have equally low compression, there's a strong possibility that the head gasket between them is blown. The appearance of coolant in the combustion chambers or the crankcase would verify this condition.

12   If one cylinder is slightly lower than the others, and the engine has a slightly rough idle, a worn lobe on the camshaft could be the cause.

13   If the compression is unusually high, the combustion chambers are probably coated with carbon deposits. If that's the case, the cylinder head(s) should be removed and decarbonized.

14   If compression is way down or varies greatly between cylinders,

3.6   Use a compression gauge with a threaded fitting for the spark plug hole, not the type that requires hand pressure to maintain the seal

it would be a good idea to have a leak-down test performed by an automotive repair shop. This test will pinpoint exactly where the leakage is occurring and how severe it is.

4   Vacuum gauge diagnostic checks

▶ Refer to illustrations 4.4 and 4.6

A vacuum gauge provides inexpensive but valuable information about what is going on in the engine. You can check for worn rings or cylinder walls, leaking head or intake manifold gaskets, incorrect carburetor adjustments, restricted exhaust, stuck or burned valves, weak valve springs, improper ignition or valve timing and ignition problems.

Unfortunately, vacuum gauge readings are easy to misinterpret, so they should be used in conjunction with other tests to confirm the diagnosis.

Both the absolute readings and the rate of needle movement are important for accurate interpretation. Most gauges measure vacuum in inches of mercury (in-Hg). The following references to vacuum assume the diagnosis is being performed at sea level. As elevation increases

(or atmospheric pressure decreases), the reading will decrease. For every 1,000 foot increase in elevation above approximately 2,000 feet, the gauge readings will decrease about one inch of mercury.

Connect the vacuum gauge directly to the intake manifold vacuum, not to ported (throttle body) vacuum (see illustration). Be sure no hoses are left disconnected during the test or false readings will result.

Before you begin the test, allow the engine to warm up completely. Block the wheels and set the parking brake. With the transaxle in Park, start the engine and allow it to run at normal idle speed.

☀☀ WARNING:

Keep your hands and the vacuum gauge clear of the fans.

Read the vacuum gauge; an average, healthy engine should normally produce about 17 to 22 in-Hg with a fairly steady needle (see illustration). Refer to the following vacuum gauge readings and what they indicate about the engine's condition:

1   A low steady reading usually indicates a leaking gasket between the intake manifold and cylinder head(s) or throttle body, a leaky vacuum hose, late ignition timing or incorrect camshaft timing. Check ignition timing with a timing light and eliminate all other possible causes, utilizing the tests provided in this Chapter before you remove the timing chain cover to check the timing marks.

2   If the reading is three to eight inches below normal and it fluctuates at that low reading, suspect an intake manifold gasket leak at an intake port or a faulty fuel injector.

3   If the needle has regular drops of about two-to-four inches at a steady rate, the valves are probably leaking. Perform a compression check or leak-down test to confirm this.

4   An irregular drop or down-flick of the needle can be caused by a sticking valve or an ignition misfire. Perform a compression check or leak-down test and read the spark plugs.

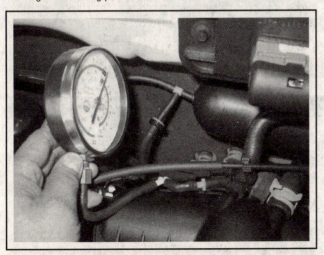

4.4   A simple vacuum gauge can be handy in diagnosing engine condition and performance

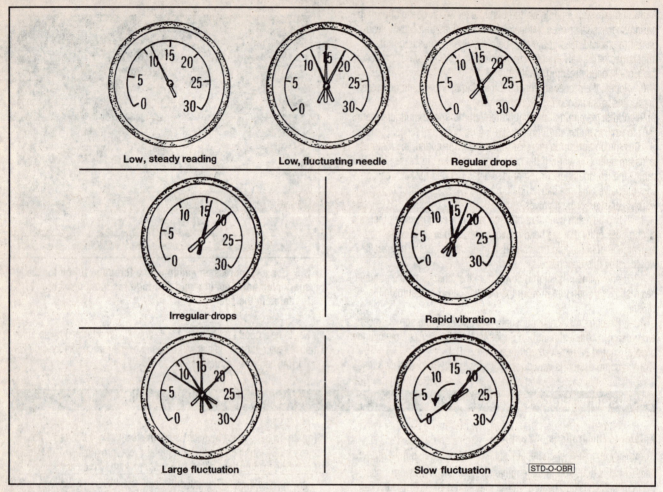

4.6 Typical vacuum gauge readings

5   A rapid vibration of about four in-Hg vibration at idle combined with exhaust smoke indicates worn valve guides. Perform a leak-down test to confirm this. If the rapid vibration occurs with an increase in engine speed, check for a leaking intake manifold gasket or head gasket, weak valve springs, burned valves or ignition misfire.

6   A slight fluctuation, say one inch up and down, may mean ignition problems. Check all the usual tune-up items and, if necessary, run the engine on an ignition analyzer.

7   If there is a large fluctuation, perform a compression or leak-down test to look for a weak or dead cylinder or a blown head gasket.

8   If the needle moves slowly through a wide range, check for a clogged PCV system, incorrect idle fuel mixture, throttle body or intake manifold gasket leaks.

9   Check for a slow return after revving the engine by quickly snapping the throttle open until the engine reaches about 2,500 rpm and let it shut. Normally the reading should drop to near zero, rise above normal idle reading (about 5 in-Hg over) and then return to the previous idle reading. If the vacuum returns slowly and doesn't peak when the throttle is snapped shut, the rings may be worn. If there is a long delay, look for a restricted exhaust system (often the muffler or catalytic converter). An easy way to check this is to temporarily disconnect the exhaust ahead of the suspected part and redo the test.

5   Engine rebuilding alternatives

The do-it-yourselfer is faced with a number of options when purchasing a rebuilt engine. The major considerations are cost, warranty, parts availability and the time required for the rebuilder to complete the project. The decision to replace the engine block, piston/connecting rod assemblies and crankshaft depends on the final inspection results of your engine. Only then can you make a cost effective decision whether to have your engine overhauled or simply purchase an exchange engine for your vehicle.

Some of the rebuilding alternatives include:

Individual parts - If the inspection procedures reveal that the engine block and most engine components are in reusable condition, purchasing individual parts and having a rebuilder rebuild your engine may be the most economical alternative. The block, crankshaft and piston/connecting rod assemblies should all be inspected carefully by a machine shop first.

Short block - A short block consists of an engine block with a crankshaft and piston/connecting rod assemblies already installed. All new bearings are incorporated and all clearances will be correct. The existing camshafts, valve train components, cylinder head and external parts can be bolted to the short block with little or no machine shop work necessary.

Long block - A long block consists of a short block plus an oil pump, oil pan, cylinder head, valve cover, camshaft and valve train components, timing sprockets and chain or gears and timing cover. All components are installed with new bearings, seals and gaskets incorporated throughout. The installation of manifolds and external parts is all that's necessary.

Low mileage used engines - Some companies now offer low

mileage used engines which is a very cost effective way to get your vehicle up and running again. These engines often come from vehicles which have been in totaled in accidents or come from other countries which have a higher vehicle turn over rate. A low mileage used engine also usually has a similar warranty like the newly remanufactured engines.

Give careful thought to which alternative is best for you and discuss the situation with local automotive machine shops, auto parts dealers and experienced rebuilders before ordering or purchasing replacement parts.

6   Engine removal - methods and precautions

▶ **Refer to illustrations 6.1, 6.2, 6.3 and 6.4**

If you've decided that an engine must be removed for overhaul or major repair work, several preliminary steps should be taken. Read all removal and installation procedures carefully prior to committing to this job.

Locating a suitable place to work is extremely important. Adequate work space, along with storage space for the vehicle, will be needed. If a shop or garage isn't available, at the very least a flat, level, clean work surface made of concrete or asphalt is required.

Cleaning the engine compartment and engine before beginning the removal procedure will help keep tools clean and organized (see illustrations 6.1 and 6.2).

An engine hoist will also be necessary. Make sure the hoist is rated in excess of the combined weight of the engine and transaxle. Safety is of primary importance, considering the potential hazards involved in removing the engine from the vehicle.

If you're a novice at engine removal, get at least one helper. One person cannot easily do all the things you need to do to remove a big heavy engine and transaxle assembly from the engine compartment. Also helpful is to seek advice and assistance from someone who's experienced in engine removal.

Plan the operation ahead of time. Arrange for or obtain all of the tools and equipment you'll need prior to beginning the job (see illustrations 6.3 and 6.4). Some of the equipment necessary to perform engine removal and installation safely and with relative ease are (in

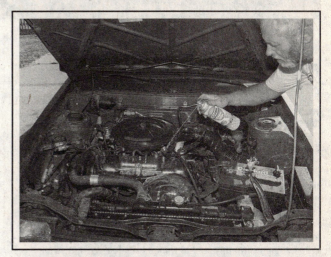

6.1 After tightly wrapping water-vulnerable components, use a spray cleaner on everything, with particular concentration on the greasiest areas, usually around the valve cover and lower edges of the block. If one section dries out, apply more cleaner

6.2 Depending on how dirty the engine is, let the cleaner soak in according to the directions and then hose off the grime and cleaner. Get the rinse water down into every area you can get at; then dry important components with a hair dryer or paper towels

6.3 Get an engine stand sturdy enough to firmly support the engine while you're working on it. Stay away from three-wheeled models: they have a tendency to tip over more easily, so get a four-wheeled unit

addition to a vehicle hoist and an engine hoist) a heavy duty floor jack (preferably fitted with a transmission jack head adapter), complete sets of wrenches and sockets as described in the front of this manual, wooden blocks, plenty of rags and cleaning solvent for mopping up spilled oil, coolant and gasoline.

Plan for the vehicle to be out of use for quite a while. A machine shop can do the work that is beyond the scope of the home mechanic. Machine shops often have a busy schedule, so before removing the engine, consult the shop for an estimate of how long it will take to rebuild or repair the components that may need work.

6.4 A clutch alignment tool is necessary if you plan to install a rebuilt engine mated to a manual transaxle

7 Engine - removal and installation

▶ **Refer to illustrations 7.8, 7.34 and 7.36**

✳✳ WARNING 1:

Gasoline is extremely flammable, so take extra precautions when you work on any part of the fuel system. Don't smoke or allow open flames or bare light bulbs near the work area, and don't work in a garage where a gas-type appliance (such as a water heater or clothes dryer) is present. Since gasoline is carcinogenic, wear fuel-resistant gloves when there's a possibility of being exposed to fuel, and, if you spill any fuel on your skin, rinse it off immediately with soap and water. Mop up any spills immediately and do not store fuel-soaked rags where they could ignite. The fuel system is under constant pressure, so, if any fuel lines are to be disconnected, the fuel pressure in the system must be relieved first (see Chapter 4 for more information). When you perform any kind of work on the fuel system, wear safety glasses and have a Class B type fire extinguisher on hand.

✳✳ WARNING 2:

The engine must be completely cool before beginning this procedure.

REMOVAL

1 Have the air conditioning system discharged by an automotive air conditioning technician.
2 Relieve the fuel system pressure (see Chapter 4).
3 Disconnect the cable from the negative battery terminal (see Chapter 5).
4 Remove the engine protective cover and the hood (see Chapter 11).
5 Remove the air filter housing (see Chapter 4).
6 Disconnect the accelerator cable, the cruise control cable, if equipped, and bracket from the engine and position them aside (see Chapter 4).
7 Remove the battery and the battery tray (see Chapter 5).
8 Clearly label and disconnect all vacuum lines, emissions hoses, wiring harness connectors, ground straps and fuel lines. Masking tape and/or a touch up paint applicator work well for marking items (see illustration). Take instant photos or sketch the locations of components and brackets.
9 Disconnect the electrical connectors from the PCM (see Chapter 6).
10 Disconnect the canister purge valve on V6 models (see Chapter 6).

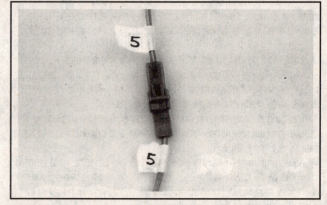

7.8 Label both ends of each wire and hose before disconnecting it

11 Detach the positive cables and the electrical connectors from the engine compartment fuse/relay box and the ground cable from the vehicle.
12 Detach the electrical connectors from the battery tray support. Also detach any other electrical connectors between the engine and the vehicle.
13 Disconnect the power steering pump return hose from the power steering pump (see Chapter 10).
14 Disconnect the fuel lines from the fuel rail (see Chapter 4).
15 Loosen the front wheel lug nuts, then raise the vehicle and secure it on jackstands.
16 Drain the cooling system (see Chapter 1).
17 Drain the engine oil and remove the drivebelts (see Chapter 1).
18 Detach the lower radiator hose from the engine (see Chapter 3).
19 Lower the vehicle and detach the heater hoses at the firewall (see Chapter 3).
20 Remove the upper radiator hose (see Chapter 3).
21 Remove the cooling fan(s) and shroud(s) (see Chapter 3).
22 Remove the radiator (see Chapter 3).
23 Remove the cruise control actuator mounting bolts and position it off to the side of the engine compartment.
24 Disconnect the shift cable(s) from the transaxle (see Chapter 7A or 7B). Also disconnect any wiring harness connectors from the transaxle.
25 Remove the clutch release cylinder and hydraulic line on manual transaxles (see Chapter 8).
26 Disconnect the air conditioning lines from the condenser.

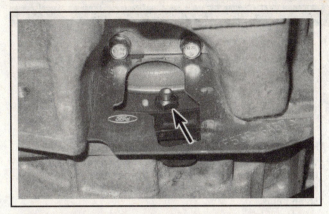

7.34 Remove the torque converter bolts through the access hole under the transaxle driveplate

27 Raise the vehicle and secure it on jackstands. Remove the front wheels and the inner fender splash shields (see Chapter 11).

28 Disconnect the air conditioning lines at the compressor. Remove the air conditioning compressor (see Chapter 3).

29 Remove the driveaxles and intermediate shaft (see Chapter 8).

30 Remove the transfer case on 4WD models (see Chapter 7C).

31 Unplug the oxygen sensor electrical connector(s).

32 Detach the exhaust pipe from the exhaust manifold(s) (see Chapter 4).

33 If equipped with an automatic transaxle, remove the torque converter bolts and remove the inspection cover from the bellhousing on the transaxle (see illustration).

34 Remove the starter motor (see Chapter 5).

35 If you're working on a V6 model, support the engine with a floor jack and block of wood positioned underneath the oil pan, then remove the engine mount (see Chapter 2A or 2B).

➡Note: This is only necessary if the engine is not equipped with two lifting brackets; the engine mount bracket on the engine can be used as a lifting point.

36 Roll the engine hoist into position and attach it to the engine with a couple pieces of heavy-duty chain (see illustrations). If the engine is equipped with lifting brackets, use them. If not, you'll have to fasten the chain to some substantial part of the engine - one that is strong enough to take the weight, but in a location that will provide good balance. If you're attaching the chain to a stud on the engine, or are using a bolt

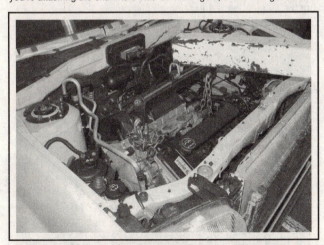

7.36 The engine hoist chains have been connected to the engine mount bracket at the right end (front) of the engine and to the lifting hook at the left end of the engine (V6 engine shown)

passing through the chain and into a threaded hole, place a washer between the nut or bolt head and the chain, and tighten the nut or bolt securely. Take up the slack in the chain, but don't lift the engine.

✳✳ WARNING:

DO NOT place any part of your body under the engine when it's supported only by a hoist or other lifting device.

37 Remove the forward and rear transaxle mounts (see Chapter 7).

38 Remove the transaxle (see Chapter 7).

39 Remove the engine mount fasteners (see Chapter 2A or 2B).

40 Recheck to be sure nothing is still connecting the engine to the vehicle. Disconnect anything still remaining.

41 Raise the engine slightly and then inspect it thoroughly once more to make sure that nothing is still attached, then slowly raise the engine out of the engine compartment. Check carefully to make sure nothing is hanging up.

✳✳ WARNING:

When raising the engine, never place any part of your body underneath it or between the engine and the engine compartment.

42 Remove the flywheel/driveplate (see Chapter 2A or 2B) and mount the engine on an engine stand (see illustration 6.3).

43 Inspect the engine and transaxle mounts (see Chapter 2A or 2B). If they're worn or damaged, replace them.

INSTALLATION

44 Install the flywheel/driveplate (see Chapter 2A or 2B).

45 If you're working on a vehicle with a manual transaxle, install the clutch and pressure plate (see Chapter 8). Now is a good time to install a new clutch.

46 Carefully lower the engine into the engine compartment and then reattach it to the engine mounts.

➡Note: If you're working on a V6 model and have attached the hoist chain to the engine mounting bracket, this won't be possible until after you've installed the transaxle.

47 Install the transaxle (see Chapter 7). If you're working on a manual transaxle equipped vehicle, apply a dab of high-temperature grease to the input shaft and guide it into the crankshaft pilot bearing until the bellhousing is flush with the engine block. If you're working on a vehicle with an automatic transaxle, guide the torque converter into the crankshaft following the procedure outlined in Chapter 7B. Install the transaxle-to-engine bolts and tighten them securely.

✳✳ CAUTION:

DO NOT use the bolts to force the transaxle and engine together!

48 Reinstall the remaining components in the reverse order of removal.

49 Add coolant, oil and transaxle fluid as needed (see Chapter 1).

50 Run the engine and check for leaks and proper operation of all accessories, then install the hood and test drive the vehicle. The Powertrain Control Module (PCM) must relearn its idle and fuel trim strategy for optimum driveability and performance (see Chapter 5, Section 1).

51 Have the air conditioning system re-charged and leak tested by the shop that discharged it.

8   Engine overhaul - disassembly sequence

1   It's much easier to remove the external components if it's mounted on a portable engine stand. A stand can often be rented quite cheaply from an equipment rental yard. Before the engine is mounted on a stand, the flywheel/driveplate should be removed from the engine.

2   If a stand isn't available, it's possible to remove the external engine components with it blocked up on the floor. Be extra careful not to tip or drop the engine when working without a stand.

3   If you're going to obtain a rebuilt engine, all external components must come off first, to be transferred to the replacement engine. These components include:

Clutch and flywheel (models with manual transaxle)
Driveplate (models with automatic transaxle)
Ignition system components
Emissions-related components
Engine mounts and mount brackets
Engine rear cover (spacer plate between flywheel/driveplate and engine block)

Intake/exhaust manifolds
Fuel injection components
Oil filter
Spark plug wires (or ignition coils) and spark plugs
Thermostat and housing assembly
Water pump

➡**Note: When removing the external components from the engine, pay close attention to details that may be helpful or important during installation. Note the installed position of gaskets, seals, spacers, pins, brackets, washers, bolts and other small items.**

4   If you're going to obtain a short block (assembled engine block, crankshaft, pistons and connecting rods), remove the timing belt, cylinder head, oil pan, oil pump pick-up tube, oil pump and water pump from your engine so that you can turn in your old short block to the rebuilder as a core. See *Engine rebuilding alternatives* for additional information regarding the different possibilities to be considered.

9   Pistons and connecting rods - removal and installation

REMOVAL

♦ **Refer to illustrations 9.1, 9.3 and 9.4**

➡**Note: Prior to removing the piston/connecting rod assemblies, remove the cylinder head and oil pan (see Chapter 2A).**

1   Use your fingernail to feel if a ridge has formed at the upper limit of ring travel (about 1/4-inch down from the top of each cylinder). If carbon deposits or cylinder wear have produced ridges, they must be completely removed with a special tool (see illustration). Follow the manufacturer's instructions provided with the tool. Failure to remove the ridges before attempting to remove the piston/connecting rod assemblies may result in piston breakage.

2   After the cylinder ridges have been removed, turn the engine so the crankshaft is facing up.

3   Before the main bearing cap assembly and connecting rods are removed, check the connecting rod endplay with feeler gauges. Slide

them between the first connecting rod and the crankshaft throw until the play is removed (see illustration). Repeat this procedure for each connecting rod. The endplay is equal to the thickness of the feeler gauge(s). Check with an automotive machine shop for the endplay service limit (a typical end play limit should measure between 0.005 to 0.015 inch [0.127 to 0.369 mm]). If the play exceeds the service limit, new connecting rods will be required. If new rods (or a new crankshaft) are installed, the endplay may fall under the minimum allowable. If it does, the rods will have to be machined to restore it. If necessary, consult an automotive machine shop for advice.

4   Check the connecting rods and caps for identification marks. If they aren't plainly marked, use paint or marker to clearly identify each rod and cap (1, 2, 3, etc., depending on the cylinder they're associated with) (see illustration).

5   Loosen each of the connecting rod cap bolts 1/2-turn at a time until they can be removed by hand.

➡**Note: New connecting rod cap bolts must be used when reassembling the engine, but save the old bolts for use when checking the connecting rod bearing oil clearance.**

9.1 Before you try to remove the pistons, use a ridge reamer to remove the raised material (ridge) from the top of the cylinders

9.3 Checking the connecting rod endplay (side clearance)

9.4 If the connecting rods and caps are not marked, use permanent ink or paint to mark the caps to the rods by cylinder number (for example, this would be the No. 4 connecting rod)

9.13 Install the piston ring into the cylinder then push it down into position using a piston so the ring will be square in the cylinder

9.14 With the ring square in the cylinder, measure the ring end gap with a feeler gauge

6   Remove the number one connecting rod cap and bearing insert. Don't drop the bearing insert out of the cap.

7   Remove the bearing insert and push the connecting rod/piston assembly out through the top of the engine. Use a wooden or plastic

9.15 If the ring end gap is too small, clamp a file in a vise as shown and file the piston ring ends - be sure to remove all raised material

hammer handle to push on the upper bearing surface in the connecting rod. If resistance is felt, double-check to make sure that all of the ridge was removed from the cylinder.

8   Repeat the procedure for the remaining cylinders.

9   After removal, reassemble the connecting rod caps and bearing inserts in their respective connecting rods and install the cap bolts finger tight. Leaving the old bearing inserts in place until reassembly will help prevent the connecting rod bearing surfaces from being accidentally nicked or gouged.

10 The pistons and connecting rods are now ready for inspection and overhaul at an automotive machine shop.

PISTON RING INSTALLATION

♦ **Refer to illustrations 9.13, 9.14, 9.15, 9.19a, 9.19b and 9.22**

11 Before installing the new piston rings, the ring end gaps must be checked. It's assumed that the piston ring side clearance has been checked and verified correct.

12 Lay out the piston/connecting rod assemblies and the new ring sets so the ring sets will be matched with the same piston and cylinder during the end gap measurement and engine assembly.

13 Insert the top (number one) ring into the first cylinder and square it up with the cylinder walls by pushing it in with the top of the piston (see illustration). The ring should be near the bottom of the cylinder, at the lower limit of ring travel.

14 To measure the end gap, slip feeler gauges between the ends of the ring until a gauge equal to the gap width is found (see illustration). The feeler gauge should slide between the ring ends with a slight amount of drag. A typical ring gap should fall between 0.010 and 0.020 inch [0.25 to 0.50 mm] for compression rings and up to 0.030 inch [0.76 mm] for the oil ring steel rails. If the gap is larger or smaller than specified, double-check to make sure you have the correct rings before proceeding.

15 If the gap is too small, it must be enlarged or the ring ends may come in contact with each other during engine operation, which can cause serious damage to the engine. If necessary, increase the end gaps by filing the ring ends very carefully with a fine file. Mount the file in a vise equipped with soft jaws, slip the ring over the file with the ends contacting the file face and slowly move the ring to remove material from the ends. When performing this operation, file only by pushing the ring from the outside end of the file towards the vise (see illustration).

9.19a Installing the spacer/expander in the oil ring groove

9.19b DO NOT use a piston ring installation tool when installing the oil control side rails

16 Excess end gap isn't critical unless it's greater than 0.040 inch (1.01 mm). Again, double-check to make sure you have the correct ring type.

17 Repeat the procedure for each ring that will be installed in the first cylinder and for each ring in the remaining cylinders. Remember to keep rings, pistons and cylinders matched up.

18 Once the ring end gaps have been checked/corrected, the rings can be installed on the pistons.

19 The oil control ring (lowest one on the piston) is usually installed first. It's composed of three separate components. Slip the spacer/expander into the groove (see illustration). If an anti-rotation tang is used, make sure it's inserted into the drilled hole in the ring groove. Next, install the upper side rail in the same manner (see illustration). Don't use a piston ring installation tool on the oil ring side rails, as they may be damaged. Instead, place one end of the side rail into the groove between the spacer/expander and the ring land, hold it firmly in place and slide a finger around the piston while pushing the rail into the groove. Finally, install the lower side rail.

20 After the three oil ring components have been installed, check to make sure that both the upper and lower side rails can be rotated smoothly inside the ring grooves.

21 The number two (middle) ring is installed next. It's usually

9.22 Use a piston ring installation tool to install the number 2 and the number 1 (top) rings - be sure the directional mark on the piston ring(s) is facing toward the top of the piston

stamped with a mark which must face up, toward the top of the piston. Do not mix up the top and middle rings, as they have different cross-sections.

➡**Note: Always follow the instructions printed on the ring package or box - different manufacturers may require different approaches.**

22 Use a piston ring installation tool and make sure the identification mark is facing the top of the piston, then slip the ring into the middle groove on the piston (see illustration). Don't expand the ring any more than necessary to slide it over the piston.

23 Install the number one (top) ring in the same manner. Make sure the mark is facing up. Be careful not to confuse the number one and number two rings.

24 Repeat the procedure for the remaining pistons and rings.

INSTALLATION

25 Before installing the piston/connecting rod assemblies, the cylinder walls must be perfectly clean, the top edge of each cylinder bore must be chamfered, and the crankshaft must be in place.

26 Remove the cap from the end of the number one connecting rod (refer to the marks made during removal). Remove the original bearing inserts and wipe the bearing surfaces of the connecting rod and cap with a clean, lint-free cloth. They must be kept spotlessly clean.

Connecting rod bearing oil clearance check

▶ **Refer to illustrations 9.30, 9.35, 9.37 and 9.41**

27 Clean the back side of the new upper bearing insert, then lay it in place in the connecting rod.

28 Make sure the tab on the bearing fits into the recess in the rod. Don't hammer the bearing insert into place and be very careful not to nick or gouge the bearing face. Don't lubricate the bearing at this time.

29 Clean the back side of the other bearing insert and install it in the rod cap. Again, make sure the tab on the bearing fits into the recess in the cap, and don't apply any lubricant. It's critically important that the mating surfaces of the bearing and connecting rod are perfectly clean and oil free when they're assembled.

30 Position the piston ring gaps at 90-degree intervals around the piston as shown (see illustration).

31 Lubricate the piston and rings with clean engine oil and attach a piston ring compressor to the piston. Leave the skirt protruding about

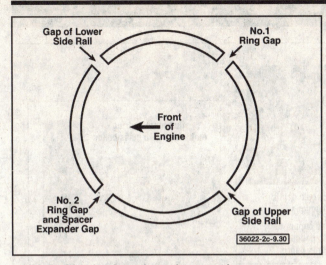

9.30 **Position the piston ring end gaps as shown**

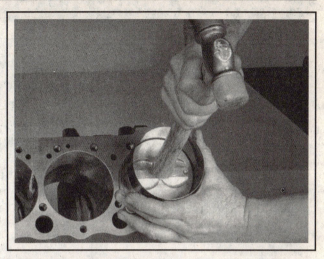

9.35 **Use a plastic or wooden hammer handle to push the piston into the cylinder**

1/4-inch to guide the piston into the cylinder. The rings must be compressed until they're flush with the piston.

32 Rotate the crankshaft until the number one connecting rod journal is at BDC (bottom dead center) and apply a liberal coat of engine oil to the cylinder walls.

33 With the mark on top of the piston facing the front (timing belt or chain end) of the engine, gently insert the piston/connecting rod assembly into the number one cylinder bore and rest the bottom edge of the ring compressor on the engine block.

34 Tap the top edge of the ring compressor to make sure it's contacting the block around its entire circumference.

35 Gently tap on the top of the piston with the end of a wooden or plastic hammer handle (see illustration) while guiding the end of the connecting rod into place on the crankshaft journal. The piston rings may try to pop out of the ring compressor just before entering the cylinder bore, so keep some downward pressure on the ring compressor. Work slowly, and if any resistance is felt as the piston enters the cylinder, stop immediately. Find out what's hanging up and fix it before proceeding. Do not, for any reason, force the piston into the cylinder - you might break a ring and/or the piston.

36 Once the piston/connecting rod assembly is installed, the connecting rod bearing oil clearance must be checked before the rod cap is permanently installed.

37 Cut a piece of the appropriate size Plastigage slightly shorter

than the width of the connecting rod bearing and lay it in place on the number one connecting rod journal, parallel with the journal axis (see illustration).

38 Clean the connecting rod cap bearing face and install the rod cap. Make sure the mating mark on the cap is on the same side as the mark on the connecting rod (see illustration 9.4).

39 Install the old rod bolts, at this time, and tighten them to the torque listed in this Chapter's Specifications.

➡**Note: Use a thin-wall socket to avoid erroneous torque readings that can result if the socket is wedged between the rod cap and the bolt head. If the socket tends to wedge itself between the fastener and the cap, lift up on it slightly until it no longer contacts the cap. DO NOT rotate the crankshaft at any time during this operation.**

40 Remove the fasteners and detach the rod cap, being very careful not to disturb the Plastigage.

41 Compare the width of the crushed Plastigage to the scale printed on the Plastigage envelope to obtain the oil clearance (see illustration). The connecting rod oil clearance is usually about 0.001 to 0.002 inch (0.025 to 0.05 mm). Consult an automotive machine shop for the clearance specified for the rod bearings on your engine.

9.37 **Place Plastigage on each connecting rod bearing journal parallel to the crankshaft centerline**

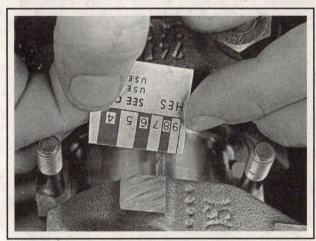

9.41 **Use the scale on the Plastigage package to determine the bearing oil clearance - be sure to measure the widest part of the Plastigage and use the correct scale; it comes with both standard and metric scales**

ENGINE BEARING ANALYSIS

Debris

Babbitt bearing embedded with debris from machinings

Microscopic detail of debris

Microscopic detail of gouges

Overplated copper alloy bearing gouged by cast iron debris

Aluminum bearing embedded with glass beads

Microscopic detail of glass beads

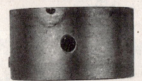

Damaged lining caused by dirt left on the bearing back

Misassembly

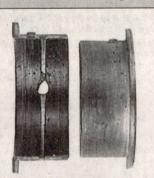

Result of a lower half assembled as an upper - blocking the oil flow

Excessive oil clearance is indicated by a short contact arc

Polished and oil-stained backs are a result of a poor fit in the housing bore

Result of a wrong, reversed, or shifted cap

Overloading

Damage from excessive idling which resulted in an oil film unable to support the load imposed

Damaged upper connecting rod bearings caused by engine lugging; the lower main bearings (not shown) were similarly affected

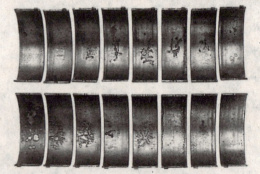

The damage shown in these upper and lower connecting rod bearings was caused by engine operation at a higher-than-rated speed under load

Misalignment

A warped crankshaft caused this pattern of severe wear in the center, diminishing toward the ends

A poorly finished crankshaft caused the equally spaced scoring shown

A tapered housing bore caused the damage along one edge of this pair

A bent connecting rod led to the damage in the "V" pattern

Lubrication

Result of dry start: The bearings on the left, farthest from the oil pump, show more damage

Corrosion

Microscopic detail of corrosion

Corrosion is an acid attack on the bearing lining generally caused by inadequate maintenance, extremely hot or cold operation, or inferior oils or fuels

Microscopic detail of cavitation

Example of cavitation - a surface erosion caused by pressure changes in the oil film

Result of a low oil supply or oil starvation

Severe wear as a result of inadequate oil clearance

Damage from excessive thrust or insufficient axial clearance

Bearing affected by oil dilution caused by excessive blow-by or a rich mixture

42 If the clearance is not as specified, the bearing inserts may be the wrong size (which means different ones will be required). Before deciding that different inserts are needed, make sure that no dirt or oil was between the bearing inserts and the connecting rod or cap when the clearance was measured. Also, recheck the journal diameter. If the Plastigage was wider at one end than the other, the journal may be tapered. If the clearance still exceeds the limit specified, the bearing will have to be replaced with an undersize bearing.

✳✳ CAUTION:

When installing a new crankshaft always use a standard size bearing.

Final installation

43 Carefully scrape all traces of the Plastigage material off the rod journal and/or bearing face. Be very careful not to scratch the bearing - use your fingernail or the edge of a plastic card.

44 Make sure the bearing faces are perfectly clean, then apply a uniform layer of clean moly-base grease or engine assembly lube to both of them. You'll have to push the piston into the cylinder to expose the face of the bearing insert in the connecting rod.

✳✳ CAUTION:

Install new connecting rod cap bolts. Do NOT reuse old bolts - they have stretched and cannot be reused.

45 Slide the connecting rod back into place on the journal, install the rod cap, install the new bolts and tighten them to the torque listed in this Chapter's Specifications. Again, work up to the torque in three steps.

46 Repeat the entire procedure for the remaining pistons/connecting rods.

47 The important points to remember are:

a) Keep the back sides of the bearing inserts and the insides of the connecting rods and caps perfectly clean when assembling them.

b) Make sure you have the correct piston/rod assembly for each cylinder.

c) The mark on the piston must face the front (timing belt end [four-cylinder engine] or timing chain [V6 engine] end) of the engine.

d) Lubricate the cylinder walls liberally with clean oil.

e) Lubricate the bearing faces when installing the rod caps after the oil clearance has been checked.

48 After all the piston/connecting rod assemblies have been correctly installed, rotate the crankshaft a number of times by hand to check for any obvious binding.

49 As a final step, check the connecting rod endplay, as described in Step 3. If it was correct before disassembly and the original crankshaft and rods were reinstalled, it should still be correct. If new rods or a new crankshaft were installed, the endplay may be inadequate. If so, the rods will have to be removed and taken to an automotive machine shop for resizing.

10 Crankshaft - removal and installation

REMOVAL

▶ **Refer to illustrations 10.1 and 10.3**

➡**Note: The crankshaft can be removed only after the engine has been removed from the vehicle. It's assumed that the flywheel or driveplate, crankshaft pulley, timing belt, oil pan, oil pump body, oil filter and piston/connecting rod assemblies have**

already been removed. The rear main oil seal retainer must be unbolted and separated from the block before proceeding with crankshaft removal.

1 Before the crankshaft is removed, measure the endplay. Mount a dial indicator with the indicator in line with the crankshaft and just touching the end of the crankshaft as shown (see illustration).

2 Pry the crankshaft all the way to the rear and zero the dial indicator. Next, pry the crankshaft to the front as far as possible and check the reading on the dial indicator. The distance traveled is the endplay. A typical crankshaft endplay will fall between 0.003 to 0.010 inch (0.076 to 0.254 mm). If it is greater than that, check the crankshaft thrust surfaces for wear after it's removed. If no wear is evident, new main bearings should correct the endplay.

3 If a dial indicator isn't available, feeler gauges can be used. Gently pry the crankshaft all the way to the front of the engine. Slip feeler gauges between the crankshaft and the front face of the thrust bearing

10.1 Checking crankshaft endplay with a dial indicator

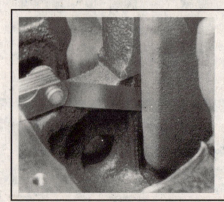

10.3 Checking the crankshaft endplay with feeler gauges at the thrust bearing journal

or washer to determine the clearance (see illustration).

4 Loosen the main bearing cap bolts (four-cylinder engines) or lower cylinder block (bedplate) bolts 1/4-turn at a time each, until they can be removed by hand. Loosen the bolts in the reverse of the tightening sequence (see illustrations 10.19a and 10.19b)

5 If you're working on a four-cylinder engine, remove the main bearing caps. If you're working on a V6 engine, gently tap the lower cylinder block with a soft-face hammer around it's perimeter. Pull the lower cylinder block straight up and off the cylinder block. Try not to drop the bearing inserts if they come out with the assembly.

6 Carefully lift the crankshaft out of the engine. It may be a good idea to have an assistant available, since the crankshaft is quite heavy and awkward to handle. With the bearing inserts in place inside the engine block and main bearing caps or lower cylinder block, reinstall the main bearing caps or lower cylinder block onto the engine block and tighten the bolts finger tight. If you're working on a four-cylinder engine, make sure you install the caps with the arrows pointing towards the front (timing belt end) of the engine.

INSTALLATION

7 Crankshaft installation is the first step in engine reassembly. It's assumed at this point that the engine block and crankshaft have been cleaned, inspected and repaired or reconditioned.

8 Position the engine block with the bottom facing up.

9 Remove the bolts and lift off the main bearing caps or lower cylinder block.

10 If they're still in place, remove the original bearing inserts from the block and from the main bearing cap assembly. Wipe the bearing surfaces of the block and main bearing cap assembly with a clean, lint-free cloth. They must be kept spotlessly clean. This is critical for determining the correct bearing oil clearance.

MAIN BEARING OIL CLEARANCE CHECK

▶ **Refer to illustrations 10.11, 10.17, 10.19a, 10.19b and 10.21**

11 Without mixing them up, clean the back sides of the new upper main bearing inserts (with grooves and oil holes) and lay one in each main bearing saddle in the engine block. Each upper bearing (engine block) has an oil groove and oil hole in it.

✳✳ CAUTION:

The oil holes in the block must line up with the oil holes in the upper bearing inserts.

→Note: The thrust bearing on the four-cylinder engine is located on the engine block number 3 journal. The thrust bearing on the V6 engine is located on the 4th journal on the lower cylinder block. The thrust washer on the V6 engine is located on the 4th journal (upper).

Clean the back sides of the lower main bearing inserts and lay them in the corresponding location in the main bearing caps or the lower cylinder block. Make sure the tab on the bearing insert fits into the recess in the block or lower cylinder block.

✳✳ CAUTION:

Do not hammer the bearing insert into place and don't nick or gouge the bearing faces. DO NOT apply any lubrication at this time.

10.17 Place the Plastigage onto the crankshaft bearing journal as shown

12 Clean the faces of the bearing inserts in the block and the crankshaft main bearing journals with a clean, lint-free cloth.

13 Check or clean the oil holes in the crankshaft, as any dirt here can go only one way - straight through the new bearings.

14 Once you're certain the crankshaft is clean, carefully lay it in position in the cylinder block.

15 Before the crankshaft can be permanently installed, the main bearing oil clearance must be checked.

16 Cut several strips of the appropriate size of Plastigage. They must be slightly shorter than the width of the main bearing journal.

17 Place one piece on each crankshaft main bearing journal, parallel with the journal axis as shown (see illustration).

18 Clean the faces of the bearing inserts in the main bearing caps or the lower cylinder block. Hold the bearing inserts in place and install the caps or the lower cylinder block onto the crankshaft and cylinder block. DO NOT disturb the Plastigage.

19 Apply clean engine oil to all bolt threads prior to installation, then install all bolts finger-tight. Tighten the bolts in the sequence shown (see illustrations) progressing in steps, to the torque listed in this Chapter's Specifications. DO NOT rotate the crankshaft at any time during this operation.

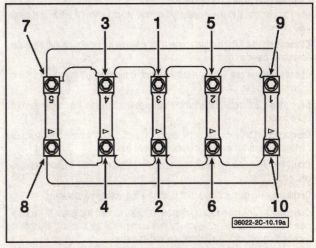

10.19a Main bearing cap bolt tightening sequence - four-cylinder engines

GLOSSARY

B

Backlash - The amount of play between two parts. Usually refers to how much one gear can be moved back and forth without moving the gear with which it's meshed.

Bearing Caps - The caps held in place by nuts or bolts which, in turn, hold the bearing surface. This space is for lubricating oil to enter.

Bearing clearance - The amount of space left between shaft and bearing surface. This space is for lubricating oil to enter.

Bearing crush - The additional height which is purposely manufactured into each bearing half to ensure complete contact of the bearing back with the housing bore when the engine is assembled.

Bearing knock - The noise created by movement of a part in a loose or worn bearing.

Blueprinting - Dismantling an engine and reassembling it to EXACT specifications.

Bore - An engine cylinder, or any cylindrical hole; also used to describe the process of enlarging or accurately refinishing a hole with a cutting tool, as to bore an engine cylinder. The bore size is the diameter of the hole.

Boring - Renewing the cylinders by cutting them out to a specified size. A boring bar is used to make the cut.

Bottom end - A term which refers collectively to the engine block, crankshaft, main bearings and the big ends of the connecting rods.

Break-in - The period of operation between installation of new or rebuilt parts and time in which parts are worn to the correct fit. Driving at reduced and varying speed for a specified mileage to permit parts to wear to the correct fit.

Bushing - A one-piece sleeve placed in a bore to serve as a bearing surface for shaft, piston pin, etc. Usually replaceable.

C

Camshaft - The shaft in the engine, on which a series of lobes are located for operating the valve mechanisms. The camshaft is driven by gears or sprockets and a timing chain. Usually referred to simply as the cam.

Carbon - Hard, or soft, black deposits found in combustion chamber, on plugs, under rings, on and under valve heads.

Cast iron - An alloy of iron and more than two percent carbon, used for engine blocks and heads because it's relatively inexpensive and easy to mold into complex shapes.

Chamfer - To bevel across (or a bevel on) the sharp edge of an object.

Chase - To repair damaged threads with a tap or die.

Combustion chamber - The space between the piston and the cylinder head, with the piston at top dead center, in which air-fuel mixture is burned.

Compression ratio - The relationship between cylinder volume (clearance volume) when the piston is at top dead center and cylinder volume when the piston is at bottom dead center.

Connecting rod - The rod that connects the crank on the crankshaft with the piston. Sometimes called a con rod.

Connecting rod cap - The part of the connecting rod assembly that attaches the rod to the crankpin.

Core plug - Soft metal plug used to plug the casting holes for the coolant passages in the block.

Crankcase - The lower part of the engine in which the crankshaft rotates; includes the lower section of the cylinder block and the oil pan.

Crank kit - A reground or reconditioned crankshaft and new main and connecting rod bearings.

Crankpin - The part of a crankshaft to which a connecting rod is attached.

Crankshaft - The main rotating member, or shaft, running the length of the crankcase, with offset throws to which the connecting rods are attached; changes the reciprocating motion of the pistons into rotating motion.

Cylinder sleeve - A replaceable sleeve, or liner, pressed into the cylinder block to form the cylinder bore.

D

Deburring - Removing the burrs (rough edges or areas) from a bearing.

Deglazer - A tool, rotated by an electric motor, used to remove glaze from cylinder walls so a new set of rings will seat.

E

Endplay - The amount of lengthwise movement between two parts. As applied to a crankshaft, the distance that the crankshaft can move forward and back in the cylinder block.

F

Face - A machinist's term that refers to removing metal from the end of a shaft or the face of a larger part, such as a flywheel.

Fatigue - A breakdown of material through a large number of loading and unloading cycles. The first signs are cracks followed shortly by breaks.

Feeler gauge - A thin strip of hardened steel, ground to an exact thickness, used to check clearances between parts.

Free height - The unloaded length or height of a spring.

Freeplay - The looseness in a linkage, or an assembly of parts, between the initial application of force and actual movement. Usually perceived as slop or slight delay.

Freeze plug - See Core plug.

G

Gallery - A large passage in the block that forms a reservoir for engine oil pressure.

Glaze - The very smooth, glassy finish that develops on cylinder walls while an engine is in service.

H

Heli-Coil - A rethreading device used when threads are worn or damaged. The device is installed in a retapped hole to reduce the thread size to the original size.

I

Installed height - The spring's measured length or height, as installed on the cylinder head. Installed height is measured from the spring seat to the underside of the spring retainer.

J

Journal - The surface of a rotating shaft which turns in a bearing.

K

Keeper - The split lock that holds the valve spring retainer in position on the valve stem.

Key - A small piece of metal inserted into matching grooves machined into two parts fitted together - such as a gear pressed onto a shaft - which prevents slippage between the two parts.

Knock - The heavy metallic engine sound, produced in the combustion chamber as a result of abnormal combustion - usually detonation. Knock is usually caused by a loose or worn bearing. Also referred to as detonation, pinging and spark knock. Connecting rod or main bearing knocks are created by too much oil clearance or insufficient lubrication.

L

Lands - The portions of metal between the piston ring grooves.

Lapping the valves - Grinding a valve face and its seat together with lapping compound.

Lash - The amount of free motion in a gear train, between gears, or in a mechanical assembly, that occurs before movement can begin. Usually refers to the lash in a valve train.

Lifter - The part that rides against the cam to transfer motion to the rest of the valve train.

M

Machining - The process of using a machine to remove metal from a metal part.

Main bearings - The plain, or babbitt, bearings that support the crankshaft.

Main bearing caps - The cast iron caps, bolted to the bottom of the block, that support the main bearings.

O

O.D. - Outside diameter.

Oil gallery - A pipe or drilled passageway in the engine used to carry engine oil from one area to another.

Oil ring - The lower ring, or rings, of a piston; designed to prevent excessive amounts of oil from working up the cylinder walls and into the combustion chamber. Also called an oil-control ring.

Oil seal - A seal which keeps oil from leaking out of a compartment. Usually refers to a dynamic seal around a rotating shaft or other moving part.

O-ring - A type of sealing ring made of a special rubberlike material; in use, the O-ring is compressed into a groove to provide the sealing action.

Overhaul - To completely disassemble a unit, clean and inspect all parts, reassemble it with the original or new parts and make all adjustments necessary for proper operation.

P

Pilot bearing - A small bearing installed in the center of the flywheel (or the rear end of the crankshaft) to support the front end of the input shaft of the transmission.

Pip mark - A little dot or indentation which indicates the top side of a compression ring.

Piston - The cylindrical part, attached to the connecting rod, that moves up and down in the cylinder as the crankshaft rotates. When the fuel charge is fired, the piston transfers the force of the explosion to the connecting rod, then to the crankshaft.

Piston pin (or wrist pin) - The cylindrical and usually hollow steel pin that passes through the piston. The piston pin fastens the piston to the upper end of the connecting rod.

Piston ring - The split ring fitted to the groove in a piston. The ring contacts the sides of the ring groove and also rubs against the cylinder wall, thus sealing space between piston and wall. There are two types of rings: Compression rings seal the compression pressure in the combustion chamber; oil rings scrape excessive oil off the cylinder wall.

Piston ring groove - The slots or grooves cut in piston heads to hold piston rings in position.

Piston skirt - The portion of the piston below the rings and the piston pin hole.

Plastigage - A thin strip of plastic thread, available in different sizes, used for measuring clearances. For example, a strip of plastigage is laid across a bearing journal and mashed as parts are assembled. Then parts are disassembled and the width of the strip is measured to determine clearance between journal and bearing. Commonly used to measure crankshaft main-bearing and connecting rod bearing clearances.

Press-fit - A tight fit between two parts that requires pressure to force the parts together. Also referred to as drive, or force, fit.

Prussian blue - A blue pigment; in solution, useful in determining the area of contact between two surfaces. Prussian blue is commonly used to determine the width and location of the contact area between the valve face and the valve seat.

R

Race (bearing) - The inner or outer ring that provides a contact surface for balls or rollers in bearing.

Ream - To size, enlarge or smooth a hole by using a round cutting tool with fluted edges.

Ring job - The process of reconditioning the cylinders and installing new rings.

Runout - Wobble. The amount a shaft rotates out-of-true.

S

Saddle - The upper main bearing seat.

Scored - Scratched or grooved, as a cylinder wall may be scored by abrasive particles moved up and down by the piston rings.

Scuffing - A type of wear in which there's a transfer of material between parts moving against each other; shows up as pits or grooves in the mating surfaces.

Seat - The surface upon which another part rests or seats. For example, the valve seat is the matched surface upon which the valve face rests. Also used to refer to wearing into a good fit; for example, piston rings seat after a few miles of driving.

Short block - An engine block complete with crankshaft and piston and, usually, camshaft assemblies.

Static balance - The balance of an object while it's stationary.

Step - The wear on the lower portion of a ring land caused by excessive side and back-clearance. The height of the step indicates the ring's extra side clearance and the length of the step projecting from the back wall of the groove represents the ring's back clearance.

Stroke - The distance the piston moves when traveling from top dead center to bottom dead center, or from bottom dead center to top dead center.

Stud - A metal rod with threads on both ends.

T

Tang - A lip on the end of a plain bearing used to align the bearing during assembly.

Tap - To cut threads in a hole. Also refers to the fluted tool used to cut threads.

Taper - A gradual reduction in the width of a shaft or hole; in an engine cylinder, taper usually takes the form of uneven wear, more pronounced at the top than at the bottom.

Throws - The offset portions of the crankshaft to which the connecting rods are affixed.

Thrust bearing - The main bearing that has thrust faces to prevent excessive endplay, or forward and backward movement of the crankshaft.

Thrust washer - A bronze or hardened steel washer placed between two moving parts. The washer prevents longitudinal movement and provides a bearing surface for thrust surfaces of parts.

Tolerance - The amount of variation permitted from an exact size of measurement. Actual amount from smallest acceptable dimension to largest acceptable dimension.

U

Umbrella - An oil deflector placed near the valve tip to throw oil from the valve stem area.

Undercut - A machined groove below the normal surface.

Undersize bearings - Smaller diameter bearings used with re-ground crankshaft journals.

V

Valve grinding - Refacing a valve in a valve-refacing machine.

Valve train - The valve-operating mechanism of an engine; includes all components from the camshaft to the valve.

Vibration damper - A cylindrical weight attached to the front of the crankshaft to minimize torsional vibration (the twist-untwist actions of the crankshaft caused by the cylinder firing impulses). Also called a harmonic balancer.

W

Water jacket - The spaces around the cylinders, between the inner and outer shells of the cylinder block or head, through which coolant circulates.

Web - A supporting structure across a cavity.

Woodruff key - A key with a radiused backside (viewed from the side).

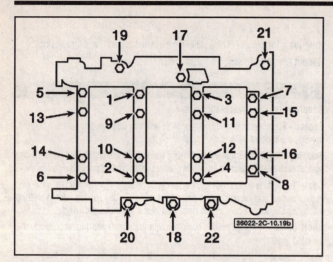

10.19b Lower cylinder block bolt tightening sequence - V6 engines

10.21 Use the scale on the Plastigage package to determine the bearing oil clearance - be sure to measure the widest part of the Plastigage and use the correct scale; it comes with both standard and metric scales

20 Remove the bolts in the reverse order of the tightening sequence and carefully lift the caps or the lower cylinder block straight up and off the block. Do not disturb the Plastigage or rotate the crankshaft.

21 Compare the width of the crushed Plastigage on each journal to the scale printed on the Plastigage envelope to determine the main bearing oil clearance (see illustration). Check with an automotive machine shop for the oil clearance for your engine.

22 If the clearance is not as specified, the bearing inserts may be the wrong size (which means different ones will be required). Before deciding if different inserts are needed, make sure that no dirt or oil was between the bearing inserts and the cap assembly or block when the clearance was measured. If the Plastigage was wider at one end than the other, the crankshaft journal may be tapered. If the clearance still exceeds the limit specified, the bearing insert(s) will have to be replaced with an undersize bearing insert(s).

✳✳ CAUTION:

When installing a new crankshaft always install a standard bearing insert set.

23 Carefully scrape all traces of the Plastigage material off the main bearing journals and/or the bearing insert faces. Be sure to remove all residue from the oil holes. Use your fingernail or the edge of a plastic card - don't nick or scratch the bearing faces.

FINAL INSTALLATION

▶ **Refer to illustration 10.28**

24 Carefully lift the crankshaft out of the cylinder block.

25 Clean the bearing insert faces in the cylinder block, then apply a thin, uniform layer of moly-base grease or engine assembly lube to each of the bearing surfaces. Be sure to coat the thrust faces as well as the journal face of the thrust bearing.

26 Make sure the crankshaft journals are clean, then lay the crankshaft back in place in the cylinder block.

27 Clean the bearing insert faces and apply the same lubricant to them. Clean the engine block and the bearing caps/lower cylinder block thoroughly. The surfaces must be free of oil residue.

28 On V6 engines, apply a bead of RTV to the engine block before installing the lower cylinder block. Be sure the bead is the correct thick-

ness (see illustration).

29 On V6 engines, install the lower cylinder block onto the crankshaft and cylinder block. If you're working on a four-cylinder engine, install the main bearing caps in their proper locations, with the arrows on the caps facing the front of the engine.

30 Prior to installation, apply clean engine oil to all bolt threads wiping off any excess, then install all bolts finger-tight.

31 Tighten the lower cylinder block (V6 engines) or caps (four cylin-

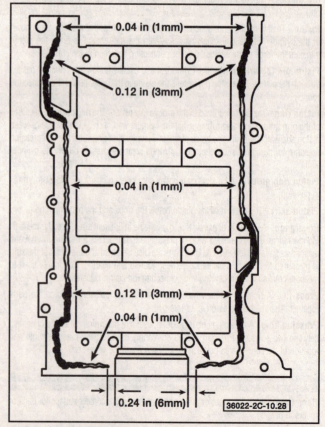

10.28 Apply RTV sealant to the cylinder block mating surface - make sure the bead of sealant is the correct diameter

der engines) following the correct torque sequence (see illustrations 10.19a and 10.19b). Torque the bolts to the Specifications listed in this Chapter.

32 Recheck the crankshaft endplay with a feeler gauge or a dial indicator. The endplay should be correct if the crankshaft thrust faces aren't worn or damaged and if new bearings have been installed.

33 Rotate the crankshaft a number of times by hand to check for any obvious binding. It should rotate with a running torque of 50 in-lbs or less. If the running torque is too high, correct the problem at this time.

34 Install a new rear main oil seal (see Chapter 2A or 2B).

11 Engine overhaul - reassembly sequence

1 Before beginning engine reassembly, make sure you have all the necessary new parts, gaskets and seals as well as the following items on hand:

Common hand tools
A 1/2-inch drive torque wrench
New engine oil
Gasket sealant
Thread locking compound

2 If you obtained a short block it will be necessary to install the cylinder head, the oil pump and pick-up tube, the oil pan, the water pump, the timing belt and timing cover, and the valve cover (see Chapter 2A or 2B). In order to save time and avoid problems, the external

components must be installed in the following general order:

Thermostat and housing cover
Water pump
Intake and exhaust manifolds
Fuel injection components
Emission control components
Spark plug wires and spark plugs
Ignition coils
Oil filter
Engine mounts and mount brackets
Clutch and flywheel (manual transaxle)
Driveplate (automatic transaxle)

12 Initial start-up and break-in after overhaul

✳✳ WARNING:

Have a fire extinguisher handy when starting the engine for the first time.

1 Once the engine has been installed in the vehicle, double-check the engine oil and coolant levels.

2 With the spark plugs out of the engine and the ignition system and fuel pump disabled, crank the engine until oil pressure registers on the gauge or the light goes out.

3 Install the spark plugs, hook up the plug wires and restore the ignition system and fuel pump functions.

4 Start the engine. It may take a few moments for the fuel system to build up pressure, but the engine should start without a great deal of effort.

5 After the engine starts, it should be allowed to warm up to nor-

mal operating temperature. While the engine is warming up, make a thorough check for fuel, oil and coolant leaks.

6 Shut the engine off and recheck the engine oil and coolant levels.

7 Drive the vehicle to an area with minimum traffic, accelerate from 30 to 50 mph, then allow the vehicle to slow to 30 mph with the throttle closed. Repeat the procedure 10 or 12 times. This will load the piston rings and cause them to seat properly against the cylinder walls. Check again for oil and coolant leaks.

8 Drive the vehicle gently for the first 500 miles (no sustained high speeds) and keep a constant check on the oil level. It is not unusual for an engine to use oil during the break-in period.

9 At approximately 500 to 600 miles, change the oil and filter.

10 For the next few hundred miles, drive the vehicle normally. Do not pamper it or abuse it.

11 After 2,000 miles, change the oil and filter again and consider the engine broken in.

Specifications

General

Displacement	
Four-cylinder models	121 cubic inches (2.0 liters)
V6 models	182 cubic inches (3.0 liters)
Bore and Stroke	
Four-cylinder models	3.34 x 3.46 inches (84.8 x 88.0 mm)
V6 models	3.50 x 3.13 inches (89.0 x 79.5 mm)
Cylinder compression	Lowest cylinder must be within 75 percent of highest cylinder
Oil pressure (at operating temperature)	
Four-cylinder models	54 to 80 psi (370 to 550 kPa) @ 4000 rpm
V6 models	45 psi (310 kPa) @ 800 rpm

Torque specifications

	Ft-lbs (unless otherwise indicated)	Nm

➡ **Note: One foot-pound (ft-lb) of torque is equivalent to 12 inch-pounds (in-lbs) of torque. Torque values below approximately 15 ft-lbs are expressed in inch-pounds, since most foot-pound torque wrenches are not accurate at these smaller values.**

	Ft-lbs (unless otherwise indicated)	Nm
Connecting rod bearing cap bolts		
Four-cylinder models		
Step 1	26	35
Step 2	Tighten an additional 90-degrees	
V6 models		
Step 1	17	23
Step 2	32	43
Main bearing caps (four-cylinder models) (in sequence - see illustration 10.19a)		
Step 1	18	25
Step 2	Tighten an additional 60-degrees	
Main bearing assembly (V6 models) (in sequence - see illustration 10.19b)		
Step 1 Bolts 1 through 8	18	25
Step 2 Bolts 9 through 16	30	40
Step 3 Bolts 1 through 16	Tighten an additional 90-degrees	
Step 4 Bolts 17 through 22	18	25

Section

1 General information
2 Antifreeze - general information
3 Thermostat - check and replacement
4 Engine cooling fans - check and replacement
5 Coolant expansion tank - removal and installation
6 Radiator - removal and installation
7 Water pump - check
8 Water pump - replacement
9 Coolant temperature sending unit - check and replacement
10 Blower motor resistor and blower motor - replacement
11 Heater/air conditioner control assembly - removal and installation
12 Heater core - replacement
13 Air conditioning and heating system - check and maintenance
14 Air conditioning compressor - removal and installation
15 Air conditioning accumulator - removal and installation
16 Air conditioning condenser - removal and installation
17 Air conditioning pressure cycling switch - replacement
18 Air conditioning orifice tube - removal and installation
19 Oil cooler - removal and installation

Reference to other Chapters

Coolant level check - See Chapter 1
Cooling system check - See Chapter 1
Cooling system servicing (draining, flushing and refilling) - See Chapter 1
Drivebelt check, adjustment and replacement - See Chapter 1
Underhood hose check and replacement - See Chapter 1

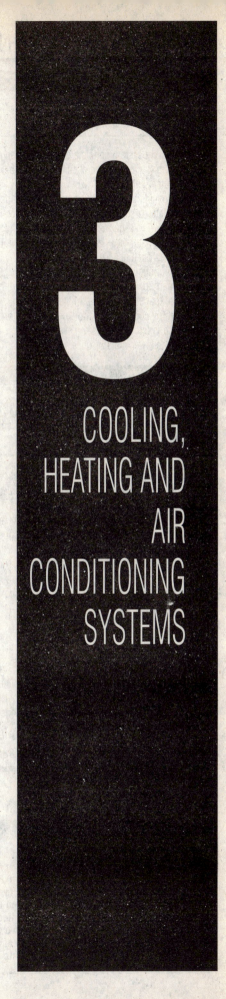

3

COOLING, HEATING AND AIR CONDITIONING SYSTEMS

1   General information

ENGINE COOLING SYSTEM

The cooling system consists of a radiator, an expansion tank, a pressure cap (located on the expansion tank), a thermostat, a cooling fan and clutch, and a belt-driven water pump.

The expansion tank (referred to by the manufacturer as a "degas bottle") functions somewhat differently than a conventional recovery tank. Designed to separate any trapped air in the coolant, it is pressurized by the radiator and has a pressure cap on top. The radiator on these models does not have a pressure cap. When the thermostat is closed, no coolant flows in the expansion tank, but when the engine is fully warmed up, coolant flows from the top of the radiator through a small hose that enters the top of the expansion tank, where the air separates and the coolant falls into a coolant reservoir in the bottom of the tank, which is fed to the cooling system through a larger hose connected to the lower radiator hose.

✳✳ WARNING:

Unlike a conventional coolant recovery tank, the pressure cap on the expansion tank should never be opened after the engine has warmed up, because of the danger of severe burns caused by steam or scalding coolant.

Coolant in the left side of the radiator circulates through the lower radiator hose to the water pump, where it is forced through coolant passages in the cylinder block. The coolant then travels up into the cylinder head, circulates around the combustion chambers and valve seats, travels out of the cylinder head past the open thermostat into the upper radiator hose and back into the radiator.

When the engine is cold, the thermostat restricts the circulation of coolant to the engine. When the minimum operating temperature is reached, the thermostat begins to open, allowing coolant to return to the radiator.

TRANSAXLE COOLING SYSTEMS

Vehicles with an automatic transaxle are equipped with a transaxle cooler, located inside the radiator, which cools the transaxle fluid. The transaxle is connected to the cooler by a pair of hoses: one delivers hot transaxle fluid to the radiator and the other brings the cooled fluid back to the transaxle. Some automatics are also equipped with an auxiliary external cooler, located in front of the air conditioning condenser and the radiator.

For more information on transaxle oil coolers, refer to Chapter 7.

ENGINE OIL COOLING SYSTEM

Besides the engine and transaxle cooling systems described above, engine heat is also dissipated through an external oil cooler that's integrated into the lubrication system. The oil cooler helps keep engine and oil temperatures within design limits under extreme load conditions.

The oil cooling system on these models consists of a cylindrical housing (oil cooler) mounted inline between the oil filter and the engine block, a heat exchanger inside the oil cooler and a pair of coolant hoses that deliver coolant from the radiator to the oil cooler housing.

HEATING SYSTEM

The heating system consists of the heater controls, the heater core, the heater blower assembly (which houses the blower motor and the blower motor resistor), and the hoses connecting the heater core to the engine cooling system. Hot engine coolant is circulated through the heater core. When the heater mode is activated, a flap door opens to expose the heater box to the passenger compartment. A fan switch on the heater controls activates the blower motor, which forces air through the core, heating the air.

AIR CONDITIONING SYSTEM

The air conditioning system consists of the condenser, which is mounted in front of the radiator, the evaporator case assembly under the dash, a compressor mounted on the engine, and the plumbing connecting all of the above components.

A blower fan forces the warmer air of the passenger compartment through the evaporator core (sort of a radiator-in-reverse), transferring the heat from the air to the refrigerant. The liquid refrigerant boils off into low pressure vapor, taking the heat with it when it leaves the evaporator.

2   Antifreeze - general information

▸ **Refer to illustration 2.5**

✳✳ WARNING:

Do not allow antifreeze to come in contact with your skin or painted surfaces of the vehicle. Rinse off spills immediately with plenty of water. Antifreeze is highly toxic if ingested. Never leave antifreeze lying around in an open container or in puddles on the floor; children and pets are attracted by its sweet smell and may drink it. Check with local authorities about disposing of used antifreeze. Many communities have collection centers which will see that antifreeze is disposed of safely. Never dump used antifreeze on the ground or pour it into drains.

✳✳ CAUTION:

Do not mix coolants of different colors. Doing so might damage the cooling system and/or the engine. The manufacturer specifies either a green colored coolant or a yellow colored coolant to be used in these systems. Read the warning label in the engine compartment for additional information.

➡**Note: Non-toxic antifreeze is now manufactured and available at local auto parts stores, but even this type must be disposed of properly.**

The cooling system should be filled with a water/ethylene glycol based antifreeze solution, which will prevent freezing down to at

2.5 Use a hydrometer (available at auto parts stores) to test the condition of your coolant

least -20-degrees F (even lower in cold climates). It also provides protection against corrosion and increases the coolant boiling point. The engines in these vehicles have aluminum heads. Depending on the engine and model year, the specified coolant varies (see the Chapter 1 Specifications). The manufacturer recommends that the correct type of coolant be used and strongly urges that coolant types not be mixed.

Drain, flush and refill the cooling system at least every other year (see Chapter 1). The use of antifreeze solutions for periods of longer than two years is likely to cause damage and encourage the formation of rust and scale in the system.

Before adding antifreeze to the system, inspect all hose connections. Antifreeze can leak through very minute openings.

The exact mixture of antifreeze to water which you should use depends on the relative weather conditions. The mixture should contain at least 50-percent antifreeze, but should never contain more than 70-percent anti-freeze. Consult the mixture ratio chart on the container before adding coolant.

Hydrometers are available at most auto parts stores to test the coolant (see illustration). Use antifreeze that meets Ford specifications for engines with aluminum heads.

✻✻ WARNING:

Do not remove the coolant tank cap, drain the coolant or perform any service procedures on the cooling system until the engine has cooled completely.

3 Thermostat - check and replacement

CHECK

1   Before assuming the thermostat is to blame for a cooling system problem, check the coolant level, drivebelt tension (see Chapter 1) and temperature gauge operation.

2   If the engine seems to be taking a long time to warm up, based on heater output or temperature gauge operation, the thermostat is probably stuck open. Replace the thermostat with a new one.

3   If the engine runs hot, use your hand to check the temperature of the lower radiator hose. If the hose isn't hot, but the engine is, the thermostat is probably stuck closed, preventing the coolant inside the engine from escaping to the radiator. Replace the thermostat.

✻✻ CAUTION:

Don't drive the vehicle without a thermostat. The computer may stay in open loop and emissions and fuel economy will suffer.

4   If the lower radiator hose is hot, it means that the coolant is flowing and the thermostat is open. Consult the *Troubleshooting* Section at the front of this manual for cooling system diagnosis.

REPLACEMENT

♦ **Refer to illustrations 3.8a and 3.8b**

✻✻ WARNING:

Wait until the engine is completely cool before performing this procedure.

➡**Note: The thermostat and thermostat housing on 2.3L engine models are replaced as an assembly.**

5   Disconnect the cable from the negative battery terminal (see Chapter 5).

6   Drain the cooling system (see Chapter 1). If the coolant is relatively new and still in good condition, save it and reuse it.

7   Follow the lower radiator hose to the engine to locate the thermostat housing.

8   Loosen the hose clamp, then detach the hose from the fitting (see illustrations). If it's stuck, grasp it near the end with a pair of adjustable pliers and twist it to break the seal, then pull it off. If the hose is old or if it has deteriorated, cut it off and install a new one.

3.8a Disconnect the radiator hose from the thermostat housing cover - four-cylinder engine shown

9   If the outer surface of the thermostat housing cover, which mates with the hose, is already corroded, pitted, or otherwise deteriorated, it might be damaged even more by hose removal. If it is, replace the thermostat housing cover.

Four-cylinder models

▶ **Refer to illustrations 3.10 and 3.11**

10   Remove the fasteners and detach the thermostat cover (see illustration). If the cover is stuck, tap it with a soft-face hammer to jar it loose. Be prepared for some coolant to spill as the gasket seal is broken.

11   Note how it's installed, which end is facing up, or out and then remove the thermostat (see illustration).

V6 models

▶ **Refer to illustrations 3.12, 3.13a and 3.13b**

12   Remove the fasteners and detach the thermostat housing cover (see illustration). If the cover is stuck, tap it with a soft-face hammer to jar it loose. Be prepared for some coolant to spill as the gasket seal is broken.

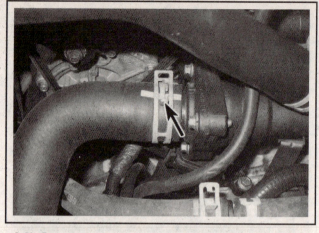

3.8b Remove the spring clamp from the radiator hose at the thermostat housing cover - V6 engine shown

13   Note how it's installed, which end is facing up, or out, and then remove the thermostat (see illustrations).

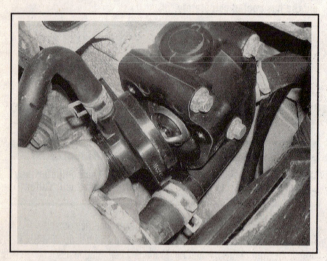

3.10 Remove the thermostat housing cover to access the thermostat

3.11 Remove the thermostat from the housing, but note that the jiggle valve on the thermostat is located in the 12 o'clock position

3.12 Remove the three mounting bolts to separate the thermostat housing cover from the housing

3.13a Lift off the thermostat housing cover . . .

3.13b . . . and remove the thermostat - V6 engine shown

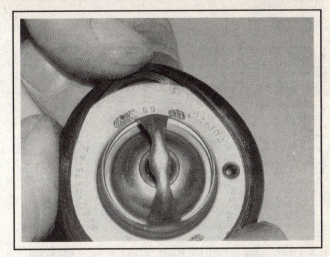

3.15 Install a new rubber seal around the perimeter of the thermostat

All models

▶ Refer to illustration 3.15

14 Remove all traces of old gasket material and sealant from the housing and cover with a gasket scraper.

15 Install a new rubber gasket on the thermostat (see illustration) and then install the thermostat in the housing, spring-end first. Make sure that you install the thermostat with the "jiggle valve" at 12 o'clock (see illustration 3.11). If the thermostat housing cover uses a paper gasket, dip the new gasket in water and position it on the thermostat housing with the holes in the gasket aligned with the bolt holes in the housing.

16 Install the thermostat housing cover and bolts and then tighten the bolts to the torque listed in this Chapter's Specifications.

17 Reattach the radiator hose to the thermostat housing cover. Make sure that the hose clamp is still tight. If it isn't, replace it.

18 Refill the cooling system (see Chapter 1).

19 Reconnect the battery. After you're done, the Powertrain Control Module (PCM) must relearn its idle and fuel trim strategy for optimum driveability and performance (see Chapter 5, Section 1).

20 Start the engine and allow it to reach normal operating temperature, then check for leaks and proper thermostat operation (as described in Steps 2 through 4).

4 Engine cooling fans - check and replacement

❊❊ WARNING:

To avoid possible injury or damage, DO NOT operate the engine with a damaged fan. Do not attempt to repair fan blades - replace a damaged fan with a new one.

➡Note 1: Always be sure to check for blown fuses before attempting to diagnose an electrical circuit problem.

➡Note 2: Four-cylinder models are equipped with a high, a medium and a low speed cooling fan relay. V6 models are equipped with a low speed relay, a medium speed relay and two high speed fan relays that are controlled by the PCM.

CHECK

▶ Refer to illustrations 4.1, 4.3 and 4.5

1 If the engine is overheating and the cooling fan is not coming on when the engine temperature rises to an excessive level, unplug the fan motor electrical connector(s) (see illustration) and connect the motor directly to the battery with fused jumper wires. If the fan motor doesn't come on, replace the motor.

2 If the radiator fan motor is okay, but it isn't coming on when the engine gets hot, the fan relay might be defective. A relay is used to

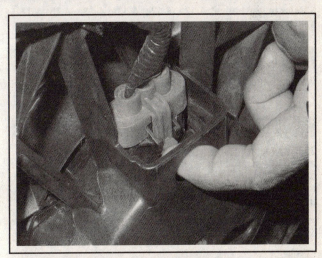

4.1 Lift up on the tab lock to release the cooling fan connector

control a circuit by turning it on and off in response to a control decision by the Powertrain Control Module (PCM). These control circuits are fairly complex, and checking them should be left to a qualified automotive technician. Sometimes, the control system can be fixed by simply identifying and replacing a bad relay.

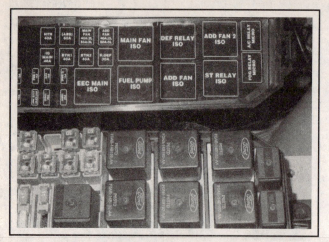

4.3 Locate the cooling fan relays in the fuse/relay box in the engine compartment

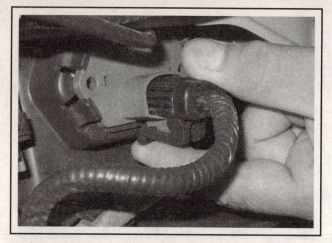

4.5 The fan motor resistor is located above the left cooling fan

3   Locate the fan relays in the engine compartment fuse/relay box (see illustration).

4   Test the relay (see Chapter 12).

5   If the relay is okay, check all wiring and connections to the fan motor. Refer to the wiring diagrams at the end of Chapter 12. If no obvious problems are found, the problem could be the Engine Coolant Temperature (ECT) sensor or the Powertrain Control Module (PCM). Have the cooling fan system and circuit diagnosed by a dealer service department or repair shop with the proper diagnostic equipment.

➡**Note: These models are equipped with a cooling fan motor resistor. Have the resistor checked if the fan motor does not respond to the speed variations signaled by the PCM (see illustration).**

REPLACEMENT

♦ **Refer to illustrations 4.12a, 4.12b, 4.13a, 4.13b, 4.15, 4.17 and 4.18**

❊❊ **WARNING 1:**

Wait until the engine is completely cool before performing this procedure.

❊❊ **WARNING 2:**

2005 and later models have a Supplemental Restraint System, or Airbag sensor, mounted in the center of the radiator support bracket. It will be necessary to disarm the system prior to performing any work around the radiator, fans or other components in this area (see Chapter 12)

6   Disconnect the cable from the negative battery terminal (see Chapter 5).

7   Disconnect the fan motor electrical connector(s) (see illustration 4.1).

8   Raise the vehicle and secure it on jackstands.

9   Drain the cooling system (see Chapter 1). If the coolant is relatively new and still in good condition, save it and reuse it.

10 Remove the hood latch (see Chapter 11).

11 Remove the upper radiator hose (see illustration 6.7). Loosen the hose clamp by squeezing the ends together. Hose clamp pliers work

4.12a Remove the bolts from the center support (upper bolt shown) . . .

best, but regular pliers will work also. If the radiator hose is stuck, grasp it near the end with a pair of adjustable pliers and twist it to break the seal, then pull it off. If the hose is old or if it has deteriorated, cut it off and install a new one.

12 Remove the center support bolts (see illustrations) and lift the center support from the engine compartment.

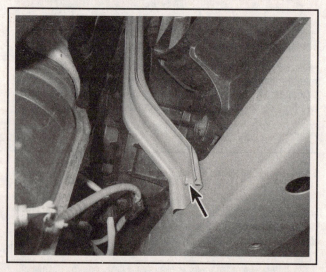

4.12b . . . and the lower section of the center support

4.13a Remove the right side radiator support bracket bolts . . .

4.13b . . . and the left side radiator support bracket bolts

13 Remove the left and right upper radiator support brackets (see illustrations).

14 Tilt the radiator forward to make additional clearance for fan removal.

15 Detach the wire harness from the fan shroud, remove the upper and lower fan shroud mounting bolts (see illustration) and then carefully lift the fan motor and shroud out of the engine compartment as a single assembly.

16 Remove the fan mounting screws.

17 To detach the fan blade from the motor, remove the nut or retaining clip from the motor shaft (see illustration). Remove the fan blade from the motor.

18 To detach the motor from the shroud, remove the retaining bolts (see illustration). Remove the motor from the shroud.

19 Installation is the reverse of removal.

➡Note: When reinstalling the fan assembly, make sure the rubber air shields around the shroud are still in place - without them, the cooling system may not work efficiently.

20 Reconnect the battery and refill the cooling system (see Chapter 1). After you're done, the Powertrain Control Module (PCM) must relearn its idle and fuel trim strategy for optimum driveability and per-

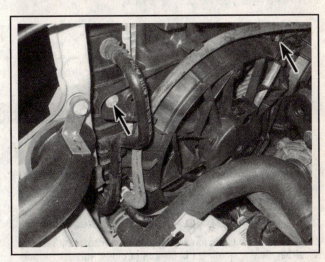

4.15 Remove the cooling fan shroud bolts - lower bolt not visible

formance (see Chapter 5, Section 1).

21 Start the engine and allow it to reach normal operating temperature, then check for leaks and proper operation.

4.17 Use a flat-bladed screwdriver and drive the locking washer off the fan motor shaft

4.18 Remove the fan motor mounting bolts

5 Coolant expansion tank - removal and installation

♦ Refer to illustration 5.3

※ WARNING:

Wait until the engine is completely cool before beginning this procedure.

1   Drain the cooling system (see Chapter 1).
2   Disconnect the expansion tank hose.
3   Remove the expansion tank mounting nuts (see illustration). Lift the tank out of the engine compartment.
4   Clean out the tank with soapy water and a brush to remove any deposits inside. Inspect the reservoir carefully for cracks. If you find a crack, replace the reservoir.
5   Installation is the reverse of removal.

5.3 Location of the expansion tank mounting nuts

6 Radiator - removal and installation

※ WARNING 1:

Wait until the engine is completely cool before beginning this procedure.

※ WARNING 2:

2005 and later models have a Supplemental Restraint System, or airbag sensor, mounted in the center of the radiator support bracket. It will be necessary to disarm the system prior to performing any work around the radiator, fans or other components in this area (see Chapter 12)

REMOVAL

♦ Refer to illustration 6.6, 6.7 and 6.8

1   Disconnect the cable from the negative battery terminal (see Chapter 5).
2   Raise the vehicle and place it securely on jackstands. Remove the lower splash shields.
3   Drain the cooling system (see Chapter 1). If the coolant is relatively new and in good condition, save it and reuse it.
4   Unbolt the cooling fan shrouds from the radiator (see Section 4).
5   Remove the hood latch and the center support (see illustrations 4.12a and 4.12b).
6   Disconnect the lower radiator hose and expansion tank hose from the left side tank of the radiator (see illustration). If the vehicle is

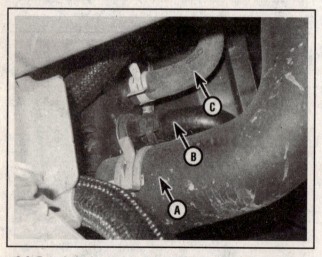

6.6 Detach the hoses from the lower left side of the radiator

A   Lower radiator hose
B   Transaxle fluid cooler hose
C   Expansion tank hose

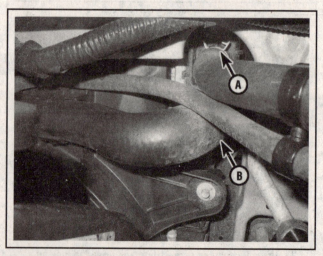

6.7 Detach the expansion tank hose (A) and the upper radiator hose (B) from the upper right side of the radiator

equipped with an automatic transaxle, also detach the cooler hose from its fitting on the side tank.

7   Lower the vehicle and disconnect the expansion tank hose and upper radiator hose from the right side of the radiator (see illustration). Also, if the vehicle is equipped with an automatic transaxle, disconnect the other fluid cooler hose from the upper left side of the radiator.

8   Remove the radiator support brackets from the radiator support beam and the radiator (see illustration).

9   Carefully lift out the radiator. Don't spill coolant on the vehicle or scratch the paint. Make sure the rubber radiator insulators that fit on the bottom of the radiator and into the sockets in the body remain in place in the body for proper reinstallation of the radiator.

10 Remove bugs and dirt from the radiator with compressed air and a soft brush. Don't bend the cooling fins. Inspect the radiator for leaks and damage. If it needs repair, have a radiator shop or a dealer service department do the work.

INSTALLATION

11 Inspect the rubber insulators in the lower crossmember for cracks and deterioration. Make sure that they're free of dirt and gravel. When installing the radiator, make sure that it's correctly seated on the insulators before fastening the top brackets.

12 Installation is otherwise the reverse of the removal procedure. After installation, fill the cooling system with the correct mixture of antifreeze and water (see Chapter 1).

13 Reconnect the battery. After you're done, the Powertrain Control

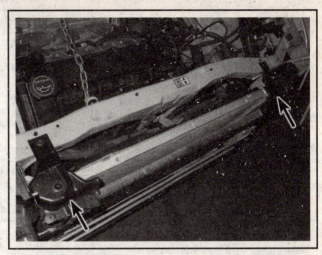

6.8 Remove the radiator support brackets and lift out the radiator

Module (PCM) must relearn its idle and fuel trim strategy for optimum driveability and performance (see Chapter 5, Section 1).

14 Start the engine and check for leaks. Allow the engine to reach normal operating temperature, indicated by the upper radiator hose becoming hot. Recheck the coolant level and add more if required.

15 If you're working on an automatic transaxle equipped vehicle, check and add fluid as needed.

7   Water pump - check

1   A failure in the water pump can cause serious engine damage due to overheating.

2   If a failure occurs in the pump seal, coolant will leak from the front cover (four-cylinder models) or the water pump housing (V6 models).

➡ **Note: The water pump on four-cylinder engines is mounted in the front cover and on V6 engines in a water pump housing near the thermostat housing.**

3   Water pumps are equipped with weep or vent holes. It is possible to check the water pump weep hole using a flashlight. If a failure occurs in the pump seal, coolant will leak from the hole. Use the flashlight to find the vent hole on the water pump and check for leaks.

➡ **Note: Some slight black staining around the weep hole is normal. If the stain is heavy brown or actual coolant is evident, replace the pump.**

4   If the water pump shaft bearings fail, there may be a howling sound near the water pump while it's running. With the engine off, shaft wear can be felt if the water pump pulley is rocked up-and-down. Don't mistake drivebelt slippage, which causes a squealing sound, for water pump bearing failure.

5   A quick water pump performance check is to put the heater on. If the pump is failing, it won't be able to efficiently circulate hot water all the way to the heater core as it should.

8   Water pump - replacement

✳✳ WARNING:

Wait until the engine is completely cool before beginning this procedure.

REMOVAL

1   Disconnect the cable from the negative battery terminal (see Chapter 5).

2   Drain the cooling system (see Chapter 1).

3   Remove the drivebelt on four-cylinder models or the water pump drivebelt on V6 models (see Chapter 1).

Four-cylinder models

▶ **Refer to illustration 8.6, 8.7 and 8.8**

4   Loosen the right front wheel lug nuts. Raise the vehicle and secure it on jackstands.

5   Remove the right front wheel and the fender splash shield.

6   Remove the water pump pulley (see illustration).

7   Remove the bolts attaching the water pump to the engine block and remove the pump from the engine (see illustration). If the water pump is stuck, gently tap it with a soft-faced hammer to break the seal.

8   Clean the bolt threads and the threaded holes in the engine (see illustration) and remove all corrosion and sealant. Remove all traces of old gasket material from the sealing surfaces.

8.6 Remove the bolts and separate the water pump pulley from the pump

8.7 Remove the water pump bolts

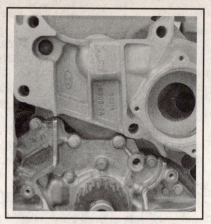

8.8 Clean the water pump bolt threads, the threaded holes in the housing and the pump mating surface of the housing

V6 models

▶ Refer to illustrations 8.10, 8.11a, 8.11b and 8.12

9   Remove the air filter housing (see Chapter 4).

10 Remove the water pump drivebelt tensioner (see illustration). If you're working on a 2006 or later model, remove the water pump pulley.

➡**Note: This requires a special puller that bolts to the hub of the pulley.**

11 Remove the water pump mounting bolts (see illustrations).

12 Clean all the gasket and O-ring surfaces on the pump (see illustration) and the housing.

8.10 Remove the water pump drivebelt tensioner bolt

ALL MODELS

13 Compare the new pump to the old one to make sure that they're identical.

14 Apply a thin film of RTV sealant to hold the new gasket in place during installation.

❋❋ **CAUTION:**

Make sure that the gasket is correctly positioned on the water pump and the mating surfaces are clean and free of old gasket material. Carefully mate the pump to the water pump housing.

15 Install the water pump bolts and tighten them to the torque listed in this Chapter's Specifications.

16 The remainder of installation is the reverse of removal. Refill the cooling system (see Chapter 1) when you're done.

17 Reconnect the battery. After you're done, the Powertrain Control Module (PCM) must relearn its idle and fuel trim strategy for optimum driveability and performance (see Chapter 5, Section 1).

18 Operate the engine to check for leaks.

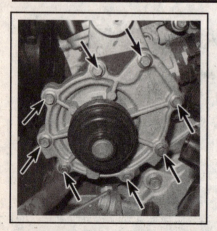

8.11a Remove the water pump bolts

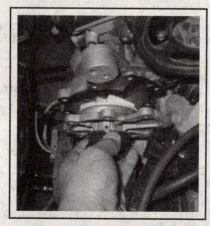

8.11b Separate the water pump from the housing

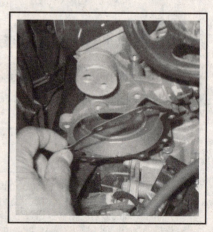

8.12 Remove the water pump gasket

9 Coolant temperature sending unit - check and replacement

❄❄ WARNING:

Wait until the engine is completely cool before beginning this procedure.

➡Note: Four-cylinder models are equipped with a cylinder head temperature sensor instead of a coolant temperature sensor (V6 models). Refer to Chapter 6 for additional information.

CHECK

1   The coolant temperature indicator system consists of a warning light or a temperature gauge on the dash and a coolant temperature sending unit mounted on the engine. On the models covered by this manual, the Cylinder Head Temperature (CHT) sensor (four cylinder models) or Engine Coolant Temperature (ECT) sensor (V6 models), which is an information sensor for the Powertrain Control Module (PCM), also functions as the coolant temperature sending unit.

2   If an overheating indication occurs, check the coolant level in the system and then make sure all connectors in the wiring harness between the sending unit and the indicator light or gauge are tight.

3   When the ignition switch is turned to START and the starter motor is turning, the indicator light (if equipped) should come on. This doesn't mean the engine is overheated; it just means that the bulb is good.

4   If the light doesn't come on when the ignition key is turned to START, the bulb might be burned out, the ignition switch might be faulty or the circuit might be open.

5   As soon as the engine starts, the indicator light should go out and remain off, unless the engine overheats. If the light doesn't go out, the wire between the sending unit and the light could be grounded, the sending unit might be defective, or the ignition switch might be faulty (see Chapter 12). Check the coolant to make sure it's correctly mixed; plain water, with no antifreeze, or coolant that's mainly water, might have too low a boiling point to activate the sending unit (see Chapter 1).

REPLACEMENT

6   See Chapter 6.

10 Blower motor resistor and blower motor - replacement

❄❄ WARNING:

The models covered by this manual are equipped with Supplemental Restraint systems (SRS), more commonly known as airbags. Always disable the airbag system before working in the vicinity of any airbag system component to avoid the possibility of accidental deployment of the airbag, which could cause personal injury (see Chapter 12).

BLOWER MOTOR RESISTOR

▶ Refer to illustration 10.2

1   Remove the lower trim panel from below the glovebox (see Chapter 11).

2   Disconnect the electrical connector from the blower motor resistor (see illustration).

3   Remove the blower motor resistor mounting screws and remove the resistor from the evaporator housing.

4   Installation is the reverse of removal.

BLOWER MOTOR

▶ Refer to illustrations 10.6 and 10.7

5   Remove the lower trim panel from below the glovebox (see Chapter 11).

6   Disconnect the blower motor electrical connector (see illustration).

7   Remove the blower motor mounting screws (see illustration) and remove the blower motor.

8   Installation is the reverse of removal.

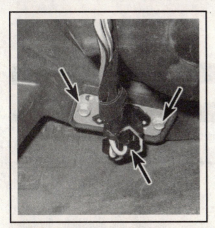

10.2 Unplug the blower motor resistor connector, then remove the mounting screws

10.6 Location of the blower motor electrical connector

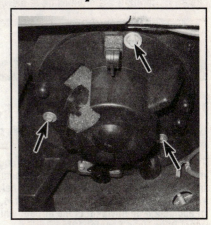

10.7 Location of the blower motor mounting screws

11   Heater/air conditioner control assembly - removal and installation

▶ **Refer to illustrations 11.3, 11.4a and 11.4b**

⁑ WARNING:

The models covered by this manual are equipped with Supplemental Restraint systems (SRS), more commonly known as airbags. Always disable the airbag system before working in the vicinity of any airbag system component to avoid the possibility of accidental deployment of the airbag, which could cause personal injury (see Chapter 12).

1   Disconnect the cable from the negative battery terminal (see Chapter 5).

2   Remove the dashboard center trim panel (see Chapter 11).

3   Remove the heater/air conditioner control assembly retaining screws (see illustration).

4   Disconnect the temperature blend door control cables, the blower motor switch and temperature control switch connectors (see illustrations).

5   Installation is the reverse of removal.

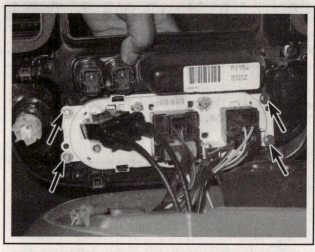

11.3 Location of the heater/air conditioner control assembly mounting screws

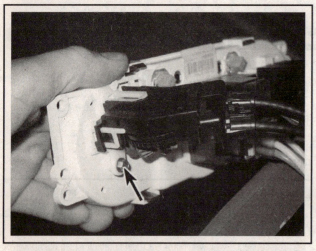

11.4a Remove the temperature blend door control cable mounting screw and separate the cable assembly from the control assembly

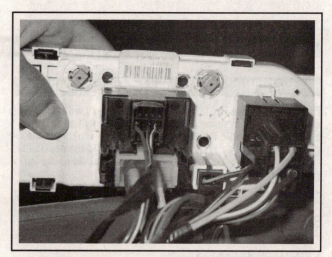

11.4b Release the tabs and disconnect the blower switch and temperature control switch connectors

12   Heater core - replacement

▶ **Refer to illustrations 12.2, 12.4, 12.5, 12.6 and 12.7**

⁑ WARNING 1:

The models covered by this manual are equipped with Supplemental Restraint systems (SRS), more commonly known as airbags. Always disarm the airbag system before working in the vicinity of any airbag system component to avoid the possibility of accidental deployment of the airbag, which could cause personal injury (see Chapter 12).

⁑ WARNING 2:

Wait until the engine is completely cool before beginning this procedure.

1   Disconnect the cable from the negative battery terminal (see Chapter 5).

2   Drain the cooling system (see Chapter 1), then disconnect the heater hoses from the heater core inlet and outlet pipes at the firewall (see illustration).

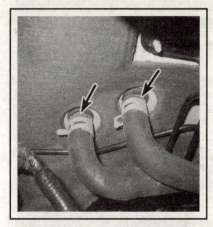

12.2 To disconnect the heater hoses from the heater core pipes, squeeze the tabs on the spring clamps together with a pair of pliers and slide them up the hoses

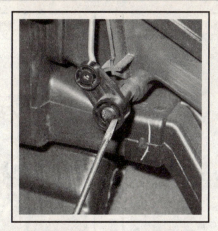

12.4 Carefully pry the lever off the blend door shaft

12.5 Remove the actuating rod from the lever

3   Remove the instrument panel (see Chapter 11).

4   Remove the lever from the heater blend door shaft (see illustration).

5   Remove the actuating rod from the lever (see illustration).

6   Remove the heater core cover screws (see illustration).

7   Pull the heater core out of the housing (see illustration).

8   Installation is the reverse of removal. Don't forget to reconnect the heater core inlet and outlet hoses at the firewall.

9   Refill the cooling system (see Chapter 1) when you're done.

12.6 Remove the screws and detach the cover from the HVAC housing

12.7 Slide the heater core from the housing

13   Air conditioning and heating system - check and maintenance

▶ Refer to illustration 13.1

✳✳ WARNING:

The air conditioning system is under high pressure. Do not loosen any hose fittings or remove any components until after the system has been discharged by a dealer service department or service station. Always wear eye protection when disconnecting air conditioning system fittings.

1   The following maintenance checks should be performed on a regular basis to ensure the air conditioner continues to operate at peak efficiency.

a) *Check the compressor drivebelt. If it's worn or deteriorated, replace it (see Chapter 1).*

b) *Check the drivebelt tension and, if necessary, adjust it (see Chapter 1).*

c) *Check the system hoses. Look for cracks, bubbles, hard spots and deterioration. Inspect the hoses and all fittings for oil bubbles and seepage. If there's any evidence of wear, damage or leaks, replace the hose(s).*

d) *Inspect the condenser fins for leaves, bugs and other debris. Use a "fin comb" or compressed air to clean the condenser.*

e) *Make sure the system has the correct refrigerant charge.*

f) *Check the evaporator housing drain tube (see illustration) for blockage.*

13.1 Look for the evaporator drain hose on the firewall; make sure it isn't plugged

13.7 If the air conditioning system is properly charged, the refrigerant line from the condenser to the evaporator should feel warm right before the orifice tube (A) and cold near the evaporator (B)

2   It's a good idea to operate the system for about 10 minutes at least once a month, particularly during the winter. Long term non-use can cause hardening, and subsequent failure, of the seals.

3   Because of the complexity of the air conditioning system and the special equipment necessary to service it, in-depth troubleshooting and repairs are not included in this manual. However, simple checks and component replacement procedures are provided in this Chapter.

4   The most common cause of poor cooling is simply a low system refrigerant charge. If a noticeable drop in cool air output occurs, the following quick check will help you determine if the refrigerant level is low.

CHECKING THE REFRIGERANT CHARGE

▸ **Refer to illustration 13.7**

5   Warm the engine up to normal operating temperature.

6   Place the air conditioning temperature selector at the coldest setting and the blower at the highest setting. Open the vehicle doors (to make sure the air conditioning system doesn't cycle off as soon as it cools the passenger compartment).

7   With the compressor engaged - the clutch will make an audible click and the center of the clutch will rotate - feel the refrigerant line in front of the orifice tube and also right before the evaporator (see illustration). The line should feel warm at the orifice tube and cold near the evaporator. If so, the system is properly charged.

8   Place a thermometer in the dashboard vent nearest the evaporator and operate the system until the indicated temperature is around 40 to 45 degrees F. If the ambient (outside) air temperature is very high, say 110 degrees F, the duct air temperature may be as high as 60 degrees F, but generally the air conditioning is 30-50 degrees F cooler than the ambient air.

➡**Note: Humidity of the ambient air also affects the cooling capacity of the system. Higher ambient humidity lowers the effectiveness of the air conditioning system.**

ADDING REFRIGERANT

▸ **Refer to illustrations 13.12 and 13.15**

9   Buy an automotive charging kit at an auto parts store. A charging kit includes a 14-ounce can of refrigerant, a tap valve and a short section of hose that can be attached between the tap valve and the system

low side service valve. Because one can of refrigerant may not be sufficient to bring the system charge up to the proper level, it's a good idea to buy an additional can. Make sure that one of the cans contains red refrigerant dye. If the system is leaking, the red dye will leak out with the refrigerant and help you pinpoint the location of the leak.

❊❊ CAUTION:

There are two types of refrigerant used in automotive systems; R-12 - which has been widely used on earlier models and the more environmentally-friendly R-134a used in all models covered by this manual. These two refrigerants (and their appropriate refrigerant oils) are not compatible and must never be mixed or components will be damaged. Use only R-134a refrigerant in the models covered by this manual.

10 Hook up the charging kit by following the manufacturer's instructions.

❊❊ WARNING:

DO NOT hook the charging kit hose to the system high side! The fittings on the charging kit are designed to fit only on the low side of the system.

11 Back off the valve handle on the charging kit and screw the kit onto the refrigerant can, making sure first that the O-ring or rubber seal inside the threaded portion of the kit is in place.

❊❊ WARNING:

Wear protective eyewear when dealing with pressurized refrigerant cans.

12 Remove the dust cap from the low-side charging connection and attach the quick-connect fitting on the kit hose (see illustration).

13 Warm up the engine and turn on the air conditioner. Keep the charging kit hose away from the fan and other moving parts.

➡**Note: The charging process requires the compressor to be running. Your compressor may cycle off if the pressure is low due to a low charge. If the clutch cycles off, you can pull the low-pres-**

13.12 Cans of R-134A refrigerant (available at auto parts stores) can be added to the low side of the air conditioning system with a simple recharging kit (V6 engine shown)

13.15 Insert a thermometer in the center vent, turn on the air conditioning system and wait for it to cool down; depending on the humidity, the output air should be 30 to 40 degrees cooler than the ambient air temperature

13.23 Remove the glove box (see Chapter 11) and insert the nozzle of the disinfectant can into the evaporator housing by shoving it through the air recirculation door

sure cycling switch plug and attach a jumper wire to the terminals in the connector. **This will keep the compressor ON.**

14 Turn the valve handle on the kit until the stem pierces the can, then back the handle out to release the refrigerant. You should be able to hear the rush of gas. Allow stabilization time between each addition.

15 If you have an accurate thermometer, place it in the center air conditioning vent (see illustration) and then note the temperature of the air coming out of the vent. A fully-charged system which is working correctly should cool down to about 40 degrees F. Generally, an air conditioning system will put out air that is 30 to 40 degrees F cooler than the ambient air. For example, if the ambient (outside) air temperature is very high (over 100 degrees F), the temperature of air coming out of the registers should be 60 to 70 degrees F.

16 When the can is empty, turn the valve handle to the closed position and release the connection from the low-side port. Replace the dust cap.

❊❊ CAUTION:

Never add more than one can of refrigerant to the system. If more refrigerant than that is required, the system should be evacuated and leak tested.

17 Remove the charging kit from the can and store the kit for future use with the piercing valve in the UP position, to prevent inadvertently piercing the can on the next use.

HEATING SYSTEMS

18 If the carpet under the heater core is damp, or if antifreeze vapor or steam is coming through the vents, the heater core is leaking. Remove it (see Section 12) and install a new unit (most radiator shops will not repair a leaking heater core).

19 If the air coming out of the heater vents isn't hot, the problem could stem from any of the following causes:

a) *The thermostat is stuck open, preventing the engine coolant from warming up enough to carry heat to the heater core. Replace the thermostat (see Section 3).*

b) *There is a blockage in the system, preventing the flow of coolant through the heater core. Feel both heater hoses at the firewall.*

They should be hot. If one of them is cold, there is an obstruction in one of the hoses or in the heater core, or the heater control valve is shut. Detach the hoses and back flush the heater core with a water hose. If the heater core is clear but circulation is impeded, remove the two hoses and flush them out with a water hose.

c) *If flushing fails to remove the blockage from the heater core, the core must be replaced (see Section 12).*

ELIMINATING AIR CONDITIONING ODORS

◆ **Refer to illustration 13.23**

20 Unpleasant odors that often develop in air conditioning systems are caused by the growth of a fungus, usually on the surface of the evaporator core. The warm, humid environment there is a perfect breeding ground for mildew to develop.

21 The evaporator core on most vehicles is difficult to access, and factory dealerships have a lengthy, expensive process for eliminating the fungus by opening up the evaporator case and using a powerful disinfectant and rinse on the core until the fungus is gone. You can service your own system at home, but it takes something much stronger than basic household germ-killers or deodorizers.

22 Aerosol disinfectants for automotive air conditioning systems are available in most auto parts stores, but remember when shopping for them that the most effective treatments are also the most expensive. The basic procedure for using these sprays is to start by running the system in the RECIRC mode for ten minutes with the blower on its highest speed. Use the highest heat mode to dry out the system and keep the compressor from engaging by disconnecting the wiring connector at the compressor (see Section 14).

23 Make sure that the disinfectant can comes with a long spray hose. Point the nozzle through the air recirculation door so that it protrudes inside the evaporator housing (see illustration), and then spray according to the manufacturer's recommendations. Try to cover the whole surface of the evaporator core, by aiming the spray up, down and sideways. Follow the manufacturer's recommendations for the length of spray and waiting time between applications.

24 Once the evaporator has been cleaned, the best way to prevent the mildew from coming back again is to make sure your evaporator housing drain tube is clear (see illustration 13.1).

14 Air conditioning compressor - removal and installation

※ **WARNING:**

The air conditioning system is under high pressure. DO NOT loosen any fittings or remove any components until after the system has been discharged. Air conditioning refrigerant must be properly discharged into an EPA-approved container at a dealer service department or an automotive air conditioning repair facility. Always wear eye protection when disconnecting air conditioning system fittings.

➡Note: If you are replacing the compressor, you must also replace the accumulator (see Section 16) and the orifice tube (see Section 18).

REMOVAL

▶ **Refer to illustration 14.5**

1   Have the air conditioning system discharged by a dealer service department or by an automotive air conditioning shop before proceeding (see **Warning** above).
2   Loosen the right front wheel lug nuts. Raise the vehicle and secure it on jackstands. Remove the right front wheel.
3   Remove the right front fender splash shield.
4   Remove the drivebelt (see Chapter 1).
5   Disconnect the electrical connector from the compressor clutch field coil (see illustration).

Four-cylinder models

6   Disconnect the compressor inlet and outlet line manifold from the compressor. Remove and discard the old O-rings.
7   Remove the compressor mounting bolts and remove the compressor.

V6 models

▶ **Refer to illustrations 14.9 and 14.10**

8   Disconnect the engine block heater electrical connector, if equipped.

14.5 Disconnect the connector from the compressor clutch field coil

9   Disconnect the compressor inlet and outlet line manifold from the compressor (see illustration). Remove and discard the old O-rings.
10 Remove the compressor mounting bolts (see illustration) and remove the compressor.

INSTALLATION

11 If a new compressor is being installed, follow the directions with the compressor regarding the draining of excess oil prior to installation.
12 The clutch may have to be transferred from the original to the new compressor.
13 Before reconnecting the inlet and outlet lines to the compressor, replace all manifold O-rings and lubricate them with refrigerant oil.
14 Installation is otherwise the reverse of removal.
15 Replace the orifice tube (see Section 18).
16 Have the system evacuated, recharged and leak tested by the shop that discharged it.

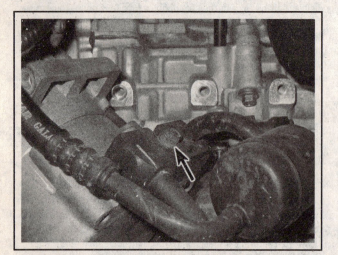

14.9 Remove the inlet and outlet line manifold bolt from the compressor and separate the lines from the compressor

14.10 Location of the air conditioning compressor bolts (V6 model shown)

15 Air conditioning accumulator - removal and installation

▶ Refer to illustration 15.3a, 15.3b, 15.4 and 15.5

❄❄ WARNING:

The air conditioning system is under high pressure. DO NOT loosen any fittings or remove any components until after the system has been discharged. Air conditioning refrigerant must be properly discharged into an EPA-approved container at a dealer service department or an automotive air conditioning repair facility. Always wear eye protection when disconnecting air conditioning system fittings.

1   Have the air conditioning system discharged by a dealer service department or by an automotive air conditioning shop before proceeding (see **Warning** above).
2   Disconnect the air conditioning pressure cycling switch electrical connector (see Section 17).
3   Disconnect the condenser line from the accumulator (see illustrations). Use special spring lock coupling tools to disconnect the air conditioning line. Cap the line to prevent contamination. Remove and discard the old O-ring.
4   Disconnect the line from the accumulator to the evaporator (see illustration). Cap the line to prevent contamination. Remove and discard the old O-ring.
5   Remove the accumulator mounting bracket nuts (see illustration)

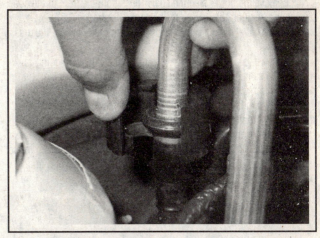

15.3a Install the air conditioning line spring lock tool with the lip of the tool towards the spring inside the coupling

and remove the accumulator.
6   Replace all old O-rings. Before installing the new O-rings, coat them with refrigerant oil.
7   Installation is otherwise the reverse of removal.
8   Take the vehicle to the shop that discharged it and have the system evacuated and recharged.

15.3b Lift up on the spring lock tool to release the coupling

15.4 Remove the protective cover from the evaporator line coupler, then use the spring lock tool to disconnect the line

15.5 Location of the accumulator mounting nuts

16 Air conditioning condenser - removal and installation

▶ Refer to illustration 16.3, 16.4 and 16.6

❄❄ WARNING:

The air conditioning system is under high pressure. DO NOT loosen any fittings or remove any components until after the system has been discharged. Air conditioning refrigerant must be pronerly discharged into an EPA-approved container at a dealer service department or an automotive air conditioning repair facility. Always wear eye protection when disconnecting air conditioning system fittings.

➡Note: The accumulator should be replaced if the condenser was damaged, causing the system to be open for some time (see Section 15).

1   Have the air conditioning system discharged by a dealer service department or an automotive air conditioning shop before proceeding (see **Warning** above).
2   Remove the front bumper cover (see Chapter 11).
3   Disconnect the refrigerant inlet and outlet lines from the condenser (see illustration). Cap the lines to prevent contamination.

4   Remove the power steering cooler lines from the front of the condenser and position them off to the side (see illustration 6.8).

5   Remove the left and right radiator support brackets (see illustration).

6   Remove the condenser (see illustration 6.8). If you're going to reinstall the same condenser, store it with the line fittings facing up to prevent oil from draining out.

7   If you're going to install a new condenser, pour one ounce of refrigerant oil of the correct type into it prior to installation.

8   Before reconnecting the refrigerant lines to the condenser, be sure to coat a pair of new O-rings with refrigerant oil, install them in the refrigerant line fittings and then tighten the condenser inlet and outlet nuts to the torque listed in this Chapter's Specifications.

9   Installation is otherwise the reverse of removal.

10   Have the system evacuated, recharged and leak tested by the shop that discharged it.

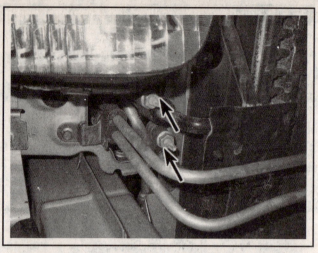

16.3 Remove the nuts and disconnect the inlet and outlet refrigerant lines from the condenser

16.4 Remove the bracket bolts and position the power steering fluid cooler off to the side

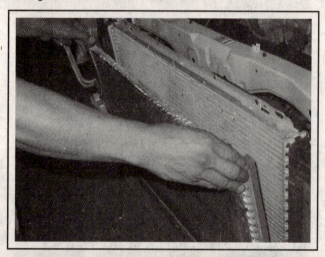

16.6 Lift the condenser away from the radiator, being careful not to damage the fins on the radiator

17   Air conditioning pressure cycling switch - replacement

▶ **Refer to illustration 17.1**

➡**Note:** The pressure cycling switch is located on top of the accumulator. The pressure cycling switch detects low refrigerant line pressure at 22 to 28 psi, switches the A/C system off, then back on again at 40 to 47 psi. If the pressure increases over 550 psi, the pressure cut-off switch, located in the high pressure line between the compressor and the accumulator, shuts the system off. A Schrader valve in the accumulator prevents refrigerant loss during pressure cycling switch replacement.

1   Unplug the electrical connector from the pressure cycling switch (see illustration).

2   Unscrew the pressure cycling switch from the accumulator.

3   Lubricate the switch O-ring with clean refrigerant oil of the correct type.

4   Screw the new switch onto the accumulator threads until hand tight, then tighten it securely.

5   Reconnect the electrical connector.

17.1 The air conditioning pressure cycling switch is mounted on top of the accumulator

18 Air conditioning orifice tube - removal and installation

18.2a Remove the protective cover from the air conditioning line coupling

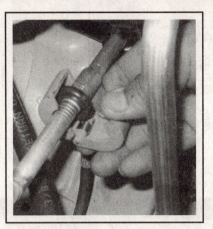

18.2b Install the special spring lock tool . . .

18.2c . . . and release the coupler by pressing the tool into the spring

▶ Refer to illustrations 18.2a, 18.2b, 18.2c and 18.3

※ WARNING:

The air conditioning system is under high pressure. DO NOT loosen any hose fittings or remove any components until the system has been discharged. Air conditioning refrigerant must be properly discharged into an EPA-approved recovery/recycling unit by a dealer service department or an automotive air conditioning repair facility. Always wear eye protection when disconnecting air conditioning system fittings.

➡Note: The orifice tube is located in the condenser to evaporator line. The orifice tube changes the high pressure liquid refrigerant into a low pressure liquid.

1 Have the air conditioning system discharged by a dealer service department or by an automotive air conditioning shop before proceeding (see **Warning** above).
2 Disconnect the refrigerant line from the condenser to the evaporator (see illustrations).
3 Using a pair of needle-nose pliers pull the orifice tube from the line (see illustration).
4 Installation is the reverse of removal. Be sure to remove and dis-

18.3 Remove the orifice tube using needle nose pliers

card the old O-rings.
5 Take the vehicle back to the shop that discharged it. Have the system evacuated, recharged and leak tested.

19 Oil cooler - removal and installation

※ WARNING:

Wait until the engine is completely cool before beginning this procedure.

1 Raise the vehicle and place it securely on jackstands.
2 Drain the engine coolant and the engine oil (see Chapter 1).
3 Remove the oil filter (see Chapter 1).

FOUR-CYLINDER MODELS

4 Disconnect the two coolant hoses from the oil cooler.

5 Remove the oil cooler mounting bolt and detach the oil cooler from the engine block.
6 Be sure to install a new O-ring.
7 Installation is the reverse of removal. Tighten the oil cooler mounting bolt to the torque listed in this Chapter's Specifications.

V6 MODELS

8 Remove the two coolant hoses from the oil cooler.
9 Unscrew the oil cooler from the engine block.
10 Be sure to use a new O-ring.
11 Installation is the reverse of removal.

Specifications

General

Expansion tank cap pressure rating	13 to 18 psi (90 to 123 kPa)
Thermostat rating (opening to fully open temperature range)	194 to 223 degrees F (90 to 106 degrees C)
Cooling system capacity	See Chapter 1
Refrigerant type	R-134a
Refrigerant capacity	Refer to HVAC specification tag

Torque specifications	Ft-lbs (unless otherwise indicated)	Nm

➡**Note: One foot-pound (ft-lb) of torque is equivalent to 12 inch-pounds (in-lbs) of torque. Torque values below approximately 15 ft-lbs are expressed in inch-pounds, since most foot-pound torque wrenches are not accurate at these smaller values.**

Condenser inlet and outlet nuts	71 in-lbs	8
Engine oil cooler mounting bolt (four-cylinder engine)	43	58
Radiator bracket support bolts	89 in-lbs	10
Thermostat housing cover bolts	89 in-lbs	10
Water pump bolts	89 in-lbs	10
Water pump drivebelt tensioner bolt	89 in-lbs	10

Section

Reference to other Chapters

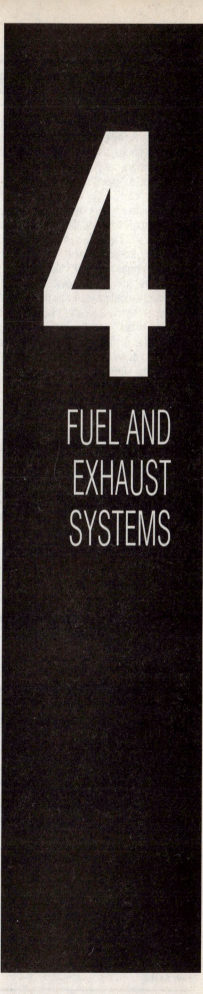

4

FUEL AND EXHAUST SYSTEMS

1   General information and precautions

This Chapter covers the removal and installation procedures for the important parts of the air intake, fuel and exhaust systems. Because emission-control systems are integral parts of the engine management system, there are many cross-references to Chapter 6. Information on the engine management system, information sensors and output actuators is in Chapter 6.

The air intake system consists of the air filter housing, the air intake duct, the throttle body and the intake manifold. Incoming air passes through the air filter element, the Mass Air Flow (MAF) sensor, the throttle body, the intake manifold plenum and the intake manifold "runners" before being mixed with fuel sprayed into the intake ports by the fuel injectors. This Chapter covers removal of the air filter housing; the replacement procedure for the air filter element is in Chapter 1. The MAF sensor measures the mass (volume) of air entering the engine and sends an analog (continuously variable) voltage signal to the Powertrain Control Module (PCM), which uses this data to determine how much fuel to deliver for the correct air/fuel ratio. The replacement procedure for the MAF sensor is in Chapter 6. The removal and installation procedure for the throttle body is in this Chapter. The removal and installation procedure for the intake manifold is in Chapter 2.

The Multiport Fuel Injection (MFI) system consists of the fuel tank, an electric fuel pump/fuel level sending unit module mounted inside the tank, the fuel rail, the pulsation damper (dampens the pulsations produced by the pumping action of the electric fuel pump), the fuel injectors and the metal and plastic fuel lines that connect the various components of the MFI system. The electric fuel pump/fuel level sending unit module can be replaced (the procedure is in this Chapter) but you cannot replace the fuel pump, the fuel level sending unit or any other part of the module separately. If any part of the module is defective, you must replace the entire unit. You'll also find removal and installation procedures for the fuel rail and injectors and for the pulsation damper in this Chapter.

All vehicles covered by this manual are equipped with a "returnless" fuel system. Four-cylinder models use an Electronic Returnless Fuel System (ERFS). There is no fuel pressure regulator and no fuel return line on ERFS-equipped models. Instead, the fuel pressure is regulated by controlling the fuel pump speed. The fuel pump is controlled by the Fuel Pump Driver Module (FPDM) inside the Powertrain Control Module (PCM).

V6 models use a Mechanical Returnless Fuel System (MRFS). These models have a fuel pressure regulator, which is located on the fuel pump/fuel level sending unit module inside the tank. They also have a short return line between a junction in the fuel supply line and the fuel pump/fuel level sending unit module. The junction is located just downstream from, and to the left of, the fuel filter. Both the fuel supply line and the short fuel return line are pressurized. When the fuel pressure exceeds the upper threshold of the system's normal operating pressure, the fuel pressure regulator opens and fuel returns to the tank via the return line.

The exhaust system consists of the exhaust manifold(s), the catalytic converters, the muffler and the exhaust pipes connecting these components. The system is suspended from the vehicle pan by rubber hangers. You'll find the removal and installation procedures for the exhaust manifold(s) in Chapter 2, and for the rest of the exhaust system in this Chapter. There is also more information about catalytic converters in Chapter 6.

The exhaust system is another area that you should service carefully, particularly when the engine is running, because the exhaust system reaches very high operating temperatures. Even brief contact with any part of the exhaust system can cause serious burns if the engine is running or has just been turned off. The catalytic converters run at even higher temperatures than the rest of the exhaust system, so be extremely cautious when working around them.

2   Fuel pressure relief procedure

▶ Refer to illustration 2.3

✳✳ WARNING:

Gasoline is extremely flammable, so take extra precautions when you work on any part of the fuel system. Don't smoke or allow open flames or bare light bulbs near the work area, and don't work in a garage where a gas-type appliance (such as a water heater or a clothes dryer) is present. Since gasoline is carcinogenic, wear latex gloves when there's a possibility of being exposed to fuel, and, if you spill any fuel on your skin, rinse it off immediately with soap and water. Mop up any spills immediately and do not store fuel-soaked rags where they could ignite. The fuel system is under constant pressure, so, if any fuel lines are to be disconnected, the fuel pressure in the system must be relieved first. When you perform any kind of work on the fuel system, wear safety glasses and have a Class B type fire extinguisher on hand.

✳✳ CAUTION:

After the fuel pressure has been relieved, it's a good idea to lay a shop towel over any fuel connection to be disassembled, to absorb the residual fuel that may leak out when servicing the fuel system.

2.3 The fuel pump relay is located in the engine compartment fuse and relay box

1   The fuel system referred to in this Chapter is defined as the fuel tank and tank-mounted fuel pump/fuel gauge sender unit, the fuel filter, the fuel injectors and the metal pipes and flexible hoses of the fuel lines between these components. All these contain fuel, which will be under pressure while the engine is running and/or while the ignition is switched on.

2   The pressure will also remain for some time after the ignition has been switched off, and it *must* be relieved before any fuel lines are disconnected.

3   To relieve fuel system pressure, start the engine and then remove the fuel pump relay (see illustration). The engine will run briefly, then stall. Turn the engine over once or twice to verify that all fuel system pressure has been released, then switch off the ignition.

✸✸ WARNING:

This procedure will merely relieve the increased pressure necessary for the engine to run. Remember that fuel will still be present in the system components, and take precautions accordingly before disconnecting any of them. Disconnect the cable from the negative terminal of the battery before performing any work on the fuel system.

4   Don't forget to install the relay when your work is completed. Note that, once the fuel system has been depressurized and drained (even partially), it will take significantly longer to restart the engine - perhaps several seconds of cranking - before the system is refilled and pressure restored.

3   Fuel pump/fuel pressure - check

✸✸ WARNING:

Gasoline is extremely flammable, so take extra precautions when you work on any part of the fuel system. See the Warning in Section 2.

FUEL PUMP OPERATION CHECK

1   The fuel pump is located inside the fuel tank, which muffles its sound when the engine is running. But you can actually hear the fuel pump if you sit inside the vehicle with the windows closed, turn the ignition key to ON (*not* START) and listen carefully for the whirring sound made by the fuel pump as it's briefly turned on to pressurize the fuel system prior to starting the engine (the sound will come from under the rear seat, because the fuel tank is located below it). You will only hear a soft whirring sound for a second or two, but that sound tells you that the pump is working. If you can't hear the pump, remove the fuel filler cap, depress the spring-loaded door inside the fuel filler neck, then have an assistant turn the ignition switch to ON while you listen for the sound of the pump being primed.

2   If the pump does not come on when the ignition key is turned to ON, check the fuel pump fuse and relay (both of which are located in the engine compartment fuse and relay box). If the fuse and relay are okay, check the wiring back to the fuel pump (see Section 5 for information on how to access the fuel pump electrical connector). If the fuse, relay and wiring are okay, the fuel pump is probably defective. If the pump runs *continuously* with the ignition key in its ON position, the Powertrain Control Module (PCM) is probably defective. Have the PCM checked by a dealer service department or other qualified repair shop.

FUEL PRESSURE CHECK

▶ **Refer to illustrations 3.3a, 3.3b, 3.3c, 3.4a, 3.4b, 3.4c,**

3   To check the fuel pressure on a V6 engine, you'll need a fuel pressure gauge with an adapter that fits the Schrader valve on the left end of the fuel rail (see illustration). Four-cylinder engines do not have a Schrader valve, so you will need to obtain a fuel pressure gauge (see illustration) with which you can tee into the fuel system at a suitable fuel line fitting.

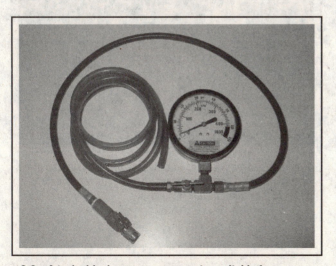

3.3a A typical fuel pressure gauge setup suitable for checking the fuel pressure on V6 models

3.3b On V6 models, the fuel pressure test port is a Schrader valve located on the left end of the fuel rail

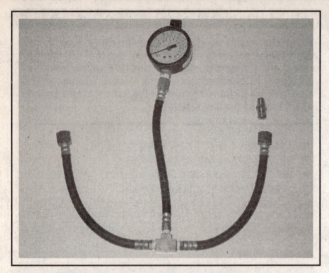

3.3c A typical fuel pressure gauge setup suitable for checking the fuel pressure on four-cylinder models; these models don't have a Schrader valve test port on the fuel rail, so you'll have to disconnect the fuel supply line at the fuel rail (or at some other fuel supply line connection in the engine compartment) and tee into it

4   Relieve the fuel pressure (see Section 2). If you're using a pressure gauge with a bleeder valve, make sure that the valve is closed. On V6 models, it's easy to connect a fuel pressure gauge to the Schrader valve test port (see illustrations). On four-cylinder models, you'll have to tee into the fuel system at the connection between the fuel supply line and the fuel rail.

5   Start the engine and allow it to idle. Note the gauge reading as soon as the pressure stabilizes, and compare it with the pressure listed in this Chapter's Specifications.

a) *If the pressure is lower than specified, check the fuel lines and hoses for kinks, blockages and leaks. Remove the fuel pump*

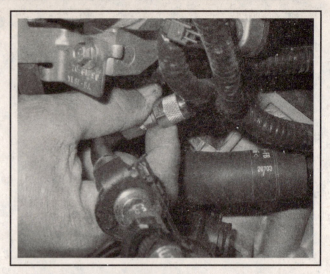

3.4a First, screw on the adapter . . .

module (see Section 5) and check the fuel strainer for restrictions. If all these components are okay, the fuel filter could be clogged or the fuel pump module could be defective.

b) *If the fuel pressure is higher than specified, replace the fuel pump module (the pressure regulator, part of the fuel pump module, is not available separately).*

6   Turn off the engine. Verify that the fuel pressure stays at the specified level for five minutes after the engine is turned off.

7   Relieve the fuel pressure (see Section 2), then disconnect the fuel pressure gauge. Be sure to cover the fitting with a rag before loosening it. Mop up any spilled gasoline.

8   Start the engine and verify that there are no fuel leaks.

3.4b . . . then hook up the fuel pressure gauge . . .

3.4c . . . and you're ready to check the fuel pressure on a V6 engine (this setup won't work on four-cylinder models because they don't have a test port)

4   Fuel lines and fittings - general information

✳✳ WARNING 1:

Gasoline is extremely flammable, so take extra precautions when you work on any part of the fuel system. See the Warning in Section 2.

✳✳ WARNING 2:

Before disconnecting any fuel line couplings, relieve the residual pressure in the fuel system (see Section 2) and equalize tank pressure by removing the fuel filler cap. This procedure will merely relieve the increased pressure necessary for the engine to run - remember that fuel will still be present in the system components, so you should be ready to mop up fuel spills when disconnecting fuel line couplings.

1   Ford uses three kinds of fuel line "couplings" (connectors):

"R-clip" (also known as "duck-bill clip" or "horseshoe clip") quick-release couplings
Push-connect quick-release couplings
Spring-lock couplings

The procedure for releasing each type of coupling is different. But a few rules of thumb apply to all Ford couplings. First, always disconnect all fuel line couplings from a fuel system component before loosening the component for removal. Second, when you disconnect an R-clip or push-connect quick-release coupling, always inspect the condition of the clip and the coupling *before reconnecting the coupling*. And when you disconnect a spring-lock coupling, always inspect the O-rings and the garter spring before reconnecting the coupling. Most of these couplings are under the same pressure as the rest of the fuel system, so to avoid leaks (and fires!) make very sure that the clip and coupling are in good condition. At one time, the clips for these couplings were generally available, at least at Ford dealerships (for example, factory fuel filter kits included new clips for the couplings connecting the fuel lines to the inlet and outlet sides of the filter). Now that is no longer the case. Even if a clip is the only part of the coupling that's damaged, you might not be able to obtain a new clip without buying a new coupling. And in most cases, the coupling itself is a non-removable part of the fuel line, so you might have to replace an entire fuel line just to get that new clip!

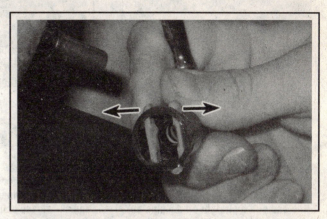

4.3a To disconnect an R-clip type fuel line coupling (this one is the connector on the *inlet* side of the fuel filter), *spread* the two legs of the clip *apart* . . .

ALL COUPLINGS

2   Inspect the visible internal parts of the coupling for dirt. If more than a light coating of dust is present, clean off the coupling before disassembling it. The seals in the coupling will stick to the fuel line as they age. Twist the coupling on the line, then push and pull the coupling until it moves freely.

R-CLIP QUICK-RELEASE COUPLINGS

▶ Refer to illustrations 4.3a through 4.3e

3   Relieve the fuel system pressure (see Section 2), then remove the clip from the coupling by bending the shipping tab down until it clears the coupling. Then, using only your hands, spread the two legs apart (or squeeze them together, depending on the type of R-clip coupling) to disengage the coupling, then pull the clip down until it protrudes from the coupling body. Do not use any tools for this part of the procedure. Finally, pull lightly on the wide part of the clip and work it clear of the line and the coupling (see illustrations). Finally, grasp the coupling and pull it straight off.

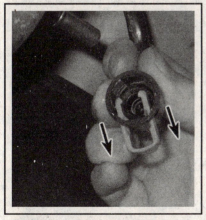

4.3b . . . then pull the clip out and detach the coupling from the component (coupling removed for clarity)

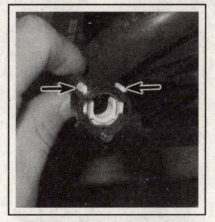

4.3c Here's another type of R-clip fuel line coupling (this one is the connector on the *outlet* side of the fuel filter); to disconnect it, *squeeze* the two legs of the clip *toward each other* . . .

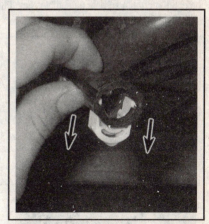

4.3d . . . pull the clip down (coupling removed for clarity) . . .

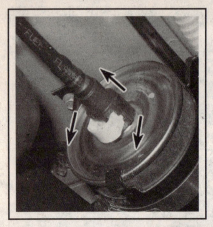

4.3e . . . then grasp the coupling and line and pull it straight off the pipe on the filter (this type of R-clip coupling is also referred to as a "horseshoe clip" coupling because of the shape of the clip)

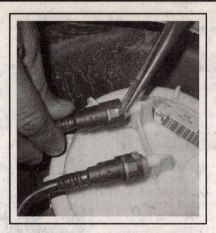

4.5a To disconnect a push-connect quick-release coupling, squeeze the two white locking tabs with a pair of needle-nose pliers . . .

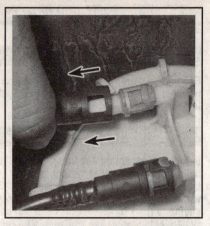

4.5b . . . then pull off the coupling (notice that the locking tab part of the coupling remains on the other fuel line (or, in this case, the pipe on top of the fuel pump/fuel level sending unit module)

4   Before reinstalling the coupling on the line, wipe off the end of the line with a clean cloth. Inspect the inside of the coupling and make sure that it's free of dirt. To reinstall the coupling on the line, align the coupling and line and push the coupling into place. When the coupling engages, you will hear an audible click. Pull on the coupling to verify that it's completely engaged. When installing the clip, carefully guide the legs into their respective holes, then push the clip up until the legs snap into place. The coupling is now locked on.

PUSH-CONNECT QUICK-RELEASE COUPLINGS

▶ Refer to illustrations 4.5a and 4.5b

5   To disconnect this type of coupling, relieve the fuel system pressure (see Section 2), then squeeze the locking tabs together with a pair of needle-nose pliers (see illustration) and pull off the coupling (see illustration).

6   Before reconnecting the coupling, wipe off the end of the line with a clean cloth. Inspect the inside of the coupling and make sure that it's free of dirt. To reconnect the coupling, insert the fuel line into the coupling until you hear an audible click. Pull on the coupling to verify that it's fully engaged.

SPRING-LOCK COUPLINGS

▶ Refer to illustrations 4.9, 4.10a, 4.10b, 4.10c, 4.10d and 4.10e

7   The fuel supply line is connected to the fuel rail by a spring-lock coupling. The male side of the spring-lock coupling, which is sealed by two O-rings, is inserted into the flared female side. The coupling is secured by a garter spring which prevents disengagement by gripping the flared end of the female fitting. A safety cover clips onto the coupling to provide additional security.

8   To disconnect a spring-lock coupling, you will need to obtain a spring-lock coupling tool, available at most auto parts stores. Be aware that 3/8-inch and 1/2-inch couplings (and other sizes) require different tools. These tools are inexpensive, and are usually sold in sets anyway.

9   First, relieve the fuel system pressure (see Section 2), then remove the safety cover (see illustration).

10 Install the spring-lock coupling tool (see illustrations). Then push the coupling tool firmly toward the garter spring housing (see illustration) to disengage the garter spring from the flared end of the female side of the connection. Now pull the two fuel lines apart (see illustrations).

4.9 Before disconnecting a spring-lock coupling, remove the safety cover

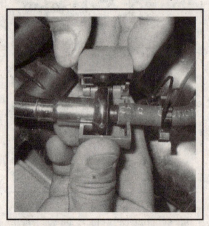

4.10a Install the special tool on the spring-lock coupling exactly as shown (the tool only fits one way) . . .

4.10b . . . close the clamshell halves of the tool around the coupling . . .

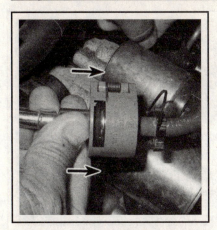

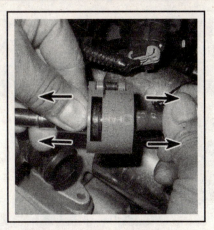

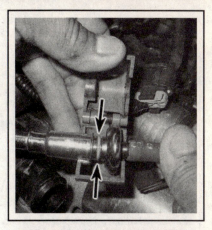

4.10c . . . push the tool to the right to disengage the garter spring from the flared end on the female side of the coupling . . .

4.10d . . . hold the tool in that position and pull the two fuel lines apart

4.10e Open the clamshell halves of the tool and you should see at least one of the O-rings on the male side of the coupling exposed. This indicates that the coupling is disconnected, so you can remove the tool and pull the two lines apart

11 Before reconnecting the coupling, wipe off the ends of both fuel lines with a clean cloth. Inspect the condition of the O-rings and the garter spring. If either O-ring or the garter spring is damaged or worn, replace it.

12 To reconnect a spring-lock coupling, press the two sides of the connection together until the flared end of the male side of the fitting is locked into place by the garter spring. Pull on the coupling to verify that it's fully engaged. Be sure to install the safety clamp.

13 When you're done, turn the ignition key to ON (not START) and re-pressurize the fuel system, which will take a moment, then check for fuel leakage around the coupling. If there are no signs of leaks, start the engine and check again.

5 Fuel pump/fuel level sending unit module - removal and installation

▶ **Refer to illustrations 5.4a, 5.4b, 5.5, 5.7 and 5.8**

✳✳ WARNING:

Gasoline is extremely flammable, so take extra precautions when you work on any part of the fuel system. See the Warning in Section 2.

1 Relieve the residual pressure in the fuel system (see Section 2), and equalize tank pressure by removing the fuel filler cap.

2 Disconnect the cable from the negative battery terminal (see Chapter 5, Section 1).

3 Fold the rear seat cushion forward (see Chapter 11 if necessary).

4 Remove the carpeting covering the fuel pump/fuel level sending unit module access cover (see illustration), then remove the access cover (see illustration). To reduce the risk of introducing water, dirt and dust into the tank while it is open, use a vacuum cleaner to clean the carpeting surrounding the access cover hole. Also blow (or wipe) off any dirt from the top of the fuel pump/fuel level sending unit and from the surface of the tank surrounding the module.

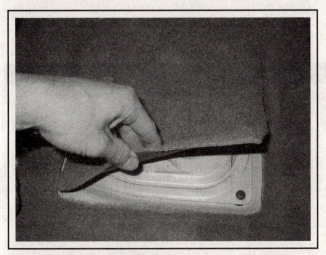

5.4a Pull back the carpeting covering the fuel pump/fuel level sending unit access cover . . .

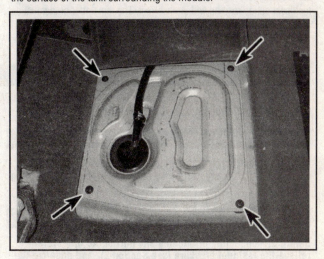

5.4b . . . remove the access cover screws and remove the cover

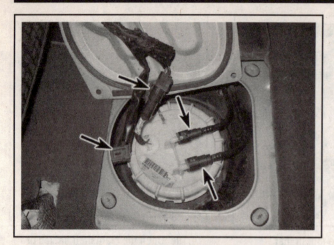

5.5 Disconnect the electrical connectors for the fuel pump/fuel level sending unit module and for the fuel pressure sensor, then disconnect the fuel line connection(s) (see Section 4)

5.7 To unscrew the fuel pump/fuel level sending unit module retaining ring, turn it counterclockwise; If it's tight, loosen it with a hammer and a brass punch

5   Disconnect the fuel pump/fuel level sending unit module electrical connector (see illustration). Also disconnect the electrical connector for the fuel pressure sensor. Set the connectors and the electrical harnesses aside.

6   Disconnect the fuel supply and return lines from the fuel pump/fuel level sending unit module (see Section 4). Use a rag to soak up any spilled fuel.

7   Unscrew the fuel pump/fuel level sending unit module retaining ring by turning it counterclockwise. If the ring is tight, use a hammer and a brass punch to loosen it (see illustration).

8   Remove the fuel pump/fuel level sending unit module, taking care not to bend the sending unit float arm (see illustration).

9   Before installing the pump, inspect the neoprene gasket (see illustration 5.8) for cracks, tears and deterioration. If it's worn or damaged, replace it. Also inspect the fuel pump inlet filter at the base of the pump. Make sure that it's clean and free of debris and dirt. If it's dirty, try washing it with carburetor cleaner spray. If this filter is seriously damaged, you'll have to replace the fuel pump/fuel level sending unit module. The filter is not available separately.

10 Align the fuel pump/fuel level sending unit module with its hole in the tank and *carefully* insert it into the tank. Make sure that you don't damage the float arm during installation. If the float arm is bent, the fuel level gauge reading will be incorrect. The remainder of installation is the reverse of removal.

11 After you've reconnected the battery, the Powertrain Control

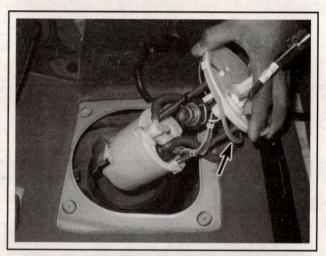

5.8 Carefully remove the fuel pump/fuel level sending unit module from the fuel tank; angle the pump as shown so that the fuel level sending unit float arm clears the edge of the access hole. Be sure to inspect the neoprene gasket for wear and damage while the pump is out

Module (PCM) must relearn its idle and fuel trim strategy for optimum driveability and performance (see Chapter 5, Section 1 for this procedure).

6   Fuel tank - removal and installation

▶ **Refer to illustrations 6.5, 6.7, 6.8, 6.11, 6.12 and 6.13**

❊❊ **WARNING 1:**

Gasoline is extremely flammable, so take extra precautions when you work on any part of the fuel system. See the Warning in Section 2.

❊❊ **WARNING 2:**

Before disconnecting or opening any part of the fuel system, relieve the residual pressure (see Section 2), and equalize the pressure inside the fuel tank by removing the fuel filler cap.

1   There is no fuel tank drain plug, so it's easier to remove the fuel tank when it's nearly empty. If that's not possible, try to siphon out the fuel in the tank before removing the tank (see Step 5).

2   Relieve the fuel system pressure (see Section 2).

3   Disconnect the cable from the negative battery terminal (see Chapter 5, Section 1).

4   Working inside the vehicle, disconnect the electrical connectors from the fuel pump/fuel level sending unit module and from the fuel pressure sensor (see Section 5). Also disconnect the fuel line(s) (some models have two, others only have one). If you don't need to siphon any fuel from the tank, it's not necessary to remove the module to remove the tank (as long as everything is disconnected from the module!).

6.5 A typical setup for siphoning fuel from the tank; siphoning kits are available at most auto parts stores

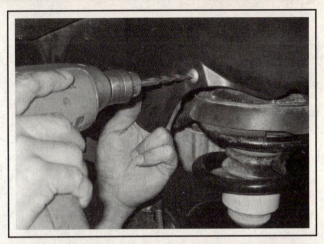

6.7 Drill out the rivets that attach the fuel filler hose shield and then remove the shield

6.8 Loosen the hose clamps and disconnect the fuel filler hose and the fuel filler vent hose

5   If there's still a lot of fuel in the tank, siphon or hand-pump the remaining fuel from the tank now (see illustration). We recommend that you siphon the fuel out of the tank through the hole in the top of the tank for the fuel pump/fuel level sending unit module, but you can also siphon it out through the fuel filler neck or through the fuel filler neck pipe (at the tank), after you have disconnected the fuel filler neck hose from the fuel tank.

✳✳ WARNING:

Don't start the siphoning action by mouth! Use a siphoning kit (available at most auto parts stores).

6   Loosen the left rear wheel lug nuts, raise the vehicle and place it securely on jackstands. Remove the left rear wheel.

7   Drill out the rivets that attach the fuel filler hose shield (see illustration) and then remove the shield.

8   Disconnect the fuel tank filler hose and the fuel tank filler vent hose from the fuel tank filler tube (see illustration).

9   Remove the muffler (see Section 15).

10   On 4WD models, remove the driveshaft, remove the differential mounting bracket-to-subframe mounting bolt, remove the differential-to-bracket bolts, loosen the differential mounting bracket-to-subframe mounting bolts, rotate the brackets and position the axle assembly to the rear (see Chapter 8).

6.11 Support the fuel tank with a transmission jack (shown) or a floor jack; if you're using a floor jack, be sure to put a sturdy piece of plywood between the jack head and the fuel tank to protect the tank; to detach the fuel tank straps, remove the bolts at rear end of each strap

11   Support the fuel tank with a transmission jack (see illustration) or a floor jack. If you're going to use a floor jack, place a sturdy piece of plywood between the jack head and the tank to protect the tank.

12   Disconnect the EVAP hose (see illustration).

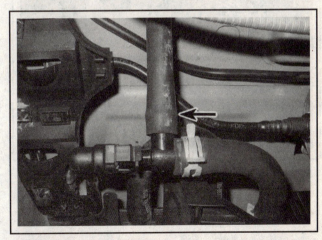

6.12 Disconnect this EVAP hose

13 Disconnect the pin-type retainer that attaches the parking brake to the left fuel tank strap (see illustration) and reposition the parking brake cable so that it's out of the way.

14 On 4WD models, disconnect the wiring harness clip from the rear of the left fuel tank strap.

15 Remove the fuel tank strap bolts (see illustration 6.11) and swing the fuel tank straps down and out of the way (the straps are hinged at the front; there are no front strap bolts).

16 Lower the tank enough to have a look at the top of the tank and unclip or detach any remaining cables, hoses or lines.

17 Lower the tank the rest of the way.

18 Installation is the reverse of the removal procedure.

19 After you've reconnected the battery, the Powertrain Control Module (PCM) must relearn its idle and fuel trim strategy for optimum driveability and performance (see Chapter 5, Section 1 for this procedure).

6.13 Detach this pin-type retainer from the front of the left fuel tank strap and reposition the parking brake cable so that it's out of the way

7 Fuel tank cleaning and repair - general information

⁂ WARNING:

Gasoline is extremely flammable, so take extra precautions when you work on any part of the fuel system. See the Warning in Section 2.

1 Any repairs to the fuel tank or filler neck should be carried out by a professional who has experience in this critical and potentially dangerous work. Even after cleaning and flushing of the fuel system, explosive fumes can remain and ignite during repair of the tank.

2 If the fuel tank is removed from the vehicle, it should not be placed in an area where sparks or open flames could ignite the fumes coming out of the tank. Be especially careful inside garages where a gas-type appliance is located, because it could cause an explosion.

8 Air filter housing - removal and installation

AIR FILTER HOUSING

♦ Refer to illustrations 8.2a, 8.2b, 8.3, 8.5a, 8.5b and 8.6

➡Note: The accompanying photos (except illustration 8.2a) depict the air filter housing on a V6 model, but except for the air intake duct, which is slightly different on four-cylinder models, the actual air filter housing is virtually identical on all models.

1 Disconnect the cable from the negative battery terminal (see Chapter 5, Section 1)

2 Disconnect the electrical connector from the Mass Air Flow (MAF) sensor (see illustrations).

3 On four-cylinder models, detach the accelerator cable from the air intake duct (see illustration 8.2a). On V6 models, disconnect the

8.2a Air intake duct installation details (four-cylinder models)

1 *Mass Air Flow (MAF) sensor electrical connector*
2 *Accelerator cable clip*
3 *Fresh air intake hose*
4 *Hose clamp at MAF sensor*
5 *Hose clamp at throttle body*

8.2b On V6 models, disconnect the electrical connector from the Mass Air Flow (MAF) sensor and loosen the air intake duct hose clamp screw

8.3 On V6 models, disconnect the crankcase vent hose from the air intake duct

8.5a To detach the air filter housing from the vehicle, remove this bolt

crankcase vent hose from the air intake duct (see illustration).

4   Loosen the air intake duct hose clamp screw at the MAF sensor end of the air intake duct (four-cylinder models, see illustration 8.2a; V6 models, see illustration 8.2b) and disconnect the air intake duct from the air filter housing.

5   Remove the air filter housing retaining bolt (see illustration). To disengage the air filter housing from its grommets (see illustration), pull it straight up. You'll also have to pull the housing to the rear far enough to disengage it from the fresh air inlet duct.

6   Inspect the rubber grommets before installing the air filter housing. If they're cracked, torn or otherwise damaged, replace them. Installation is otherwise the reverse of removal. Make sure that the air filter housing locator pins are correctly seated in their grommets, and that the air intake mouth of the filter housing is correctly seated inside the fresh air inlet duct (see illustration).

7   After you've reconnected the battery, the Powertrain Control Module (PCM) must relearn its idle and fuel trim strategy for optimum driveability and performance (see Chapter 5, Section 1 for this procedure).

FRESH AIR INLET DUCT

▶ **Refer to illustration 8.10**

8   Remove the battery and the battery tray (see Chapter 5).

9   Remove the air filter housing (see Steps 1 through 6).

10   Remove the fresh air inlet duct retaining bolt (see illustration) and remove the inlet duct.

11   Installation is the reverse of removal.

12   After you've reconnected the battery, the Powertrain Control Module (PCM) must relearn its idle and fuel trim strategy for optimum driveability and performance (see Chapter 5, Section 1 for this procedure).

FRESH AIR INLET DUCT RESONATOR

▶ **Refer to illustrations 8.14 and 8.15**

13   Loosen the left front wheel lug nuts. Raise the front of the vehicle and place it securely on jackstands. Remove the left front wheel.

14   Remove the pin-type retainers and screws, then remove the left inner fender splash shield (see illustration).

8.5b To disengage the air filter housing from these two grommets, pull it straight up (air filter housing cover and air filter element removed for clarity)

8.6 When installing the air filter housing, make sure that the air intake mouth of the housing is correctly seated

8.10 To detach the fresh air inlet duct from the vehicle body, remove this bolt

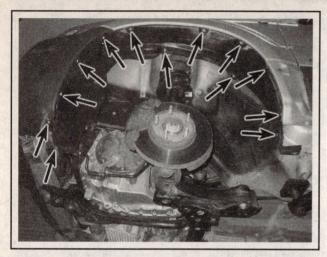

8.14 To detach the left inner fender splash shield, remove these fasteners (the shield uses a combination of screws and pin-type retainers; if any of them are damaged or missing, be sure to replace them when installing the shield)

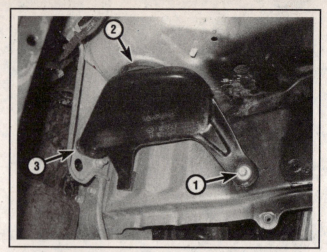

8.15 To detach the fresh air inlet duct resonator from the vehicle body, remove the bolt (1), then disengage the resonator from the fresh air inlet insulator (2) and from the locator pin grommet (3); inspect both the insulator and the grommet and make sure that they're in good condition

15 Remove the resonator retaining bolt (see illustration) and remove the resonator.

16 Inspect the rubber insulator between the resonator and the fresh air inlet duct and the rubber grommet for the locator pin. If either is damaged or worn, replace it.

17 Installation is otherwise the reverse of removal.

9   Accelerator cable - removal and installation

▶ **Refer to illustrations 9.2, 9.3, 9.4a, 9.4b, 9.5, 9.6, 9.7a and 9.7b**

1 Disconnect the cable from the negative battery terminal (see Chapter 5, Section 1).

2 On V6 models, remove the engine cover (see illustration).

3 On four-cylinder models, detach the accelerator cable from the air intake duct (see illustration 8.2a). On V6 models, detach the accelerator cable bracket from the intake manifold (see illustration).

4 Disengage the accelerator cable from the cable bracket (see illustration).

5 Disconnect the accelerator cable from the throttle body (see illustration).

6 Working inside the passenger compartment, disengage the lower end of the accelerator cable from the accelerator pedal (see illustration).

7 Returning to the engine compartment, pull the cable through the firewall until the cable's lower end plug reaches the grommet, then remove the grommet and pull the cable through the hole (see illustrations).

8 Installation is the reverse of the removal procedure.

9 Have an assistant depress and release the accelerator pedal while you verify that the throttle valve moves smoothly and easily from the fully closed to the fully open position and back again.

10 After you've reconnected the battery, the Powertrain Control Module (PCM) must relearn its idle and fuel trim strategy for optimum driveability and performance (see Chapter 5, Section 1 for this procedure).

9.2 To detach the engine cover from a V6 model, remove these three nuts

9.3 On V6 models, remove this bolt to detach the accelerator cable bracket from the intake manifold

9.4a To disengage the accelerator cable housing (1) from the cable bracket, rotate the cable housing 90 degrees to the left or right and pull the housing out of its slot in the bracket; to disconnect the cable from the throttle linkage, remove the retainer clip (2) and pull the cable end off the pin on the linkage (four-cylinder models)

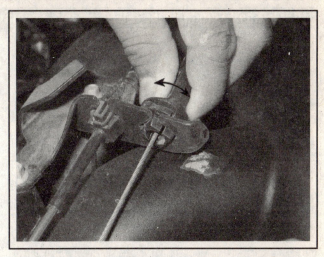

9.4b To disengage the accelerator cable from the cable bracket, rotate the cable housing 90 degrees to the left or right, then pull the housing out of its slot in the bracket

9.5 To disconnect the end of the accelerator cable from the throttle body on a V6 model, slide the end plug out of its slot in the throttle lever cam

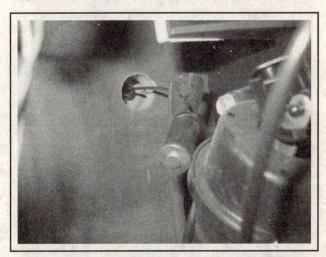

9.6 To disengage the lower end of the accelerator cable from the top of the accelerator pedal, pull firmly on the plug at the end of the cable to free it from the top of the pedal, then slide the cable out of the slot

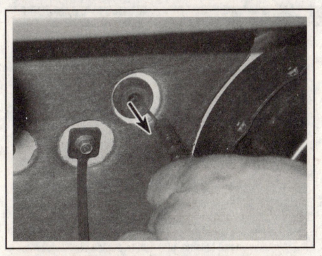

9.7a Pull out the cable from the engine compartment side . . .

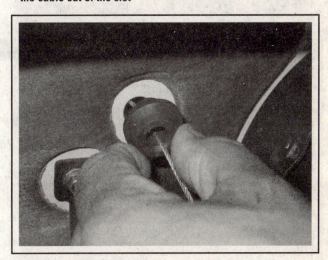

9.7b . . . until the cable's lower end plug reaches the grommet, then pry out the grommet and remove the cable and grommet from the vehicle

10 Multiport Fuel Injection (MFI) system - general information

These models are equipped with a Multiport Fuel Injection (MFI) system. The MFI system consists of three basic sub-systems: the air induction system, the fuel system and the electronic control system.

➥Note: Refer to Chapter 6 for further information on the components of the electronic control system.

AIR INDUCTION SYSTEM

The air induction system consists of the fresh air inlet duct and resonator, the air filter housing, the Mass Air Flow (MAF) sensor, the air intake duct, the throttle body, the air intake plenum and the intake manifold. The MAF sensor is an information sensor for the Powertrain Control Module (PCM). The MAF sensor uses a heated wire system to send the PCM a constantly varying (analog) voltage signal corresponding to the volume of air passing into the engine. Another sensor measures intake air temperature. The PCM uses these signals to calculate the mass (density) of air entering the engine.

The throttle valve inside the throttle body is controlled by the driver, through the accelerator pedal. As the valve opens, the amount of air that can pass through the system increases. The Throttle Position (TP) sensor opens further, the MAF sensor's signal alters and the PCM opens each injector for a longer duration to increase the amount of fuel delivered to the inlet ports.

FUEL SYSTEM

An electric fuel pump located inside the fuel tank supplies fuel under pressure to the fuel rail, which distributes fuel evenly to all injectors. A filter between the fuel pump and the fuel rail protects the components of the system. From the fuel rail, fuel is injected into the intake ports, just above the intake valves, by a fuel injector.

All vehicles covered by this manual are equipped with a "returnless" fuel system. Four-cylinder models use an Electronic Returnless Fuel System (ERFS). There is no fuel pressure regulator and no fuel return line on ERFS-equipped models. Instead, the fuel pressure is regulated by controlling the fuel pump speed. The fuel pump is controlled by the Fuel Pump Driver Module (FPDM) inside the Powertrain Control Module (PCM).

V6 models use a Mechanical Returnless Fuel System (MRFS).

These models have a fuel pressure regulator, which is located on the fuel pump/fuel level sending unit module inside the tank. They also have a short return line between a junction in the fuel supply line and the fuel pump/fuel level sending unit module. The junction is located just downstream from, and to the left of, the fuel filter. Both the fuel supply line and the short fuel return line are pressurized. When the fuel pressure exceeds the upper threshold of the system's normal operating pressure, the fuel pressure regulator opens and fuel returns to the tank via the return line.

The amount of fuel supplied by the injectors is precisely controlled by injector "drivers" inside the PCM. The PCM uses signals from the Crankshaft Position (CKP) sensor and the Camshaft Position (CMP) sensor to determine when to trigger each injector in cylinder firing order (sequential injection), with benefits in terms of better fuel economy and lower exhaust emissions.

ELECTRONIC CONTROL SYSTEM

The PCM controls the MFI system and the other sub-systems of the entire engine management system. It receives signals from a number of information sensors, which monitor such variables as intake air mass and temperature, coolant temperature, engine speed and position, acceleration/deceleration, and exhaust gas oxygen content. These signals help the PCM determine the injection duration necessary for the optimum air/fuel ratio. These sensors and associated PCM-controlled relays are located throughout the engine compartment. For further information regarding the PCM and its control of the engine management system, see Chapter 6.

IDLE SPEED AND MIXTURE ADJUSTMENT

Both the idle speed and mixture are under the control of the Powertrain Control Module (PCM) and neither can be adjusted. Not only can they not be adjusted, they cannot even be checked, except with the use of special diagnostic equipment, which makes this a task for a specialist. Do not attempt to "adjust" these settings in any way without such equipment. If you think that the idle speed and mixture are incorrect, take the vehicle to a dealer service department an have the system tested.

11 Fuel injection system - general check

◆ Refer to illustrations 11.7 and 11.8

✳✳ WARNING:

Gasoline is extremely flammable, so take extra precautions when you work on any part of the fuel system. See the Warning in Section 2.

1   Check all electrical connectors that are related to the system. Check the ground wire connections for tightness. Loose connectors and poor grounds can cause many problems that resemble more serious malfunctions.

2   Check to see that the battery is fully charged, as the control unit and sensors depend on an accurate supply voltage in order to properly meter the fuel.

3   Check the air filter element. A dirty or partially blocked filter will severely impede performance and economy (see Chapter 1).

4   Check the related fuses. If a blown fuse is found, replace it and see if it blows again. If it does, search for a wire shorted to ground in the harness.

5   Check the air intake duct to the intake manifold for leaks, which will result in an excessively lean mixture. Also check the condition of all vacuum hoses connected to the intake manifold and/or throttle body.

6   Remove the air intake duct from the throttle body and check for dirt, carbon, varnish, or other residue in the throttle body, particularly around the throttle plate. If it's dirty, clean it with carburetor cleaner spray, a toothbrush and shop towel.

7   With the engine running, place an automotive stethoscope against each injector, one at a time, and listen for a clicking sound that

11.7 Use a stethoscope to listen to the injectors: they should be making a smooth and steady clicking sound as they open and close

11.8 Use an ohmmeter to measure the resistance of the inductive coil winding inside each injector

indicates operation (see illustration). If you don't have a stethoscope, you can place the tip of a long screwdriver against the injector and listen through the handle. If you hear the injectors operating but there is a misfire condition present, the electrical circuits are functioning, but the injectors may be dirty or fouled from carbon deposits - commercial cleaning products may help, or the injectors may require replacement.

8   If you can't hear the injector operating, disconnect the injector

electrical connector and measure the resistance across the terminals of each injector connector with an ohmmeter (see illustration). Compare your measurement with the resistance value listed in this Chapter's Specifications. Replace any injector whose resistance value does not fall within the specifications.

9   If the injector is not operating, but the resistance reading is within specifications, the PCM or the circuit between the PCM and the injector might be faulty.

12 Throttle body - inspection, removal and installation

INSPECTION

▶ Refer to illustrations 12.2a and 12.2b

1   Verify that the throttle linkage operates smoothly.

2   Remove the air intake duct from the throttle body, open the throttle plate and inspect the throttle body bore for carbon and residue build-up. If it's dirty, clean it with solvent or carburetor cleaner (see illustrations). Make sure that the solvent or carb cleaner is safe for oxygen sensor systems and catalytic converters.

❋❋ CAUTION:

Do not clean the Throttle Position (TP) sensor or the Idle Air Control (IAC) motor with the solvent. Also, do NOT use a metal brush to clean the bore of the throttle body, which is protected by a special coating. Scrubbing the bore with a stiff brush could ruin the coating. Instead, wipe out the bore with a clean shop rag and a little solvent.

12.2a Over time, the area right behind the throttle plate is prone to a build-up of sludge because of the crankcase vapors vented to the intake manifold by the PCV system; if the build-up becomes excessive, it can prevent the throttle plate from closing at idle (throttle body removed for clarity)

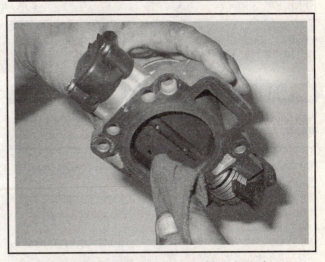

12.2b Wipe the sludge from this area with a clean shop rag and a small amount of solvent; do NOT scrub it with a stiff metal brush or you will damage the protective coating in the throttle bore (throttle body removed for clarity)

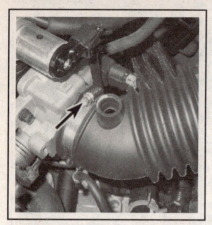

12.5 To detach the air intake duct from the throttle body, loosen this hose clamp screw (V6 model shown, four-cylinder models similar)

12.7 To disconnect the cruise control cable from its pin on the throttle lever, pull the end of the cable (V6 model shown, four-cylinder models similar)

12.8 Disconnect the electrical connector from the Throttle Position (TP) sensor (V6 model shown, four-cylinder models similar)

12.9a Disconnect the electrical connector from the Idle Air Control (IAC) valve (V6 model shown, four-cylinder models similar)

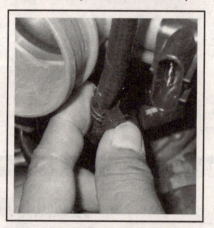

12.9b On V6 models, detach the IAC valve harness clip from the throttle body mounting stud located near the Throttle Position (TP) sensor

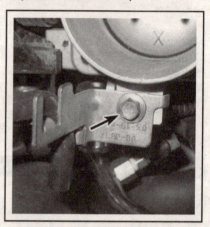

12.10 To detach the transaxle vent tube bracket from the throttle body, remove this bolt

REMOVAL

▶ Refer to illustrations 12.5, 12.7, 12.8, 12.9a, 12.9b, 12.10, 12.11a, 12.11b, 12.11c and 12.12

❊❊❊ WARNING:

Wait until the engine is completely cool before beginning this procedure.

3   Disconnect the cable from the negative battery terminal (see Chapter 5, Section 1).

4   On four-cylinder models, detach the accelerator cable from the air intake duct. On V6 models, disconnect the crankcase vent hose from the air intake duct (see illustration 8.3).

5   Disconnect the air intake duct from the throttle body (see illustration).

6   Disconnect the accelerator cable from the throttle body (see Section 9).

7   If the vehicle is equipped with cruise control, disconnect the cruise control cable from the throttle body (see illustration).

8   Disconnect the electrical connector from the Throttle Position (TP) sensor (see illustration).

12.11a To detach the throttle body from the air intake manifold on a four-cylinder model, remove these four bolts

12.11b To detach the throttle body from the air intake manifold on a V6 model, remove these two bolts

12.11c Remove the throttle body from the intake manifold (four-cylinder model shown)

12.12 Remove the throttle body gasket and discard it; when installing the throttle body, be sure to use a NEW gasket

9 Disconnect the electrical connector from the Idle Air Control (IAC) valve (see illustration). On V6 models, detach the IAC harness from the throttle body mounting stud located near the TP sensor (see illustration).

10 On V6 models, remove the transaxle vent tube bracket from the throttle body (see illustration).

11 Remove the throttle body mounting bolts (see illustrations) and then remove the throttle body (see illustration) from the manifold.

12 Remove the throttle body gasket (see illustration) and discard it.

13 If necessary, clean the throttle body as outlined in Step 2.

INSTALLATION

14 Using a NEW gasket, install the throttle body and tighten the throttle body mounting bolts to the torque listed in this Chapter's Specifications.

15 The remainder of installation is the reverse of removal.

16 After you've reconnected the battery, the Powertrain Control Module (PCM) must relearn its idle and fuel trim strategy for optimum driveability and performance (see Chapter 5, Section 1 for this procedure).

17 Start the engine and verify that the throttle body operates correctly and that there are no air leaks.

13 Fuel pulsation damper - removal and installation

◆ Refer to illustrations 13.4, 13.6a, 13.6b and 13.7

※※ WARNING:

Gasoline is extremely flammable, so take extra precautions when you work on any part of the fuel system. See the Warning in Section 2.

1 Relieve the fuel system pressure (see Section 2).

2 Disconnect the cable from the negative battery terminal.

3 On V6 models, remove the throttle body (see Section 12).

4 Disconnect the vacuum line from the pulsation damper (see illustration).

5 On four-cylinder models, remove the two bolts that attach the pulsation damper to the fuel rail and then remove the damper.

6 On V6 models, remove the fuel pulsation damper snap-ring and then remove the damper (see illustrations).

13.4 Disconnect the vacuum line from the pulsation damper (V6 model shown)

13.6a On V6 models, remove the pulsation damper snap-ring . . .

13.6b . . . and remove the pulsation damper

7   Before installing the pulsation damper, be sure to remove the old O-ring (see illustration) and discard it. Install a new O-ring on the pulsation damper (even if you're planning to reuse the old damper).

8   Installation is the reverse of removal. On four-cylinder models, be sure to tighten the pulsation damper bolts to the torque listed in this Chapter's Specifications.

9   After you've reconnected the battery, the Powertrain Control Module (PCM) must relearn its idle and fuel trim strategy for optimum driveability and performance (see Chapter 5, Section 1 for this procedure).

10 Start the engine and verify that there are no fuel leaks.

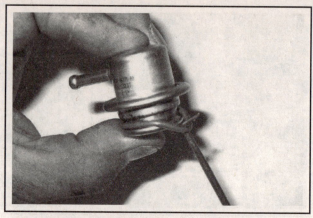

13.7 Remove the old O-ring from the pulsation damper (V6 model shown)

14 Fuel rail and injectors - removal and installation

1   Relieve the fuel system pressure (see Section 2) and equalize tank pressure by removing the fuel filler cap.

2   Disconnect the cable from the negative battery terminal (see Chapter 5, Section 1).

FOUR-CYLINDER MODELS

♦ **Refer to illustrations 14.10 and 14.11**

3   Remove the air intake duct.

4   Disconnect the accelerator cable from the throttle lever cam. If equipped, also disconnect the cruise control cable.

5   Disconnect the fuel supply line from the fuel rail.

6   Disconnect the vacuum line from the fuel pulsation damper.

7   Disconnect the electrical connectors from the fuel injectors.

8   Remove the fuel rail mounting bolts.

9   Remove the fuel rail and injectors as a single assembly.

10 Remove the clamp that secures each fuel injector to the fuel rail and pull out the injector (see illustration).

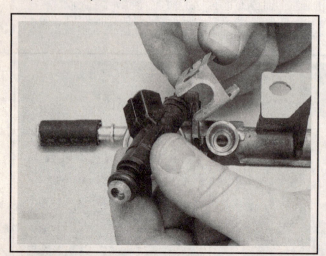

14.10 To disengage an injector from the fuel rail on a four-cylinder model, remove this clamp and pull the injector straight out of the fuel rail (wiggle and pull at the same time if the O-ring is stuck to the injector bore)

11 Remove the old O-rings from each injector (see illustration) and discard them. Always install new O-rings on the injectors before reassembling the injectors and the fuel rail.

12 Installation is otherwise the reverse of removal. To ensure that the new injector O-rings are not damaged when the injectors are installed into the fuel rail and into the intake manifold, lubricate them with clean engine oil. And be sure to tighten the fuel rail mounting bolts to the torque listed in this Chapter's Specifications.

13 After you've reconnected the battery, the Powertrain Control Module (PCM) must relearn its idle and fuel trim strategy for optimum driveability and performance (see Chapter 5, Section 1 for this procedure).

14 Start the engine and verify that there are no fuel leaks.

V6 MODELS

♦ **Refer to illustrations 14.18a, 14.18b, 14.18c, 14.19, 14.20, 14.21 and 14.22**

15 Remove the upper intake manifold (see Chapter 2B).

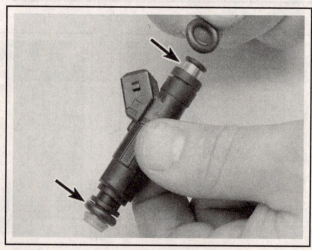

14.11 Always remove and discard the old injector O-rings and install new O-rings on each injector (four-cylinder models)

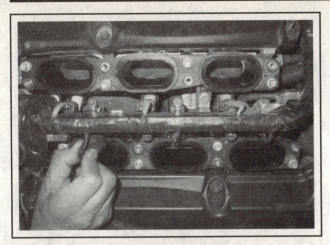

14.18a Disconnect the electrical connectors from the injectors . . .

16 Disconnect the vacuum line from the fuel pulsation damper (see illustration 13.4).

17 Disconnect the fuel supply line from the fuel rail (see Section 4).

18 Disconnect the electrical connectors from the injectors (see illustration) and detach the fuel injector harness from the brackets at the left and right ends of the vee (see illustration). Then trace the harness to each electrical device to which it's connected and disconnect the electrical connectors from those devices (see illustration) and set the harness aside.

19 Remove the fuel rail mounting bolts (see illustration).

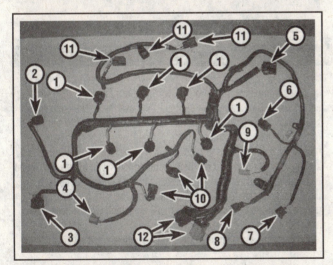

14.18c Electrical connector guide for main engine wiring harness (V6 models)

1   Fuel injector connectors
2   Idle Air Control (IAC) valve connector
3   Throttle Position (TP) sensor connector
4   Engine Coolant Temperature (ECT) sensor connector
5   Power Steering Pressure (PSP) switch connector
6   Camshaft Position (CMP) sensor connector
7   Oil pressure sending unit connector
8   Crankshaft Position (CKP) sensor connector
9   Noise suppressor connector
10   Ignition coil connectors (rear cylinder head)
11   Ignition coil connectors (front cylinder head)
12   Powertrain Control Module (PCM) connectors

14.18b . . . detach the injector wiring harness from the two brackets located in the vee between the cylinder heads (other bracket not visible in this photo), then trace the harness to each electrical device to which it's connected, disconnect it and set it aside (V6 models)

20 Carefully disengage the injectors from the lower intake manifold and lift the fuel rail and all six injectors from the engine as a single assembly (see illustration).

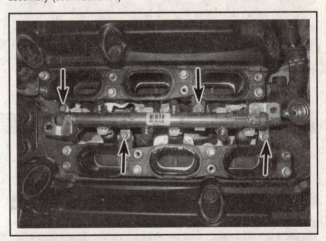

14.19 To detach the fuel rail from the engine, remove these four bolts (V6 models)

14.20 Remove the fuel rail and the injectors as a single assembly (V6 models)

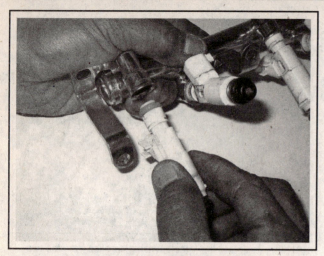

14.21 To detach an injector from the fuel rail, simply wiggle it side to side a little to loosen the O-ring and then pull it straight out as shown (V6 models)

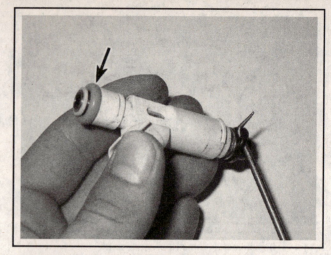

14.22 Remove the old O-rings from each injector and discard them; always install new O-rings when installing the injectors (V6 models)

21 Remove the injectors from the fuel rail (see illustration).

22 Remove and discard the old injector O-rings (see illustration). Always install new O-rings on the injectors before reassembling the injectors and the fuel rail.

23 Installation is the reverse of the removal procedure. To ensure that the new injector O-rings are not damaged when the injectors are installed into the fuel rail and into the intake manifold, lubricate them with clean engine oil. Be sure to tighten the fuel rail mounting bolts to the torque listed in this Chapter's Specifications.

24 After you've reconnected the battery, the Powertrain Control Module (PCM) must relearn its idle and fuel trim strategy for optimum driveability and performance (see Chapter 5, Section 1 for this procedure).

25 Start the engine and verify that there are no fuel leaks.

15 Exhaust system - inspection and component replacement

INSPECTION

✳✳ WARNING:

Inspect and repair exhaust system components only after allowing the exhaust components to cool completely. This applies particularly to the catalytic converter, which operates at very high temperatures. Also, when working under the vehicle, make sure it is securely supported on jackstands.

1 The exhaust system consists of the exhaust manifold(s), the catalytic converter(s), the exhaust pipes, the resonator (V6 models), the muffler and all brackets, hangers and clamps. Inspect the exhaust system regularly to ensure that it remains safe and quiet. Look for any damaged or bent parts, open seams, holes, loose connections, excessive corrosion or other defects which could allow exhaust fumes to enter the vehicle. Also check the catalytic converter(s) when you inspect the exhaust system. Inspect the catalytic converter heat shield(s) for cracks, dents and loose or missing fasteners. If a heat shield is damaged, the converter might also be damaged. Have the converter inspected by a dealer service department. Damaged or deteriorated exhaust system components should not be repaired; they should be replaced with new parts.

2 Before trying to disassemble any exhaust components, spray the fasteners with a penetrating oil to help ease removal. If the exhaust system components are extremely corroded or rusted together, welding equipment will probably be required to remove them. The convenient way to accomplish this is to have a muffler repair shop remove the corroded sections with a cutting torch. If, however, you want to save money by doing it yourself (and you don't have a welding outfit with a cutting torch), simply cut off the old components with a hacksaw. If you have compressed air, special pneumatic cutting chisels can also be used. If you decide to tackle the job at home, be sure to wear safety goggles to protect your eyes from metal chips and work gloves to protect your hands.

3 Here are some simple guidelines to follow when repairing the exhaust system:

   a) *Work from the back to the front when removing exhaust system components.*
   b) *Apply penetrating oil to the exhaust system component fasteners to make them easier to remove.*
   c) *Use new gaskets, hangers and clamps when installing exhaust systems components.*
   d) *Apply anti-seize compound to the threads of all exhaust system fasteners at reassembly.*
   e) *Be sure to allow sufficient clearance between newly installed parts and all points on the underbody to avoid overheating the floor pan and possibly damaging the interior carpet and insulation. Pay particularly close attention to the catalytic converter and heat shield.*

15.4a A typical rubber exhaust hanger; to remove an exhaust hanger, simply disengage it from the bracket attached to the floorpan and from the bracket attached to the exhaust pipe, catalytic converter, muffler, etc. If the hanger is difficult to remove, use a large prybar as a lever to pry it off

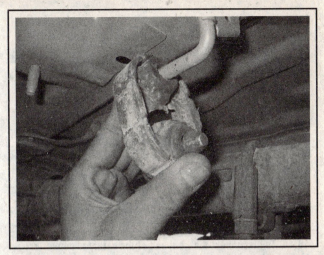

15.4b To install a new rubber exhaust hanger, simply push it onto the bracket attached to the floorpan and the bracket attached to the exhaust pipe, catalytic converter, muffler, etc. If the hanger is difficult to install, use a little talcum powder to help it slide onto the brackets more easily

COMPONENT REPLACEMENT

Rubber exhaust hangers

▶ Refer to illustrations 15.4a and 15.4b

4   The exhaust system is attached to the body with mounting brackets and rubber hangers. Because of the intense heat generated by the exhaust system, these hangers should be inspected regularly and often. Anytime you must raise the vehicle to perform any under-vehicle service, make sure that you inspect the rubber exhaust hangers. Look for cracks, tears and deterioration. If a hanger is worn or damaged, replace it (see illustrations). If a hanger breaks or becomes disconnected from its hanger bracket or from the bracket on the part that it supports, the exhaust system will transmit excessive noise and vibration to the vehicle body.

Catalytic converters

❋❋ WARNING:

The catalytic converters get extremely hot during operation, and can remain very hot for hours after the engine has been turned off. Make sure that a converter has cooled down before you touch it.

Four-cylinder models

▶ Refer to illustration 15.9

5   Four-cylinder models are equipped with a three-way catalytic converter (TWC) that's bolted to the exhaust manifold.

➥**Note: See Chapter 6 for more information on the function and operation of the catalytic converter.**

6   Remove the exhaust manifold heat shield (see "Exhaust manifold - removal and installation" in Chapter 2A).

7   Disconnect the electrical connectors for the upstream and downstream oxygen sensors and then remove the upstream sensor (see "Oxygen sensors - replacement" in Chapter 6).

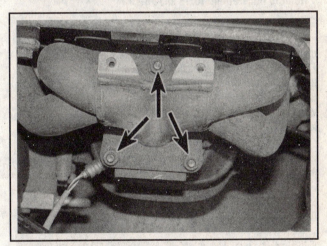

15.9 To detach the upper end of the catalytic converter from the exhaust manifold on a four-cylinder model, remove these three nuts

8   Disconnect the Exhaust Gas Recirculation (EGR) pipe (see "Exhaust Gas Recirculation system - component replacement" in Chapter 6).

9   Remove the three nuts from the exhaust manifold flange (see illustration).

10   Raise the vehicle and place it securely on jackstands.

11   Remove the downstream oxygen sensor (see "Oxygen sensors - replacement" in Chapter 6).

12   Remove the two bolts from the clamp that attaches the catalyst to the engine block. (It's not necessary to unbolt the clamp bracket from the engine block.)

13   Remove (and discard) the nuts from the flange at the lower end of the short section of exhaust pipe below the converter. Discard the old flange gasket.

14   Remove the catalytic converter assembly.

15   Installation is the reverse of removal. Apply anti-seize compound to the threads of all bolts and studs. Be sure to use new fasteners at both ends of the converter and a new flange gasket. Tighten all fasteners securely.

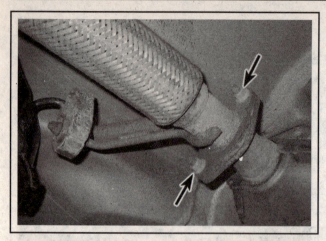

15.18 To disconnect the front end of the catalytic converter from the crossover and flexible exhaust pipe, remove these two flange nuts

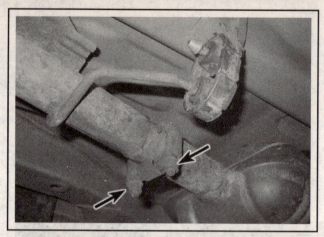

15.19 To disconnect the rear end of the catalytic converter from the exhaust pipe behind it, loosen the two nuts on this clamp and slide the clamp to the rear

V6 models

▶ **Refer to illustrations 15.18 and 15.19**

16 V6 models are equipped with three converters: an upstream "fast-light-off" catalyst directly below each exhaust manifold (and an integral part of the manifold), and a conventional three-way catalytic converter (TWC) located behind the junction between the two exhaust pipes for the front and rear cylinder heads. The following procedure applies to the larger catalyst underneath the vehicle. To replace an upstream converter, refer to "Exhaust manifold - removal and installation" in Chapter 2B.

17 Raise the vehicle and place it securely on jackstands.

18 Remove the nuts from the flange located in front of the catalytic converter (see illustration).

19 Loosen the clamp located behind the converter (see illustration).

20 Disengage the two catalytic converter hanger brackets from their rubber exhaust hangers and then remove the catalytic converter.

21 Be sure to inspect both rubber hangers (see Step 1). Installation is the reverse of removal. Apply anti-seize compound to the threads of all bolts and studs. Be sure to use new fasteners at both ends of the converter and a new flange gasket. Tighten all fasteners securely.

Crossover and flexible exhaust pipe (V6 models)

▶ **Refer to illustrations 15.23 and 15.24**

22 Raise the vehicle and place it securely on jackstands.

23 Remove the nuts that attach the forward crossover flange to the front exhaust manifold/catalytic converter (see illustration). Discard the nuts and the old flange gasket.

24 Remove the nuts that attach the rear crossover flange to the rear exhaust manifold/catalytic converter (see illustration). Discard the nuts and the old flange gasket.

25 Remove the nuts that attach the flange behind the flexible exhaust pipe to the front end of the downstream catalytic converter (see illustration 15.18). Discard the nuts and the old flange gasket.

26 Remove the crossover and flexible exhaust pipe assembly.

27 Installation is the reverse of removal. Be sure to use new flange nuts and flange gaskets. Apply anti-seize compound to the threads of all bolts and studs. Tighten all fasteners securely.

Resonator (V6 models)

▶ **Refer to illustrations 15.28 and 15.31**

28 The resonator (see illustration) is a small auxiliary muffler that

15.23 To disconnect the front flange of the crossover and flexible exhaust pipe from the exhaust manifold/catalytic converter for the front cylinder head, remove these two nuts

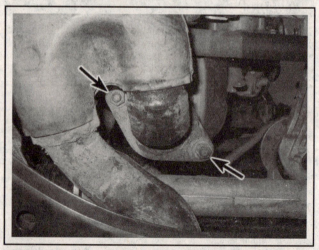

15.24 To disconnect the rear flange of the crossover and flexible exhaust pipe from the exhaust manifold/catalytic converter for the rear cylinder head, remove these two nuts

15.28 The resonator is a small muffler that helps the muffler to reduce exhaust noise (V6 models only)

15.31 To disconnect the resonator flange from the muffler flange, remove these two nuts

helps the main muffler reduce exhaust noise. (Usually, the resonator reduces noise in one frequency, the muffler reduces noise in another frequency.)

29 Raise the vehicle and place it securely on jackstands.

30 Loosen the clamp ahead of the resonator (see illustration 15.19) and slide the clamp out of the way. Discard the nuts.

31 Remove the two nuts from the flange behind the resonator (see illustration). Discard the nuts.

32 Remove the resonator.

33 Installation is the reverse of removal. Be sure to use new flange nuts and a new flange gasket at the front, and new nuts for the clamp at the rear, of the resonator. Apply anti-seize compound to the threads of all bolts and studs. Tighten all fasteners securely.

Muffler (all models)

▶ Refer to illustrations 15.36a and 15.36b

34 Raise the vehicle and place it securely on jackstands.

35 Remove the two nuts from the flange behind the resonator (see illustration 15.31) and discard the nuts. (On 2.0L models, there's no resonator, just a straight exhaust pipe, but the flange is still there.)

36 Disengage the muffler hanger brackets from the front and rear muffler exhaust hangers (see illustrations) and remove the muffler.

37 Inspect the condition of the rubber exhaust hangers. Replace them if they're worn or damaged.

38 Installation is the reverse of removal. Be sure to use new fasteners and tighten all fasteners securely.

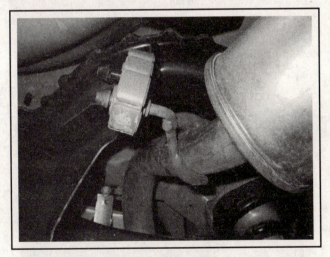

15.36a Front muffler hanger (all models)

15.36b Rear muffler hanger (all models)

Specifications

Fuel pressure
    2001 (both engines) — 35 to 65 psi (240 to 448 kPa)
    2002
        Four-cylinder engine — 35 to 65 psi (240 to 448 kPa)
        V6 engine — 39 to 55 psi (270 to 380 kPa)
    2003 and 2004 (both engines) — 50 to 65 psi (345 to 448 kPa)
    2005 and later (both engines) — 39 psi (270 kpa)
Fuel injector resistance
    2001
        Four-cylinder engine — 11.4 to 12.6 ohms
        V6 engine — 10.3 to 17.3 ohms
    2002 through 2004
        Four-cylinder engine — 13.8 to 15.2 ohms
        V6 engine — 13.1 to 14.5 ohms
    2005 and later — 11 to 18 ohms

Torque specifications	Ft-lbs (unless otherwise indicated)	Nm

➡ **Note: One foot-pound (ft-lb) of torque is equivalent to 12 inch-pounds (in-lbs) of torque. Torque values below approximately 15 ft-lbs are expressed in inch-pounds, since most foot-pound torque wrenches are not accurate at these smaller values.**

	Ft-lbs	Nm
Throttle body-to-intake manifold bolts		
Four-cylinder engine	62 in-lbs	7 Nm
V6 engine	89 in-lbs	10 Nm
Fuel rail mounting bolts	89 in-lbs	10 Nm
Fuel pulsation damper bolts (four-cylinder engine)	53 in-lbs	6 Nm

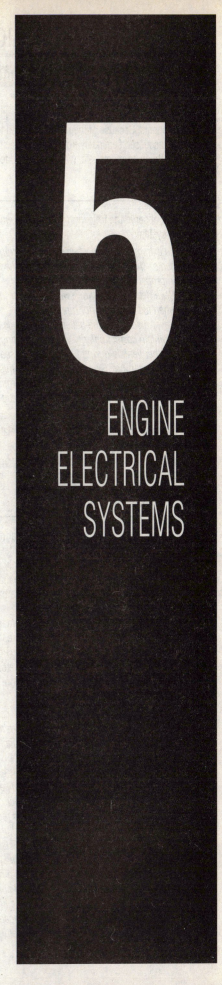

5

ENGINE
ELECTRICAL
SYSTEMS

Section

1   General information, precautions and battery disconnection

The engine electrical systems include all ignition, charging and starting components. Because of their engine-related functions, these components are discussed separately from chassis electrical devices such as the lights, the instruments, etc. (which are included in Chapter 12).

PRECAUTIONS

Always observe the following precautions when working on the electrical system:

a) *Be extremely careful when servicing engine electrical components. They are easily damaged if checked, connected or handled improperly.*

b) *Never leave the ignition switched on for long periods of time when the engine is not running.*

c) *Never disconnect the battery cables while the engine is running.*

d) *Maintain correct polarity when connecting battery cables from another vehicle during jump starting - see the* "Booster battery (jump) starting" *Section at the front of this manual.*

e) *Always disconnect the negative cable from the battery before working on the electrical system, but read the following battery disconnection procedure first.*

It's also a good idea to review the safety-related information regarding the engine electrical systems located in the "Safety first!" Section at the front of this manual, before beginning any operation included in this Chapter.

BATTERY DISCONNECTION

The battery is located in the engine compartment on all vehicles covered by this manual. To disconnect the battery for service procedures that require battery disconnection, simply disconnect the cable from the negative battery terminal. Make sure that you isolate the cable to prevent it from coming into contact with the battery negative terminal.

Some vehicle systems (radio, alarm system, power door locks, windows, etc.) require battery power all the time, either to enable their operation or to maintain control unit memory (Powertrain Control Module, automatic transaxle control module, etc.), which would be lost if the battery were to be disconnected. So before you disconnect the battery, note the following points:

a) *Before connecting or disconnecting the cable from the negative battery terminal, make sure that you turn the ignition key and the lighting switch to their OFF positions. Failure to do so could damage semiconductor components.*

b) *On a vehicle with power door locks, it is a wise precaution to remove the key from the ignition and to keep it with you, so that it does not get locked inside if the power door locks should engage accidentally when the battery is reconnected!*

c) *After the battery has been disconnected, then reconnected (or a new battery has been installed) on vehicles with an automatic transaxle, the Transaxle Control Module (TCM) will need some time to relearn its adaptive strategy. As a result, shifting might feel firmer than usual. This is a normal condition and will not adversely affect the operation or service life of the transaxle. Eventually, the TCM will complete its adaptive learning process and the shift feel of the transaxle will return to normal.*

d) *The engine management system's PCM will lose some of the information stored in its "map" (program) when the battery is disconnected. Whenever the battery has been disconnected, the Powertrain Control Module (PCM) must relearn its idle and fuel trim strategy before the vehicle returns to its optimal driveability and performance. To initiate this process, refer to* "Relearning the idle and fuel trim strategy after battery disconnection" *below.*

MEMORY SAVERS

Devices known as "memory savers" (typically, small 9-volt batteries) can be used to avoid some of the above problems. A memory saver is usually plugged into the cigarette lighter, and then you can disconnect the vehicle battery from the electrical system. The memory saver will deliver sufficient current to maintain security alarm codes and - maybe, but don't count on it! - PCM memory. It will also run "unswitched" (always on) circuits such as the clock and radio memory, while isolating the car battery in the event that a short circuit occurs while the vehicle is being serviced.

✳✳ WARNING:

If you're going to work around any airbag system components, disconnect the battery and do not use a memory saver. If you do, the airbag could accidentally deploy and cause personal injury.

✳✳ CAUTION:

Because memory savers deliver current to operate unswitched circuits when the battery is disconnected, make sure that the circuit that you're going to service is actually open before working on it!

RELEARNING THE IDLE AND FUEL TRIM STRATEGY AFTER BATTERY DISCONNECTION

✳✳ CAUTION:

Failure to perform the following procedure after battery reconnection could adversely affect the idle quality of the engine until it eventually relearns its idle trim.

1   With the vehicle stationary, apply the parking brake.

2   Put the shift lever in PARK, turn off all accessories and then start the engine.

3   Allow the engine to warm up to its normal operating temperature.

4   Allow the engine to idle for at least one minute.

5   Turn on the air conditioning system and allow the engine to idle for at least another minute.

6   Drive the vehicle at least 10 miles.

7   The vehicle should now have relearned its idle and fuel trim strategy.

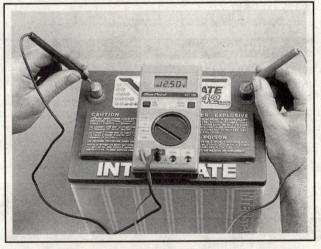

2   Battery - emergency jump starting

Refer to the *Booster battery (jump) starting* procedure at the front of this manual.

3   Battery - check, removal and installation

❊❊ WARNING:

Hydrogen gas is produced by the battery, so keep open flames and lighted cigarettes away from it at all times. Always wear eye protection when working around a battery. Rinse off spilled electrolyte immediately with large amounts of water.

CHECK

▶ **Refer to illustrations 3.1a, 3.1b and 3.1c**

1   A battery cannot be accurately tested until it is at or near a fully charged state. Disconnect the negative battery cable from the battery and perform the following tests:

   a) *Battery state of charge test - Visually inspect the indicator eye (if equipped) on the top of the battery. If the indicator eye is dark in color, charge the battery as described in Chapter 1. If the battery is equipped with removable caps, check the battery electrolyte. The electrolyte level should be above the upper edge of the plates. If the level is low, add distilled water. DO NOT OVERFILL. The excess electrolyte may spill over during periods of heavy charging. Test the specific gravity of the electrolyte using a hydrometer (see illustration). Remove the caps and extract a sample of the electrolyte and observe the float inside the barrel of the hydrometer. Follow the instructions from the tool manufacturer and determine the specific gravity of the electrolyte for each cell. A fully charged battery will indicate approximately 1.270 (green zone) at 68-degrees F (20-degrees C). If the specific gravity of the electrolyte is low (red zone), charge the battery as described in Chapter 1.*

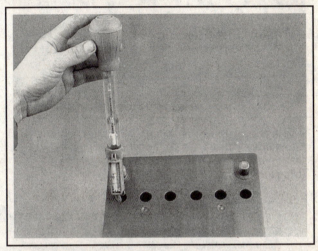

3.1a Use a battery hydrometer to draw electrolyte from the battery cell; this hydrometer is equipped with a thermometer to make temperature corrections

   b) *Open circuit voltage test - Using a digital voltmeter, perform an open circuit voltage test (see illustration). Connect the negative probe of the voltmeter to the negative battery post and the positive probe to the positive battery post. The battery voltage should be greater than 12.5 volts. If the battery is less than the specified voltage, charge the battery before proceeding to the next test. Do not proceed with the battery load test until the battery is fully charged.*

   c) *Battery load test - An accurate check of the battery condition can only be performed with a load tester (available at most auto parts*

3.1b To test the open-circuit voltage of the battery, connect the black probe of a voltmeter to the negative terminal and the red probe to the positive terminal of the battery; if the battery is fully charged, the voltmeter should indicate about 12.5 volts (depending on the outside air temperature)

3.1c Some battery load testers are equipped with an ammeter, which enables you to impose a precise load on the battery (less expensive testers have only a load switch and a voltmeter)

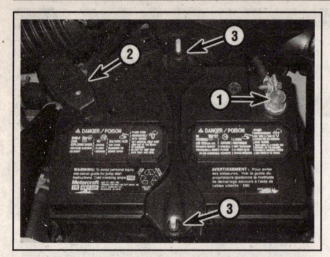

3.2 To remove the battery from the battery tray, disconnect the negative battery cable (1), then the positive cable (2); then remove the two hold-down nuts (3) and remove the hold-down bracket

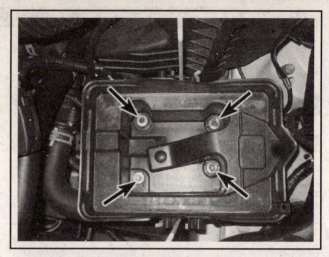

3.5 To remove the battery tray, remove these four mounting bolts

REPLACEMENT

▶ **Refer to illustrations 3.2 and 3.5**

2   Remove the protective cover from the positive battery terminal. Then disconnect both cables from the battery terminals (see illustration).

❋❋ **WARNING:**

Always disconnect the negative cable first and connect it last, or you might accidentally short the battery with the tool you're using to loosen the cable clamps.

3   Remove the hold-down nuts and the hold-down bracket (see illustration 3.2).
4   Lift out the battery. Use a battery lifting strap that attaches to the battery posts to lift the battery safely and easily.
5   If you need to access components located underneath the battery tray, remove the four bolts that secure the battery tray (see illustration) and remove the tray.
6   Installation is the reverse of removal.

❋❋ **WARNING:**

When connecting the battery cables, always connect the positive cable first and the negative cable last to avoid a short circuit caused by the tool used to tighten the cable clamps.

7   After you're done, the Powertrain Control Module (PCM) must relearn its idle and fuel trim strategy for optimum driveability and performance (see Section 1 for this procedure).

stores). This test evaluates the ability of the battery to operate the starter and other accessories during periods of heavy amperage draw (load). Install a special battery load-testing tool onto the battery terminals (see illustration). Load test the battery according to the tool manufacturer's instructions. This tool utilizes a carbon pile to increase the load demand (amperage draw) on the battery. Maintain the load on the battery for 15 seconds and observe that the battery voltage does not drop below 9.6 volts. If the battery condition is weak or defective, the tool will indicate this condition immediately.

➥**Note: Cold temperatures will cause the minimum voltage requirements to drop slightly. Follow the chart given in the tool manufacturer's instructions to compensate for cold climates. Minimum load voltage for freezing temperatures (32-degrees F/0-degrees C) should be approximately 9.1 volts.**

d) Battery drain test - This test will indicate whether there's a constant drain on the vehicle's electrical system that can cause the battery to discharge. Make sure all accessories are turned Off. If the vehicle has an underhood light, verify it's working properly, then disconnect it. Connect one lead of a digital ammeter to the disconnected negative battery cable clamp and the other lead to the negative battery post. A drain of approximately 100 milliamps or less is considered normal (due to the engine control computers, clocks, digital radios and other components that normally cause a key-off battery drain). An excessive drain (approximately 500 milliamps or more) will cause the battery to discharge. The problem circuit or component can be located by removing the fuses, one at a time, until the excessive drain stops and normal drain is indicated on the meter.

---

4   Battery cables - replacement

▶ **Refer to illustrations 4.2, 4.4a, 4.4b and 4.4c**

1   Periodically inspect the entire length of each battery cable for damage, cracked or burned insulation and corrosion. Poor battery

cable connections can cause starting problems and decreased engine performance.
2   Check the cable-to-terminal connections at the ends of the cables for cracks, loose wire strands and corrosion (see illustration).

The presence of white, fluffy deposits under the insulation at the cable terminal connection is a sign that the cable is corroded and should be replaced. Check the terminals for distortion, missing mounting bolts and corrosion (see Chapter 1 for further information regarding battery cable maintenance).

3   When removing the cables always disconnect the negative cable from the negative battery post first and hook it up last or the tool used to loosen the cable clamps may short the battery. Even if only the positive cable is being replaced, be sure to disconnect the negative cable from the negative battery post first.

4   Disconnect the old cables from the battery (see Section 3), then disconnect each of them at the other end. It might also be necessary to detach the cables from cable brackets or clips before they can be removed. Trace each cable from the battery all the way down to its opposite end and detach the cables from any cable brackets or clips as necessary (see illustrations). If either cable is bundled together with other wiring harnesses, look for the other end of the cable where it comes out of the harness. The negative or ground cable is usually bolted to the engine or transaxle and the positive cable is connected to the starter motor solenoid. (If you're unable to trace the ground cable to its lower end, you might have to remove the protective sheath from the harness and separate the cable from the other wires.) Note the routing of both cables to ensure correct installation.

5   Positive cables are almost always red and larger in cross-section; ground cables are usually black and smaller in cross-section. But if you're replacing either or both of the cables, take them with you when buying new cables. It is vitally important that you replace the cables with the identical parts.

6   Clean the threads of the starter solenoid and/or ground connection with a wire brush to remove rust and corrosion. Apply a light coat of battery terminal corrosion inhibitor or petroleum jelly to the threads to prevent future corrosion.

7   Attach the lower ends of the cables first, then connect the positive cable to the positive battery post (don't reconnect the ground cable to the negative battery post until you're completely finished). Before connecting a new cable to the battery, make sure that it reaches the battery post without having to be stretched.

8   If either cable is supposed to be secured to the engine compartment by any brackets or clips, make sure that you reattach them.

9   After both cables are completely installed, reconnect the ground cable to the negative battery post.

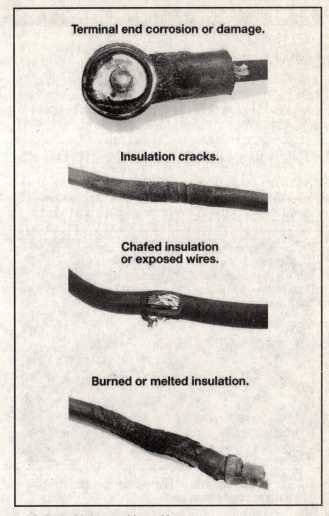

4.2 Typical battery cable problems

10 After you're done, the Powertrain Control Module (PCM) must relearn its idle and fuel trim strategy for optimum driveability and performance (see Section 1 for this procedure).

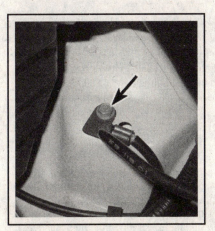

4.4a To detach the ground cable from the left fender, remove this bolt

4.4b To detach the lower end of the ground cable from the transaxle, remove this bolt (V6 model shown, other models similar)

4.4c To disconnect the lower end of the positive battery cable from the starter solenoid, remove this nut (V6 model shown, other models similar)

5   Ignition system - general information

◗ **Refer to illustration 5.2**

The ignition system consists of the ignition coils, the Crankshaft Position (CKP) sensor, the Camshaft Position (CMP) sensor, the Powertrain Control Module (PCM), the spark plug wires and the spark plugs. None of the vehicles covered by this manual are equipped with a distributor nor do any of these vehicles use a separate ignition control module. "Coil drivers" inside the PCM handle the control module function based on data from the CKP and CMP sensors. (For more information on the CKP and CMP sensors, refer to Chapter 6.)

2.0L four-cylinder models employ a coil pack (see illustration) mounted at the left end of the valve cover, consisting of two ignition

5.2 The ignition coil pack on four-cylinder models is located at the left end of the valve cover

coils. Each coil supplies ignition voltage to two cylinders. The firing order of a four-cylinder engine is 1-3-4-2. The PCM fires one coil for each pair of cylinders (1 and 4, or 3 and 2) that are at Top Dead Center (TDC) at the same time. These cylinder pairs are known as "companion cylinders," or "running mates." Each time either coil fires, it sends ignition voltage to both of its paired cylinders. One cylinder is on its compression stroke, so that cylinder gets most of the voltage (because pressure, and therefore resistance, is higher in that cylinder). The other cylinder is on its exhaust stroke, so it gets very little of the voltage (because pressure, and therefore resistance, is low in that cylinder). In effect, the spark in the cylinder on its exhaust stroke is wasted. So this type of ignition system is known as a "waste spark" system.

Each waste-spark coil is in series with its two spark plugs. As the coil fires, secondary current creates a high-voltage spark across the gaps of both plugs. One plug fires with the traditional forward polarity of an ignition system: negative (−) to positive (+). The other plug fires with opposite polarity: positive (+) to negative (−). Thus, one plug always fires with what has always been called "reversed polarity." The voltage capacity of a the coil pack is high enough, however, to ensure that the available voltage is always high enough to fire the plug with reversed polarity when it is on the compression stroke.

2.3L four-cylinder models and 3.0L V6 engines use an individual coil for each cylinder. Each coil is mounted directly above the plug that it fires, and is connected to the plug by a coiled high-tension lead housed inside a long rubber boot that protects it from the elements. When the engine is first cranked over, the PCM fires two cylinders at once, one on compression and one as a waste spark, just like the coil-pack on the four-cylinder engine. However, once the engine starts, cylinders are only fired one at a time, on their compression stroke.

Base ignition timing for all models is nominally 8 to 12 degrees Before Top Dead Center (BTDC), but it cannot be checked or adjusted.

6   Ignition system - check

◗ **Refer to illustration 6.3**

✳✳ WARNING:

Because of the very high voltage generated by the ignition system (approximately 40,000 volts), use extreme care whenever performing an operation involving ignition components. This not only includes the coil and spark plug wires, but related items connected to the system as well, such as the electrical connectors, tachometer and any test equipment.

➠**Note: The ignition system components on these models are difficult to diagnose. In the event of ignition system failure, if the checks do not clearly indicate the source of the ignition system problem, have the vehicle tested by a dealer service department or other qualified auto repair facility.**

1   If a malfunction occurs and the vehicle won't start, do not immediately assume that the ignition system is causing the problem. First, check the following items:

a)   *Make sure the battery cable clamps, where they connect to the battery, are clean and tight.*

b)   *Test the condition of the battery (see Section 3). If it does not pass all the tests, replace it with a new battery.*

c)   *Check the external ignition coil (if equipped) wiring and connections.*

d)   *Check the related fuses inside the fuse box (see Chapter 12). If they're burned, determine the cause and repair the circuit.*

2   If the engine turns over but won't start, make sure there is sufficient secondary ignition voltage to fire the spark plug.

3   Disconnect the spark plug wire (four-cylinder models) or ignition coil (V6 models) from a spark plug and attach it to a calibrated ignition tester (available at most auto parts stores) (see illustration). Connect the clip on the tester to a bolt or metal bracket on the engine.

➠**Note: On 2.0L four-cylinder models, each ignition coil fires two cylinders (see Section 5 for a complete description of this type of ignition system). Because the coil assembly actually fires two spark plugs simultaneously, you must check the spark at both high-tension terminals to test for sufficient secondary voltage. Testing at only one terminal will not conclusively tell you that one of these coils is operating correctly because there could be an open, or high resistance, in the circuit between the winding and the high tension terminal that you didn't test. So be sure to test both terminals of each coil on these models.**

4   Relieve the fuel pressure (see Chapter 4). Keep the fuel system disabled while performing the ignition system checks.

5   Crank the engine and watch the end of the tester to see if bright blue, well-defined sparks occur (weak spark or intermittent spark is the same as no spark).

6   If sparks occur, sufficient voltage is reaching the spark plug to fire it (repeat the check at the remaining spark plug wires or ignition coils to verify that all the ignition coils are functioning). However, the plugs themselves may be fouled, so remove and check them as described in Chapter 1 or install new ones.

7   If no sparks or intermittent sparks occur, check for battery voltage to the ignition coils (refer to the wiring diagrams at the end of Chapter 12). If battery voltage is present, the ignition coils are probably defective. Have the coils tested by a dealer service department.

8   Also, if no sparks or intermittent sparks occur, check the ignition wires to each spark plug (four-cylinder models) (see Chapter 1).

9   If the checks are all correct, the Camshaft Position (CMP) sensor or Crankshaft Position (CKP) sensor might be defective (see Chapter 6 for CMP and CKP sensor replacement procedures).

6.3 To use a spark tester, disconnect a spark plug wire (or on V6 models, as shown, an ignition coil), clip the tester to a convenient ground (like a valve cover bolt), and operate the starter. If enough voltage is present to fire the plug, sparks will be visible between the electrode tip and the tester body

7   Ignition coils - replacement

2.0L FOUR-CYLINDER ENGINES

▸ **Refer to illustrations 7.2 and 7.3**

1   Disconnect the cable from the negative battery terminal (see Section 1).

2   Disconnect the ignition coil pack electrical connector (see illustration).

3   Disconnect all the spark plug wires from the ignition coil pack (see illustration). Pull on the spark plug wire boots, not on the wires.

4   Remove the four bolts that secure the coil pack to its mounting bracket and remove the coil pack.

5   Installation is the reverse of the removal procedure with the following additions:

a) *Before installing the spark plug wire connector into the ignition coil, coat the entire interior of the rubber boot with silicone dielectric compound.*

b) *Insert each spark plug wire into the proper terminal of the ignition coil. Push the wire into the terminal and make sure the boots are fully seated and both locking tabs are engaged properly.*

c) *After you're done, the Powertrain Control Module (PCM) must relearn its idle and fuel trim strategy for optimum driveability and performance (see Section 1 for this procedure).*

7.2 Disconnect the electrical connector from the coil pack (four-cylinder models)

7.3 Disconnect the spark plug wires from the coil pack (four-cylinder models)

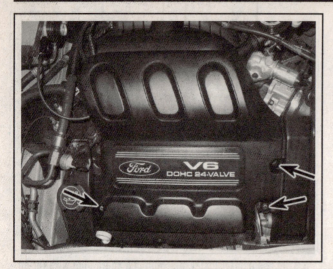

7.7 To detach the engine cover, remove these three nuts (V6 models)

7.8 Disconnect the electrical connector from the ignition coil

2.3L FOUR-CYLINDER AND 3.0L V6 ENGINES

♦ **Refer to illustrations 7.7, 7.8, 7.9, 7.10 and 7.11**

6   Disconnect the cable from the negative battery terminal (see Section 1).

7   Remove the engine cover (see illustration). And, if you're going to remove an ignition coil from the rear valve cover, remove the upper intake manifold (see Chapter 2B).

8   Disconnect the electrical connector from the ignition coil (see illustration).

9   Remove the coil mounting bolt (see illustration).

10   Remove the ignition coil (see illustration).

11   Coat the inside of the spark plug boot with silicone dielectric compound (see illustration).

12   Installation is otherwise the reverse of removal.

13   After you're done, the Powertrain Control Module (PCM) must relearn its idle and fuel trim strategy for optimum driveability and performance (see Section 1 for this procedure).

7.9 To detach an ignition coil from the valve cover, remove this bolt

7.10 To remove an ignition coil from the valve cover, pull it straight up

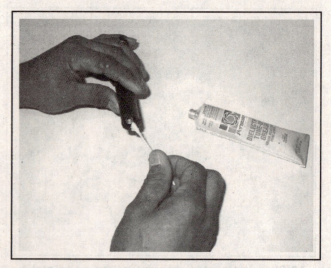

7.11 Before pushing the spark plug boot back onto the spark plug, coat the inside of the boot with silicone dielectric compound

8 Charging system - general information and precautions

♦ **Refer to illustration 8.2**

The charging system supplies electrical power for the ignition system, the lights, the radio, the electronic control systems and all other electrical components on the car. The charging system consists of the battery, the alternator (with an integral voltage regulator), a charge indicator or warning lamp on the instrument panel, a 120-amp main fuse (located in the engine compartment fuse and relay box) and the wiring

8.2 The alternator is located behind the right end of the engine on all models (four-cylinder model shown)

between all the components. The 120-amp fuse is the main circuit protection device for the entire vehicle electrical system. There's another smaller (15-amp) fuse in the engine compartment fuse and relay box and, on V6 models, a third fuse (also 15 amps) in the passenger compartment fuse and relay box inside the vehicle. These smaller fuses protect the circuits between the alternator and the fuse and relay boxes.

The alternator generates alternating current (ac) that is rectified to direct current (dc) to charge the battery and supply power to other electrical systems. The alternator is driven by a drivebelt at the front of the engine (right side of the vehicle). On four-cylinder models, the alternator is located on the backside of the engine (see illustration). It's also located in the same place on V6 models. The voltage regulator limits the alternator charging voltage by regulating the current supplied to the alternator field circuit. The regulator is a solid-state electronic assembly mounted inside the alternator. The regulator is not separately replaceable on these vehicles. If it's defective, you must replace the alternator.

The alternator drivebelt, the battery, and all charging system wires and connections should be inspected at the intervals listed in Chapter 1.

Be very careful when making any circuit connections and note the following:

a) *Never start the engine with a battery charger connected.*
b) *Always disconnect both battery cables before using a battery charger: negative cable first, positive cable last. After you're done, the Powertrain Control Module (PCM) must relearn its idle and fuel trim strategy for optimum driveability and performance (see Section 1 for this procedure).*

9 Charging system - check

♦ **Refer to illustration 9.2**

1 If the charging system malfunctions, don't immediately assume that the alternator is causing the problem. First check the following items:

a) *Ensure that the battery cable connections at the battery are clean and tight.*
b) *If the battery is not a maintenance-free type, check the electrolyte level and specific gravity. If the electrolyte level is low, add clean, mineral-free tap water. If the specific gravity is low, charge the battery.*
c) *Check the alternator wiring and connections.*
d) *Check the drivebelt condition and tension (see Chapter 1).*
e) *Check the alternator mounting bolts for looseness.*
f) *Run the engine and check the alternator for abnormal noise.*

2 Use a voltmeter to check the battery voltage with the engine off. It should be at least 12 volts (see illustration).

3 Start the engine and check the battery voltage again. It should now be approximately 14 to 15 volts.

4 If the voltage reading is less than the specified charging voltage, check the charging system fuses in the engine compartment and passenger compartment fuse and relay boxes. If a fuse is blown, replace it. If all three fuses are OK, the voltage regulator is defective. Replace the alternator (the voltage regulator cannot be replaced separately).

5 If the voltage reading is more than the specified charging voltage, the voltage regulator is defective. Replace the alternator (the voltage regulator cannot be replaced separately).

6 Some models have an ammeter on the instrument panel that indicates charge or discharge. With all electrical equipment on and the engine idling, the gauge needle may show a discharge condition. At fast idle or normal driving speeds, the needle should stay on the charge side of the gauge. The state of charge of the battery determines the amount of charging current shown by the ammeter. (The lower the

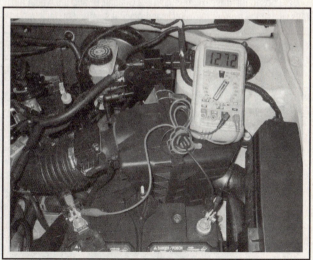

9.2 Battery voltage should be at least 12 volts with the engine off. When the engine is running, regulated voltage should be 13.5 to 15 volts

battery state of charge, the farther the needle should move toward the charge side.)

7 Some models have a voltmeter on the instrument panel that indicates battery voltage with the key on and engine off and alternator charging voltage when the engine is running.

8 The charge lamp on the instrument panel lights with the key on and engine not running and should go out when the engine runs.

9 If the ammeter or voltmeter does not show a charge when it should, or the alternator light remains on, there is a fault in the system. Before inspecting the brushes or replacing the voltage regulator or the alternator, check the battery condition, alternator belt tension, and electrical cable connections.

10 If replacing the regulator doesn't restore voltage to the specified range, the problem may be in the alternator. Have the alternator tested by an automotive electrical specialist.

10 Alternator - removal and installation

FOUR-CYLINDER MODELS

1 Disconnect the cable from the negative battery terminal (see Section 1).

2 Remove the alternator drivebelt (see Chapter 1).

3 Disconnect the electrical connectors from the alternator.

4 Raise the front of the vehicle and place it securely on jackstands.

5 Remove the lower alternator bolts.

6 *Unscrew* the upper alternator bolt. (There's not enough clearance to remove the upper alternator bolt; it comes off with the alternator.)

7 Move the alternator to the rear, then lift it up and remove it from the engine compartment.

8 Before installing the alternator, insert the upper alternator bolt into its hole in the alternator mounting boss (you can't install the bolt once the alternator is in place).

9 Installation is otherwise the reverse of removal.

10 After you've reconnected the battery, the Powertrain Control Module (PCM) must relearn its idle and fuel trim strategy for optimum driveability and performance (see Section 1 for this procedure).

V6 MODELS

▶ Refer to illustrations 10.13, 10.16a, 10.16b, 10.17, 10.18, 10.20, 10.21 and 10.23

11 Disconnect the cable from the negative battery terminal (see Section 1).

12 Loosen the driveaxle hub nut (see Chapter 8) and the wheel lug nuts. Raise the front of the vehicle and place it securely on jackstands.

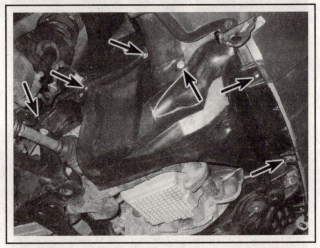

10.13 To detach the right engine splash shield from the vehicle, remove these fasteners (V6 models)

Remove the wheel.

13 Remove the right lower engine splash shield (see illustration).

14 Remove the right driveaxle (see Chapter 8). (You will also need to remove the intermediate shaft before you can remove the alternator, but don't actually remove it at this time, or gear lubricant will leak out of the transaxle!)

15 Remove the drivebelt (see Chapter 1).

16 Remove the alternator splash shield (see illustrations).

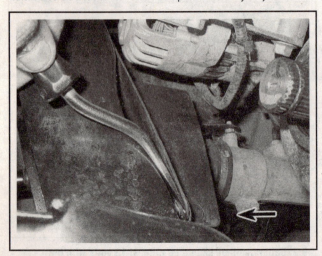

10.16a To detach the alternator splash shield, remove this push fastener . . .

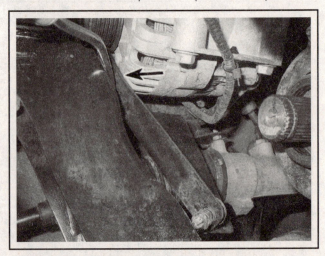

10.16b . . . and this one, then remove the splash shield (V6 models)

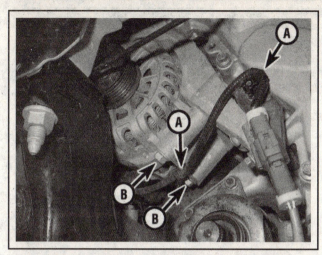

10.17 Detach the two wiring harness clips (A) and position the harness out of the way; to detach the lower part of the alternator from its mounting bracket, remove these two bolts (B) (V6 models)

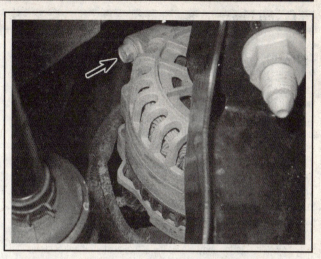

10.18 Remove the upper alternator bolt (V6 models)

17 Detach the wiring harness clips (see illustration) and position the harness out of the way.

18 Remove the upper alternator mounting bolt (see illustration).

19 Remove the lower alternator mounting bolts (see illustration 10.17) and position the alternator out of the way so that you can remove the alternator mounting bracket.

20 Remove the alternator mounting bracket (see illustration).

21 Disconnect the electrical connectors from the alternator (see illustration).

22 Remove the driveaxle intermediate shaft (see Chapter 8). When you detach the inner splined end of the intermediate shaft from the transaxle, some gear lubricant will leak out, so put a drain pan underneath to catch the spilled fluid.

23 Remove the alternator (see illustration) and then install the intermediate shaft immediately to prevent the loss of any more transaxle gear lube.

24 Be sure to check the fluid level inside the transaxle and refill as necessary (see Chapter 1). Installation is otherwise the reverse of removal.

25 After you've reconnected the battery, the Powertrain Control Module (PCM) must relearn its idle and fuel trim strategy for optimum driveability and performance (see Section 1 for this procedure).

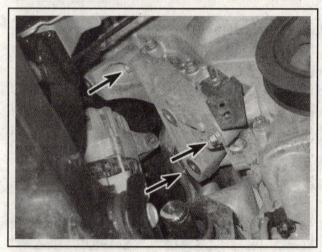

10.20 To detach the alternator mounting bracket from the engine block, remove these bolts (V6 models)

10.21 Disconnect the electrical connector from the alternator, remove the nut from the battery positive (B+) terminal and disconnect the cable from the terminal (V6 models)

10.23 To remove the alternator, lift it out through the space normally occupied by the right driveaxle and intermediate shaft (V6 models)

11 Starting system - general information and precautions

The starting system consists of the battery, the ignition switch, the starter relay, the starter relay diode, the clutch start switch (manual transaxles), the Transmission Range (TR) sensor (automatic transaxles), the starter motor solenoid, the starter motor and the wires that connect these components. The solenoid is located on the starter motor, which is located on the back side of the engine block (four-cylinder models) and on top of the transaxle (V6 models).

The starter motor on a vehicle with a manual transaxle can be operated only when the clutch pedal is depressed. The starter on a vehicle with an automatic transaxle can be operated only when the shift lever is in PARK or NEUTRAL. When the ignition key is turned to the START position, it closes the starter control circuit, which energizes the starter relay. (The starter relay is located in the engine compartment fuse and relay box.) The starter relay closes the actual starter circuit between the battery and the starter solenoid, which energizes the solenoid, which moves a lever that engages the starter pinion gear with the flywheel ring gear to crank the engine.

Always observe the following precautions when working on the starting system:

a) Excessive cranking of the starter motor can overheat it and cause serious damage. Never operate the starter motor for more than 15 seconds at a time without pausing for at least two minutes to allow it to cool.

b) The starter is connected directly to the battery and could arc or cause a fire if mishandled, overloaded or short-circuited.

c) Always detach the cable from the negative battery terminal before working on the starting system.

12 Starter motor and circuit - check

♦ **Refer to illustrations 12.3 and 12.4**

1   If a malfunction occurs in the starting circuit, do not immediately assume that the starter is causing the problem. First, check the following items:

a) Make sure that the battery cable clamps are clean and tight where they connect to the battery.

b) Check the condition of the battery cables (see Section 4). Replace any defective battery cables with new parts.

c) Test the condition of the battery (see Section 3). If it does not pass all the tests, replace it with a new battery.

d) Check the starter solenoid wiring and connections. Refer to the wiring diagrams at the end of Chapter 12.

e) Check the starter mounting bolts for tightness.

f) Make sure that the shift lever is in PARK or NEUTRAL (automatic transaxle) or the clutch pedal is pressed (manual transaxle).

g) Check the adjustment of the Transmission Range (TR) sensor on vehicles with an automatic transaxle (see Chapter 6). On vehicles with a manual transaxle, make sure that the Clutch Pedal Position (CPP) switch is correctly installed.

h) Check the operation of the starter relay (located in the engine compartment fuse and relay box). Refer to Chapter 12 for the relay testing procedure.

2   If the starter does not actuate when the ignition switch is turned to the start position, check for battery voltage to the solenoid. This will determine if the solenoid is receiving the correct voltage signal from the ignition switch. Connect a test light or voltmeter to the starter solenoid switched terminal (the small wire) and while an assistant turns the ignition switch to the start position. If voltage is not available, refer to the wiring diagrams in Chapter 12 and check all the fuses and relays in series with the starting system. If voltage is available but the starter motor does not operate, remove the starter from the engine compartment (see Section 13) and bench test the starter (see Step 4).

3   If the starter turns over slowly, check the starter cranking voltage and the current draw from the battery. This test must be performed with the starter assembly on the engine. Crank the engine over (for 10 seconds or less) and observe the battery voltage. It should not drop below 8.0 volts on manual transaxle models or 8.5 volts on automatic transaxle models. Also, observe the current draw using an amp meter

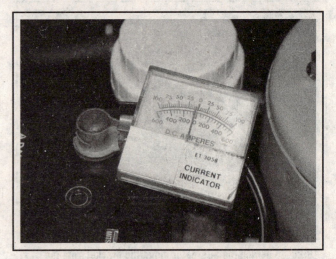

12.3 To use an inductive ammeter, simply hold the ammeter over the positive or negative cable (whichever cable has better clearance)

(see illustration). It should not exceed 400 amps or drop below 250 amps.

❊❊ CAUTION:

The battery cables might overheat because of the large amount of current being drawn from the battery. Discontinue the testing until the starting system has cooled down.

If the starter motor cranking amp values are not within the correct range, replace it with a new unit. There are several conditions that may affect the starter cranking potential. The battery must be in good condition and the battery cold-cranking rating must not be under-rated for the particular application. Be sure to check the battery specifications carefully. The battery terminals and cables must be clean and not corroded. Also, in cases of extreme cold temperatures, make sure the battery and/or engine block is warmed before performing the tests.

4   If the starter is receiving voltage but does not activate, remove

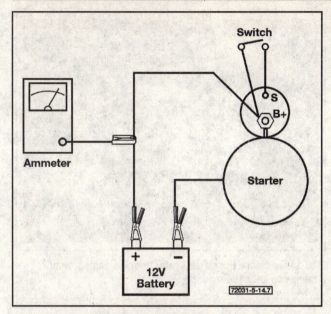

12.4 Starter motor bench testing details

and check the starter/solenoid assembly on the bench. Most likely the solenoid is defective. In some rare cases, the engine may be seized so be sure to try and rotate the crankshaft pulley (see Chapter 2) before proceeding. With the starter/solenoid assembly mounted in a vise on the bench, install one jumper cable from the negative battery terminal to the body of the starter. Install the other jumper cable from the positive battery terminal to the B+ terminal on the starter. Install a starter switch and apply battery voltage to the solenoid S terminal (for 10 seconds or less) and see if the solenoid plunger, shift lever and overrunning clutch extends and rotates the pinion drive (see illustration). If the pinion drive extends but does not rotate, the solenoid is operating but the starter motor is defective. If there is no movement but the solenoid clicks, the solenoid and/or the starter motor is defective. If the solenoid plunger extends and rotates the pinion drive, the starter/solenoid assembly is working properly.

13 Starter motor - removal and installation

FOUR-CYLINDER MODELS

1 Disconnect the cable from the negative battery terminal (see Section 1).

2 Remove the three starter motor mounting bolts.

3 Raise the front of the vehicle and place it securely on jackstands.

4 Remove the bolts from the support bracket for the intermediate shaft center bearing (see Chapter 8). (It's not necessary to remove either the right driveaxle or the intermediate shaft, but detaching the center bearing support bracket will give you enough room to pull out the starter.)

5 Disconnect the battery cable (the large cable) and the starter control electrical connector from the starter motor solenoid terminals.

6 Remove the starter.

7 Installation is the reverse of removal.

8 After you've reconnected the battery, the Powertrain Control Module (PCM) must relearn its idle and fuel trim strategy for optimum driveability and performance (see Section 1 for this procedure).

V6 MODELS

▶ Refer to illustration 13.12, 13.13 and 13.14

✶✶ WARNING:

Wait until the engine is completely cool before beginning this procedure.

9 Disconnect the cable from the negative battery terminal (see Section 1).

10 Remove the air intake duct (see Chapter 4), then remove the air filter housing and Mass Air Flow (MAF) sensor as a single assembly (see Chapter 4). (It's not necessary to detach the MAF sensor from the air filter housing.)

11 Drain the cooling system (see Chapter 1).

12 Remove the coolant hoses located above the starter motor (see illustration).

13.12 To gain access to the starter motor on V6 models, disconnect these coolant hoses and position them out of the way (have some rags handy to catch any residual coolant that might drip onto the engine)

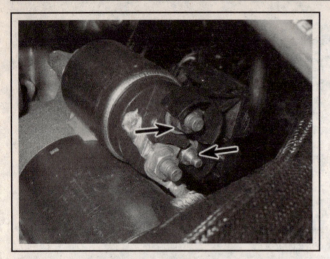

13.13 Disconnect the battery starter cable from the big terminal and the starter control cable from the smaller terminal (V6 models)

13.14 To detach the starter motor from the engine, remove these two bolts (V6 models)

13 Disconnect the battery cable (the large cable) and the starter control electrical connector from the starter motor solenoid terminals (see illustration).

14 Remove the starter motor mounting bolts (see illustration) and remove the starter from the engine.

15 Installation is the reverse of removal.

16 After you've reconnected the battery, the Powertrain Control Module (PCM) must relearn its idle and fuel trim strategy for optimum driveability and performance (see Section 1 for this procedure).

Specifications

General

Firing order	
Four-cylinder engine	1-3-4-2
V6 engine	1-4-2-5-3-6
Cylinder numbering (from drivebelt end to transaxle end)	
Four-cylinder engine	1-2-3-4
V6 engine	
Rear bank	1-2-3
Front bank	4-5-6
Ignition timing	Not adjustable

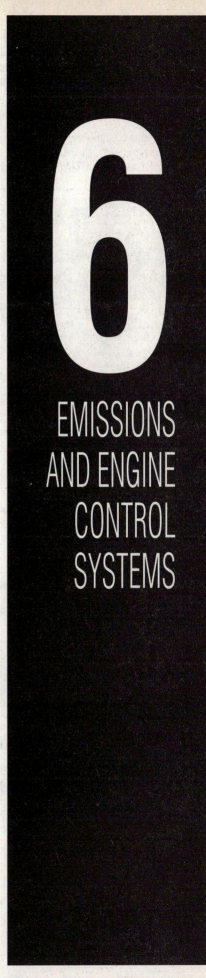

6

EMISSIONS AND ENGINE CONTROL SYSTEMS

1 General information

♦ **Refer to illustrations 1.1a, 1.1b, 1.1c and 1.7**

The emission control systems and components (see illustrations) are an integral part of the engine management system, which is called the Multiport Fuel Injection (MFI) system (see Chapter 4 for more information on the MFI system). The MFI system also includes all the government-mandated diagnostic features of the second generation of on-board diagnostics, which is known as On-Board Diagnostics II (OBD-II).

At the center of the MFI and OBD-II operations is the Powertrain Control Module (PCM), or on-board computer. The PCM controls not only engine operation but also the automatic transaxle. The PCM receives engine operating information as input signals from a number of sensors and provides output commands to actuators such as the ignition coil(s), the fuel injectors and various solenoids and relays for the engine and automatic transaxle. Other emission controls included in the overall engine control system are:

Catalytic converter(s)
Evaporative Emission Control (EVAP) system
Exhaust Gas Recirculation (EGR) system
Positive Crankcase Ventilation (PCV) system

The Sections in this Chapter include general descriptions and component replacement procedures for most of the information sensors and output actuators, as well as other components that are part of the systems listed above. Refer to Chapter 4 for more information on the air intake, fuel and exhaust systems, and to Chapter 5 for information on the ignition system. Also refer to Chapter 1 for scheduled maintenance procedures for emission-related systems and components.

The procedures in this Chapter are intended to be practical, affordable and within the capabilities of the home mechanic. The diagnosis of most engine and emission control functions and driveability problems requires specialized tools, equipment and training. When checking or servicing become too difficult or require special test equipment, consult a dealer service department or other qualified repair shop.

Although engine and emission control systems are very sophisticated on late-model vehicles, you can perform many checks and do most of the regular maintenance at home with common tune-up and hand tools and relatively inexpensive meters. Because of the Federally mandated warranty that covers the emission control system, check with a dealer about warranty coverage before working on any emission-related systems. After the warranty has expired, you may wish to perform

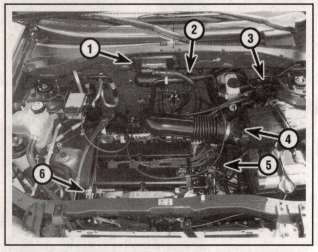

1.1a Emissions and engine control component locations (four-cylinder models)

1   *Powertrain Control Module (PCM)*
2   *EGR vacuum regulator valve*
3   *Evaporative Emissions Control (EVAP) system canister purge valve*
4   *Mass Air Flow (MAF) sensor*
5   *Differential pressure feedback EGR system sensor*
6   *Oxygen sensor electrical connectors*

1.1b Emissions and engine control component locations, left side (V6 models)

1   *Mass Air Flow (MAF) sensor*
2   *Crankcase vent tube*
3   *Idle Air Control (IAC) valve*
4   *EGR vacuum regulator valve*
5   *Exhaust Gas Recirculation (EGR) valve*
6   *Differential pressure feedback EGR system sensor*
7   *Evaporative Emissions Control (EVAP) system canister purge valve*
8   *Throttle Position (TP) sensor*

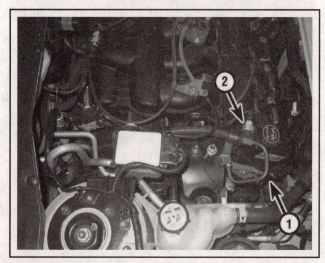

1.1c Emission control component locations, right side (V6 models)

1   *Camshaft Position (CMP) sensor*
2   *Power Steering Pressure (PSP) switch*

some of the component replacement procedures in this Chapter to save money. Remember, the most frequent cause of emission and driveability problems is a loose electrical connector, or a broken wire or vacuum hose, so always check the electrical connections, the electrical wiring and the vacuum hoses first.

Pay close attention to any special precautions given in this Chapter. Remember that illustrations of various systems might not exactly match the system installed on the vehicle on which you're working because of changes made by the manufacturer during production or from year to year.

A Vehicle Emission Control Information (VECI) label (see illustration) is located in the engine compartment (on the underside of the hood on our project vehicle, although it might be located somewhere else, like the upper radiator crossmember, on your vehicle). This label contains emission-control and engine tune-up specifications and adjustment information. It also includes a vacuum hose routing diagram for emission-control components. When servicing the engine or emission systems, always check the VECI label in your vehicle. If any information in this manual contradicts what you read on the VECI label on your vehicle, always defer to the information on the VECI label.

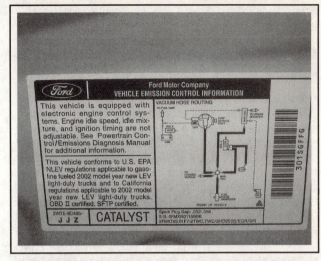

1.7 The VECI label in the engine compartment identifies the emission control devices on a particular engine and includes a vacuum hose routing diagram

---

2 On-Board Diagnostic (OBD) system and Diagnostic Trouble Codes (DTCs)

SCAN TOOL INFORMATION

▶ **Refer to illustrations 2.1 and 2.2**

1 Hand-held scanners are the most powerful and versatile tools for analyzing engine management systems used on later model vehicles (see illustration). Early model scanners handle codes and some diagnostics for many systems. Each brand scan tool must be examined carefully to match the year, make and model of the vehicle you are working on. Often, interchangeable cartridges are available to access the particular manufacturer (Ford, GM, Chrysler, Toyota etc.). Some manufacturers will specify by continent (Asia, Europe, USA, etc.).

➡**Note: An aftermarket generic scanner should work with any model covered by this manual. Before purchasing a generic**

scan tool, contact the manufacturer of the scanner you're planning to buy and verify that it will work properly with the OBD-II system you want to scan. If necessary, of course, you can always have the codes extracted by a dealer service department or an independent repair shop with a professional scan tool.

2 With the arrival of the Federally mandated emission control system (OBD-II), a specially designed scanner has been developed. Several tool manufacturers have released OBD-II scan tools for the home mechanic (see illustration).

OBD SYSTEM GENERAL DESCRIPTION

3 All models are equipped with the second generation OBD-II system. This system consists of an on-board computer known as the Powertrain Control Module (PCM), and information sensors, which monitor various functions of the engine and send data to the PCM. This system

2.1 Scanners like these from Actron and AutoXray are powerful diagnostic aids - they can tell you just about anything you want to know about your engine management system

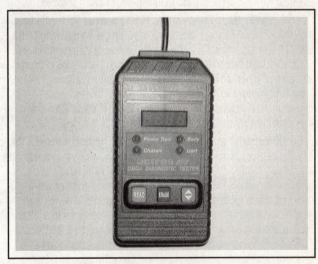

2.2 Trouble code readers like the Actron OBD-II diagnostic tester simplify the task of extracting the trouble codes

incorporates a series of diagnostic monitors that detect and identify fuel injection and emissions control systems faults and store the information in the computer memory. This updated system also tests sensors and output actuators, diagnoses drive cycles, freezes data and clears codes. This powerful diagnostic computer must be accessed using the new OBD-II scan tool and 16 pin Data Link Connector (DLC) located under the driver's dash area.

4   The PCM is the "brain" of the electronically controlled fuel and emissions system. It receives data from a number of sensors and other electronic components (switches, relays, etc.). Based on the information it receives, the PCM generates output signals to control various relays, solenoids (i.e. fuel injectors) and other actuators. The PCM is specifically calibrated to optimize the emissions, fuel economy and driveability of the vehicle.

5   It isn't a good idea to attempt diagnosis or replacement of the PCM or emission control components at home while the vehicle is under warranty. Because of a Federally mandated warranty which covers the emissions system components and because any owner-induced damage to the PCM, the sensors and/or the control devices may void this warranty, take the vehicle to a dealer service department if the PCM or a system component malfunctions.

INFORMATION SENSORS

6   **Camshaft Position (CMP) sensor** - The CMP sensor produces a signal that the PCM uses to identify the number 1 cylinder and to time the firing sequence of the fuel injectors. On four-cylinder models, the CMP sensor is located at the left rear corner of the cylinder head. On V6 models, the CMP sensor is located on the right end of the front cylinder head.

7   **Clutch Pedal Position (CPP) switch** (manual transaxle models) - The CPP switch, which is located at the top of the clutch pedal, provides a voltage input to the PCM which indicates whether the clutch pedal is depressed (no load on the engine) or not depressed (load on the engine). The PCM uses this information (along with data from other sensors) to help it determine the load on the engine so that it can alter the air/fuel mixture ratio accordingly.

8   **Crankshaft Position (CKP) sensor** - The CKP sensor produces a signal that the PCM uses to determine the position of the crankshaft. The CKP sensor is located on the right (drivebelt) end of all engines, adjacent to the crankshaft timing belt or chain sprocket.

9   **Cylinder Heat Temperature (CHT) sensor** (four-cylinder models) - The CHT sensor, which is located on the right (timing belt) end of the cylinder head, is a "thermistor," a type of variable resistor in which the resistance changes in accordance with the change in temperature. The CHT is known as a "negative temperature coefficient" (NTC) thermistor because as the temperature increases, the resistance decreases, and vice versa. The PCM uses the CHT sensor to monitor the operating temperature of the engine.

10   **Differential pressure feedback EGR system sensor** - The differential pressure feedback EGR system sensor, which is located near the firewall, to the right of the brake master cylinder reservoir, is a pressure transducer that monitors the pressure differential across a metering orifice located in the sensor. (A transducer is a device that receives a signal from one system and transfers that signal to another system, often in a different form.) The differential pressure feedback EGR system sensor outputs a voltage signal that's proportional to the pressure drop across its metering orifice. The PCM uses this data to calculate the EGR flow rate.

11   **Engine Coolant Temperature (ECT) sensor (V6 models)** - The ECT sensor is a thermistor (temperature-sensitive variable resistor) that sends a voltage signal to the PCM, which uses this data to determine the temperature of the engine coolant. The ECT sensor helps the PCM control the air/fuel mixture ratio and ignition timing, and it also helps the PCM determine when to turn the Exhaust Gas Recirculation (EGR) system on and off. The ECT sensor is located on the thermostat housing, right below the throttle body.

12   **Fuel tank pressure sensor** - The fuel tank pressure sensor, which is located above the fuel tank, near the fuel pump/fuel level sending unit module, measures the fuel tank pressure when the PCM tests the EVAP system, and it's also used to control fuel tank pressure by signaling the EVAP system to purge the tank when the pressure becomes excessive.

13   **Knock sensor** - The knock sensor is a "piezoelectric" crystal that oscillates in proportion to engine vibration. (The term *piezoelectric* refers to the property of certain crystals that produce a voltage when subjected to a mechanical stress.) The oscillation of the piezoelectric crystal produces a voltage output that is monitored by the PCM, which retards the ignition timing when the oscillation exceeds a certain threshold. When the engine is operating normally, the knock sensor oscillates consistently and its voltage signal is steady. When detonation occurs, engine vibration increases, and the oscillation of the knock sensor exceeds a design threshold. (Detonation is an uncontrolled explosion, after the spark occurs at the spark plug, which spontaneously combusts the remaining air/fuel mixture, resulting in a "pinging" or "slapping" sound.) If allowed to continue, detonation is annoying, and engine performance is diminished. On four-cylinder engines, the knock sensor is located on the right end of the rear side of the engine block. On V6 models, the knock sensor is located on the left rear side of the engine block.

14   **Mass Air Flow (MAF) sensor** - The MAF sensor is located on the air intake duct, right at the air filter housing. The MAF sensor is the principal means by which the Powertrain Control Module (PCM) monitors intake airflow. It uses a hot-wire sensing element to measure the amount of air entering the engine. The wire is maintained at a temperature of 392 degrees F (200-degrees C) above the ambient temperature by electrical current. As intake air passes through the MAF sensor and over the hot wire, it cools the wire, and the control system immediately corrects the temperature back to its constant value. The current required to maintain the constant value is used by the PCM as an indicator of airflow.

15   **Output Shaft Speed (OSS) sensor** (automatic transaxle models) - The OSS sensor, a magnetic pick-up coil which is located on the backside of the transaxle, provides the Powertrain Control Module (PCM) with information about the rotational speed of the output shaft in the transaxle. The PCM uses this information to control and diagnose powertrain behavior and to determine vehicle speed (instead of the Vehicle Speed Sensor, or VSS, which is used on manual transaxles).

16   **Oxygen sensors** - An oxygen sensor is a galvanic battery that generates a small variable voltage signal in proportion to the difference between the oxygen content in the exhaust stream and the oxygen content in the ambient air. The PCM uses the voltage signal from the upstream oxygen sensor to maintain a "stoichiometric" air/fuel ratio of 14.7:1 by constantly adjusting the "on-time" of the fuel injectors. There are *two* oxygen sensors on four-cylinder models: one *upstream* sensor (ahead of the catalytic converter) and a *downstream* oxygen sensor (after the catalyst). There are *four* oxygen sensors, one upstream and

one downstream sensor for each cylinder bank, on V6 models. On these models, there are three catalysts: a smaller "fast-light-off" cat right below each exhaust manifold (the catalysts are actually an integral part of the exhaust manifolds) and another larger downstream catalyst. The oxygen sensors are located upstream and downstream in relation to the two smaller catalysts.

17 Power Steering Pressure (PSP) switch - The PSP sensor monitors the pressure inside the power steering system. When the front wheels are being turned at low speed there is more friction between the rubber tire treads and the road, so the pressure required to turn the wheels increases. The PCM uses the PSP sensor to determine when to increase engine idle speed during low-speed vehicle maneuvers. The PSP switch is located on the high-pressure side of the power steering system, near the right end of the front cylinder head valve cover.

18 Throttle Position (TP) sensor - The TP sensor, which is located on the throttle body, on the end of the throttle valve shaft, is a potentiometer that produces a variable voltage signal in accordance with the opening angle of the throttle valve. This voltage signal tells the PCM when the throttle is closed, in a cruise position, or wide open, or anywhere in between. The PCM uses this information, along with data from a number of other sensors, to calculate injector on-time.

19 Transmission Range (TR) sensor - The TR sensor, which is located at the manual lever on top of the automatic transaxle, functions like a conventional Park/Neutral Position (PNP) switch: it prevents the engine from starting in any gear other than Park or Neutral, and it closes the circuit for the back-up lights when the shift lever is moved to Reverse. The PCM also sends a voltage signal to the TR sensor, which uses a series of step-down resistors that act as a voltage divider. The PCM monitors the TR sensor's voltage output, which corresponds to the position of the manual lever. Thus the PCM is able to determine the gear selected and is able to determine the correct pressure for the electronic pressure control system of the transaxle.

20 Turbine Shaft Speed (TSS) sensor (automatic transaxle models) - The TSS sensor, a magnetic pick-up coil which is located on the left side of the transaxle, provides the Powertrain Control Module (PCM) with information about the rotational speed of the turbine (input) shaft. The PCM uses this information to determine control strategies for the Torque Converter Clutch (TCC) and to determine the static Electronic Pressure Control (EPC) pressure setting during shifts.

21 Vehicle Speed Sensor (VSS) - The VSS, which is located on the transaxle, provides information to the PCM to indicate vehicle speed. Manual transaxles are equipped with one VSS. Automatics are equipped with an input and an output VSS (the PCM compares the difference, if any, between the two signals to predict transaxle failure).

OUTPUT ACTUATORS

22 EVAP canister purge valve - The EVAP canister purge valve, which is located in the engine compartment, near the master cylinder, is normally closed. But when ordered to do so by the PCM, it allows fuel vapors from the EVAP canister to be drawn into the intake manifold for combustion under certain operating conditions. The PCM-controlled EVAP canister purge valve also controls this vapor flow.

23 EVAP canister vent solenoid - The EVAP canister vent solenoid, which is located underneath the vehicle, near the EVAP canister, seals the EVAP system for inspection and maintenance tests and for OBD-II leak and pressure tests.

24 Exhaust Gas Recirculation (EGR) vacuum regulator valve - When the engine is put under a load (hard acceleration, pass-

ing, going up a steep hill, pulling a trailer, etc.), combustion chamber temperatures increase. When combustion chamber temperature exceeds 2500 degrees, excessive amounts of oxides of nitrogen (NOx) are produced. NOx is a precursor of photochemical smog. When combined with hydrocarbons (HC), other "reactive organic compounds" (ROCs) and sunlight, it forms ozone, nitrogen dioxide and nitrogen nitrate and other nasty stuff. The vacuum-controlled EGR valve allows exhaust gases to be recirculated back to the intake manifold where they dilute the incoming air/fuel mixture, which lowers the combustion chamber temperature and decreases the amount of NOx produced during high-load conditions. The amount of exhaust gases recirculated to the intake is determined by the strength of the vacuum signal delivered to the EGR valve. The PCM-controlled EGR vacuum regulator valve is the electromagnetic device that regulates the supply of vacuum to the EGR valve. The EGR vacuum regulator valve is located near the EGR valve.

25 Fuel injectors - The fuel injectors, which spray a fine mist of fuel into the intake ports, where it is mixed with incoming air, are inductive coils under PCM control. For more information about the injectors, see Chapter 4.

26 Idle Air Control (IAC) valve - The IAC valve controls the amount of air allowed to bypass the throttle valve when the throttle valve is at its (nearly closed) idle position. The IAC valve is controlled by the PCM. When the engine is placed under an additional load at idle (low-speed maneuvers or the air conditioning compressor, for example), the engine can run roughly, stumble and even stall. To prevent this from happening, the PCM opens the IAC valve to increase the idle speed enough to overcome the extra load imposed on the engine. The IAC valve is mounted on the intake manifold, near the throttle body.

27 Ignition coil(s) - The ignition coil(s) is/are under the control of the Powertrain Control Module (PCM). There is no ignition control module. Instead, "coil drivers" inside the PCM turn the primary side of the coil(s) on and off. For more information about the ignition coil(s), see Chapter 5.

OBTAINING AND CLEARING DIAGNOSTIC TROUBLE CODES (DTCS)

28 All models covered by this manual are equipped with on-board diagnostics. When the PCM recognizes a malfunction in a monitored emission control system, component or circuit, it turns on the CHECK ENGINE light, also known as the Malfunction Indicator Light (MIL), on the dash. The PCM will continue to display the MIL until the problem is fixed and the Diagnostic Trouble Code (DTC) is cleared from the PCM's memory. You'll need a scan tool to access any DTCs stored in the PCM.

29 Before outputting any DTCs stored in the PCM, thoroughly inspect ALL electrical connectors and hoses. Make sure that all electrical connections are tight, clean and free of corrosion. And make sure that all hoses are correctly connected, fit tightly and are in good condition (no cracks or tears). Also, make sure that the engine is tuned up. A poorly running engine is probably one of the biggest causes of emission-related malfunctions. Often, simply giving the engine a good tune-up will correct the problem.

Accessing the DTCs

▶ **Refer to illustration 2.30**

30 On these models, all of which are equipped with On-Board Diagnostic II (OBD-II) systems, the Diagnostic Trouble Codes (DTCs) can only be accessed with a scan tool. Simply plug the connector of the

scan tool into the diagnostic connector (see illustration), which is located under the left side of the dash, then follow the instructions

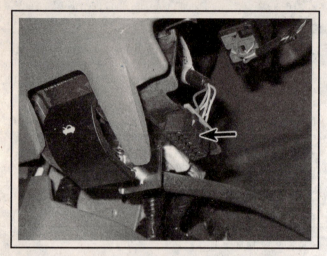

2.30 Location of the 16-pin Data Link Connector (DLC)

included with the scan tool to extract the DTCs.

31 Once you have outputted all of the stored DTCs, look them up on the accompanying DTC chart.

32 After troubleshooting the source of each DTC, make any necessary repairs or replace the defective component(s).

Clearing the DTCs

33 Clear the DTCs with the scan tool in accordance with the instructions provided by the scan tool's manufacturer.

DIAGNOSTIC TROUBLE CODES

34 The accompanying tables are a list of the Diagnostic Trouble Codes (DTCs) that can be accessed by a do-it-yourselfer working at home (there are many, many more DTCs available to dealerships with proprietary scan tools and software, but those codes cannot be accessed by a generic scan tool). If, after you have checked and repaired the connectors, wire harness and vacuum hoses (if applicable) for an emission-related system, component or circuit, the problem persists, have the vehicle checked by a dealer service department or a qualified repair shop.

OBD-II TROUBLE CODES

➡**Note: Not all trouble codes apply to all models.**

Code	Probable cause
P0040	Upstream oxygen sensors swapped (crossed wiring harnesses)
P0041	Downstream oxygen sensors swapped (crossed wiring harnesses)
P0068	Throttle Position (TP) sensor inconsistent with Mass Air Flow sensor
P0102	Mass Air Flow (MAF) sensor circuit, low input
P0103	Mass Air Flow (MAF) sensor circuit, high input
P0106	Barometric (BARO) pressure sensor circuit, performance problem
P0107	Barometric (BARO) pressure sensor/MAP sensor circuit, low voltage
P0108	Barometric (BARO) pressure sensor/MAP sensor circuit, high voltage
P0109	BARO/MAP sensor circuit intermittent
P0112	Intake Air Temperature (IAT) sensor circuit, low input
P0113	Intake Air Temperature (IAT) sensor circuit, high input
P0116	Engine Coolant Temperature (ECT) circuit range/performance problem
P0117	Engine Coolant Temperature (ECT) sensor circuit, low input
P0118	Engine Coolant Temperature (ECT) sensor circuit, high input
P0121	Throttle Position (TP) circuit out of range or performance problem
P0122	Throttle Position (TP) sensor circuit, low input
P0123	Throttle Position (TP) sensor circuit, high input
P0125	Insufficient coolant temperature for closed loop fuel control
P0128	Coolant temperature below thermostat regulated temperature
P0131	Upstream oxygen sensor circuit problem (rear cylinder bank on V6)
P0132	Upstream oxygen sensor circuit, high voltage (rear cylinder bank on V6)

Code	Probable cause
P0133	Upstream oxygen sensor circuit, slow response (rear cylinder bank on V6)
P0135	Upstream oxygen sensor heater circuit problem (rear cylinder bank on V6)
P0136	Downstream oxygen sensor circuit problem (rear cylinder bank on V6)
P0138	Downstream oxygen sensor circuit, high voltage (rear cylinder bank on V6)
P0141	Downstream oxygen sensor heater circuit problem (rear cylinder bank on V6)
P0148	Fuel delivery error
P0151	Upstream oxygen sensor circuit, low voltage (front cylinder bank on V6)
P0152	Upstream oxygen sensor circuit, high voltage (front cylinder bank on V6)
P0153	Upstream oxygen sensor circuit, slow response (front cylinder bank on V6)
P0155	Upstream oxygen sensor heater circuit problem (front cylinder bank on V6)
P0156	Downstream oxygen sensor circuit problem (front cylinder bank on V6)
P0158	Downstream oxygen sensor circuit, high voltage (front cylinder bank on V6)
P0161	Downstream oxygen sensor heater circuit problem (front cylinder bank on V6)
P0171	System too lean (rear cylinder bank on V6)
P0172	System too rich (rear cylinder bank on V6)
P0174	System too lean (front cylinder bank on V6)
P0175	System too rich (front cylinder bank on V6)
P0176	Flexible Fuel (FF) sensor circuit malfunction
P0180	Engine Fuel Temperature (EFT) sensor A circuit, low input
P0181	Engine Fuel Temperature (EFT) sensor A circuit, range/performance
P0183	Engine Fuel Temperature (EFT) sensor circuit, high input
P0190	Fuel Rail Pressure (FRP) sensor circuit malfunction
P0191	Fuel Rail Pressure (FRP) sensor circuit performance
P0192	Fuel Rail Pressure (FRP) sensor circuit, low input
P0193	Fuel Rail Pressure (FRP) sensor circuit, high input
P0196	Engine Oil Temperature sensor circuit range/performance problem
P0197	Engine Oil Temperature sensor circuit, low input
P0198	Engine Oil Temperature sensor circuit, high input
P0201	Injector no. 1 circuit malfunction
P0202	Injector no. 2 circuit malfunction
P0203	Injector no. 3 circuit malfunction
P0204	Injector no. 4 circuit malfunction
P0205	Injector no. 5 circuit malfunction
P0206	Injector no. 6 circuit malfunction
P0219	Engine overspeed condition
P0221	Throttle Position (TP) sensor B circuit range/performance problem
P0222	Throttle Position (TP) sensor B circuit, low input
P0223	Throttle Position (TP) sensor B circuit, high input

Code	Probable cause
P0230	Fuel pump primary circuit malfunction
P0231	Fuel pump secondary circuit low
P0232	Fuel pump secondary circuit high
P0297	Vehicle overspeed condition
P0298	Engine oil over temperature condition
P0300	Random misfire detected
P0301	Cylinder no. 1 misfire detected
P0302	Cylinder no. 2 misfire detected
P0303	Cylinder no. 3 misfire detected
P0304	Cylinder no. 4 misfire detected
P0305	Cylinder no. 5 misfire detected
P0306	Cylinder no. 6 misfire detected
P0315	PCM unable to learn crankshaft pulse wheel tooth spacing
P0316	Misfire occurred during first 1000 engine revolutions
P0320	Ignition engine speed input circuit malfunction
P0325	Knock sensor 1 circuit malfunction
P0326	Knock sensor 1 circuit range/performance
P0330	Knock sensor 2 circuit malfunction
P0331	Knock sensor 2 circuit range/performance
P0340	Camshaft Position (CMP) sensor circuit malfunction
P0345	Camshaft Position (CMP) sensor circuit malfunction
P0350	Ignition coil primary or secondary circuit malfunction (four-cylinder)
P0351	Ignition coil A primary or secondary circuit malfunction (V6 engine)
P0352	Ignition coil B primary or secondary circuit malfunction (V6 engine)
P0353	Ignition coil C primary or secondary circuit malfunction (V6 engine)
P0354	Ignition coil D primary or secondary circuit malfunction (V6 engine)
P0355	Ignition coil E primary or secondary circuit malfunction (V6 engine)
P0356	Ignition coil F primary or secondary circuit malfunction (V6 engine)
P0400	EGR flow failure (outside the minimum or maximum limits)
P0401	Exhaust Gas Recirculation (EGR) valve, insufficient flow detected
P0402	Exhaust Gas Recirculation (EGR) valve, excessive flow detected
P0403	EEGR electric motor windings or circuits to PCM shorted or open
P0405	DPF EGR sensor circuit, low voltage detected
P0406	DPF EGR sensor circuit, high voltage detected
P0411	Secondary Air Injection (AIR) system, upstream flow
P0412	Secondary Air Injection (AIR) system, circuit malfunction
P0420	Catalyst system efficiency below threshold (rear catalyst on V6)
P0430	Catalyst system efficiency below threshold (front catalyst on V6)

Code	Probable cause
P0442	EVAP control system, small leak detected
P0443	EVAP control system, canister purge valve circuit malfunction
P0446	EVAP control system canister vent solenoid circuit malfunction
P0451	Fuel tank pressure sensor circuit out of range or performance problem
P0452	Fuel tank pressure sensor circuit, low input
P0453	Fuel tank pressure sensor circuit, high input
P0455	EVAP control system, big leak detected
P0456	EVAP control system, very small leak detected
P0457	EVAP control system, leak detected (fuel filler neck cap loose or off)
P0460	Fuel level sensor circuit malfunction
P0462	Fuel level sensor circuit, low input
P0463	Fuel level sensor circuit, high input
P0480	Visctronic Drive Fan (VDF) primary circuit malfunction
P0481	High Fan Control (HFC) primary circuit failure
P0500	Vehicle Speed Sensor (VSS) malfunction
P0501	Vehicle Speed Sensor (VSS) range/performance problem
P0503	Vehicle Speed Sensor (VSS), intermittent malfunction
P0505	Idle Air Control (IAC) system malfunction
P0506	Idle Air Control (IAC) rpm lower than expected
P0507	Idle Air Control (IAC) rpm higher than expected
P0511	Idle Air Control (IAC) circuit malfunction
P0528	Visctronic Drive Fan (VDF) speed sensor circuit malfunction
P0534	Low air conditioning cycling period
P0537	Air conditioning evaporator temperature circuit, low input
P0538	Air conditioning evaporator temperature circuit, high input
P0552	Power Steering Pressure (PSP) sensor circuit malfunction
P0553	Power Steering Pressure (PSP) sensor circuit malfunction
P0602	Control module programming error
P0603	Powertrain Control Module (PCM) Keep-Alive-Memory (KAM) test error
P0605	Powertrain Control Module (PCM) Read-Only-Memory (ROM) error
P0606	Powertrain Control Module (PCM) internal communication error
P0703	Brake switch circuit input malfunction
P0704	Clutch pedal position switch malfunction
P0720	Insufficient input from Output Shaft Speed (OSS) sensor
P0721	Noise interference on Output Shaft Speed (OSS) sensor signal
P0722	No signal from Output Shaft Speed (OSS) sensor
P0723	Output Shaft Speed (OSS) sensor circuit, intermittent failure
P0812	Reverse Switch (RS) input circuit malfunction

3   Camshaft Position (CMP) sensor - replacement

FOUR-CYLINDER MODELS

▶ **Refer to illustrations 3.3 and 3.5**

1   Disconnect the cable from the negative battery terminal (see Chapter 5, Section 1).

2   Locate the CMP sensor at the left rear corner of the cylinder head.

3   Disconnect the electrical connector from the CMP sensor (see illustration).

4   Remove the CMP sensor retaining bolt.

5   Remove the CMP sensor (see illustration).

6   Installation is the reverse of removal. Be sure to tighten the CMP sensor bolt to the torque listed in this Chapter's Specifications.

7   After you've reconnected the battery, the Powertrain Control Module (PCM) must relearn its idle and fuel trim strategy for optimum driveability and performance (see Chapter 5, Section 1 for this procedure).

V6 MODELS

▶ **Refer to illustration 3.9**

8   Disconnect the cable from the negative battery terminal (see Chapter 5, Section 1).

9   Locate the CMP sensor at the right end of the front cylinder head (see illustration).

10   Disconnect the electrical connector from the CMP sensor.

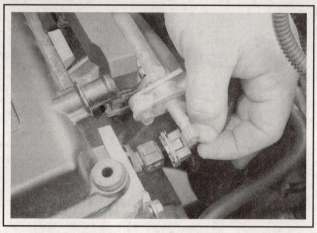

3.3 Disconnect the electrical connector from the CMP sensor (four-cylinder models)

11   Remove the CMP sensor retaining bolt.

12   Remove the CMP sensor.

13   Installation is the reverse of removal. Be sure to tighten the CMP sensor bolt to the torque listed in this Chapter's Specifications.

14   After you've reconnected the battery, the Powertrain Control Module (PCM) must relearn its idle and fuel trim strategy for optimum driveability and performance (see Chapter 5, Section 1 for this procedure).

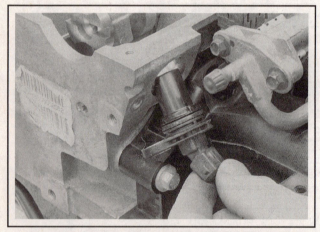

3.5 Remove the CMP sensor retaining bolt, then remove the CMP sensor from the cylinder head (four-cylinder models)

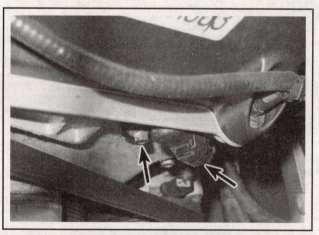

3.9 On V6 models, the CMP sensor is located at the right end of the front cylinder head; to remove the CMP sensor, disconnect the electrical connector and remove the retaining bolt

4   Clutch Pedal Position (CPP) switch - replacement

▶ **Refer to illustration 4.2**

1   Disconnect the cable from the negative battery terminal (see Chapter 5, Section 1).
2   Locate the CPP switch at the top of the clutch pedal (see illustration).
3   Disconnect the electrical connector from the CPP switch.
4   Unscrew the CPP switch locknut.
5   Remove the CPP switch.
6   Installation is the reverse of removal.
7   After you've reconnected the battery, the Powertrain Control Module (PCM) must relearn its idle and fuel trim strategy for optimum driveability and performance (see Chapter 5, Section 1 for this procedure).

4.2 On models with a manual transaxle, the Clutch Pedal Position (CPP) switch is located at the top of the clutch pedal

1   Electrical connector
2   Clutch Pedal Position (CPP) switch
3   Locknut

5   Crankshaft Position (CKP) sensor - replacement

2.0L FOUR-CYLINDER MODELS

▶ **Refer to illustrations 5.5 and 5.6**

1   Disconnect the cable from the negative battery terminal (see Chapter 5, Section 1).
2   Remove the exhaust manifold (see Chapter 2A).
3   Locate the CKP sensor on the front of the engine near the flywheel end of the block.

4   Disconnect the electrical connector from the CKP sensor.
5   Unscrew the CKP sensor mounting bolt (see illustration).
6   Remove the CKP sensor (see illustration).
7   Installation is the reverse of removal. Be sure to tighten the CKP sensor mounting bolt to the torque listed in this Chapter's Specifications.
8   After you've reconnected the battery, the Powertrain Control Module (PCM) must relearn its idle and fuel trim strategy for optimum driveability and performance (see Chapter 5, Section 1 for this procedure).

5.5 On 2.0L four-cylinder models, the CKP sensor is located on the front side of the block, near the flywheel; to remove the CKP sensor, disconnect the electrical connector and remove the mounting bolt

5.6 Remove the CKP sensor (four-cylinder models)

V6 MODELS

◗ **Refer to illustration 5.12**

9   Disconnect the cable from the negative battery terminal (see Chapter 5, Section 1).

10   Loosen the right front wheel lug nuts. Raise the front of the vehicle and place it securely on jackstands. Remove the right front wheel.

11   Remove the lower right splash shield (see illustration 10.13 in Chapter 5).

12   Locate the CKP sensor (see illustration) next to the crankshaft pulley.

13   Disconnect the electrical connector from the CKP sensor.

14   Remove the CKP sensor mounting bolt.

15   Remove the CKP sensor.

16   Installation is the reverse of removal. Be sure to tighten the CKP sensor mounting bolt to the torque listed in this Chapter's Specifications.

17   After you've reconnected the battery, the Powertrain Control Module (PCM) must relearn its idle and fuel trim strategy for optimum driveability and performance (see Chapter 5, Section 1 for this procedure).

2.3L FOUR-CYLINDER ENGINE

Note: The CKP sensor for this engine must be replaced with a new one whenever it is removed because there is a special alignment tool that must be used to install the sensor that can only be obtained with the purchase of a new sensor - the tool is not sold separately.

18   Disconnect the cable from the negative battery terminal (see

5.12 On V6 models, the CKP sensor is located near the crankshaft pulley; to remove the CKP sensor, disconnect the electrical connector and remove the sensor mounting bolt

Chapter 5).

19   The CKP sensor is mounted right next to the crankshaft pulley.

20   Disconnect the electrical connector to the CKP sensor.

21   Set the engine at TDC (see Chapter 2B).

22   With the special timing pin and crankshaft pulley alignment tool in place, remove the mounting bolts for the CKP sensor.

23   To install the CKP sensor, install the mounting bolts - but do not tighten them.

24   Adjust the CKP sensor by using the CKP sensor alignment tool, then tighten the mounting bolts securely.

---

6   Cylinder Head Temperature (CHT) sensor - replacement

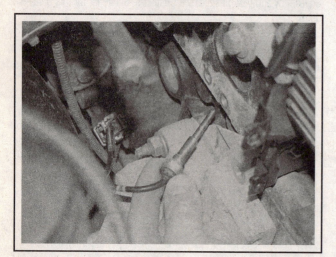

6.4 To remove the CHT sensor from a 2.0L four-cylinder engine, disconnect the electrical connector, then unscrew the sensor. On 2.3L four-cylinder engines, the sensor is located between the number 2 and number 3 spark plugs. (V6 engines do not use a CHT sensor, they use an ECT sensor)

◗ **Refer to illustration 6.4**

➡**Note: This procedure applies to four-cylinder models only.**

1   Disconnect the cable from the negative battery terminal (see Chapter 5, Section 1).

2   Remove the alternator (see Chapter 5).

3   Disconnect the CHT sensor electrical connector.

4   Unscrew and remove the CHT sensor (see illustration).

5   Installation is the reverse of removal. Be sure to tighten the CHT sensor to the torque listed in this Chapter's Specifications.

6   After you've reconnected the battery, the Powertrain Control Module (PCM) must relearn its idle and fuel trim strategy for optimum driveability and performance (see Chapter 5, Section 1 for this procedure).

7   Engine Coolant Temperature (ECT) sensor - replacement

◆ Refer to illustrations 7.4, 7.6 and 7.8

❉❉ WARNING:

Wait until the engine is completely cool before beginning this procedure.

➡Note: This procedure applies to V6 models only.

1 Disconnect the cable from the negative battery terminal (see Chapter 5, Section 1).

2 Drain the cooling system (see Chapter 1).

3 Remove the air intake duct (see Chapter 4).

4 Locate the ECT sensor on the thermostat housing (see illustration).

5 Disconnect the electrical connector from the ECT sensor.

6 Remove the ECT sensor retaining clip (see illustration) by pulling it straight up.

7 Remove the ECT sensor.

8 Remove the ECT sensor O-ring (see illustration) and discard it. Always use a new O-ring when installing the ECT sensor, even if you're planning to reuse the old ECT sensor.

9 Installation is the reverse of removal.

10 Refill the cooling system (see Chapter 1).

11 After you've reconnected the battery, the Powertrain Control Mod-

7.4 On V6 models, the ECT sensor is located on the thermostat housing (four-cylinder models don't use an ECT sensor; they use a CHT sensor); to remove the ECT sensor, disconnect the electrical connector and remove the retaining clip, then pull out the sensor

ule (PCM) must relearn its idle and fuel trim strategy for optimum driveability and performance (see Chapter 5, Section 1 for this procedure).

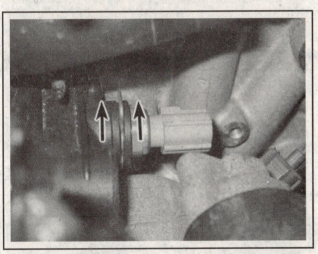

7.6 To remove the ECT sensor retaining clip, pull it straight up

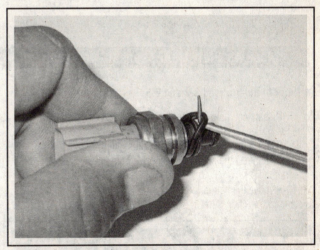

7.8 Remove and discard the old ECT sensor O-ring; always use a new O-ring when installing the ECT sensor, even if you plan to reuse the old sensor

8   Knock sensor - replacement

FOUR-CYLINDER MODELS

1 Disconnect the cable from the negative battery terminal (see Chapter 5, Section 1).

2 Raise the front of the vehicle and place it securely on jackstands.

3 Locate the knock sensor on the back side of the block, near the alternator. If you're working on a 2.3L four-cylinder model, remove the intake manifold (see Chapter 2A).

4 The knock sensor electrical connector is attached to a bracket by two push fasteners. Detach the connector from the bracket and then

disconnect it.

5 Remove the knock sensor retaining nut.

6 Remove the knock sensor.

7 Installation is the reverse of removal. Be sure to tighten the knock sensor retaining nut to the torque listed in this Chapter's Specifications.

8 After you've reconnected the battery, the Powertrain Control Module (PCM) must relearn its idle and fuel trim strategy for optimum driveability and performance (see Chapter 5, Section 1 for this procedure).

8.11 On V6 models, the knock sensor is located on the rear side of the block, near the transaxle; to detach the knock sensor from the block, trace the electrical lead up to the connector (see next illustration) and disconnect it, then remove the knock sensor retaining bolt and remove the sensor

V6 MODELS

⏵ **Refer to illustrations 8.11 and 8.12**

9   Disconnect the cable from the negative battery terminal (see Chapter 5, Section 1).

10   Raise the front of the vehicle and place it securely on jackstands.

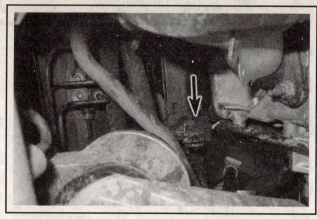

8.12 Trace the electrical lead from the knock sensor up to the sensor electrical connector and disconnect it

11   Locate the knock sensor on the rear side of the block (see illustration).

12   Disconnect the knock sensor electrical connector (see illustration).

13   Remove the knock sensor retaining bolt.

14   Remove the knock sensor.

15   Installation is the reverse of removal. Be sure to tighten the knock sensor retaining bolt to the torque listed in this Chapter's Specifications.

16   After you've reconnected the battery, the Powertrain Control Module (PCM) must relearn its idle and fuel trim strategy for optimum driveability and performance (see Chapter 5, Section 1 for this procedure).

9   Mass Air Flow (MAF) sensor - replacement

⏵ **Refer to illustrations 9.2 and 9.5**

1   Disconnect the cable from the negative battery terminal (see Chapter 5, Section 1).

2   Remove the air intake duct (see illustration).

3   Disconnect the electrical connector from the MAF sensor (see illustration 9.2).

4   Remove the half of the air filter housing that includes the MAF sensor (see Section 8 in Chapter 4).

5   Remove the four MAF sensor retaining nuts (see illustration) and remove the MAF sensor.

6   Installation is the reverse of removal. Be sure to tighten the MAF sensor retaining nuts securely.

7   After you've reconnected the battery, the Powertrain Control Module (PCM) must relearn its idle and fuel trim strategy for optimum driveability and performance (see Chapter 5, Section 1 for this procedure).

9.2 Loosen the air intake duct hose clamp screw and pull off the duct, then disconnect the electrical connector from the MAF sensor (V6 model shown, four-cylinder models similar)

9.5 To detach the MAF sensor from the air filter housing cover, remove these nuts (V6 model shown, four-cylinder models similar)

10 Output Shaft Speed (OSS) sensor - replacement

◆ Refer to illustrations 10.3, 10.4, 10.6 and 10.7

➡Note: This sensor is used only on models with an automatic transaxle.

1   Disconnect the cable from the negative battery terminal (see Chapter 5, Section 1).

2   Raise the front of the vehicle and place it securely on jackstands.

3   Remove the lower left splash shield (see illustration).

4   Locate the OSS sensor on the left side of the transaxle (see illustration).

5   Disconnect the electrical connector from the OSS sensor (see illustration 10.4).

6   Remove the OSS sensor retaining bolt (see illustration) and remove the OSS sensor.

7   Remove the old O-ring from the OSS sensor (see illustration) and discard it. Be sure to use a new O-ring when installing the OSS sensor (even if you're planning to reuse the old OSS sensor).

8   Installation is the reverse of removal. Be sure to tighten the OSS sensor retaining bolt to the torque listed in this Chapter's Specifications.

9   After you've reconnected the battery, the Powertrain Control Module (PCM) must relearn its idle and fuel trim strategy for optimum driveability and performance (see Chapter 5, Section 1 for this procedure).

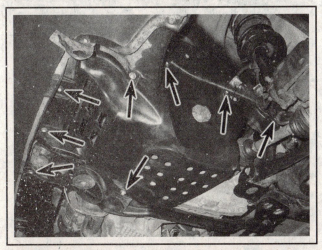

10.3 To detach the lower left splash shield, remove these fasteners

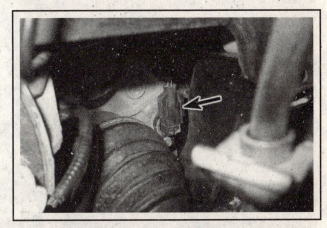

10.4 The OSS sensor is located on the left side of the automatic transaxle

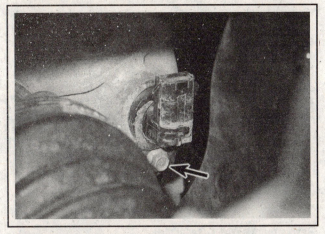

10.6 To detach the OSS sensor from the transaxle, remove this bolt

10.7 Be sure to replace the OSS sensor O-ring (even if you're planning to reuse the same OSS sensor)

11 Oxygen sensors - general information and replacement

GENERAL INFORMATION

1   An oxygen sensor is a galvanic battery that produces a very small voltage output in response to the amount of oxygen in the exhaust gases. This voltage signal is the "input" side of the feedback loop between the oxygen sensor and the Powertrain Control Module (PCM). Without it, the PCM would be unable to correct the injector on-time (which determines the air/fuel ratio) to maintain the "perfect" (known as *stoichiometric*) air/fuel ratio of 14.7:1 that the catalyst needs for optimal operation.

ON-BOARD DIAGNOSTICS II (OBD-II)

2   All vehicles covered by this manual have On-Board Diagnostics II (OBD-II) engine management systems, which means they have the ability to verify the accuracy of the basic feedback loop between the oxygen sensor and the PCM. They accomplish this by using an oxygen sensor *ahead* of the catalytic converter and another oxygen sensor *behind* the catalytic converter. By comparing the amount of oxygen in the post-catalyst exhaust gas to the oxygen content of the exhaust gas before it enters the catalyst, the PCM can determine the efficiency of the converter.

Four-cylinder models

3   All four-cylinder vehicles covered by this manual have *two* heated oxygen sensors: one *upstream* sensor (ahead of the catalytic converter) and a *downstream* oxygen sensor (after the catalyst).

V6 models

4   There are *four* heated oxygen sensors, one upstream and one downstream sensor for each cylinder head, on V6 models. On these models, there are three catalysts: a smaller "fast-light-off" cat right below each exhaust manifold (the catalysts are actually an integral part of the exhaust manifolds) and another larger downstream catalyst. The oxygen sensors are located upstream and downstream in relation to the two smaller catalysts.

All models

5   The upstream and downstream oxygen sensors on all models are heated to speed up the warm-up time during which the sensors are unable to produce an accurate voltage signal. The circuit for each oxygen sensor heater is controlled by the PCM, which opens the ground side of the circuit to shut off the heater as soon as the sensor reaches its normal operating temperature.

6   Special care must be taken whenever a sensor is serviced.

a) *Oxygen sensors have a permanently attached pigtail and an electrical connector that cannot be removed. Damaging or removing the pigtail or electrical connector will render the sensor useless.*

b) *Keep grease, dirt and other contaminants away from the electrical connector and the louvered end of the sensor.*

c) *Do not use cleaning solvents of any kind on an oxygen sensor.*

d) *Oxygen sensors are extremely delicate. Do not drop a sensor or throw it around or handle it roughly.*

e) *Make sure that the silicone boot on the sensor is installed in the correct position. Otherwise, the boot might melt and it might prevent the sensor from operating correctly.*

REPLACEMENT

➠**Note: Because it is installed in the exhaust manifold or pipe, both of which contract when cool, an oxygen sensor might be very difficult to loosen when the engine is cold. Rather than risk damage to the sensor or its mounting threads, start and run the engine for a minute or two, then shut it off. Be careful not to burn yourself during the following procedure.**

Four-cylinder models

Upstream oxygen sensor

▶ **Refer to illustration 11.9**

7   Disconnect the cable from the negative battery terminal (see Chapter 5, Section 1).

11.9 On four-cylinder models, the electrical connectors for the oxygen sensors are located at the right front corner of the valve cover

1   *Electrical connector for upstream oxygen sensor*
2   *Electrical connector for downstream oxygen sensor*

8   Remove the exhaust manifold heat shield (see Chapter 2A).

9   Disconnect the upstream oxygen sensor electrical connector (see illustration), which is located near the right front corner of the valve cover. There are two oxygen sensor connectors at this location: one is for the upstream oxygen sensor and the other connector is for the downstream sensor. Trace the electrical harness from the upstream oxygen sensor back to its connector to ensure that you're unplugging the correct connector.

10   Using an oxygen sensor socket (available at most automotive retailers), unscrew the upstream oxygen sensor. If the sensor is difficult to loosen, spray some penetrant onto the sensor threads and allow it to soak in for awhile.

11   If you're going to install the old sensor, apply anti-seize compound to the threads of the sensor to facilitate future removal. If you're going to install a new oxygen sensor, it's not necessary to apply anti-seize compound to the threads. The threads on new sensors already have anti-seize compound on them.

12   Installation is otherwise the reverse of removal. Be sure to tighten the sensor to the torque listed in this Chapter's Specifications.

13   After you've reconnected the battery, the Powertrain Control Module (PCM) must relearn its idle and fuel trim strategy for optimum driveability and performance (see Chapter 5, Section 1 for this procedure).

Downstream oxygen sensor

▶ **Refer to illustration 11.17**

14   Disconnect the cable from the negative battery terminal (see Chapter 5, Section 1).

15   Disconnect the oxygen sensor electrical connector (see illustration 11.9), which is located near the right front corner of the valve cover. There are two identical oxygen sensor connectors at this location: one is for the upstream oxygen sensor and the other connector is for the downstream sensor. Trace the electrical harness from the upstream oxygen sensor back to its connector (with the vehicle still on the ground, it's easier to trace the harness from the upstream sensor)

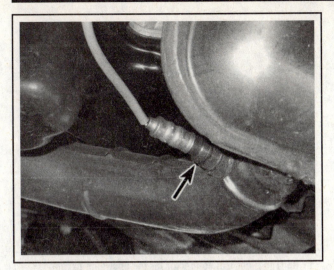

11.17 The downstream oxygen sensor on four-cylinder models is located right below the catalytic converter

11.22 The electrical connectors for the upstream oxygen sensor (1) and the downstream sensor (2) for the front cylinder bank are located at the front engine mount (water pump removed for clarity, but you can disconnect either connector without removing the pump) (V6 models)

and then disconnect the *other* connector, which is the connector for the *downstream* sensor.

16 Raise the front of the vehicle and place it securely on jackstands.

17 Unscrew the downstream oxygen sensor (see illustration), which is located right below the catalytic converter. If the sensor is difficult to loosen, spray some penetrant onto the sensor threads and allow it to soak in for awhile.

18 If you're going to install the old sensor, apply anti-seize compound to the threads of the sensor to facilitate future removal. If you're going to install a new oxygen sensor, it's not necessary to apply anti-seize compound to the threads. The threads on new sensors already have anti-seize compound on them.

19 Installation is otherwise the reverse of removal. Be sure to tighten the sensor to the torque listed in this Chapter's Specifications.

20 After you've reconnected the battery, the Powertrain Control Module (PCM) must relearn its idle and fuel trim strategy for optimum driveability and performance (see Chapter 5, Section 1 for this procedure).

V6 models

Upstream oxygen sensor (front cylinder bank)

► **Refer to illustrations 11.22 and 11.23**

21 Disconnect the cable from the negative battery terminal (see Chapter 5, Section 1).

22 Disconnect the upstream oxygen sensor electrical connector (see illustration).

23 Locate the upstream oxygen sensor for the front cylinder bank (see illustration). Using an oxygen sensor socket (available at most automotive retailers), unscrew the upstream oxygen sensor. If the sensor is difficult to loosen, spray some penetrant onto the sensor threads and allow it to soak in for awhile.

24 If you're going to install the old sensor, apply anti-seize compound to the threads of the sensor to facilitate future removal. If you're going to install a new oxygen sensor, it's not necessary to apply anti-seize compound to the threads. The threads on new sensors already have anti-seize compound on them.

25 Installation is otherwise the reverse of removal. Be sure to tighten the sensor to the torque listed in this Chapter's Specifications.

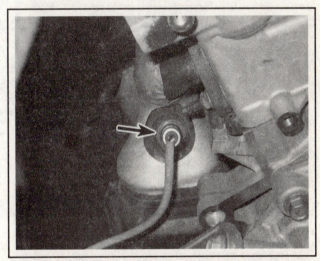

11.23 The upstream oxygen sensor for the front cylinder bank is located on the left side of the exhaust manifold, right above the catalytic converter; use an oxygen sensor socket to remove it (V6 models)

26 After you've reconnected the battery, the Powertrain Control Module (PCM) must relearn its idle and fuel trim strategy for optimum driveability and performance (see Chapter 5, Section 1 for this procedure).

Downstream oxygen sensor (front cylinder bank)

► **Refer to illustration 11.30**

27 Disconnect the cable from the negative battery terminal (see Chapter 5, Section 1).

28 Disconnect the downstream oxygen sensor electrical connector (see illustration 11.22).

29 Raise the front of the vehicle and place it securely on jackstands.

30 Locate the downstream oxygen sensor for the front cylinder bank (see illustration), then unscrew the downstream oxygen sensor. If the

11.30 The downstream oxygen sensor for the front cylinder bank is located between the catalytic converter and the exhaust pipe flange; it's not necessary to use an oxygen sensor socket on to remove this sensor because there's enough room to put a wrench on it (V6 models)

sensor is difficult to loosen, spray some penetrant onto the sensor threads and allow it to soak in for awhile.

31 If you're going to install the old sensor, apply anti-seize compound to the threads of the sensor to facilitate future removal. If you're going to install a new oxygen sensor, it's not necessary to apply anti-seize compound to the threads. The threads on new sensors already have anti-seize compound on them.

32 Installation is otherwise the reverse of removal. Be sure to tighten the sensor to the torque listed in this Chapter's Specifications.

33 After you've reconnected the battery, the Powertrain Control Module (PCM) must relearn its idle and fuel trim strategy for optimum driveability and performance (see Chapter 5, Section 1 for this procedure).

Upstream oxygen sensor (rear cylinder bank)

▶ **Refer to illustrations 11.35 and 11.38**

34 Disconnect the cable from the negative battery terminal (see Chapter 5, Section 1).

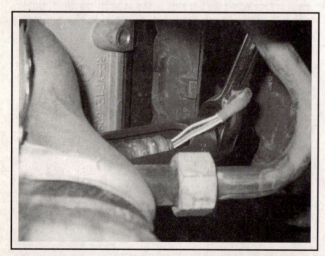

11.38 Use an oxygen sensor socket to unscrew the upstream oxygen sensor for the rear cylinder bank (V6 models)

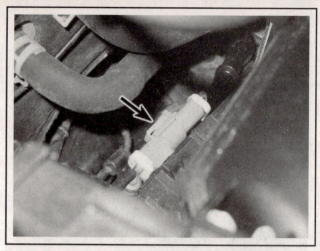

11.35 The electrical connector for the upstream oxygen sensor for the rear cylinder bank is located behind the rear cylinder head, near the heater hoses; if you find it difficult to unplug the connector, detach it from the plastic wiring harness protector, then unplug it (V6 models)

35 Disconnect the upstream oxygen sensor electrical connector (see illustration), which is located behind the rear cylinder head, near the heater hoses.

36 Raise the front of the vehicle and place it securely on jackstands.

37 Locate the upstream oxygen sensor on the rear cylinder head exhaust manifold, right above the EGR pipe.

38 Using an oxygen sensor socket, unscrew the oxygen sensor (see illustration). If the sensor is difficult to loosen, spray some penetrant onto the sensor threads and allow it to soak in awhile.

39 If you're going to install the old sensor, apply anti-seize compound to the threads of the sensor to facilitate future removal. If you're going to install a new oxygen sensor, it's not necessary to apply anti-seize compound to the threads. The threads on new sensors already have anti-seize compound on them.

40 Installation is otherwise the reverse of removal. Be sure to tighten the sensor to the torque listed in this Chapter's Specifications.

41 After you've reconnected the battery, the Powertrain Control Module (PCM) must relearn its idle and fuel trim strategy for optimum driveability and performance (see Chapter 5, Section 1 for this procedure).

Downstream oxygen sensor (rear cylinder bank)

▶ **Refer to illustrations 11.45 and 11.46**

42 Disconnect the cable from the negative battery terminal (see Chapter 5, Section 1).

43 Loosen the right front wheel lug nuts. Raise the vehicle and place it securely on jackstands. Remove the right front wheel.

44 Remove the right lower engine splash shield (see illustration 10.13 in Chapter 5).

45 Disconnect the downstream oxygen sensor electrical connector (see illustration).

46 Using a wrench, unscrew and remove the downstream oxygen sensor (see illustration). If the sensor is difficult to loosen, spray some penetrant onto the sensor threads and allow it to soak in for awhile.

➡**Note: In the accompanying photo, the alternator has been removed for clarity. You shouldn't have to actually remove the alternator to remove the downstream sensor, but it is a very**

11.45 The electrical connector for the downstream oxygen sensor for the rear cylinder bank is located near the crankshaft pulley

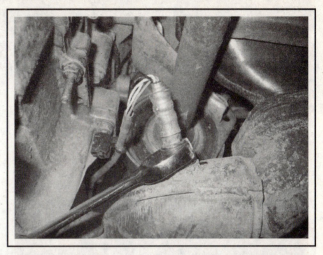

11.46 You should be able to remove the downstream oxygen sensor for the rear cylinder bank with a regular wrench (alternator removed for clarity) (V6 models)

tight fit, so if the sensor proves difficult to remove, you might have to remove the alternator (see Chapter 5) to give yourself more room to work.

47 If you're going to install the old sensor, apply anti-seize compound to the threads of the sensor to facilitate future removal. If you're going to install a new oxygen sensor, it's not necessary to apply anti-seize compound to the threads. The threads on new sensors already have anti-seize compound on them.

48 Installation is otherwise the reverse of removal. Be sure to tighten the downstream oxygen sensor to the torque listed in this Chapter's Specifications.

49 After you've reconnected the battery, the Powertrain Control Module (PCM) must relearn its idle and fuel trim strategy for optimum driveability and performance (see Chapter 5, Section 1 for this procedure).

12 Power Steering Pressure (PSP) switch - replacement

▶ **Refer to illustrations 12.2 and 12.4**

➡**Note: This procedure applies to V6 models only.**

1 Disconnect the cable from the negative battery terminal (see Chapter 5, Section 1).

2 Locate the PSP switch on the power steering pressure line, right behind the oil filler cap (see illustration).

3 Disconnect the electrical connector from the PSP switch.

4 Using a wrench, unscrew the PSP switch (see illustration) and remove it.

5 Installation is the reverse of removal.

6 After you've reconnected the battery, the Powertrain Control Module (PCM) must relearn its idle and fuel trim strategy for optimum driveability and performance (see Chapter 5, Section 1 for this procedure).

12.2 The PSP switch is located on the power steering pressure line, near the oil filler cap (V6 models)

12.4 Unscrew the PSP switch with a wrench

13 Throttle Position (TP) sensor - replacement

▶ Refer to illustrations 13.2 and 13.3

➡Note: This procedure applies to all V6 models and to 2003 four-cylinder models (the TP sensor is not removable on 2001 and 2002 2.0L models; it's part of the throttle body).

1   Disconnect the cable from the negative battery terminal (see Chapter 5, Section 1).
2   On V6 models, remove the engine cover (see illustration).
3   Disconnect the TP sensor electrical connector (see illustration).

13.2   To detach the engine cover from a V6 engine, remove these fasteners

4   Remove the TP sensor mounting screws (see illustration 13.3) and remove the TP sensor.
5   When installing the TP sensor screws on a 2003 four-cylinder model, be sure to hand start the screws. They're self-threading, so failure to hand-start them could damage the throttle body. Installation is otherwise the reverse of removal.
6   After you've reconnected the battery, the Powertrain Control Module (PCM) must relearn its idle and fuel trim strategy for optimum driveability and performance (see Chapter 5, Section 1 for this procedure).

13.3   To remove the TP sensor, disconnect the electrical connector and remove the TP sensor mounting screws (V6 model shown, 2003 four-cylinder TP sensor similar)

14 Transmission Range (TR) sensor - replacement

▶ Refer to illustration 14.6

❊❊ **WARNING:**

Wait until the engine is completely cool before beginning this procedure.

14.6   Disconnect the electrical connector from the TR sensor, then remove the mounting bolts

➡Note 1: This procedure applies to V6 models only.

➡Note 2: A special tool (Ford tool no. 307-351, or equivalent) is required for this procedure - without it, chances are you won't be able to adjust the sensor properly, and a trouble code will then be set (along with driveability problems). If you don't have access to the special tool, have this procedure performed at a dealer service department or other qualified repair shop.

REMOVAL

1   Set the parking brake, then place the shift lever in Neutral.
2   Remove the battery and the battery tray (see Chapter 5).
3   Remove the air filter housing and air intake duct (see Chapter 4).
4   Drain the engine coolant (see Chapter 1).
5   Remove the thermostat housing (see Chapter 3).
6   Disconnect the electrical connector from the TR sensor (see illustration).
7   Unscrew the bolts and remove the sensor.

INSTALLATION

8   Fit the special tool onto the sensor, engaging the two prongs on the tool with the two notches in the rotating ring of the sensor. The

large tang on the other end of the tool fits into the notch in the sensor housing.

9   Place the sensor onto the transaxle, making sure the projections on the rotating ring of the sensor align with the slots in the shaft.

10 Install the sensor mounting bolts and tighten them to the torque listed in this Chapter's Specifications. Remove the special tool, then reconnect the electrical connector.

11 The remainder of installation is the reverse of the removal procedure.

12 Refill the cooling system (see Chapter 1).

13 After you've reconnected the battery, the Powertrain Control Module (PCM) must relearn its idle and fuel trim strategy for optimum driveability and performance (see Chapter 5, Section 1 for this procedure).

15   Turbine Shaft Speed (TSS) sensor - replacement

▶ **Refer to illustrations 15.4 and 15.7**

➡**Note: This procedure applies to models with an automatic transaxle.**

1   Disconnect the cable from the negative battery terminal (see Chapter 5, Section 1).

2   Loosen the left front wheel lug nuts. Raise the vehicle and place it securely on jackstands. Remove the left front wheel.

3   Remove the lower left splash shield (see illustration 10.3).

4   Locate the TSS sensor on the left side of the transaxle (see illustration).

5   Disconnect the TSS sensor electrical connector.

6   Put a drain pan under the TSS sensor to catch any spilled automatic transmission fluid. Then remove the TSS sensor mounting bolt and remove the sensor.

7   Remove the old TSS sensor O-ring (see illustration) and discard it. Be sure to use a new O-ring when installing the TSS sensor (whether you're reusing the old sensor or installing a new one).

8   Installation is the reverse of removal. Be sure to tighten the TSS sensor mounting bolt to the torque listed in this Chapter's Specifications. Tighten the wheel lug nuts to the torque listed in the Chapter 1 Specifications.

9   After you've reconnected the battery, the Powertrain Control Module (PCM) must relearn its idle and fuel trim strategy for optimum driveability and performance (see Chapter 5, Section 1 for this procedure).

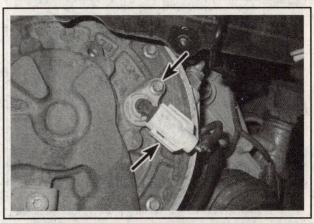

15.4 The TSS sensor is located on the left side of the automatic transaxle; to remove the TSS sensor, disconnect the electrical connector and remove the sensor mounting bolt (models with an automatic transaxle)

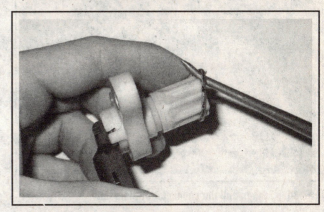

15.7 Be sure to remove and discard the old TSS sensor O-ring; always use a new O-ring when installing the TSS sensor whether you're reusing the old sensor or installing a new one (models with an automatic transaxle)

16   Vehicle Speed Sensor (VSS) - replacement

➡**Note: This procedure applies to models with a manual transaxle.**

1   Disconnect the cable from the negative battery terminal (see Chapter 5, Section 1).

2   On 2002 4WD models, raise the vehicle and place it securely on jackstands. (The VSS is accessed from underneath the vehicle on these models.)

3   Locate the VSS on top of the rear part of the transaxle, near the inner CV joints.

4   Disconnect the VSS electrical connector.

5   Remove the VSS hold-down bolt.

6   Remove the VSS.

7   Installation is the reverse of removal. Be sure to tighten the VSS hold-down bolt to the torque listed in this Chapter's Specifications.

8   After you've reconnected the battery, the Powertrain Control Module (PCM) must relearn its idle and fuel trim strategy for optimum driveability and performance (see Chapter 5, Section 1 for this procedure).

17 Powertrain Control Module (PCM) - replacement

♦ Refer to illustration 17.3a, 17.3b, 17.4a, 17.4b and 17.5

※ CAUTION:

To avoid electrostatic discharge damage to the PCM, handle the PCM only by its case. Do not touch the electrical terminals during removal and installation. If available, ground yourself to the vehicle with an anti-static ground strap, available at computer supply stores.

➥Note: The PCM is a highly reliable component and rarely requires replacement. Because the PCM is the most expensive part of the engine management system, you should be absolutely positive that it has failed before replacing it. If in doubt, have the system tested by an experienced driveability technician at a dealer service department or other qualified repair shop.

1   Disconnect the cable from the negative terminal of the battery (see Chapter 5, Section 1).

2   The PCM is installed in the center of the upper firewall, and can be accessed from the engine compartment side.

3   Disconnect the electrical connector retaining bolt, then disconnect the electrical connector from the PCM (see illustrations).

4   Remove the PCM cover nuts and remove the cover (see illustrations).

5   Carefully remove the PCM from its receptacle (see illustration).

6   Installation is the reverse of removal.

7   After you've reconnected the battery, the Powertrain Control Module (PCM) must relearn its idle and fuel trim strategy for optimum driveability and performance (see Chapter 5, Section 1 for this procedure).

17.3a The Powertrain Control Module (PCM) is located in the firewall, on the engine compartment side; to disconnect the electrical connector, remove this bolt . . .

17.3b . . . then pull the connector straight out

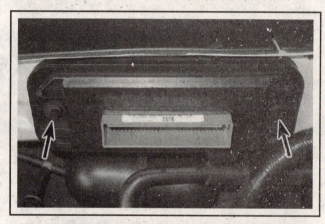

17.4a To remove the PCM cover, remove these two nuts . . .

17.4b . . . and remove the cover

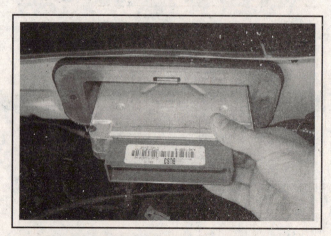

17.5 Carefully remove the PCM from its receptacle in the firewall

18 Idle Air Control (IAC) valve - replacement

FOUR-CYLINDER MODELS

▶ **Refer to illustration 18.3**

1 Disconnect the cable from the negative terminal of the battery (see Chapter 5, Section 1).

2 Raise the front of the vehicle and place it securely on jackstands.

3 Locate the IAC valve on the underside of the intake manifold (see illustration).

4 Disconnect the electrical connector from the IAC valve.

5 Remove the IAC mounting bolts.

6 Remove the IAC valve and discard the old gasket.

7 Using a new gasket, install the IAC valve and tighten the bolts to the torque listed in this Chapter's Specifications.

8 Reconnect the IAC valve electrical connector.

9 Lower the vehicle and reconnect the cable to the negative battery terminal.

10 After you've reconnected the battery, the Powertrain Control Module (PCM) must relearn its idle and fuel trim strategy for optimum drive-ability and performance (see Chapter 5, Section 1 for this procedure).

V6 MODELS

▶ **Refer to illustrations 18.13, 18.14 and 18.16**

11 Disconnect the cable from the negative terminal of the battery (see Chapter 5, Section 1).

12 The IAC valve is located on top of the intake manifold, near the throttle body.

13 Disconnect the electrical connector (see illustration) from the IAC valve.

14 Remove the IAC valve mounting bolts (see illustration).

15 Remove the IAC valve.

16 Remove and discard the old IAC valve gasket (see illustration)

17 Install a new IAC valve gasket. Make sure that the gasket is fully seated in its groove before installing the IAC valve.

18 Install the IAC valve. Be sure to tighten the IAC valve mounting bolts to the torque listed in this Chapter's Specifications.

19 The remainder of installation is the reverse of removal. Reconnect the cable to the negative battery terminal.

20 After you've reconnected the battery, the Powertrain Control Mod-

18.3 On four-cylinder models, the IAC valve is located underneath the intake manifold (manifold removed for clarity); to detach the IAC valve from the manifold, disconnect the electrical connector and remove the two mounting bolts

18.13 Disconnect the IAC valve electrical connector (V6 models)

ule (PCM) must relearn its idle and fuel trim strategy for optimum drive-ability and performance (see Chapter 5, Section 1 for this procedure).

18.14 To detach the IAC valve from the intake manifold, remove these two bolts

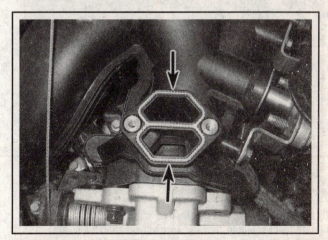

18.16 Be sure to remove the old IAC valve gasket and install a new one before reinstalling the IAC valve

19 Catalytic converters

➡**Note: Because of a Federally-mandated extended warranty which covers emission-related components such as the catalytic converter, check with a dealer service department before replacing the converter at your own expense.**

GENERAL DESCRIPTION

1   A catalytic converter (or catalyst) is an emission control device in the exhaust system that reduces certain pollutants in the exhaust gas stream. There are two types of converters. An oxidation catalyst reduces hydrocarbons (HC) and carbon monoxide (CO). A reduction catalyst reduces oxides of nitrogen (NOx). Catalysts that can reduce *all three pollutants* are known as "three-way catalysts." The models covered by this manual are equipped with three-way catalysts.

CHECK

2   The test equipment for a catalytic converter (a "loaded-mode" dynamometer and a 5-gas analyzer) is expensive. If you suspect that the converter on your vehicle is malfunctioning, take it to a dealer or authorized emission inspection facility for diagnosis and repair.

3   Whenever you raise the vehicle to service underbody components, inspect the converter for leaks, corrosion, dents and other damage. Carefully inspect the welds and/or flange bolts and nuts that attach the front and rear ends of the converter to the exhaust system. If you note any damage, replace the converter.

4   Although catalytic converters don't break too often, they can become clogged or even plugged up. The easiest way to check for a restricted converter is to use a vacuum gauge to diagnose the effect of a blocked exhaust on intake vacuum.

a) *Connect a vacuum gauge to an intake manifold vacuum source (see Chapter 2).*

b) *Warm the engine to operating temperature, place the transaxle in Park (automatic models) or Neutral (manual models) and apply the parking brake.*

c) *Note the vacuum reading at idle and jot it down.*

d) *Quickly open the throttle to near its wide-open position and then quickly get off the throttle and allow it to close. Note the vacuum reading and jot it down.*

e) *Do this test three more times, recording your measurement after each test.*

f) *If your fourth reading is more than one in-Hg lower than the reading that you noted at idle, the exhaust system might be restricted (the catalytic converter could be plugged, OR an exhaust pipe or muffler could be restricted).*

REPLACEMENT

5   See "Exhaust system servicing - general information" in Chapter 4 for the catalytic converter replacement procedures for both four-cylinder and V6 models.

20 Evaporative emissions control (EVAP) system - general information and component replacement

GENERAL DESCRIPTION

▶ **Refer to illustration 20.2**

1   The **Evaporative Emissions Control (EVAP) system** prevents fuel system vapors (which contain unburned hydrocarbons) from

20.2 The EVAP canister, check valve, dust separator and canister vent solenoid, and the hoses connecting them, are located underneath the vehicle, near the left side; to replace any of these components, you must first remove the entire assembly

escaping into the atmosphere. On warm days, vapors trapped inside the fuel tank expand until the pressure reaches a certain threshold, at which point the fuel vapors are routed from the fuel tank through the fuel vapor vent valve and the fuel vapor control valve to the EVAP canister, where they're stored temporarily, until they can be consumed by the engine during normal operation. When the conditions are right (engine warmed up, vehicle up to speed, moderate or heavy load on the engine, etc.) the Powertrain Control Module (PCM) opens the canister purge valve, which allows the fuel vapors to be drawn from the canister into the intake manifold, where they mix with the air/fuel mixture before being consumed in the combustion chambers. This system is complex and virtually impossible to troubleshoot without the right tools and training. However, the following description should give you a good idea of how it works:

2   The **EVAP canister** (see illustration) is located under the vehicle, near the left side of the vehicle. The EVAP canister, which contains activated carbon, is the repository for storing the fuel vapors. You'll have to raise the vehicle to inspect or replace the canister or any other part of the EVAP system except for the canister purge valve (which is located in the engine compartment) but the canister is designed to be maintenance-free and should last the life of the vehicle. There are several other important components located near the EVAP canister: the check valve, the dust separator and the canister vent solenoid.

3   The **fuel tank pressure sensor**, which is located near the in-tank fuel pump/fuel level sending unit module on top of the fuel tank, monitors the pressure inside the tank, and transmits its measurement to the PCM during an OBD-II leak test.

4   The **fuel vapor vent (FVV) valve**, which is mounted on top of the fuel tank, controls the flow of fuel vapors entering the EVAP system. On vehicles with composite fuel tanks, the FVV valve cannot be removed or repaired.

5   The **fuel vapor control valve** (V6 models only) prevents liquid fuel from entering the EVAP canister or the canister purge valve during refueling. It also prevents liquid fuel from flooding the fuel vapor hoses if the fuel tank is overfilled.

6   The **canister vent solenoid**, which is mounted on the EVAP canister, is normally open. But it seals off the EVAP system for inspection and maintenance (I/M 240) testing and for OBD-II leak and pressure tests.

7   The **evaporative emission (EVAP) check valve**, which is mounted on the EVAP canister mounting bracket, is normally closed. But it opens during refueling, which allows the air inside the fuel tank to vent to the atmosphere through a more direct and lower-resistance path as it's displaced by the rising fuel level in the tank.

8   The **evaporative emission (EVAP) canister purge valve**, which is under the control of the Powertrain Control Module (PCM), regulates the flow of vapors being purged from the EVAP canister into the intake manifold. The canister purge valve is normally closed. It opens only when directed to do so by the PCM, which uses the availability of intake manifold vacuum and data from various information sensor inputs to determine when and how long to open the valve. The interval of time during which the purge valve is opened by the PCM is known as its "duty cycle." The purge valve is located in the engine compartment, on a bracket near the brake master cylinder.

9   The **evaporative emission (EVAP) dust separator**, which is attached to the EVAP canister mounting bracket, prevents dust and dirt particles suspended in the atmosphere from entering the EVAP system.

General system checks

10   The most common symptom of a faulty EVAP system is a strong fuel odor (particularly during hot weather). If you smell fuel while driving or (more likely) right after you park the vehicle and turn off the engine, check the fuel filler cap first. Make sure that it's screwed onto the fuel filler neck all the way. If the odor persists, inspect all EVAP hose connections, both in the engine compartment and under the vehi-

cle. You'll have to raise the vehicle and place it securely on jackstands to inspect most of the EVAP system, since it's located under the vehicle. Be sure to inspect each hose attached to the canister for damage and leakage along its entire length. Repair or replace as necessary. Inspect the canister for damage and look for fuel leaking from the bottom. If fuel is leaking or the canister is otherwise damaged, replace it.

11   Poor idle, stalling, and poor driveability can be caused by a defective fuel vapor vent valve or canister purge valve, a damaged canister, cracked hoses, or hoses connected to the wrong tubes. Fuel loss or fuel odor can be caused by fuel leaking from fuel lines or hoses, a cracked or damaged canister, or a defective vapor valve.

12   To check for excessive fuel vapor pressure in the fuel tank, remove the gas cap and listen for the sound of pressure release. If the fuel tank emits a "whooshing" sound when you open the filler cap, fuel tank vapor pressure is excessive. Inspect the canister vapor hoses and the canister inlet port for blockage or collapsed hoses. Also inspect the vapor vent valve. A complete test can only be done with a proprietary OBD-II scan tool (see Section 2), which will run a series of checks using the fuel tank pressure sensor and other output actuators to detect excessive pressure. You'll have to take the vehicle to a dealer service department to have the EVAP system professionally diagnosed.

COMPONENT REPLACEMENT

EVAP canister purge valve

⬦ **Refer to illustrations 20.15, 20.17a, 20.17b and 20.18**

➡**Note: The EVAP canister purge valve depicted in the accompanying photos shows the purge valve on a V6 model, but the purge valve on four-cylinder models is identical in location and design to the unit you see here.**

13   Disconnect the cable from the negative terminal of the battery (see Chapter 5, Section 1).

14   The EVAP canister purge valve is located in the engine compartment, on a bracket near the master cylinder.

15   Disconnect the purge valve electrical connector (see illustration).

16   Disconnect the vacuum line from the purge valve (see illustration 20.15). Cap the vacuum line to prevent dirt or moisture from entering it while it's disconnected.

17   Disconnect the EVAP canister return line and outlet line (see illustrations). Cap the tubes to prevent dirt, dust and moisture from

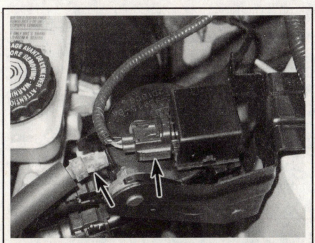

20.15 Disconnect the electrical connector and the vacuum line from the EVAP canister purge valve; be sure to cap the vacuum line to prevent dirt and moisture from entering the line while it's disconnected (V6 model shown, four-cylinder models similar)

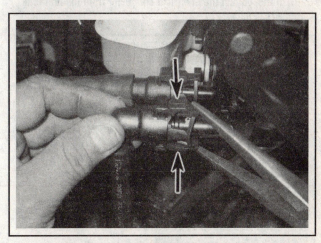

20.17a To disconnect the EVAP canister return line, squeeze the two tabs on the fitting together and pull off the line (V6 model shown, four-cylinder models similar)

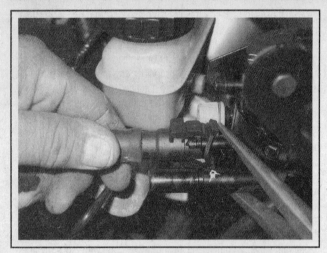

20.17b Disconnect the EVAP canister outlet line the same way (V6 model shown, four-cylinder models similar)

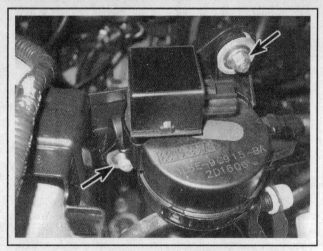

20.18 To detach the EVAP canister purge valve from its mounting bracket, remove these two nuts (V6 model shown, four-cylinder models similar)

entering the EVAP system while the lines are open. (It's not really necessary to mark the two lines because the lines and the fittings are different diameters.)

18 Remove the two purge valve mounting nuts (see illustration) and

remove the purge valve from its mounting bracket (it's not necessary to remove the bracket).

19 Installation is the reverse of removal.

20 After you've reconnected the battery, the Powertrain Control Module (PCM) must relearn its idle and fuel trim strategy for optimum driveability and performance (see Chapter 5, Section 1 for this procedure).

Fuel tank pressure sensor

▶ **Refer to illustrations 20.24, 20.25a and 20.25b**

21 Disconnect the cable from the negative terminal of the battery (see Chapter 5, Section 1).

22 Remove the rear seat cushion (see Chapter 11).

23 Pull back the carpeting and remove the fuel pump/fuel level sending unit module access cover (see illustrations 5.4a and 5.4b in Chapter 4).

24 Disconnect the electrical connector from the fuel tank pressure sensor (see illustration).

25 Pull the fuel tank pressure sensor out from under the floorpan and cut the two crimped hose clamps (see illustrations).

26 Note which way the fuel tank pressure sensor is oriented before disconnecting the inlet and outlet hoses.

27 Installation is the reverse of removal. Be sure to secure the hoses

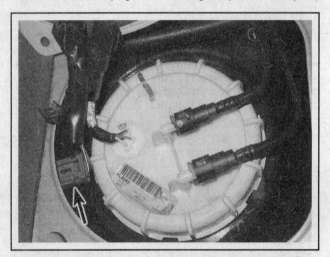

20.24 Disconnect the electrical connector from the fuel tank pressure sensor

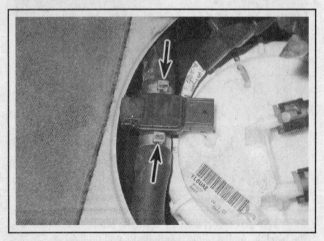

20.25a Pull the fuel tank pressure sensor out from under the floorpan and cut the two crimped hose clamps . . .

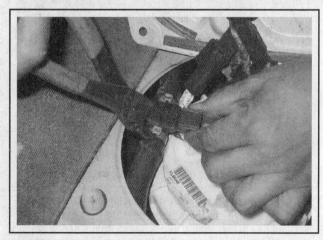

20.25b . . . with a pair of diagonal cutters

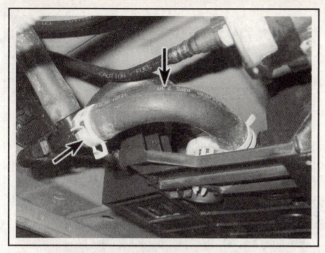

20.31 To disconnect the EVAP canister outlet hose, loosen this hose clamp, slide it back and pull off the hose

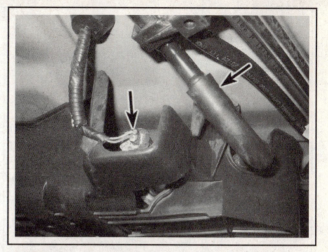

20.32 Disconnect the canister vent solenoid electrical connector and the canister vent hose

to the sensor with new hose clamps (it's not necessary to use crimp-style clamps).

28 After you've reconnected the battery, the Powertrain Control Module (PCM) must relearn its idle and fuel trim strategy for optimum drive-ability and performance (see Chapter 5, Section 1 for this procedure).

EVAP canister, check valve, dust separator and canister vent solenoid

⬥ **Refer to illustrations 20.31, 20.32, 20.33a, 20.33b, 20.33c, 20.34a, 20.34b, 20.34c, 20.35a, 20.35b, 20.36a and 20.36b**

29 Disconnect the cable from the negative terminal of the battery (see Chapter 5, Section 1).

30 Raise the vehicle and place it securely on jackstands.

31 On the back side of the EVAP canister assembly, disconnect the EVAP canister outlet hose (see illustration).

32 On the front side of the EVAP canister assembly, disconnect the canister vent solenoid electrical connector and the canister vent hose (see illustration).

33 Remove the EVAP canister mounting bracket nuts and bolts (see illustrations) and lower the EVAP canister, its mounting bracket and the rest of the EVAP components as a single assembly (see illustration).

20.33a To detach the EVAP canister mounting bracket from the underside of the vehicle, remove these two nuts from the left side . . .

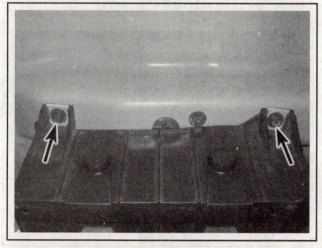

20.33b . . . remove these two bolts from the right side . . .

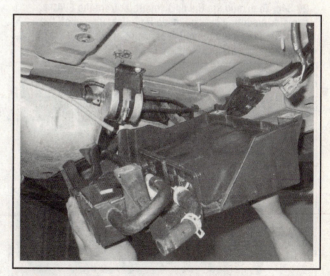

20.33c . . . and then lower the EVAP canister, the mounting bracket and the rest of the EVAP system components as a single assembly

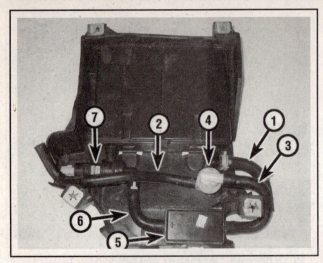

20.34a EVAP canister and related EVAP components

1	EVAP canister outlet hose	5	Dust separator
2	Remote canister vent hose	6	Dust separator-to-canister
3	Remote canister vent hose		vent solenoid hose
4	EVAP check valve	7	Canister vent solenoid

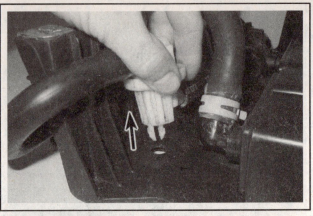

20.34b To detach the check valve from the EVAP canister mounting bracket, disengage the check valve mounting tangs from the hole in the bracket by pulling it straight up

34 Remove the remote canister vent hoses, the check valve, the dust separator and the dust separator-to-canister vent solenoid hose (see illustrations). To disengage the dust separator from the EVAP canister mounting bracket, simply pull it straight up to slide it off the retaining tab on the mounting bracket (see illustration).

35 To detach the EVAP canister from its mounting bracket, pry up

20.34c To disengage the dust separator from the EVAP canister mounting bracket, slide it straight up and off the retaining tab on the mounting bracket

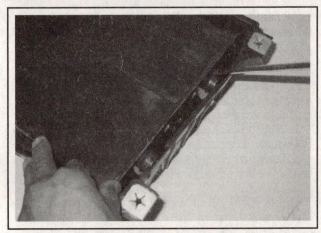

20.35a To disengage the EVAP canister from its mounting bracket, pry up the right side of the canister . . .

20.35b . . . and then slide the two mounting tabs on the left side of the canister out of their slots in the mounting bracket

20.36a To separate the vent solenoid from the EVAP canister, simply pull the solenoid straight out

the right side of the canister and then slide the two mounting tabs on the left side of the canister out from their slots in the mounting bracket (see illustrations).

36 If you're replacing the EVAP canister or the canister vent solenoid, separate the two components (see illustration). After you've separated the canister and the vent solenoid, inspect the solenoid O-ring and replace it if it's damaged or worn (see illustration).

37 Installation is the reverse of removal.

38 After you've reconnected the battery, the Powertrain Control Module (PCM) must relearn its idle and fuel trim strategy for optimum driveability and performance (see Chapter 5, Section 1 for this procedure).

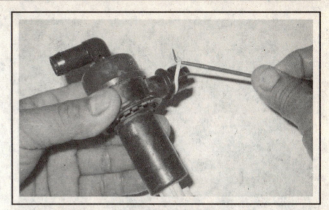

20.36b Always inspect the vent solenoid O-ring for cracks, tears and deterioration; if it's damaged or worn, replace it

21 Exhaust Gas Recirculation (EGR) system - general information and component replacement

GENERAL DESCRIPTION

1 Exhaust gas recirculation (EGR) systems on late-model vehicles have two equally important functions: they reduce oxides of nitrogen (NOx) emissions and they reduce engine detonation, or pinging. Recirculating a small amount of exhaust back to the intake system reduces combustion temperatures because exhaust is a mixture of inert gases and does not contribute to the combustion process. Because high combustion temperature is a major factor in both NOx emissions and detonation, EGR effectively reduces both.

2 When the combustion chambers reach about 2500-degrees F, they begin to produce excessive quantities of oxides of nitrogen (NOx). NOx, when combined with unburned hydrocarbons (HC), other volatile organic compounds and sunlight, forms ozone, nitrogen dioxide and nitrogen nitrate, otherwise known as photochemical smog. The Exhaust Gas Recirculation (EGR) system reduces (NOx) by recirculating exhaust gases from the exhaust ports through the EGR valve and back into the intake manifold, from which they're recycled back through the combustion chambers, which lowers the temperature during the combustion process.

3 The EGR system on the vehicles covered by this manual is known as a "differential pressure feedback" EGR system. The differential pressure feedback system consists of the pipe connecting the exhaust manifold to the EGR valve, the EGR valve itself, the differential pressure feedback EGR system sensor and the EGR vacuum regulator valve (or solenoid), as well as the Powertrain Control Module (PCM) and several information sensors, including the Crankshaft Position (CKP) sensor, the Engine Coolant Temperature (ECT) sensor, the Intake Air Temperature (IAT) sensor, the Mass Air Flow (MAF) sensor and the Throttle Position (TP) sensor. Before the PCM will activate the EGR system, the engine must be fully warmed up, stable and operating under a moderate load and rpm. The PCM will deactivate the EGR when the engine is at idle, during extended wide-open-throttle conditions and whenever it detects a malfunction in the EGR system or in one of its monitored components or circuits.

4 Here's how the differential pressure feedback EGR system works: The PCM determines the correct amount of EGR flow for the conditions, then it calculates the appropriate pressure drop across the metering orifice, inside the differential pressure feedback sensor, that's needed to achieve that flow rate, and then it sends a voltage signal to the EGR vacuum regulator solenoid. This signal is known as the "duty cycle." The EGR vacuum regulator solenoid receives a variable duty

cycle signal that can be anywhere from 0 per cent to 100 per cent. The higher the duty cycle percentage, the stronger the vacuum signal diverted by the vacuum regulator solenoid to the EGR valve.

5 Inside the EGR valve, a spring-loaded diaphragm in a vacuum chamber is connected to a pintle valve by a rod. Normally, the pintle valve is kept closed by spring pressure pushing down against the diaphragm. When the vacuum signal from the vacuum regulator solenoid becomes strong enough to overcome the pressure of the spring, the diaphragm begins to lift upward, which pulls up the rod and lifts the pintle valve off its seat, allowing exhaust gases to flow through the EGR valve and be recirculated back into the intake manifold.

6 The exhaust gases flowing through the EGR valve must first pass through the EGR metering orifice. One side of the orifice is connected to exhaust backpressure and the other side leads to the intake manifold. Whenever there is EGR flow, it creates a pressure drop across the orifice. When the EGR valve closes, EGR flow through the orifice ceases, and the pressure on both sides of the orifice is equal. The PCM tries to maintain a pressure drop across the orifice that's appropriate to the operating conditions. The differential pressure feedback sensor measures the actual pressure drop across the metering orifice and sends a voltage signal (between 0 and 5 volts) to the PCM that's proportional to the measured pressure drop. This feedback signal from the differential pressure feedback sensor is used by the PCM to make constant corrections to the EGR flow rate.

7 Typically, EGR systems are trouble-free. If the EGR valve ever fails, it will do so while it's either closed or open. If the EGR valve is closed when it fails the EGR system will no longer work, but there will be no obvious symptom, other than the fact that the engine might detonate (or "ping"), or run a little hotter, under a load on a hot day (acceleration, passing, going up a hill or pulling a trailer). And when your vehicle is subjected to a biennial "loaded-mode" (dynamometer-type) smog test, the EGR system will fail. If the EGR valve is open when it fails, the symptom will be obvious. Exhaust gases metered into the combustion chambers during idle will cause the engine to run roughly and might even cause it to run so roughly that it stalls.

COMPONENT REPLACEMENT

EGR valve and pipe

2.0L four-cylinder models

8 Raise the vehicle and place it securely on jackstands.

21.26 Disconnect the vacuum line from the EGR valve (V6 models)

21.27 To disconnect the EGR pipe from the EGR valve, unscrew this big nut and then carefully pull out the pipe just enough to clear the valve (V6 models)

9   Remove the right lower splash shield (see illustration 10.13 in Chapter 5).

10   Unscrew the tube nut fitting and disconnect the EGR pipe from the exhaust manifold. This fitting might be difficult to loosen because of the intense heat to which it has been repeatedly subjected. If so, spray some penetrant on the threads of the fitting and then try again later. (The penetrant manufacturer will specify how long you should wait for the penetrant to loosen things up.)

11   In the engine compartment, remove the air intake duct (see Chapter 4).

12   Unscrew the big nut at the upper end of the EGR pipe and disconnect the pipe from the EGR valve.

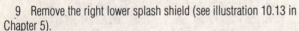

CAUTION:

The manufacturer says that anytime you disconnect the EGR pipe from the EGR valve, you MUST replace the old EGR pipe. Do NOT reuse the old EGR pipe! The manufacturer also says that you must inspect the (aluminum) threads inside the EGR valve for damage. If the threads are damaged, you MUST replace the EGR valve.

13   Remove the two EGR pipe bracket bolts.

14   Carefully remove the differential pressure feedback EGR sensor from the EGR pipe.

15   Remove the EGR pipe and discard it (see **Caution** in Step 12).

16   Disconnect the vacuum line from the EGR valve.

17   Remove the two EGR valve mounting bolts.

18   Remove the EGR valve and remove and discard the old gasket.

19   Scrape all exhaust deposits and old gasket material from the EGR valve mounting surface on the manifold and, if you plan to use the same valve, from the mounting surface of the valve. Carefully remove carbon deposits from the valve port and pintle with a small screwdriver.

CAUTION:

Do not try to wash the valve in solvent or sandblast it. If the EGR passage contains excessive deposits, clean it out with a small scraper and a vacuum. Make sure that all loose particles are removed to keep them from clogging the EGR valve or from being drawn into the engine.

20   Installation is the reverse of removal. Be sure to tighten the EGR valve mounting bolts to the torque listed in this Chapter's Specifications. And don't forget to use a new EGR pipe and tighten the EGR pipe fittings securely.

2.3L four-cylinder models

WARNING:

Wait until the engine is completely cool before beginning this procedure.

21   The EGR is located on the left side of the cylinder head. Engine coolant passes through the valve.

22   Drain the engine coolant.

23   Remove the upper radiator hose from the thermostat outlet, then remove the coolant hose from the EGR valve.

24   Remove the two EGR mounting bolts and remove the valve. Discard the old gasket.

25   Installation is the reverse of removal.

21.28 To detach the EGR valve from its mounting bracket, remove these two bolts (V6 models)

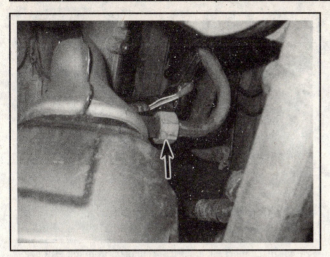

21.30 To disconnect the EGR pipe from the exhaust manifold, unscrew this big nut

V6 models

▶ **Refer to illustrations 21.26, 21.27, 21.28 and 21.30**

26 Disconnect the vacuum line from the EGR valve (see illustration).

27 Disconnect the EGR pipe from the EGR valve (see illustration).

28 Remove the bolts securing the EGR valve to its mounting bracket on the intake manifold (see illustration) and remove the EGR valve. Remove and discard the old gasket.

29 Remove the differential pressure feedback EGR sensor from the EGR pipe (see Step 28).

30 Disconnect the EGR pipe from the exhaust manifold (see illustration).

31 Scrape all exhaust deposits and old gasket material from the EGR valve mounting surface on the mounting bracket at the intake manifold and, if you plan to use the same valve, from the mounting surface of the valve. Carefully remove carbon deposits from the valve port and pintle with a small screwdriver.

❋❋ CAUTION:

Do not try to wash the valve in solvent or sandblast it. If the EGR passage contains excessive deposits, clean it out with a small scraper and a vacuum. Make sure that all loose particles are removed to keep them from clogging the EGR valve or from being drawn into the engine.

32 Installation is the reverse of removal. Attach the EGR pipe nuts loosely at the valve and at the exhaust manifold until the EGR valve is tightened on the intake manifold. Tighten the pipe fittings securely. Be sure to tighten the EGR valve mounting bolts to the torque listed in this Chapter's Specifications.

Differential pressure feedback EGR system sensor

▶ **Refer to illustrations 21.34a, 21.34b and 21.35**

33 Disconnect the cable from the negative terminal of the battery (see Chapter 5, Section 1).

34 Disconnect the electrical connector from the differential pressure feedback EGR system sensor (see illustrations).

35 Carefully disconnect the differential pressure feedback EGR system sensor from the two hoses that connect it to the two small metal pipes welded to the EGR pipe (four-cylinder models, see illustration 21.34a; V6 models, see accompanying illustration).

36 While the differential pressure feedback EGR system sensor is

21.34a On four-cylinder models, the differential pressure feedback EGR system sensor is located at the left end of the cylinder head, near the ignition coil

1	Electrical connector	3	Differential pressure
2	Rubber hoses		feedback EGR system sensor
		4	EGR pipe

21.34b Disconnect the electrical connector from the differential pressure feedback EGR system sensor (V6 models)

21.35 To disconnect the differential pressure feedback EGR system sensor from the two hoses that connect it to the two small metal pipes welded to the EGR pipe, carefully pull it straight up; be sure to inspect the hoses before installing the sensor (V6 model shown, four-cylinder models similar)

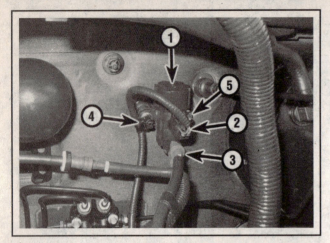

21.40 EGR vacuum regulator valve (four-cylinder models)

1   *EGR vacuum regulator valve*
2   *Electrical connector*
3   *Vacuum hose connector*
4   *Right mounting nut (remove harness clip from stud first, then remove nut)*
5   *Left mounting nut*

21.41 Disconnect the electrical connector from the EGR vacuum regulator valve (V6 model shown, four-cylinder models similar)

removed, inspect the condition of the two small hoses. Look for cracks, tears and deterioration. If the hoses are worn or damaged, replace them.

37 Installation is the reverse of removal.

38 After you've reconnected the battery, the Powertrain Control Module (PCM) must relearn its idle and fuel trim strategy for optimum driveability and performance (see Chapter 5, Section 1 for this procedure).

EGR vacuum regulator valve

▶ **Refer to illustrations 21.40, 21.41, 21.42, 21.43 and 21.44**

39 Disconnect the cable from the negative terminal of the battery (see Chapter 5, Section 1).

40 On four-cylinder models, locate the EGR vacuum regulator valve on the firewall (see illustration), to the right of the brake master cylin-

der. On V6 models, it's on the intake manifold.

41 Disconnect the electrical connector from the EGR vacuum regulator valve (2.0L four-cylinder models, see illustration 21.40; V6 models, see accompanying illustration).

42 Disconnect the vacuum hoses from the EGR vacuum regulator valve (2.0L four-cylinder models, see illustration 21.40; V6 models, see accompanying illustration).

43 On V6 models, detach the PCM wiring harness bracket (see illustration) and set it aside.

44 Remove the EGR vacuum regulator valve mounting nuts (2.0L four-cylinder models, see illustration 21.40) or bolts (V6 models, see accompanying illustration) and remove the valve from the firewall (four-cylinder models) or from the intake manifold (V6 models).

45 Installation is the reverse of removal. Be sure to tighten the vacuum regulator valve mounting nuts or bolts securely.

46 After you've reconnected the battery, the Powertrain Control Module (PCM) must relearn its idle and fuel trim strategy for optimum driveability and performance (see Chapter 5, Section 1 for this procedure).

21.42 Disconnect the vacuum lines from the EGR vacuum regulator valve (V6 model shown, four-cylinder models similar)

21.43 On V6 models, remove this nut, detach the PCM wiring harness bracket from the stud and push the harness out of the way

21.44 To detach the EGR vacuum regulator valve, remove these two bolts; be careful not to damage the threads on the stud (on the right bolt) that secures the PCM wiring harness bracket (V6 model shown, four-cylinder models similar, except that there's no stud on either bolt)

22 Positive Crankcase Ventilation (PCV) system - general information and component replacement

GENERAL DESCRIPTION

➡**Note: Refer to Chapter 1 for scheduled maintenance on the PCV system for four-cylinder models. (The only scheduled maintenance for the PCV valve on V6 models is replacement every 100,000 miles).**

1   The Positive Crankcase Ventilation (PCV) system reduces hydrocarbon emissions by scavenging crankcase vapors. It does this by circulating fresh air from the air cleaner through the crankcase, where it mixes with blow-by gases and is then rerouted through a PCV valve to the intake manifold. The PCV system uses intake manifold vacuum to draw crankcase vapors from the crankcase into the intake manifold. The PCV valve varies the amount of blow-by gases that can be returned to the intake manifold in proportion to the amount of intake manifold vacuum available, but in the event of a backfire it prevents the entry of combustion gases into the manifold. To maintain idle quality, the PCV valve restricts the flow when intake manifold vacuum is high.

2   The PCV system consists of a fresh-air inlet hose between the air intake duct and the crankcase (see illustration), the PCV valve itself and the PCV hose (also referred to as the crankcase ventilation hose), which connects the PCV valve to the intake manifold. Both the four-cylinder engine and the V6 also use a crankcase vent oil separator to which the PCV valve is attached. The crankcase vent oil separator acts as a baffle to prevent oil in the crankcase from entering the PCV valve.

3   Inspect the fresh-air inlet hose and the PCV valve hose (crankcase ventilation hose) for cracks, leaks and other damage. Disconnect the hose from the crankcase vent oil separator and the intake manifold and check the inside for obstructions. If a hose is clogged, replace it. If the PCV valve is clogged or otherwise not working properly, replace it, do not try to clean it.

COMPONENT REPLACEMENT

Four-cylinder models

Fresh air inlet hose

▶ **Refer to illustration 22.4**

4   Disconnect the fresh air inlet hose from the air intake duct (see illustration).

5   Remove the air intake duct (see Chapter 4).

6   Disconnect the fresh air inlet hose from the pipe at the left rear corner of the valve cover.

7   Thoroughly clean the fresh air inlet hose and inspect the condition of the hose. Look for cracks, tears and other deterioration. If it's damaged or worn, replace it. Also inspect the grommet at the air intake duct. Make sure that it's not cracked or torn. If it's worn or damaged, replace it. A leaking fresh air inlet hose or grommet will result in an unmetered air leak ("false air") that will lean out the air/fuel mixture ratio, which will cause a lean misfire and other driveability problems.

8   Installation is the reverse of removal.

PCV hose (crankcase ventilation hose)

▶ **Refer to illustration 22.10**

9   Disconnect the PCV hose from the PCV valve, which is located at the upper left corner of the crankcase vent oil separator, which in turn is located on the front side of the engine block, behind the exhaust manifold and the crankcase vent oil separator.

10   Disconnect the PCV hose from the intake manifold (see illustration).

22.4 The fresh-air inlet hose on four-cylinder models connects the air intake duct (1) to the crankcase via a pipe on the valve cover (2) (valve cover pipe not visible in this photo; it's below the accordion pleats in the air intake duct)

22.10 The PCV hose, or crankcase ventilation hose, begins at the PCV valve (which is located on the left end of the crankcase vent oil separator) and ends here at the intake manifold, downstream from the throttle plate in the throttle body, so that the pressure differential caused by intake manifold vacuum will pull the crankcase vapors into the manifold (four-cylinder models)

11   Thoroughly clean the PCV hose and inspect the condition of the hose. Look for cracks, tears and other deterioration. If it's damaged or worn, replace it. Also inspect the grommet at the air intake duct. Make sure that it's not cracked or torn. If it's worn or damaged, replace it. A leaking PCV hose result in an unmetered air leak ("false air") that will lean out the air/fuel mixture ratio, which will cause a lean misfire and other driveability problems.

12   Installation is the reverse of removal.

PCV valve

13   See Chapter 1.

22.16a To detach the crankcase vent oil separator from the engine block on a four-cylinder model, remove these three bolts . . .

Crankcase vent oil separator

▶ **Refer to illustrations 22.16a, 22.16b and 22.18**

➡**Note: The PCV valve and oil separator on the 2.3L four-cylinder engine is located under the intake manifold, requiring its removal (see Chapter 2A).**

14 The crankcase vent oil separator is located on the front side of

22.18 Before installing the crankcase vent oil separator on a four-cylinder model, be sure to install a new gasket

22.20 Disconnect the fresh air inlet hose from the front valve cover and from the air intake duct (V6 models)

22.16b . . . and pull off the separator and the old gasket

the engine block, behind the exhaust manifold and the catalytic converter. To access the separator, remove the catalytic converter (see "Exhaust system - inspection and component replacement" in Chapter 4) and remove the exhaust manifold (see Chapter 2A).

15 Disconnect the PCV hose from the PCV valve or remove the PCV valve from the crankcase vent oil separator (see Chapter 1).

16 Remove the crankcase vent oil separator mounting bolts and remove the separator (see illustrations). Remove and discard the old oil separator gasket.

17 Remove the PCV valve from the oil separator if you haven't already done so. Then wash out the oil separator with a suitable solvent. Blow it out with compressed air (be sure to wear safety goggles during this procedure!) and make sure that the passages are clear.

18 Install a new crankcase vent oil separator gasket (see illustration).

19 Installation is otherwise the reverse of removal. Be sure to tighten the oil separator mounting bolts to the torque listed in this Chapter's Specifications.

V6 models

Fresh air inlet hose

▶ **Refer to illustrations 22.20 and 22.22**

20 Disconnect the fresh air inlet hose from the front valve cover (see illustration).

21 Disconnect the fresh air inlet hose from the air intake duct (see illustration 22.20).

22.22 Disconnect the fresh air inlet hose from the rear valve cover (V6 models)

22.24a Disconnect the PCV hose from the PCV valve, which is located in the left end of the valley between the cylinder heads (V6 models)

22 Disconnect the fresh air inlet hose from the rear valve cover (see illustration).

23 Installation is the reverse of removal.

PCV hose (crankcase ventilation hose)

▶ **Refer to illustrations 22.24a, 22.24b and 22.25**

24 Disconnect the PCV hose from the PCV valve (see illustrations).

25 Disconnect the PCV hose from the intake manifold (see illustration).

26 Carefully note the routing the PCV hose and then pull it out and remove it.

27 Installation is the reverse of removal. Make sure that you route the hose exactly the same way that it was routed before removal. Make sure that there are no kinks in the hose.

PCV valve

▶ **Refer to illustration 22.29**

28 Disconnect the PCV hose from the PCV valve (see illustrations 22.24a and 22.24b).

29 Disconnect the PCV valve from the crankcase vent oil separator

22.25 To disconnect the PCV hose (crankcase ventilation hose) from the intake manifold, loosen this hose clamp, slide it back and pull off the hose

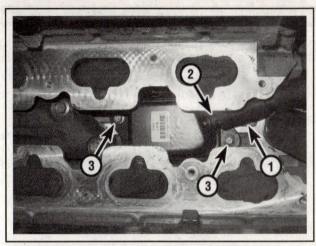

22.24b PCV hose, PCV valve and crankcase vent oil separator installation details (intake manifold removed for clarity) (V6 models)

1 PCV hose
2 PCV valve
3 Crankcase vent oil separator mounting bolts

(see illustration). *Unscrew* the PCV valve - don't try to just pull it out.

30 Inspect the PCV valve (see Chapter 1).

31 Installation is the reverse of removal.

Crankcase vent oil separator

32 Remove the intake manifold (see Chapter 2B)

33 Disconnect the PCV hose from the PCV valve (see illustration 22.24b).

34 Remove the PCV valve (see illustration 22.29).

35 Remove the front cylinder head (see Chapter 2B). (You can't remove the crank-case vent oil separator without removing the front cylinder head.)

36 Remove the crankcase vent oil separator mounting bolts (see illustration 22.24b).

37 Remove the crankcase vent oil separator. Remove the old oil separator gasket.

38 Wash out the oil separator with a suitable solvent. Blow it out with compressed air (be sure to wear safety goggles during this procedure!) and make sure that the passages are clear.

39 Installation is the reverse of removal. Be sure to use a new gasket and tighten the crankcase vent oil separator bolts to the torque listed in this Chapter's Specifications.

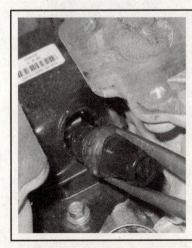

22.29 Unscrew the PCV valve to remove it from the crankcase vent oil separator (V6 models)

Torque specifications	Ft-lbs (unless otherwise indicated)	Nm

➡️**Note: One foot-pound (ft-lb) of torque is equivalent to 12 inch-pounds (in-lbs) of torque. Torque values below approximately 15 ft-lbs are expressed in inch-pounds, since most foot-pound torque wrenches are not accurate at these smaller values.**

Camshaft Position (CMP) sensor mounting bolt		
Four-cylinder engine	180 in-lbs	20
V6 engine	89 in-lbs	10
Crankshaft Position (CKP) sensor mounting bolt		
Four-cylinder engine	62 in-lbs	7
V6 engine	89 in-lbs	10
Cylinder Head Temperature (CHT) sensor	89 in-lbs	10
Exhaust Gas Recirculation (EGR) valve mounting bolts		
Four-cylinder engine	80 in-lbs	9
V6 engine	18	25
Idle Air Control (IAC) valve mounting bolts		
2.0L four-cylinder and 3.0L V6 engines	89 in-lbs	10
2.3L four-cylinder engine	35 in-lbs	4
Knock sensor retaining nut/bolt		
Four-cylinder engine (retaining nut)	180 in-lbs	20
V6 engine (retaining bolt)	18	25
Output Shaft Speed (OSS) sensor mounting bolt	120 in-lbs	13
Oxygen sensors (all oxygen sensors, all models)	30	40
Transmission Range (TR) sensor mounting bolts	108 in-lbs	12
Turbine Shaft Speed (TSS) sensor mounting bolt	120 in-lbs	13
Vehicle Speed Sensor (VSS) (2WD and 4WD)	62 in-lbs	7

Section

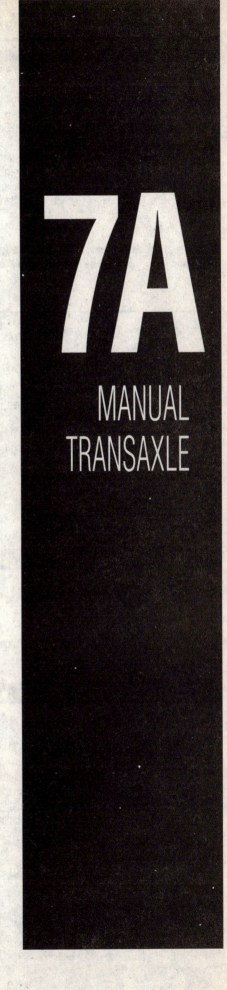

7A

MANUAL
TRANSAXLE

1 General information

The vehicles covered by this manual are equipped with either a 5-speed manual or a 4-speed automatic transaxle. This Part of Chapter 7 contains information on the manual transaxle. Service procedures for the automatic transaxle are contained in Part B. Information on the transfer case used on 4WD models can be found in Part C.

The transaxle is contained in a cast-aluminum alloy casing bolted to the engine's left-hand end, and consists of the gearbox and final drive differential - often called a transaxle. The transaxle unit type is stamped on a plate attached to the transaxle.

TRANSAXLE OVERHAUL

Because of the complexity of the assembly, possible unavailability of replacement parts and special tools necessary, internal repair procedures for the transaxle are not recommended for the home mechanic. The bulk of the information in this Chapter is devoted to removal and installation procedures.

2 Shift lever - removal and installation

2WD MODELS

1 Apply the Parking brake. Place the shift lever in Neutral. Unscrew and remove the shift lever knob.
2 Remove the center console trim panel and rubber shift lever boot.
3 Use a pair of snap-ring pliers to remove the steel snap-ring. Remove the plastic clip from under the steel snap-ring.
4 Remove the rubber O-ring.
5 Raise the vehicle and support it securely on jackstands.
6 Remove the nut and through-bolt securing the shift linkage rod to the shift lever.
7 Lift the gearshift lever from the housing.
8 Installation is the reverse of removal.

4WD MODELS

9 Apply the Parking brake. Place the shift lever in Neutral. Unscrew the shift lever knob.
10 Remove the center console trim panel and rubber shift lever boot.
11 Disconnect the shift cables from the shift lever by prying them off of the ballstuds.
12 Using a pair of pliers, remove the spring clips securing the cables to the shifter base.
13 Pull the shift cables forward to release them from the base, then position them out of the way.
14 Remove the four bolts securing the shifter base to the floor, then remove the shifter.
15 Installation is the reverse of removal.

3 Shift linkage (2WD models) - removal and installation

1 Raise the vehicle and support it securely on jackstands.
2 Remove the nut and through-bolt securing the shift linkage rod to the transaxle shift lever.
3 At the shift lever, remove the nut and through-bolt connecting the shift lever to the shift linkage rod.
4 Remove the shift linkage rod from the vehicle.
5 Installation is the reverse of removal.

4 Shift cables (4WD models) - removal and installation

1 Remove the gear shift lever (see Section 2).
2 Remove the center console (see Chapter 11).
3 Trace the cables to the floor and unbolt the interior grommet.
4 Working inside the engine compartment, remove the shift cable retaining clips then remove the shift cables from the transaxle levers.
5 Disconnect the cable retainer from the retainer bracket by pulling on the black pin then lifting the cable from the bracket.

6 Raise the front of the vehicle and support it securely on jackstands.
7 Remove the nuts securing the shift cable retaining bracket.
8 Inside the engine compartment, carefully remove the shift cables one at a time from the vehicle.
9 Installation is the reverse of removal.

5 Driveaxle oil seals - replacement

1 Oil leaks frequently occur due to wear of the driveaxle oil seals. Replacement of these seals is relatively easy, since the repair can be performed without removing the transaxle from the vehicle.
2 Driveaxle oil seals are located at the sides of the transaxle, where the driveaxles are attached. If leakage at the seal is suspected, raise the vehicle and support it securely on jackstands. If the seal is leaking, lubricant will be found on the sides of the transaxle, below the seals.
3 Refer to Chapter 8 and remove the driveaxles.

4   Use a screwdriver or prybar to carefully pry the oil seal out of the transaxle bore.

5   If the oil seal cannot be removed with a screwdriver or prybar, a special oil seal removal tool (available at auto parts stores) will be required.

6   Using a large section of pipe or a large deep socket (slightly smaller than the outside diameter of the seal) as a drift, install the new oil seal. Drive it into the bore squarely and make sure it's completely seated. Coat the seal lip with transaxle lubricant.

7   Install the driveaxle(s). Be careful not to damage the lip of the new seal.

6   Manual transaxle - removal and installation

REMOVAL

1   Disconnect the cable from the negative terminal of the battery (see Chapter 5).

2   Remove the air filter housing (see Chapter 4).

3   Disconnect the electrical connector for the back-up light switch.

4   If you're working on a 4WD model, disconnect the shift cables from the transaxle shift levers (see Section 4).

5   Remove the transaxle front and rear wire harness brackets from the transaxle.

6   Disconnect the electrical connector for the vehicle speed sensor (see Chapter 6).

7   Attach an engine support fixture to the lifting hook at the transaxle end of the engine. If no hook is provided, use a bolt of the proper size and thread pitch to attach the support fixture chain to a hole at the end of the cylinder head.

➡**Note: Engine support fixtures can be obtained at most equipment rental yards and some auto parts stores.**

8   Disconnect the clutch release cylinder and line from the transaxle (see Chapter 8).

9   Remove the left side transaxle mount and bracket.

10 Remove the front transaxle mount and bracket.

11 Remove the rear transaxle mount through bolt.

12 Remove the starter (see Chapter 5).

13 Remove the four upper transaxle-to-engine mounting bolts.

14 Loosen the driveaxle/hub nuts and the wheel lug nuts, raise the front of the vehicle and support it securely on jackstands. Remove the wheels.

15 Remove the driveaxles (see Chapter 8).

16 Drain the transaxle lubricant (see Chapter 1).

17 Remove the three bolts securing the transaxle support insulator bracket, then remove the bracket.

18 If you're working on a 2WD model, disconnect the shift linkage bar (see Section 3) and support bar.

19 Remove the subframe crossmember.

20 Remove the longitudinal crossmember.

21 Remove the upper and lower left-side splash shields.

22 If you're working on a 4WD model, remove the transfer case (see Chapter 7 Part C).

23 Support the transaxle with a jack - preferably a jack made for this purpose (available at most tool rental yards). Safety chains will help steady the transaxle on the jack.

24 Remove the seven remaining bolts securing the transaxle to the engine.

25 Move the transaxle to the rear to disengage it from the engine block dowel pins. Then carefully remove the transaxle.

INSTALLATION

26 Lubricate the input shaft with a light coat of high-temperature grease. With the transaxle secured to the jack, raise it into position behind the engine and carefully slide it forward, engaging the input shaft with the clutch. Do not use excessive force to install the transaxle - if the input shaft won't slide into place, readjust the angle of the transaxle or turn the input shaft so the splines engage properly with the clutch.

27 Once the transaxle is flush with the engine, install the transaxle-to-engine bolts. Tighten the bolts to the torque listed in this Chapter's Specifications.

✳✳ CAUTION:

Don't use the bolts to force the transaxle and engine together.

28 The remainder of installation of the transaxle is a reversal of the removal procedure, but note the following points:

   a) Tighten the suspension crossmember mounting bolts to the torque values listed in this Chapter's Specifications.
   b) Tighten the driveaxle/hub nuts to the torque value listed in the Chapter 8 Specifications.
   c) Tighten the starter mounting bolts to the torque value listed in the Chapter 5 Specifications.
   d) If installing the transfer case, refer to Chapter 7, Part C.
   e) Tighten the wheel lug nuts to the torque listed in the Chapter 1 Specifications.
   f) Fill the transaxle with the correct type and amount of transaxle fluid as described in Chapter 1.

7   Manual transaxle overhaul - general information

1   Overhauling a manual transaxle is a difficult job for the do-it-yourselfer. It involves the disassembly and reassembly of many small parts. Numerous clearances must be precisely measured and, if necessary, changed with select-fit spacers and snap-rings. As a result, if transaxle problems arise, it can be removed and installed by a competent do-it-yourselfer, but overhaul should be left to a transmission repair shop. Rebuilt transaxles may be available - check with your dealer parts department and auto parts stores. At any rate, the time and money involved in an overhaul is almost sure to exceed the cost of a rebuilt unit.

2   Nevertheless, it's not impossible for an inexperienced mechanic to rebuild a transaxle if the special tools are available and the job is done in a deliberate step-by-step manner so nothing is overlooked.

3   The tools necessary for an overhaul include internal and external

snap-ring pliers, a bearing puller, a slide hammer, a set of pin punches, a dial indicator and possibly a hydraulic press. In addition, a large, sturdy workbench and a vise or transaxle stand will be required.

4   During disassembly of the transaxle, make careful notes of how each piece comes off, where it fits in relation to other pieces and what holds it in place.

5   Before taking the transaxle apart for repair, it will help if you have some idea what area of the transaxle is malfunctioning. Certain problems can be closely tied to specific areas in the transaxle, which can make component examination and replacement easier. Refer to the *Troubleshooting* Section at the front of this manual for information regarding possible sources of trouble.

8   Transaxle mount - replacement

1   Insert a large screwdriver or prybar between the mount and the transaxle and pry up.

2   The transaxle should not move excessively away from the mount. If it does, replace the mount.

3   If you're working on a four-cylinder model, remove the battery (see Chapter 5).

4   Remove the air filter housing cover and air intake tube (see Chapter 4).

5   Support the transaxle with a jack, remove the nuts and bolts and remove the mount. It may be necessary to raise the transaxle slightly to provide enough clearance to remove the mount.

6   Installation is the reverse of removal.

➡**Note: Install all of the mount fasteners before tightening any of them.**

Specifications

General

Transaxle oil type	See Chapter 1
Transaxle oil capacity	See Chapter 1

Torque specifications

	Ft-lbs (unless otherwise indicated)	Nm

➡**Note: One foot-pound (ft-lb) of torque is equivalent to 12 inch-pounds (in-lbs) of torque. Torque values below approximately 15 ft-lbs are expressed in inch-pounds, since most foot-pound torque wrenches are not accurate at these smaller values.**

	Ft-lbs	Nm
Transaxle-to-engine mounting bolts	33	45
Crossmember-to-subframe bolts	85	115
Longitudinal crossmember-to-subframe bolts	66	90

Section

Reference to other Chapters

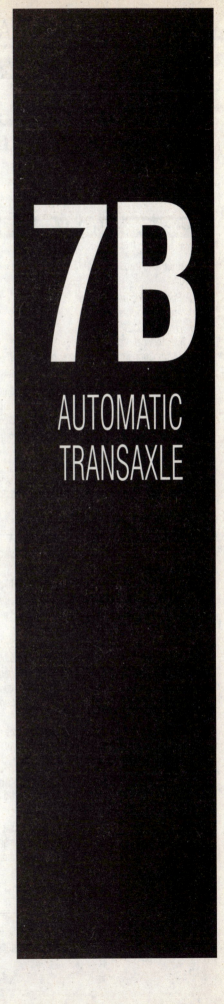

7B

AUTOMATIC TRANSAXLE

1 General information

All information on the automatic transaxle is included in this Part of Chapter 7. Information for the manual transaxle can be found in Part A of this Chapter.

Because of the complexity of the automatic transaxles and the specialized equipment necessary to perform most service operations, this Chapter contains only those procedures related to general diagnosis, routine maintenance, adjustment and removal and installation.

If the transaxle requires major repair work, it should be left to a dealer service department or an automotive or transmission repair shop. Once properly diagnosed you can, however, remove and install the transaxle yourself and save the expense, even if the repair work is done by a transmission shop.

2 Diagnosis - general

1   Automatic transaxle malfunctions may be caused by five general conditions:

   a) *Poor engine performance*
   b) *Improper adjustments*
   c) *Hydraulic malfunctions*
   d) *Mechanical malfunctions*
   e) *Malfunctions in the computer or its signal network*

2   Diagnosis of these problems should always begin with a check of the easily repaired items: fluid level and condition (see Chapter 1), shift cable adjustment and shift lever installation. Next, perform a road test to determine if the problem has been corrected or if more diagnosis is necessary. If the problem persists after the preliminary tests and corrections are completed, additional diagnosis should be performed by a dealer service department or other qualified transmission repair shop. Refer to the *Troubleshooting* Section at the front of this manual for information on symptoms of transaxle problems.

PRELIMINARY CHECKS

3   Drive the vehicle to warm the transaxle to normal operating temperature.

4   Check the fluid level as described in Chapter 1:

   a) *If the fluid level is unusually low, add enough fluid to bring the level within the designated area of the dipstick, then check for external leaks (see following).*
   b) *If the fluid level is abnormally high, drain off the excess, then check the drained fluid for contamination by coolant. The presence of engine coolant in the automatic transmission fluid indicates that a failure has occurred in the internal radiator oil cooler walls that separate the coolant from the transmission fluid (see Chapter 3).*
   c) *If the fluid is foaming, drain it and refill the transaxle, then check for coolant in the fluid, or a high fluid level.*

5   Check the engine idle speed.

➡**Note: If the engine is malfunctioning, do not proceed with the preliminary checks until it has been repaired and runs normally.**

6   Check and adjust the shift cable, if necessary (see Section 4).

7   If hard shifting is experienced, inspect the shift cable under the steering column and at the manual lever on the transaxle (see Section 4).

FLUID LEAK DIAGNOSIS

8   Most fluid leaks are easy to locate visually. Repair usually consists of replacing a seal or gasket. If a leak is difficult to find, the following procedure may help.

9   Identify the fluid. Make sure it's transmission fluid and not engine oil or brake fluid (automatic transmission fluid is a deep red color).

10   Try to pinpoint the source of the leak. Drive the vehicle several miles, then park it over a large sheet of cardboard. After a minute or two, you should be able to locate the leak by determining the source of the fluid dripping onto the cardboard.

11   Make a careful visual inspection of the suspected component and the area immediately around it. Pay particular attention to gasket mating surfaces. A mirror is often helpful for finding leaks in areas that are hard to see.

12   If the leak still cannot be found, clean the suspected area thoroughly with a degreaser or solvent, then dry it thoroughly.

13   Drive the vehicle for several miles at normal operating temperature and varying speeds. After driving the vehicle, visually inspect the suspected component again.

14   Once the leak has been located, the cause must be determined before it can be properly repaired. If a gasket is replaced but the sealing flange is bent, the new gasket will not stop the leak. The bent flange must be straightened.

15   Before attempting to repair a leak, check to make sure that the following conditions are corrected or they may cause another leak.

➡**Note: Some of the following conditions cannot be fixed without highly specialized tools and expertise. Such problems must be referred to a qualified transmission shop or a dealer service department.**

Gasket leaks

16   Check the pan periodically. Make sure the bolts are tight, no bolts are missing, the gasket is in good condition and the pan is flat (dents in the pan may indicate damage to the valve body inside).

17   If the pan gasket is leaking, the fluid level or the fluid pressure may be too high, the vent may be plugged, the pan bolts may be too tight, the pan sealing flange may be warped, the sealing surface of the transaxle housing may be damaged, the gasket may be damaged or the transaxle casting may be cracked or porous. If sealant instead of gasket material has been used to form a seal between the pan and the transaxle housing, it may be the wrong type of sealant.

Seal leaks

18   If a transaxle seal is leaking, the fluid level or pressure may be too high, the vent may be plugged, the seal bore may be damaged, the seal itself may be damaged or improperly installed, the surface of the shaft protruding through the seal may be damaged or a loose bearing may be causing excessive shaft movement.

19   Make sure the dipstick tube seal is in good condition and the tube is properly seated. Periodically check the area around the sensors for leakage. If transmission fluid is evident, check the seals for damage.

Case leaks

20 If the case itself appears to be leaking, the casting is porous and will have to be repaired or replaced.

21 Make sure the oil cooler hose fittings are tight and in good condition.

Fluid comes out vent pipe or fill tube

22 If this condition occurs the possible causes are, the transaxle is overfilled, there is coolant in the fluid, the case is porous, the dipstick is incorrect, the vent is plugged or the drain-back holes are plugged.

3   Shift lever - replacement

COLUMN-MOUNTED SHIFTER

♦ **Refer to illustration 3.7**

❈❈ WARNING 1:

These models are equipped with a Supplemental Restraint System (SRS), more commonly known as airbags. Always disable the airbag system before working in the vicinity of any airbag system component to avoid the possibility of accidental deployment of the airbag(s), which could cause personal injury (see Chapter 12).

❈❈ WARNING 2:

Do not use a memory saving device to preserve the PCM or radio memory when working on or near airbag system components.

1 Disconnect the cable from the negative battery terminal (see Chapter 5). Wait at least two minutes before proceeding.

2 Remove the steering wheel/airbag module (see Chapter 10).

3 Remove the steering column covers (see Chapter 11).

4 Remove the clockspring (see Chapter 10, Section 12).

5 Remove the multi-function switch and ignition switch (see Chapter 12).

6 Remove the shift cable from the steering column shift lever (see Section 4).

7 Disconnect the electrical connector and wiring harness (see illustration).

8 Remove the three shift lever mounting fasteners, then remove the lever.

9 Installation is the reverse of removal. After you've reconnected the battery, the Powertrain Control Module (PCM) must relearn its idle

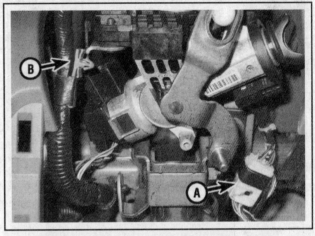

3.7 Disconnect the electrical connector (A) and wiring harness (B)

and fuel mixture trim strategy for optimum drivability and performance (see Chapter 5, Section 1 for this procedure).

CONSOLE-MOUNTED SHIFTER

10 Remove the shift lever trim ring by gently prying up on the four trim ring clips.

11 Remove the finish plate, then disconnect the electrical connector.

12 Disconnect the shift cable from the ball stud, then remove the cable from the shifter assembly.

13 Disconnect any remaining electrical connectors from the shifter.

14 Remove the four bolts, then lift the assembly out of the console.

15 Installation is the reverse of removal.

4   Shift cable - replacement and adjustment

COLUMN-MOUNTED SHIFTER

❈❈ WARNING 1:

These models are equipped with a Supplemental Restraint System (SRS), more commonly known as airbags. Always disable the airbag system before working in the vicinity of any airbag system component to avoid the possibility of accidental deployment of the airbag(s), which could cause personal injury (see Chapter 12).

❈❈ WARNING 2:

Do not use a memory saving device to preserve the PCM or radio memory when working on or near airbag system components.

Replacement

♦ **Refer to illustrations 4.3, 4.4 and 4.5**

1 Disconnect the cable from the negative battery terminal (see Chapter 5). Wait at least two minutes before proceeding.

2 Remove the steering column shrouds (see Chapter 11).

3 Disconnect the shift cable from the shift lever and steering column bracket (see illustration).

4 Working inside the engine compartment, remove the nuts securing the cable to the firewall (see illustration).

5 Disconnect the shift cable from the shift lever and transaxle mounting bracket (see illustration), then remove the cable from the vehicle.

6 Installation is the reverse of removal. Before installing the steering column shrouds and connecting the battery, be sure to adjust the cable as specified.

4.3 Remove the C-clip (A) and pull the cable end off the lever, then squeeze the tabs to remove the cable from the bracket (B)

Adjustment

▶ **Refer to illustrations 4.7 and 4.9**

7   With the steering column covers removed, place a 0.023 in. (0.6mm) feeler gauge between the shift lever and shift lever detent (see illustration).

8   Put the shift lever in the DRIVE position, then have an assistant hold it firmly in position.

9   Inside the engine compartment, remove the cable from the selector ballstud, then loosen the cable adjuster and adjust the cable (see illustration). Be sure the transaxle selector lever is in the DRIVE position, then connect the cable to the ballstud.

10 Tighten the cable adjuster then remove the feeler gauge and test the shift lever operation in each gear selection position.

11 Replace the steering column shrouds.

12 After you've reconnected the battery, the Powertrain Control Module (PCM) must relearn its idle and fuel mixture trim strategy for optimum drivability and performance (see Chapter 5, Section 1 for this procedure).

CONSOLE-MOUNTED SHIFTER

Replacement

13 Disconnect the cable from the negative battery terminal (see

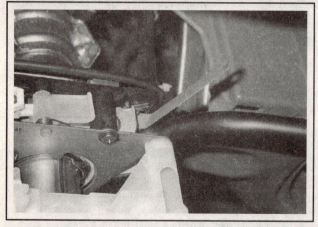

4.7 Insert a feeler gauge between the shift lever and the shift lever detent

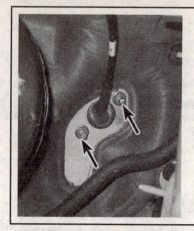

4.4 Inside the engine compartment, remove the two mounting nuts to release the cable from the firewall

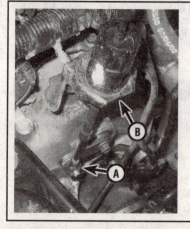

4.5 Using a small screwdriver, carefully pry the shift cable from the lever ballstud (A), then squeeze the release tabs under the mounting bracket and slide the cable from the bracket (B)

Chapter 5).

14 Raise the vehicle and securely support it on jackstands

15 Remove the left splash shield.

16 Place the shifter in drive

17 Remove the snow shield from the transaxle.

18 Remove the adjustment bolts from the transaxle shift cable and disconnect the cable from the shifter lever adjustment screw.

19 Disconnect the cable retainers along the length of the cable.

20 Remove the floor console finish panel.

21 Remove the cable body pass through grommet nuts, disconnect the cable from the shifter ball stud and release the cable housing from the shifter.

22 Installation is the reverse of removal. Be certain to adjust the new cable after installation.

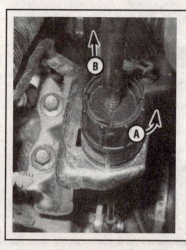

4.9 Turn the adjuster counterclockwise to loosen the adjuster (A); the cable can then be adjusted by moving it up or down (B)

Adjustment

23 Disconnect the cable from the negative battery terminal (see Chapter 5)

24 Raise the vehicle and securely support it on jackstands

25 Remove the left splash shield.

26 Place the shifter in drive.

27 Loosen the shifter cable adjustment screw and cable bracket nuts

enough to allow easy movement of the cable

28 Align the shifter lever between the two ribs on the transaxle.

29 With the transmission shifter still in Drive, tighten the cable bracket nuts, then tighten the shifter cable adjustment screw.

30 After installing any remaining components, apply the parking brake, lower the vehicle and operate the vehicle in each range to verify the adjustment is correct.

5 Auxiliary cooler - removal and installation

▶ Refer to illustration 5.2

1 To gain access to the cooler, remove the front bumper cover (see Chapter 11).

2 Disconnect the cooler lines and the bolts securing the cooler (see illustration).

3 Remove the cooler from the vehicle.

4 Installation is the reverse of removal. Be sure to tighten all fasteners securely.

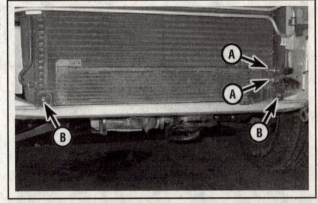

5.2 Using a pair of pliers, disconnect the clamps securing the hoses (A), then remove the two cooler mounting bolts (B)

6 Automatic transaxle - removal and installation

▶ **Refer to illustrations 6.5, 6.6, 6.8, 6.10a, 6.10b, 6.11, 6.12, 6.18, 6.22, 6.23, 6.24, 6.25a, 6.25b, 6.27 and 6.29**

REMOVAL

1 Disconnect the cable from the negative terminal of the battery (see Chapter 5).

2 Remove the air filter housing (see Chapter 4).

3 Disconnect the electrical connector for the transmission range sensor and the upstream oxygen sensor (see Chapter 6).

4 Disconnect the shift cable from the transaxle shift lever (see Section 4).

5 Remove the transaxle wire harness bracket from the transaxle (see illustration).

6 Remove the shift cable bracket from the transaxle (see illustration).

7 Remove the starter (see Chapter 5).

8 Disconnect the battery ground cable at the transaxle (see illustration).

9 Attach an engine support fixture to the lifting hook at the

6.5 Remove the nut securing the wire harness bracket to the transaxle, then pull the bracket and harness aside

6.6 Disconnect the shift cable and bracket from the transaxle

6.8 Remove the bolt securing the battery ground cable

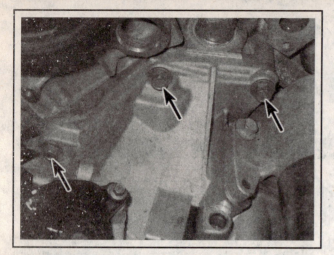

6.10a Remove the upper . . .

6.10b . . . transaxle-to-engine mounting bolts

6.11 Remove the transaxle mount bolt and plate

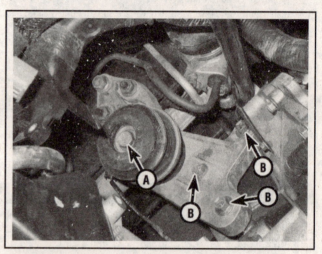

6.12 Remove the transaxle mount bolt (A) and the bracket bolts (B)

transaxle end of the engine. If no hook is provided, use a bolt of the proper size and thread pitch to attach the support fixture chain to a hole at the end of the cylinder head.

➨Note: Engine support fixtures can be obtained at most equip-

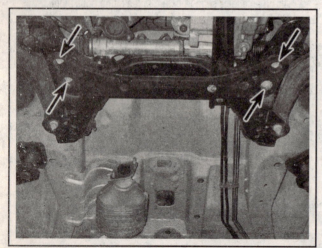

6.18 Remove the subframe crossmember bolts

ment rental yards and some auto parts stores.

10 Remove the transaxle-to-engine bolts that are accessible from above (see illustrations).

11 Remove the upper transaxle mount (see illustration).

12 Remove the rear transaxle mount (see illustration).

13 Remove the upper engine mount bolt from the right side of the engine.

14 Loosen the driveaxle/hub nuts and the wheel lug nuts, raise the front of the vehicle and support it securely on jackstands. Remove the wheels.

15 Remove the under-vehicle splash shield(s).

16 Drain the transaxle lubricant (see Chapter 1).

17 Remove the driveaxles (see Chapter 8).

18 Remove the subframe crossmember (see illustration).

19 Remove the front section of the exhaust system (see Chapter 4).

20 Remove the dampener from the longitudinal crossmember, then remove the crossmember.

21 On 4WD models, remove the transfer case (see Chapter 7, Part C).

22 Remove the torque converter inspection cover (see illustration).

23 Mark the relationship of the torque converter to the driveplate (see illustration).

6.22 Remove the inspection cover for access to the torque converter retaining nuts

6.23 Mark the relationship of the torque converter to the driveplate

6.24 Remove the four driveplate-to-torque converter nuts

6.25a Disconnect the transaxle cooler lines . . .

24 Remove the four driveplate-to-torque converter nuts (see illustration). Turn the crankshaft for access to each nut. Turn the crankshaft in a clockwise direction only (as viewed from the front).

25 Disconnect the fluid cooler hoses from the transaxle (see illustrations). Be prepared for spillage, and plug the hoses and the lines on the transaxle.

26 Mark and disconnect any electrical connectors accessible from

below.

27 Remove the transaxle vent tube (see illustration).

28 Support the transaxle with a jack - preferably a jack made for this purpose (available at most tool rental yards). Safety chains will help steady the transaxle on the jack.

29 Remove the remaining bolts securing the transaxle to the engine (see illustration).

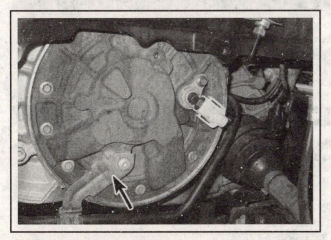

6.25b . . . and mounting bracket

6.27 Remove the transaxle vent tube from the valve body cover

30 Move the transaxle to the rear to disengage it from the engine block dowel pins and make sure the torque converter is detached from the driveplate. Lower the transaxle with the jack. Clamp a pair of locking pliers on the bellhousing case. The pliers will prevent the torque converter from falling out while you're removing the transaxle.

INSTALLATION

31 Installation of the transaxle is a reversal of the removal procedure, but note the following points:

a) As the torque converter is reinstalled, ensure that the drive tangs at the center of the torque converter hub engage with the recesses in the automatic transaxle fluid pump inner gear. This can be confirmed by turning the torque converter while pushing it towards the transaxle. If it isn't fully engaged, it will "clunk" into place.

b) When installing the transaxle, make sure the matchmarks you made on the torque converter and driveplate line up.

c) Install all of the driveplate-to-torque converter nuts before tightening any of them.

d) Tighten the driveplate-to-torque converter nuts to the specified torque.

e) Tighten the transaxle mounting bolts to the specified torque.

f) Tighten the suspension crossmember mounting bolts to the torque values listed in this Chapter's Specifications.

g) Tighten the driveaxle/hub nuts to the torque value listed in the Chapter 8 Specifications.

h) Tighten the wheel lug nuts to the torque listed in the Chapter 1

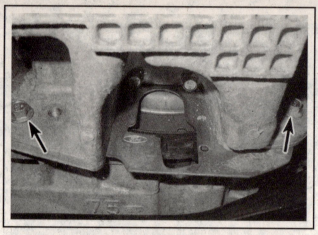

6.29 With the transaxle jack in place remove the remaining transaxle-to-engine mounting bolts

Specifications.

i) Fill the transaxle with the correct type and amount of automatic transmission fluid as described in Chapter 1.

j) On completion, adjust the shift cable as described in Section 4.

k) After you've reconnected the battery, the Powertrain Control Module (PCM) must relearn its idle and fuel mixture trim strategy for optimum driveability and performance (see Chapter 5, Section 1 for this procedure).

7 Automatic transaxle overhaul - general information

In the event of a problem occurring, it will be necessary to establish whether the fault is electrical, mechanical or hydraulic in nature, before repair work can be contemplated. Diagnosis requires detailed knowledge of the transaxle's operation and construction, as well as access to specialized test equipment, and so is deemed to be beyond the scope of this manual. It is therefore essential that problems with the automatic transaxle are referred to a dealer service department or other qualified repair facility for assessment.

Note that a faulty transaxle should not be removed before the vehicle has been diagnosed by a knowledgeable technician equipped with the proper tools, as troubleshooting must be performed with the transaxle installed in the vehicle.

Specifications

General

Fluid type and capacity	See Chapter 1

Torque specifications	Ft-lbs (unless otherwise indicated)	Nm

➡**Note: One foot-pound (ft-lb) of torque is equivalent to 12 inch-pounds (in-lbs) of torque. Torque values below approximately 15 ft-lbs are expressed in inch-pounds, since most foot-pound torque wrenches are not accurate at these smaller values.**

Crossmember mounting bolts	35	48
Longitudinal crossmember mounting bolts	96	130
Longitudinal crossmember dampener	30	40
Torque converter-to-driveplate nuts	27	36
Transaxle-to-engine mounting bolts	30	40

Section

7C

TRANSFER CASE

1   General information

Due to the complexity of the transfer case covered in this manual and the need for specialized equipment to perform most service operations, this chapter contains only routine maintenance and removal and installation procedures.

If the transfer case requires major repair work, it should be taken to a dealer service department or an automotive or transmission repair shop. You can, however, remove and install the transfer case yourself and save the expense of that labor, even if the repair work is done by a transmission shop.

2   Transfer case rear output shaft oil seal - removal and installation

1   Raise the vehicle and support it securely on jackstands.

2   Drain the transfer case lubricant (see Chapter 1).

3   Remove the driveshaft (see Chapter 8).

4   Mark the relative positions of the pinion, nut and flange.

5   Use a beam- or dial-type inch-pound torque wrench to determine the torque required to rotate the pinion. Record it for use later.

6   Count the number of threads visible between the end of the nut and the end of the pinion shaft and record it for use later.

7   Remove the flange mounting nut using a chain wrench to hold the pinion flange while loosening the locknut.

8   Remove the companion flange; a small puller may be required for removal.

9   Pry out the seal with a screwdriver or a seal removal tool. Don't damage the seal bore.

10   Lubricate the lips of the new seal with multi-purpose grease and tap it evenly into position with a seal installation tool or a large socket. Make sure it enters the housing squarely and is tapped into its full depth.

11   Align the mating marks made before disassembly and install the companion flange. If necessary, tighten the pinion nut to draw the flange into place.

12   Tighten the nut carefully until the original number of threads are exposed and the marks are aligned.

13   Measure the torque required to rotate the pinion and tighten the nut in small increments until it matches the figure recorded in Step 5.

14   Connect the driveshaft, add the specified lubricant to the transfer case (see Chapter 1) and lower the vehicle.

3   Transfer case driveaxle oil seal (right side) - removal and installation

1   Remove the wheel cover or hub cap. Break the hub nut loose with a socket and large breaker bar.

2   Loosen the wheel lug nuts, raise the vehicle and support it securely on jackstands. Remove the wheel.

3   Remove the right driveaxle and intermediate shaft (see Chapter 8).

4   Remove the exhaust crossover pipe (see Chapter 4).

5   Remove the three bolts securing the heat shield then remove the heat shield.

6   Remove the dust shield.

7   Carefully pry out the oil seal with a seal removal tool or a large screwdriver; make sure you don't scratch the seal bore.

8   Using a seal installer or a large deep socket as a drift, install the new oil seal. Drive it into the bore squarely and make sure it's completely seated.

9   Lubricate the lip of the new seal with multi-purpose grease, then install a new dust shield.

10   Install the intermediate shaft and driveaxle (see Chapter 8).

11   The remainder of installation is the reverse of removal. Check the transfer case lubricant level and add some, if necessary, to bring it to the appropriate level (see Chapter 1).

4   Transfer case - removal and installation

FOUR-CYLINDER MODELS

1   Loosen the right front wheel lug nuts. Raise the front of the vehicle and support it securely on jackstands. Remove the wheel.

2   Unbolt the front portion of the driveshaft (see Chapter 8) and suspend it from a piece of wire (don't let it hang from the center support bearing). Remove the right driveaxle and intermediate shaft (see Chapter 8).

3   Remove the four bolts securing the crossmember and remove the crossmember.

4   Working on the right side of the transfer case, remove the upper two mounting nuts and two lower mounting bolts. Remove the transfer case from the vehicle.

5   Installation is the reverse of removal, noting the following points:

a)   Install a new O-ring seal to the case.

b)   Tighten the driveshaft fasteners to the torque listed in the Chapter 8 Specifications.

c)   Tighten the transfer case and crossmember fasteners to the torque listed in this Chapter's Specifications.

d)   Refill the transfer case with the proper type and amount of fluid (see Chapter 1).

e)   Tighten the wheel lug nuts to the torque listed in the Chapter 1 Specifications.

V6 MODELS

6   Remove the wheel cover or hub cap. Break the hub nut loose with a socket and large breaker bar. Loosen the wheel lug nuts.

7   Raise the front of the vehicle and support it securely on jackstands. Remove the wheel.

8   Unbolt the front portion of the driveshaft (see Chapter 8), sus-

pend it from a piece of wire (don't let it hang from the center support bearing).

9   Remove the right driveaxle and intermediate shaft (see Chapter 8). Then remove the exhaust system crossover pipe and rear exhaust manifold (see Chapter 4).

10 Remove the four bolts securing the crossmember and remove the crossmember.

11 Remove the alternator (see Chapter 5).

12 Remove the six bolts securing the transfer case bracket to the engine block.

13 Working on the right side of the transfer case, remove the three transfer case mounting bolts.

14 Working on the left side, remove the final mounting bolt then remove the transfer case from the vehicle.

15 Installation is the reverse of removal, noting the following points:

   a) *Install a new O-ring seal to the case.*
   b) *Tighten the exhaust system fasteners to the torque listed in the Chapter 4 Specifications.*
   c) *Tighten the driveshaft fasteners to the torque listed in Chapter 8 Specifications*
   d) *Tighten the transfer case and crossmember fasteners to the torque listed in this Chapter's Specifications.*
   e) *Refill the transfer case with the proper type and amount of fluid (see Chapter 1).*
   f) *Tighten the wheel lug nuts to the torque listed in the Chapter 1 Specifications.*

5   Mode select switch - replacement

▶ **Refer to illustration 5.1**

1   Pull the switch knob straight off (see illustration).
2   Remove the instrument center trim panel (see Chapter 11).
3   Disconnect the switch electrical connector.
4   Remove the two mounting screws then remove the switch.
5   Installation is the reverse of removal.

5.1 Pull the knob straight off from the mode select switch

Specifications

Transfer case fluid type	See Chapter 1

Torque specifications

➡**Note: One foot-pound (ft-lb) of torque is equivalent to 12 inch-pounds (in-lbs) of torque. Torque values below approximately 15 ft-lbs are expressed in inch-pounds, since most foot-pound torque wrenches are not accurate at these smaller values.**

	Ft-lbs (unless otherwise indicated)	Nm
Crossmember mounting bolts	30	40
Transfer case-to-transaxle bolts/nuts	33	45
Transfer case bracket-to-engine block mounting bolts	30	40

Notes

Section

Reference to other Chapters

8

CLUTCH AND DRIVELINE

The information in this Chapter deals with the components from the rear of the engine to the drive wheels, except for the transaxle, which is dealt with in the previous Chapter.

Since nearly all the procedures covered in this Chapter involve working under the vehicle, make sure it's securely supported on sturdy jackstands or on a hoist where the vehicle can be easily raised and lowered.

1   All vehicles with a manual transaxle have a single dry plate, diaphragm spring-type clutch. The clutch disc has a splined hub which allows it to slide along the splines of the transaxle input shaft. The clutch and pressure plate are held in contact by spring pressure exerted by the diaphragm in the pressure plate.

2   The clutch release system is operated by hydraulic pressure. The hydraulic release system consists of the clutch pedal, a master cylinder and a shared common reservoir with the brake master cylinder, a release (or slave) cylinder and the hydraulic line connecting the two components.

3   When the clutch pedal is depressed, a pushrod pushes against brake fluid inside the master cylinder, applying hydraulic pressure to the release cylinder, which pushes the release bearing against the diaphragm fingers of the clutch pressure plate.

4   Terminology can be a problem when discussing the clutch components because common names are in some cases different from those used by the manufacturer. For example, the driven plate is also called the clutch plate or disc, the clutch release bearing is sometimes called a throwout bearing, the release cylinder is sometimes called the slave cylinder.

5   Unless you're replacing components with obvious damage, do these preliminary checks to diagnose clutch problems:

a) *The first check should be of the fluid level in the clutch master cylinder. If the fluid level is low, add fluid as necessary and inspect the hydraulic system for leaks. If the master cylinder reservoir is dry, bleed the system as described in Section 8 and recheck the clutch operation.*

b) *To check "clutch spin-down time," run the engine at normal idle speed with the transaxle in Neutral (clutch pedal up - engaged). Disengage the clutch (pedal down), wait several seconds and shift the transaxle into Reverse. No grinding noise should be heard. A grinding noise would most likely indicate a bad pressure plate or clutch disc.*

c) *To check for complete clutch release, run the engine (with the parking brake applied to prevent vehicle movement) and hold the clutch pedal approximately 1/2-inch from the floor. Shift the transaxle between 1st gear and Reverse several times. If the shift is rough, component failure is indicated.*

d) *Visually inspect the pivot bushing at the top of the clutch pedal to make sure there's no binding or excessive play.*

REMOVAL

1   Working under the dashboard, disconnect the clutch master cylinder pushrod from the pedal and unscrew the clutch master cylinder bracket nut.

2   Clamp a pair of locking pliers onto the clutch fluid feed hose, a couple of inches downstream of the brake fluid reservoir (the clutch master cylinder is supplied with fluid from the brake fluid reservoir). The pliers should be just tight enough to prevent fluid flow when the hose is disconnected. Disconnect the reservoir hose from the clutch master cylinder.

3   Using a flare-nut wrench, disconnect the hydraulic line fitting at the cylinder. Have rags handy, as some fluid will be lost as the line is removed. Cap or plug the ends of the line to prevent fluid leakage and the entry of contaminants.

4   Remove the remaining mounting nut and detach the cylinder from the firewall.

❈ CAUTION:

Don't allow brake fluid to come into contact with the paint, as it will damage the finish.

INSTALLATION

5   Place the master cylinder in position on the firewall and install the mounting nut finger tight.

6   Connect the hydraulic line fitting to the clutch master cylinder and tighten it finger tight (since the cylinder is still a bit loose, it'll be easier to start the threads into the cylinder).

7   Tighten the mounting nut to the torque listed in this Chapter's Specifications, then tighten the hydraulic line fitting securely.

8   Attach the fluid feed hose from the reservoir to the clutch master cylinder and tighten the hose clamp. Remove the locking pliers.

9   Working under the dash, install the remaining mounting nut and tighten it to the torque listed in this Chapter's Specifications. Connect the pushrod to the clutch pedal.

10 Fill the reservoir with brake fluid conforming to DOT 3 specifications and bleed the clutch system as outlined in Section 5.

4   Clutch release cylinder - removal and installation

REMOVAL

1   Disconnect the hydraulic line at the release cylinder using a flare-nut wrench. Have a small can and rags handy, as some fluid will be spilled as the line is removed. Plug the line to prevent excessive fluid loss and contamination.

2   Remove the release cylinder mounting bolts.

3   Remove the release cylinder.

INSTALLATION

4   Connect the hydraulic line fitting to the release cylinder, using your fingers only at this time (since the cylinder is still a bit loose, it'll be easier to start the threads into the cylinder).

5   Tighten the mounting bolts to the torque listed in this Chapter's Specifications.

6   Tighten the hydraulic fitting securely, using a flare-nut wrench.

7   Check the fluid level in the brake fluid reservoir, adding brake fluid conforming to DOT 3 specifications until the level is correct.

8   Bleed the system as described in Section 5, then recheck the brake fluid level.

5   Clutch hydraulic system - bleeding

1   Bleed the hydraulic system whenever any part of the system has been removed or the fluid level has fallen so low that air has been drawn into the master cylinder. The bleeding procedure is very similar to bleeding a brake system.

2   Fill the brake master cylinder reservoir with new brake fluid conforming to DOT 3 specifications.

✳✳ CAUTION:

Do not re-use any of the fluid coming from the system during the bleeding operation or use fluid which has been inside an open container for an extended period of time.

3   Have an assistant depress the clutch pedal and hold it. Open the bleeder valve on the release cylinder, allowing fluid and any air to escape. Close the bleeder valve when the flow of fluid (and bubbles) ceases. Once closed, have your assistant release the pedal.

4   Continue this process until all air is evacuated from the system, indicated by a solid stream of fluid being ejected from the bleeder valve each time with no air bubbles. Keep a close watch on the fluid level inside the brake master cylinder reservoir - if the level drops too far, air will get into the system and you'll have to start all over again.

➡Note: **Wash the area with water to remove any excess brake fluid.**

5   Check the brake fluid level again, and add some, if necessary, to bring it to the appropriate level. Check carefully for proper operation before placing the vehicle into normal service.

6   Clutch components - removal, inspection and installation

✳✳ WARNING:

Dust produced by clutch wear is hazardous to your health. DO NOT blow it out with compressed air and DO NOT inhale it. DO NOT use gasoline or petroleum-based solvents to remove the dust. Brake system cleaner should be used to flush the dust into a drain pan. After the clutch components are wiped clean with a rag, dispose of the contaminated rags and cleaner in a covered, marked container.

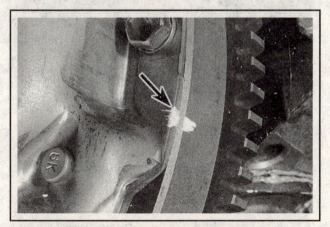

6.5 Mark the relationship of the pressure plate to the flywheel (if you're planning to re-use the old pressure plate)

REMOVAL

♦ **Refer to illustration 6.5**

1   Access to the clutch components is normally accomplished by removing the transaxle, leaving the engine in the vehicle. If the engine is being removed for major overhaul, check the clutch for wear and replace worn components as necessary. However, the relatively low cost of the clutch components compared to the time and trouble spent gaining access to them warrants their replacement anytime the engine or transaxle is removed, unless they are new or in near-perfect condition. The following procedures are based on the assumption the engine will stay in place.

2   Remove the transaxle from the vehicle (see Chapter 7, Part A). Support the engine while the transaxle is out. Preferably, an engine support fixture or a hoist should be used to support it from above.

3   The clutch fork and release bearing can remain attached to the transaxle housing for the time being.

4   To support the clutch disc during removal, install a clutch alignment tool through the clutch disc hub.

5   Carefully inspect the flywheel and pressure plate for indexing marks. The marks are usually an X, an O or a white letter. If they cannot be found, scribe or paint marks yourself so the pressure plate and the flywheel will be in the same alignment during installation (see illustration).

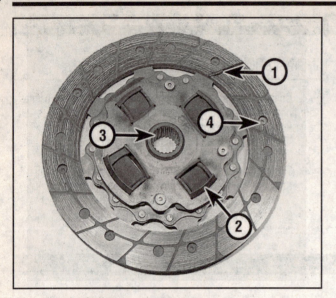

6.9 The clutch disc

1   *Lining* - this will wear down in use
2   *Springs or dampers* - check for cracking and deformation
3   *Splined hub* - the splines must not be worn and should slide smoothly on the transaxle input shaft splines
4   *Rivets* - these secure the lining and will damage the flywheel or pressure plate if allowed to contact the surfaces

6   Turning each bolt a little at a time, loosen the pressure plate-to-flywheel bolts. Work in a criss-cross pattern until all spring pressure is relieved. Then hold the pressure plate securely and completely remove the bolts, followed by the pressure plate and clutch disc.

INSPECTION

▶ **Refer to illustrations 6.9, 6.11a and 6.11b**

7   Ordinarily, when a problem occurs in the clutch, it can be attributed to wear of the clutch driven plate assembly (clutch disc). However, all components should be inspected at this time.

8   Inspect the flywheel for cracks, heat checking, grooves and other obvious defects. If the imperfections are slight, a machine shop can machine the surface flat and smooth, which is highly recommended regardless of the surface appearance. Refer to Chapter 2 for the flywheel removal and installation procedure.

9   Inspect the lining on the clutch disc. There should be at least 1/16-inch of lining above the rivet heads. Check for loose rivets, distortion, cracks, broken springs and other obvious damage (see illustration). As mentioned above, ordinarily the clutch disc is routinely replaced, so if in doubt about the condition, replace it with a new one.

10   The release bearing should also be replaced along with the clutch disc (see Section 7).

11   Check the machined surfaces and the diaphragm spring fingers of the pressure plate (see illustrations). If the surface is grooved or otherwise damaged, replace the pressure plate. Also check for obvious

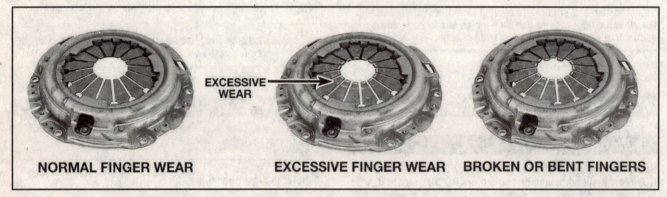

NORMAL FINGER WEAR   **EXCESSIVE FINGER WEAR**   **BROKEN OR BENT FINGERS**

6.11a Replace the pressure plate if excessive wear or damage are noted

6.11b Inspect the pressure plate surface for excessive score marks, cracks and signs of overheating

6.16 Center the clutch disc in the pressure plate with a clutch alignment tool

damage, distortion, cracking, etc. Light glazing can be removed with emery cloth or sandpaper. If a new pressure plate is required, new and re-manufactured units are available.

12 Check the pilot bearing in the end of the crankshaft for excessive wear, scoring, dryness, roughness and any other obvious damage. If any of these conditions are noted, replace the bearing.

13 Removal can be accomplished with a slide hammer and puller attachment, which are available at most auto parts stores or tool rental yards. Refer to Chapter 2 for the flywheel removal procedure (it must be removed before the pilot bearing is removed).

INSTALLATION

▶ Refer to illustration 6.16

14 To install a new pilot bearing, lightly lubricate the outside surface with grease, then drive it into the recess with a bearing driver or a socket (see illustration). Install the flywheel (see Chapter 2).

15 Before installation, clean the flywheel and pressure plate machined surfaces with brake cleaner, lacquer thinner or acetone. It's important that no oil or grease is on these surfaces or the lining of the clutch disc. Handle the parts only with clean hands.

16 Position the clutch disc and pressure plate against the flywheel with the clutch held in place with an alignment tool (see illustration). Make sure the disc is installed properly (most replacement clutch discs will be marked "flywheel side" or something similar - if not marked, install the clutch disc with the damper springs toward the transaxle).

17 Tighten the pressure plate-to-flywheel bolts only finger tight, working around the pressure plate.

18 Center the clutch disc by ensuring the alignment tool extends through the splined hub and into the pilot bearing in the crankshaft. Wiggle the tool up, down or side-to-side as needed to center the disc. Tighten the pressure plate-to-flywheel bolts a little at a time, working in a criss-cross pattern to prevent distorting the cover. After all of the bolts are snug, tighten them to the torque listed in this Chapter's Specifications. Remove the alignment tool.

19 Using high-temperature grease, lubricate the inner groove of the release bearing (see Section 7). Also place a small amount of grease on the release lever contact areas and the transaxle input shaft bearing retainer.

20 Install the clutch release bearing (see Section 7).

21 Install the transaxle and all components removed previously.

---

7   Clutch release bearing and lever - removal, inspection and installation

☀ WARNING:

Dust produced by clutch wear is hazardous to your health. DO NOT blow it out with compressed air and DO NOT inhale it. DO NOT use gasoline or petroleum-based solvents to remove the dust. Brake system cleaner should be used to flush the dust into a drain pan. After the clutch components are wiped clean with a rag, dispose of the contaminated rags and cleaner in a covered, marked container.

REMOVAL

1 Remove the transaxle (see Chapter 7A).

2 Pull the clutch release fork off the ballstud and slide the release bearing off the input shaft along with the release fork.

INSPECTION

▶ Refer to illustration 7.4

3 Wipe off the bearing with a clean rag and inspect it for damage, wear and cracks. Don't immerse the bearing in solvent - it's sealed for life and immersion in solvent will ruin it.

4 Hold the center of the bearing and rotate the outer portion while applying pressure (see illustration). If the bearing doesn't turn smoothly or if it's noisy or rough, replace it.

➡Note: Considering the difficulty involved with replacing the release bearing, we recommend replacing the release bearing whenever the clutch components are replaced.

7.4 To check the bearing, hold it by the outer race and rotate the inner race while applying pressure; if the bearing doesn't turn smoothly or if it is noisy, replace the bearing

INSTALLATION

5 Lightly lubricate the friction surfaces of the release bearing, ballstud and the input shaft bearing retainer with high-temperature grease.

6 Install the release lever and bearing onto the input shaft.

7 The remainder of installation is the reverse of removal.

8 Driveaxles - removal and installation

FRONT

Removal

▶ Refer to illustrations 8.1 and 8.7

1   Remove the wheel cover or hub cap. Break the driveaxle/hub nut loose with a socket and large breaker bar (see illustration).

2   Loosen the wheel lug nuts, raise the vehicle and support it securely on jackstands. Remove the wheel.

3   Separate the lower control arm from the steering knuckle (see Chapter 10).

4   Remove the driveaxle/hub nut from the axle and discard it. If equipped with antilock brakes, remove the wheel speed sensor and set it aside.

5   Swing the knuckle/hub assembly out (away from the vehicle) until the end of the driveaxle is free of the hub.

➡**Note: If the driveaxle splines stick in the hub, tap on the end of the driveaxle with a plastic hammer. Support the outer end of the driveaxle with a piece of wire to avoid unnecessary strain on the inner CV joint.**

6   If you're removing the right driveaxle, carefully pry the inner CV joint off the intermediate shaft using a large screwdriver or prybar positioned between the CV joint housing and the intermediate shaft bearing support.

7   If you're removing the left driveaxle, pry the inner CV joint out of the transaxle using a large screwdriver or prybar positioned between the transaxle and the CV joint housing (see illustration). Be careful not to damage the differential seal.

8   Support the CV joints and carefully remove the driveaxle from the vehicle.

Installation

9   Pry the old spring clip from the inner end of the driveaxle (left side) or outer end of the intermediate shaft (right side) and install a new one. Lubricate the differential or intermediate shaft seal with multipurpose grease and raise the driveaxle into position while supporting the CV joints.

➡**Note: Position the spring clip with the opening facing down; this will ease insertion of the driveaxle and prevent damage to the clip.**

10   Push the splined end of the inner CV joint into the differential side gear (left side) or onto the intermediate shaft (right side) and make sure the spring clip locks in its groove.

11   Apply a light coat of multi-purpose grease to the outer CV joint splines, pull out on the steering knuckle assembly and install the stub axle into the hub.

12   Insert the balljoint stud into the steering knuckle and tighten the pinch bolt to the torque listed in the Chapter 10 Specifications.

13   Install a new driveaxle/hub nut. Tighten the hub nut securely, but don't try to tighten it to the actual torque specification until you've lowered the vehicle to the ground.

14   Grasp the inner CV joint housing (not the driveaxle) and pull out to make sure the driveaxle has seated securely in the transaxle or on the intermediate shaft.

15   Install the wheel and lug nuts, then lower the vehicle. Tighten the lug nuts to the torque listed in the Chapter 1 Specifications.

16   Tighten the driveaxle/hub nut to the torque listed in this Chapter's Specifications. Install the hub cap or wheel cover.

INTERMEDIATE SHAFT

Removal

▶ Refer to illustration 8.23

17   Remove the right side wheel cover or hub cap. Break the hub nut loose with a socket and large breaker bar.

18   Loosen the wheel lug nuts, raise the vehicle and support it securely on jackstands. Remove the wheel.

19   Separate the lower control arm from the steering knuckle (see Chapter 10).

20   Remove the driveaxle/hub nut from the axle and discard it.

21   Swing the knuckle/hub assembly out (away from the vehicle) until the end of the driveaxle is free of the hub.

➡**Note: If the driveaxle splines stick in the hub, tap on the end of the driveaxle with a plastic hammer. Support the outer end of the driveaxle with a piece of wire to avoid unnecessary strain on the inner CV joint.**

22   Remove the driveaxle (see Step 6).

23   Remove the bearing support nuts (see illustration) and slide the intermediate shaft out of the transaxle. Be careful not to damage the

8.1 Loosen the driveaxle/hub nut with a long breaker bar

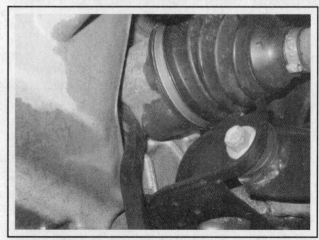

8.7 Carefully pry the inner end of the driveaxle from the transaxle

8.23 Remove the nuts securing the intermediate shaft bearing support

8.32 Carefully pry the inner end of the driveaxle from the differential

differential seal when pulling the shaft out.

24 Check the support bearing for smooth operation by turning the shaft while holding the bearing. If you feel any roughness, take the intermediate shaft to an automotive machine shop or other qualified repair facility to have a new bearing installed.

Installation

25 Lubricate the lips of the transaxle seal with multi-purpose grease. Carefully guide the intermediate shaft into the transaxle side gear then install the mounting nuts for the bearing support. Tighten the nuts to the torque listed in this Chapter's Specifications.

26 The remainder of installation is the reverse of removal.

REAR (4WD MODELS)

Removal

▶ **Refer to illustration 8.32**

27 Remove the wheel cover or hub cap. Break the driveaxle/hub nut loose with a socket and large breaker bar (see illustration 8.1).

28 Block the front wheels to prevent the vehicle from rolling. Loosen the wheel lug nuts, raise the rear of the vehicle and support it securely on jackstands. Remove the wheel.

29 Remove the driveaxle/hub nut and discard it.

30 Remove the coil spring (see Chapter 10).

31 Remove the nut and detach the trailing arm from the lower suspension arm balljoint (see Chapter 10), then pry the trailing arm outward and remove the outer end of the driveaxle from the hub.

Don't let the driveaxle hang by the inner CV joint.

32 Pry the inner end of the driveaxle out of the differential and remove it from the vehicle (see illustration).

Installation

33 Pry the old spring clip from the inner end of the driveaxle and install a new one.

34 Apply a light film of grease to the area on the inner CV joint stub shaft where the seal rides, then insert the splined end of the inner CV joint into the differential. Make sure the spring clip locks in its groove.

35 Apply a light film of grease to the outer CV joint splines, pry the trailing arm outward and insert the outer end of the driveaxle into the hub.

36 Install the coil spring see Chapter 10.

37 Connect the trailing arm to the lower suspension arm and install the nut. Using a floor jack, raise the trailing arm to simulate normal ride height, then tighten the nut to the torque listed in the Chapter 10 Specifications.

38 Install a new driveaxle/hub nut. Tighten the hub nut securely, but don't try to tighten it to the actual torque specification until you've lowered the vehicle to the ground.

39 Install the wheel and lug nuts, then lower the vehicle. Tighten the lug nuts to the torque listed in the Chapter 1 Specifications.

40 Tighten the driveaxle/hub nut to the torque listed in this Chapter's Specifications. Install the wheel cover or hub cap.

9 Driveaxle boot - replacement

➡Note 1: If the CV joints are worn, indicating the need for an overhaul (usually due to torn boots), explore all options before beginning the job. Complete rebuilt driveaxles are available on an exchange basis, which eliminates much time and work.

➡Note 2: Some auto parts stores carry "split" type replacement boots, which can be installed without removing the driveaxle from the vehicle. This is a convenient alternative; however, the driveaxle should be removed and the CV joint disassembled and cleaned to ensure the joint is free from contaminants such as

moisture and dirt which will accelerate CV joint wear.

➡Note 3: Models equipped with ABS are equipped with ABS sensor rings on the outer CV joints. Be sure to inspect the sensor rings for chipped or missing teeth. Replace the sensor ring if necessary.

1 Remove the driveaxle from the vehicle (see Section 8).

2 Mount the driveaxle in a vise. The jaws of the vise should be lined with wood or rags to prevent damage to the driveaxle.

FRONT

Inner CV joint and boot

▶ **Refer to illustrations 9.3, 9.4, 9.5, 9.6a, 9.6b, 9.7, 9.11, 9.14, 9.16, 9.17a, 9.17b, 9.17c, 9.17d and 9.17e**

Removal

3   Remove the boot clamps (see illustration).

4   Pull the boot back from the inner CV joint and slide the joint housing off. Be sure to mark the relationship of the tri-pod to the outer race (see illustration).

5   Use a center punch to mark the tri-pod and axleshaft to ensure that they are reassembled properly (see illustration).

6   Spread the ends of the stop-ring apart, slide it towards the center of the shaft, then remove the retainer clip from the end of the axleshaft (see illustration).

7   Use a hammer and a brass punch to drive the tri-pod joint from the driveaxle (see illustration).

8   Remove the stop-ring from the axleshaft and discard it.

Inspection

9   Clean the old grease from the outer race and the tri-pod bearing assembly. Carefully disassemble each section of the tri-pod assembly, one at a time so as not to mix up the parts, and clean the needle bearings with solvent.

10   Inspect the rollers, tri-pod, bearings and outer race for scoring, pitting or other signs of abnormal wear, which will warrant the replacement of the inner CV joint.

Reassembly

11   Slide the clamps and boot onto the axleshaft. It's a good idea to wrap the axleshaft splines with tape to prevent damaging the boot (see illustration).

12   Install a new stop-ring on the axleshaft, but don't seat it in its groove; position it on the shaft past the groove.

13   Place the tri-pod on the shaft (making sure the marks are aligned) and install a new bearing retainer clip. Now slide the tri-pod up against the retainer clip and seat the stop-ring in its groove.

14   Apply CV joint grease to the tri-pod assembly, the inside of the joint housing and the inside of the boot (see illustration).

15   Slide the boot into place.

16   Position the CV joint mid-way through its travel, then equalize the pressure in the boot (see illustration).

17   Tighten the boot clamps (see illustrations).

18   Install the driveaxle assembly (see Section 8).

9.3 Cut off the boot clamps and discard them

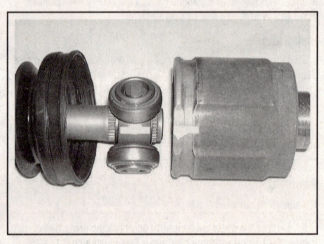

9.4 Mark the relationship of the tri-pod assembly to the outer race

9.5 Use a center punch to place marks on the tri-pod and the driveaxle to ensure that they are properly reassembled

9.6a Spread the ends of the stop-ring apart and slide it towards the center of the shaft . . .

9.6b . . . then slide the tri-pod assembly back and remove the retainer clip

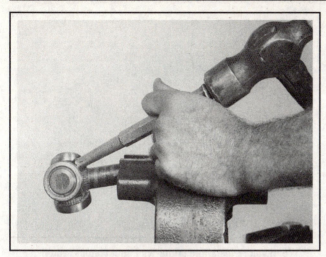

9.7 Drive the tri-pod joint from the axleshaft with a brass punch and hammer - make sure you don't damage the bearing surfaces or the splines on the shaft

9.11 Wrap the splined area of the axleshaft with tape to prevent damage to the boot(s) when installing it

9.14 Pack the outer race with CV joint grease and slide it over the tri-pod assembly - make sure the match marks on the CV joint housing and tri-pod line up

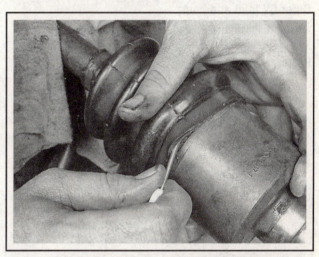

9.16 Equalize the pressure inside the boot by inserting a small, dull screwdriver between the boot and the outer race

9.17a To install new fold-over type clamps, bend the tang down . . .

9.17b . . . and flatten the tabs to hold it in place

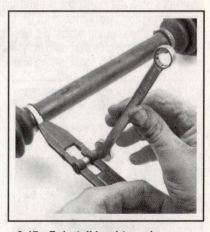

9.17c To install band-type clamps you'll need a special tool; install the band with its end pointing in the direction of axle rotation and tighten it securely, then pivot the tool up 90-degrees and tap the center of the clip with a center punch . . .

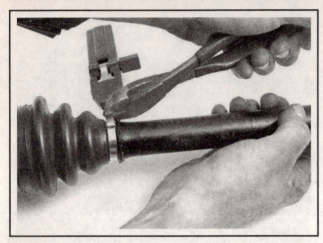

9.17d . . . then bend the end of the clamp back over the clip and cut off the excess

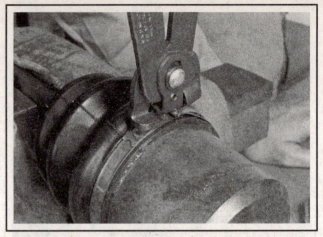

9.17e If you're installing crimp-type boot clamps, you'll need a pair of special crimping pliers (available at most auto parts stores)

Outer CV joint and boot

▶ Refer to illustration 9.20, 9.25a, 9.25b and 9.25c

Removal

19 Remove the boot clamps (see illustration 9.3).

20 Strike the edge of the CV joint housing sharply with a soft-face hammer to dislodge the outer CV joint from the axleshaft (see illustration). Remove and discard the bearing retainer clip from the axleshaft.

21 Slide the outer CV joint boot off the axle shaft.

Inspection

22 Thoroughly clean all components with solvent until the old CV grease is completely removed. Inspect the bearing surfaces of the inner tri-pods and housings for cracks, pitting, scoring, and other signs of wear. If any part of the outer CV joint is worn, you must replace the entire driveaxle assembly (inner CV joint, axleshaft and outer CV joint).

Reassembly

23 Slide a new sealing boot clamp and sealing boot onto the axleshaft. It's a good idea to wrap the axleshaft splines with tape to prevent damaging the boot (see illustration 9.11).

24 Place a new bearing retainer clip onto the axle shaft.

25 Place half the grease provided in the sealing boot kit into the outer CV joint assembly housing (see illustration). Put the remaining

9.20 Strike the edge of the CV joint housing sharply with a soft-faced hammer to dislodge the CV joint from the shaft

grease into the sealing boot (see illustrations).

26 Align the splines on the axleshaft with the splines on the outer CV joint assembly and using a soft-faced hammer, gently drive the CV joint onto the axleshaft until the CV joint is seated to the axleshaft.

9.25a Pack the outer CV joint assembly with CV grease . . .

9.25b . . . then apply grease to the inside of the boot until . . .

9.25c . . . the level is up to the end of the axle

27 Position the CV joint mid-way through its travel, then equalize the pressure in the boot (see illustration 9.16).

28 Tighten the boot clamps (see illustrations 9.17a through 9.17e).

29 Install the driveaxle as outlined in Section 8.

REAR (4WD MODELS)

→**Note: This procedure applies to both the inner and outer CV joint boots.**

Removal

30 Remove the driveaxle from the vehicle (see Section 8).

31 Mount the driveaxle in a vise. The jaws of the vise should be lined with wood or rags to prevent damage to the driveaxle.

32 Remove the boot clamps (see illustration 9.3).

33 Strike the edge of the CV joint housing sharply with a soft-face hammer to dislodge the outer CV joint from the axleshaft (see illustration 9.20).

34 Remove and discard the bearing retainer clip and snap-ring from the axleshaft.

35 Slide the CV joint boot off the axleshaft.

Inspection

36 Thoroughly clean all components with solvent until the old grease is completely removed. Inspect the bearing surfaces of the inner tri-pods and housings for cracks, pitting, scoring, and other signs of wear. If any part of the CV joint is worn, you must replace the entire driveaxle assembly (inner CV joint, axleshaft and outer CV joint).

Reassembly

37 Slide a new sealing boot clamp and sealing boot onto the axleshaft.

38 Install a new snap-ring and bearing retainer clip onto the axle shaft.

39 Place half the grease provided in the sealing boot kit into the outer CV joint assembly housing. Put the remaining grease into the sealing boot (see illustrations 9.25a through 9.25c).

40 Align the splines on the axleshaft with the splines on the CV joint assembly and using a soft-faced hammer, gently drive the CV joint onto the axleshaft until the CV joint is seated to the axleshaft.

41 Position the CV joint mid-way through its travel, then equalize the pressure in the boot (see illustration 9.16).

42 Tighten the boot clamps (see illustrations 9.17a through 9.17e).

43 Install the driveaxle as outlined in Section 8.

10 Driveshaft (4WD models) - removal and installation

REMOVAL

▸ **Refer to illustrations 10.2, 10.3, 10.4, 10.5 and 10.6**

→**Note: The manufacturer recommends replacing driveshaft fasteners with new ones when installing the driveshaft.**

1 Raise the vehicle and support it securely on jackstands, place the selector lever in Neutral.

2 Remove the bolt securing the ground strap (see illustration).

3 Use chalk or a scribe to "index" the relationship of the driveshaft to the differential pinion yoke. This ensures correct alignment when the driveshaft is reinstalled (see illustration).

4 Remove the bolts securing the universal joint clamps to the differential pinion yoke (see illustration).

5 Working at the front of the drive shaft, remove the bolts securing the driveshaft to the transaxle/transfer case (see illustration).

10.2 Remove the ground strap mounting bolt

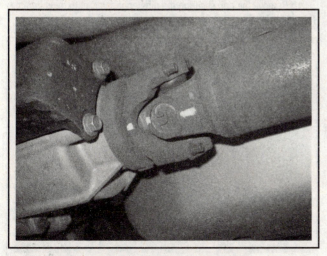

10.3 Mark the relationship of the driveshaft to the differential pinion yoke

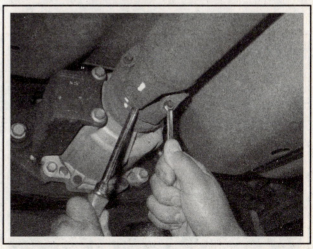

10.4 Immobilize the driveshaft by placing a screwdriver into the universal joint while loosening the bolts

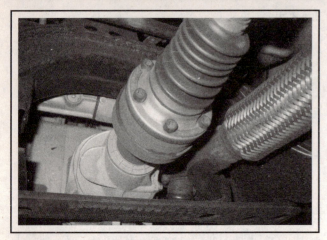

10.5 Remove the bolts securing the driveshaft to the transaxle/transfer case

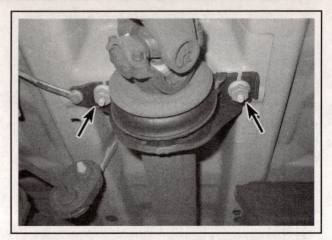

10.6 Remove the nuts securing the center support bearing

6   Remove the nuts securing the center support bearing (see illustration).

7   With the help from an assistant carefully remove the driveshaft from the vehicle.

INSTALLATION

8   Installation is the reverse of removal. Make sure the universal joint caps are properly placed in the flange seat. Tighten the fasteners to the torque listed in this Chapter's Specifications.

11 Rear driveaxle oil seals (4WD models)

1   Raise the rear of the vehicle and support it securely on jackstands. Place the transaxle in Neutral with the parking brake off. Block the front wheels to prevent the vehicle from rolling.

2   Remove the driveaxle(s) (see Section 8).

3   Carefully pry out the driveaxle oil seal with a seal removal tool or a large screwdriver. Be careful not to damage or scratch the seal bore.

4   Using a seal installer or a large deep socket as a drift, install the

new oil seal. Drive it into the bore squarely and make sure it's completely seated.

5   Lubricate the lip of the new seal with multi-purpose grease, then install the driveaxle. Be careful not to damage the lip of the new seal.

6   Check the differential lubricant level and add some, if necessary, to bring it to the appropriate level (see Chapter 1).

12 Differential (4WD models) - removal and installation

REMOVAL

▶ **Refer to illustrations 12.4, 12.5 and 12.7**

1   Raise the rear of the vehicle and support it securely on jack-

stands. Block the front wheels to prevent the vehicle from rolling.

2   Remove the driveshaft (see Section 10).

3   Remove the driveaxles (see Section 8)

4   Remove the bolt securing the differential bracket to the subframe (see illustration).

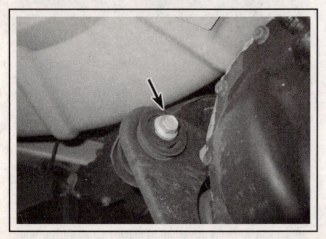

12.4 Differential mounting bracket-to-subframe mounting bolt

12.5 Mass damper mounting bolts

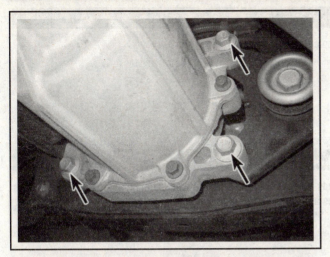

12.7 Remove the four bolts securing the differential to its mounting brackets (one bolt not visible in photo)

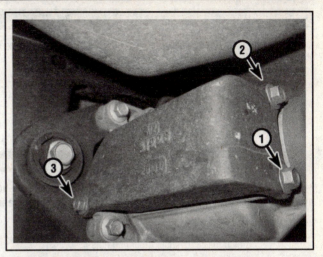

12.9 In the sequence shown, torque the bolts to the Specification listed in this Chapter

5   Remove the three bolts securing the differential mass damper (see illustration).

6   At the top of the differential, disconnect the electrical connector.

7   Support the rear of the differential with a floor jack. Remove the four bolts securing the differential to the mounting brackets (see illustration).

8   Loosen the bolts securing the brackets-to-subframe, rotate the brackets and carefully remove the differential.

INSTALLATION

▸ **Refer to illustration 12.9**

9   Installation is the reverse of removal, noting the following points:

a) *Install all the mass damper bolts finger tight first, then tighten them in the proper sequence* (see illustration).

b) *Tighten all fasteners to the torque listed in this Chapter's Specifications.*

Specifications

Clutch fluid type   See Chapter 1

Torque specifications	Ft-lbs (unless otherwise indicated)	Nm

➡ Note: One foot-pound (ft-lb) of torque is equivalent to 12 inch-pounds (in-lbs) of torque. Torque values below approximately 15 ft-lbs are expressed in inch-pounds, since most foot-pound torque wrenches are not accurate at these smaller values.

Clutch

Clutch master cylinder mounting nuts	17	23
Clutch pressure plate-to-flywheel bolts	21	29
Clutch release cylinder mounting bolts	15	20

Differential (4WD models)

Differential mass damper bolts	40	54
Differential mounting bracket-to-subframe bolts	85	115
Differential-to-bracket bolts	59	80

Driveaxles

Driveaxle/hub nut	214	290
Intermediate shaft bearing bracket nuts	20	27

Driveshafts

Center bearing mounting nuts (4X4)	35	48
Universal joint cap bolts	17	23
Front driveshaft-to-transaxle bolts	27	37

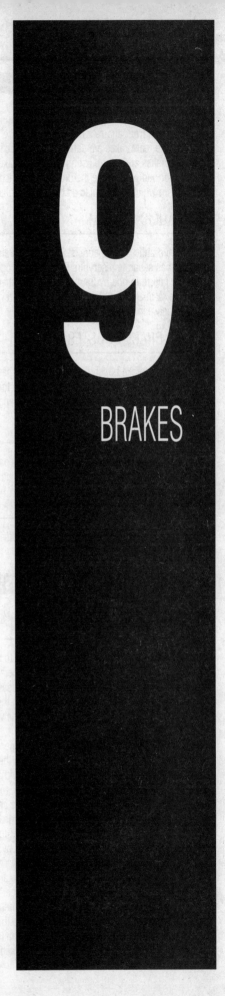

9

BRAKES

Section

Reference to other Chapters

1 General information

The vehicles covered by this manual are equipped with hydraulically operated front and rear brake systems. The front brakes are disc type and the rear brakes are either drum or disc type. Both the front and rear brakes are self adjusting. The disc brakes automatically compensate for pad wear, while the drum brakes incorporate an adjustment mechanism which is activated as the parking brake is applied.

HYDRAULIC SYSTEM

The hydraulic system consists of two separate circuits. The master cylinder has separate reservoirs for the two circuits, and, in the event of a leak or failure in one hydraulic circuit, the other circuit will remain operative. A dual proportioning valve on the firewall provides brake balance between the front and rear brakes.

POWER BRAKE BOOSTER

The power brake booster, utilizing engine manifold vacuum and atmospheric pressure to provide assistance to the hydraulically operated brakes, is mounted on the firewall in the engine compartment.

PARKING BRAKE

The parking brake operates the rear brakes only, through cable actuation. It's activated by a lever mounted in the center console.

SERVICE

After completing any operation involving disassembly of any part of the brake system, always test drive the vehicle to check for proper braking performance before resuming normal driving. When testing the brakes, perform the tests on a clean, dry, flat surface. Conditions other than these can lead to inaccurate test results.

Test the brakes at various speeds with both light and heavy pedal pressure. The vehicle should stop evenly without pulling to one side or the other. Avoid locking the brakes, because this slides the tires and diminishes braking efficiency and control of the vehicle.

Tires, vehicle load and wheel alignment are factors which also affect braking performance.

PRECAUTIONS

There are some general cautions and warnings involving the brake system on this vehicle:

a) *Use only brake fluid conforming to DOT 3 specifications.*
b) *The brake pads and linings may contain asbestos fibers which are hazardous to your health if inhaled. Whenever you work on brake system components, clean all parts with brake system cleaner. Do not allow the fine dust to become airborne. Also, wear an approved filtering mask.*
c) *Safety should be paramount whenever any servicing of the brake components is performed. Do not use parts or fasteners which are not in perfect condition, and be sure that all clearances and torque specifications are adhered to. If you are at all unsure about a certain procedure, seek professional advice. Upon completion of any brake system work, test the brakes carefully in a controlled area before putting the vehicle into normal service. If a problem is suspected in the brake system, don't drive the vehicle until it's fixed.*

2 Anti-lock Brake System (ABS) - general information

GENERAL INFORMATION

1   The anti-lock brake system is designed to maintain vehicle steerability, directional stability and optimum deceleration under severe braking conditions on most road surfaces. It does so by monitoring the rotational speed of each wheel and controlling the brake line pressure to each wheel during braking. This prevents the wheels from locking up.

2   The ABS system has three main components - the wheel speed sensors, the electronic control unit (ECU) and the hydraulic unit. Four wheel speed sensors - one at each wheel - send a variable voltage signal to the control unit, which monitors these signals, compares them to its program and determines whether a wheel is about to lock up. When a wheel is about to lock up, the control unit signals the hydraulic unit to reduce hydraulic pressure (or not increase it further) at that wheel's brake caliper. Pressure modulation is handled by electrically-operated solenoid valves.

3   If a problem develops within the system, an "ABS" warning light will glow on the dashboard. Sometimes, a visual inspection of the ABS system can help you locate the problem. Carefully inspect the ABS wiring harness. Pay particularly close attention to the harness and connections near each wheel. Look for signs of chafing and other damage caused by incorrectly routed wires. If a wheel sensor harness is damaged, the sensor must be replaced.

❋ WARNING:

Do NOT try to repair an ABS wiring harness. The ABS system is sensitive to even the smallest changes in resistance. Repairing the harness could alter resistance values and cause the system to malfunction. If the ABS wiring harness is damaged in any way, it must be replaced.

❋ CAUTION:

Make sure the ignition is turned off before unplugging or reattaching any electrical connections.

DIAGNOSIS AND REPAIR

4   If a dashboard warning light comes on and stays on while the vehicle is in operation, the ABS system requires attention. Although special electronic ABS diagnostic testing tools are necessary to properly diagnose the system, you can perform a few preliminary checks before taking the vehicle to a dealer service department.

a) *Check the brake fluid level in the reservoir.*
b) *Verify that the computer electrical connectors are securely connected.*
c) *Check the electrical connectors at the hydraulic control unit.*

d) Check the fuses.
e) Follow the wiring harness to each wheel and verify that all connections are secure and that the wiring is undamaged.

5   If the above preliminary checks do not rectify the problem, the vehicle should be diagnosed by a dealer service department or other qualified repair shop. Due to the complex nature of this system, all actual repair work must be done by a qualified automotive technician.

WHEEL SPEED SENSOR - REMOVAL AND INSTALLATION

6   Loosen the wheel lug nuts, raise the vehicle and support it

securely on jackstands. Remove the wheel.

7   Make sure the ignition key is turned to the Off position.

8   Trace the wiring back from the sensor, detaching all brackets and clips while noting its correct routing, then disconnect the electrical connector.

9   Remove the mounting bolt and carefully pull the sensor out from the knuckle or brake backing plate.

10 Installation is the reverse of the removal procedure. Tighten the mounting bolt securely.

11 Install the wheel and lug nuts, tightening them securely. Lower the vehicle and tighten the lug nuts to the torque listed in the Chapter 1 Specifications.

3   Disc brake pads - replacement

▶ Refer to illustrations 3.5 and 3.6a through 3.6o

✳✳ WARNING:

Disc brake pads must be replaced on both front or both rear wheels at the same time - never replace the pads on only one wheel. Also, the dust created by the brake system is harmful to your health. Never blow it out with compressed air and don't inhale any of it. An approved filtering mask should be worn when working on the brakes. Do not, under any circumstances, use petroleum-based solvents to clean brake parts. Use brake system cleaner only!

1   Remove the cap from the brake fluid reservoir.

2   Loosen the wheel lug nuts, raise the vehicle and support it securely on jackstands. Block the wheels at the opposite end.

3   Remove the wheels. Work on one brake assembly at a time, using the assembled brake for reference if necessary.

4   Inspect the brake disc carefully as outlined in Section 5. If machining is necessary, follow the information in that Section to remove the disc, at which time the pads can be removed as well.

5   Push the piston back into its bore to provide room for the new brake pads. A C-clamp can be used to accomplish this (see illustration). As the piston is depressed to the bottom of the caliper bore, the fluid in the master cylinder will rise. Make sure that it doesn't overflow.

3.5 Before removing the caliper, be sure to depress the piston into the bottom of its bore in the caliper with a large C-clamp to make room for the new pads

If necessary, siphon off some of the fluid.

6   Follow the accompanying photos (illustrations 3.6a through 3.6o), for the actual pad replacement procedure. Be sure to stay in order and read the caption under each illustration.

3.6a Always wash the brakes with brake cleaner before disassembling anything

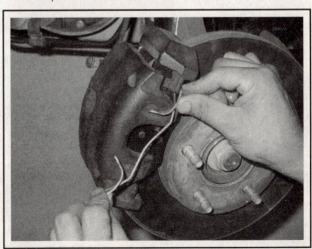

3.6b Remove the brake caliper anti-rattle clip

3.6c Pry the covers off to locate the caliper guide bolts . . .

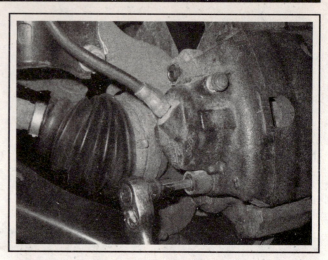

3.6d . . . then loosen and remove the bolts

7   When reinstalling the caliper, be sure to tighten the mounting bolts to the torque listed in this Chapter's Specifications. After the job has been completed, firmly depress the brake pedal a few times to bring the pads into contact with the disc. Check the level of the brake fluid, adding some if necessary. Check the operation of the brakes carefully before placing the vehicle into normal service.

3.6e Remove the caliper

3.6f Never let the caliper hang by the brake hose - use a piece of wire to tie it to the coil spring

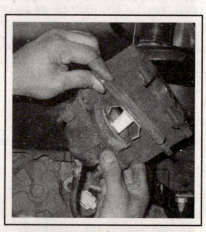

3.6g Unclip the inner pad from the piston . . .

3.6h . . . then remove the outer pad from the caliper mounting bracket

3.6i Pull out the sliding pins and clean them off, then apply a coat of high-temperature grease to the pins

3.6j Apply anti-squeal compound to the back of the pads

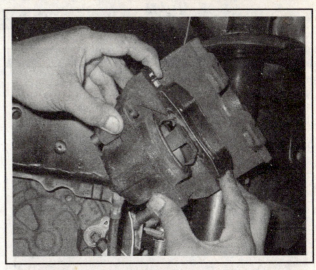

3.6k Clip the inner pad into the piston

3.6l Install the outer pad

3.6m Install the caliper and tighten the caliper mounting bolts to the torque listed in this Chapter's Specifications

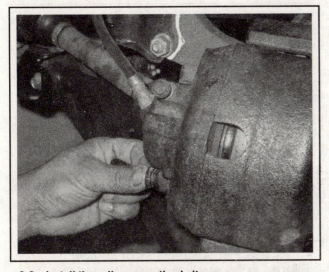

3.6n Install the caliper mounting bolt covers

3.6o Install the anti-rattle clip, then depress the brake pedal a few times to bring the pads into contact with the disc

4   Disc brake caliper - removal and installation

✳✳ WARNING:

Dust created by the brake system is harmful to your health. Never blow it out with compressed air and don't inhale any of it. An approved filtering mask should be worn when working on the brakes. Do not, under any circumstances, use petroleum-based solvents to clean brake parts. Use brake system cleaner only.

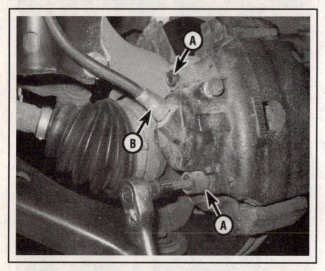

4.2 Remove the two mounting bolts (A) then unscrew the brake hose (B)

➟ Note: If replacement is indicated (usually because of fluid leakage), it is recommended that the calipers be replaced, not overhauled. New and factory rebuilt units are available on an exchange basis, which makes this job quite easy. Always replace the calipers in pairs - never replace just one of them.

REMOVAL

▶ **Refer to illustration 4.2**

1   Loosen the front wheel lug nuts, raise the front of the vehicle and place it securely on jackstands. Remove the wheel.

2   Break loose the brake hose fitting (but don't try to unscrew it yet), then remove the caliper mounting bolts (see illustration). Lift the caliper off its mounting bracket, then unscrew it from the brake hose. Plug the brake hose to keep contaminants out of the brake system and to prevent losing any more brake fluid than is necessary.

➟ Note: If the caliper is being removed for access to another component, don't disconnect the hose.

3   Remove the inner brake pad from the caliper. If the caliper is being removed for access to another component, hang it from the coil spring with a piece of wire (see illustration 3.6f).

INSTALLATION

4   Install the caliper by reversing the removal procedure. Make sure the brake hose isn't twisted.

5   Bleed the brake circuit according to the procedure in Section 10. Make sure there are no leaks from the hose connections. Test the brakes carefully before returning the vehicle to normal service.

5   Brake disc - inspection, removal and installation

INSPECTION

▶ **Refer to illustrations 5.2, 5.3, 5.4a, 5.4b, 5.5a and 5.5b**

1   Loosen the wheel lug nuts, raise the vehicle and support it securely on jackstands. Remove the wheel and install the lug nuts to hold the disc in place against the hub flange.

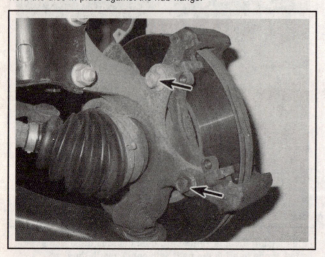

5.2 The caliper mounting bracket is retained by two bolts

➟ Note: If the lug nuts don't contact the disc when screwed on all the way, install washers under them.

2   Remove the brake caliper as outlined in Section 4. It isn't necessary to disconnect the brake hose. After removing the caliper bolts,

5.3 The brake pads on this vehicle were obviously neglected, as they wore down completely and cut deep grooves into the disc - wear this severe means the disc must be replaced

5.4a To check disc runout, mount a dial indicator as shown and rotate the disc

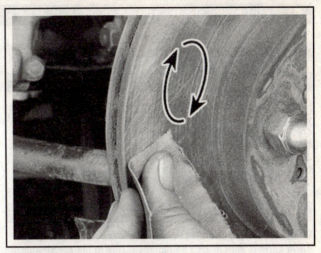

5.4b Using a swirling motion, remove the glaze from the disc surface with sandpaper or emery cloth

suspend the caliper out of the way with a piece of wire (see illustration 3.6f). If you're working on the front brakes, remove the two caliper mounting bracket-to-steering knuckle bolts (see illustration) and detach the mounting bracket.

3 Visually inspect the disc surface for score marks and other damage. Light scratches and shallow grooves are normal after use and may not always be detrimental to brake operation, but deep scoring requires disc removal and refinishing by an automotive machine shop. Be sure to check both sides of the disc (see illustration). If pulsating has been noticed during application of the brakes, suspect disc runout.

4 To check disc runout, place a dial indicator at a point about 1/2-inch from the outer edge of the disc (see illustration). Set the indicator to zero and turn the disc. The indicator reading should not exceed the specified allowable runout limit. If it does, the disc should be refinished by an automotive machine shop.

➡**Note: The discs should be resurfaced regardless of the dial indicator reading, as this will impart a smooth finish and ensure a perfectly flat surface, eliminating any brake pedal pulsation or other undesirable symptoms related to questionable discs. At the very least, if you elect not to have the discs resurfaced, remove the glaze from the surface with emery cloth or sandpaper, using a swirling motion (see illustration).**

5 It's absolutely critical that the disc not be machined to a thickness under the specified minimum thickness. The minimum (or discard) thickness is cast or stamped into the inside of the disc (see illustration). The disc thickness can be checked with a micrometer (see illustration).

REMOVAL

6 Remove the lug nuts which were installed to hold the disc in place and remove the disc from the hub.

INSTALLATION

7 Place the disc in position over the threaded studs.

8 Install the caliper mounting bracket and caliper, tightening the bolts to the torque values listed in this Chapter's Specifications.

9 Install the wheel, then lower the vehicle to the ground. Tighten the lug nuts to the torque listed in the Chapter 1 Specifications. Depress the brake pedal a few times to bring the brake pads into contact with the disc. Bleeding won't be necessary unless the brake hose was disconnected from the caliper. Check the operation of the brakes carefully before driving the vehicle.

5.5a The minimum thickness dimension is cast into the back side of the disc

5.5b Use a micrometer to measure disc thickness

6   Drum brake shoes - replacement

♦ Refer to illustrations 6.4 and 6.6a through 6.6w

❋❋ WARNING:

Drum brake shoes must be replaced on both wheels at the same time - never replace the shoes on only one wheel. Also, the dust created by the brake system is harmful to your health. Never blow it out with compressed air and don't inhale any of it. An approved filtering mask should be worn when working on the brakes. Do not, under any circumstances, use petroleum-based solvents to clean brake parts. Use brake system cleaner only!

❋❋ CAUTION:

Whenever the brake shoes are replaced, the return and hold-down springs should also be replaced. Due to the continuous heating/cooling cycle the springs are subjected to, they can lose tension over a period of time and may allow the shoes to drag on the drum and wear at a much faster rate than normal.

1   Loosen the wheel lug nuts, raise the rear of the vehicle and support it securely on jackstands. Block the front wheels to keep the vehicle from rolling.

2   Release the parking brake.
3   Remove the wheel.

➥Note: All four rear brake shoes must be replaced at the same time, but to avoid mixing up parts, work on only one brake assembly at a time.

4   Remove the brake drum.

➥Note: If the brake drum cannot be easily pulled off the axle and shoe assembly, make sure the parking brake is completely released. If the drum still cannot be pulled off, the brake shoes will have to be retracted. This is done by first removing the plug from the brake drum (see illustration). With the plug removed, pull the lever off the adjuster star wheel with a hooked tool while turning the adjuster wheel with another screwdriver, moving the shoes away from the drum. The drum should now come off.

5   Clean the brake shoe assembly with brake system cleaner before beginning work.
6   Follow the accompanying illustrations for the brake shoe replacement procedure (see illustrations 6.6a through 6.6w). Be sure to stay in order and read the caption under each illustration.
7   Before reinstalling the drum, it should be checked for cracks,

6.4   Remove this plug for access to the adjuster star wheel

6.6a   Unhook the return spring from its hole in the front shoe

6.6b   Unhook the front brake shoe hold-down clip

6.6c   Remove the front shoe and disengage the anchor spring

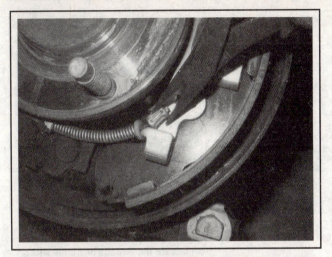

6.6d Disengage the cable from the parking brake lever

6.6e Unhook the rear brake shoe hold-down clip

score marks, deep scratches and hard spots, which will appear as small discolored areas. If the hard spots cannot be removed with fine emery cloth or if any of the other conditions listed above exist, the drum must be taken to an automotive machine shop to have it resurfaced.

➡**Note: Professionals recommend resurfacing the drums each time a brake job is done. Resurfacing will eliminate the possibility of out-of-round drums. If the drums are worn so much that they can't be resurfaced without exceeding the maximum allowable diameter (stamped or cast into the drum), then new ones**

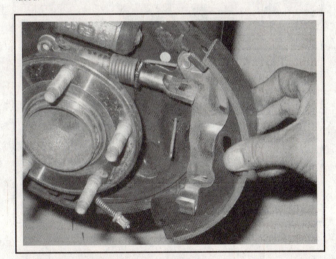

6.6f Remove the rear shoe assembly

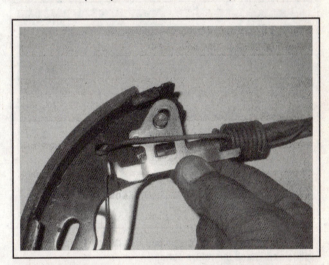

6.6g On the rear shoe, remove the self-adjust lever . . .

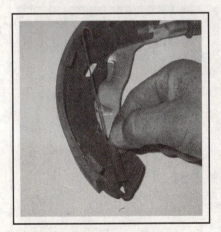

6.6h . . . and spring . . .

6.6i . . . then remove the adjuster screw and return spring

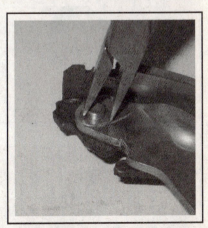

6.6j Pry open the C-clip and detach the parking brake lever from the rear shoe

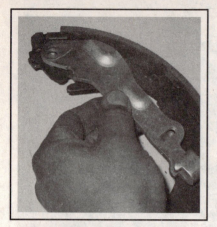

6.6k Place the parking brake lever on the new rear shoe . . .

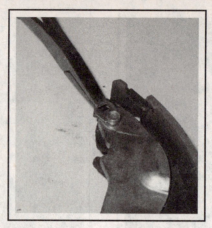

6.6l . . . and secure it in place with the C-clip

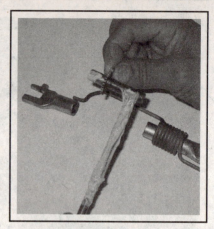

6.6m Clean the adjuster screw then lubricate the threads and ends with high-temperature grease

will be required. At the very least, if you elect not to have the drums resurfaced, remove the glaze from the surface with emery cloth using a swirling motion.

8   Install the brake drum on the axle flange. Using a screwdriver inserted through the adjusting hole in the brake drum (see illustration 6.4), turn the adjuster star wheel until the brake shoes drag on the drum as the drum is rotated, then back off the star wheel until the shoes don't drag. Reinstall the plug in the drum.

6.6n Insert the adjuster screw into into its slot on the rear shoe and attach the return spring

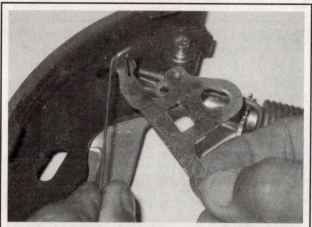

6.6o Attach the self-adjust lever and spring

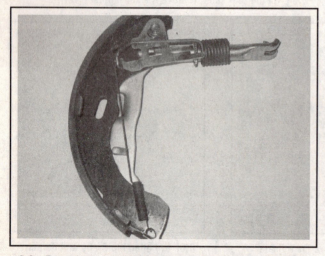

6.6p Rear view of assembled rear shoe/adjuster assembly

6.6q Apply high-temperature grease to the friction points of the backing plate

6.6r Attach the rear brake shoe hold-down clip

6.6s Attach the parking brake cable to the parking brake lever

9　Mount the wheel and install the lug nuts. Lower the vehicle and tighten the lug nuts to the torque listed in the Chapter 1 Specifications.

10　Make a number of forward and reverse stops and operate the parking brake to adjust the brakes until satisfactory pedal action

is obtained.

11　Check the operation of the brakes carefully before driving the vehicle.

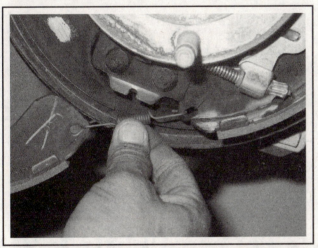

6.6t Attach the anchor spring to the bottom of each shoe

6.6u Install the adjuster screw, making sure it engages the slot in the front shoe

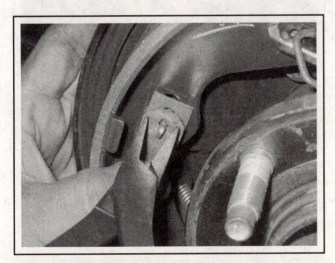

6.6v Secure the front shoe with the hold-down clip

6.6w Attach the upper return spring to the hole in the front shoe

7 Wheel cylinder - removal and installation

➡Note: If replacement is indicated (usually because of fluid leakage or sticky operation), it is recommended that the wheel cylinders be replaced, not overhauled. Always replace the wheel cylinders in pairs - never replace just one of them.

7.4 Disconnect the brake line (A) then remove the wheel cylinder mounting bolts (B)

REMOVAL

▶ **Refer to illustration 7.4**

1   Raise the rear of the vehicle and support it securely on jackstands. Block the front wheels to keep the vehicle from rolling.
2   Remove the brake shoe assembly (see Section 6).
3   Remove all dirt and foreign material from around the wheel cylinder.
4   Disconnect the brake line (see illustration). Don't pull the brake line away from the wheel cylinder.
5   Remove the wheel cylinder mounting bolts.
6   Detach the wheel cylinder from the brake backing plate and immediately plug the brake line to prevent fluid loss and contamination.

INSTALLATION

7   Place the wheel cylinder in position and install the bolts finger tight. Connect the brake line to the cylinder, being careful not to cross thread the fitting. Tighten the wheel cylinder mounting bolts to the torque listed in this Chapter's Specifications. Now tighten the brake line fitting securely.
8   Install the brake shoe assembly (see Section 6).
9   Bleed the brakes (see Section 10).
10 Check the operation of the brakes carefully before driving the vehicle.

8 Master cylinder - removal and installation

REMOVAL

▶ **Refer to illustrations 8.5 and 8.7**

1   The master cylinder is located in the engine compartment, mounted to the power brake booster.
2   Remove as much fluid as you can from the reservoir with a syringe, such as an old turkey baster.

❋❋ WARNING:

If a baster is used, never again use it for the preparation of food.

3   Place rags under the fluid fittings and prepare caps or plastic bags to cover the ends of the lines once they are disconnected.

❋❋ CAUTION:

Brake fluid will damage paint. Cover all body parts and be careful not to spill fluid during this procedure.

4   On manual transaxle models, disconnect the clutch master cylinder supply hose from the brake fluid reservoir.
5   Loosen the fittings at the ends of the brake lines where they enter the master cylinder (see illustration). To prevent rounding off the corners on these nuts, the use of a flare-nut wrench, which wraps around the nut, is preferred. Pull the brake lines slightly away from the master

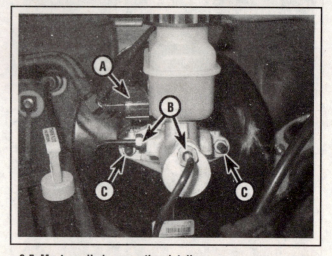

8.5 Master cylinder mounting details

A   *Fluid level warning switch connector*
B   *Brake line fittings*
C   *Mounting nuts*

cylinder and plug the ends to prevent contamination.
6   Disconnect the electrical connector at the brake fluid level switch on the master cylinder reservoir, then remove the nuts attaching the master cylinder to the power booster. Pull the master cylinder off the studs and out of the engine compartment. Again, be careful not to spill the fluid as this is done.

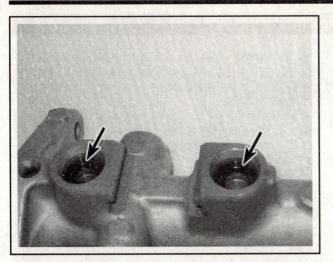

**8.7 After the reservoir has been removed, replace the
O-rings with new ones**

7   If a new master cylinder is being installed, remove the reservoir
from the master cylinder and transfer it to the new master cylinder.

→Note: Be sure to install new seals when transferring the reservoir (see illustration).

INSTALLATION

▶ **Refer to illustrations 8.9 and 8.14**

8   Bench bleed the new master cylinder before installing it. Mount
the master cylinder in a vise, with the jaws of the vise clamping on the
mounting flange.

9   Attach a pair of master cylinder bleeder tubes to the outlet ports
of the master cylinder (see illustration).

10 Fill the reservoir with brake fluid of the recommended type (see
Chapter 1).

11 Slowly push the pistons into the master cylinder (a large Phillips
screwdriver can be used for this) - air will be expelled from the pressure chambers and into the reservoir. Because the tubes are submerged
in fluid, air can't be drawn back into the master cylinder when you
release the pistons.

12 Repeat the procedure until no more air bubbles are present.

13 Remove the bleed tubes, one at a time, and install plugs in the
open ports to prevent fluid leakage and air from entering. Install the
reservoir cap.

14 Install the master cylinder over the studs on the power brake
booster and tighten the attaching nuts only finger tight at this time.

→Note: Be sure to install a new O-ring into the sleeve of the
master cylinder (see illustration).

15 Thread the brake line fittings into the master cylinder. Since the
master cylinder is still a bit loose, it can be moved slightly in order for
the fittings to thread in easily. Do not strip the threads as the fittings are
tightened.

16 Fully tighten the mounting nuts, then the brake line fittings.
Tighten the nuts to the torque listed in this Chapter's Specifications.

17 Fill the master cylinder reservoir with fluid, then bleed the master
cylinder and the brake system as described in Section 10. To bleed the
cylinder on the vehicle, have an assistant depress the brake pedal and
hold the pedal to the floor. Loosen the fitting to allow air and fluid to
escape. Repeat this procedure on both fittings until the fluid is clear of
air bubbles.

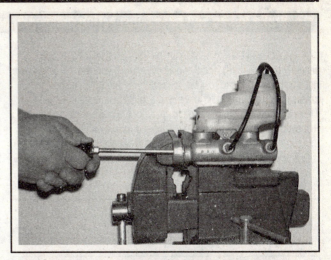

**8.9 The best way to bleed air from the master cylinder
before installing it on the vehicle is with a pair of bleeder
tubes that direct brake fluid into the reservoir during
bleeding**

✳✳ CAUTION:

**Have plenty of rags on hand to catch the fluid - brake fluid will
ruin painted surfaces. After the bleeding procedure is completed, rinse the area under the master cylinder with clean
water.**

18 Test the operation of the brake system carefully before placing the
vehicle into normal service.

✳✳ WARNING:

**Do not operate the vehicle if you are in doubt about the effec-
tiveness of the brake system. It is possible for air to become
trapped in the anti-lock brake system hydraulic control unit, so,
if the pedal continues to feel spongy after repeated bleedings or
the BRAKE or ANTI-LOCK light stays on, have the vehicle towed
to a dealer service department or other qualified shop to be
bled with the aid of a scan tool.**

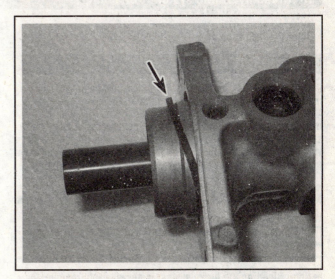

8.14 Install a new O-ring onto the master cylinder sleeve

9 Brake hoses and lines - inspection and replacement

1   About every six months, with the vehicle raised and placed securely on jackstands, the flexible hoses which connect the steel brake lines with the front and rear brake assemblies should be inspected for cracks, chafing of the outer cover, leaks, blisters and other damage. These are important and vulnerable parts of the brake system and inspection should be complete. A light and mirror will be needed for a thorough check. If a hose exhibits any of the above defects, replace it with a new one.

FLEXIBLE HOSES

▶ **Refer to illustration 9.3**

2   Clean all dirt away from the ends of the hose.

9.3 Unscrew the brake line threaded fitting with a flare-nut wrench to protect the fitting corners from being rounded off (A), then pull off the U-clips (B) with a pair of pliers (front shown, rear similar)

3   To disconnect a brake hose from the brake line, unscrew the metal tube nut with a flare nut wrench, then remove the U-clip from the female fitting at the bracket and remove the hose from the bracket (see illustration).

4   Disconnect the hose from the caliper, discarding the sealing washers on either side of the fitting.

5   Using new sealing washers, attach the new brake hose to the caliper or wheel cylinder.

6   To reattach a brake hose to the metal line, insert the end of the hose through the frame bracket, make sure the hose isn't twisted, then attach the metal line by tightening the tube nut fitting securely. Install the U-clip at the frame bracket.

➡**Note: The weight of the vehicle must be on the suspension, so the vehicle should not be raised while positioning the hose.**

7   Carefully check to make sure the suspension or steering components don't make contact with the hose. Have an assistant push down on the vehicle and also turn the steering wheel lock-to-lock during inspection.

8   Bleed the brake system (see Section 10).

METAL BRAKE LINES

9   When replacing brake lines, be sure to use the correct parts. Don't use copper tubing for any brake system components. Purchase steel brake lines from a dealer parts department or auto parts store.

10 Prefabricated brake line, with the tube ends already flared and fittings installed, is available at auto parts stores and dealer parts departments. These lines can be bent to the proper shapes using a tubing bender.

11 When installing the new line make sure it's well supported in the brackets and has plenty of clearance between moving or hot components.

12 After installation, check the master cylinder fluid level and add fluid as necessary. Bleed the brake system as outlined in Section 10 and test the brakes carefully before placing the vehicle into normal operation.

10 Brake hydraulic system - bleeding

▶ **Refer to illustration 10.8**

❊❊ WARNING 1:

If air has found its way into the hydraulic control unit, the system must be bled with the use of a scan tool. If the brake pedal feels "spongy" even after bleeding the brakes, or the ABS light on the instrument panel does not go off, or if you have any doubts whatsoever about the effectiveness of the brake system, have the vehicle towed to a dealer service department or other repair shop equipped with the necessary tools for bleeding the system.

❊❊ WARNING 2:

Wear eye protection when bleeding the brake system. If the fluid comes in contact with your eyes, immediately rinse them with water and seek medical attention.

➡**Note: Bleeding the brake system is necessary to remove any air that's trapped in the system when it's opened during removal and installation of a hose, line, caliper, wheel cylinder or master cylinder.**

1   It will be necessary to bleed the system at all four brakes if air has entered the system due to low fluid level, or if the brake lines have been disconnected at the master cylinder.

2   If a brake line was disconnected only at a wheel, then only that caliper or wheel cylinder must be bled.

3   If a brake line is disconnected at a fitting located between the master cylinder and any of the brakes, that part of the system served by the disconnected line must be bled.

4   Remove any residual vacuum (or hydraulic pressure) from the brake power booster by applying the brake several times with the engine off.

5   Remove the master cylinder reservoir cap and fill the reservoir with brake fluid. Reinstall the cap.

➡**Note: Check the fluid level often during the bleeding operation and add fluid as necessary to prevent the fluid level from falling low enough to allow air bubbles into the master cylinder.**

6   Have an assistant on hand, as well as a supply of new brake fluid, an empty clear plastic container, a length of plastic, rubber or vinyl tubing to fit over the bleeder valve and a wrench to open and close the bleeder valve.

10.8 When bleeding the brakes, a hose is connected to the bleed screw at the caliper and submerged in brake fluid - air will be seen as bubbles in the tube and container (all air must be expelled before moving to the next wheel)

7   Beginning at the right rear wheel, loosen the bleeder screw slightly, then tighten it to a point where it's snug but can still be loosened quickly and easily.

8   Place one end of the tubing over the bleeder screw fitting and submerge the other end in brake fluid in the container (see illustration).

9   Have the assistant slowly depress the brake pedal and hold it in the depressed position.

10   While the pedal is held depressed, open the bleeder screw just enough to allow a flow of fluid to leave the valve. Watch for air bubbles to exit the submerged end of the tube. When the fluid flow slows after a couple of seconds, tighten the screw and have your assistant release the pedal.

11   Repeat Steps 9 and 10 until no more air is seen leaving the tube, then tighten the bleeder screw and proceed to the left rear wheel, the right front wheel and the left front wheel, in that order, and perform the same procedure. Be sure to check the fluid in the master cylinder reservoir frequently.

12   Never use old brake fluid. It contains moisture which can boil, rendering the brake system inoperative.

13   Refill the master cylinder with fluid at the end of the operation.

14   Check the operation of the brakes. The pedal should feel solid when depressed, with no sponginess. If necessary, repeat the entire process.

✳✳ WARNING:

Do not operate the vehicle if you are in doubt about the effectiveness of the brake system. It is possible for air to become trapped in the anti-lock brake system hydraulic control unit, so, if the pedal continues to feel spongy after repeated bleedings or the BRAKE or ANTI-LOCK light stays on, have the vehicle towed to a dealer service department or other qualified shop to be bled with the aid of a scan tool.

11 Power brake booster - check, removal and installation

♦ **Refer to illustration 11.9**

OPERATING CHECK

1   Depress the brake pedal several times with the engine off and make sure that there is no change in the pedal reserve distance.

2   Depress the pedal and start the engine. If the pedal goes down slightly, operation is normal.

AIRTIGHTNESS CHECK

3   Start the engine and turn it off after one or two minutes. Depress the brake pedal several times slowly. If the pedal goes down farther the first time but gradually rises after the second or third depression, the booster is airtight.

4   Depress the brake pedal while the engine is running, then stop the engine with the pedal depressed. If there is no change in the pedal reserve travel after holding the pedal for 30 seconds, the booster is airtight.

REMOVAL AND INSTALLATION

5   Disassembly of the power unit requires special tools and is not ordinarily performed by the home mechanic. If a problem develops, it's recommended that a new or factory rebuilt unit be installed.

6   In the engine compartment, remove the nuts attaching the master cylinder to the booster and carefully pull the master cylinder forward until it clears the mounting studs. Be careful not to bend or kink the brake lines. On 3.0L models it may be necessary to disconnect the EVAP canister purge valve (see Chapter 6).

7   Disconnect the vacuum hose where it attaches to the power brake booster.

8   In the passenger compartment, remove the retaining pin and washer, then disconnect the pushrod from the top of the brake pedal.

9   Remove the nuts attaching the booster to the firewall (see illustration).

10   Carefully lift the booster unit away from the firewall and out of the engine compartment.

11   To install the booster, place it into position and tighten the retaining nuts to the torque listed in this Chapter's Specifications. Connect the pushrod to the brake pedal.

12   Install the master cylinder. Reconnect the vacuum hose.

13   Carefully test the operation of the brakes before placing the vehicle in normal service.

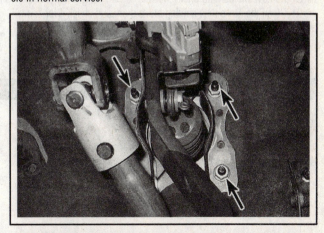

11.9 To detach the power brake booster from the firewall, remove these four nuts (one nut not visible in picture)

12 Parking brake - adjustment

DRUM BRAKES

▶ **Refer to illustration 12.3**

1   The parking brake lever, when properly adjusted, should travel three to five clicks, when a moderate pulling force is applied. If it travels less than the specified minimum number of clicks, there's a chance the parking brake might not be releasing completely and might be dragging on the drum. If the lever can be pulled up more than the specified maximum number of clicks, the parking brake may not hold adequately on an incline, allowing the car to roll.

2   To gain access to the parking brake cable adjuster, remove the center console trim panels (see Chapter 11).

3   If equipped, remove the locking clip. With a wrench, turn the adjusting nut until the desired travel is attained (see illustration).

4   Install the center console trim panels.

DISC BRAKES

5   Release the parking brake lever.

6   Remove the parking brake lever boot by squeezing inward on the bottom of the boot, then lift the boot to access the adjustment nut.

7   Adjust the nut so when the lever is pulled, you hear or feel five

12.3 Turn the adjusting nut until the desired handle travel is obtained (center console removed for clarity)

clicks of the lever's ratchet mechanism.

8   Verify the parking brake is actually holding the vehicle when applied.

13 Parking brake shoes (models with rear disc brakes) - replacement

1   Release the parking brake.

2   Loosen the rear wheel lug nuts. Raise the vehicle and support it securely on jackstands. Remove the wheels. Be sure to block the front tires.

3   Remove the brake calipers (see Section 4) and the brake discs (see Section 5).

4   Clean the parking brake assembly with brake system cleaner before beginning work.

5   Remove the brake shoe retracting spring.

6   Remove the adjusting screw spring, then remove the adjusting screw.

7   Remove the hold-down springs from the shoes.

8   Remove the parking brake shoes.

9   Clean the brake disc/parking brake drum and check it for score marks, deep grooves, hard spots (which will appear as small discolored areas) and cracks. If the disc/drum is worn, scored or out-of-

round, it can be resurfaced by an automotive machine shop.

10   Install the shoes by reversing the removal procedure. Turn the adjusting screw so the disc just fits over the new shoes. When the disc is installed, the shoes should not rub as the disc is turned. If you have a brake shoe adjusting gauge, adjust the diameter of the shoes to 0.042-inch less than that of the drum surface of the rear brake disc.

11   Repeat this procedure for the other parking brake assembly.

12   Install the brake discs (see Section 5) and the brake calipers (see Section 4).

13   Remove the rubber plug from the brake backing plate and, using a screwdriver or brake adjusting tool, turn the adjusting screw star wheel until the parking brake shoes start to drag as the disc is turned, then back off the start wheel until the shoes don't drag.

14   Install the rear wheels and lug nuts, lower the vehicle and tighten the lug nuts to the torque listed in the Chapter 1 Specifications.

14 Brake light switch - replacement

▶ **Refer to illustrations 14.1 and 14.2**

1   Disconnect the electrical connector at the switch, then rotate the switch counterclockwise and remove the switch (see illustration).

2   To unlock the new switch, rotate the knob counterclockwise

(see illustration).

3   Start the engine, depress and hold the brake pedal then install the switch turning it clockwise.

4   Connect the switch electrical connector.

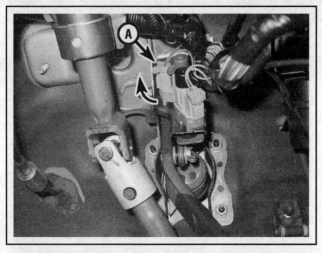

14.1 Disconnect the electrical connector (A) then rotate the switch clockwise to remove it

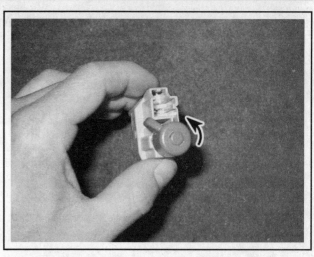

14.2 Rotate the knob counterclockwise until it stops to unlock the switch

Specifications

General

Brake fluid type	See Chapter 1

Disc brakes

Brake pad minimum thickness	See Chapter 1
Disc lateral runout limit	0.004 inch
Disc minimum thickness	Cast into disc
Minimum pad lining thickness	See Chapter 1

Drum brakes

Maximum drum diameter	Cast into drum
Shoe lining minimum thickness	See Chapter 1

Torque specifications

	Ft-lbs (unless otherwise indicated)	Nm

➡Note: One foot-pound (ft-lb) of torque is equivalent to 12 inch-pounds (in-lbs) of torque. Torque values below approximately 15 ft-lbs are expressed in inch-pounds, since most foot-pound torque wrenches are not accurate at these smaller values.

	Ft-lbs (unless otherwise indicated)	Nm
Caliper mounting bracket bolts	111	150
Caliper mounting bolts	26	35
Master cylinder mounting nuts	13	17
Power brake booster mounting nuts	17	23
Wheel cylinder mounting bolts	108 in-lbs	12
Wheel lug nuts	See Chapter 1	

Notes

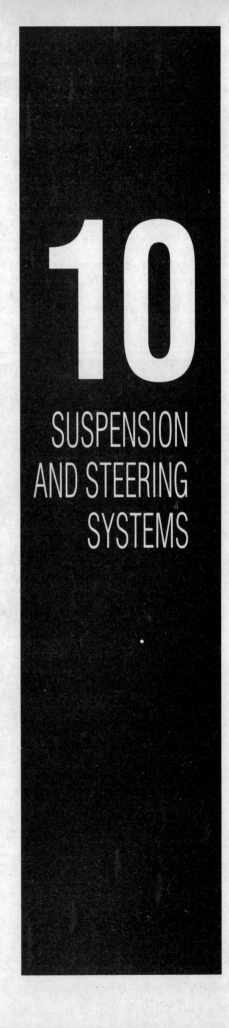

10

SUSPENSION AND STEERING SYSTEMS

Section

1 General information

◆ **Refer to illustrations 1.1a and 1.1b**

The front suspension (see illustration) is a MacPherson strut design. The upper end of each strut/coil spring assembly is attached to the vehicle's body strut support. The lower end of the strut assembly is connected to the upper end of the steering knuckle. The steering knuckle is attached to a balljoint mounted on the outer end of the suspension control arm. A stabilizer bar reduces body roll.

The rear suspension (see illustration) employs a trailing arm, two lateral suspension arms, a coil spring and shock absorber per side.

The rack-and-pinion steering gear is located behind the engine/transaxle assembly on the front suspension crossmember and actuates the tie-rods, which are attached to the steering knuckles. The inner ends of the tie-rods are protected by rubber boots which should be inspected periodically for secure attachment, tears and leaking lubricant (which would indicate a failed rack seal).

The power assist system consists of a belt-driven pump and associated lines and hoses. The fluid level in the power steering pump reservoir should be checked periodically (see Chapter 1).

The steering wheel operates the steering shaft, which actuates the steering gear through universal joints. Looseness in the steering can be caused by wear in the steering shaft universal joints, the steering gear, the tie-rod ends and loose retaining bolts.

PRECAUTIONS

Frequently, when working on the suspension or steering system components, you may come across fasteners which seem impossible

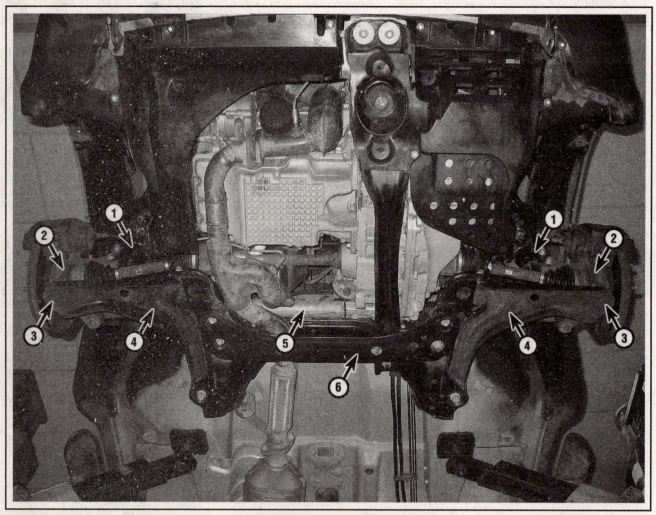

1.1a Front suspension and steering components

1	Strut/coil spring assembly	3	Balljoint	5	Steering gear
2	Steering knuckle	4	Control arm	6	Suspension crossmember

to loosen. These fasteners on the underside of the vehicle are continually subjected to water, road grime, mud, etc., and can become rusted or "frozen," making them extremely difficult to remove. In order to unscrew these stubborn fasteners without damaging them (or other components), be sure to use lots of penetrating oil and allow it to soak in for a while. Using a wire brush to clean exposed threads will also ease removal of the nut or bolt and prevent damage to the threads. Sometimes a sharp blow with a hammer and punch will break the bond between a nut and bolt threads, but care must be taken to prevent the punch from slipping off the fastener and ruining the threads. Heating the stuck fastener and surrounding area with a torch sometimes helps too, but isn't recommended because of the obvious dangers associated with fire. Long breaker bars and extension, or "cheater," pipes will increase leverage, but never use an extension pipe on a ratchet - the ratcheting mechanism could be damaged. Sometimes tightening the nut or bolt first will help to break it loose. Fasteners that require drastic measures to remove should always be replaced with new ones.

Since most of the procedures dealt with in this Chapter involve jacking up the vehicle and working underneath it, a good pair of jack-stands will be needed. A hydraulic floor jack is the preferred type of jack to lift the vehicle, and it can also be used to support certain components during various operations.

❋❋ WARNING:

Never, under any circumstances, rely on a jack to support the vehicle while working on it. Whenever any of the suspension or steering fasteners are loosened or removed they must be inspected and, if necessary, replaced with new ones of the same part number or of original equipment quality and design. Torque specifications must be followed for proper reassembly and component retention. Never attempt to heat or straighten any suspension or steering components. Instead, replace any bent or damaged part with a new one.

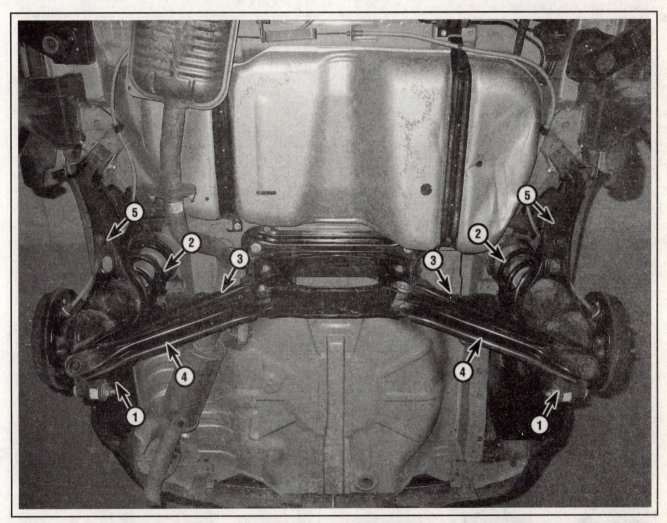

1.1b Typical rear suspension components

1	Shock absorber	3	Upper suspension arm	5	Trailing arm
2	Coil spring	4	Lower suspension arm		

2   Strut assembly (front) - removal, inspection and installation

REMOVAL

▶ **Refer to illustrations 2.3, 2.4 and 2.6**

1   Loosen the wheel lug nuts, raise the vehicle and support it securely on jackstands. Remove the wheel.

2   Unbolt the brake hose bracket from the strut. If the vehicle is equipped with ABS, detach the speed sensor wiring harness from the strut by removing the clamp bracket bolt.

3   Detach the stabilizer bar link from the bracket on the strut (see illustration).

4   Remove the strut-to-knuckle nuts (see illustration) and knock the bolts out with a hammer and punch.

5   Separate the strut from the steering knuckle. Be careful not to overextend the inner CV joint. Also, don't let the steering knuckle fall outward and strain the brake hose.

6   Mark the relationship of the outer studs-to-bearing plate (see

illustration). Support the strut and spring assembly with one hand and remove the four strut-to-body nuts. Remove the assembly out from the fenderwell.

INSPECTION

7   Check the strut body for leaking fluid, dents, cracks and other obvious damage which would warrant repair or replacement.

8   Check the coil spring for chips or cracks in the spring coating (this will cause premature spring failure due to corrosion). Inspect the spring seat for cuts, hardness and general deterioration.

9   If any undesirable conditions exist, proceed to the strut disassembly procedure (see Section 3).

INSTALLATION

10 Guide the strut assembly up into the fenderwell, align the previously made matchmarks and insert the upper mounting studs through the holes in the body. Once the studs protrude, install the nuts so the strut won't fall back through. This is most easily accomplished with the help of an assistant, as the strut is quite heavy and awkward.

11 Slide the steering knuckle into the strut flange and insert the two bolts. Install the nuts, align the previously made matchmarks and tighten them to the torque listed in this Chapter's Specifications.

12 Connect the brake hose bracket to the strut and tighten the bolt securely. If the vehicle is equipped with ABS, install the speed sensor wiring harness bracket.

13 Connect the stabilizer bar link to the strut bracket. Tighten the nut to the torque listed in this Chapter's Specifications.

14 Install the wheel and lug nuts, then lower the vehicle and tighten the lug nuts to the torque listed in the Chapter 1 Specifications.

15 Tighten the upper mounting nuts to the torque listed in this Chapter's Specifications.

16 Drive the vehicle to an alignment shop to have the front end alignment checked, and if necessary, adjusted.

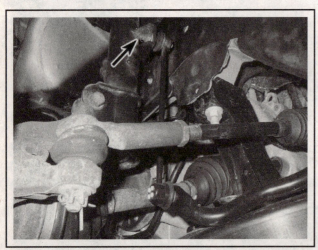

2.3 Disconnect the stabilizer bar link rod

2.4 To detach the strut from the steering knuckle, remove the two nuts, then knock out the bolts with a hammer and punch

2.6 Mark the relationship of the studs to the bearing plate, then remove the upper mounting nuts

3 Strut/spring assembly - replacement

▶ Refer to illustrations 3.3, 3.4, 3.5a, 3.5b, 3.5c, 3.5d and 3.9

✳✳ WARNING:

Before attempting to disassemble the front suspension strut, a tool to hold the coil spring in compression must be obtained. Do not attempt to use makeshift methods. Uncontrolled release of the spring could cause damage and personal injury. Use a high-quality spring compressor, and carefully follow the tool manufacturer's instructions provided with it. After removing the coil spring with the compressor still installed, place it in a safe, isolated area.

1   If the front suspension struts exhibit signs of wear (leaking fluid, loss of damping capability, sagging or cracked coil springs) then they should be disassembled and overhauled as necessary. The struts themselves cannot be serviced, and should be replaced if faulty; the springs and related components can be replaced individually. To maintain balanced characteristics on both sides of the vehicle, the components on both sides should be replaced at the same time.

2   With the strut removed from the vehicle (see Section 2), clean away all external dirt, then mount it in a vise.

3   Install the coil spring compressor tools (ensuring that they are fully engaged), and compress the spring until all tension is relieved

3.3 Make sure the spring compressor tool is on securely

from the upper mount (see illustration).

4   Hold the strut piston rod with an Allen key and unscrew the thrust bearing retaining nut with a box-end wrench (see illustration).

5   Withdraw the top mounting, thrust bearing, upper spring seat and spring, followed by the boot and the bump stop (see illustrations).

3.4 Loosen and remove the retaining nut

3.5a Remove the upper bearing and spring seat . . .

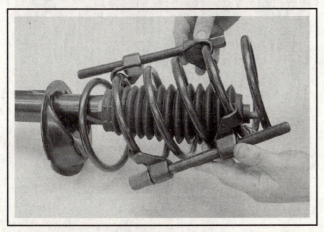

3.5b . . . then carefully remove the spring . . .

3.5c . . . followed by the boot . . .

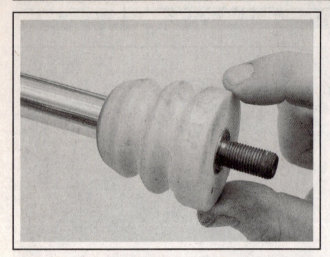

3.5d . . . and the bump stop

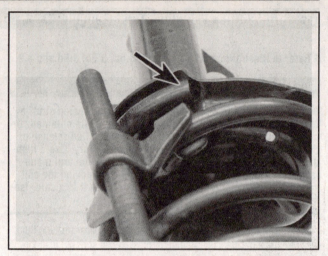

3.9 When installing the spring, make sure the ends fit into the recessed portion of the seats

6   If a new spring is to be installed, the original spring must now be carefully released from the compressor. If it is to be re-used, the spring can be left in compression.

7   With the strut assembly now completely disassembled, examine all the components for wear and damage, and check the bearing for smoothness of operation. Replace components as necessary.

8   Examine the strut for signs of fluid leakage. Check the strut piston rod for signs of pitting along its entire length, and check the strut body for signs of damage. Test the operation of the strut, while holding it in an upright position, by moving the piston through a full stroke, and then through short strokes of 2 to 4 inches. In both cases, the resistance felt should be smooth and continuous. If the resistance is jerky, uneven, or if there is any visible sign of wear or damage to the strut, replacement is necessary.

9   Reassembly is a reversal of dismantling, noting the following points:

  a) *The coil springs must be installed with the paint mark at the bottom.*
  b) *Make sure that the coil spring ends are correctly located in the upper and lower seats before releasing the compressor (see illustration).*
  c) *Check that the bearing is correctly installed on the piston rod seat.*
  d) *Tighten the thrust bearing retaining nut to the specified torque.*

4   Stabilizer bar and bushings (front) - removal and installation

REMOVAL

▶ **Refer to illustrations 4.2 and 4.3**

1   Loosen the front wheel lug nuts. Raise the front of the vehicle and support it securely on jackstands. Apply the parking brake and block the rear wheels to keep the vehicle from rolling off the stands. Remove the front wheels.

2   Detach the stabilizer bar links from the bar (see illustration). If the ballstud turns with the nut, use an Allen wrench to hold the stud.

3   Unbolt the stabilizer bar bushing clamps (see illustration). Guide the stabilizer bar out from between the crossmember and the body.

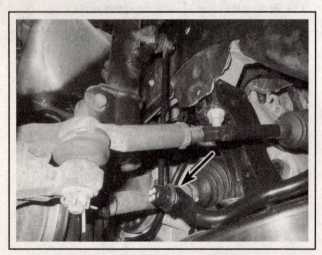

4.2 Remove the lower nut and detach the link from the bar

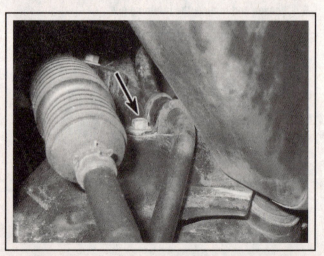

4.3 Stabilizer bar bracket bolt (other bolt not visible in photo)

4   While the stabilizer bar is off the vehicle, slide off the retainer bushings and inspect them. If they're cracked, worn or deteriorated, replace them.

5   Clean the bushing area of the stabilizer bar with a stiff wire brush to remove any rust or dirt.

INSTALLATION

6   Lubricate the inside and outside of the new bushing with vegetable oil (used in cooking) to simplify reassembly.

✳✳ CAUTION:

Don't use petroleum or mineral-based lubricants or brake fluid - they will lead to deterioration of the bushings. The slits of the bushings must face the rear of the vehicle.

7   Installation is the reverse of removal. Tighten the fasteners to the torque values listed in this Chapter's Specifications.

5   Control arm (front) - removal, inspection and installation

REMOVAL

▶ **Refer to illustrations 5.2a, 5.2b and 5.3**

1   Loosen the wheel lug nuts on the side to be dismantled, raise the front of the vehicle, support it securely on jackstands and remove the wheel.

2   Remove the pinch bolt securing the balljoint to the control arm. Use a prybar to disconnect the control arm from the steering knuckle (see illustrations).

3   Remove the control arm front pivot bolt and rear mounting bolt (see illustration).

4   Remove the control arm.

INSPECTION

5   Check the control arm for distortion and the bushings for wear, replacing parts as necessary. Do not attempt to straighten a bent control arm.

INSTALLATION

6   Installation is the reverse of removal. Tighten all of the fasteners to the torque values listed in this Chapter's Specifications.

➡**Note: Before tightening the pivot bolt and the bolt on the rear of the control arm, raise the outer end of the control arm with a floor jack to simulate normal ride height.**

7   Install the wheel and lug nuts, lower the vehicle and tighten the lug nuts to the torque listed in the Chapter 1 Specifications.

8   It's a good idea to have the front wheel alignment checked and, if necessary, adjusted after this job has been performed.

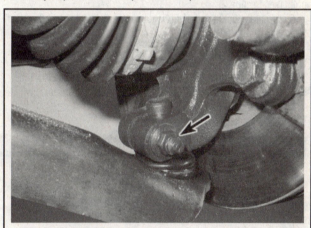

5.2a To detach the control arm from the steering knuckle balljoint, remove this nut and bolt . . .

5.2b . . . and pry the balljoint out of the steering knuckle with a large prybar or screwdriver

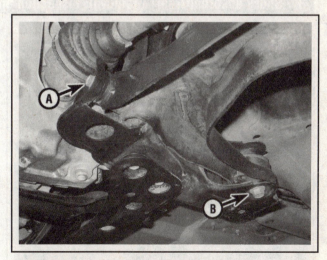

5.3 To detach the front of the control arm from the crossmember, remove the pivot bolt (A) and the rear mounting bolt (B)

6   Steering knuckle and hub - removal and installation

❄❄ WARNING:

Dust created by the brake system is harmful to your health. Never blow it out with compressed air and don't inhale any of it. Do not, under any circumstances, use petroleum-based solvents to clean brake parts. Use brake system cleaner only.

REMOVAL

1   Remove the wheel cover and loosen, but don't remove, the drive-axle/hub nut. Loosen the wheel lug nuts, raise the vehicle and support it securely on jackstands, then remove the wheel.

2   Remove the brake caliper (don't disconnect the hose) and the brake disc (see Chapter 9), and disconnect the brake hose from the strut. Hang the caliper from the coil spring with a piece of wire - don't let it hang by the brake hose.

3   If the vehicle is equipped with ABS, remove the wheel speed sensor (see Chapter 9).

4   Loosen, but don't remove the strut-to-steering knuckle nuts and bolts (see Section 2).

5   Separate the tie-rod end from the steering knuckle arm (see Section 14).

6   Remove the balljoint-to-steering knuckle pinch bolt (see Section 5).

7   Remove the driveaxle/hub nut and push the driveaxle from the hub as described in Chapter 8. Support the end of the driveaxle with a piece of wire.

8   Remove the balljoint from the steering knuckle (see Section 5).

9   The strut-to-knuckle bolts can now be removed.

10   Carefully separate the steering knuckle from the strut.

INSTALLATION

11   Guide the knuckle and hub assembly into position, inserting the driveaxle into the hub.

12   Push the knuckle into the strut flange and install the bolts and nuts, but don't tighten them yet.

13   Connect the balljoint to the knuckle and tighten the pinch bolt/nut to the torque listed in this Chapter's Specifications.

14   Attach the tie-rod to the steering knuckle arm (see Section 14). Tighten the strut bolt nuts and the tie-rod nut to the torque listed in this Chapter's Specifications.

15   Place the brake disc on the hub and install the caliper as outlined in Chapter 9.

16   Install the driveaxle/hub nut and tighten it securely, but not completely yet.

17   Install the wheel and lug nuts. Lower the vehicle and tighten the lug nuts to the torque listed in the Chapter 1 Specifications.

18   Tighten the driveaxle/hub nut to the torque listed in the Chapter 8 Specifications. Install the wheel cover.

19   Have the front-end alignment checked and, if necessary, adjusted.

7   Hub and bearing assembly (front) - removal and installation

Due to the special tools and expertise required to press the hub and bearing from the steering knuckle, this job should be left to a professional mechanic. However, the steering knuckle and hub may be removed and the assembly taken to an automotive machine shop or other qualified repair facility equipped with the necessary tools. See Section 6 for the steering knuckle and hub removal procedure.

8   Shock absorber (rear) - removal, inspection and installation

8.3a Remove the fasteners securing the rear trim cover . . .

▸ **Refer to illustrations 8.3a, 8.3b, 8.3c and 8.4**

1   Loosen the wheel lug nuts, raise the vehicle and support it securely on jackstands. Block the front wheels to prevent the vehicle from rolling. Remove the wheel.

2   Support the rear end of the trailing arm with a floor jack. Raise the jack slightly to take the spring pressure off the shock absorber lower mount.

❄❄ WARNING:

The jack must remain in this position throughout the entire procedure.

3   Working inside the vehicle, remove the rear quarter trim panel

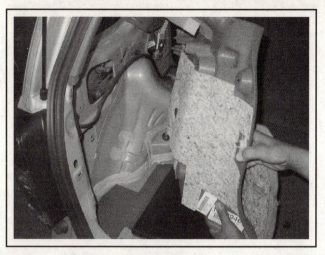

8.3b . . . followed by the trim cover . . .

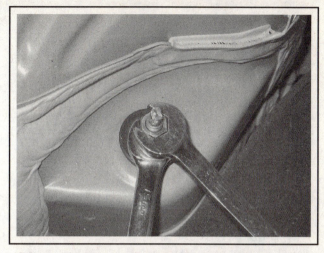

8.3c . . . then unscrew the two upper shock mounting nuts

for access to the shock absorber upper mounting nut. Remove the nuts, upper retainer, bushing and lower retainer (see illustrations).

4   Unscrew the shock absorber lower mounting nut, then pull the shock off the mounting pin (see illustration). Note how the retainers are positioned.

5   Installation is the reverse of the removal procedure. Tighten the mounting fasteners to the torque listed in this Chapter's Specifications.

8.4 Shock absorber lower mounting bolt

9   Suspension arms (rear) - removal and installation

1   Loosen the wheel lug nuts, raise the vehicle and support it securely on jackstands. Block the front wheels to prevent the vehicle from rolling. Remove the wheel.

UPPER SUSPENSION ARM

▸ **Refer to illustrations 9.2 and 9.3**

2   Remove the nut from the upper ballstud at the outer end of the arm (see illustration), then separate the arm from the boss on the trailing arm. If the ballstud sticks in its boss, a two-jaw puller or balljoint removal tool can be used to force it out.

9.2 Remove the nut from the upper ballstud

9.3 Remove the upper pivot bolt from the inner end of the upper suspension arm

9.5 Remove the nut from the lower ballstud

3   Remove the pivot bolt from the inner end of the arm (see illustration). Remove the arm from the vehicle.

4   Installation is the reverse of removal. Tighten the fasteners to the torque listed in this Chapter's Specifications.

LOWER SUSPENSION ARM

▶ Refer to illustrations 9.5 and 9.6

5   Remove the nut from the lower ballstud at the outer end of the arm (see illustration), then separate the arm from the boss on the trailing arm. If the ballstud sticks in its boss, use a balljoint removal tool to force it out.

6   Remove the pivot bolt from the inner end of the arm (see illustration). Remove the arm from the vehicle.

7   Installation is the reverse of removal. Tighten the fasteners to the torque listed in this Chapter's Specifications.

TRAILING ARM

▶ Refer to illustration 9.13

8   Remove the coil spring (see Section 10).
9   Remove the brake shoe assembly (see Chapter 9).
10 Unbolt the brake hose and brake line brackets from the trailing

arm. Unbolt the parking brake cable brackets from the trailing arm.

11 If equipped, remove the ABS wheel speed sensor and unbolt the harness brackets from the trailing arm.

12 Remove the hub and bearing assembly (see Section 11). Separate the brake backing plate from the trailing arm and suspend it out of the way with a piece of wire or string.

13 Mark the relationship of the toe adjusting cam to the trailing arm mounting bracket (see illustration).

14 Unscrew the pivot bolt and separate the trailing arm from the vehicle.

15 Inspect the trailing arm pivot bushing for signs of deterioration. If it is in need of replacement, take the trailing arm to an automotive machine shop to have the bushing replaced.

16 Installation is the reverse of removal, noting the following points:

a) *Align the matchmarks on the toe adjusting cam and the mounting bracket.*
b) *Before fully tightening the trailing arm pivot bolt, raise the rear end of the trailing arm with a floor jack to simulate normal ride height.*
c) *Tighten all fasteners to the proper torque specifications.*
d) *It won't be necessary to bleed the brakes unless a hydraulic fitting was loosened.*
e) *Have the rear wheel alignment checked and, if necessary, adjusted.*

9.6 Remove the lower pivot bolt from the inner end of the lower suspension arm

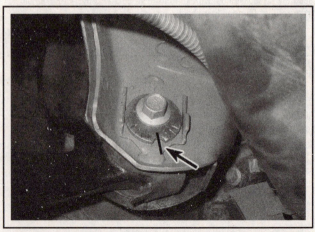

9.13 Mark the relationship of the toe adjusting cam to the trailing arm mounting bracket

10 Coil spring (rear) - removal and installation

♦ **Refer to illustration 10.2, 10.3 and 10.7**

❊❊ WARNING:

Always replace the springs as a set - never replace just one of them.

1   Loosen the wheel lug nuts, raise the vehicle and support it securely on jackstands. Block the front wheels to prevent the vehicle from rolling. Remove the wheel.

2   Unclip the brake line from the body and trailing arm mounting brackets (see illustration).

➡**Note: On models with rear disc brakes, remove the caliper and set it aside.**

3   Support the trailing arm with a floor jack (see illustration).

4   If equipped, remove the ABS wheel speed sensor and unbolt the harness brackets from the trailing arm.

5   Remove the pivot bolt on the inner end of the upper suspension arm and loosen the pivot bolt on the inner end of the lower suspension arm.

6   Detach the lower end of the shock absorber from the trailing arm (see illustration 8.4).

7   Mark the position of the spring to the spring insulator (see illustration).

8   Slowly lower the floor jack, pull the trailing arm down and remove the coil spring.

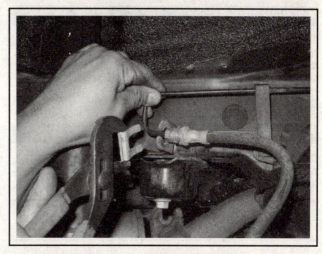

10.2 Remove the clip securing the brake line

9   Check the spring for cracks and chips, replacing the springs as a set if any defects are found. Also check the upper insulator for damage and deterioration, replacing it if necessary.

10 Installation is the reverse of removal. Be sure to position the lower end of the coil spring in the depressed area of the trailing arm. Tighten all fasteners to the proper torque specifications.

10.3 Using a floor jack, support the trailing arm

10.7 Mark the relationship of the spring to the spring insulator

11 Hub and bearing assembly (rear) - removal and installation

Due to the special tools and expertise required to press the hub and bearing from the steering knuckle, this job should be left to a professional mechanic. However, the trailing arm may be removed and the assembly taken to an automotive machine shop or other qualified repair facility equipped with the necessary tools. See Section 9 for the trailing arm removal procedure.

12 Steering wheel - removal and installation

☀ WARNING 1:

These models are equipped with a Supplemental Restraint System (SRS), more commonly known as airbags. Always disable the airbag system before working in the vicinity of any airbag system component to avoid the possibility of accidental deployment of the airbag(s), which could cause personal injury (see Chapter 12).

☀ WARNING 2:

Do not use a memory saving device to preserve the PCM or radio memory when working on or near airbag system components.

REMOVAL

▶ **Refer to illustrations 12.2, 12.3, 12.4, 12.5, and 12.7**

1 Turn the ignition key to Off, then disconnect the cable from the negative terminal of the battery. Wait at least two minutes before proceeding.

2 Turn the steering wheel so the wheels are pointing straight ahead. Open the cover on the bottom of the steering wheel (see illustration).

3 Disengage the connector lock and disconnect the airbag module electrical connector (see illustration).

4 Inside the cover, loosen the pinion shaft and release the steering wheel from the steering column (see illustration).

5 Pull the off the steering wheel and unplug the electrical connector for the horn (see illustration). Set the steering wheel/airbag module in a safe, isolated area.

☀ WARNING:

Carry the steering wheel/airbag module with the trim side facing away from you, and set the steering wheel/airbag module down with the trim side facing up. Don't place anything on top of the steering wheel/airbag module.

6 If it is necessary to remove the clockspring, remove the steering

12.2 At the bottom of the steering wheel, open the cover to gain access to the airbag harness

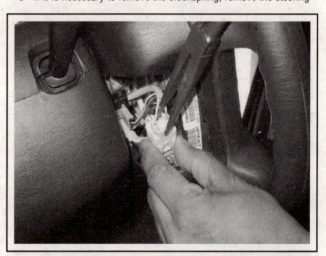

12.3 With a pair of pliers, disengage the airbag connector

12.4 Using a socket, loosen the steering wheel pinion bolt

12.5 Lift the steering wheel off the steering shaft then unplug the electrical connector

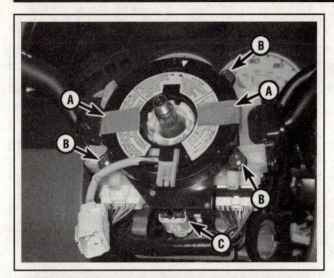

12.7 Apply two pieces of tape to the clockspring to prevent it from rotating (A), then remove the three airbag clockspring mounting screws (B) and disconnect the electrical connectors (C)

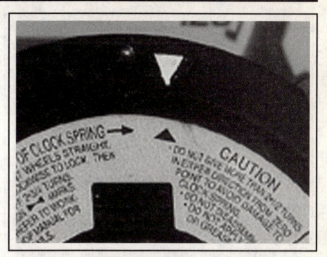

12.8 The clockspring must be centered with the arrow pointing up

column covers (see Chapter 11).

7   Unplug the clockspring electrical connector, then remove the three screws and detach it from the combination switch (see illustration).

INSTALLATION

▶ **Refer to illustration 12.8**

8   When installing the clockspring, make absolutely sure that the clockspring is centered with the arrow on the clockspring pointing up. This shouldn't be a problem as long as you taped the clockspring and you have not turned the steering shaft while the wheel was removed. If

for some reason the hub was turned, center the clockspring by turning the hub clockwise by hand until it stops (but don't force it, as the cable could break). Rotate the hub counterclockwise about 2-3/4 turns and align the two pointers (see illustration).

9   If removed, reinstall the steering column covers (see Chapter 11).

10 To install the wheel, plug in the horn connector and place the steering wheel on the steering shaft.

11 Inside the cover, tighten the pinion shaft to the torque listed in this Chapter's Specifications.

12 Plug in the electrical connector for the airbag module and close the locking device.

13 After you've reconnected the battery, the Powertrain Control Module (PCM) must relearn its idle and fuel mixture trim strategy for optimum driveability and performance (see Chapter 5, Section 1 for this procedure).

13   Steering column - removal and installation

❋❋ WARNING 1:

These models are equipped with a Supplemental Restraint System (SRS), more commonly known as airbags. Always disable the airbag system before working in the vicinity of any airbag system component to avoid the possibility of accidental deployment of the airbag(s), which could cause personal injury (see Chapter 12).

❋❋ WARNING 2:

Do not use a memory saving device to preserve the PCM or radio memory when working on or near airbag system components.

REMOVAL

▶ **Refer to illustrations 13.7, 13.8a and 13.8b**

1   Park the vehicle with the wheels pointing straight ahead. Disconnect the cable from the negative terminal of the battery (see Chapter 5).

2   Remove the steering wheel (see Section 12), then turn the ignition key to the LOCK position to prevent the steering shaft from turning.

❋❋ CAUTION:

If this is not done, the airbag clockspring could be damaged.

13.7 Mark the U-joint-to-intermediate shaft (A), then remove the pinch bolt and nut (B)

13.8a Remove the bolt at the top of the steering column . . .

3   Remove the steering column covers (see Chapter 11).

4   Remove the clockspring (see Section 12).

5   Disconnect the electrical connectors for the multi-function switch (see Chapter 12).

6   If equipped, remove the shift cable from the shift lever and cable mounting bracket (see Chapter 7 Part B).

7   Mark the relationship of the U-joint to the intermediate shaft, then remove and discard the pinch bolt and nut (see illustration).

8   Remove the steering column mounting fasteners (see illustrations), lower the column and pull it to the rear, making sure nothing is still connected, then remove the column.

INSTALLATION

9   Guide the steering column into position, then install the steering column mounting fasteners and tighten them to the torque listed in this Chapter's Specifications.

10   Connect the U-joint to the intermediate shaft. Install a new intermediate shaft pinch bolt and nut, tightening it to the torque listed in this Chapter's Specifications.

11   The remainder of installation is the reverse of removal. After

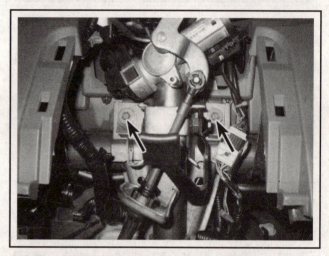

13.8b . . . and the two bolts securing the underside

you've reconnected the battery, the Powertrain Control Module (PCM) must relearn its idle and fuel mixture trim strategy for optimum driveability and performance (see Chapter 5, Section 1 for this procedure).

14   Tie-rod ends - removal and installation

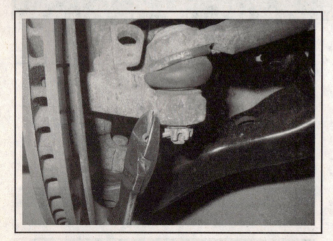

14.2 Remove the cotter pin from the castle nut and loosen - but don't remove - the nut

REMOVAL

▶ **Refer to illustrations 14.2, 14.3a, 14.3b and 14.4**

1   Loosen the front wheel lug nuts. Apply the parking brake, raise the front of the vehicle and support it securely on jackstands. Remove the front wheel.

2   Remove the cotter pin (see illustration) and loosen the nut on the tie-rod end stud.

14.3a Loosen the jam nut . . .

14.3b . . . then mark the position of the tie-rod end in relation to the threads

3   Hold the tie-rod with a pair of locking pliers or wrench and loosen the jam nut enough to mark the position of the tie-rod end in relation to the threads (see illustrations).

4   Disconnect the tie-rod end from the steering knuckle arm with a puller (see illustration). Remove the nut and detach the tie-rod end.

5   Unscrew the tie-rod end from the tie-rod.

INSTALLATION

6   Thread the tie-rod end on to the marked position and insert the stud into the steering knuckle arm. Tighten the jam nut securely.

7   Install the castle nut on the stud and tighten it to the torque listed in this Chapter's Specifications. Install a new cotter pin. If the hole for the cotter pin doesn't line up with one of the slots in the nut, tighten the nut an additional amount until it does.

8   Install the wheel and lug nuts. Lower the vehicle and tighten the lug nuts to the torque listed in the Chapter 1 Specifications.

9   Have the alignment checked and, if necessary, adjusted.

14.4 Disconnect the tie-rod end from the steering knuckle arm with a puller

15 Steering gear boots - replacement

♦ **Refer to illustrations 15.3a and 15.3b**

1   Loosen the lug nuts, raise the vehicle and support it securely on jackstands. Remove the wheel.

2   Remove the tie-rod end and jam nut (see Section 14).

3   Remove the outer steering gear boot clamp with a pair of pliers (see illustration). Cut off the inner boot clamp with a pair of diagonal cutters (see illustration). Slide off the boot.

15.3a The outer ends of the steering gear boots are secured by band-type clamps; they're easily released with a pair of pliers

15.3b The inner ends of the steering gear boots are retained by boot clamps which must be cut off and discarded

4 Before installing the new boot, wrap the threads and serrations on the end of the steering rod with a layer of tape so the small end of the new boot isn't damaged.

5 Slide the new boot into position on the steering gear until it seats in the groove in the steering rod and install new clamps.

6 Remove the tape and install the tie-rod end (see Section 14).

7 Install the wheel and lug nuts. Lower the vehicle and tighten the lug nuts to the torque listed in the Chapter 1 Specifications.

16 Steering gear - removal and installation

✳✳ WARNING:

These models are equipped with airbags. Always disable the airbag system before working in the vicinity of airbag system components (see Chapter 12). Make sure the steering column shaft is not turned while the steering gear is removed or you could damage the airbag system clockspring. To prevent the shaft from turning, turn the ignition key to the lock position before beginning work, and run the seat belt through the steering wheel and clip it into its latch.

REMOVAL

◆ Refer to illustrations 16.3, 16.8, 16.9 and 16.10

➡Note: On some vehicles equipped with the 3.0L engine, it may be necessary to remove the EGR valve (see Chapter 6).

1 Disconnect the cable from the negative terminal of the battery (see Chapter 5).

2 Remove the rear transaxle mount and bracket (see Chapter 7 Part B).

3 Detach the power steering pressure and return line bracket bolts (see illustration).

4 From inside the vehicle under the dashboard, slide the steering shaft boot up from the firewall and remove and discard the intermediate shaft pinch bolt and nut (see Section 13).

5 Drain the power steering fluid from the remote power steering reservoir. This can be accomplished with a suction gun or large syringe, or by disconnecting the fluid hose and draining the fluid into a container.

6 Loosen the front wheel lug nuts. Raise the vehicle and place it securely on jackstands. Remove both front wheels.

7 Detach the tie-rod ends from the steering knuckles (see Section 14).

8 Mark the U-joint and the steering gear input shaft with alignment markings for later installation, then separate the U-joint from the steering gear input shaft (see illustration).

16.3 Remove the fasteners securing the pressure and return line brackets

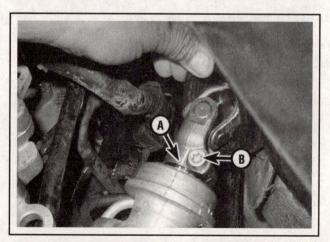

16.8 Remove the universal joint cover, then mark the relationship of the universal joint to the steering gear input shaft (A) and remove the U-joint pinch bolt (B)

16.9 Remove the bolt securing the power steering pressure and return lines

9   Place a drain pan under the steering gear and detach the power steering pressure and return lines (see illustration). Cap the ends to prevent excessive fluid loss and contamination.
10 Remove the two steering gear mounting bolts (see illustration).
11 Remove the steering gear from the vehicle.

INSTALLATION

12 Installation is the reverse of removal, noting the following points:

a) When connecting the steering gear input shaft to the intermediate shaft U-joint, be sure to align the matchmarks, and install a new pinch bolt and nut

16.10 Steering gear mounting bolt (left side shown, right side similar)

b) Tighten all fasteners to the torque values listed in this Chapter's Specifications.
c) Tighten all fasteners for the rear transaxle mount and mounting bracket to the torque listed in the Chapter 7 Specifications
d) Tighten the lug nuts to the torque listed in the Chapter 1 Specifications.
e) After you've reconnected the battery, the Powertrain Control Module (PCM) must relearn its idle and fuel mixture trim strategy for optimum driveability and performance (see Chapter 5, Section 1 for this procedure).
f) Fill the power steering reservoir with the recommended fluid (see Chapter 1). Bleed the power steering hydraulic system as described in Section 18.
g) Have the front end alignment checked and, if necessary, adjusted.

17 Power steering pump - removal and installation

▶ **Refer to illustrations 17.6, 17.7, 17.8, 17.12, 17.14, 17.18a and 17.18b**

1   Disconnect the cable from the negative battery terminal (see Chapter 5).
2   Using a large syringe or suction gun, suck as much fluid out of the power steering fluid reservoir as possible. Place a drain pan under the vehicle to catch any fluid that spills out when the hoses are disconnected.

REMOVAL

Four-cylinder engine

3   Remove the drivebelt (see Chapter 1).
4   Disconnect the electrical connector at the power steering pump.
5   Unscrew and remove the bolt securing the high pressure fluid line support bracket. Using a flare-nut wrench, unscrew the pressure line fitting from the pump.
6   Disconnect the supply hose from the power steering pump (see illustration).

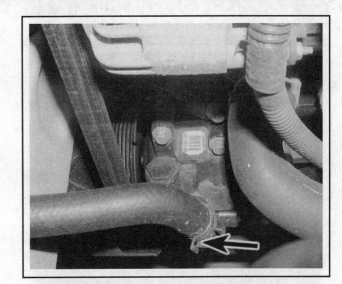

17.6 Disconnect the supply hose from the pump

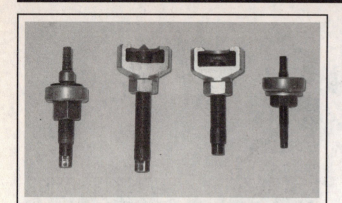

17.7 A pulley removal kit is needed to remove the power steering pulley from the four-cylinder engine pump

17.12 With the pulley secured, remove the pulley mounting nut

7   Unscrew and remove the four mounting bolts, and withdraw the power steering pump from its bracket. The pulley can be removed on the work bench, using a pulley removal tool (see illustration).

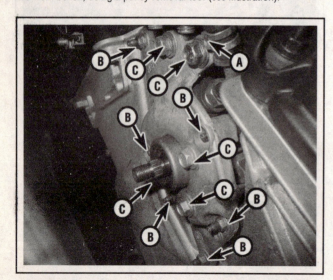

17.18a Remove the screw securing the pressure line bracket (A) followed by the six mounting nuts (B), then remove the five bolts securing the mounting bracket (C) . . .

17.8 Remove the nut securing the ground strap

17.14 Unplug the electrical connector (A), then remove the bolt securing the pressure line bracket (B)

V6 engine

8   Remove the ground wire (see illustration).

9   Loosen the right front wheel lug nuts. Raise the front the vehicle and support it securely on jackstands, then remove the wheel. Remove the drivebelt (see Chapter 1).

10   Install the wheel and lower the vehicle to the ground.

11   Support the engine with a floor jack and block of wood.

12   Remove the pulley from the power steering pump (see illustration).

13   Disconnect the fluid return hose from the pump, allowing the fluid to drain into a suitable container.

14   Unplug the electrical connector from the power steering fluid pressure switch and remove the bolt securing the pressure line bracket (see illustration).

15   Disconnect the power steering pressure hose from the pump, allowing the fluid to drain into a suitable container. Use two wrenches; a backup wrench to hold the fitting on the pump tube, the other to loosen the fitting.

16   Under the power steering reservoir, remove the refrigerant line bracket-to-body nut.

17   Remove the upper engine mount (see Chapter 2 Part B).

18   Unscrew the power steering mounting bolts, then remove the bracket and the pump (see illustrations).

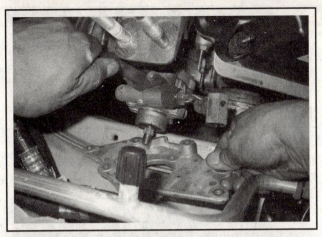

17.18b . . . and carefully remove the bracket and pump

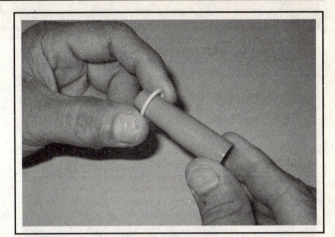

17.19a Slide the teflon seal onto the seal tool . . .

INSTALLATION

▶ **Refer to illustrations 17.19a and 17.19b**

19 Installation is the reverse of removal, noting the following points:

a) *Tighten the bolts and unions securely.*

b) *The O-ring on the high-pressure outlet should be replaced. Use a special tool or a tapered tube to slide the new O-ring onto the pipe union (see illustrations).*

c) *On 3.0L V6 models, when installing the engine mounts refer to Chapter 2 Part B.*

d) *Install the drivebelt as outlined in Chapter 1.*

e) *After you've reconnected the battery, the Powertrain Control Module (PCM) must relearn its idle and fuel mixture trim strategy for optimum driveability and performance (see Chapter 5, Section 1 for this procedure).*

f) *Fill the power steering reservoir with the recommended fluid (see Chapter 1). Bleed the power steering hydraulic system as described in Section 18.*

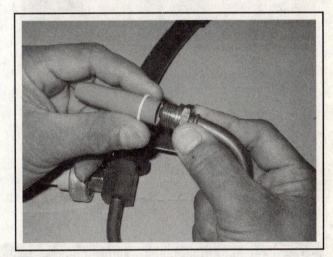

17.19b . . . then slide it onto the fitting

18 Power steering system - bleeding

1 The power steering system must be bled whenever a line is disconnected. Bubbles can be seen in power steering fluid that has air in it and the fluid will often have a tan or milky appearance. Low fluid level can cause air to mix with the fluid, resulting in a noisy pump as well as foaming of the fluid.

2 Open the hood and check the fluid level in the reservoir, adding the specified fluid necessary to bring it up to the proper level (see Chapter 1).

3 Start the engine and slowly turn the steering wheel several times from left-to-right and back again. Do not turn the wheel completely from lock-to-lock. Check the fluid level, topping it up as necessary until it remains steady and no more bubbles are visible.

19 Power steering fluid cooler - removal and installation

REMOVAL

▶ **Refer to illustrations 19.2 and 19.4**

1   Using a large syringe or suction gun, suck as much fluid out of the power steering fluid reservoir as possible. Place a drain pan under the vehicle to catch any fluid that spills out when the hoses are disconnected.

2   Disconnect the cooler hoses (see illustration).

19.2 Using a pair pliers, release the clamps securing the hoses

3   Remove the front bumper cover (see Chapter 11).

4   Unscrew the fluid cooler mounting nuts and remove the cooler from the vehicle (see illustration).

INSTALLATION

5   Installation is the reverse of removal. Fill the power steering reservoir with the recommended fluid (see Chapter 1). Bleed the power steering hydraulic system as described in Section 18.

19.4 Remove the two fasteners securing the cooler

20 Wheels and tires - general information

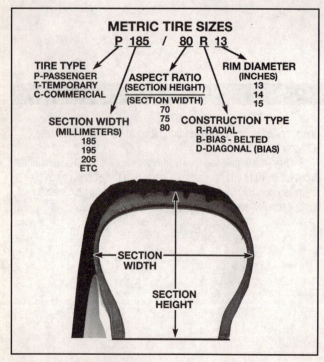

20.1 Metric tire size code

▶ **Refer to illustration 20.1**

1   All vehicles covered by this manual are equipped with metric-sized fiberglass or steel belted radial tires (see illustration). Use of other size or type of tires may affect the ride and handling of the vehicle. Don't mix different types of tires, such as radials and bias belted, on the same vehicle as handling may be seriously affected. It's recommended that tires be replaced in pairs on the same axle, but if only one tire is being replaced, be sure it's the same size, structure and tread design as the other.

2   Because tire pressure has a substantial effect on handling and wear, the pressure on all tires should be checked at least once a month or before any extended trips (see Chapter 1).

3   Wheels must be replaced if they are bent, dented, leak air, have elongated bolt holes, are heavily rusted, out of vertical symmetry or if the lug nuts won't stay tight. Wheel repairs that use welding or peening are not recommended.

4   Tire and wheel balance is important in the overall handling, braking and performance of the vehicle. Unbalanced wheels can adversely affect handling and ride characteristics as well as tire life. Whenever a tire is installed on a wheel, the tire and wheel should be balanced by a shop with the proper equipment.

21 Wheel alignment - general information

▸ **Refer to illustration 21.1**

A wheel alignment refers to the adjustments made to the wheels so they are in proper angular relationship to the suspension and the ground. Wheels that are out of proper alignment not only affect vehicle control, but also increase tire wear. The front end angles normally measured are camber, caster and toe-in (see illustration). Toe-in and camber are adjustable; if the caster is not correct, check for bent components. Rear toe-in is also adjustable.

Getting the proper wheel alignment is a very exacting process, one in which complicated and expensive machines are necessary to perform the job properly. Because of this, you should have a technician with the proper equipment perform these tasks. We will, however, use this space to give you a basic idea of what is involved with a wheel alignment so you can better understand the process and deal intelligently with the shop that does the work.

Toe-in is the turning in of the wheels. The purpose of a toe specification is to ensure parallel rolling of the wheels. In a vehicle with zero toe-in, the distance between the front edges of the wheels will be the same as the distance between the rear edges of the wheels. The actual amount of toe-in is normally only a fraction of an inch. On the front end, toe-in is controlled by the tie-rod end position on the tie-rod. On the rear end, it's controlled by a cam at the front of the suspension trailing arm. Incorrect toe-in will cause the tires to wear improperly by making them scrub against the road surface.

Camber is the tilting of the wheels from vertical when viewed from one end of the vehicle. When the wheels tilt out at the top, the camber is said to be positive (+). When the wheels tilt in at the top the camber is negative (-). The amount of tilt is measured in degrees from vertical and this measurement is called the camber angle. This angle affects the amount of tire tread which contacts the road and compensates for changes in the suspension geometry when the vehicle is cornering or traveling over an undulating surface. On the front end it is adjusted by altering the position of the strut upper mount in the strut tower.

Caster is the tilting of the front steering axis from the vertical. A tilt toward the rear is positive caster and a tilt toward the front is negative caster.

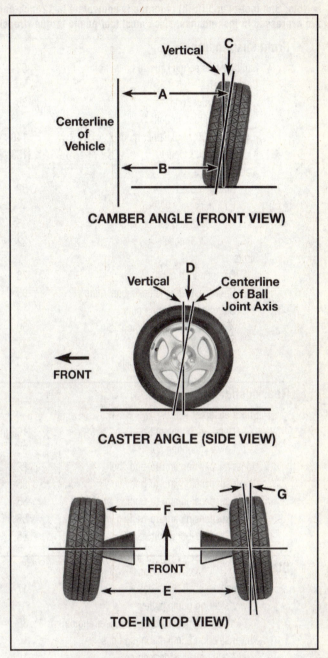

CAMBER ANGLE (FRONT VIEW)

CASTER ANGLE (SIDE VIEW)

TOE-IN (TOP VIEW)

21.1 Camber, caster and toe-in angles

A minus B = C (degrees camber)
D = degrees caster
E minus F = toe-in (measured in inches)
G = toe-in (expressed in degrees)

Torque specifications	Ft-lbs (unless otherwise indicated)	Nm

➡**Note: One foot-pound (ft-lb) of torque is equivalent to 12 inch-pounds (in-lbs) of torque. Torque values below approximately 15 ft-lbs are expressed in inch-pounds, since most foot-pound torque wrenches are not accurate at these smaller values.**

Front suspension

Balljoint-to-steering knuckle pinch bolt	52	70
Control arm		
Front pivot bolt	85	115
Rear mounting bolt		
2002 and earlier models	148	200
2003 models	133	180
Stabilizer bar		
Bracket bolts	52	70
Link nuts		
2002 and earlier models	35	48
2003 models	32	43
Struts		
Damper shaft nut	76	103
Strut-to-steering knuckle bolts/nuts	85	115
Strut upper mounting nuts		
2003 and earlier models	59	80
2004 models	41	55
2005 and later models	30	40

Rear suspension

Shock absorber		
Upper mounting nut	156 in-lbs	18
Lower mounting nut	85	115
Upper suspension arm-to-body bolt	85	115
Lower suspension arm-to-body bolt	85	115
Upper suspension arm-to-trailing arm	85	115
Lower suspension arm-to-trailing arm	85	115
Trailing arm-to-body bolt	85	115

Steering

Intermediate shaft pinch bolt	17	23
Power steering pump pulley mounting nut (2.0L four-cylinder engine)	36	49
Power steering pump mounting bolts (2.0L four-cylinder engine)	18	25
Power steering bracket-to-pump bolts (3.0L V6 engine)	18	25
Power steering pump bracket nuts (3.0L V6 engine)	89 in-lbs	10
Power steering pressure and return line-to-steering gear-bracket bolts	89 in-lbs	10
Power steering pressure and return line-to-steering-gear mounting bolt	18	25
Steering column mounting nuts	168 in-lbs	19
Steering column support bolt	144 in-lbs	16
Steering gear mounting bolts	93	126
Steering wheel-to-steering column pinion shaft	132 in-lbs	15
Tie-rod end-to-steering knuckle nut	41	55
U-joint-to-steering gear input shaft pinch bolt	18	24

Section

11

BODY

1 General information

These models feature a "unibody" layout, using a floor pan with integral side frame rails which support the body components, front and rear suspension systems and other mechanical components.

Certain components are particularly vulnerable to accident damage and can be unbolted and repaired or replaced. Among these parts are the body moldings, bumpers, front fenders, the hood and trunk lid, doors and all glass.

Only general body maintenance practices and body panel repair procedures within the scope of the do-it-yourselfer are included in this Chapter.

2 Body - maintenance

1   The condition of your vehicle's body is very important, because the resale value depends a great deal on it. It's much more difficult to repair a neglected or damaged body than it is to repair mechanical components. The hidden areas of the body, such as the wheel wells, the frame and the engine compartment, are equally important, although they don't require as frequent attention as the rest of the body.

2   Once a year, or every 12,000 miles, it's a good idea to have the underside of the body steam-cleaned. All traces of dirt and oil will be removed and the area can then be inspected carefully for rust, damaged brake lines, frayed electrical wires, damaged cables and other problems.

3   At the same time, clean the engine and the engine compartment with a steam cleaner or water-soluble degreaser.

4   The wheel wells should be given close attention, since undercoating can peel away and stones and dirt thrown up by the tires can cause the paint to chip and flake, allowing rust to set in. If rust is found, clean down to the bare metal and apply an anti-rust paint.

5   The body should be washed about once a week. Wet the vehicle thoroughly to soften the dirt, then wash it down with a soft sponge and plenty of clean soapy water. If the surplus dirt is not washed off very carefully, it can wear down the paint.

6   Spots of tar or asphalt thrown up from the road should be removed with a cloth soaked in kerosene. Scented lamp oil is available in most hardware stores and the smell is easier to work with than straight kerosene.

7   Once every six months, wax the body and chrome trim. If a chrome cleaner is used to remove rust from any of the vehicle's plated parts, remember that the cleaner also removes part of the chrome, so use it sparingly. On any plated parts where chrome cleaner is used, use a good paste wax over the plating for extra protection.

3 Vinyl trim - maintenance

Don't clean vinyl trim with detergents, caustic soap or petroleum-based cleaners. Plain soap and water works just fine, with a soft brush to clean dirt that may be ingrained. Wash the vinyl as frequently as the rest of the vehicle.

After cleaning, application of a high quality rubber and vinyl protectant will help prevent oxidation and cracks. The protectant can also be applied to weatherstripping, vacuum lines and rubber hoses, which often fail as a result of chemical degradation, and to the tires.

4 Upholstery and carpets - maintenance

1   Every three months remove the floormats and clean the interior of the vehicle (more frequently if necessary). Use a stiff whisk broom to brush the carpeting and loosen dirt and dust, then vacuum the upholstery and carpets thoroughly, especially along seams and crevices.

2   Dirt and stains can be removed from carpeting with basic household or automotive carpet shampoos available in spray cans. Follow the directions and vacuum again, then use a stiff brush to bring back the "nap" of the carpet.

3   Most interiors have cloth or vinyl upholstery, either of which can be cleaned and maintained with a number of material-specific cleaners or shampoos available in auto supply stores. Follow the directions on the product for usage, and always spot-test any upholstery cleaner on an inconspicuous area (bottom edge of a backseat cushion) to ensure that it doesn't cause a color shift in the material.

4   After cleaning, vinyl upholstery should be treated with a protectant.

➡**Note: Make sure the protectant container indicates the prod-uct can be used on seats - some products may make a seat too slippery.**

❋❋ CAUTION:

Do not use protectant on steering wheels.

5   Leather upholstery requires special care. It should be cleaned regularly with saddlesoap or leather cleaner. Never use alcohol, gasoline, nail polish remover or thinner to clean leather upholstery.

6   After cleaning, regularly treat leather upholstery with a leather conditioner, rubbed in with a soft cotton cloth. Never use car wax on leather upholstery.

7   In areas where the interior of the vehicle is subject to bright sunlight, cover leather seating areas of the seats with a sheet if the vehicle is to be left out for any length of time.

5 Body repair - minor damage

FLEXIBLE PLASTIC BODY PANELS (FRONT AND REAR BUMPER FASCIA)

The following repair procedures are for minor scratches and gouges. Repair of more serious damage should be left to a dealer service department or qualified auto body shop. Below is a list of the equipment and materials necessary to perform the following repair procedures on plastic body panels. Although a specific brand of material may be mentioned, it should be noted that equivalent products from other manufacturers may be used instead.

Wax, grease and silicone removing solvent
Cloth-backed body tape
Sanding discs
Drill motor with three-inch disc holder
Hand sanding block
Rubber squeegees
Sandpaper
Non-porous mixing palette
Wood paddle or putty knife
Curved-tooth body file
Flexible parts repair material

1   Remove the damaged panel, if necessary or desirable. In most cases, repairs can be carried out with the panel installed.

2   Clean the area(s) to be repaired with a wax, grease and silicone removing solvent applied with a water-dampened cloth.

3   If the damage is structural, that is, if it extends through the panel, clean the backside of the panel area to be repaired as well. Wipe dry.

4   Sand the rear surface about 1-1/2 inches beyond the break.

5   Cut two pieces of fiberglass cloth large enough to overlap the break by about 1-1/2 inches. Cut only to the required length.

6   Mix the adhesive from the repair kit according to the instructions included with the kit, and apply a layer of the mixture approximately 1/8-inch thick on the backside of the panel. Overlap the break by at least 1-1/2 inches.

7   Apply one piece of fiberglass cloth to the adhesive and cover the cloth with additional adhesive. Apply a second piece of fiberglass cloth to the adhesive and immediately cover the cloth with additional adhesive in sufficient quantity to fill the weave.

8   Allow the repair to cure for 20 to 30 minutes at 60-degrees to 80-degrees F.

9   If necessary, trim the excess repair material at the edge.

10 Remove all of the paint film over and around the area(s) to be repaired. The repair material should not overlap the painted surface.

11 With a drill motor and a sanding disc (or a rotary file), cut a "V" along the break line approximately 1/2-inch wide. Remove all dust and loose particles from the repair area.

12 Mix and apply the repair material. Apply a light coat first over the damaged area; then continue applying material until it reaches a level slightly higher than the surrounding finish.

13 Cure the mixture for 20 to 30 minutes at 60-degrees to 80-degrees F.

14 Roughly establish the contour of the area being repaired with a body file. If low areas or pits remain, mix and apply additional adhesive.

15 Block sand the damaged area with sandpaper to establish the actual contour of the surrounding surface.

16 If desired, the repaired area can be temporarily protected with several light coats of primer. Because of the special paints and techniques required for flexible body panels, it is recommended that the vehicle be taken to a paint shop for completion of the body repair.

STEEL BODY PANELS

♦ **See photo sequence**

Repair of minor scratches

17 If the scratch is superficial and does not penetrate to the metal of the body, repair is very simple. Lightly rub the scratched area with a fine rubbing compound to remove loose paint and built up wax. Rinse the area with clean water.

18 Apply touch-up paint to the scratch, using a small brush. Continue to apply thin layers of paint until the surface of the paint in the scratch is level with the surrounding paint. Allow the new paint at least two weeks to harden, then blend it into the surrounding paint by rubbing with a very fine rubbing compound. Finally, apply a coat of wax to the scratch area.

19 If the scratch has penetrated the paint and exposed the metal of the body, causing the metal to rust, a different repair technique is required. Remove all loose rust from the bottom of the scratch with a pocket knife, then apply rust inhibiting paint to prevent the formation of rust in the future. Using a rubber or nylon applicator, coat the scratched area with glaze-type filler. If required, the filler can be mixed with thinner to provide a very thin paste, which is ideal for filling narrow scratches. Before the glaze filler in the scratch hardens, wrap a piece of smooth cotton cloth around the tip of a finger. Dip the cloth in thinner and then quickly wipe it along the surface of the scratch. This will ensure that the surface of the filler is slightly hollow. The scratch can now be painted over as described earlier in this Section.

REPAIR OF DENTS

20 When repairing dents, the first job is to pull the dent out until the affected area is as close as possible to its original shape. There is no point in trying to restore the original shape completely as the metal in the damaged area will have stretched on impact and cannot be restored to its original contours. It is better to bring the level of the dent up to a point which is about 1/8-inch below the level of the surrounding metal. In cases where the dent is very shallow, it is not worth trying to pull it out at all.

21 If the back side of the dent is accessible, it can be hammered out gently from behind using a soft-face hammer. While doing this, hold a block of wood firmly against the opposite side of the metal to absorb the hammer blows and prevent the metal from being stretched.

22 If the dent is in a section of the body which has double layers, or some other factor makes it inaccessible from behind, a different technique is required. Drill several small holes through the metal inside the damaged area, particularly in the deeper sections. Screw long, self tapping screws into the holes just enough for them to get a good grip in the metal. Now the dent can be pulled out by pulling on the protruding heads of the screws with locking pliers.

23 The next stage of repair is the removal of paint from the damaged area and from an inch or so of the surrounding metal. This is easily done with a wire brush or sanding disk in a drill motor, although it can be done just as effectively by hand with sandpaper. To complete the preparation for filling, score the surface of the bare metal with a screwdriver or the tang of a file or drill small holes in the affected area. This will provide a good grip for the filler material. To complete the repair, see the Section on filling and painting.

These photos illustrate a method of repairing simple dents. They are intended to supplement Body repair - minor damage in this Chapter and should not be used as the sole instructions for body repair on these vehicles.

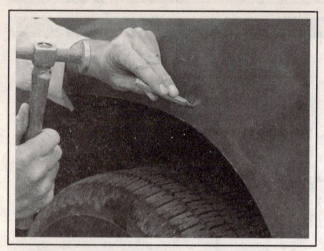

1 If you can't access the backside of the body panel to hammer out the dent, pull it out with a slide-hammer-type dent puller. In the deepest portion of the dent or along the crease line, drill or punch hole(s) at least one inch apart . . .

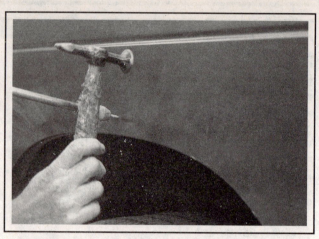

2 . . . then screw the slide-hammer into the hole and operate it. Tap with a hammer near the edge of the dent to help 'pop' the metal back to its original shape. When you're finished, the dent area should be close to its original contour and about 1/8-inch below the surface of the surrounding metal

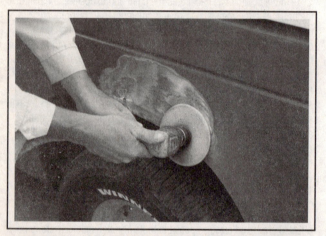

3 Using coarse-grit sandpaper, remove the paint down to the bare metal. Hand sanding works fine, but the disc sander shown here makes the job faster. Use finer (about 320-grit) sandpaper to feather-edge the paint at least one inch around the dent area

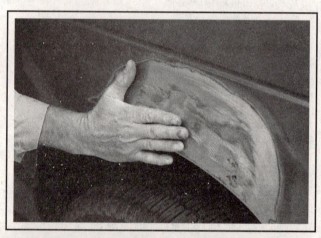

4 When the paint is removed, touch will probably be more helpful than sight for telling if the metal is straight. Hammer down the high spots or raise the low spots as necessary. Clean the repair area with wax/silicone remover

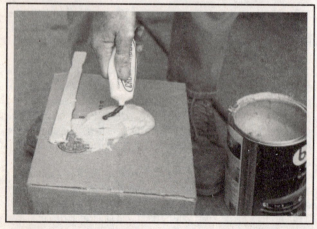

5 Following label instructions, mix up a batch of plastic filler and hardener. The ratio of filler to hardener is critical, and, if you mix it incorrectly, it will either not cure properly or cure too quickly (you won't have time to file and sand it into shape)

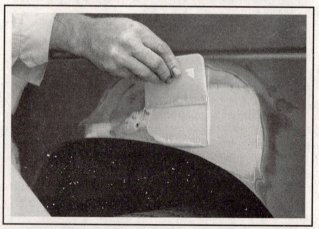

6 Working quickly so the filler doesn't harden, use a plastic applicator to press the body filler firmly into the metal, assuring it bonds completely. Work the filler until it matches the original contour and is slightly above the surrounding metal

7 Let the filler harden until you can just dent it with your fingernail. Use a body file or Surform tool (shown here) to rough-shape the filler

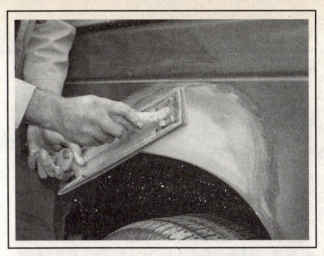

8 Use coarse-grit sandpaper and a sanding board or block to work the filler down until it's smooth and even. Work down to finer grits of sandpaper - always using a board or block - ending up with 360 or 400 grit

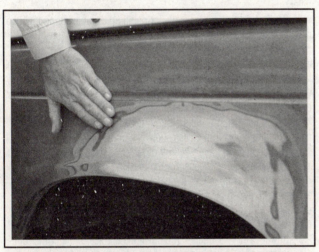

9 You shouldn't be able to feel any ridge at the transition from the filler to the bare metal or from the bare metal to the old paint. As soon as the repair is flat and uniform, remove the dust and mask off the adjacent panels or trim pieces

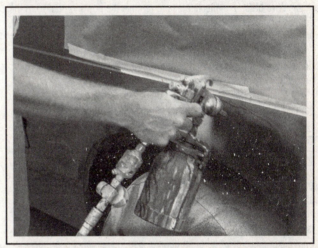

10 Apply several layers of primer to the area. Don't spray the primer on too heavy, so it sags or runs, and make sure each coat is dry before you spray on the next one. A professional-type spray gun is being used here, but aerosol spray primer is available inexpensively from auto parts stores

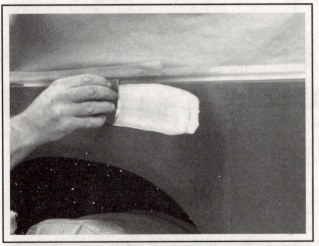

11 The primer will help reveal imperfections or scratches. Fill these with glazing compound. Follow the label instructions and sand it with 360 or 400-grit sandpaper until it's smooth. Repeat the glazing, sanding and respraying until the primer reveals a perfectly smooth surface

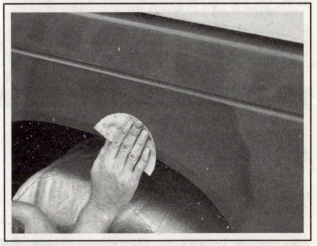

12 Finish sand the primer with very fine sandpaper (400 or 600-grit) to remove the primer overspray. Clean the area with water and allow it to dry. Use a tack rag to remove any dust, then apply the finish coat. Don't attempt to rub out or wax the repair area until the paint has dried completely (at least two weeks)

REPAIR OF RUST HOLES OR GASHES

24 Remove all paint from the affected area and from an inch or so of the surrounding metal using a sanding disk or wire brush mounted in a drill motor. If these are not available, a few sheets of sandpaper will do the job just as effectively.

25 With the paint removed, you will be able to determine the severity of the corrosion and decide whether to replace the whole panel, if possible, or repair the affected area. New body panels are not as expensive as most people think and it is often quicker to install a new panel than to repair large areas of rust.

26 Remove all trim pieces from the affected area except those which will act as a guide to the original shape of the damaged body, such as headlight shells, etc. Using metal snips or a hacksaw blade, remove all loose metal and any other metal that is badly affected by rust. Hammer the edges of the hole in to create a slight depression for the filler material.

27 Wire brush the affected area to remove the powdery rust from the surface of the metal. If the back of the rusted area is accessible, treat it with rust inhibiting paint.

28 Before filling is done, block the hole in some way. This can be done with sheet metal riveted or screwed into place, or by stuffing the hole with wire mesh.

29 Once the hole is blocked off, the affected area can be filled and painted. See the following subsection on filling and painting.

FILLING AND PAINTING

30 Many types of body fillers are available, but generally speaking, body repair kits which contain filler paste and a tube of resin hardener are best for this type of repair work. A wide, flexible plastic or nylon applicator will be necessary for imparting a smooth and contoured finish to the surface of the filler material. Mix up a small amount of filler on a clean piece of wood or cardboard (use the hardener sparingly). Follow the manufacturer's instructions on the package, otherwise the filler will set incorrectly.

31 Using the applicator, apply the filler paste to the prepared area. Draw the applicator across the surface of the filler to achieve the desired contour and to level the filler surface. As soon as a contour that approximates the original one is achieved, stop working the paste. If you continue, the paste will begin to stick to the applicator. Continue to add thin layers of paste at 20-minute intervals until the level of the filler is just above the surrounding metal.

32 Once the filler has hardened, the excess can be removed with a body file. From then on, progressively finer grades of sandpaper should be used, starting with a 180-grit paper and finishing with 600-grit wet-or-dry paper. Always wrap the sandpaper around a flat rubber or wooden block, otherwise the surface of the filler will not be completely flat. During the sanding of the filler surface, the wet-or-dry paper should be periodically rinsed in water. This will ensure that a very smooth finish is produced in the final stage.

33 At this point, the repair area should be surrounded by a ring of bare metal, which in turn should be encircled by the finely feathered edge of good paint. Rinse the repair area with clean water until all of the dust produced by the sanding operation is gone.

34 Spray the entire area with a light coat of primer. This will reveal any imperfections in the surface of the filler. Repair the imperfections with fresh filler paste or glaze filler and once more smooth the surface with sandpaper. Repeat this spray-and-repair procedure until you are satisfied that the surface of the filler and the feathered edge of the paint are perfect. Rinse the area with clean water and allow it to dry completely.

35 The repair area is now ready for painting. Spray painting must be carried out in a warm, dry, windless and dust free atmosphere. These conditions can be created if you have access to a large indoor work area, but if you are forced to work in the open, you will have to pick the day very carefully. If you are working indoors, dousing the floor in the work area with water will help settle the dust which would otherwise be in the air. If the repair area is confined to one body panel, mask off the surrounding panels. This will help minimize the effects of a slight mismatch in paint color. Trim pieces such as chrome strips, door handles, etc., will also need to be masked off or removed. Use masking tape and several thickness of newspaper for the masking operations.

36 Before spraying, shake the paint can thoroughly, then spray a test area until the spray painting technique is mastered. Cover the repair area with a thick coat of primer. The thickness should be built up using several thin layers of primer rather than one thick one. Using 600-grit wet-or-dry sandpaper, rub down the surface of the primer until it is very smooth. While doing this, the work area should be thoroughly rinsed with water and the wet-or-dry sandpaper periodically rinsed as well. Allow the primer to dry before spraying additional coats.

37 Spray on the top coat, again building up the thickness by using several thin layers of paint. Begin spraying in the center of the repair area and then, using a circular motion, work out until the whole repair area and about two inches of the surrounding original paint is covered. Remove all masking material 10 to 15 minutes after spraying on the final coat of paint. Allow the new paint at least two weeks to harden, then use a very fine rubbing compound to blend the edges of the new paint into the existing paint. Finally, apply a coat of wax.

6 Body repair - major damage

1 Major damage must be repaired by an auto body shop specifically equipped to perform unibody repairs. These shops have the specialized equipment required to do the job properly.

2 If the damage is extensive, the body must be checked for proper alignment or the vehicle's handling characteristics may be adversely affected and other components may wear at an accelerated rate.

3 Due to the fact that some of the major body components (hood, fenders, doors, etc.) are separate and replaceable units, any seriously damaged components should be replaced rather than repaired. Sometimes the components can be found in a wrecking yard that specializes in used vehicle components, often at considerable savings over the cost of new parts.

7 Hinges and locks - maintenance

Once every 3,000 miles, or every three months, the hinges and latch assemblies on the doors, hood and trunk (or liftgate) should be given a few drops of light oil or lock lubricant. The door latch strikers should also be lubricated with a thin coat of grease to reduce wear and ensure free movement. Lubricate the door and trunk (or liftgate) locks with spray-on graphite lubricant.

8 Windshield and fixed glass - replacement

Replacement of the windshield and fixed glass requires the use of special fast-setting adhesive/caulk materials and some specialized tools and techniques. These operations should be left to a dealer service department or a shop specializing in glass work.

9 Hood - removal, installation and adjustment

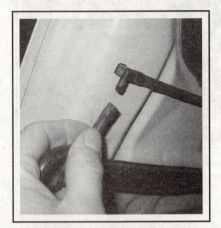

9.2 Disconnect the windshield washer fluid lines from the connectors at the hood

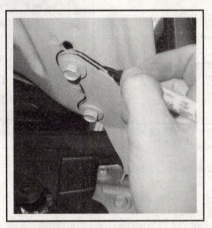

9.3 Draw alignment marks around the hood hinges to ensure proper alignment of the hood when it's reinstalled

9.9 To adjust the hood latch horizontally or vertically, draw a reference mark and loosen the latch bolts

➥Note: The hood is somewhat awkward to remove and install, at least two people should perform this procedure.

REMOVAL AND INSTALLATION

▶ **Refer to illustrations 9.2 and 9.3**

1   Open the hood, then place blankets or pads over the fenders and cowl area of the body. This will protect the body and paint as the hood is lifted off.

2   Disconnect any cables or wires that will interfere with removal. Disconnect the windshield washer tubing from the nozzles on the hood (see illustration).

3   Make marks around the hood hinge to ensure proper alignment during installation (see illustration).

4   Have an assistant support the weight of the hood and remove the hinge-to-hood bolts and lift off the hood.

5   Installation is the reverse of removal. Align the hinge bolts with the marks made in Step 3.

ADJUSTMENT

▶ **Refer to illustrations 9.9 and 9.10**

6   Fore-and-aft and side-to-side adjustment of the hood is done by moving the hinge plate slot after loosening the bolts or nuts.

7   Mark around the entire hinge plate so you can determine the amount of movement.

8   Loosen the bolts and move the hood into correct alignment. Move it only a little at a time. Tighten the hinge bolts and carefully lower the hood to check the position.

9   If necessary after installation, the entire hood latch assembly can be adjusted up-and-down as well as from side-to-side on the radiator support so the hood closes securely and flush with the fenders. Scribe a line or mark around the hood latch mounting bolts to provide a reference point, then loosen them and reposition the latch assembly, as necessary (see illustration). Following adjustment, retighten the mounting bolts.

10   Finally, adjust the hood bumpers on the radiator support so the hood, when closed, is flush with the fenders (see illustration).

11   The hood latch assembly, as well as the hinges, should be periodically lubricated with white, lithium-base grease to prevent binding and wear.

9.10 To adjust the vertical height of the leading edge of the hood so that it's flush with the fenders, turn each edge cushion clockwise (to lower the hood) or counterclockwise (to raise the hood)

10 Hood latch and release cable - removal and installation

LATCH

▶ **Refer to illustrations 10.2a and 10.2b**

1 Mark the position of the latch to aid alignment when installing, then remove the retaining bolts securing the hood latch to the radiator support (see illustration 9.9). Remove the latch.

2 Disconnect the hood release cable by disengaging the cable from the latch assembly (see illustrations).

3 Installation is the reverse of removal.

➡ **Note: Adjust the latch so the hood engages securely when closed and the hood bumpers are slightly compressed.**

CABLE

▶ **Refer to illustrations 10.5 and 10.10**

4 Working in the passenger compartment, remove the driver's side kick panel.

5 Lift the hood release handle lever upward, then rotate the cable housing end and disengage the cable from the hood release lever handle (see illustration). If the handle lever needs to be replaced, remove the handle mounting bolts to release it from the instrument panel.

6 Attach a piece of thin wire or string to the end of the cable.

7 Working in the engine compartment, disconnect the hood release cable from the latch assembly as described in Steps 1 and 2. Unclip all the cable retaining clips on the radiator support and the inner fenderwell.

8 Pull the cable forward into the engine compartment until you can see the wire or string, then remove the wire or string from the old cable and fasten it to the new cable.

9 With the new cable attached to the wire or string, pull the wire or string back through the firewall until the new cable reaches the

10.2a Depress the locking tabs on the cable housing to release the cable from the hood latch

inside handle.

10 Check that the cable grommet is properly seated in the engine compartment firewall (see illustration).

11 Working in the passenger compartment, reinstall the new cable into the hood release lever, making sure the cable housing fits snugly into the notch in the handle bracket.

➡ **Note: Pull on the cable with your fingers from the passenger compartment until the cable stop seats in the grommet on the firewall correctly.**

12 The remainder of the installation is the reverse of removal.

10.2b Remove the cable end from the slotted portion of the latch mechanism

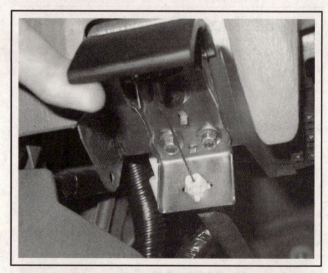

10.5 Lift upward on the handle and depress the tabs on the backside of the cable housing using needle nose pliers to release it from the base of the handle, then detach the cable end from the lever

11 Bumpers - removal and installation

1   Apply the parking brake, raise the vehicle and support it securely on jackstands.

FRONT BUMPER

▶ **Refer to illustrations 11.2, 11.4, 11.6, 11.7, 11.8, 11.9a, 11.9b and 11.10**

2   Remove the pin retainers from the inner fender splash shield (see illustration).

3   Remove the front bumper cover mounting bolts (see illustration 11.2). Pull the splash shield away from the front of the bumper area.

4   Remove the front bumper cover push-pin type retainers that retain the cover to the fender (see illustration).

5   Disconnect the fog lamp connectors, if equipped.

6   Remove the bumper cover lower bolts (see illustration).

7   Remove the pin-type retainers from the front of the bumper cover (see illustration).

8   Remove the two upper bumper cover mounting bolts (see illustration), then remove the cover.

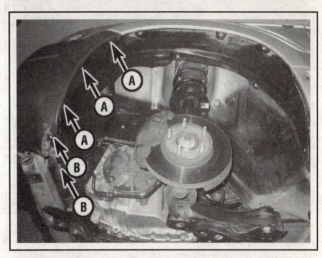

11.2 Remove the pin retainers (A) and the bolts (B) from the lower section of the inner fender splash shield from each side of the vehicle

11.4 Remove the cover-to-fender retainers from each side of the vehicle

11.6 Remove the bumper cover lower mounting bolts

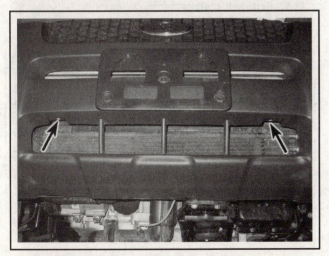

11.7 Remove the retainers from the front of the bumper cover

11.8 Remove the upper bumper cover mounting bolts - one on each side of the radiator support

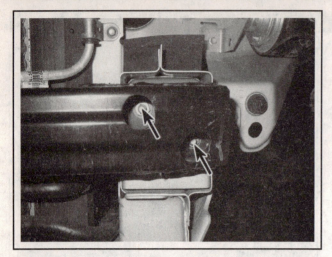

11.9a Remove the front bumper mounting nuts from the left side . . .

11.9b . . . and the right side of the vehicle

9 Remove the front bumper mounting nuts (see illustrations).
10 Remove the front bumper (see illustration).
11 Installation is the reverse of removal.

REAR BUMPER

▶ **Refer to illustrations 11.12, 11.13, 11.14, 11.15, 11.16a, 11.16b and 11.17**

12 Remove the pin retainers from the inner fender splash shield (see illustration). Pull the splash shield away from the rear bumper cover.

11.10 Lift the bumper from the front of the vehicle

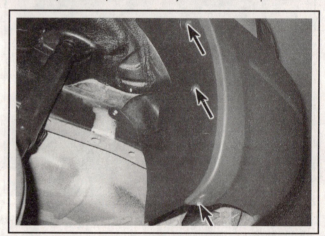

11.12 Remove the retainers from the inner fender splash shield

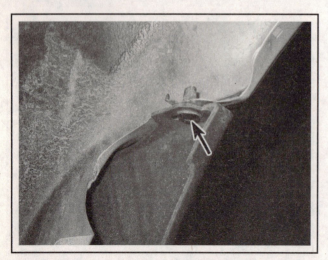

11.13 Remove the screws from the rear bumper cover and fender - one on each side of the vehicle

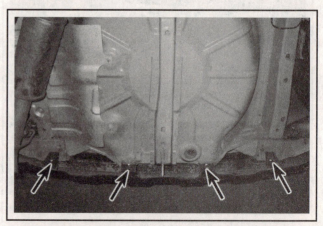

11.14 Remove the retainers from the underside of the rear bumper cover

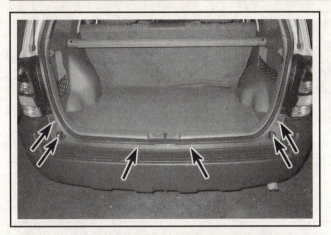

11.15 Remove the rear bumper cover mounting bolts

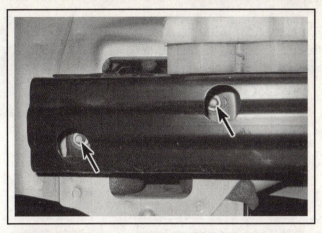

11.16a Remove the rear bumper mounting nuts from the right side . . .

13 Remove the rear bumper cover mounting screws from the quarter panel (see illustration).
14 Remove the pin-type retainers from below (see illustration).
15 Remove the rear bumper cover mounting bolts (see illustration),

then remove the cover.
16 Remove the rear bumper mounting nuts (see illustration).
17 Remove the rear bumper (see illustration).
18 Installation is the reverse of removal.

11.16b . . . and the left side of the vehicle

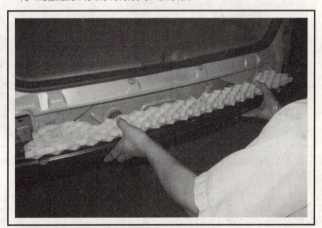

11.17 Remove the bumper from the vehicle

12 Front fender - removal and installation

▶ Refer to illustrations 12.3a, 12.3b, 12.3c, 12.6, 12.8, 12.9, 12.10a and 12.10b

1 Loosen the front wheel lug nuts. Raise the vehicle, support it securely on jackstands and remove the front wheel(s).
2 Remove the headlight housing (see Chapter 12).
3 Remove the inner fender splash shield (see illustration).

➡Note: The fender is fastened using either mounting screws or pin-type fasteners (see illustration).

4 Remove the sidemarker lights, if equipped (see Chapter 12).
5 If you're removing the passenger side fender, remove the radio antenna (see Chapter 12). If you're removing the driver side fender, remove the hood prop rod from the fender and prop the hood open.

4WD MODELS

6 Remove the fender molding (see illustration).

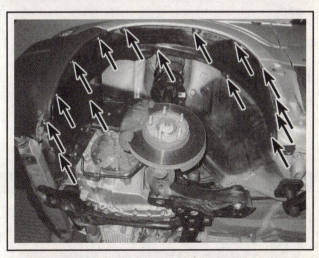

12.3a Remove the inner fender splash shield pin-type retainers and mounting screws

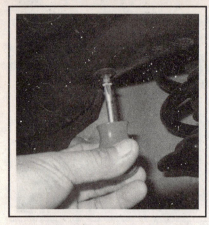

12.3b On pin-type retainers, loosen the center screw . . .

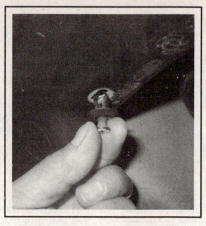

12.3c . . . then pop the assembly from the fenderwell

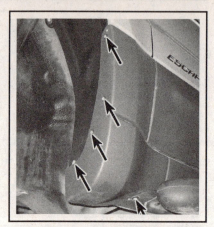

12.6 Remove the fender molding screws and detach the molding

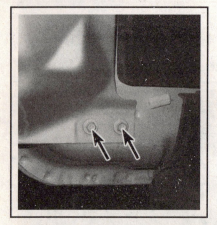

12.8 Location of the lower fender-to-body bolts

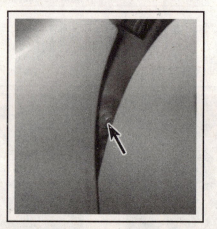

12.9 Remove the upper fender-to-body bolt

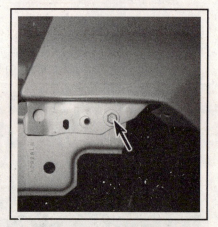

12.10a Location of the fender corner bolt

7 Remove the rocker panel molding.

➡Note: The rocker panel molding must be released from inside the door panel. Remove the door trim panel (see Section 15). The molding retainer clips are not reusable. Install new clips on reassembly.

ALL MODELS

8 Remove the lower fender-to-body bolts (see illustration).
9 Open the front door and remove the upper fender-to-body bolt (see illustration).
10 Remove the remaining fender mounting bolts (see illustrations).
11 Lift off the fender. It's a good idea to have an assistant support the fender while it's being moved away from the vehicle to prevent damage to the surrounding body panels.
12 Installation is the reverse of removal. Check the alignment of the fender to the hood and front edge of the door before final tightening of the fender fasteners.

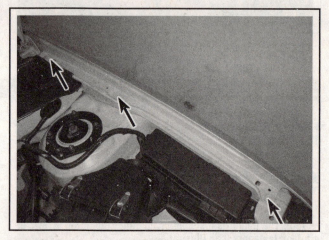

12.10b Remove the three bolts along the top of the fender

13 Radiator grille - removal and installation

♦ **Refer to illustrations 13.2 and 13.3**

1 Remove the front bumper cover (see Section 11).
2 Remove the radiator grille mounting nuts, if equipped (see illustration).

3 Release the radiator grille clips along the perimeter of the grille (see illustration). The retaining clips can be disengaged by simply pressing down on the tabs.
4 Pull the grille out and remove it.
5 Installation is the reverse of removal.

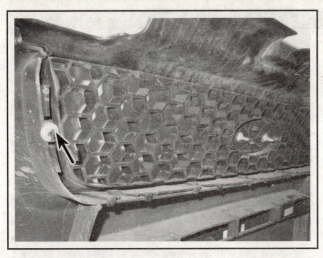

13.2 Location of the grille mounting nut - one on each side

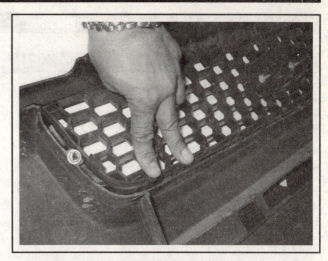

13.3 Press the radiator grille clips to release

14 Cowl cover and vent tray - removal and installation

▶ **Refer to illustrations 14.2a, 14.2b, 14.2c and 14.3**

1   Remove the wiper arms (see Chapter 12).

2   Remove the push pin fasteners and mounting screws securing the cowl cover (see illustrations).

➡**Note: Use a small screwdriver to pop the screw covers up to access the cowl cover mounting screws (see illustration).**

3   If the vent tray needs to be removed, first remove the wiper motor linkage assembly as described in Chapter 12, then remove the vent tray mounting bolts (see illustration).

4   Installation is the reverse of removal.

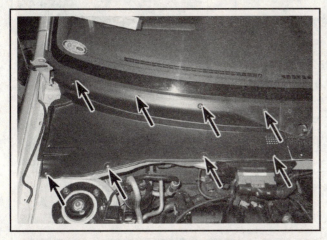

14.2a Location of the right cowl cover fasteners

14.2b Location of the left cowl cover fasteners

14.2c Remove the screw covers to access the upper fasteners

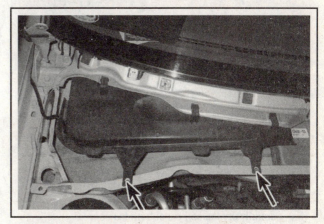

14.3 Location of the vent tray mounting screws

15 Door trim panels - removal and installation

REMOVAL

Front and rear doors

▶ Refer to illustrations 15.1a, 15.1b, 15.2, 15.3, 15.4a, 15.4b, 15.4c, 15.5, 15.6a, 15.6b, 15.7a, 15.7b and 15.7c

1   Remove the bezel from the door latch release handle (see illustrations).

2   Remove the screw from the door pull cup (see illustration).

3   On the rear door, remove the sail panel (see illustration).

4   Remove the door trim panel retaining screws (see illustrations), then carefully pry the panel out until the clips disengage (see illustration). Work slowly and carefully around the outer edge of the trim panel until it's free.

➡Note: The front doors use two screws to secure the door trim panels, one near the outer edge and one along the inside panel. The rear door panel is not secured with screws.

5   Using a screwdriver or trim panel tool, carefully pry around the perimeter of the panel to disengage the retaining clips (see illustration).

6   Unplug any wiring harness connectors (see illustrations) and remove the panel.

7   For access to the door outside handle or the door window regulator inside the door, raise the window fully, then carefully peel back the plastic watershield (see illustrations).

Liftgate

▶ Refer to illustrations 15.8 and 15.9

8   Remove the liftgate panel mounting screws (see illustration).

15.1a Remove the screw from the bezel . . .

15.1b . . . then remove the bezel from the handle

15.2 Remove the cup screw

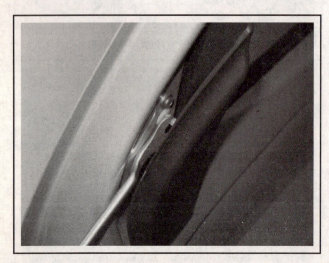

15.3 Carefully pry the sail panel from the door

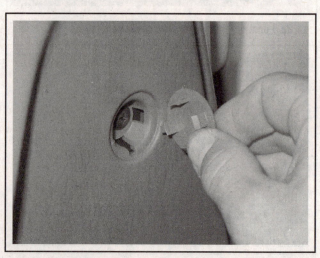

15.4a Carefully pry the screw cover off the door panel and remove the door panel mounting screw

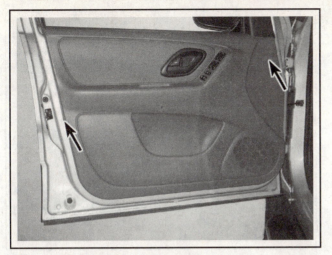

15.4b Location of the front door panel screws

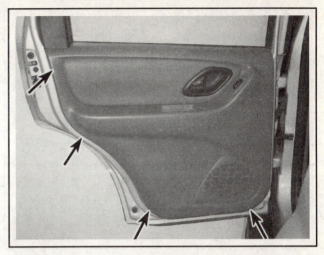

15.4c The rear door panel is not secured with mounting screws - carefully pry the door panel using a flat-bladed screwdriver or door panel tool until the door clips release

15.5 Using a panel tool, pry the door panel where the clips are located

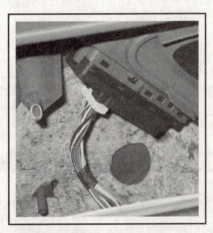

15.6a Unplug the door panel window and lock switch connector - front door shown

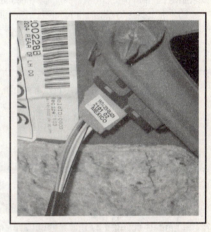

15.6b Unplug the rear door window and lock switch connector

15.7a Remove the door panel bracket screw

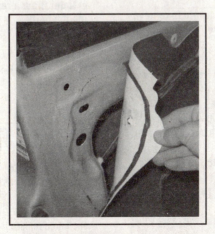

15.7b Peel back the plastic watershield

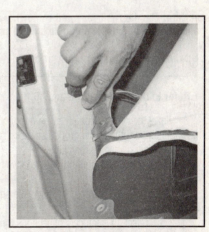

15.7c Use a scraper or razor blade to cut through the old sealant

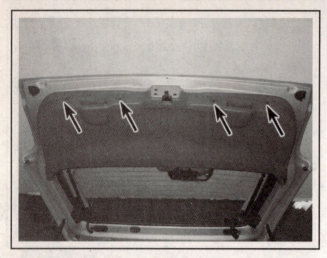

15.8 Remove the screws from the liftgate panel

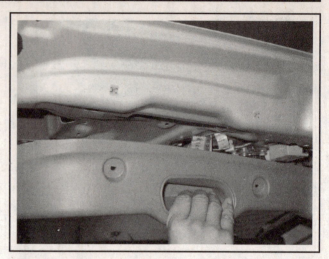

15.9 Lower the panel and separate it from the upper door rim

9   Using a screwdriver or trim panel tool, pry out the clips and remove the trim panel from the liftgate (see illustration).

10   For access to other components inside the door, carefully peel back the plastic watershield.

INSTALLATION

11   Prior to installation of the door trim panel, be sure to reinstall any clips in the panel which may have come out when you removed the panel.

12   Position the wire harness connectors for the power door lock switch and the power window switch (if equipped) on the back of the panel, then place the panel in position in the door. Press the door panel into place until the clips are seated.

13   The remainder of the installation is the reverse of removal.

16 Door - removal, installation and adjustment

✳✳ WARNING:

The models covered by this manual are equipped with Supplemental Restraint systems (SRS), more commonly known as airbags. Always disarm the airbag system before working in the vicinity of any airbag system component to avoid the possibility of accidental deployment of the airbag, which could cause personal injury (see Chapter 12).

➡Note: The door is heavy and somewhat awkward to remove and install - at least two people should perform this procedure.

REMOVAL AND INSTALLATION

▶ **Refer to illustrations 16.6 and 16.8**

1   Raise the window completely in the door. Open the door all the way and support it from the ground on jacks or blocks covered with rags to prevent damaging the paint.

2   Disconnect the cable from the negative battery terminal (see Chapter 5).

3   Remove the door trim panel and watershield as described in Section 15.

4   Disconnect all electrical connections, ground wires and harness retaining clips from the door.

➡Note: It is a good idea to label all connections to aid the reassembly process.

5   From the door side, detach the rubber conduit between the body and the door. Then pull the wiring harness through the conduit hole and remove it from the door.

6   Remove the door stop strut bolt(s) (see illustration).

7   Mark around the door hinges with a pen or a scribe to facilitate realignment during reassembly.

8   With an assistant holding the door, remove the hinge-to-door bolts (see illustration) and lift the door off.

➡Note: Draw a reference line around the hinges before removing the bolts.

9   Installation is the reverse of removal.

10   Reconnect the battery. After you're done, the Powertrain Control Module (PCM) must relearn its idle and fuel trim strategy for optimum driveability and performance (see Chapter 5, Section 1).

ADJUSTMENT

▶ **Refer to illustration 16.14**

11   Having proper door-to-body alignment is a critical part of a well-functioning door assembly. First check the door hinge pins for excessive play. Fully open the door and lift up and down on the door without lifting the body. If a door has 1/16-inch or more play, the hinges should be replaced.

12   Door-to-body alignment adjustments are made by loosening the hinge-to-body bolts or hinge-to-door bolts and moving the door. Proper body alignment is achieved when the top of the doors are paral-

16.6 Remove the bolt from the door stop strut

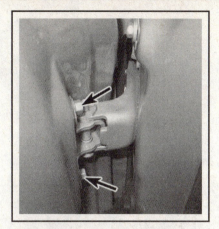

16.8 Remove the door hinge bolts with the door supported (bottom hinge similar)

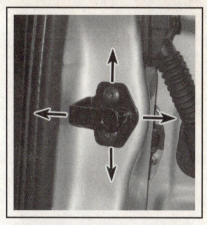

16.14 Adjust the door lock striker by loosening the mounting screws and gently tapping the striker in the desired direction

lel with the roof section, the front door is flush with the fender, the rear door is flush with the rear quarter panel and the bottom of the doors are aligned with the lower rocker panel. If these goals can't be reached by adjusting the hinge-to-body or hinge-to-door bolts, body alignment shims may have to be purchased and inserted behind the hinges to achieve correct alignment.

13 To adjust the door-closed position, scribe a line or mark around the striker plate to provide a reference point, then check that the door latch is contacting the center of the latch striker. If not adjust the up and down position first.

14 Finally adjust the latch striker sideways position, so that the door panel is flush when closed and provides positive engagement with the latch mechanism (see illustration).

17 Door latch, lock cylinder and handles - removal and installation

✳ CAUTION:

Wear gloves when working inside the door openings to protect against cuts from sharp metal edges.

FRONT HANDLES AND DOOR LATCH ASSEMBLY

▶ **Refer to illustrations 17.2, 17.3, 17.4a, 17.4b, 17.5, 17.6, 17.7, 17.8, 17.10, 17.11a and 17.11b**

1 Raise the window, then remove the door trim panel and watershield (see Section 15).

2 Working inside the door, remove the screw that secures the door latch assembly (see illustration).

3 Remove the door handle cover from the exterior of the door (see illustration).

✳ CAUTION:

Take care not to scratch the paint on the outside of the door. Wide masking tape applied around the handle opening before beginning the procedure can help avoid scratches.

4 Remove the door handle by sliding it toward the rear of the vehicle (see illustrations).

5 Working inside the door panel, remove the screw (see illustra-

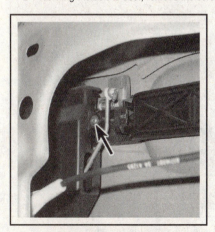

17.2 Loosen this door latch screw

17.3 Remove the door handle cover

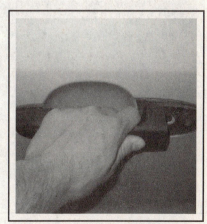

17.4a Slide the door handle toward the rear of the vehicle to remove it . . .

17.4b . . . and remove the rubber insulators

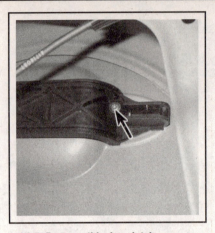

17.5 Remove this door latch assembly screw

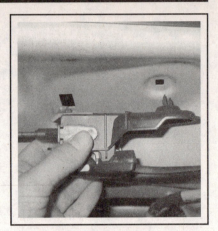

17.6 Pull the door handle from the door

17.7 Remove the door latch screws (install new ones when reinstalling the latch)

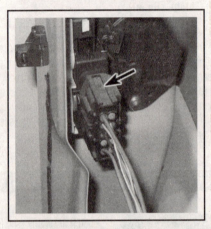

17.8 Release the clip and disconnect the electrical connector

17.10 Remove the anti-theft guard assembly from the latch

tion) and loosen the remote control assembly.

6 Release the clip and position the interior door handle to the side (see illustration).

7 Remove the door latch screws (see illustration). The door latch screws must not be reused. Always install new door latch screws on reassembly.

8 Disconnect the door latch electrical connector (see illustration).

9 Slide the door latch remote control assembly toward the front of the vehicle.

10 Remove the anti-theft guard from the latch assembly (see illustration).

11 Release the clip and and disconnect the exterior door handle actuating rod (see illustrations).

12 Installation is the reverse of removal.

17.11a Release the clip . . .

17.11b . . . then remove the actuating rod from the door handle

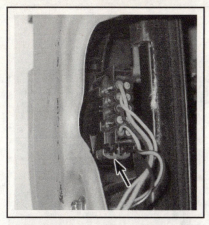

17.14 Release the clip for the electrical connector and unplug it from the door latch assembly

17.15 Remove the screws on the door glass top run

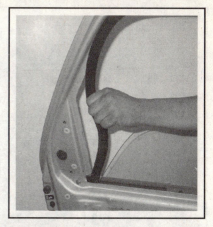

17.16 Lift the door glass top run from the door

REAR HANDLES AND DOOR LATCH ASSEMBLY

▶ **Refer to illustrations 17.14, 17.15, 17.16, 17.18, 17.19, 17.21, 17.22, 17.24a, 17.24b, 17.25a and 17.25b**

13 Raise the window, then remove the door trim panel and watershield (see Section 15).

14 Remove the electrical connector from the rear door latch (see illustration).

15 Remove the bolts that retain the door glass top run (see illustration).

16 Separate the door glass top run from the door (see illustration).

17 Remove the door handle screws from inside the door panel.

18 Remove the cover from the outside of the door (see illustration).

✳✳ CAUTION:

Take care not to scratch the paint on the outside of the door. Wide masking tape applied around the handle opening before beginning the procedure can help avoid scratches.

19 Remove the door handle by sliding it toward the rear of the vehicle (see illustration).

20 Working inside the door panel, remove the screw and loosen the

17.18 Remove the cover from the rear door handle

remote control assembly.

21 Disconnect the door handle actuating rod (see illustration).

22 Remove the door latch screws (see illustration). The door latch screws must not be reused. Always install new door latch screws on reassembly.

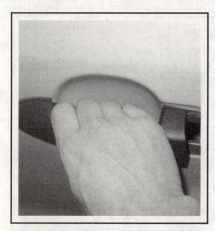

17.19 Slide the door handle toward the rear of the vehicle

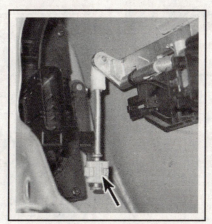

17.21 Release the clip from the actuating rod

17.22 Remove the door latch screws but do not reuse them

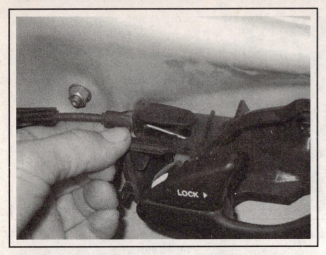

17.24a Release the door handle cable conduit by lifting . . .

23 Remove the rear door latch.
24 Release the cable conduit and disconnect the interior door handle cable (see illustrations).

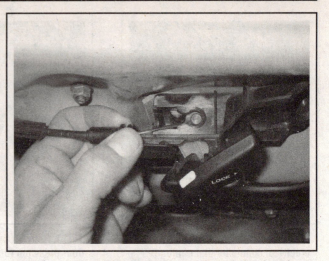

17.24b . . . then sliding the cable end through the slotted portion of the handle casting

25 Remove the rear door handle assembly (see illustrations).
26 Installation is the reverse of removal.

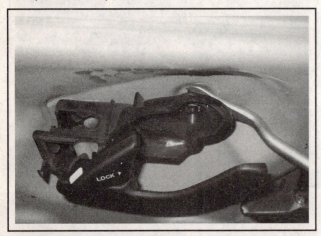

17.25a Pry the door handle clips . . .

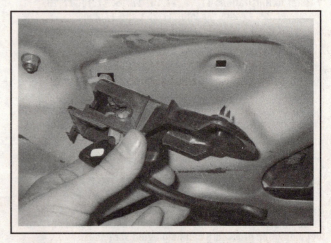

17.25b . . . and separate the door handle from the door

18 Door window glass - removal and installation

�֎ CAUTION:

Wear gloves when working inside the door openings to protect against cuts from sharp metal edges.

FRONT DOOR GLASS

▶ **Refer to illustrations 18.3, 18.4 and 18.6**

1 Remove the door trim panel and the plastic watershield (see Section 15).
2 Lower the window glass all the way down into the door.
3 Remove the weatherstrip from the front door interior glass channel (see illustration).
4 Raise the window just enough to access the window retaining bolts through the holes in the door frame (see illustration).

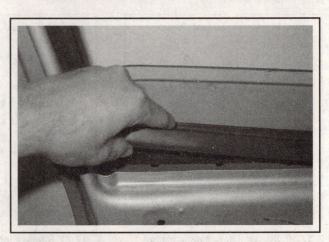

18.3 Remove the weatherstrip from the front door glass channel

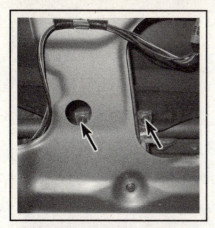

18.4 Access the window retaining bolts through the holes in the door frame

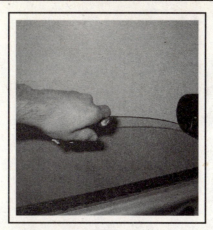

18.6 Lift the window glass from the door

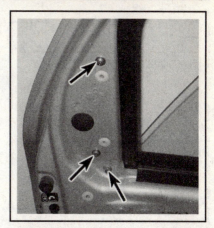

18.11 Remove the exterior sail panel mounting screws

5   Place a rag over the glass to help prevent scratching the glass and remove the two glass mounting bolts.

6   Remove the glass by pulling it up and out (see illustration).

7   Installation is the reverse of removal.

REAR DOOR GLASS

♦ **Refer to illustrations 18.11, 18.12, 18.13, 18.14 and 18.16**

8   Remove the door panel and watershield (see Section 15).

9   Remove the door window regulator (see Section 19).

10 Lower the window glass all the way down into the door.

11 Remove the interior sail panel (see illustration 15.3) and the exterior sail panel (see illustration).

12 Remove the weatherstrip from the rear door glass channel (see illustration).

13 Remove the door belt line molding (see illustration).

14 Remove the door glass top run mounting bolts (see illustration).

15 Position the door glass down and forward, tilting it slightly.

16 Remove the door glass top run (see illustration).

17 Remove the glass by pulling it up and out.

18 Installation is the reverse of the removal procedure.

LIFTGATE GLASS

♦ **Refer to illustrations 18.19, 18.20, 18.21, 18.22a, 18.22b and 18.23**

19 Open the liftgate and remove the two rubber access covers (see illustration).

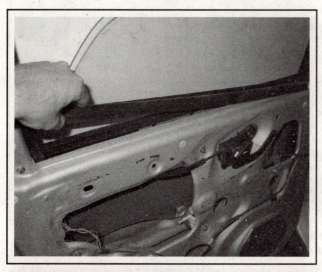

18.12 Remove the weatherstrip from the rear door glass channel

18.13 Remove the door belt line molding piece

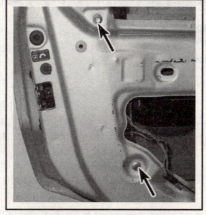

18.14 Remove the bolts that retain the door glass top run

18.16 Lift the door glass top run from the door interior

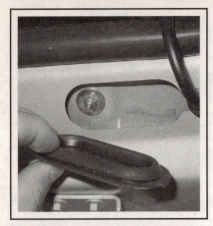

18.19 Remove the rubber access cover and slide the harness from the slotted portion of the access hole

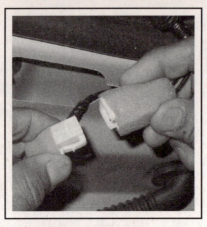

18.20 Disconnect the liftgate electrical connector

18.21 Disconnect the heated grid wire

20 Disconnect the liftgate electrical connector (see illustration).

21 Disconnect the heated grid wire electrical connector (see illustration).

22 Have an assistant support the liftgate and remove the two liftgate support struts (see illustrations).

23 Remove the two liftgate window hinge nuts (see illustration).

24 Installation is the reverse of removal.

18.22a Using the tip of a small screwdriver, pry the release clip . . .

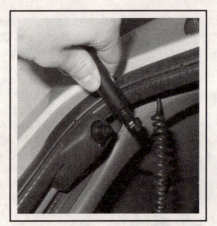

18.22b . . . and slide the the connector forward and off the ballstud

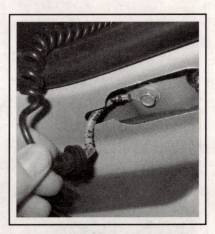

18.23 Location of the liftgate hinge nut on the left side of the vehicle

19 Door window glass regulator - removal and installation

☀ CAUTION:

Wear gloves when working inside the door openings to protect against cuts from sharp metal edges.

FRONT

1 Remove the door trim panel and the plastic watershield (see Section 15).

2 Lower the window glass all the way down.

Power window regulator

▶ **Refer to illustrations 19.6 and 19.7**

3 Disconnect the cable from the negative battery terminal (see Chapter 5).

4 Remove the screws that retain the door window glass (see illustration 18.4).

5 Lift the door glass and have an assistant hold the door glass upright.

6 Disconnect the electrical connector from the window regulator motor (see illustration).

7 Remove the regulator/motor assembly mounting bolts (see illustration).

8 Remove the window regulator/motor assembly from the door.

9 Reconnect the battery. After you're done, the Powertrain Control Module (PCM) must relearn its idle and fuel trim strategy for optimum driveability and performance (see Chapter 5, Section 1).

10 Installation is the reverse of removal. Lubricate the rollers and wear points on the regulator with white grease before installation.

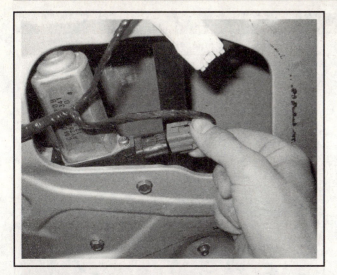

19.6 Disconnect the window regulator motor connector

19.7 Location of the window regulator/motor mounting bolts

Manual window regulator

11 Remove the five mounting bolts and nuts and remove the regulator assembly through the service hole in the door frame.

12 Installation is the reverse of removal. Lubricate the rollers and wear points on the regulator with white grease before installation.

REAR
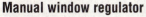

13 Remove the door trim panel and the plastic watershield (see Section 15).

14 Lower the window glass all the way down.

Power window regulator

▶ **Refer to illustrations 19.16 and 19.19**

15 Disconnect the cable from the negative battery terminal (see Chapter 5).

16 Remove the screws that retain the door window glass (see illustration).

17 Lift the door glass and have an assistant hold the door glass upright.

18 Disconnect the electrical connector from the window regulator motor.

19 Remove the regulator/motor assembly mounting bolts (see illustration).

20 Remove the window regulator/motor assembly from the door.

21 Installation is the reverse of removal. Lubricate the rollers and wear points on the regulator with white grease before installation.

22 Reconnect the battery. After you're done, the Powertrain Control Module (PCM) must relearn its idle and fuel trim strategy for optimum driveability and performance (see Chapter 5, Section 1).

Manual window regulator

23 Remove the five mounting bolts and nuts and remove the regulator assembly through the service hole in the door frame.

24 Installation is the reverse of removal. Lubricate the rollers and wear points on the regulator with white grease before installation.

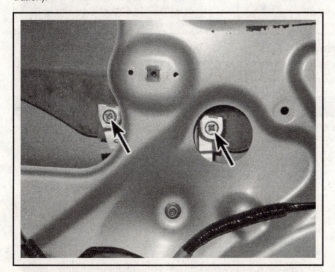

19.16 Location of the rear window glass mounting bolts

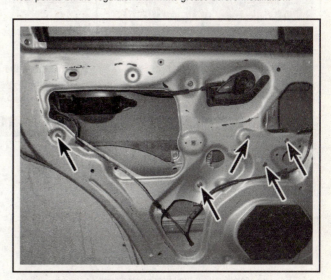

19.19 Location of the power window regulator/motor mounting bolts

20 Mirrors - removal and installation

OUTSIDE MIRRORS

◆ **Refer to illustrations 20.2, 20.4 and 20.5**

1   Remove the front door trim panel (see Section 15).

2   Remove the front door interior sail panel (see illustration).

3   Disconnect the speaker electrical connector, if equipped (see Chapter 12).

4   Disconnect the electrical connector from the mirror (see illustration).

5   Remove the three mirror retaining bolts and detach the mirror from the vehicle (see illustration).

6   Installation is the reverse of removal.

INSIDE MIRROR

◆ **Refer to illustration 20.8**

7   Disconnect the auto-dimmer electrical connector, if equipped.

8   Pry the tension clip at the base of the mirror stalk with a screwdriver (see illustration). Push the screwdriver out, using leverage to release the mirror from the bracket.

9   To install the mirror, insert the mirror into the bracket, pushing downward until the mirror is secured.

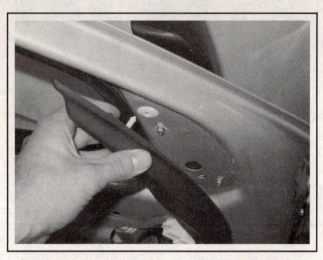

20.2 Pry the front door interior sail panel with a panel tool or flat-bladed screwdriver and separate it from the door

10 If the mount plate itself has come off the windshield, adhesive kits are available at auto parts stores to resecure it. Follow the instructions included with the kit.

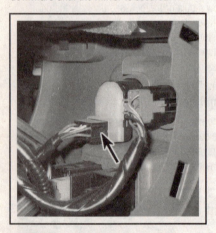

20.4 Disconnect the power mirror electrical connector

20.5 Remove the mirror retaining bolts

20.8 Use a screwdriver to release the mirror clip

21 Liftgate - removal, installation and adjustment

➡**Note: The back door is heavy and somewhat awkward to remove and install - at least two people should perform this procedure.**

REMOVAL AND INSTALLATION

◆ **Refer to illustrations 21.3a, 21.3b, 21.4a, 21.4b and 21.6**

1   Have an assistant hold the liftgate in the open position.

2   Disconnect all electrical connections, ground wires and harness retaining clips from the liftgate.

➡**Note: It is a good idea to label all connections to aid the reassembly process.**

3   From the liftgate side, detach the rubber conduit between the body and the liftgate (see illustrations). Then pull the wiring harness through the conduit hole and remove it from the liftgate.

4   Remove the liftgate support struts (see illustrations).

5   Mark around the liftgate hinges with a pen or a scribe to facilitate realignment during reassembly.

6   With an assistant holding the liftgate, remove the hinge-to-liftgate bolts and lift the door off (see illustration).

➡**Note: Draw a reference line around the hinges before removing the bolts.**

7   Installation is the reverse of removal.

21.3a Detach the rubber conduit from the door cavities to expose the wiring harness

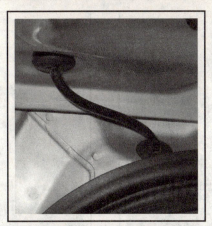

21.3b Remove the rubber conduit from the body and the liftgate to expose the heater grid ground wire

21.4a Release the clip and slide it forward to release the liftgate support strut from the ballstud (lower strut clip shown)

ADJUSTMENT

▶ **Refer to illustration 21.11**

8 Having proper liftgate-to-body alignment is a critical part of a well-functioning liftgate assembly. First check the liftgate hinge pins for excessive play. Fully open the liftgate and move it side-to-side. If it has 1/16-inch or more play, the hinges should be replaced.

9 Liftgate-to-body alignment adjustments are made by loosening the hinge-to-body bolts or hinge-to-liftgate bolts and moving the door. Proper body alignment is achieved when the top of the liftgate is paral-

lel with the roof section, the sides of the liftgate are flush with the rear quarter panels and the bottom of the liftgate is aligned with the lower sill panel. If these goals can't be reached by adjusting the hinge-to-body or hinge-to-liftgate bolts, body alignment shims may have to be purchased and inserted behind the hinges to achieve correct alignment.

10 To adjust the liftgate-closed position, scribe a line or mark around the striker plate to provide a reference point, then check that the liftgate latch is contacting the center of the latch striker. If not adjust the up and down position first.

11 Finally adjust the latch striker sideways position, so that the liftgate panel is flush with the rear quarter panel and provides positive engagement with the latch mechanism (see illustration).

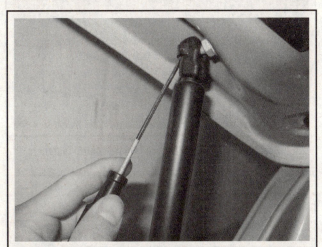

21.4b Release the upper support strut clip and release it from the ballstud

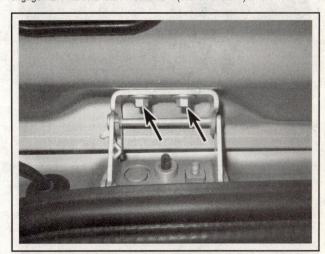

21.6 Location of the hinge-to-liftgate bolts

22 Liftgate latch remote control, latch and window latch - removal and installation

LIFTGATE LATCH REMOTE CONTROL

▶ **Refer to illustrations 22.2a, 22.2b, 22.3 and 22.4**

1 Open the liftgate and remove the trim panel and watershield as described in Section 15.

2 Disconnect the actuating rods from the liftgate latch remote control (see illustrations).

➡**Note: All door lock rods are attached by plastic clips. The plastic clips can be removed by unsnapping the portion engaging the connecting rod and then pulling the rod out of its locating hole.**

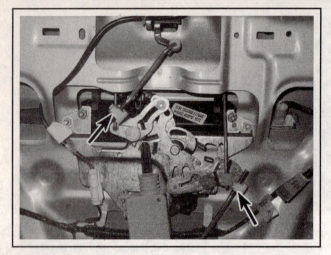

22.2a Disconnect the actuating rods from the liftgate latch remote control

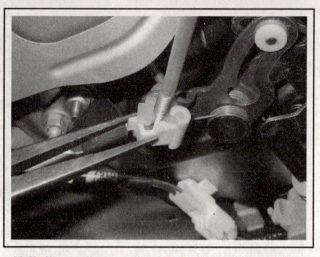

22.2b Use needle-nose pliers to release the locking tab from the clip

3   Remove the liftgate latch remote control electrical connectors (see illustration).
4   Remove the screw and nuts securing the latch to the door (see

illustration). Remove the latch assembly through the door opening.
5   Installation is the reverse of removal.

22.3 Remove the liftgate latch remote control connectors

22.4 Location of the liftgate latch remote control fasteners

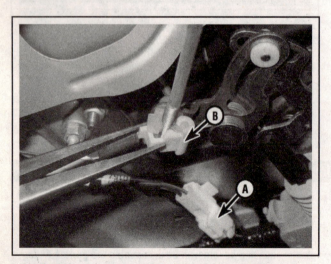

22.7 Disconnect the liftgate window ajar switch (A) and release the actuating rod from the window latch (B)

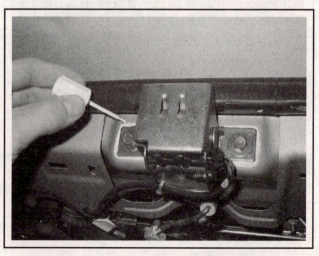

22.9 Mark the location of the liftgate window latch

LIFTGATE LATCH AND WINDOW LATCH

♦ **Refer to illustrations 22.7 and 22.9**

6   Open the back door and remove the door trim panel and watershield as described in Section 15.

7   Disconnect the liftgate window ajar switch (see illustration).

8   Disconnect the liftgate window latch actuating rod (see illustration 22.7).

9   Mark the location of the liftgate window latch to insure correct alignment (see illustration).

10 Remove the liftgate window latch mounting bolts. Separate the assembly from the liftgate.

11 Remove the liftgate latch mounting bolts and the liftgate latch.

12 The remainder of the installation is the reverse of removal.

23 Center console - removal and installation

✷✷ WARNING:

The models covered by this manual are equipped with Supplemental Restraint systems (SRS), more commonly known as airbags. Always disarm the airbag system before working in the vicinity of any airbag system component to avoid the possibility of accidental deployment of the airbag, which could cause personal injury (see Chapter 12).

23.3 Remove the finish panel from the console by carefully lifting the edges out of the locking tabs

AUTOMATIC TRANSAXLE MODELS

♦ **Refer to illustrations 23.3, 23.4a, 23.4b, 23.5 and 23.6**

1   Disconnect the cable from the negative battery terminal (see Chapter 5).

2   Raise the emergency brake handle.

3   Remove the floor console finish panel from the console (see illustration).

4   Remove the front bolts from the floor console (see illustrations).

5   Remove the bolts from the rear section of the center console (see illustration).

6   Lift the center console from the vehicle (see illustration).

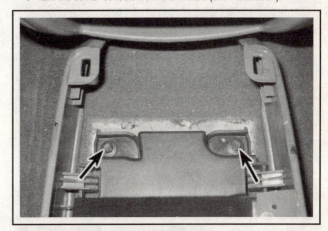

23.4a Location of the floor console front bolts

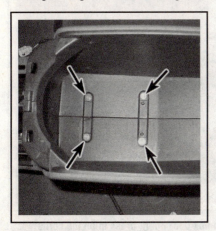

23.4b Location of the floor console interior mounting bolts

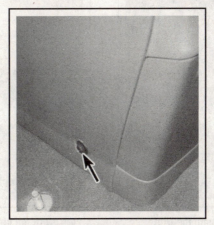

23.5 Location of the floor console rear bolts - one on each side

23.6 Lift the center console from the vehicle

7 Installation is the reverse of removal.

8 Reconnect the battery. After you're done, the Powertrain Control Module (PCM) must relearn its idle and fuel trim strategy for optimum driveability and performance (see Chapter 5, Section 1).

MANUAL TRANSAXLE MODELS

9 Remove the manual transaxle shift knob from the shift lever (see Chapter 7A).

10 Remove the floor console front finish panel.

11 Raise the parking brake handle.

12 Remove the floor console rear finish panel.

13 Remove the floor console front and rear bolts.

14 Lift the center console from the vehicle.

15 Installation is the reverse of removal.

24 Dashboard trim panels

✳✳ WARNING:

The models covered by this manual are equipped with Supplemental Restraint systems (SRS), more commonly known as airbags. Always disarm the airbag system before working in the vicinity of any airbag system component to avoid the possibility of accidental deployment of the airbag, which could cause personal injury (see Chapter 12).

INSTRUMENT CLUSTER BEZEL

▶ **Refer to illustration 24.3**

1 Disconnect the cable from the negative battery terminal (see Chapter 5).

2 Remove the steering wheel (see Chapter 10).

3 Remove the screws at the top of the instrument cluster bezel (see illustration).

4 Grasp the bezel with both hands and pull straight out to disengage the bezel from the instrument panel.

5 Installation is the reverse of the removal procedure. Make sure the clips are engaged properly before pushing the bezel firmly into place.

6 Reconnect the battery. After you're done, the Powertrain Control Module (PCM) must relearn its idle and fuel trim strategy for optimum driveability and performance (see Chapter 5, Section 1).

24.3 Remove the screws from the top of the instrument cluster bezel

LOWER TRIM PANEL

▶ **Refer to illustration 24.7**

7 Release the locking tabs from the upper latches, swing the trim panel down and remove it from the instrument panel (see illustration).

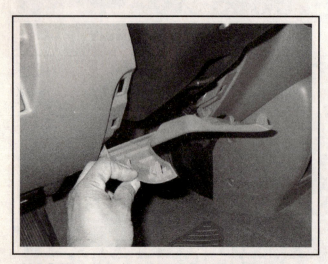

24.7 Release the upper locking tabs and swing the trim panel down

24.9 With the glove box door open, press in on the corner tabs and pull down to drop the door

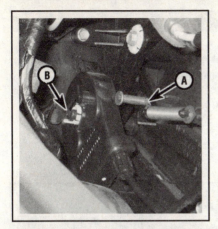

24.10 Drop the lever, install a dowel into the lock position (A) and release the temperature control cable assembly by pulling the release tab (B) away from the selector shaft

24.11 Remove the climate control knobs from the control assembly

24.12 Use a panel tool to pry the center trim panel from the instrument panel

CENTER TRIM PANEL

8   Disconnect the cable from the negative battery terminal (see Chapter 5).

9   Open the glove box door. Press the release tabs toward the interior of the glove box while pulling down on the door (see illustration).

10 Disconnect the temperature control cable from the heater/air conditioner housing (see illustration).

11 Remove the climate control knobs from the center control assembly (see illustration).

12 Use a panel tool to pry the center trim panel out slightly (see illustration).

13 Disconnect the electrical connectors from the accessories (see illustration).

➡**Note: It will be necessary to pull the center trim panel out**

slightly to gain access to the remaining electrical connectors.

14 Remove the climate control assembly mounting screws (see illustration).

15 Remove the center trim panel from the dash area.

16 Installation is the reverse of removal. Make sure the clips are engaged properly before pushing the bezel firmly into place.

17 Reconnect the battery. After you're done, the Powertrain Control Module (PCM) must relearn its idle and fuel trim strategy for optimum driveability and performance (see Chapter 5, Section 1).

GLOVE BOX

18 Open the glove box and squeeze the sides in to allow the compartment to drop, then remove the mounting screws (see illustration 24.9).

24.13 Disconnect the electrical connectors from the center trim panel control assembly

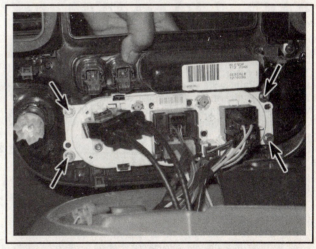

24.14 Location of the climate control assembly mounting screws

25 Steering column covers - removal and installation

▶ Refer to illustrations 25.2a and 25.2b

✳✳ WARNING:

The models covered by this manual are equipped with Supplemental Restraint systems (SRS), more commonly known as airbags. Always disarm the airbag system before working in the vicinity of any airbag system component to avoid the possibility of accidental deployment of the airbag, which could cause personal injury (see Chapter 12).

1   On tilt steering columns, move the column to the lowest position. Refer to Chapter 12 and remove the ignition key lock cylinder.

2   Remove the screws, then separate the halves and remove the upper and lower steering column covers (see illustrations).

3   Installation is the reverse of the removal procedure.

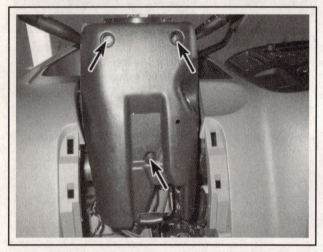

25.2a Location of the steering column cover screws

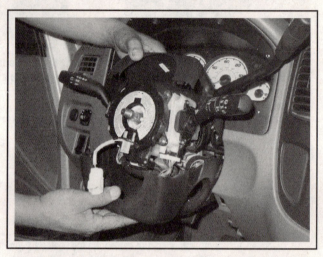

25.2b Separate the upper and lower steering column covers (steering wheel removed for clarity)

26 Instrument panel - removal and installation

▶ Refer to illustrations 26.6, 26.7a. 26.7b, 26.8, 26.10, 26.14, 26.15, 26.16, 26.17, 26.22a, 26.22b, 26.23, 26.24, 26.27a, 26.27b, 26.28a and 26.28b

✳✳ WARNING:

The models covered by this manual are equipped with Supplemental Restraint systems (SRS), more commonly known as airbags. Always disarm the airbag system before working in the vicinity of any airbag system component to avoid the possibility of accidental deployment of the airbag, which could cause personal injury (see Chapter 12).

1   Disconnect the cable from the negative battery terminal (see Chapter 5).

2   On tilt steering columns, move the column to the lowest position. Refer to Chapter 10 and remove the steering wheel.

3   Remove the passenger's side airbag (see Chapter 12).

4   Remove the audio unit from the center of the dashboard (see Chapter 12).

5   Remove the heater/air conditioner control assembly (see Chapter 3).

6   Remove the pin-type retainers from the front door scuff plates (see illustration).

7   Remove the pin-type retainers from the A-pillar lower trim panels (see illustration), then remove the panels.

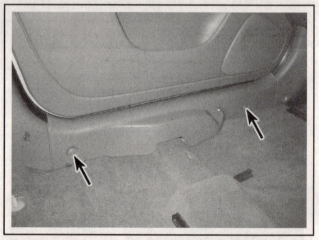

26.6 Remove the front door scuff plate fasteners and covers from the driver's and passenger's side of the vehicle

8   Disconnect the instrument panel harness connectors located by the cowl (see illustration).

9   Remove the hood latch bolts and position the assembly off to the side without disconnecting the cable (see Section 10).

10 Remove the utility compartment (see illustration).

11 Remove the steering column covers (see Section 25).

26.7a Remove the fasteners from the A-pillar lower trim panels - left side shown

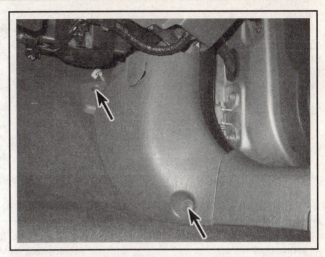

26.7b Right side A-pillar trim panel fasteners

12 On manual transaxle models, disconnect the shift cable (see Chapter 7).

13 Disconnect the steering column intermediate shaft U-joint (see Chapter 10).

14 Remove the cover panel (see illustration).

15 Disconnect the harness connectors (see illustration).

26.8 Location of the instrument panel connectors

26.10 Remove the utility compartment mounting screws - two each side

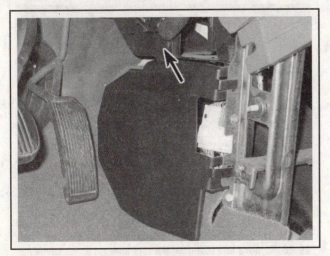

26.14 Remove the cover panel fastener

26.15 Disconnect the instrument panel connectors below the center dash

26.16 Disconnect the vacuum harness connector

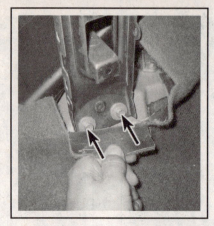

26.17 Remove the instrument panel center brace mounting bolts

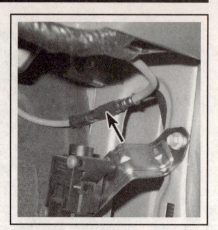

26.21 Disconnect the antenna connector

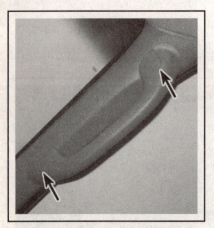

26.22a Remove the screw covers . . .

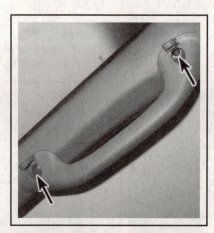

26.22b . . . and remove the A-pillar assist handle mounting bolts

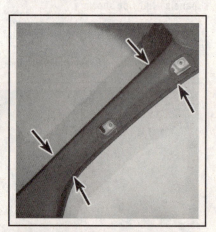

26.23 Remove the garnish molding by prying the edges with a panel tool

16 Disconnect the climate control vacuum harness (see illustration).
17 Remove the instrument panel center brace (see illustration).
18 Disconnect the temperature control cable from the heater/air con-

ditioner assembly (see Section 24).

19 Press the glove box tabs toward the interior of the glove box and pull the door down (see Section 24).

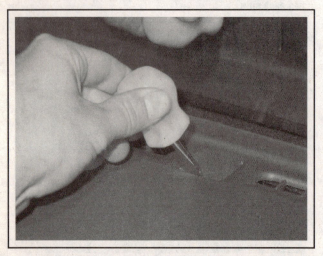

26.24 Pry off this cover from the center of the instrument panel and remove the bolt underneath

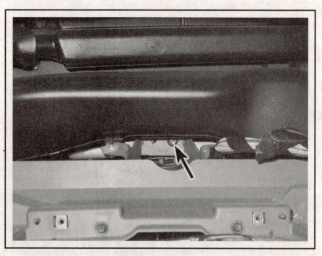

26.26 Remove this bolt from the instrument cluster cavity

26.27a Remove the finish panel from the left . . .

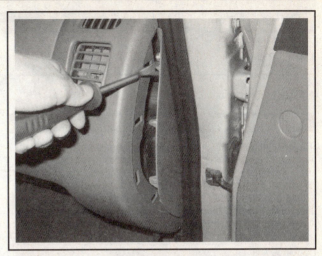

26.27b . . . and right side of the instrument panel

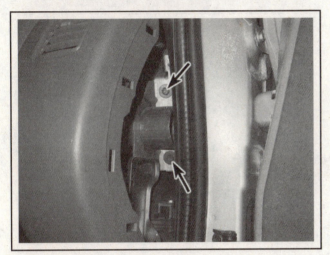

26.28a Remove the bolts from the support structure on the left . . .

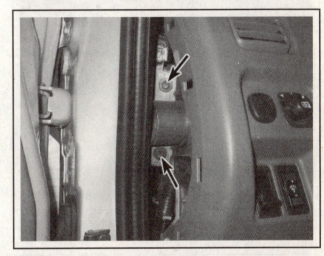

26.28b . . . and right side of the instrument panel

20 Disconnect the blower electrical connectors (see Chapter 3).

21 Disconnect the interior antenna cable connection (see illustration).

22 Remove the A-pillar passenger assist handle (see illustrations).

23 Remove the windshield side garnish moldings (see illustration).

24 Remove the small cover from the center of the instrument panel (near the windshield), then unscrew the bolt (see illustration).

25 Remove the instrument cluster (see Chapter 12).

26 Working in the instrument cluster cavity, remove the instrument panel bolt (see illustration).

27 Remove the finish panels from each side of the instrument panel (see illustrations).

28 Remove the instrument panel mounting bolts from the support structure (see illustrations).

29 Remove the center floor console (see Section 23).

30 Remove the lower trim panel (see Section 24). Then detach the bolts securing the steering column and lower it away from the instrument panel (see Chapter 10).

31 A number of electrical connectors must be disconnected in order to remove the instrument panel. Most are designed so that they will only fit on the matching connector (male or female), but if there is any doubt, mark the connectors with masking tape and a marking pen before disconnecting them.

32 Once all the fasteners are removed, lift the instrument panel then pull it away from the windshield and take it out through the driver's door opening.

➡ **Note: This is a two-person job.**

33 Installation is the reverse of removal.

27 Seats - removal and installation

FRONT SEAT

▶ **Refer to illustrations 27.2a, 27.2b and 27.3**

❋❋ **WARNING:**

These vehicles are equipped with side-impact airbags located in the outboard sides of the front seat backs, and most models are also equipped with seat belt pre-tensioners, which are also explosive devices. Always disarm the airbag system before working in the vicinity of any airbag system component to avoid the possibility of accidental deployment of the airbag, which could cause personal injury (see Chapter 12).

1 Pry out the plastic covers to access the seat tracks and their mounting bolts.
2 Remove the retaining bolts (see illustrations).
3 Tilt the seat upward to access the underside, then disconnect any electrical connectors (see illustration) and lift the seat from the vehicle.
4 Installation is the reverse of removal.

REAR SEAT

▶ **Refer to illustration 27.6**

5 Fold the seat forward.
6 Remove the hinge retaining bolts and detach the seat from the vehicle (see illustration).
7 Installation is the reverse of removal.

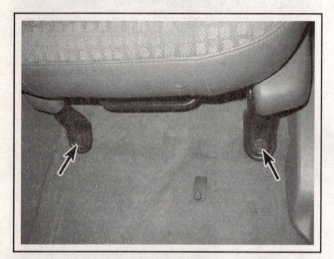

27.2a Location of the forward mounting bolts

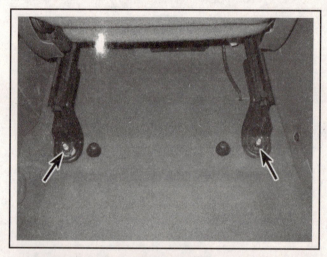

27.2b Location of the rear mounting bolts

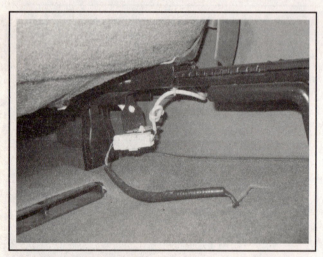

27.3 Disconnect any electrical connectors under the seat

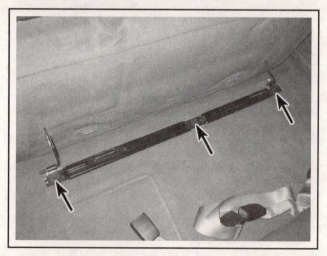

27.6 Location of the rear seat hinge bolts

Section

12

CHASSIS ELECTRICAL SYSTEM

1 General information

The electrical system is a 12-volt, negative ground type. Power for the lights and all electrical accessories is supplied by a lead/acid-type battery, which is charged by the alternator.

This Chapter covers repair and service procedures for the various electrical components not associated with the engine. Information on the battery, alternator and starter motor can be found in Chapter 5.

It should be noted that when portions of the electrical system are serviced, the negative battery cable should be disconnected from the battery to prevent electrical shorts and/or fires.

2 Electrical troubleshooting - general information

▶ **Refer to illustrations 2.5a and 2.5b**

1   A typical electrical circuit consists of an electrical component, any switches, relays, motors, fuses, fusible links or circuit breakers related to that component and the wiring and connectors that link the component to both the battery and the chassis. To help you pinpoint an electrical circuit problem, wiring diagrams are included at the end of this Chapter.

2   Before tackling any troublesome electrical circuit, first study the appropriate wiring diagrams to get a complete understanding of what makes up that individual circuit. Trouble spots, for instance, can often be narrowed down by noting if other components related to the circuit are operating properly. If several components or circuits fail at one time, chances are the problem is in a fuse or ground connection, because several circuits are often routed through the same fuse and ground connections.

3   Electrical problems usually stem from simple causes, such as loose or corroded connections, a blown fuse, a melted fusible link or a failed relay. Visually inspect the condition of all fuses, wires and connections in a problem circuit before troubleshooting the circuit.

4   If test equipment and instruments are going to be utilized, use the diagrams to plan ahead of time where you will make the necessary connections in order to accurately pinpoint the trouble spot.

5   The basic tools needed for electrical troubleshooting include a circuit tester or voltmeter (a 12-volt bulb with a set of test leads can also be used), a continuity tester, which includes a bulb, battery and set of test leads, and a jumper wire, preferably with a circuit breaker incorporated, which can be used to bypass electrical components (see illustrations). Before attempting to locate a problem with test instruments, use the wiring diagram(s) to decide where to make the connections.

VOLTAGE CHECKS

▶ **Refer to illustration 2.6**

6   Voltage checks should be performed if a circuit is not functioning properly. Connect one lead of a circuit tester to either the negative battery terminal or a known good ground. Connect the other lead to a

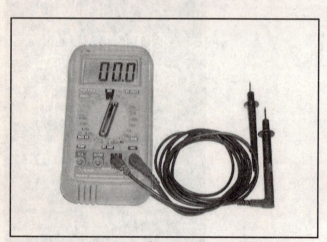

2.5a The most useful tool for electrical troubleshooting is a digital multimeter that can check volts, amps, and test continuity

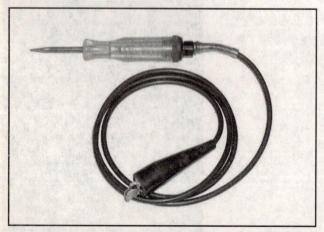

2.5b A simple test light is a very handy tool for testing voltage

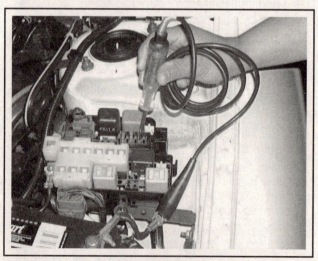

2.6 In use, a basic test light's lead is clipped to a known good ground, then the pointed probe can test connectors, wires or electrical sockets - if the bulb lights, the circuit being tested has battery voltage

connector in the circuit being tested, preferably nearest to the battery or fuse (see illustration). If the bulb of the tester lights, voltage is present, which means that the part of the circuit between the connector and the battery is problem free. Continue checking the rest of the circuit in the same fashion. When you reach a point at which no voltage is present, the problem lies between that point and the last test point with voltage. Most of the time the problem can be traced to a loose connection.

➡**Note: Keep in mind that some circuits receive voltage only when the ignition key is in the Accessory or Run position.**

FINDING A SHORT

7   One method of finding shorts in a live circuit is to remove the fuse and connect a test light in place of the fuse terminals (fabricate two jumper wires with small spade terminals, plug the jumper wires into the fuse box and connect the test light). There should be voltage present in the circuit. Move the suspected wiring harness from side-to-side while watching the test light. If the bulb goes off, there is a short to ground somewhere in that area, probably where the insulation has rubbed through.

GROUND CHECK

8   Perform a ground test to check whether a component is properly grounded. Disconnect the battery and connect one lead of a continuity tester or multimeter (set to the ohm scale), to a known good ground. Connect the other lead to the wire or ground connection being tested. If the resistance is low (less than 5 ohms), the ground is good. If the bulb on a self-powered test light does not go on, the ground is not good.

CONTINUITY CHECK

▶ **Refer to illustration 2.9**

9   A continuity check is done to determine if there are any breaks in a circuit - if it is passing electricity properly. With the circuit off (no power in the circuit), a self-powered continuity tester or multimeter can be used to check the circuit. Connect the test leads to both ends of the circuit (or to the "power" end and a good ground), and if the test light comes on the circuit is passing current properly (see illustration). If the resistance is low (less than 5 ohms), there is continuity; if the reading is 10,000 ohms or higher, there is a break somewhere in the circuit. The same procedure can be used to test a switch, by connecting the continuity tester to the switch terminals. With the switch turned to ON, the test light should come on (or low resistance should be indicated on a meter).

FINDING AN OPEN CIRCUIT

10   When diagnosing for possible open circuits, it is often difficult to locate them by sight because the connectors hide oxidation or terminal misalignment. Merely wiggling a connector on a sensor or in the wiring harness may correct the open circuit condition. Remember this

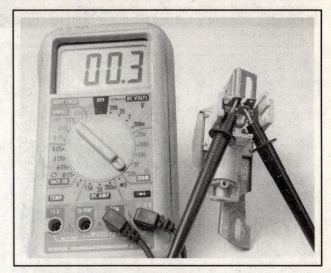

2.9 With a multimeter set to the ohm scale, resistance can be checked across two terminals - when checking for continuity, a low reading indicates continuity, a high reading or infinity indicates high resistance or lack of continuity

when an open circuit is indicated when troubleshooting a circuit. Intermittent problems may also be caused by oxidized or loose connections.

11   Electrical troubleshooting is simple if you keep in mind that all electrical circuits are basically electricity running from the battery, through the wires, switches, relays, fuses and fusible links to each electrical component (light bulb, motor, etc.) and to ground, from which it is passed back to the battery. Any electrical problem is an interruption in the flow of electricity to and from the battery.

CONNECTORS

12   Most electrical connections on these vehicles are made with multiwire plastic connectors. The mating halves of many connectors are secured with locking clips molded into the plastic connector shells. The mating halves of large connectors, such as some of those under the instrument panel, are held together by a bolt through the center of the connector.

13   To separate a connector with locking clips, use a small screwdriver to pry the clips apart carefully, then separate the connector halves. Pull only on the shell, never pull on the wiring harness as you may damage the individual wires and terminals inside the connectors. Look at the connector closely before trying to separate the halves. Often the locking clips are engaged in a way that is not immediately clear. Additionally, many connectors have more than one set of clips.

14   Each pair of connector terminals has a male half and a female half. When you look at the end view of a connector in a diagram, be sure to understand whether the view shows the harness side or the component side of the connector. Connector halves are mirror images of each other, and a terminal that is shown on the right side end-view of one half will be on the left side end view of the other half.

3 Fuses and fusible links - general information

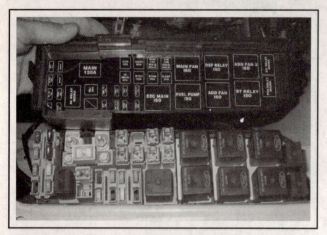

3.1a The fuse/relay box is mounted on the left side of the engine compartment; it contains diodes (for the starter relay and for the air conditioning compressor clutch), fuses and relays, all of which are listed by location and function on the underside of the fuse/relay box cover

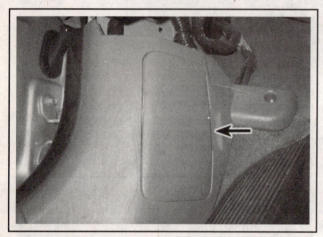

3.1b To open the fuse panel cover from the left kick panel, pull here, then disengage the two cover locator tabs and remove the cover

3.1c The passenger compartment fuse/relay box is located either in the left kick panel as shown, or on the right-hand side of the center console. It contains fuses and relays

FUSES

◆ **Refer to illustrations 3.1a, 3.1b, 3.1c and 3.3**

The electrical circuits of the vehicle are protected by a combination of fuses, circuit breakers and fusible links. Fuse blocks are located under the instrument panel and in the engine compartment (see illustrations). Each of the fuses is designed to protect a specific circuit, and the various circuits are identified on the fuse panel cover. If the fuse panel cover is difficult to read, or missing, you can also refer to your owner's manual, which includes a complete guide to all fuses and relays in both fuse/relay boxes.

Miniaturized fuses are employed in the fuse blocks. These compact fuses, with blade terminal design, allow fingertip removal and replacement. If an electrical component fails, always check the fuse first. The best way to check a fuse is with a test light. Check for power at the exposed terminal tips of each fuse. If power is present on one side of the fuse but not the other, the fuse is blown. A blown fuse can also be confirmed by visually inspecting it (see illustration).

Be sure to replace blown fuses with the correct type. Fuses of different ratings are physically interchangeable, but only fuses of the proper rating should be used. Replacing a fuse with one of a higher or lower value than specified is not recommended. Each electrical circuit needs a specific amount of protection. The amperage value of each fuse is molded into the fuse body.

If the replacement fuse immediately fails, don't replace it again until the cause of the problem is isolated and corrected. In most cases, this will be a short circuit in the wiring caused by a broken or deteriorated wire.

FUSIBLE LINKS

Some circuits are protected by fusible links. The links are used in circuits which are not ordinarily fused, or which carry high current, such as the starter circuit. If your vehicle uses any fusible links, they'll be located in the engine compartment fuse/relay box. Cartridge-type fusible links are similar in appearance to a large fuse. After disconnecting the cable from the negative battery terminal (see Chapter 5, Section 1), simply unplug (or unbolt) and replace a fusible link with one of the same amperage.

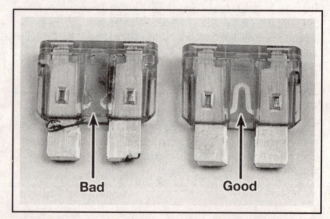

3.3 When a fuse blows, the element between the terminals melts - the fuse on the left is blown, the fuse on the right is good

4   Circuit breakers - general information

Circuit breakers protect certain circuits, such as the power windows or heated seats. Depending on the vehicle's accessories, there may be one or two circuit breakers, located in the fuse/relay box in the engine compartment.

Because the circuit breakers reset automatically, an electrical overload in a circuit-breaker-protected system will cause the circuit to fail momentarily, then come back on. If the circuit does not come back on, check it immediately.

For a basic check, pull the circuit breaker up out of its socket on the fuse panel, but just far enough to probe with a voltmeter. The breaker should still contact the sockets.

With the voltmeter negative lead on a good chassis ground, touch each end prong of the circuit breaker with the positive meter probe. There should be battery voltage at each end. If there is battery voltage only at one end, the circuit breaker must be replaced.

Some circuit breakers must be reset manually.

5   Relays - general information and testing

GENERAL INFORMATION

1   Several electrical accessories in the vehicle, such as the fuel injection system, horns, starter, and fog lamps use relays to transmit the electrical signal to the component. Relays use a low-current circuit (the control circuit) to open and close a high-current circuit (the power circuit). If the relay is defective, that component will not operate properly. Most relays are mounted in the engine compartment fuse/relay box, with some specialized relays located above the interior fuse box in the dash (see illustrations 3.1a and 3.1c). If a faulty relay is suspected, it can be removed and tested using the procedure below or by a dealer service department or a repair shop. Defective relays must be replaced as a unit.

TESTING

♦ **Refer to illustrations 5.2a and 5.2b**

2   Most of the relays used in these vehicles are of a type often called "ISO" relays, which refers to the International Standards Organization. The terminals of ISO relays are numbered to indicate their usual circuit connections and functions. There are two basic layouts of termi-

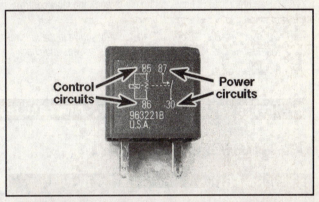

5.2a Most relays are marked on the outside to easily identify the control circuits and the power circuits - four terminal type shown

nals on the relays used in these vehicles (see illustrations).

3   Refer to the wiring diagram for the circuit to determine the proper connections for the relay you're testing. If you can't determine the correct connection from the wiring diagrams, however, you may be able to determine the test connections from the information that follows.

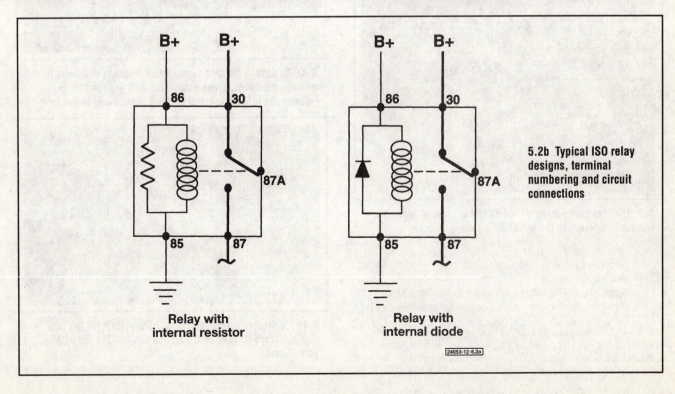

5.2b Typical ISO relay designs, terminal numbering and circuit connections

Relay with internal resistor

Relay with internal diode

24053-12-5.2a

4   Two of the terminals are the relay control circuit and connect to the relay coil. The other relay terminals are the power circuit. When the relay is energized, the coil creates a magnetic field that closes the larger contacts of the power circuit to provide power to the circuit loads.

5   Terminals 85 and 86 are normally the control circuit. If the relay contains a diode, terminal 86 must be connected to battery positive (B+) voltage and terminal 85 to ground. If the relay contains a resistor, terminals 85 and 86 can be connected in either direction with respect to B+ and ground.

6   Terminal 30 is normally connected to the battery voltage (B+) source for the circuit loads. Terminal 87 is connected to the circuit leading to the component being powered. If the relay has several alternate terminals for load or ground connections, they usually are numbered 87A, 87B, 87C, and so on.

7   Use an ohmmeter to check continuity through the relay control coil.

   a) *Connect the meter according to the polarity shown in the illustration for one check; then reverse the ohmmeter leads and check continuity in the other direction.*

   b) *If the relay contains a resistor, resistance will be indicated on the meter, and should be the same value with the ohmmeter in either direction.*

   c) *If the relay contains a diode, resistance should be higher with the ohmmeter in the forward polarity direction than with the meter leads reversed.*

   d) *If the ohmmeter shows infinite resistance in both directions, replace the relay.*

8   Remove the relay from the vehicle and use the ohmmeter to check for continuity between the relay power circuit terminals. There should be no continuity between terminal 30 and 87 with the relay de-energized.

9   Connect a fused jumper wire to terminal 86 and the positive battery terminal. Connect another jumper wire between terminal 85 and ground. When the connections are made, the relay should click.

10 With the jumper wires connected, check for continuity between the power circuit terminals. Now, there should be continuity between terminals 30 and 87.

11 If the relay fails any of the above tests, replace it.

6   Turn signal and hazard flasher - check and replacement

♦ **Refer to illustrations 6.1, 6.4a, 6.4b and 6.4c**

❋❋ WARNING:

The models covered by this manual are equipped with Supplemental Restraint systems (SRS), more commonly known as airbags. Always disarm the airbag system before working in the vicinity of any airbag system component to avoid the possibility of accidental deployment of the airbag, which could cause personal injury (see Section 25).

1   The turn signal and hazard flashers are controlled from a single electronic flasher unit which is mounted to the left of the steering column under the instrument panel (see illustration).

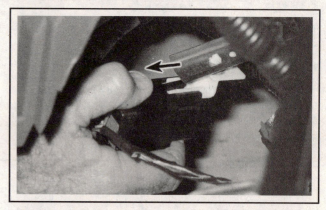

6.4a To detach the turn signal/hazard flasher unit from its mounting bracket, press down here with your thumb to release the locking tab and pull the flasher unit to the rear

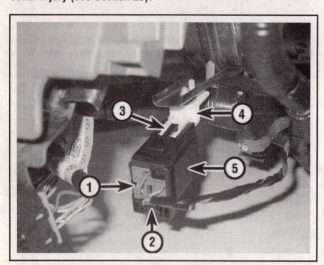

6.1 The turn signal/hazard flasher unit is located under the instrument panel, to the left of the steering column

1   *Electrical connector*
2   *Electrical connector release (located underneath the flasher unit, not visible in this photo)*
3   *Mounting tab (lift up with a small pocket screwdriver to release)*
4   *Plastic mounting bracket (it's not necessary to remove this part, but if you have difficulty releasing the mounting tab, you can pull the bracket down to separate it from the metal bracket above)*
5   *Turn signal/hazard flasher unit*

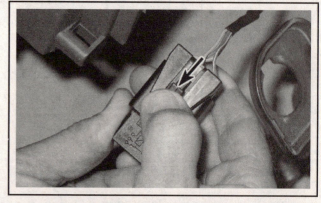

6.4b To disconnect the electrical connector from the turn signal/hazard flasher unit, depress this locking tab with your thumb . . .

2   When the flasher unit is functioning properly, an audible click can be heard during its operation. If the turn signal indicator (on the instrument panel) on one side of the vehicle flashes much more rapidly than normal, a faulty turn signal bulb is indicated.

3   If both turn signals fail to blink, the problem may be due to a blown fuse, a faulty flasher unit, a broken switch or a loose or open connection. If a quick check of the fuse box indicates that the turn signal fuse has blown, check the wiring for a short before installing a new fuse.

4   To replace the flasher, remove the flasher from its mounting bracket and then disconnect the electrical connector (see illustrations). (It's easier to detach the flasher unit first, and *then* disconnect the electrical connector.)

5   Make sure that the replacement unit is identical to the original. Compare the old one to the new one before installing it.

6   Installation is the reverse of removal.

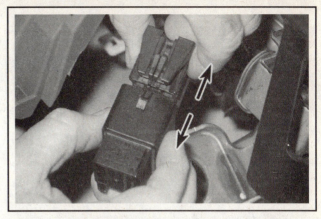

6.4c . . . and separate the connector from the turn signal/ hazard flasher unit

7   Ignition switch and key lock cylinder - replacement

❋❋ WARNING:

All models covered by this manual are equipped with a Supplemental Restraint System (SRS), more commonly known as airbags. Always disarm the airbag system before working in the vicinity of any airbag system component to avoid the possibility of accidental deployment of the airbag, which could cause personal injury (see Section 25).

KEY LOCK CYLINDER

▶ **Refer to illustrations 7.3a, 7.3b, 7.3c, 7.4a and 7.4b**

1   Disconnect the cable from the negative battery terminal (see Chapter 5, Section 1).

2   Turn the ignition key lock cylinder to the ON position.

3   Insert a 1/8-inch awl or punch through the hole in the lower steering column cover, insert it through the hole in the steering column housing and then simultaneously depress the release button on the lock cylinder and pull the lock cylinder out of the steering column housing (see illustrations).

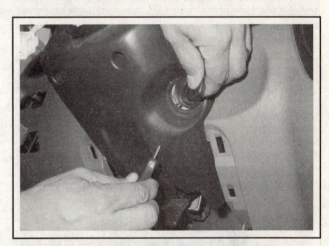

7.3a To release the key lock cylinder from the steering column assembly, insert a 1/8-inch awl or punch through this hole in the steering column cover . . .

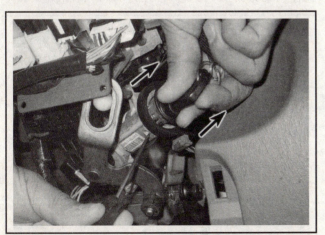

7.3b . . . through this hole in the steering column housing, then depress the release button on the lock cylinder and pull out the lock cylinder (steering column cover removed for clarity)

7.3c Key lock cylinder removal and installation details

1   *Release button*
2   *When installing the key lock cylinder, align the edge of the key with the release button to put the key in the ON position*

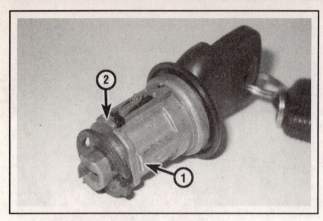

7.4a Key lock cylinder installation details

1   *Narrow ridge (other narrow ridge, on other side of cylinder, not visible)*
2   *Wide ridge*

4   To install the lock cylinder, make sure that the ignition key is still in the ON position (see illustration 7.3c), then insert the lock cylinder into the steering column housing with the wide ridge and two narrow ridges on the lock cylinder aligned with the wide groove and narrow

7.11a To detach the steering column covers, remove these three screws . . .

7.11b . . . then pull the upper and lower halves of the steering column cover apart and remove them (steering wheel removed for clarity)

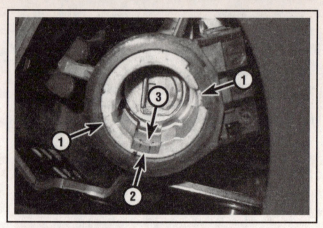

7.4b Key lock cylinder receptacle in steering column housing

1   *Narrow grooves*
2   *Wide groove*
3   *Release button locating hole in steering column housing*

grooves inside the lock cylinder receptacle (see illustrations).
5   Rotate the key back to the OFF position. This will allow the release button to extend itself back into the locating hole in the steering column housing.
6   Turn the lock to ensure that operation is correct in all positions.
7   Reconnect the cable to the negative battery terminal.
8   After you've reconnected the battery, the Powertrain Control Module (PCM) must relearn its idle and fuel trim strategy for optimum driveability and performance (see Chapter 5, Section 1 for this procedure).

IGNITION SWITCH

▶ **Refer to illustration 7.11a, 7.11b, 7.12a, 7.12b, 7.14a, 7.14b and 7.14c**

9   Disconnect the cable from the negative battery terminal (see Chapter 5, Section 1).
10   Remove the key lock cylinder (see Steps 1 through 3).
11   Remove the upper and lower steering column covers (see illustrations).
12   Disconnect the ignition switch electrical connector (see illustrations).

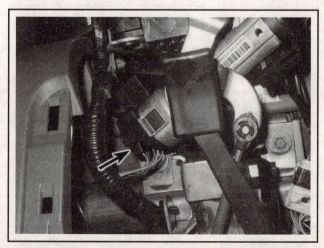

7.12a To disconnect the electrical connector from the ignition switch . . .

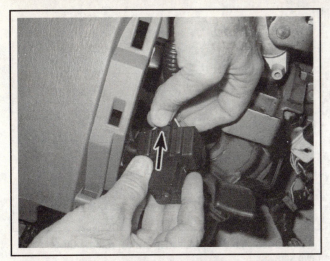

7.12b . . . depress this lock and pull out the connector

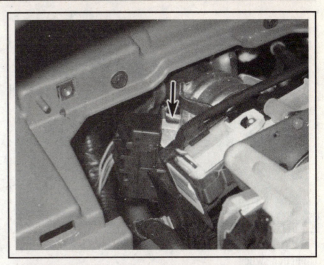

7.14a To remove the ignition switch from the steering column housing, release this button on top . . .

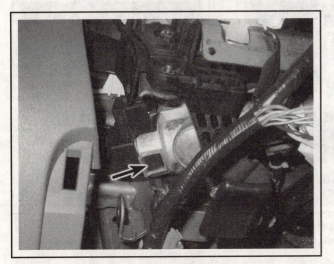

7.14b . . . and this button on the bottom . . .

7.14c . . . then pull the ignition switch to the left to disengage it from the steering column housing

13 Lower the steering column to its lowest tilt position.
14 Remove the ignition switch (see illustrations).
15 Installation is the reverse of removal.
16 After you've reconnected the battery, the Powertrain Control Module (PCM) must relearn its idle and fuel trim strategy for optimum driveability and performance (see Chapter 5, Section 1 for this procedure).

17 Verify that the ignition switch operates correctly in the LOCK, ON, START and ACC positions.

8 Steering column switches - replacement

⁂ WARNING:

The models covered by this manual are equipped with Supplemental Restraint systems (SRS), more commonly known as airbags. Always disarm the airbag system before working in the vicinity of any airbag system component to avoid the possibility of accidental deployment of the airbag, which could cause personal injury (see Section 25).

MULTI-FUNCTION SWITCH

♦ **Refer to illustrations 8.4, 8.5a and 8.5b**

1 Disconnect the cable from the negative battery terminal (see Chapter 5, Section 1).
2 Remove the key lock cylinder (see Section 7).
3 Remove the steering column covers (see illustrations 7.11a and 7.11b).

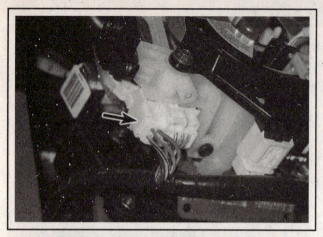

8.4 Disconnect the electrical connector from the multi-function switch

8.5a To detach the multi-function switch, remove these two screws . . .

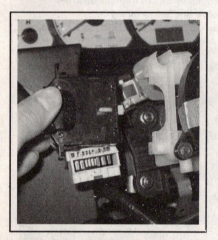

8.5b . . . then remove the switch from the steering column assembly

8.10 Disconnect the electrical connector from the windshield wiper/washer switch

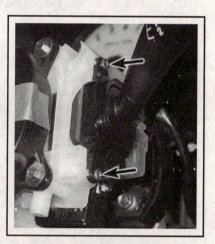

8.11a To detach the windshield wiper/washer switch, remove these two retaining screws . . .

4   Disconnect the electrical connector from the multi-function switch (see illustration).

5   Remove the multi-function switch retaining screws, then detach the switch from the steering column (see illustrations).

6   Installation is the reverse of removal.

7   After you've reconnected the battery, the Powertrain Control Module (PCM) must relearn its idle and fuel trim strategy for optimum driveability and performance (see Chapter 5, Section 1 for this procedure).

WINDSHIELD WIPER/WASHER SWITCH

▶ **Refer to illustrations 8.10, 8.11a and 8.11b**

8   Disconnect the cable from the negative battery terminal (see Chapter 5, Section 1).

9   Remove the key lock cylinder (see Section 7) and the steering column covers (see illustrations 7.11a and 7.11b).

10   Disconnect the electrical connector from the windshield wiper/washer switch (see illustration).

11   Remove the windshield wiper/washer switch retaining screws, then detach the switch from the steering column (see illustrations).

12   Installation is the reverse of removal.

13   After you've reconnected the battery, the Powertrain Control Module (PCM) must relearn its idle and fuel trim strategy for optimum driveability and performance (see Chapter 5, Section 1 for this procedure).

8.11b . . . then remove the switch from the steering column

9   Instrument panel switches - replacement

✳✷ WARNING:

The models covered by this manual are equipped with Supplemental Restraint systems (SRS), more commonly known as airbags. Always disarm the airbag system before working in the vicinity of any airbag system component to avoid the possibility of accidental deployment of the airbag, which could cause personal injury (see Section 25).

LEFT/RIGHT POWER MIRROR ADJUSTMENT SWITCH

▶ **Refer to illustrations 9.2 and 9.3**

1   Disconnect the cable from the negative battery terminal (see Chapter 5, Section 1).
2   Carefully pry the power window switch from the instrument panel (see illustration).
3   Disconnect the electrical connector (see illustration) and remove the switch.
4   Installation is the reverse of removal.
5   After you've reconnected the battery, the Powertrain Control Module (PCM) must relearn its idle and fuel trim strategy for optimum driveability and performance (see Chapter 5, Section 1 for this procedure).

INSTRUMENT PANEL DIMMER SWITCH

▶ **Refer to illustrations 9.7 and 9.8**

6   Disconnect the cable from the negative battery terminal (see Chapter 5, Section 1).
7   Carefully pry the switch from the instrument panel (see illustration).
8   Disconnect the electrical connector (see illustration) and remove the switch.
9   Installation is the reverse of removal.
10 After you've reconnected the battery, the Powertrain Control Module (PCM) must relearn its idle and fuel trim strategy for optimum driveability and performance (see Chapter 5, Section 1 for this procedure).

9.2 Carefully pry the left/right power mirror adjustment switch from the dash with a small screwdriver (the switch is secured to the dash by a small metal tab on each side)

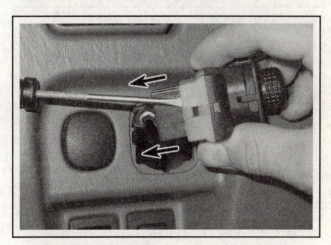

9.3 Disconnect the electrical connector from the left/right power mirror adjustment switch; if the connector is difficult to separate from the switch, use a small screwdriver to carefully pry it loose

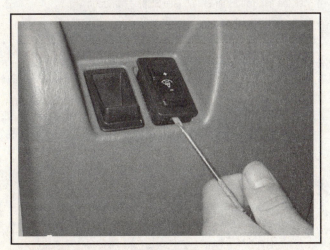

9.7 Carefully pry the instrument panel dimmer switch from the dash

9.8 Disconnect the electrical connector from the instrument panel dimmer switch and remove the switch

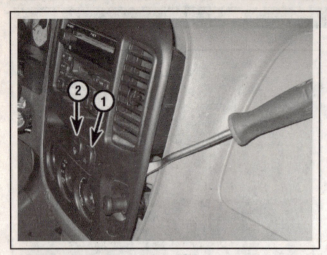

9.12 Carefully pry the center trim panel loose (it's not necessary to remove it)

1   Hazard flasher switch
2   Rear window defogger switch

9.14a To detach the hazard flasher switch from the center trim panel, squeeze these two locking tangs . . .

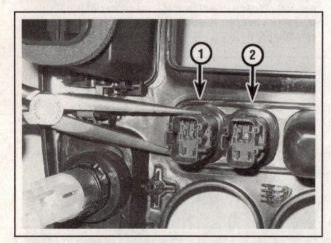

9.14b . . . with a pair of needle-nose pliers and push the switch out of the trim panel; push it out *from the rear side*; **don't try to push the switch through the trim panel from the front (center trim panel removed for clarity)**

1   Hazard flasher switch
2   Rear window defogger switch (remove the same way)

9.13 Disconnect the electrical connector from the hazard flasher switch

HAZARD FLASHER SWITCH

▶ **Refer to illustrations 9.12, 9.13, 9.14a and 9.14b**

11 Disconnect the cable from the negative battery terminal (see Chapter 5, Section 1).

12 Pry the center trim panel loose from the dash (see illustration). (It's not necessary to actually remove it.)

13 Disconnect the hazard flasher electrical connector (see illustration).

14 To remove the hazard flasher switch, squeeze the two locking tangs (see illustrations) and push the switch out of the center trim panel.

15 Installation is the reverse of removal.

16 After you've reconnected the battery, the Powertrain Control Module (PCM) must relearn its idle and fuel trim strategy for optimum driveability and performance (see Chapter 5, Section 1 for this procedure).

REAR WINDOW DEFOGGER SWITCH

17 The rear window defogger switch, which is located to the left of the hazard flasher switch, is removed and installed exactly the same way as the hazard flasher switch (see Steps 11 through 16).

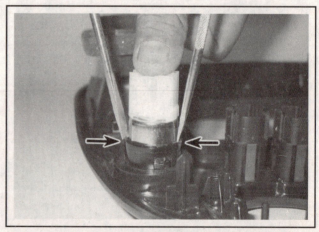

9.20a To release the cigarette lighter from the center trim panel, pry these two locking tangs out . . .

CIGARETTE LIGHTER

▶ **Refer to illustrations 9.20a and 9.20b**

18 Disconnect the cable from the negative battery terminal (see Chapter 5, Section 1).

19 Remove the center trim panel (see Chapter 11).

20 Pry open the two locking tangs and push the cigarette lighter out of the trim panel (see illustrations).

21 When installing the cigarette lighter in the center trim panel, be sure to push the lighter into the trim panel until it snaps into place, indicating that it's fully seated.

22 Installation is otherwise the reverse of removal.

23 After you've reconnected the battery, the Powertrain Control Module (PCM) must relearn its idle and fuel trim strategy for optimum driveability and performance (see Chapter 5, Section 1 for this procedure).

9.20b . . . and push the cigarette lighter out of the trim panel from the back side; when installing the cigarette lighter, make sure that the dimpled area (A) on each side of the lighter is aligned with a locking tang, or the lighter won't be securely fastened to the trim panel

10 Instrument cluster - removal and installation

▶ **Refer to illustrations 10.3, 10.4a and 10.4b**

❊❊ WARNING:

The models covered by this manual are equipped with Supplemental Restraint systems (SRS), more commonly known as airbags. Always disarm the airbag system before working in the vicinity of any airbag system component to avoid the possibility of accidental deployment of the airbag, which could cause personal injury (see Section 25).

➡Note: This procedure is intended for removing the instrument cluster for access to other components (such as during instrument panel removal) only. If the instrument cluster requires replacement, the job will have to be performed at a dealer service department or other qualified repair shop equipped with the special scan tool that is required to upload the module configuration data and download this data into the new cluster.

1 Disconnect the cable from the negative battery terminal (see Chapter 5, Section 1).

2 Tilt the steering wheel to its lowest position and move the transaxle shift lever out of the way.

3 Remove the instrument cluster finish panel screws (see illustration) and remove the cluster finish panel.

4 Remove the instrument cluster retaining screws (see illustration),

10.3 To detach the instrument cluster finish panel, remove these two screws

then pull out the cluster and disconnect the electrical connectors from the back side (see illustration).

5 Installation is the reverse of removal.

6 After you've reconnected the battery, the Powertrain Control Module (PCM) must relearn its idle and fuel trim strategy for optimum driveability and performance (see Chapter 5, Section 1 for this procedure).

10.4a To detach the instrument cluster, remove these four screws . . .

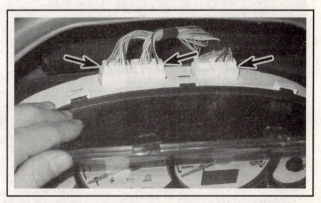

10.4b . . . pull out the cluster and disconnect the electrical connectors from the back side

11 Wiper motors - check and replacement

WIPER MOTOR CIRCUIT CHECK

➡Note: Refer to the wiring diagrams at the end of this Chapter for wire colors in the following checks. When checking for voltage, probe a grounded 12-volt test light to each terminal at a connector until it lights; this verifies voltage (power) at the terminal. If the following checks fail to locate the problem, have the system diagnosed by a dealer service department or other properly equipped repair facility.

1   If the wipers work slowly, make sure the battery is in good condition and has a strong charge (see Chapter 5). If the battery is in good condition, remove the wiper motor (see below) and operate the wiper arms by hand. Check for binding linkage and pivots. Lubricate or repair the linkage or pivots as necessary. Reinstall the wiper motor. If the wipers still operate slowly, check for loose or corroded connections, especially the ground connection. If all connections look OK, replace the motor.

11.7a Remove each windshield wiper arm retaining nut . . .

2   If the wipers fail to operate when activated, check the fuse (see Section 3). If the fuse is OK, connect a jumper wire between the wiper motor's ground terminal and ground, then retest. If the motor works now, repair the ground connection. If the motor still doesn't work, turn the wiper switch to the HI position and check for voltage at the motor.

➡Note: The cowl cover will have to be removed to access the electrical connector (see Steps 7 and 8).

3   If there's voltage at the connector, remove the motor and check it off the vehicle with fused jumper wires from the battery. If the motor now works, check for binding linkage (see Step 1). If the motor still doesn't work, replace it. If there's no voltage to the motor, check for voltage at the wiper control relays. If there's voltage at the wiper control relays and no voltage at the wiper motor, have the switch tested. If the switch is OK, the wiper control relay is probably bad. See Section 5 for relay testing.

4   If the interval (delay) function is inoperative, check the continuity of all the wiring between the switch and wiper control module.

5   If the wipers stop at the position they're in when the switch is turned off (fail to park), check for voltage at the park feed wire of the wiper motor connector when the wiper switch is OFF but the ignition is ON. If no voltage is present, check for an open circuit between the wiper motor and the fuse panel.

WIPER MOTOR REPLACEMENT

Windshield wiper motor

▸ **Refer to illustrations 11.7a, 11.7b, 11.7c, 11.8a, 11.8b, 11.8c, 11.9, 11.10 and 11.12**

6   Disconnect the cable from the negative battery terminal (see Chapter 5, Section 1).

7   Remove the windshield wiper retaining nuts (see illustration). Mark the positions of the wiper arm on the windshield, then remove the wiper arm (see illustrations).

8   Remove the windshield cowl cover (see illustrations). Store all the trim caps, Phillips screws and pin-type retainers in a plastic bag.

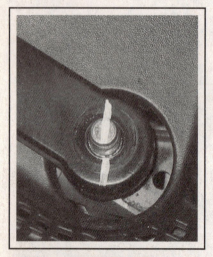

11.7b . . . mark the relationship of the wiper arm to the shaft . . .

11.7c . . . then pull the windshield wiper arm off the shaft

11.8a Remove the trim caps that cover up the rear cowl fasteners (the ones nearer the windshield)

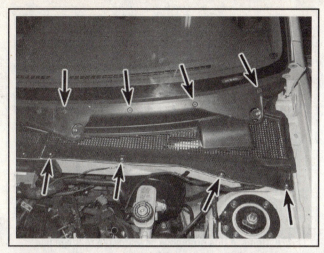

11.8b To detach the left cowl vent panel, remove these fasteners (the rear fasteners are Phillips screws; the front fasteners are pin-type retainers, also referred to as pop fasteners)

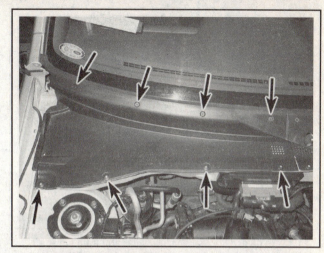

11.8c To detach the right cowl vent panel, remove these fasteners (the rear fasteners are Phillips screws; the front fasteners are pin-type retainers, also referred to as pop fasteners)

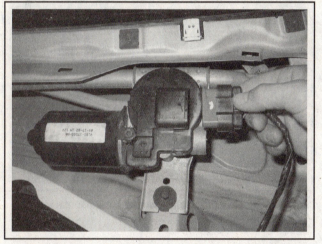

11.9 Disconnect the electrical connector from the windshield wiper motor

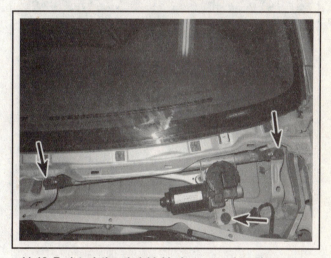

11.10 To detach the windshield wiper motor from the vehicle, remove these bolts

9   Disconnect the wiper motor harness connector from the windshield wiper motor (see illustration).

10 Remove the windshield wiper motor/linkage assembly mounting bolts (see illustration).

11 Lift the windshield wiper motor assembly from the cowl area.

12 Remove the windshield wiper motor mounting bolts (see illustration) and separate the motor from its mounting bracket.

13 Installation is the reverse of removal. Be sure to align the marks you made on the windshield wiper arms and the wiper arm shafts.

14 After you've reconnected the battery, the Powertrain Control Module (PCM) must relearn its idle and fuel trim strategy for optimum driveability and performance (see Chapter 5, Section 1 for this procedure).

Rear window wiper motor

◆ **Refer to illustrations 11.16, 11.17a, 11.17b, 11.18, 11.19a, 11.19b and 11.20**

15 Disconnect the cable from the negative battery terminal (see Chapter 5, Section 1).

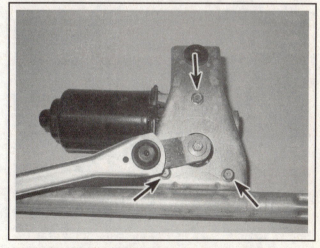

11.12 To detach the windshield wiper motor from its mounting bracket, remove these three bolts

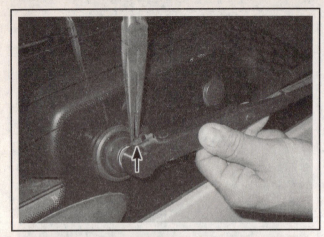

11.16 To detach the rear window wiper arm from the shaft, pull this locking tab straight up with a pair of needle-nose pliers, then pull the wiper arm straight off the shaft

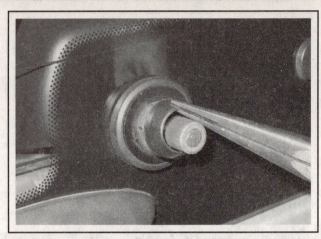

11.17a Remove this protective cover for the rear window wiper motor shaft nut . . .

11.17b . . . then unscrew the nut

11.18 To remove the plastic cover for the wiper motor, simply pop it off

16 Remove the rear window wiper arm (see illustration).

17 Remove the protective cover for the rear window wiper motor shaft nut, then remove the nut (see illustrations).

18 Open the liftgate and remove the plastic cover for the rear window

wiper motor (see illustration).

19 Disconnect the electrical connector from the rear window wiper motor (see illustrations).

11.19a Using a panel removal tool or a screwdriver, detach the electrical connector from its bracket . . .

11.19b . . . then release this locking tab with a small screwdriver and unplug the connector

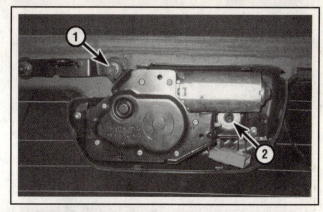

20 Remove the mounting nut and bolt (see illustration) and remove the rear window wiper motor.

21 Installation is the reverse of removal.

22 After you've reconnected the battery, the Powertrain Control Module (PCM) must relearn its idle and fuel trim strategy for optimum driveability and performance (see Chapter 5, Section 1 for this procedure).

11.20 To detach the rear window wiper motor from the rear window, remove the mounting nut (1) and bolt (2)

12 Radio and speakers - removal and installation

❄❄ WARNING:

The models covered by this manual are equipped with Supplemental Restraint systems (SRS), more commonly known as airbags. Always disable the airbag system before working in the vicinity of any airbag system component to avoid the possibility of accidental deployment of the airbag, which could cause personal injury (see Section 25).

RADIO

▶ **Refer to illustration 12.2a, 12.2b, 12.3, 12.4a and 12.4b**

1 Disconnect the cable from the negative battery terminal (see Chapter 5, Section 1).

2 For theft protection, the radio receiver is retained in the instrument panel by special clips. Releasing these clips requires the use of a pair of special radio removal tools, available at most auto parts stores, or two short lengths of coat hanger wire bent into U-shapes (see illustration). Insert the tools into the holes at the corners of the radio assembly (see illustration). Insert the tools until you feel the internal retaining clips release.

3 Push outward on both removal tools and simultaneously pull the radio assembly out of the instrument panel (see illustration).

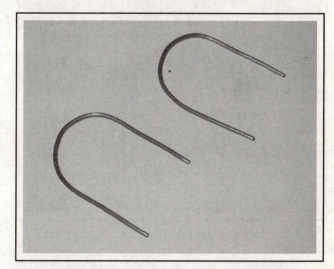

12.2a You'll need a pair of special radio removal tools (available at most auto parts stores) or make your own from a couple of pieces of coat hanger wire bent into a U-shape as shown

12.2b Insert the special radio removal tools into the holes at each end of the radio as shown, then push them in until you feel the internal clips release

12.3 Push outward on both radio removal tools and simultaneously pull out the radio

12.4a When the radio has been pulled out far enough to access the back side, disconnect the antenna cable . . .

12.4b . . . and the electrical connector from the radio

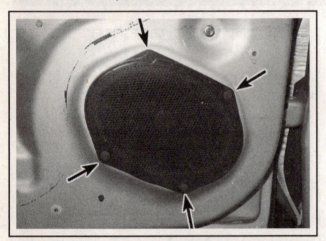

12.8 To detach a speaker from a front door, remove these four screws

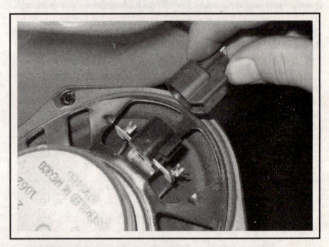

12.9 Before removing the speaker from the front door, disconnect the electrical connector

4   Disconnect the antenna and the electrical connector from the back of the radio (see illustrations) and remove the radio from the vehicle.

5   Installation is the reverse of removal. After reconnecting the electrical connector and antenna cable, insert the radio into the dash and slide it into place until you feel and/or hear the retaining clips snapping into place.

6   After you've reconnected the battery, the Powertrain Control Module (PCM) must relearn its idle and fuel trim strategy for optimum driveability and performance (see Chapter 5, Section 1 for this procedure).

SPEAKERS

Front door speakers

▶ Refer to illustrations 12.8 and 12.9

7   Remove the door trim panel (see Chapter 11).

8   Remove the speaker mounting screws (see illustration) and pull the speaker out of its receptacle in the door.

9   Disconnect the electrical connector (see illustration) and remove the speaker from the vehicle.

10 Installation is the reverse of removal.

Rear door speakers

▶ Refer to illustrations 12.12 and 12.13

11 Remove the door trim panel (see Chapter 11).

12 Remove the speaker mounting screws (see illustration) and pull

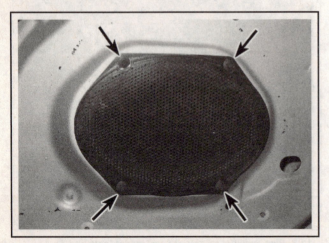

12.12 To detach a speaker from a rear door, remove these four screws

12.13 Before removing the speaker from the rear door, disconnect the electrical connector

the speaker out of its receptacle in the door.

13 Disconnect the electrical connector (see illustration) and remove the speaker from the vehicle.

14 Installation is the reverse of removal.

13 Antenna and cable - removal and installation

✳ WARNING:

The models covered by this manual are equipped with Supplemental Restraint systems (SRS), more commonly known as airbags. Always disable the airbag system before working in the vicinity of any airbag system component to avoid the possibility of accidental deployment of the airbag, which could cause personal injury (see Section 25).

ANTENNA (AND OUTSIDE ANTENNA CABLE)

♦ Refer to illustrations 13.1, 13.3a, 13.3b and 13.6

→Note: The antenna cable actually has two sections. This procedure describes the removal procedure for the antenna mast, the antenna mounting base and the outside part of the antenna cable, which begins at the connector below the blower motor housing and extends to the antenna mounting base in the right fender. For the removal procedure for the rest of the antenna cable (the part from the connector to the back of the radio, see Step 9).

1 Remove the antenna mast (see illustration) from its mounting base.

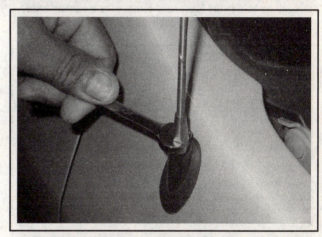

13.1 Unscrew the antenna mast with a 10 mm wrench

2 Remove the right scuff plate and the right lower A-pillar trim panel (see "Instrument panel - removal and installation" in Chapter 11).

3 Working under the right end of the dash, detach the two antenna cable clips and disconnect the antenna cable connector (see illustrations).

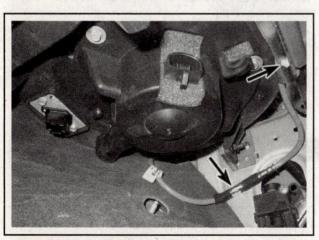

13.3a Detach these two cable clips . . .

13.3b . . . and disconnect the antenna cable connector

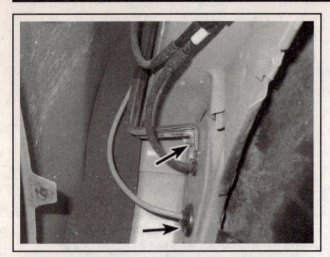

13.6 Remove the antenna cable grommet, pull the antenna cable into the fender area, remove the antenna support bracket nut, then pull the antenna mounting base down through its hole in the fender and remove the mounting base, support bracket and antenna cable as a single assembly

13.13 Detach these two pin-type retainers from the vertical support brace located at the right side of the radio recess

4   Loosen the right front wheel lug nuts. Raise the vehicle and place it securely on jackstands. Remove the right front wheel.

5   Remove the right inner fender splash shield (see "Front fender - removal and installation" in Chapter 11).

6   Working inside the fender area, remove the antenna cable grommet (see illustration), pull the antenna cable into the fender area, remove the antenna support bracket nut, then pull the antenna mount-

13.12 After removing the glove box, detach these three pin-type retainers from the support brace running along the lower edge of the glove box recess

ing base down through its hole in the fender and remove the mounting base, support bracket and antenna cable as a single assembly

7   Remove the electrical tape securing the antenna cable to the support bracket and discard the old antenna base and cable.

8   Installation is the reverse of removal.

(INSIDE) ANTENNA CABLE

▶ **Refer to illustrations 13.12 and 13.13**

➡**Note: This procedure describes the removal procedure for the rest of the antenna cable, which begins at the connector shown in illustration 13.3b and extends to the back of the radio. If you want to remove the outside part of the antenna cable, refer to Steps 1 through 8 above.**

9   Remove the radio (see Section 12).

10   Remove the right scuff plate and kick panel (see "Front fender - removal and installation" in Chapter 11), then disconnect the inside part of the antenna cable from the outside cable (see illustrations 13.3a and 13.3b).

11   Remove the glove box (see Chapter 11).

12   Detach the three pin-type retainers that secure the cable to the horizontal support brace located on the lower edge of the glove box recess (see illustration).

13   There are two more pin-type retainers (see illustration) securing the antenna cable to the vertical support brace that's located on the right side of the radio recess. Detach both of them.

14   Remove the inside antenna cable.

15   Installation is the reverse of removal.

14 Rear window defogger - check and repair

1   The rear window defogger consists of a number of horizontal elements baked onto the glass surface.

2   Small breaks in the element can be repaired without removing the rear window.

CHECK

▶ **Refer to illustrations 14.4, 14.5 and 14.7**

3   Turn the ignition switch and defogger system switches to the ON

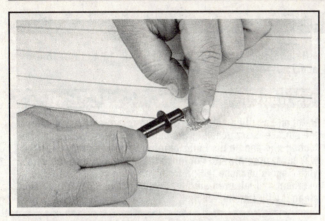

14.4 When measuring the voltage at the rear window defogger grid, wrap a piece of aluminum foil around the positive probe of a voltmeter and press the foil against the wire with your finger

position. Using a voltmeter, place the positive probe against the defogger grid positive terminal and the negative probe against the ground terminal. If battery voltage is not indicated, check the fuse, defogger switch and related wiring. If voltage is indicated, but all or part of the defogger doesn't heat, proceed with the following tests.

4   When measuring voltage during the next two tests, wrap a piece of aluminum foil around the tip of the voltmeter positive probe and press the foil against the heating element with your finger (see illustration). Place the negative probe on the defogger grid ground terminal.

5   Check the voltage at the center of each heating element (see illustration). If the voltage is 5 or 6-volts, the element is okay (there is no break). If the voltage is zero, the element is broken between the center of the element and the positive end. If the voltage is 10 to 12-volts the element is broken between the center of the element and ground. Check each heating element.

6   Connect the negative lead to a good body ground. The reading should stay the same. If it doesn't, the ground connection is bad.

7   To find the break, place the voltmeter negative probe against the defogger ground terminal. Place the voltmeter positive probe with the foil strip against the heating element at the positive terminal end and slide it toward the negative terminal end. The point at which the voltmeter deflects from several volts to zero is the point at which the heating element is broken (see illustration).

REPAIR

▶ **Refer to illustration 14.13**

8   Repair the break in the element using a repair kit specifically recommended for this purpose, available at most auto parts stores. Included in this kit is plastic conductive epoxy.

9   Prior to repairing a break, turn off the system and allow it to cool off for a few minutes.

10   Lightly buff the element area with fine steel wool, then clean it thoroughly with rubbing alcohol.

11   Use masking tape to mask off the area being repaired.

12   Thoroughly mix the epoxy, following the instructions provided with the repair kit.

13   Apply the epoxy material to the slit in the masking tape, overlapping the undamaged area about 3/4-inch on either end (see illustration).

14   Allow the repair to cure for 24 hours before removing the tape and using the system.

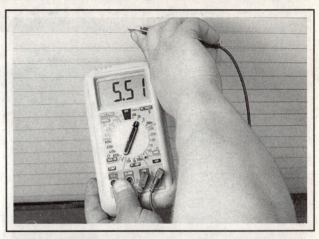

14.5 To determine whether a heating element has broken, check the voltage at the center of each element; if the voltage is five or six volts, the element is unbroken, but if the voltage is 10 or 12 volts, the element is broken between the center and the ground side; if there's no voltage, the element is broken between the center and the positive side

14.7 To find the break, place the voltmeter negative lead against the defogger ground terminal, place the voltmeter positive lead with the foil strip against the heating element at the positive terminal end and slide it toward the negative terminal end; the point at which the voltmeter reading changes abruptly is the point at which the element is broken

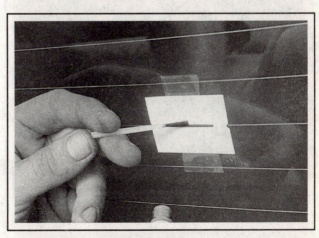

14.13 To use a defogger repair kit, apply masking tape to the inside of the window at the damaged area, then brush on the special conductive coating

15 Headlight bulb - replacement

15.2a To disconnect the electrical connector from the headlight, squeeze the two locking tabs on the side . . .

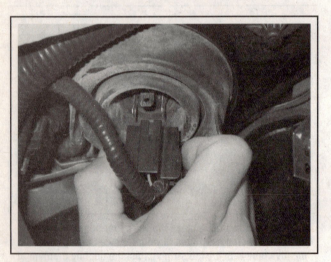

15.2b . . . and pull off the connector

15.4 To disengage the bulb retainer spring, press each end of the spring forward and unhook it, then swing the retainer out of the way

▶ Refer to illustration 15.2a, 15.2b, 15.3, 15.4, 15.5, 15.6 and 15.7

❋❋ WARNING:

Halogen gas filled bulbs are under pressure and may shatter if the surface is scratched or the bulb is dropped. Wear eye protection and handle the bulbs carefully, grasping only the base whenever possible. Do not touch the surface of the bulb with your fingers because the oil from your skin could cause it to overheat and fail prematurely. If you do touch the bulb surface, clean it with rubbing alcohol.

1 Make sure that the headlight switch and the ignition switch are both turned off, then open the hood.
2 Disconnect the electrical connector from the headlight assembly (see illustrations).
3 Remove the rubber boot from the headlight assembly (see illustration).
4 Disengage the headlight bulb retainer spring (see illustration).
5 Remove the bulb from the headlight assembly (see illustration).

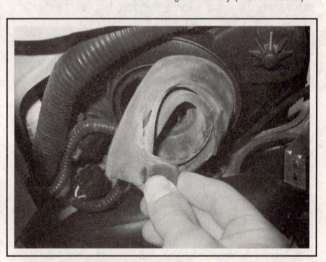

15.3 Remove the protective rubber boot from the headlight assembly

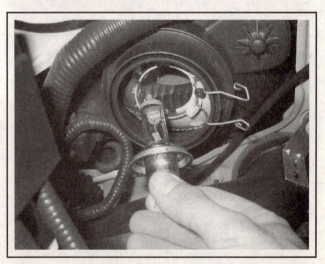

15.5 Carefully remove the bulb from the headlight assembly

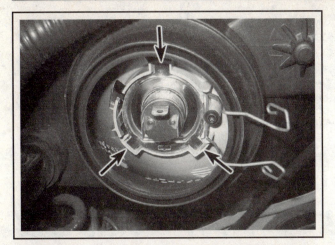

15.6 When installing the new bulb, make sure that the three metal tabs on the new bulb are aligned with the three grooves in the plastic base, and that the bulb's metal base is fully seated against the plastic base, before securing it with the spring retainer

15.7 When reconnecting the spring retainer, make sure that the retainer ends are correctly engaged with the hooks

6   Without touching the glass part of the new bulb with your fingers, insert the bulb into the headlight assembly. Make sure that the three metal tabs on the new bulb are aligned with the three grooves in the plastic base (see illustration), then push the bulb into the headlight assembly

until the bulb's metal base is fully seated against the plastic base.

7   Swing the spring retainer back into place and engage the spring ends with their respective hooks on the headlight assembly (see illustration).

8   Install the protective rubber boot on the headlight assembly.

9   Plug in the electrical connector.

10 Test the headlight operation, then close the hood.

16 Headlights - adjustment

♦ Refer to illustrations 16.1 and 16.3

➡Note: The headlights must be aimed correctly. If adjusted incorrectly they could blind the driver of an oncoming vehicle and cause a serious accident or seriously reduce your ability to see the road. The headlights should be checked for proper aim every 12 months and any time a new headlight is installed or front end body work is performed. It should be emphasized that the following procedure is only an interim step that will provide temporary adjustment until the headlights can be adjusted by a properly equipped shop.

1   The vertical adjustment screws are located behind each headlight (see illustration). (There are no horizontal adjustment screws.)

2   There are several methods for adjusting the headlights. The sim-

plest method requires masking tape, a blank wall and a level floor.

3   Position masking tape vertically on the wall in reference to the vehicle centerline and the centerlines of both headlights (see illustration).

16.1 Headlight vertical adjustment screw location (there is no horizontal adjustment screw)

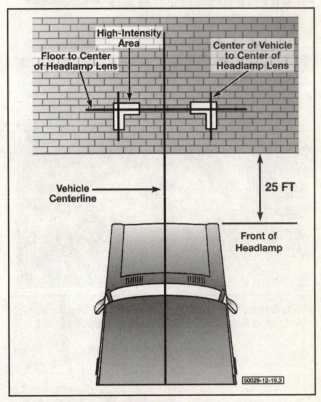

16.3 Headlight adjustment details

4   Position a horizontal tape line in reference to the centerline of all the headlights.

➡Note: It may be easier to position the tape on the wall with the vehicle parked only a few inches away.

5   Adjustment should be made with the vehicle parked 25 feet from the wall, sitting level, the gas tank half-full and no heavy load in the vehicle.

6   Starting with the low beam adjustment, position the high intensity zone so it is two inches below the horizontal line. Adjustment is made by turning the adjusting screw clockwise to raise the beam and counterclockwise to lower the beam.

7   With the high beams on, the high intensity zone should be vertically centered with the exact center just below the horizontal line.

➡Note: It may not be possible to position the headlight aim exactly for both high and low beams. If a compromise must be made, keep in mind that the low beams are the most used and have the greatest effect on safety.

8   Have the headlights adjusted by a dealer service department or service station at the earliest opportunity.

17 Headlight housing - replacement

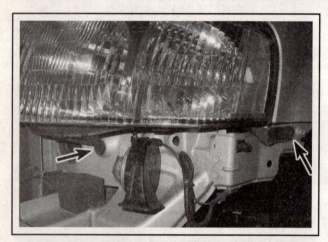

17.4 To detach the lower part of the headlight housing from the vehicle, remove these two bolts

◆ **Refer to illustrations 17.4, 17.5 and 17.6**

1   Make sure that the headlight switch and the ignition switch are turned off.

2   Remove the front bumper cover (see Chapter 11).

3   Disconnect the electrical connector from the headlight housing (see illustrations 15.2a and 15.2b).

➡Note: It's not necessary to remove the rubber protective boot or the bulb to remove the headlight housing. Of course, if you're planning to replace the headlight housing, and therefore need to remove the boot and bulb, it's easier to do so after you have removed the headlight housing.

4   Remove the two lower headlight housing mounting bolts (see illustration).

5   Remove the upper headlight housing mounting bolt and nut (see illustration).

6   Remove the headlight housing (see illustration).

7   Installation is the reverse of removal.

17.5 To detach the upper part of the headlight housing from the upper radiator crossmember, remove this bolt and nut

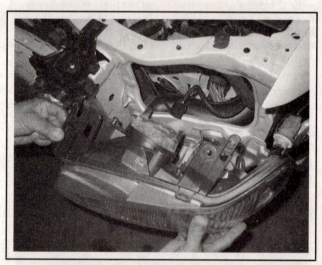

17.6 Carefully remove the headlight housing from the vehicle

18 Horn - replacement

► **Refer to illustration 18.3**

1   Loosen the left front wheel lug nuts. Raise the vehicle and secure it on jackstands. Remove the left front wheel.
2   Remove the front bumper cover (see Chapter 11).
3   Disconnect the electrical connector from the horn (see illustration).
4   Remove the horn mounting nut and separate the horn from its mounting bracket.
5   Installation is the reverse of removal.

18.3 To remove the horn, disconnect the electrical connector and remove the mounting nut

.19 Bulb replacement

FRONT TURN SIGNAL BULBS

► **Refer to illustrations 19.3 and 19.4**

1   Loosen the left or right front wheel lug nuts. Raise the front of the vehicle and place it securely on jackstands. Remove the left or right front wheel.
2   Remove the left inner fender splash shield (see "Front fender - removal and installation" in Chapter 11).
3   Locate the turn signal bulb holder (see illustration). To remove the bulb holder, simply turn it counterclockwise 1/4-turn and pull it out of the front turn signal assembly. (It's not necessary to disconnect the electrical connector from the bulb holder.)
4   Remove the turn signal bulb from the bulb holder (see illustration).
5   Installation is the reverse of removal.

HIGH-MOUNT BRAKE LIGHT BULBS

► **Refer to illustrations 19.6a, 19.6b, 19.7a, 19.7b and 19.8**

6   Remove the high-mount brake light assembly mounting screws (see illustration) and washers, pull the assembly out and disconnect

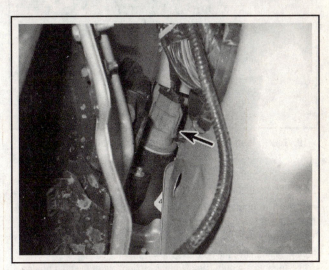

19.3 To remove the turn signal bulb holder, turn it counterclockwise 1/4-turn and pull it out of the front turn signal housing

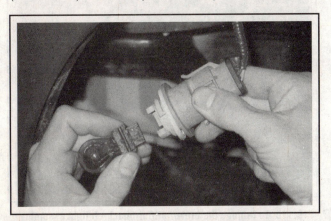

19.4 To remove the turn signal bulb from the bulb holder, pull it straight out of the holder

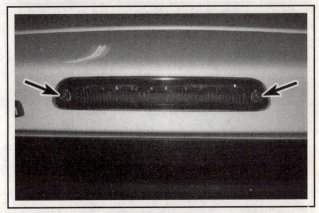

19.6a To detach the high-mount brake light assembly from the roof, remove these two screws and washers; discard the old screws and washers and use new ones when you install the high-mount brake light unit

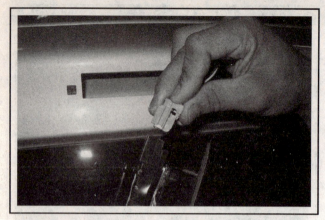

19.6b Pull out the high-mount brake light assembly and disconnect the electrical connector

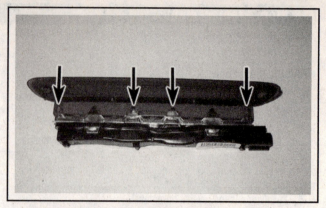

19.7a To separate the high-mount brake light bulb holder assembly from the lens, use a small screwdriver to disengage all six retaining snaps (two, on other side, not visible) . . .

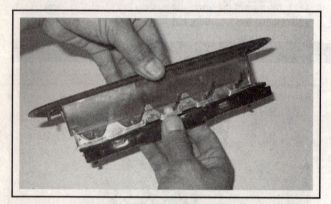

19.7b . . . then pull the bulb holder assembly out of the lens

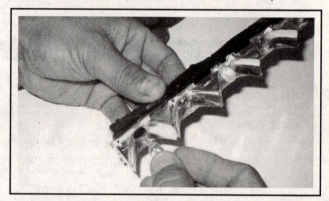

19.8 To replace a high-mount brake light bulb, simply pull it straight out of the bulb holder

the electrical connector (see illustration). Then place the high-mount brake light assembly on a work bench.

➡**Note: The manufacturer recommends that you discard the old mounting screws and washers.**

7 Separate the bulb holder assembly from the lens (see illustrations), then remove the bulb assembly from the housing.

8 To replace a bulb, simply pull it straight out of the bulb holder (see illustration).

9 To install a new bulb, push it straight into the bulb holder.

10 Installation is the reverse of removal. The manufacturer recommends that you use new mounting screws and washers.

BRAKE/TAIL/TURN/BACK-UP LIGHT BULBS

▶ **Refer to illustrations 19.11a, 19.11b, 19.12a, 19.12b and 19.13**

11 Remove the two brake/tail/turn/back-up assembly mounting screws (see illustration). To remove the assembly, pull it to the rear to

19.11a To detach the brake/tail/turn/back-up light assembly from the rear quarter panel, remove these two screws

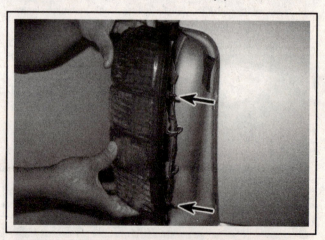

19.11b To remove the brake/tail/turn/back-up light assembly from the rear quarter panel, pop loose these two locator pins from their respective grommets in the rear quarter panel

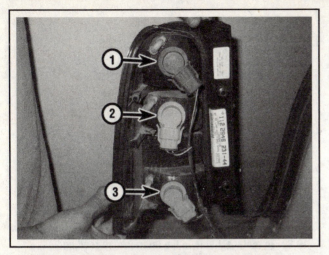

19.12a Brake/tail/turn signal/back-up light assembly

1   *Brake/tail light bulb*   3   *Back-up light bulb*
2   *Turn signal light bulb*

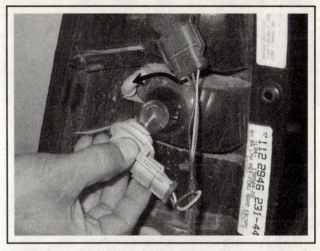

19.12b To remove a brake/tail light, turn signal or back-up light bulb socket, turn it counterclockwise 1/4-turn and pull it out

disengage the two locator pins on the outer edge of the lens from their corresponding grommets in the rear quarter panel (see illustration).

12 To replace a bulb, rotate the bulb socket counterclockwise and remove the bulb socket (see illustrations).

13 To remove a bulb from its socket, pull it straight out (see illustration).

14 To install a bulb in its socket, push it straight into the socket.

15 Installation is the reverse of removal.

LICENSE PLATE LIGHT BULBS

▸ **Refer to illustrations 19.16, 19.17 and 19.18**

16 Pry the license plate light assembly from the liftgate (see illustration).

17 To remove the bulb socket from the license plate light assembly, turn it counterclockwise a 1/4-turn and pull it out (see illustration).

18 To remove the bulb from the socket, pull it straight out (see illustration).

19.13 To remove a brake/tail light, turn signal or back-up light bulb, simply pull it straight out of the socket; to install a bulb, simply push it straight into the socket until it stops

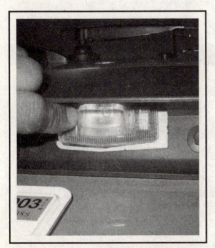

19.16 Pry the license plate light assembly from the liftgate

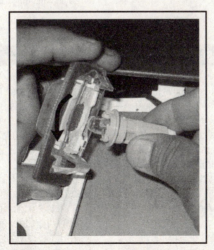

19.17 To remove the bulb socket from the license plate light assembly, turn it counterclockwise a 1/4-turn and pull it out

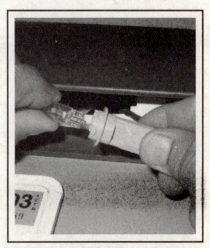

19.18 To remove the bulb from the socket, pull it straight out

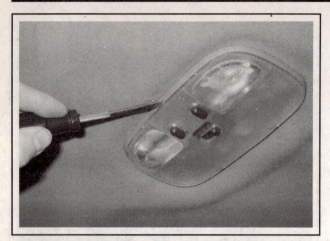

19.21 To remove the interior/map reading light lens, carefully pry it off with a small screwdriver inserted into this slot, which is provided for this purpose (prying off the lens elsewhere might damage or scratch the housing)

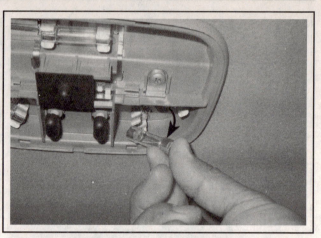

19.22 To replace a bulb in the interior/map reading light assembly, simply pull it out

19 To install a new bulb in the socket, push it straight into the socket.

20 Installation is the reverse of removal.

INTERIOR/MAP READING LIGHT

▶ **Refer to illustrations 19.21 and 19.22**

21 Carefully pry the interior/map reading light lens loose from the light assembly (see illustration).

22 To replace one of the light bulbs in the interior/map reading light assembly, simply pull it out (see illustration).

23 Installation is the reverse of removal.

CARGO LIGHT

▶ **Refer to illustration 19.25**

24 To remove the cargo light assembly from the headliner, simply pry it loose. Be careful not to damage the headliner.

25 To remove the cargo light bulb (see illustration), turn it counterclockwise a 1/4-turn and pull it out. To install a new bulb, insert it into the bulb holder and turn it clockwise until it locks into place.

26 Installation is the reverse of removal.

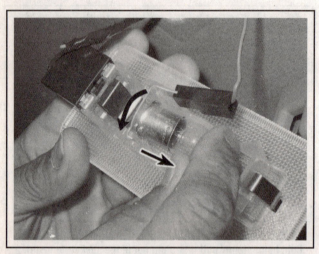

19.25 To replace the cargo light bulb, turn it counterclockwise and pull it out; to install a new bulb, insert it into the bulb holder and turn it clockwise until it locks into place

20 Electric side view mirrors - description

1 Most electric rear view mirrors use two motors to move the glass; one for up and down adjustments and one for left-right adjustments.

2 The control switch has a selector portion that sends voltage to the left or right side mirror. With the ignition ON but the engine OFF, roll down the windows and operate the mirror control switch through all functions (left-right and up-down) for both the left and right side mirrors.

3 Listen carefully for the sound of the electric motors running in the mirrors.

4 If the motors can be heard but the mirror glass doesn't move, there's a problem with the drive mechanism inside the mirror.

5 If the mirrors do not operate and no sound comes from the mir-

rors, check the fuse (see Section 3).

6 If the fuse is OK, remove the mirror control switch. Have the switch continuity checked by a dealership service department or other qualified automobile repair facility.

7 Test the ground connections. Refer to the wiring diagrams at the end of Chapter 12.

8 If the mirror still doesn't work, remove the mirror and check the wires at the mirror for voltage.

9 If there's not voltage in each switch position, check the circuit between the mirror and control switch for opens and shorts.

10 If there's voltage, remove the mirror and test it off the vehicle with jumper wires. Replace the mirror if it fails this test.

21 Cruise control system - description

1   The cruise control system maintains vehicle speed with an electrically-operated motor located in the engine compartment, which is connected to the throttle body by a cable. The system consists of the Powertrain Control Module, the speed control actuator, the speed control cable, the speed control indicator light, the speed control actuator switches, the Brake Pedal Position (BPP) switch, the Clutch Pedal Position (CPP) switch (models with a manual transaxle) or the Transmission Range (TR) sensor (models with an automatic transaxle). The cruise control system requires diagnostic procedures that are beyond the scope of this manual. Listed below are some general procedures that may be used to locate common problems.

2   Check the fuses (see Section 3).

3   Have an assistant operate the brake lights while you check their operation (voltage from the brake light switch deactivates the cruise control).

4   If the brake lights don't come on or stay on all the time, correct the problem and retest the cruise control system.

5   Visually inspect the control cable between the cruise control motor and the throttle linkage for free movement. Replace it if necessary.

6   Test drive the vehicle to determine if the cruise control is now working. If it isn't, take it to a dealer service department or an automotive electrical specialist for further diagnosis.

22 Power window system - description

1   The power window system operates electric motors, mounted in the doors, which lower and raise the windows. The system consists of the control switches, the motors, regulators, glass mechanisms and associated wiring.

2   The power windows can be lowered and raised from the master control switch by the driver or by remote switches located at the individual windows. Each window has a separate motor, which is reversible. The position of the control switch determines the polarity and therefore the direction of operation.

3   The circuit is protected by a fuse and a circuit breaker. Each motor is also equipped with an internal circuit breaker, this prevents one stuck window from disabling the whole system.

4   The power window system will only operate when the ignition switch is ON. In addition, many models have a window lockout switch at the master control switch which, when activated, disables the switches at the rear windows and, sometimes, the switch at the passenger's window also. Always check these items before troubleshooting a window problem.

5   These procedures are general in nature, so if you can't find the problem using them, take the vehicle to a dealer service department or other properly equipped repair facility.

6   If the power windows won't operate, always check the fuse and circuit breaker first.

7   If only the rear windows are inoperative, or if the windows only operate from the master control switch, check the rear window lockout switch for continuity in the unlocked position. Replace it if it doesn't have continuity.

8   Check the wiring between the switches and fuse panel for continuity. Repair the wiring, if necessary.

9   If only one window is inoperative from the master control switch, try the other control switch at the window.

➡**Note: This doesn't apply to the driver's door window.**

10   If the same window works from one switch, but not the other, check the switch for continuity.

11   If the switch tests OK, check for a short or open in the circuit between the affected switch and the window motor.

12   If one window is inoperative from both switches, remove the trim panel from the affected door and check for voltage at the switch and at the motor while the switch is operated.

13   If voltage is reaching the motor, disconnect the glass from the regulator (see Chapter 11). Move the window up and down by hand while checking for binding and damage. Also check for binding and damage to the regulator. If the regulator is not damaged and the window moves up and down smoothly, replace the motor. If there's binding or damage, lubricate, repair or replace parts, as necessary.

14   If voltage isn't reaching the motor, check the wiring in the circuit for continuity between the switches and motors. You'll need to consult the wiring diagram for the vehicle. If the circuit is equipped with a relay, check that the relay is grounded properly and receiving voltage.

23 Power door lock system - description

1   A power door lock system operates the door lock actuators mounted in each door. The system consists of the switches, actuators, a control unit and associated wiring. Diagnosis can usually be limited to simple checks of the wiring connections and actuators for minor faults that can be easily repaired.

2   Power door lock systems are operated by bi-directional solenoids located in the doors. The lock switches have two operating positions: Lock and Unlock. When activated, the switch sends a ground signal to the door lock control unit to lock or unlock the doors. Depending on which way the switch is activated, the control unit reverses polarity to the solenoids, allowing the two sides of the circuit to be used alternately as the feed (positive) and ground side.

3   Some vehicles may have an anti-theft system incorporated into the power locks. If you are unable to locate the trouble using the following general Steps, consult a dealer service department or other qualified repair shop.

4   Always check the circuit protection first. Some vehicles use a combination of circuit breakers and fuses.

5   Operate the door lock switches in both directions (Lock and Unlock) with the engine off. Listen for the click of the solenoids operating.

6   Test the switches for continuity. Remove the switches and have them checked by a dealer service department or other qualified automobile repair facility.

7   Check the wiring between the switches, control unit and solenoids for continuity. Repair the wiring if there's no continuity.

8   Check for a bad ground at the switches or the control unit.

9   If all but one lock solenoids operate, remove the trim panel from the affected door (see Chapter 11) and check for voltage at the solenoid while the lock switch is operated. One of the wires should have voltage in the Lock position; the other should have voltage in the Unlock position.

10 If the inoperative solenoid is receiving voltage, replace the solenoid.

11 If the inoperative solenoid isn't receiving voltage, check the relay for an open or short in the wire between the lock solenoid and the control unit.

➡**Note: It's common for wires to break in the portion of the harness between the body and door (opening and closing the door fatigues and eventually breaks the wires).**

24 Daytime Running Lights (DRL) - general information

The Daytime Running Lights (DRL) system illuminates the headlights whenever the engine is running. The only exception is with the engine running and the parking brake engaged. Once the parking brake is released, the lights will remain on as long as the ignition switch is on, even if the parking brake is later applied.

The DRL system supplies reduced power to the headlights so they won't be too bright for daytime use, while prolonging headlight life.

25 Airbag system - general information and precautions

GENERAL INFORMATION

▶ **Refer to illustration 25.1**

1   All models are equipped with a Supplemental Restraint System (SRS), more commonly known as airbags. This system is designed to protect the driver, and the front seat passenger, from serious injury in the event of a head-on or frontal collision and side impacts. It uses an electronic crash sensor, which is referred to by the manufacturer as the Restraints Control Module (RCM) and a side-impact sensor in each B-pillar. The airbag assemblies are mounted on the steering wheel and inside the passenger's side of the dash (see illustration), and in the side of each front seat back. Some 2001 models and all 2002 and later models are equipped with seat belt pre-tensioners. These are pyrotechnic devices controlled by the Restraints Control Module (RCM) that reduce the slack in the seat belts during an impact of sufficient force to trigger the airbags.

AIRBAG MODULE

Driver's airbag

2   The airbag inflator module contains a housing incorporating the cushion (airbag) and inflator unit, mounted in the center of the steering wheel. The inflator assembly is mounted on the back of the housing over a hole through which gas is expelled, inflating the bag almost instantaneously when an electrical signal is sent from the system. A "clockspring" on the steering column under the steering wheel carries this signal to the module. This clockspring assembly can transmit an electrical signal regardless of steering wheel position. The igniter in the airbag converts the electrical signal to heat and ignites the powder, which inflates the bag.

3   For information on how to remove and install the driver's side airbag, refer to "Steering wheel - removal and installation" in Chapter 10.

Passenger's airbag

4   The airbag is mounted above the glove compartment. It consists of an inflator containing an igniter, a reaction housing/airbag assembly and a trim cover.

25.1 The passenger side airbag module is located inside the dash, right above the glove box

5   The passenger's side airbag is considerably larger than the steering wheel-mounted unit and is supported by the steel reaction housing. The trim cover is textured and painted to match the instrument panel and has a molded seam, which splits when the bag inflates.

Side impact airbags

6   These airbags are mounted on the outboard side of the front seat back frames. In the event of a side impact of sufficient force they inflate, ripping open the front seat back trim covers and deploy to protect the occupant.

RESTRAINTS CONTROL MODULE (RCM)

7   This unit supplies the current to the airbag system (and seat belt pre-tensioners, on models so equipped) in the event of the collision, even if battery power is cut off. It checks this system every time the vehicle is started, causing the "SRS" light to go on, then off, if the system is operating properly. If there is a fault in the system, the light will go on and stay on, or it will flash or the dash will make a beeping sound. If this happens, take the vehicle to your dealer immediately for service.

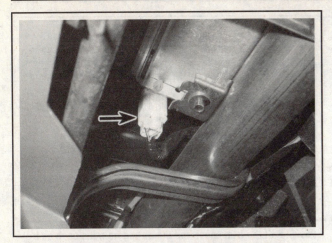

25.11 The electrical connector for the passenger's side airbag is located above the glove box recess, to the left of the airbag module (glove box removed for clarity)

DISARMING THE SYSTEM AND OTHER PRECAUTIONS

▶ **Refer to illustration 25.10**

✳✳ WARNING 1:

Failure to follow these precautions could result in accidental deployment of the airbag and personal injury.

✳✳ WARNING 2:

Never probe the connectors of the SRS. Do not move or remount from the original position any SRS component. Never Move an SRS component with the key in the ON position. Do not use any memory saver devices.

8 Whenever working in the vicinity of the steering wheel, instrument panel or any of the other SRS system components, the system must be disarmed. To disarm the system:

2004 and earlier models

   a) *Point the wheels straight ahead and turn the key to the Lock position.*
   b) *Disconnect the cable from the negative battery terminal. Refer to Chapter 5, Section 1 for the disconnecting procedure.*
   c) *Wait at least two minutes for the back-up power supply to be depleted.*

2005 and later models

De-powering procedure

Note: The airbag warning lamp illuminates when the Restraint Control Module fuse is removed and the ignition switch is ON. This is normal operation and does not indicate a fault in the SRS.

   a) *Turn all accessories OFF.*
   b) *Turn the ignition to OFF.*
   c) *At the Smart Junction Box, located at the right side of the center console, remove the cover.*
   d) *With the cover off, locate and remove the Restraints Control Module (RCM) fuse.*
   e) *Turn the ignition ON and monitor the airbag warning light for a*

minimum of 30 seconds. If the correct RCM fuse has been removed the light will remain lit continuously without flashing. If the airbag warning light does not remain lit continuously, STOP and remove the correct fuse and monitor the light as outlined.
   f) *Turn the ignition switch OFF.*
   g) *Disconnect the cable from the negative terminal of the battery and wait at least one minute before proceeding.*

Re-powering procedure

✳✳ WARNING:

Make sure that there is no one in the vehicle and that nothing is blocking any airbag module while performing the Re-power procedure.

   a) *Turn the ignition switch from OFF to ON.*
   b) *Reinstall the RCM fuse in the Smart Junction Box, then install the cover*
   c) *Connect the cable to the negative terminal of the battery.*
   d) *Check the system by turning the ignition switch from ON to OFF.*
   e) *Wait 10 seconds, then turn the key back to the ON position.*
   f) *Visually monitor the airbag warning light. The light should remain lit for about 6 seconds, then turn off.*
   g) *It may take 30 seconds or more for the RCM to complete the self tests. If any fault is present in the system, the light will either fail to light, remain lit or flash.*
   h) *If the airbag warning light is inoperative and a fault exists, a chime will sound in a series of 5 sets of 5 beeps.*
   i) *If there is any fault in the system, bring the vehicle to a professional automotive repair facility for proper diagnosis and repair.*

9 Whenever handling an airbag module, always keep the airbag opening (the trim side) pointed away from your body. Never place the airbag module on a bench or other surface with the airbag opening facing the surface. Always place the airbag module in a safe location with the airbag opening facing up.

10 Never measure the resistance of any SRS component or use any electrical test equipment on any of the wiring or components. An ohmmeter has a built-in battery supply that could accidentally deploy the airbag.

11 Never use electrical welding equipment on a vehicle equipped with an airbag without first disconnecting the airbag electrical connectors, located behind a panel on the underside of the steering wheel (driver's airbag) (see Chapter 10) and above the glove box (passenger's airbag) (see illustration) and under each front seat (side-impact airbags). On models with seat belt pre-tensioners, the pre-tensioner electrical connectors are also located under the seats.

12 Never dispose of a live airbag module or seat belt pre-tensioner. Return it to a dealer service department or other qualified repair shop for safe deployment and disposal.

AIRBAG MODULE REMOVAL AND INSTALLATION

Driver's airbag module and clockspring

13 Refer to Chapter 10, "Steering wheel - removal and installation", for the driver's side airbag module and clockspring removal and installation procedures.

Passenger's airbag module

▶ **Refer to illustrations 25.16 and 25.17**

14 Disarm the airbag system as described previously in this Section.

25.17 To detach the passenger side airbag from the dash, remove these four bolts, then carefully but firmly push on the airbag module to disengage the trim cover from the top of the dash

15 Remove the glove box (see "Instrument panel - removal and installation" in Chapter 11).

16 Disconnect the electrical connector (see illustration 25.11).

17 Remove the airbag module mounting bolts (see illustration). After removing the bolts, carefully but firmly push up on the airbag module to disengage the trim cover from the top of the dash (the airbag module and trim cover are attached and are removed as a single assembly). Do NOT try to pry open the trim cover from up top, or you will damage the surface of the dash and/or the trim cover.

18 Working from above, pull the airbag trim cover and airbag module out of the dash (see illustration). Be sure to heed the precautions

25.18 Pull the trim cover and the airbag from the dash as a single assembly. Be sure to keep your body positioned to the side of the airbag

outlined previously in this Section.

19 Installation is the reverse of the removal procedure. Tighten the airbag module mounting bolts securely.

20 After you've reconnected the battery, the Powertrain Control Module (PCM) must relearn its idle and fuel trim strategy for optimum driveability and performance (see Chapter 5, Section 1 for this procedure).

Side-impact airbag

21 Under normal circumstances there would never be a reason to remove a seat airbag. However, if it has been determined that there is a problem with the side-impact airbag module, the work must be left to a dealer service department or other qualified repair shop.

26 Wiring diagrams - general information

Since it isn't possible to include all wiring diagrams for every year covered by this manual, the following diagrams are those that are typical and most commonly needed.

Prior to troubleshooting any circuits, check the fuse and circuit breakers (if equipped) to make sure they're in good condition. Make

sure the battery is properly charged and check the cable connections (see Chapter 1).

When checking a circuit, make sure that all connectors are clean, with no broken or loose terminals. When unplugging a connector, do not pull on the wires. Pull only on the connector housings themselves.

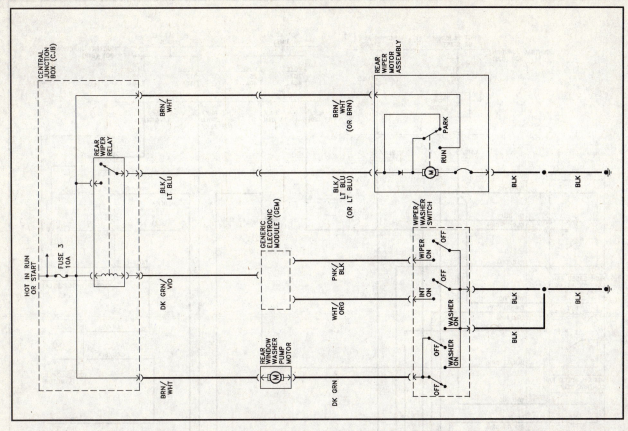

Rear wiper/washer system

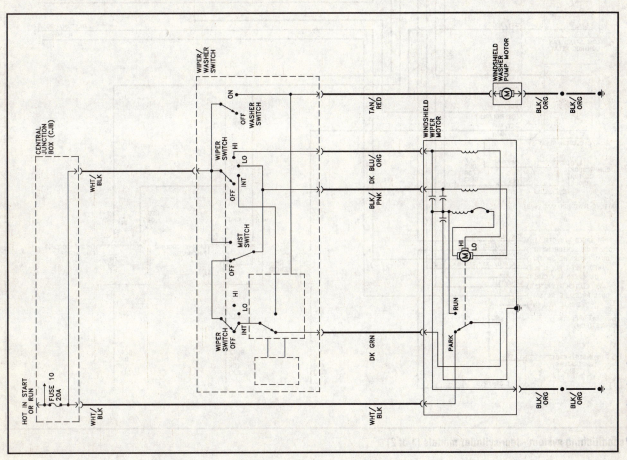

Front wiper/washer system

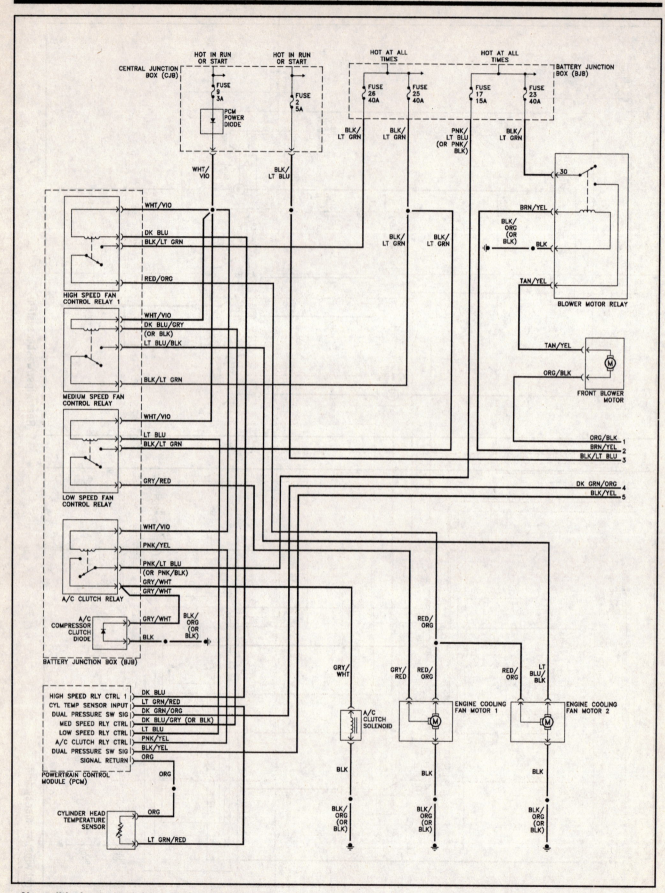

Air conditioning system - four-cylinder models (1 of 2)

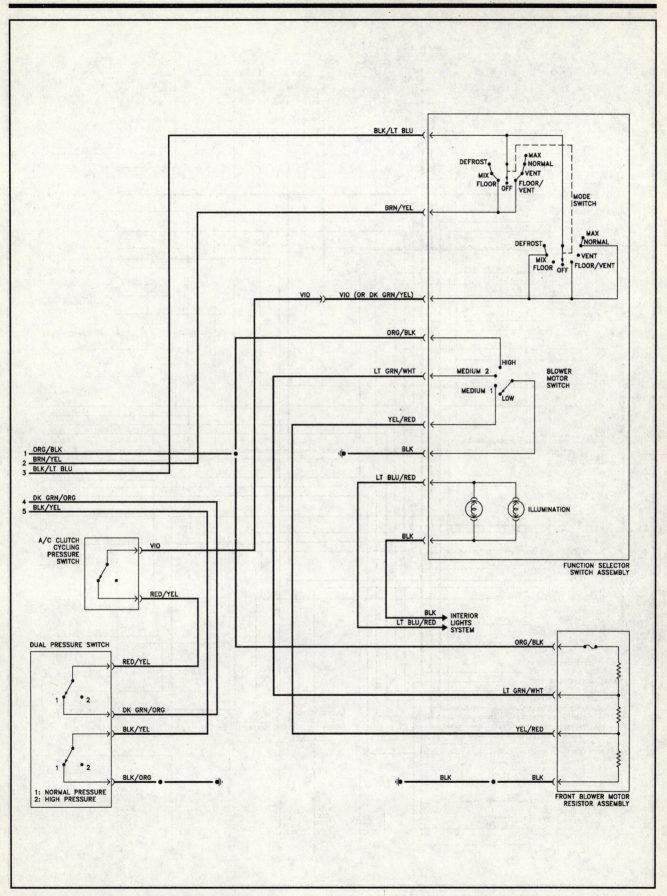

Air conditioning system - four-cylinder models (2 of 2)

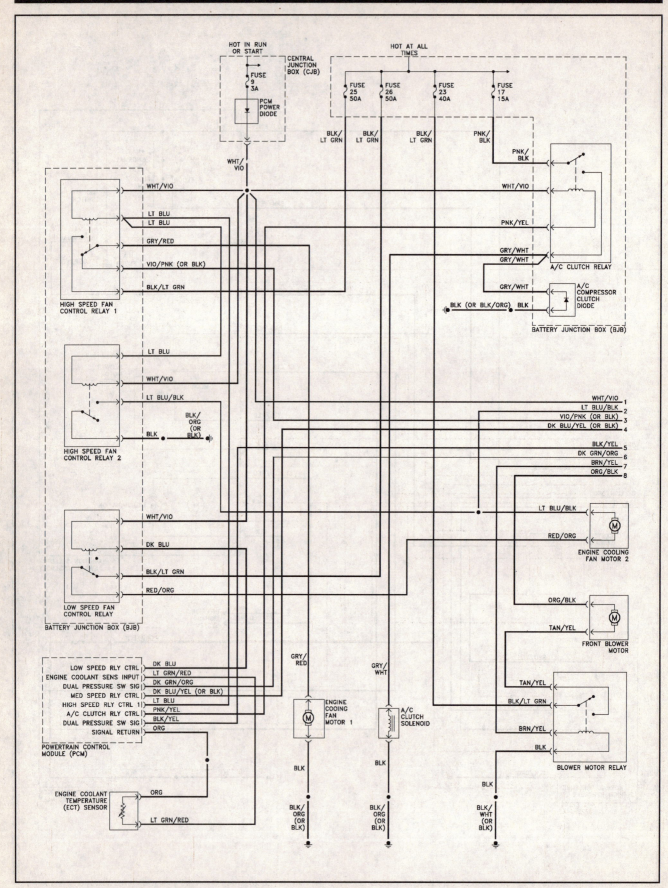

Air conditioning system - V6 models (1 of 2)

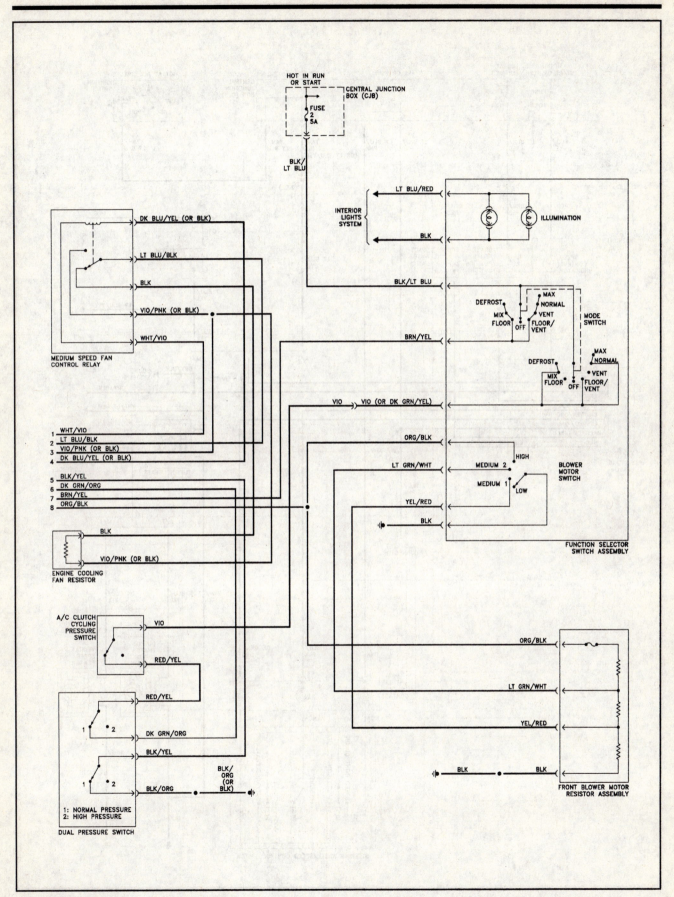

Air conditioning system - V6 models (2 of 2)

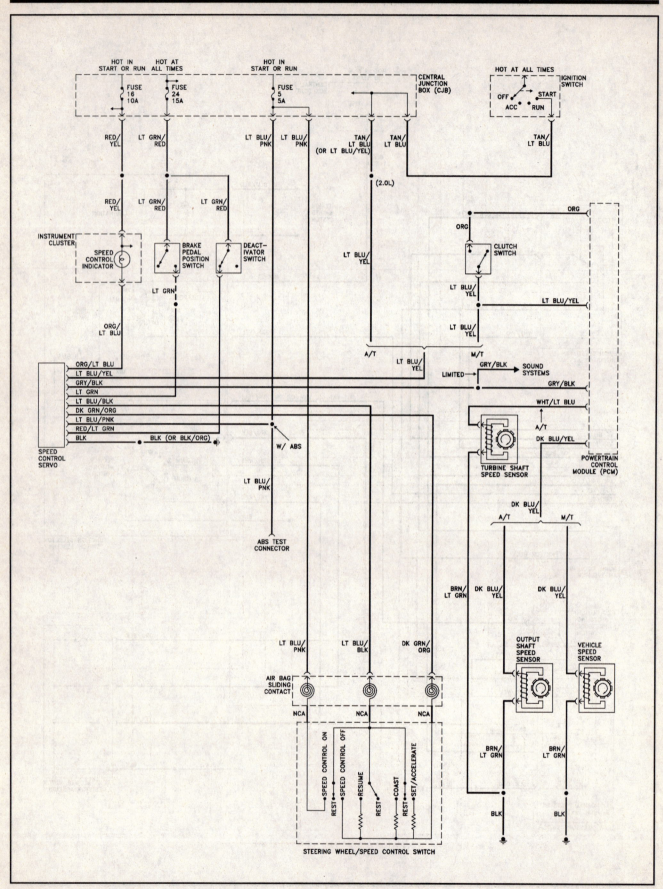

Cruise control system

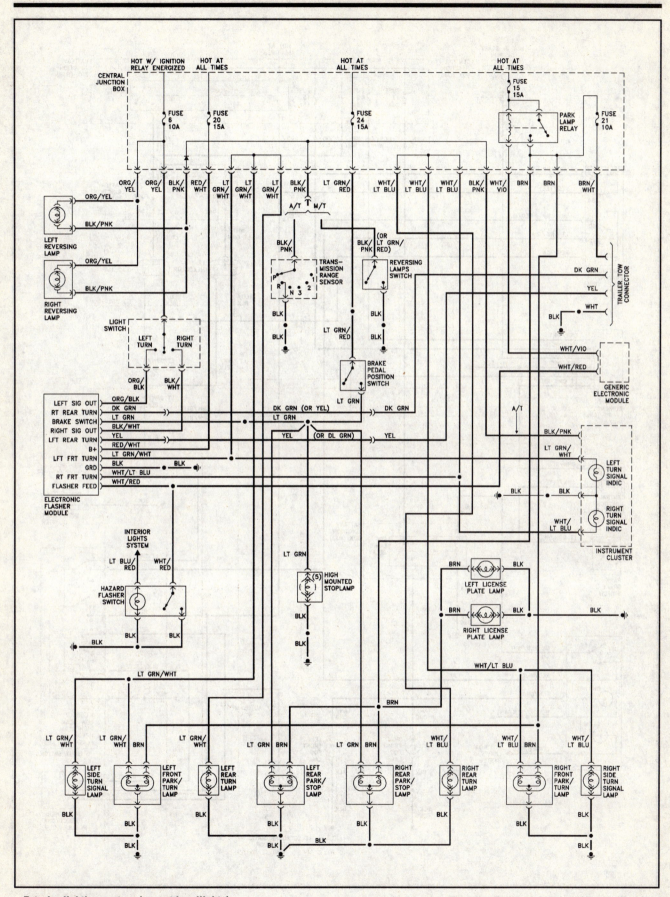

Exterior lighting system (except headlights)

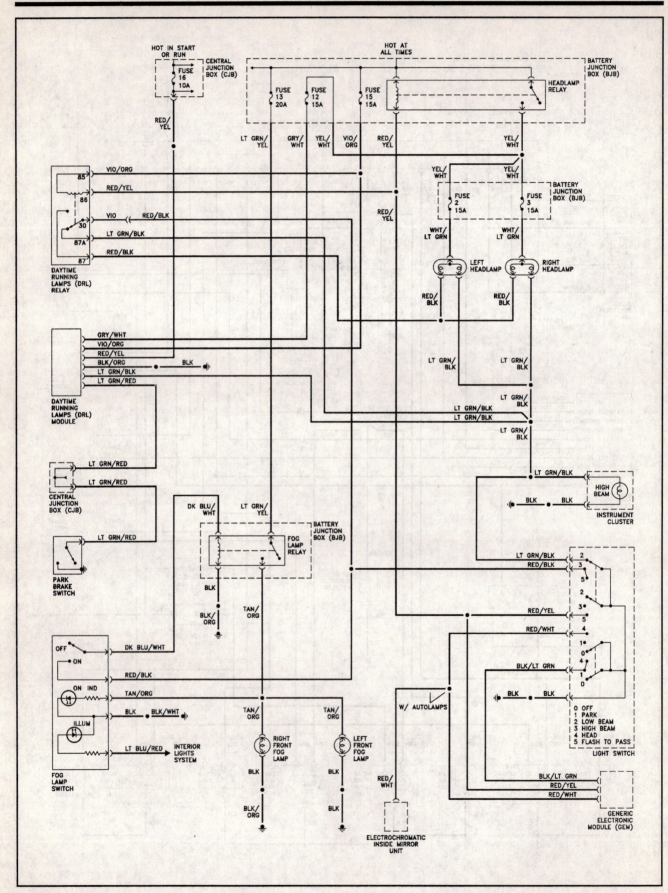

Headlight system (models with Daytime Running Lights)

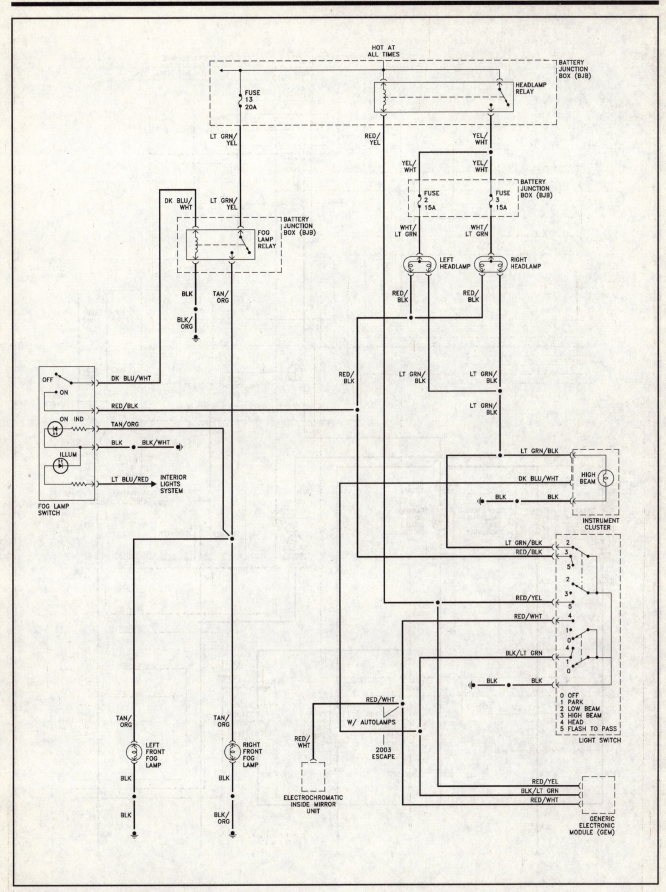

Headlight system (models without Daytime Running Lights)

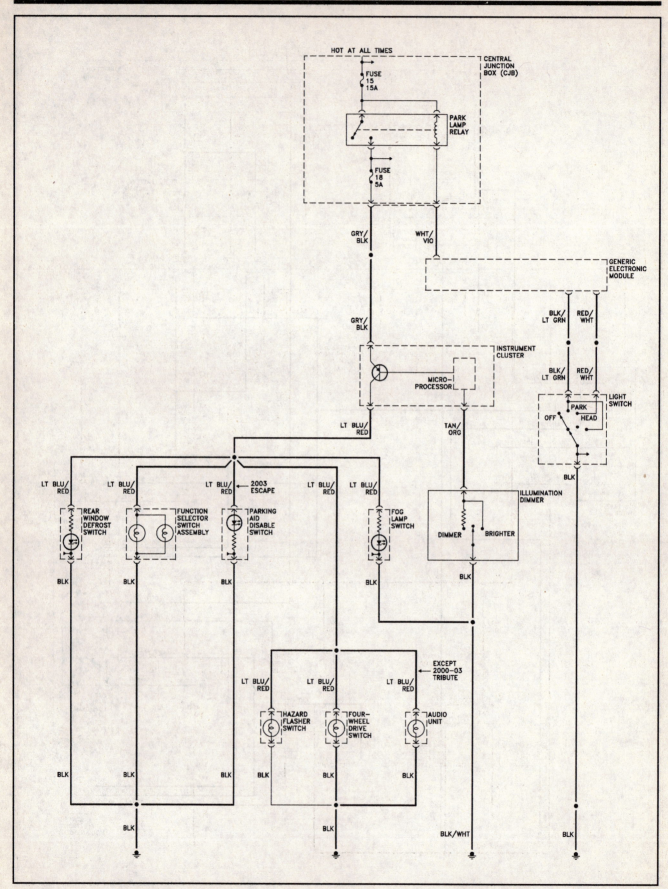

Instrument panel and switch illumination system

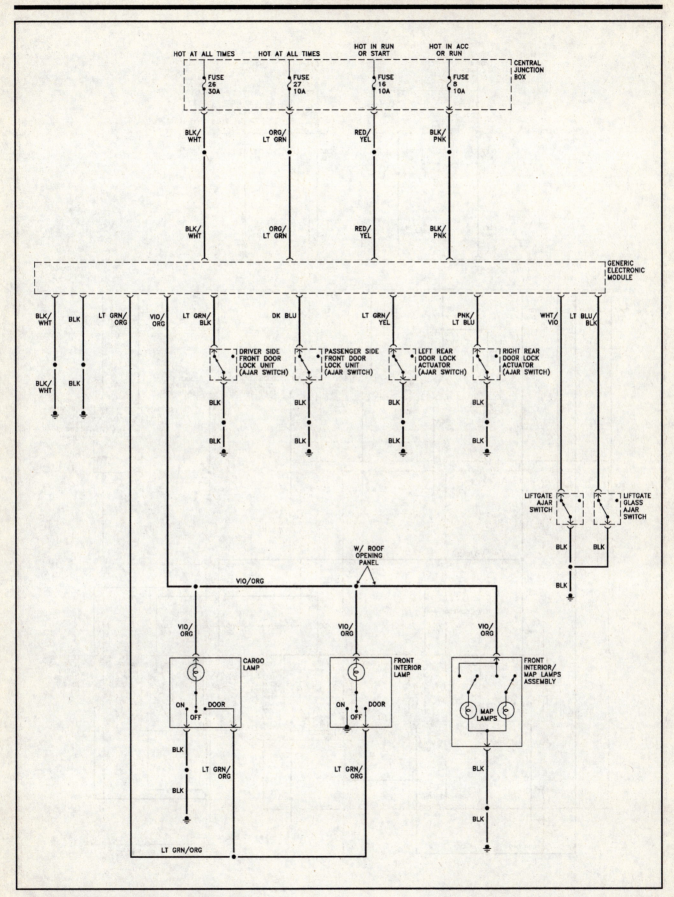

Interior lighting system (2001 and 2002 models)

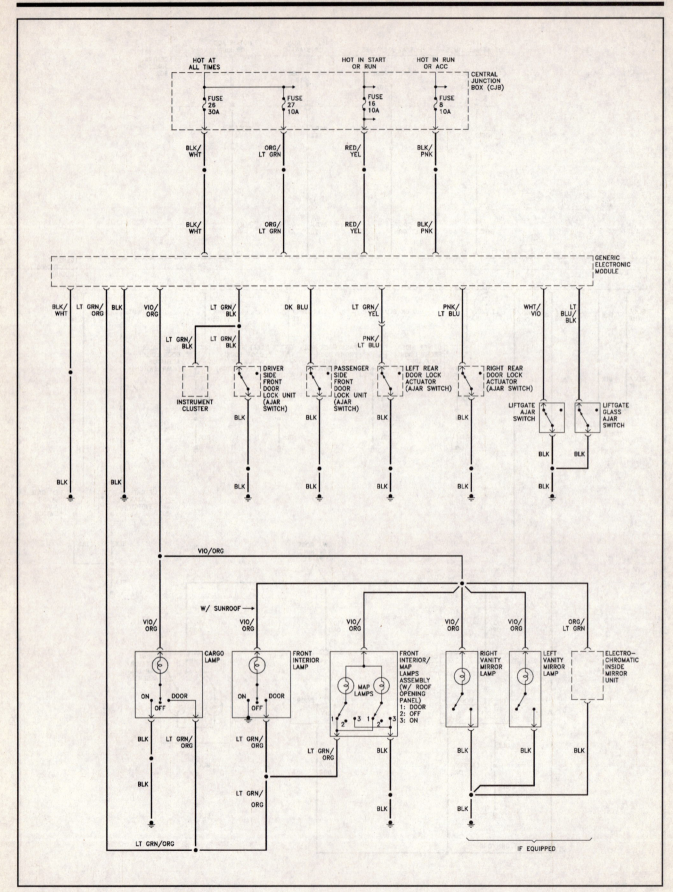

Interior lighting system (2003 models)

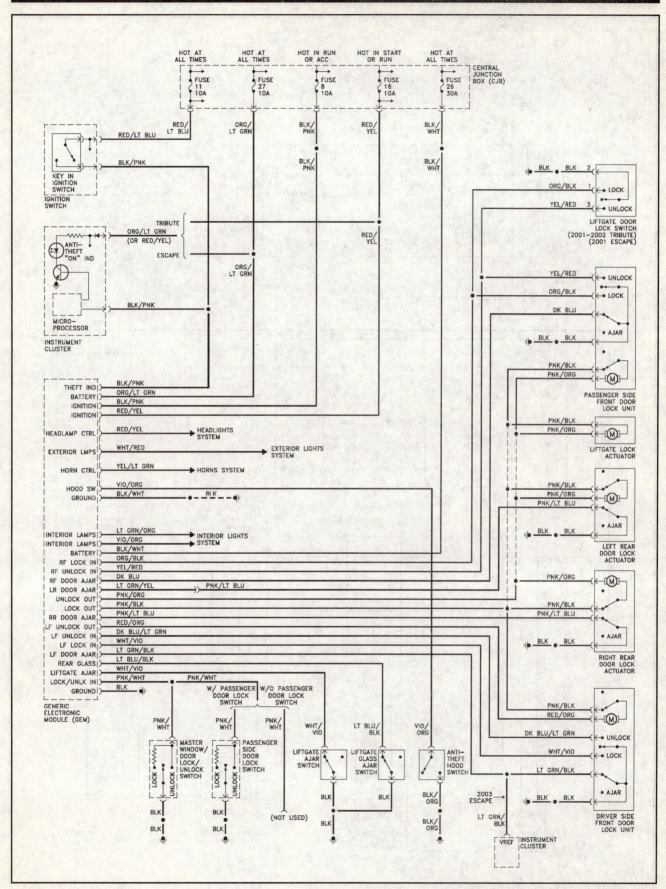

Power door lock system

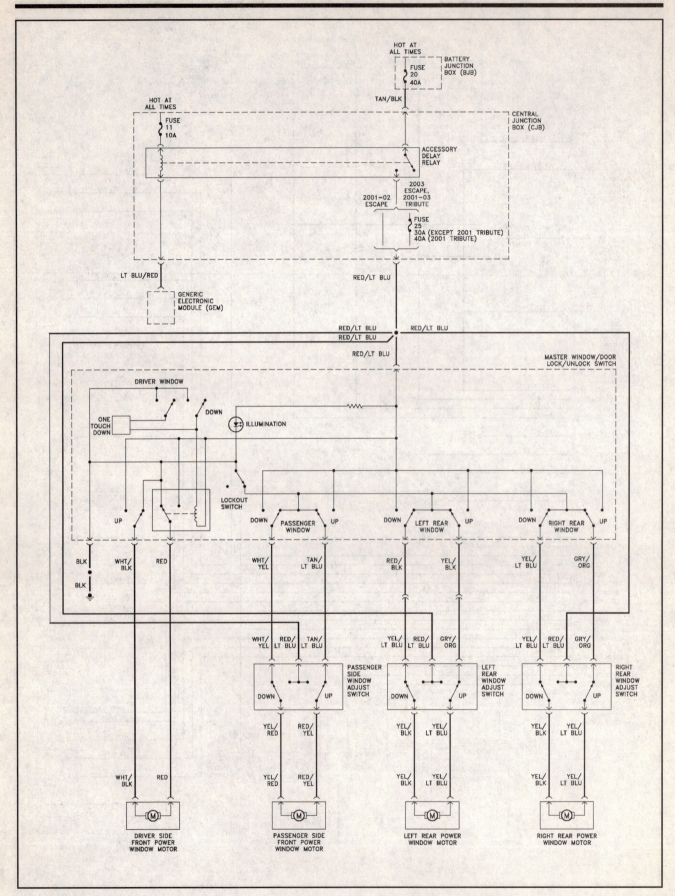

Power window system

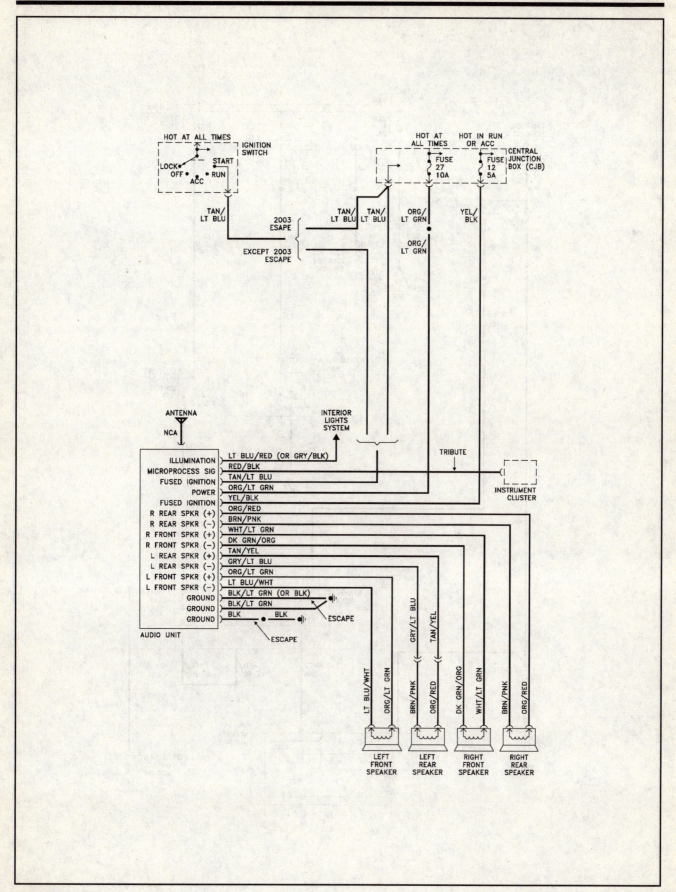

Audio system

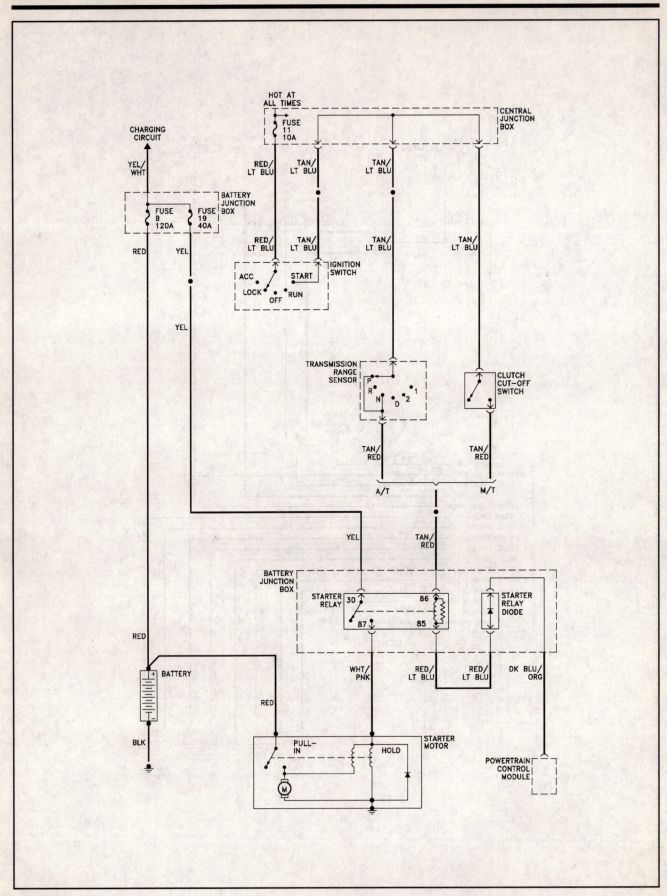

Starting system

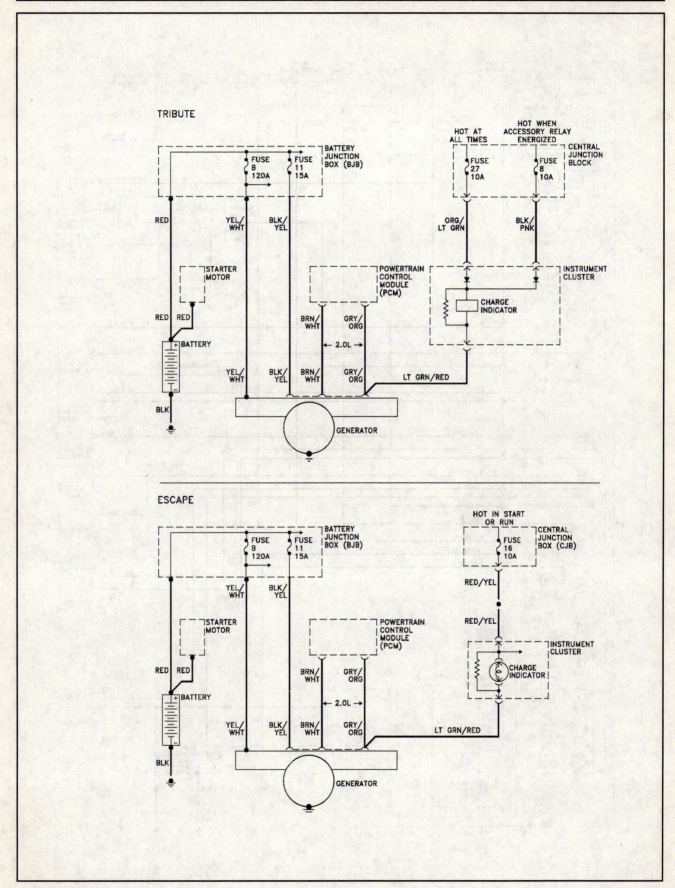

Charging system

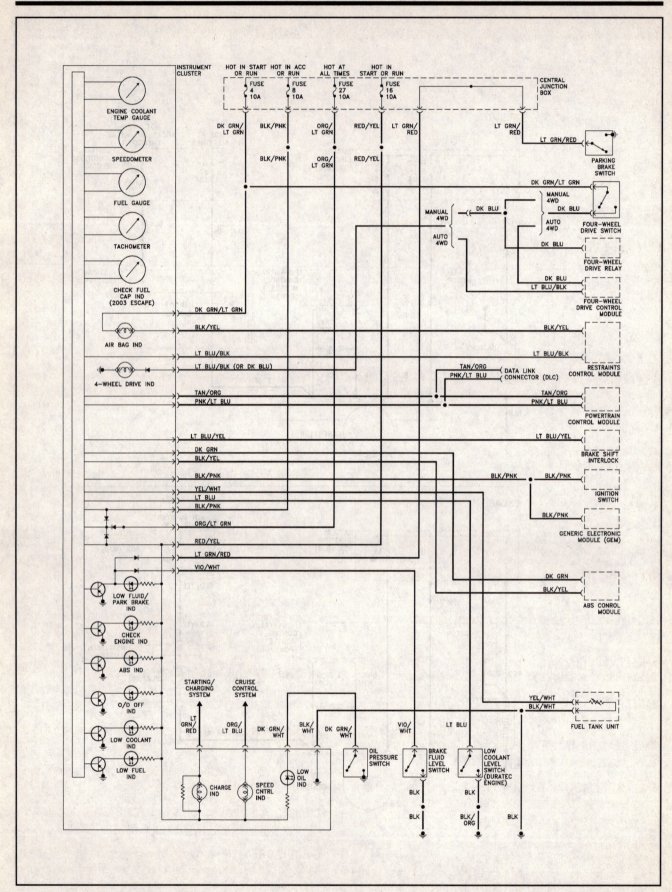

Instrument cluster and related circuits

GLOSSARY

AIR/FUEL RATIO: The ratio of air-to-gasoline by weight in the fuel mixture drawn into the engine.

AIR INJECTION: One method of reducing harmful exhaust emissions by injecting air into each of the exhaust ports of an engine. The fresh air entering the hot exhaust manifold causes any remaining fuel to be burned before it can exit the tailpipe.

ALTERNATOR: A device used for converting mechanical energy into electrical energy.

AMMETER: An instrument, calibrated in amperes, used to measure the flow of an electrical current in a circuit. Ammeters are always connected in series with the circuit being tested.

AMPERE: The rate of flow of electrical current present when one volt of electrical pressure is applied against one ohm of electrical resistance.

ANALOG COMPUTER: Any microprocessor that uses similar (analogous) electrical signals to make its calculations.

ARMATURE: A laminated, soft iron core wrapped by a wire that converts electrical energy to mechanical energy as in a motor or relay. When rotated in a magnetic field, it changes mechanical energy into electrical energy as in a generator.

ATMOSPHERIC PRESSURE: The pressure on the Earth's surface caused by the weight of the air in the atmosphere. At sea level, this pressure is 14.7 psi at 32°F (101 kPa at 0°C).

ATOMIZATION: The breaking down of a liquid into a fine mist that can be suspended in air.

AXIAL PLAY: Movement parallel to a shaft or bearing bore.

BACKFIRE: The sudden combustion of gases in the intake or exhaust system that results in a loud explosion.

BACKLASH: The clearance or play between two parts, such as meshed gears.

BACKPRESSURE: Restrictions in the exhaust system that slow the exit of exhaust gases from the combustion chamber.

BAKELITE: A heat resistant, plastic insulator material commonly used in printed circuit boards and transistorized components.

BALL BEARING: A bearing made up of hardened inner and outer races between which hardened steel balls roll.

BALLAST RESISTOR: A resistor in the primary ignition circuit that lowers voltage after the engine is started to reduce wear on ignition components.

BEARING: A friction reducing, supportive device usually located between a stationary part and a moving part.

BIMETAL TEMPERATURE SENSOR: Any sensor or switch made of two dissimilar types of metal that bend when heated or cooled due to the different expansion rates of the alloys. These types of sensors usually function as an on/off switch.

BLOWBY: Combustion gases, composed of water vapor and unburned fuel, that leak past the piston rings into the crankcase during normal engine operation. These gases are removed by the PCV system to prevent the buildup of harmful acids in the crankcase.

BRAKE PAD: A brake shoe and lining assembly used with disc brakes.

BRAKE SHOE: The backing for the brake lining. The term is, however, usually applied to the assembly of the brake backing and lining.

BUSHING: A liner, usually removable, for a bearing; an anti-friction liner used in place of a bearing.

CALIPER: A hydraulically activated device in a disc brake system, which is mounted straddling the brake rotor (disc). The caliper contains at least one piston and two brake pads. Hydraulic pressure on the piston(s) forces the pads against the rotor.

CAMSHAFT: A shaft in the engine on which are the lobes (cams) which operate the valves. The camshaft is driven by the crankshaft, via a belt, chain or gears, at one half the crankshaft speed.

CAPACITOR: A device which stores an electrical charge.

CARBON MONOXIDE (CO): A colorless, odorless gas given off as a normal byproduct of combustion. It is poisonous and extremely dangerous in confined areas, building up slowly to toxic levels without warning if adequate ventilation is not available.

CARBURETOR: A device, usually mounted on the intake manifold of an engine, which mixes the air and fuel in the proper proportion to allow even combustion.

CATALYTIC CONVERTER: A device installed in the exhaust system, like a muffler, that converts harmful byproducts of combustion into carbon dioxide and water vapor by means of a heat-producing chemical reaction.

CENTRIFUGAL ADVANCE: A mechanical method of advancing the spark timing by using flyweights in the distributor that react to centrifugal force generated by the distributor shaft rotation.

CHECK VALVE: Any one-way valve installed to permit the flow of air, fuel or vacuum in one direction only.

CHOKE: A device, usually a moveable valve, placed in the intake path of a carburetor to restrict the flow of air.

CIRCUIT: Any unbroken path through which an electrical current can flow. Also used to describe fuel flow in some instances.

CIRCUIT BREAKER: A switch which protects an electrical circuit from overload by opening the circuit when the current flow exceeds a predetermined level. Some circuit breakers must be reset manually, while most reset automatically.

COIL (IGNITION): A transformer in the ignition circuit which steps up the voltage provided to the spark plugs.

COMBINATION MANIFOLD: An assembly which includes both the intake and exhaust manifolds in one casting.

COMBINATION VALVE: A device used in some fuel systems that routes fuel vapors to a charcoal storage canister instead of venting them into the atmosphere. The valve relieves fuel tank pressure and allows fresh air into the tank as the fuel level drops to prevent a vapor lock situation.

COMPRESSION RATIO: The comparison of the total volume of the cylinder and combustion chamber with the piston at BDC and the piston at TDC.

CONDENSER: 1. An electrical device which acts to store an electrical charge, preventing voltage surges. 2. A radiator-like device in the air conditioning system in which refrigerant gas condenses into a liquid, giving off heat.

CONDUCTOR: Any material through which an electrical current can be transmitted easily.

CONTINUITY: Continuous or complete circuit. Can be checked with an ohmmeter.

COUNTERSHAFT: An intermediate shaft which is rotated by a mainshaft and transmits, in turn, that rotation to a working part.

CRANKCASE: The lower part of an engine in which the crankshaft and related parts operate.

CRANKSHAFT: The main driving shaft of an engine which receives reciprocating motion from the pistons and converts it to rotary motion.

CYLINDER: In an engine, the round hole in the engine block in which the piston(s) ride.

CYLINDER BLOCK: The main structural member of an engine in which is found the cylinders, crankshaft and other principal parts.

CYLINDER HEAD: The detachable portion of the engine, usually fastened to the top of the cylinder block and containing all or most of the combustion chambers. On overhead valve engines, it contains the valves and their operating parts. On overhead cam engines, it contains the camshaft as well.

DEAD CENTER: The extreme top or bottom of the piston stroke.

DETONATION: An unwanted explosion of the air/fuel mixture in the combustion chamber caused by excess heat and compression, advanced timing, or an overly lean mixture. Also referred to as "ping".

DIAPHRAGM: A thin, flexible wall separating two cavities, such as in a vacuum advance unit.

DIESELING: A condition in which hot spots in the combustion chamber cause the engine to run on after the key is turned off.

DIFFERENTIAL: A geared assembly which allows the transmission of motion between drive axles, giving one axle the ability to turn faster than the other.

DIODE: An electrical device that will allow current to flow in one direction only.

DISC BRAKE: A hydraulic braking assembly consisting of a brake disc, or rotor, mounted on an axle, and a caliper assembly containing, usually two brake pads which are activated by hydraulic pressure. The pads are forced against the sides of the disc, creating friction which slows the vehicle.

DISTRIBUTOR: A mechanically driven device on an engine which is responsible for electrically firing the spark plug at a predetermined point of the piston stroke.

DOWEL PIN: A pin, inserted in mating holes in two different parts allowing those parts to maintain a fixed relationship.

DRUM BRAKE: A braking system which consists of two brake shoes and one or two wheel cylinders, mounted on a fixed backing plate, and a brake drum, mounted on an axle, which revolves around the assembly.

DWELL: The rate, measured in degrees of shaft rotation, at which an electrical circuit cycles on and off.

ELECTRONIC CONTROL UNIT (ECU): Ignition module, module, amplifier or igniter. See Module for definition.

ELECTRONIC IGNITION: A system in which the timing and firing of the spark plugs is controlled by an electronic control unit, usually called a module. These systems have no points or condenser.

END-PLAY: The measured amount of axial movement in a shaft.

ENGINE: A device that converts heat into mechanical energy.

EXHAUST MANIFOLD: A set of cast passages or pipes which conduct exhaust gases from the engine.

FEELER GAUGE: A blade, usually metal, or precisely predetermined thickness, used to measure the clearance between two parts.

FIRING ORDER: The order in which combustion occurs in the cylinders of an engine. Also the order in which spark is distributed to the plugs by the distributor.

FLOODING: The presence of too much fuel in the intake manifold and combustion chamber which prevents the air/fuel mixture from firing, thereby causing a no-start situation.

FLYWHEEL: A disc shaped part bolted to the rear end of the crankshaft. Around the outer perimeter is affixed the ring gear. The starter drive engages the ring gear, turning the flywheel, which rotates the crankshaft, imparting the initial starting motion to the engine.

FOOT POUND (ft. lbs. or sometimes, ft.lb.): The amount of energy or work needed to raise an item weighing one pound, a distance of one foot.

FUSE: A protective device in a circuit which prevents circuit overload by breaking the circuit when a specific amperage is present. The device is constructed around a strip or wire of a lower amperage rating than the circuit it is designed to protect. When an amperage higher than that stamped on the fuse is present in the circuit, the strip or wire melts, opening the circuit.

GEAR RATIO: The ratio between the number of teeth on meshing gears.

GENERATOR: A device which converts mechanical energy into electrical energy.

HEAT RANGE: The measure of a spark plug's ability to dissipate heat from its firing end. The higher the heat range, the hotter the plug fires.

HUB: The center part of a wheel or gear.

HYDROCARBON (HC): Any chemical compound made up of hydrogen and carbon. A major pollutant formed by the engine as a byproduct of combustion.

HYDROMETER: An instrument used to measure the specific gravity of a solution.

INCH POUND (inch lbs.; sometimes in.lb. or in. lbs.): One twelfth of a foot pound.

INDUCTION: A means of transferring electrical energy in the form of a magnetic field. Principle used in the ignition coil to increase voltage.

INJECTOR: A device which receives metered fuel under relatively low pressure and is activated to inject the fuel into the engine under relatively high pressure at a predetermined time.

INPUT SHAFT: The shaft to which torque is applied, usually carrying the driving gear or gears.

INTAKE MANIFOLD: A casting of passages or pipes used to conduct air or a fuel/air mixture to the cylinders.

JOURNAL: The bearing surface within which a shaft operates.

KEY: A small block usually fitted in a notch between a shaft and a hub to prevent slippage of the two parts.

MANIFOLD: A casting of passages or set of pipes which connect the cylinders to an inlet or outlet source.

MANIFOLD VACUUM: Low pressure in an engine intake manifold formed just below the throttle plates. Manifold vacuum is highest at idle and drops under acceleration.

MASTER CYLINDER: The primary fluid pressurizing device in a hydraulic system. In automotive use, it is found in brake and hydraulic clutch systems and is pedal activated, either directly or, in a power brake system, through the power booster.

MODULE: Electronic control unit, amplifier or igniter of solid state or integrated design which controls the current flow in the ignition primary circuit based on input from the pick-up coil. When the module opens the primary circuit, high secondary voltage is induced in the coil.

NEEDLE BEARING: A bearing which consists of a number (usually a large number) of long, thin rollers.

OHM: (Ω) The unit used to measure the resistance of conductor-to-electrical flow. One ohm is the amount of resistance that limits current flow to one ampere in a circuit with one volt of pressure.

OHMMETER: An instrument used for measuring the resistance, in ohms, in an electrical circuit.

OUTPUT SHAFT: The shaft which transmits torque from a device, such as a transmission.

OVERDRIVE: A gear assembly which produces more shaft revolutions than that transmitted to it.

OVERHEAD CAMSHAFT (OHC): An engine configuration in which the camshaft is mounted on top of the cylinder head and operates the valve either directly or by means of rocker arms.

OVERHEAD VALVE (OHV): An engine configuration in which all of the valves are located in the cylinder head and the camshaft is located in the cylinder block. The camshaft operates the valves via lifters and pushrods.

OXIDES OF NITROGEN (NOx): Chemical compounds of nitrogen produced as a byproduct of combustion. They combine with hydrocarbons to produce smog.

OXYGEN SENSOR: Use with the feedback system to sense the presence of oxygen in the exhaust gas and signal the computer which can reference the voltage signal to an air/fuel ratio.

PINION: The smaller of two meshing gears.

PISTON RING: An open-ended ring with fits into a groove on the outer diameter of the piston. Its chief function is to form a seal between the piston and cylinder wall. Most automotive pistons have three rings: two for compression sealing; one for oil sealing.

PRELOAD: A predetermined load placed on a bearing during assembly or by adjustment.

PRIMARY CIRCUIT: the low voltage side of the ignition system which consists of the ignition switch, ballast resistor or resistance wire, bypass, coil, electronic control unit and pick-up coil as well as the connecting wires and harnesses.

PRESS FIT: The mating of two parts under pressure, due to the inner diameter of one being smaller than the outer diameter of the other, or vice versa; an interference fit.

RACE: The surface on the inner or outer ring of a bearing on which the balls, needles or rollers move.

REGULATOR: A device which maintains the amperage and/or voltage levels of a circuit at predetermined values.

RELAY: A switch which automatically opens and/or closes a circuit.

RESISTANCE: The opposition to the flow of current through a circuit or electrical device, and is measured in ohms. Resistance is equal to the voltage divided by the amperage.

RESISTOR: A device, usually made of wire, which offers a preset amount of resistance in an electrical circuit.

RING GEAR: The name given to a ring-shaped gear attached to a differential case, or affixed to a flywheel or as part of a planetary gear set.

ROLLER BEARING: A bearing made up of hardened inner and outer races between which hardened steel rollers move.

ROTOR: 1. The disc-shaped part of a disc brake assembly, upon which the brake pads bear; also called, brake disc. 2. The device mounted atop the distributor shaft, which passes current to the distributor cap tower contacts.

SECONDARY CIRCUIT: The high voltage side of the ignition system, usually above 20,000 volts. The secondary includes the ignition coil, coil wire, distributor cap and rotor, spark plug wires and spark plugs.

SENDING UNIT: A mechanical, electrical, hydraulic or electro-magnetic device which transmits information to a gauge.

SENSOR: Any device designed to measure engine operating conditions or ambient pressures and temperatures. Usually electronic in nature and designed to send a voltage signal to an on-board computer, some sensors may operate as a simple on/off switch or they may provide a variable voltage signal (like a potentiometer) as conditions or measured parameters change.

SHIM: Spacers of precise, predetermined thickness used between parts to establish a proper working relationship.

SLAVE CYLINDER: In automotive use, a device in the hydraulic clutch system which is activated by hydraulic force, disengaging the clutch.

SOLENOID: A coil used to produce a magnetic field, the effect of which is to produce work.

SPARK PLUG: A device screwed into the combustion chamber of a spark ignition engine. The basic construction is a conductive core inside of a ceramic insulator, mounted in an outer conductive base. An electrical charge from the spark plug wire travels along the conductive core and jumps a preset air gap to a grounding point or points at the end of the conductive base. The resultant spark ignites the fuel/air mixture in the combustion chamber.

SPLINES: Ridges machined or cast onto the outer diameter of a shaft or inner diameter of a bore to enable parts to mate without rotation.

TACHOMETER: A device used to measure the rotary speed of an engine, shaft, gear, etc., usually in rotations per minute.

THERMOSTAT: A valve, located in the cooling system of an engine, which is closed when cold and opens gradually in response to engine heating, controlling the temperature of the coolant and rate of coolant flow.

TOP DEAD CENTER (TDC): The point at which the piston reaches the top of its travel on the compression stroke.

TORQUE: The twisting force applied to an object.

TORQUE CONVERTER: A turbine used to transmit power from a driving member to a driven member via hydraulic action, providing changes in drive ratio and torque. In automotive use, it links the driveplate at the rear of the engine to the automatic transmission.

TRANSDUCER: A device used to change a force into an electrical signal.

TRANSISTOR: A semi-conductor component which can be actuated by a small voltage to perform an electrical switching function.

TUNE-UP: A regular maintenance function, usually associated with the replacement and adjustment of parts and components in the electrical and fuel systems of a vehicle for the purpose of attaining optimum performance.

TURBOCHARGER: An exhaust driven pump which compresses intake air and forces it into the combustion chambers at higher than atmospheric pressures. The increased air pressure allows more fuel to be burned and results in increased horsepower being produced.

VACUUM ADVANCE: A device which advances the ignition timing in response to increased engine vacuum.

VACUUM GAUGE: An instrument used to measure the presence of vacuum in a chamber.

VALVE: A device which control the pressure, direction of flow or rate of flow of a liquid or gas.

VALVE CLEARANCE: The measured gap between the end of the valve stem and the rocker arm, cam lobe or follower that activates the valve.

VISCOSITY: The rating of a liquid's internal resistance to flow.

VOLTMETER: An instrument used for measuring electrical force in units called volts. Voltmeters are always connected parallel with the circuit being tested.

WHEEL CYLINDER: Found in the automotive drum brake assembly, it is a device, actuated by hydraulic pressure, which, through internal pistons, pushes the brake shoes outward against the drums.

MASTER INDEX